jewelry of our time

jewelry of our time

art, ornament and obsession

**Helen W. Drutt English
and Peter Dormer**

with 586 illustrations,
458 in colour

RIZZOLI NEW YORK

*For my mother Blossom P. Williams, the memory of
my father Harry Williams, all the artists and the memory of
Stella Kramrisch, who made the impossible possible and
taught me that the eyes hold history.* HWDE

Frontispiece:
Olaf Skoogfors. American.
Brooch. 1966
Sterling silver, ivory, pearls 5.2 x 4.6 x 0.6 cm.
Estate of Olaf Skoogfors, USA. Courtesy Helen Drutt
Photo Olaf Skoogfors

First published in the United States of America in 1995 by
RIZZOLI INTERNATIONAL PUBLICATIONS, INC.
300 Park Avenue South, New York, NY 10010

First published in Great Britain in 1995 by
Thames and Hudson Ltd, London

© 1995 Helen W. Drutt English

Library of Congress Cataloging-in-Publication Data

Drutt, Helen Williams.
    Jewelry of our time: art, ornament, and obsession/Helen
Drutt and Peter Dormer.
        P.   cm.
    Includes bibliographical references and index.
    ISBN 0-8478-1914-0
    1. Jewelry—History—20th Century.   I. Dormer, Peter.   II. Title.
    NK7310.D78 1995
    739.27'09'045—dc20   95-21636
                                                          CIP

Designed by Liz Rudderham

Printed and bound in Singapore

contents

acknowledgments

acknowledgments

authors' note

authors' note

I should like to thank my co-author Peter Dormer for his continuous encouragement, and Martha Flood and Brenda Moore whose extraordinary efforts helped to give birth to this book. Janine Mileaf and Lauren Brandt served as research assistants in preparing the Biographies, Chronology and Bibliography, and Mary Hujsak of the American Craft Council Library lent guidance. The artists have generously answered numerous queries during all stages of preparation. I am also particularly grateful to Marianne Aav, Ulla Paakkunainen, Jarno Peltonen of the Taideteollisuusmuseo in Helsinki; Ivy Barsky; Gijs Bakker; Dr Sigrid Barten of the Museum Bellerive in Zurich; the late Edna S. Beron; Lois Boardman; Liesbeth Crommelin and Rudi Fuchs of the Stedelijk Museum in Amsterdam; John Freyaldenhoven; Patricia Harner; Yvonne Joris; Jennifer Lipman; Gert Staal; Merrily Tompkins who provided material from the estates of Ken Cory and Don Tompkins, and Nancy Worden from the estate of Ken Cory. I thank my children, Ilene Weiss and Matthew Drutt, for their continuous understanding, and the staff of Thames and Hudson whose patient support has made this publication possible.

HWDE

Much of the material for this publication has been drawn from the archives of Helen Williams Drutt English, Philadelphia, PA, USA.

The text of Chapters 1 to 4 were written by Peter Dormer, Eastern Arts Fellow in the Critical Appreciation of the Applied Arts, 1993-94, at the University of East Anglia, who had access to the same source material, which led him into direct communication with many of the artists. All works illustrated in Chapters 1 to 4 are fabricated, unique and drawn from the Helen Williams Drutt Collection, Philadelphia, unless otherwise noted.

Measurements in the captions to the illustrations are given in the following order where appropriate: height, width, depth.

introduction
introduction

The artist appeals to that part of our being…which is a gift and not an acquisition – and, therefore, more permanently enduring.

Joseph Conrad

The resurgence of the modern craft movement after World War II signalled great changes in the field of contemporary jewelry. Although exhibitions exploring new movements in the fine arts were part of the early 1960s, information heralding avant-garde concepts – and approaches diametrically opposed to the prevalent ideas of ornamentation – were rarely part of this public forum. The works awaited discovery, the artists awaited recognition.

Can I ever forget the first moment that an electro-formed Stanley Lechtzin brooch captured my eye, changing forever my concept of jewelry, or a discussion with Olaf Skoogfors about the *Dimsdale Machine*, which for me, reflected Antonioni's *The Red Desert*, a film that explored the postwar Italian industrial landscape and was *there* in the brooch? These are the signs and symbols of the passion which ensued, and were among the first works acquired.

Most of the images in this publication document a visual journey that began in 1960, in Philadelphia – discovering work, visiting artists, organizing exhibitions, teaching, and learning to see – and was expanded beyond the city with the increasing interest in the field. This experience was paralleled by individuals in other cities – Amsterdam, London, and Vienna – where contemporary jewelry was being acquired and exhibited by a few individuals.

The formation of a collection was not intentional, nor was it a primary concern. The founding of the Philadelphia Council of Professional Craftsmen in 1967 and the development of a Modern Craft History Course in 1973 led to the establishment of the Helen Drutt Gallery in 1974, which placed me in contact with artists and significant works that had received little response. Acquiring work to hold history became essential. Traditionally it is the role of the art historian and critic to recognize and preserve the work of their age; the independent observer, free from politics and board restrictions, also affords the artist freedom from oblivion. Our museums, therefore, are filled with objects donated by those whose spirit of adventure and passion have recorded the taste of their time. By wearing the jewelry, these individuals stimulate queries from museum administrators, acquaintances, students and strangers. A golden triangle is formed – artist, object, observer – bound together by pioneering galleries and a few visionary institutions.

The artists illustrated and included in the biographies in this book represent selections from the holdings of the Helen Williams Drutt Collection, and their works have been augmented from other sources to broaden the scope of this book. *Jewelry of Our Time* documents my experiences during the last thirty-five years. Works were drawn from five continents; the collection includes pieces by established and emerging artists and by those who, little known at the time of acquisition, have since gained international recognition. Some have moved into other fields of contemporary art, industrial design and architecture. Many died young from accidents or illness, including AIDS. Their history is bound within these pages.

Other collections embrace a different selection of artists and works, also central to the field, reflecting the activities of their collectors and the artists who were connected with them. Different cities, different artists and different stimuli – they will some day form another chapter in the chronicles of 20th-century art.

As these artists moved through this revolutionary period, each developed a unique visual identity that removed the work from 'social' jewelry. Their place has been secured by public and private collectors. Who were they and how did their support form the roots of this movement?

In 1961, Graham Hughes, director of the Worshipful Company of Goldsmiths, organized the first international exhibition of modern jewelry, at Goldsmiths' Hall in London. Dominated by artists who enjoyed a greater reputation in the fine arts, the inclusion of goldsmiths made it a landmark exhibition. This was followed three years later, by the *Internationale Ausstellung: Schmuck – Jewellery – Bijoux*, in Darmstadt, Germany, which kindled the interest of two Dutch collectors, Ida and the late Rom Boelen, in the European-trained goldsmiths; the Boelens then went on to encourage the publication of a seminal text entitled *Schmuck als Künstlerische Aussage unserer Zeit* in 1971. As patrons they also supported Claus Bury's first trip to the USA in 1973, which had important reverberations throughout the craft community.

In 1965 Lechtzin and Skoogfors travelled to Europe, visiting Freidrich Becker, Reinhold Reiling, Claus Bury, Max Fröhlich, Sigurd Persson, Wendy Ramshaw and David Watkins. In 1968 Miyé Matsukata's important link with Japan introduced work from North America to Tokyo. A dialogue was beginning.

Benno Premsela, the prominent designer and applied arts activist, organized *Objects To Wear* in 1969. Touring the United States, it brought Dutch avant-garde jewelry to our attention. Shortly before, *Tendenzen* had been initiated at the Schmuckmuseum in 1967, and these wellspring exhibitions continued through the decades under the direction of Fritz Falk. *Objects USA* (1969), the first major national survey of contemporary American crafts, cited the seminal metalsmiths, and the inaugural exhibition sponsored by the Society of North American Goldsmiths (SNAG), *Goldsmith '70* at the Minnesota Museum of Art, St Paul, created a national exchange of ideas. It was there that Dr Harry Bober, eminent medievalist, gave the keynote address, announcing that SNAG spelled backwards was Gans, which in German means 'goose', and they had at last, as in the days of Cellini, come together to lay the golden egg.

In 1970, energy was global. The Japan Jewellery Association initiated a triennial. In 1971 in Nuremberg,

Gold und Silber, Gerät und Schmuck celebrated the five-hundredth anniversary of Dürer's birth with an international exhibition of metalsmiths, and included two Americans – Lechtzin and Skoogfors. These catalogues stirred the American craft and design community, and opened our doors to European and Japanese work.

Electrum, Barbara Cartlidge's gallery in London, founded in 1971, was the first devoted exclusively to exhibiting contemporary jewelry. A year later, Inge Asenbaum established Galerie am Graben in Vienna. Her interest in the Secessionists and Jungendstiel (the Viennese and German movements related to Art Nouveau) took a leap over the decades into the world of the contemporary goldsmith. Asenbaum's catalogues and collection are rare evidence, documenting the dynamic changes during this period. From 1976, Paul Derrez's Galerie Ra in Amsterdam also created a major centre for these works. All understood the importance of forming collections while the world was being educated.

In 1973 Stanley Lechtzin had a solo exhibition at Goldsmiths' Hall, and the first American exhibition of Wendy Ramshaw and David Watkins took place in Philadelphia. The seeds for those events were sown in Dublin at the World Crafts Council (WCC) in 1970, where I initially met Graham Hughes.

In 1971, government-sponsored programmes helped establish a stronger national and international network, as universities, colleges and non-profitmaking bodies organized exhibitions and encouraged exchanges among the artists. Gijs Bakker and Emmy van Leersum's lecture tour in 1975, sponsored by the WCC, was part of this energy. In 1980, the WCC meeting in Vienna created a dynamic forum for international crafts, heralded by Peter Skubic's *Schmuck International*. It was there that I first met Skubic, Martinazzi, Maierhofer and Inge Asenbaum,

among others. The many encounters with Martinazzi in the decade that followed eventually led to the introduction of his work to the American audience. Here is an artist who uses symbols in the form of golden lips and eyes to point out the relationships between human beings and events. Through the exhibitions, the exchange between Europe and the USA was being strengthened and continued as meetings with Breon O'Casey in 1981 and Peter Chang in 1989 broadened the gallery's commitments.

The role of the collector has been paramount. *The Jewelry Project* exhibition of 1983 records the support of Malcolm, Sue and Abigail Knapp for the documentation of an exciting period of transition and experimentation. Initiated in 1976, the Mieke and Jan Teunen collection, *Schmuck der Avantgarde, (1967–88)* was exhibited at the Wilhelm-Hack-Museum in Germany from 1990 to 1991, and has since been acquired by the Museum für Kunst und Gewerbe in Hamburg. In 1993, the Stedelijk Museum, in Amsterdam, presented *Voorzien*, Benno Premsela's collection of applied arts, which included a major selection of jewelry. The role of the jewelry collector during these decades was akin to that of the artists' patrons of the early 20th century – Kahnweiler, Gertrude Stein, Arensberg and Barnes – symbiotic relationships developed between the maker and the active observer and created the legacy of the moment. The collector has played a vital part in developing our knowledge and preserving the evidence of this vibrant movement.

Before the 1980s brought a fresh infusion of collective energy, there were few who had ventured into the realm of the goldsmith. Among them were Robert L. Pfannebecker and Sandy and Lou Grotta, whose dedicated support of the American craft movement is well documented. The new generation of collectors, many of whose acquisitions were homogenized by the marketplace, bypassed the field of contemporary jewelry which demands a singular view. Though the collecting audience has been sparse, a growing number of collectors developed in the 1980s into the 1990s, some of whom, such as Lois Boardman and Daphne Farago, have been cited on these pages. Their interest has been reinforced by the private galleries.

Through seeing and discovering, one dissolves the act of acquisition into the greater notion of caretaking and securing history for the artist. This concept defines the Helen Williams Drutt Collection.

In 1984 the Musée des Arts Décoratifs, Montreal, exhibited works from the collection which have since travelled throughout the USA and Europe. This journey has been augmented by lecturing, supporting exhibitions, as well as attending events which expand the dialogue, such as *Ornamenta I* in Pforzheim 1989 and the annual SNAG conferences in America – all of which reinforce Bober's image of the goose that laid the golden egg.

Jewelry of Our Time moves beyond ornament, and explores the sweeping changes in which the artists on these pages celebrate freedom and expansion of expression. In a world where traditional art categories are no longer applicable, they have joined forces with mainstream art and moved into the territory formerly held by the 'artist' of our time.

Helen W. Drutt English
Philadelphia, 1995

1 the new movement

1 the new movement

1 the new movement

Previous page
Hermann Jünger
German

Brooch. 1986
Gold, silver, aquamarine,
coral, sapphire, enamel
36 x 40 cm
Private collection

Jewelry in north-west Europe and North America under-went a great change between the early 1960s and the late 1980s. During these years it became possible and accept-able within the metals and jewelry world for artists to use jewelry as a means for making individualistic art. Like many other visual arts in the 20th century, jewelry is characterized by the desire of each artist to present to the world his or her singular view.

However, three points should be noted. To begin with, the generations of artists considered in this book did not appear from nowhere. They were preceded by talented, inventive men and women, prominent in the 1940s and 1950s who, by the quality of their work and through their teaching, established the foundation for 'new jewelry's' subsequent renaissance.

Secondly, the period we are examining is not open-ended. That is to say, the thirty-five years covered by this book (1960–1995 approximately) are interesting because so much innovation occurred, but like all passages of creative energy the momentum of innovation could not continue for ever. The new jewelry was formed in our period in the same sense that, arguably, 'new painting' was formed in Europe between 1880 and 1910, or in the United States from 1940 to 1960. The dates have to be approximate because beginnings and endings in art are not like railway timetables.

Thirdly, although the jewelry we are looking at is characterized by individuality, it is quite clear that several groups of artists share similar interests in content or in style, or have had the same teachers, or have simply grown up in similar cultures, with the result that their work has aspects in common.

Neither this book nor this essay in four chapters is definitive or complete; the history is too recent and too complicated. We are trying to present a coherent picture of what has happened in the new jewelry and why it is worth studying and enjoying.

art and ornament

art and ornament

It would be misleading to pretend that ornament and decoration are no longer important goals in jewelry. For some jewelers the creation of ornamental work is their central goal, and this commitment to decoration is welcome. The creation of decorative objects has never been so hard; 20th-century technology has radically subverted the quality and the status of decoration. Every two-bit 'factory' can produce and reproduce decorative objects that appear to become cruder in each successive generation of manufacture. Technology has also removed the practical application of decoration in areas such as architecture. The industrialized, mass production of components in building, together with an approach to building that relies on standardized 'kit' construction, has eliminated many opportunities for applied art. Consequently the continuation of intelligent, contemporary decoration in fields such as metalware and jewelry becomes especially precious.

Decoration is not necessarily a background art on the margins of our awareness, because it can command attention by being witty, sentimental, ironic, teasing and tantalizing. Decoration is, however, a commercial activity in so far as it is generally understood that to be successful it should appeal to other people, and that to be complete it should be bought and owned by others. To that extent, decoration is different from art.

Art brings a certain freedom from the constraints of commerce and, in the sense in which art is practised in the 20th century, it provides a licence to question ortho-doxies. The Austrian architect and designer Adolf Loos (1870-1933) clarified the implications of this when he said that a house should appeal to everybody, as distinct from works of art 'which do not have to appeal to anyone'. This distinction can be applied to all kinds of aesthetic disciplines such as furniture, textiles and jewelry. If the intention is to create a practical art – literally an applied art – then it should have wide appeal, and not only to a specialist audience.

There is a problem in calling jewelry an art which we will state and then set aside. In one important sense, it is not in the power of jewelers or those of us who attempt a description of contemporary jewelry to call it an art. The term 'art' confers a status upon an object that is currently higher than and different from the status of craft or design. Jewelry does not have the status of art in the wider art community. That is to say, the major art institutions, collectors and critics who 'run' the art world do not, whatever the rest of us might claim, regard jewelry as an art in the same way as painting or sculpture. Jewelry does not, for example, figure strongly in the Museum of Modern Art in New York, it does not appear at the Venice Biennale, and it seldom, if at all, appears in the professional literature of magazines such as *Art Forum*.

When we say that jewelry is an art, we are stating simply that many jewelers now have the same expectations and claim the same freedom of subject matter and the same relationship with their work that can be observed in other art-like activities. But what we also observe is that institutionally the art world still, by and large, regards jewelry and other 'applied' arts as not-Art. We have chosen to set this aside in this book for the purposes of exploring modern jewelry.

The Australian jeweler, artist and writer Margaret West (b.1936) believes that jewelers have been reclaiming a freedom from the constraints imposed by the Industrial Revolution – a revolution which made most design rather predictable. The jeweler has taken it upon herself or himself to be, as West describes it, 'a pourer-in of meaning'. The role of 'pourer-in of meaning' is an interesting one. It may have arisen because 20th-century technological society is so extraordinarily prolific in producing objects that there is a need for artists to tell us what our obsession with manufacture and possession means. We have turned the design, manufacture and consumption of objects into a language and a ritual. We have made production and consumption into a way of life. Artists have been commenting upon this phenomenon, and some of these artists have used jewelry as their vehicle.

Jewelry has a rich and complex subject matter: it has a long history of being intertwined with people's imaginations. Jewelry is present in familiar rituals and institutions: engagement, marriage, the church, the military (medals and 'decorations'), coming of age, declarations of personal status and group identity. Jewelry is its own social anthropology and when one adds to the notion of ritual (with all the metaphor, symbolism and design vocabulary that each ritual generates) the further meanings and associations that are attendant upon materials, and different ways of working materials, then the contemporary jeweler has an embarrassment of riches. These riches are embedded in connections between people. All those Main-Street-store silver and gold crosses, engagement, wedding and eternity rings, christening gifts, signet rings may be banal in design, but the content of the ritual surrounding each of these objects lifts them above most other mass-manufactured design.

Making small things with large meanings confers a different image of 'the artist' from the one most current in late 20th-century art – that of the artist as hero or heroine working on the large scale. The artist making jewelry may pore over the small artwork in such a way that the centre of his or her world temporarily shrinks to a physical space measured in centimetres, but the metaphorical and imaginative space may be vast: a whole world of symbolism and emotion.

It is probably true that often the objects produced in jewelry have aspects known only to their makers and their owners – only the maker/owner knows the full richness of a piece of jewelry and understands its other life, for when it is not being worn then it becomes a private work of art.

The 'smallness' of jewelry can be misleading. It is to be noted that there has evolved in the last thirty years a range of sculptural or small 'architectural works' that have the spatial, textural, volumetric and perspectival complexities of larger works together with a sense of intimacy and modesty. This is discussed more fully in Chapter 2.

Jewelry can encourage a different attitude towards viewing and contemplation. You need to wear it, or, when not wearing it, to leave it where it can be seen, or pick it up and turn it over in your hands. In this sense the visual, tactile and metaphorical complexity of the private reverie between a piece of jewelry art and the individual owner can create a powerful relationship. And, as hinted earlier, there is yet another level of pleasure that resides in the secret life of the jewel – the object that you own, you value and you keep hidden away until that special event or memory or desire causes you to visit it once again.

The image of the artist-jeweler poring over her or his work may seem overly romantic, and, indeed, an inaccurate account of the way some contemporary jewelers work, but it raises the matter of 'craft'.

One of the aspects that makes the art of jewelry as a whole an art distinguishable from that of several of the other visual arts, such as late 20th-century painting, sculpture, video and performance art, is that for some, perhaps many, jewelers, the possession and use of a substantial body of craft knowledge provides the means through which ideas are discovered, as well as made visible. For these jewelers it is important to recognize that their ideas have been, and continue to be, developed through making.

However, some jewelers, such David Watkins (b.UK 1940) argue that innovative jewelry design is not necessarily dependent on a craft-making technology. Many jewelers do not evolve their ideas through making, although they do realize them in this way. But advances in computer design and manufacture may make 'craft' an obsolete notion for art-jewelers.

Some people believe that computer-aided design and manufacture will soon be available to all but the poorest of small workshops, and that one of the effects of computer-aided manufacture will be the elimination of handwork. This technology will allow the creation of three-dimensional designs on computer, that are then manufactured by automated milling machines and a technology known to industry as rapid automated prototyping.

Such technology is largely (although not wholly) irrelevant to our period, because it has not been available. Yet – even setting technology aside – handcraft has been a contentious issue for some jewelers. Craft is out of fashion in art criticism, and it is an embarrassing term, even to craftspersons, especially to those anxious about their status as artists. The attitude of both artists and critics is to prefix the term 'craft' with the word 'mere' and then to hurry on to a consideration of the ideas. But there are many artists whose work has both beauty and intellectual value because it is thoughtfully crafted and because the work has been conceived through the process of making.

An interesting explanation of what this means is offered by Francesco de Bartolomeis in the catalogue entitled *Materia e Tempo,* which is a presentation and discussion of the work of the goldsmith and sculptor in stone, Bruno Martinazzi (b.Italy 1923). What follows is a description of Martinazzi's work in stone, but it is intended also as an analogous description of all his work, including his goldsmithing – a relationship between thinking and making:

There is always a direct relationship with stone, consisting of thought and action…one does not want to compromise with projectional predetermination a work of art that will keep you occupied for more than a month…there is a difference between making a small model to be handed over to the stone masons so that they will carry out their work…the scientist and the artist don't test or research into the *implementation* of a project and so the implementation is itself part of the research…spending so much time with the material brings the whole process back to mental factors….The artist may produce things that machines, stone masons or someone else could do more rapidly and better, but the artist does them because he thinks, because when he does these things he really does them…he does not translate, with an extension of time, something that was completely in place from the beginning.

For those jewelers who share Martinazzi's way of thinking, the history of making that centuries of metalware presents is of immense importance. And for all jewelry artists interested in re-investing modern jewelry with some of its historical symbolic or ritualistic power, there is the history of metaphor and symbolism in metalware. And there is more than one history, of course. Most of the civilizations and cultures that exist or have existed appear to possess a richly entwined history of ceremony, ornament and metalware.

the dialogue with modernism

the dialogue with modernism

A number of jewelers, however, and especially those who came to prominence in north-west Europe in the 1960s and 1970s, appeared to turn away from a history that was only to do with jewelry or metalware, and looked to the broader and specifically Western movement we call 'modernism'.

Modernism is a slippery word. It embraces many theories and practices. A book on modernism would need to consider the far-reaching effects of political and allegedly scientific analyses such as Marxism and psycho-analytic theory, as well as the principles of industrial manufacture and the organization and integration of labour and machinery. But this is not that book. The notion of modernism that is applicable here is the over-simple but powerful one that rests in the images of modernism: Cubist painting by Picasso and Braque, the early skyscrapers of Chicago and New York, the glass and steel architecture of the famous and now iconic German art and design school – the Bauhaus. It is the furniture of Gerrit Rietveld, the stark geometry of Russian painters, such as Kasimir Malevich, and the primary-coloured grids of Piet Mondrian. But it is also the later, more organic shapes that occurred in the architecture of Le Corbusier and the sculpture of Henry Moore, as well as the furniture of

Charles Eames or the technology-led, streamlined forms of successive generations of aircraft beginning with the DC3.

In this collection of images, modernism begins around 1904 and continues to the present in the electricity pylons and the industrial machinery of our age. It has its metaphorical counterpart in the early work of such contemporary artists as Walter Kelley Morris (b.USA 1945), Anton Cepka (b.Czechoslovakia 1936), Eva Eisler (b.Czechoslovakia 1952), Lisa Gralnick (b.USA 1956), Gary Griffin (b.USA 1945).

These images of modernism and their metaphorical application in jewelry have in common an emphasis upon simple clean forms, clarity of line, and an absence of elaborate detailing, except for the detailing that occurs through the repetition of elements required through the function of the design (such as the rivets, bolts or welds required to hold together a plane, ship, building or piece of metalware). These images also share an unfolding of 20th-century materials, either those particular to this century including acrylics and aluminium, or materials that, while not new, are used in ways specific to our century, as in the application of large areas of glass or concrete. Jewelers have adapted both a range of 'new'

materials and 20th-century technological imagery to their work, and they also have embraced the sense of logic and rational purpose that underlies this technology.

Specifically, there is a range of modernist jewelry from countries such as the Czech Republic and Slovakia, the Netherlands, Britain and Germany that has made a metaphor out of the engineering detailing that is used in modernism. Junctions between pieces of metal, rivets and the repetition of components are redolent of the decoration that modern technological design spawned naturally. The use of such devices is a way for jewelers to be both rigorous in design and decorative. It allows a person both to renounce ornament and yet to make ornamental work.

But modernism is not all straight or streamlined lines and reductivist forms. Modernism also includes movements such as Dada and Surrealism whose images are complex, multi-layered, rooted in metaphor, symbol and dream. Strange images, apparently simple, but potent have lasted for decades – Man Ray's clothes-iron with a line of nails embedded in its base, Meret Oppenheim's fur cup-and-saucer and Salvador Dali's melting watch. The images of Dada and Surrealism do not translate so easily into steel, glass and concrete, but thrive in the flexible media of paint, photography and film – media that can cheat the reality of gravity and physics, and match the fluidity of the human imagination and its fears and dreams.

Dada and Surrealism may yet prove to be the most long-lasting inventions of modernism because they flourish in the arts of film and advertising, and seem set to have a deep influence upon the shaping of computer-centred media. The most powerful of Dada and Surrealism's strategies is also one of the simplest – the putting-together of contrary or disparate objects or images. The result may be amusing or merely peculiar, but sometimes it can be profound.

However, there are caveats, and the jewelry artist Kiff Slemmons (b.USA 1944) is clear about them. In her work in the 1990s she has, like Ken Cory (b.USA, 1943–94) and Laurie Hall (b.USA 1944), used materials such as rulers, zippers and pencils for, as she puts it, 'their metaphoric possibilities'. She is not the first artist by any means to have recognized the power of this strategy, and in the world of jewelry one of the pioneers of the use of found objects was Ramona Solberg (b.USA 1921). Slemmons says, 'It is my purpose that the tension set up between the recognized objects and their unexpected implications will lead to seeing and thinking of jewelry in new ways.' But she knows that simply putting disparate objects together does not in itself create meaning. In an interview in *Metalsmith* magazine, Summer 1993, she explained the pitfalls of the unthinking approach to 'Surrealism' by quoting from René Magritte, who, after Salvador Dali, is possibly the most well-known of Surrealist painters. Magritte, talking here of his 1933 painting, *Effective Strategies,* said:

We are familiar with a bird in a cage. Our interest is quickened if the bird is replaced by a fish or a shoe but although these images are interesting they are unfortunately accidental, arbitrary. It is possible to arrive at a new image that will stand up to examination through its definitiveness, its rightness – the image which shows an egg in the cage.

The rightness is *so* obvious when stated – although more pleasing and tantalizing as an image – an egg is a future bird, but an egg needs no caging.

But as Slemmons comments, what Magritte is talking about is imagery and how it works: 'I think he's making an important point. Just because you choose to put two objects, two images next to each other – which I think is being done a lot these days – doesn't necessarily mean there is any further meaning.'

For people for whom the art of jewelry is a new field there may be surprise at just how much contemporary jewelry art appears to deal with the narrative possibilities opened up by the surreal. Sometimes the narrative exists as a potential story — the artists supply a variety of figures and symbols, you supply the meaning. This is true of Kim Overstreet (b.USA 1955) and Robin Kranitzky (b.USA 1956), and Manfred Bischoff (b.Germany 1947). The more direct visual, vaguely surreal pun, however, as practised so often by René Magritte, surfaces quite frequently in modern jewelry. Here one encounters a contemporary 'folk art' in which the surreal, Magritte-like visual pun is used to effect. One such example is Merrily Tompkins's (b. USA 1947) *Snatch Purse,* which she wears around her waist. It is a real bag, displaying the photo-image of her thighs with a brush of beaver fur hanging between them. At the top of the bag there is an image of a railway engine and a tunnel – when the bag is opened or shut, the railway engine moves in and out of the tunnel. Freud would doubtless have bought one.

Dada and Surrealism in its more light-hearted mode entered jewelry well before the war by way of fashion and the creation of accessories. In the 1930s, for example, the Italian fashion designer Elsa Schiaparelli (1896–1973) worked with Salvador Dali to produce hats in the form of shoes, ice-cream cones and lamb cutlets. She designed a clear plastic necklace crawling with metal-coloured bugs, and developed a range of phosphorescent brooches and buttons that also functioned as paperweights.

Dada and Surrealism are important to a number of jewelers in particular and to jewelry in general because Surrealism emphasized the role of content and subject-matter in art. Consequently Surrealism has provided a counter-balance to formalism and abstraction. Moreover, because Surrealism has placed such emphasis upon the subconscious and the non-rational, it has proved continuously attractive to artists who want to explore the human-made world in terms of its values and the emotions it stimulates in us.

Putting matters simply, one might assert that the world of abstraction and formalism is a world of design and control, whereas Dada and Surrealism is about the imagination's resistance to and sometimes horror of that control. Contemporary jewelry has been shaped by both.

Other tendencies have had an effect upon contemporary jewelry. It is most interesting just how important figuration, storytelling and the invention of a modern folk art have been in North American jewelry. And this work seems rooted in the particular American talent for caricature, cartoon and animation. America's contribution to 20th-century visual culture may prove to have been at its most skilled, inventive, creative and subversive in cartoon and animation work – work that has its parallel in American jewelry. What is extraordinary, and this is discussed below, is how effective American cartoon or 'folk' art can be. Witty artists can use the commonplace and the cheap to wring the emotions.

abstractionism

In north-west Europe, North America and Australia the thirty-five years of new jewelry (1960–95) have not been dominated by one movement. Even in the Netherlands, where one sees a certain modernist aesthetic dominating the development of jewelry in the 1960s and 1970s, there are contradictions. There is a conflict of values regarding the nature of modern jewelry and its functions. This conflict is represented by individuals. On the one hand there is the artist/goldsmith Robert Smit (b.Netherlands 1941) who by the mid-1980s was pouring scorn on the 'experimentation' of Dutch rationalists, on the other hand there is the artist/designer Gijs Bakker (b.Netherlands 1942), famous as one of the contributors to the radicalization of modern jewelry, and known to be a jewelry creator who does not much like jewelry. Indeed, half the 'Young Turks' of the new jewelry movement in the 1960s and 1970s in the Netherlands were reluctant jewelers. Their attitude to the traditions of the preceding generation of jewelers was a form of parricide.

To understand the range of jewelry that may be placed under the heading of abstractionism, we can begin by considering the work that has been produced by people such as Max Fröhlich (b.Switzerland 1908), Olaf Skoogfors (b.Sweden, 1930–75) and Emmy van Leersum (b.Netherlands, 1930–84).

Max Fröhlich is one of the masters of modern jewelry and an eminent European teacher. Fröhlich's father was a textile manufacturer with a factory in a long, narrow, Swiss Alpine valley; he designed and produced textiles for Africa. As a child, Fröhlich did not like school, but he liked making things, and he was enrolled, as a fifteen-year-old boy, in the metal department of the Ecole des Beaux Arts in Geneva. Fröhlich had no particular ambition to be a metalsmith – he did not like textiles, but his mother, who was English, liked silver and, he says, 'I think my parents just thought, "Let's try. Let's try." ' He learned many metal-working skills – he learned to raise holloware, he learned to polish and planish and chase. In 1924 Geneva was still a city of Art Deco, whereas Zurich, where Fröhlich went the following year, was 'more Bauhaus than the Bauhaus'. The philosophy of the art school in Zurich was 'Form without Ornament'.

Fröhlich completed his training when he was nineteen, and during those years he became completely converted to the Zurich school's anti-ornamental thinking. But, although the school took a harsh line against decoration, its students were encouraged to make as many things in as many different ways as they could.

In 1988 Fröhlich told Richard Polsky (*Oral History Project*, Columbia University, New York): 'My aim was to become a good silversmith. I never thought to become an artist. I have the ambition to make a good thing. And good in proportion, and good in drawing, good in design.... I never thought to become an artist.' Fröhlich has never pretended that his small abstractions are philosophy: they are about vanity.

As a silversmith you do not make jewelry but I had to make jewelry. I couldn't live on silversmithing. And jewelry has to do with vanity. And my philosophy of making jewelry is to embellish people.... To give him or her a special aspect. I think it is a very good, or simple way of helping people...most of the clientele were women above fifty years. And, you see, they are not spoiled people, generally. Women older than forty-five, fifty years, are not generally spoiled people. And I tried to give them a feeling, really, of their personality, because each man or woman, as mankind,...is unique in this way.

In North America, one of the central figures in the evolution of the abstractionist, formal approach in new jewelry was Olaf Skoogfors who, although he was born in Sweden, had lived in the USA since the age of four. The following quotations are from Skoogfors, taken from the catalogue to *The American Contemporary Jewelry Exhibition*, Tokyo, 1968:

I consider myself to be an artist as well as a craftsperson. The same efforts that go into painting or sculpture go into my jewelry. If this medium is a lesser art, then I am a lesser artist....

The forms and imagery of my jewelry often occur with minimum pre-planning. One cast form suggests additional forms or stones, and pieces are added much in the manner of a collage. I never feel limited by a preconceived idea, but need freedom to make alterations based on my response to the piece.

I feel that good jewelry must act as decoration, but it should also reach beyond these limits to satisfy greater aesthetic needs. Thus, another aim in my jewelry is to make a meaningful statement about forms, texture, colour, balance, etc., in common with other art forms.

Skoogfors brought to his work a range of ideas generated from his interests in music, film, literature and nature. He has been described as sponge-like – absorbing ideas and images and then expelling them again with his own explanations and interpretations. He examined the Scandinavian, Benin, pre-Columbian, Celtic and Viking traditions, and he explored the aesthetic concerns of contemporary sculptural trends. In later years he referred to himself as a constructivist – liking to work and build directly with the metal. He worked primarily in silver, and frequently gold-plated silver. He was particularly interested in working through ideas over a series of related objects. Skoogfors had a talent for the nuances of texture as well as the overall shape and composition of a form.

In the winter of 1987, *Metalsmith* magazine published a discussion with Stanley Lechztin on Skoogfors and his work. Lechztin explains the synthesis of ideas in the late 1950s and early 1960s, and how they moulded the attitudes of the late 1960s and early 1970s. He said:

I think the attitude of direct work in the medium was one that pervaded the art community. It wasn't Abstract Expressionism *per se* that affected our work as much as that attitude, which you found in all the schools and all the studios, the feeling that you need not make careful models and careful drawings and precise plans, but you can just walk into the studio and begin making art. And that is a break from the industrial design attitude that permeated in the 50s and 60s, and when I talk about industrial design, I lump Scandinavian design into it, because the Scandinavian stuff that so influenced us at that time was designed by and large by architects…

On the other hand, it is important to note that drawing was an important part of Skoogfors's work and many of his jewelry pieces were preceded by sketches and drawings.

The belief in the power of formal abstraction, sensitively organized and made, was one that Skoogfors shared with many 'abstract' artists, although, as the 20th century draws to a close, it is a belief that is probably out of fashion. Skoogfors's work was not (any more than Fröhlich's) ostensibly 'about' the world. Rather it was about the material rather than the social fabric of the world, its nature, its texture and the way it felt. Lechztin put it thus:

I think Olaf [who was a committed, active socialist] agreed with me that he would no way use his work for social comment. There are much better media for effecting social change than jewelry. Olaf was involved in aesthetics when he sat down at the bench.

Skoogfors once said, 'I think of my pieces as compositions, in some cases in alliance with the human body, but often as independent objects. This is particularly true in my pins which by their very nature allow this freedom.' He also said:

In more recent times I have been interested in the strength/vitality of barbaric, primitive and peasant design, and in my own way am trying to capture that vitality in my work. I believe jewelry must be wearable, but have a strong, forceful image as well. It should not just be casual decoration, but a reflection of the creator and the wearer.

In the early part of our period, the early to mid-1960s, the influence of Scandinavian design was still quite strong although it was beginning to wane after its all-conquering successes in north-west Europe and the United States in the 1940s and 1950s. Scandinavian design as represented by Danish furniture and silverware or Swedish or Finnish ceramics, glass and textiles was influential because it offered uncluttered modernity and 'soft' organic forms. It was domesticated modernism. The USA, although it hosted several exhibitions of Scandinavian design, including jewelry, in the 1950s, already possessed its own version of domestic abstract modernism, partly as a result of the Scandinavian bias built into the highly influential design and applied arts school at Cranbrook, and partly because of such talents as furniture designers Charles and Ray Eames.

The European aesthetic (Dada, Surrealism and German Expressionism notwithstanding) is often concerned with removing content and throwing elements out of a design;

American aesthetic, as befits the whole culture, is concerned with 'freeing' up.

A good example of what this means in practice is demonstrated by the work of Albert Paley (b.USA 1944). Paley began by making jewelry, but is now known for work ranging from large-scale architectural works to sculpture, his jewelry acting as a catalyst for his works for public places in the second half of the 1970s.

The Art in Public Places movement has, since the mid-1960s, become a huge source of commissions and patronage (often enshrined in state and national law). The availability of funds, the argument that this is art for the public good, and the freedom from the orthodoxies of taste that shape the curatorial policies of contemporary art galleries and museums, has encouraged hybrid artists, such as jewelers, to make sculpture as art for public places.

In the beginning, as Paley moved towards a greater interest in the aesthetics of forged metalwork, the ideas that were later to be developed in his larger work were explored by him in his jewelry. Albert Paley's departure from jewelry (he ceased making it in 1977) is regrettable. His jewelry was extremely labour-intensive and the economics of such work made it unviable as commissions for his architectural work increased. Many of his jewelry pieces brought to the small scale a complexity, richness and drama that exist only in the work of Richard Mawdsley (b.USA 1945), although with an entirely different aesthetic and content. Paley exploited the drama in Art Nouveau; for all its decorative associations, Art Nouveau is theatrical, and offers visually the kind of highs and lows we normally associate with baroque architecture, and which post-modern architecture (which promised so much) failed to provide. Paley is regarded as an artist whose definitions have broadened towards a larger scale, which includes architectural, ornamental and functional iron work, as well as site-specific sculpture.

But, again, even in his very large works, there is that element of preciousness. He knows an enormous amount about the way metal works, what it can be made to do and what each technique will offer him. Paley is one of the artists who deserve the description 'practical philosopher' in that he makes choices grounded in his knowledge of the craft, but uses this knowledge as a part of his aesthetic philosophy. This aspect is illuminated in an essay on his work by Penelope Hunter-Stiebel:

Paley has written a treatise…in his discussion of each technique he has delved into the natural laws to which it relates and evaluated it according to its degree of conformity to those laws. In the section on riveting he declares that the process can be more than just a technological necessity. In order that the metal will 'record the raw energy of its own formation' he recommends punching instead of drilling out a hole. The metal is thus dislocated rather than removed, and a swelling remains to document the action. Looking at examples in Paley's metalwork, one sees how details like the punched rivet convey animation, while a drilled version would appear mechanical and, in consequence, lifeless.

In the 1960s and the early 1970s the developments in the new jewelry were marked by several self-conscious attempts at changing other people's perception of jewelry, especially that of other artists. In the Netherlands there was a desire to get jewelry discussed, or at least understood, in terms of its contemporary ideas as distinct from its traditional values. One strategy for achieving this was to make jewelry in non-traditional materials. This was the one into which Emmy van Leersum evolved. By producing work in non-precious materials and with a minimum of craft, it was thought that this would emphasize the idea and the design of the work as the bearers of value, rather than the skill or the material in which those ideas were presented. In this sense jewelry could be 'conceptual'.

Emmy van Leersum did not invent conceptual jewelry, but she pursued it with single-mindedness. Her earliest work used precious metals and stones; these materials were dropped but were not finally banished – she did occasionally use gold in some of her later pieces. The work that began to distinguish her as an artist was based on simple Euclidean geometry – distorted cylinders, mostly, in paper-thin sheet metal such as stainless steel. She and Gijs Bakker became interested in developing series of works. In these, one can see the development of a design through several pieces. Each development is simple and the sequence unfolds as a rhythm of nuances. It is very much like the Systems painters and artists who emerged in Britain in the late 1960s – artists such as Michael Kidner, or Mary and Kenneth Martin, who used arithmetical systems to dictate the design of a sculpture or a painting and to set up the parameters for the next work in the series.

There are several texts quoting Emmy van Leersum on the nature of her work, and a surprising proportion of it describes process. What she appeared to want and what she accomplished was jewelry that was rich in its simplicity and which broke with past conventions.

The 1960s was the first decade in many to celebrate youth. The children born in the early 1950s were growing up, healthier and more confident than preceding generations. A cult of 'the body' was emerging, and Van Leersum's beautifully nuanced jewelry is set off to best advantage when worn by athletic, young, lean, good-looking bodies. She is quoted in the catalogue *Emmy van Leersum in het Stedelijk* (1979) as saying:

I am now involved with the human body, so I wanted to dismantle all the old conventions and start afresh, from the beginning: there is the human arm, and it needs a covering. An arm has, roughly, the shape of a cylinder, so I took standard cylinders as my basic form.

Undoubtedly it is a cliché to say that the Dutch culture is in a constant tension between its Calvinist roots – a Puritan religious heritage with a strong fear of a masterful and avenging God – and its hedonistic urges. For although it has until recently been a God-fearing society (unlike England where God has been of marginal interest to the mass of the population for nearly two centuries), it is also a comfortable, self-indulgent culture which has been more or less prosperous for nearly three centuries. The culture has also over this period fostered a widespread sensibility to good design. Perhaps the reasons are rooted in the fact that the Netherlands has, from the 17th century onwards, turned domesticity – the home, design for the home, design for living – into an art that is widely shared throughout the country. People grow up in an ordered, society in which ordinary artefacts are designed in an attitude of respect for both quality and restraint. But it is also a design culture with some quirks, and Van Leersum's early neckpieces are a good example: they are cleanly and rationally designed, yet look a little ridiculous. Some of the aluminium neckpieces which hold the model's head in a type of metal halter look embarrassingly like sci-fi film props, a mixture of the space suit and the biblical imagery of St John's head served on a platter, but once this rather sensationalist period in her work was over, her series of simple bracelets and neckpieces and her works combining jewelry with clothing provide substantial evidence to support the architect Mies van der Rohe's notorious maxim: Less is More.

A contributor to the catalogue accompanying the 1980 exhibition of Van Leersum's work at the Stedelijk Museum, Benno Premsela, identified in her work three starting-points for the new jewelry. First, the monetary value of the material became irrelevant; second, once the value of jewelry as a status symbol had been deflated, the relation between the ornament and the human body once again assumed a dominant position – jewelry became body-conscious; third, jewelry lost its exclusiveness to one sex or age – it could be worn by men, women and children.

From the way Emmy van Leersum described her work, it is evident that ideas came through the process as much if not more than before the work began. Her 'new jewelry' could not exist without the work itself – it was not a fully conceptual art in which the idea was typed out on a piece of paper and the viewer left to imagine what the object would look like or what it would feel like to wear.

Consider the following description quoted in the 1979 Stedelijk catalogue of her work:

As a logical way of drawing and cutting lines in synthetic materials, I started treating the line autonomously, notably in the opposition of two diagonal sections of the square, in both cases the result was a different division of the square. By using the segments horizontally and then vertically – and this was very remarkable – not only the division but also the horizontal-vertical principle gave rise to totally different form…

Gijs Bakker's work is more diverse than that of Emmy van Leersum, and he has, in any case, pursued a career as an artist, jeweler and designer embracing most methods of craft, art and industrial manufacture. His work is discussed more fully in Chapter 3.

One of the fashions in art education and art practice in the mid to late 1960s and in the 1970s was 'problem solving'. In north-west European art schools, especially the Netherlands and Britain, students were expected to invent a 'problem' and then solve it: the problem and the solution thus became the subject matter around which the process of designing and making an object was hung.

A good example of this approach is to be found in the work of Hans Appenzeller (b.Netherlands, 1949). Since 1969 he had been working with simple geometry, especially the tube, and materials such as aluminium and then rubber. His approach was orientated around engineering. In 1976, with his working partner Jan Aarntez, he presented a collection at the Stedelijk. This was described in 1982 by Gert Staal as follows:

Both employed the same formal limitations in their designs, namely the use of the triangle as the starting point. It was not new for Appenzeller to intentionally impose a design restriction upon his design freedom but in no other collection had the basic premise been so difficult to unite with the demands of wearability and the idea that there must be a relationship between the form of the jewelry and the body form.

As the 1980s progressed, Appenzeller was able to find a wider public wanting to buy his annual jewelry collections. The imposing of design restrictions was a familiar strategy for many avant-garde artists and designers because the restriction, however 'artificial', provides a rule, or set of rules, and a subject matter. It makes up for not being given a specific commission or a particular function to fulfil. It is almost impossible to create without a subject matter.

In the Netherlands and elsewhere in Europe there were other conceptualists, rationalists and 'problem-solvers' prominent in the 1970s and 1980s, such as Joke Brakman (b.Netherlands, 1946), Caroline Broadhead (b.UK 1950), Johanna Dahm (b.Switzerland 1947), Paul Derrez (b.Netherlands 1950), George Dobler (b.Germany 1952), Marion Herbst (b.Netherlands, 1944–95), Herman Hermsen (b.Netherlands 1953),

Otto Künzli (b. Switzerland 1948), Eric Spiller (b. UK 1946) and David Watkins.

One of the Europeans most credited with exporting the 'intellectual' approach to jewelry to America was Claus Bury (b.Germany 1946). This is emphatically not to imply that American metalsmiths were or are any less interested in ideas and conceptual content than their European counterparts but to suggest that in Europe a skill had been developed for turning intellectualism into style as well as content.

Bury's influence upon jewelers in North America in the early 1970s was considerable because he brought with him a preciousness of a specific kind: intellectual precision. He introduced the idea of producing careful drawings prior to making a work of jewelry, and also of exhibiting these drawings with the jewelry, as a part of the finished arte-fact. His considered, intellectual, approach, as much as his carefully composed abstractions, made of gold, acrylic or coloured metal alloys, made Bury celebrated in the USA. His classical, constructivist works were a contrast to some of the more ebullient jewelry that was and remains charac-teristic of the USA. He was also a bridge between engineering and jewelry in the same sense that he has now become a bridge between architecture and sculpture.

Claus Bury began to leave jewelry at about the same time as Paley. The transitional works between his architec-tonic rings of the early 1970s to his barn-sized architec-tonic sculptures of the late 1980s were site-specific works – drawings in the earth – in Israel, the USA and Australia. These temporary structures were an extension of the Land Art/Earth Art movement that emerged in the late 1960s. Today, his sculptures are like non-functional buildings; they have the jeweler's refinement and the modernist's classicism, and they present an irony about the 20th-century development of architecture in the West.

The irony is this. Modernists often had an idealistic vision of the virtues of mass machine-directed manufacture. They thought that machine production would generate not just precision but preciousness – that the machined edge, the machined plane and the machined form would necessarily include finesse. But in fact, and this is borne out by the technology used for the rapid construction of modern buildings, what machine production generates is an economical form of 'good-enough production'. It does not often deliver the quality of high finesse, that special aesthetic finish that we want to call precious. In industry 'the best is the enemy of the good'.

Only in art can modernism's perfection usually be afforded and created. Jewelers have a heightened sense of 'the precious'; it is a part of their job, and when jewelers turn to sculpture or to public art or to 'useless architec-ture', as in Bury's case, then they contribute a dimension that other sculptors with different routes of learning have neglected or forgotten: the dimension of the precious.

One of the differences between American and European jewelry is alleged to centre upon the different attitude towards jewelry as design and jewelry as art that exists between the two continents. For example, Paley's approach fits a concept of jewelry as art – where much of the discovery is in the process. Whereas, an approach, such as that of Bury or Van Leersum, that works out the ideas thoroughly in drawings (or even, as we have seen, mathematical sequences) is characterized as design.

The debate about whether or not 'design' or 'art' is the appropriate approach for jewelry must strike any intelli-gent lay reader as arcane – or even pointless, especially when in reality the definitions of both approaches are so fluid. But debate holds some interest for two reasons, both of which relate to the very contemporary challenge or promise held by computer-aided design and computer-aided manufacture (CAD-CAM). First, it seems reasonable to assume that had CAD-CAM been available in the 1960s and 1970s to people such as Van Leersum and Bakker then they would have used it. They could have worked out their series on computer and then have had it made by machine. That they would have done this is implicit in the processes they used and the ways in which they worked: they worked in series solving formal problems generated through simple arithmetic and geometry. It is work that is almost ideal for the computer and computer-directed milling-machines.

In fact, David Watkins experimented with a computer in 1973. He was using a crude, early expert system: 'I developed a grammar of form and a syntax and ran it through the computer. It was done numerically. I had to translate figures into shapes and the shapes into objects.'

However, in those days computer-aided design/computer-aided manufacture was a science-fiction fantasy; now in the mid-1990s it is becoming an affordable reality for those who want it. The American artist Stanley Lechztin, is already producing formal abstract jewelry using CAD-CAM technology. Or rather he has produced a lot of 'virtual' jewelry – it exists in fully rendered forms in three dimensions in 'computer space', and he is working on computer-directed milling-machine techniques, as well as some further advances in automated rapid prototyping techniques that will enable his virtual wares to become real wares.

Lechztin is interesting both for his CAD-CAM approach, and for his earlier work, which was also technology-led and which put him at the forefront of American new jewelry throughout the 1960s and 1970s (although he had few imitators). He is not a figurative jeweler, he is an abstractionist, and, oddly enough because even as recently as the late 1980s no one would

have conceded the following to be true, Lechztin is as much a modernist as any of the most formal of formal Dutch jewelry designers. For, if one considers that one of the elements in Dutch jewelry design has been a nascent love affair with the notion of technology and machine production, then Lechztin is an example to them all: his work has been consistently led by technology. The forms Lechztin created in his first generation of work (from the mid-1960s to the mid-1980s) were barely hand-crafted; he grew them in acid baths by the process of electroforming. This technology resulted in work that is as far removed from the Dutch aesthetic as is possible: it is highly organic in form, with strong hints of Art Nouveau and the baroque. It is luxurious in its use of precious materials and it is large, opulent, showy and just about everything a young Van Leersum or Bakker would have opposed.

Electroforming produces or reproduces metallic objects by electrodeposition on a matrix. Once the process has been completed, the matrix is removed and a metal shell remains. Lechztin's early preoccupation as a metalsmith in the mid to late 1960s was the lack of dimension, of volume, in traditional jewelry making. He wanted forms with substantial body but without the weight that traditional methods of metal fabrication or casting would produce. Depositing metal on a matrix using the electroforming, electrochemical process enabled Lechztin to 'grow' his jewelry, adding depth and encrustations of metal as needed. The obvious analogy between this electrochemical growth process and the growth of plant, animal forms and geological phenomena, such as stalactites and stalagmites, was important to Lechztin. Complementing his interest in metals, Lechztin also used acrylic resins to create shapes that reciprocate those of his metal forms. The organic, baroque forms, like sea-creatures, that Lechztin generated with this process had no comparison with anything in Europe nor, for that matter, in the USA. He gave it all up in 1987 for the computer.

Lechtzin thinks handwork is nearly dead, made redundant by the computer. He switched technologies because he wants to be economically viable and because he has so many ideas and too little time to 'make' them – consequently he is happy to find a technology in which he can make on computer more quickly than by hand, and with the ability to revise his design efficiently and speedily with greater thoroughness than is practically possible by hand.

What is interesting is that what Lechtzin says in 1995 is what Van Leersum pursued in 1975: 'Once we eliminate the overwhelming physical investment [of handwork] we open up the opportunity to continue to explore the permutations of an idea until we have finished with it.' Yet what is also interesting is that Lechtzin's forms have changed radically. This is because they are determined by the technology. He has swapped organic growth for Euclidean geometry because the CAD-CAM technology favours the one and not the other (although this may change as CAD-CAM becomes more sophisticated).

In so far as a substantial part of the new jewelry movement, at least in Europe, has argued consistently that it is the idea that counts, that the craft is merely the means of execution, then Lechtzin's philosophy may be the way of the future, a way of producing unique objects in an 'endless stream'.

In Europe the leading exponent of computer-aided design and jewelry is David Watkins, working at the Royal College of Art, London, with postgraduate students. Watkins and his students are exploring the connection between CAD-CAM and craft processes, and in particular the point at which it is necessary for human craftsmanship to intervene. Watkins is trying to understand the 'pull' of the computer, explore the constraints or the lack of them.

Very few of the artists in this book have been as technology orientated as Lechtzin or Watkins; most have preferred to explore their adventures in formal aesthetics by using hand-tool processes – in part because there was no alternative, but also because they enjoyed the labour and because they found the way of designing through making intellectually and emotionally productive. Most of the jewelry that we are concerned with has necessarily been the product of handcraft. Indeed, people have gone out of their way to make an ideology out of workmanship, especially in Germany, less so in the Netherlands where there is no real 'crafts' movement.

The formalist aesthetic in Germany, as already stated, owes much of its particular quality to the craftsmanship that goes into making it. A lot of effort was (and is) expended in making the work, and this effort included a lot of hand-finishing. This leaves its signature of soft precision; which is to say that the forms are refined and often precise, but have a different kind of precision from that produced by the available technology of post-war machined work.

Among the post-war masters of German art-craft metalsmithing are Friedrich Becker (b.Germany 1922), Hermann Jünger and Peter Skubic (b.Yugoslavia 1935). Each has been influential as a teacher. Each believes in the idea of jewelry as an expressive art and has encouraged inventiveness. Much of the work that resulted from the generation of jewelers who enjoyed such distinguished tutelage was abstract and simple in its geometry: an artistic expression of the then-dominant (West) German aesthetic in industrial design. There is also a practical, economic aspect to this choice of form. Given that gold and silversmithing is labour intensive, and that this generation of jewelers wanted to work for themselves as individual artists (they were not going to employ teams of fabricators to help them), then the forms were almost bound to be fairly simple.

Among the German 'abstractionist' jewelers who appeared in the 1970s and early 80s are: Klaus Arck (b.Germany 1956) who trained in Pforzheim and later in Cologne under Peter Skubic; Axel Baumgartel (b.Germany 1956), another of Skubic's pupils; Georg Dobler (b.Germany 1952); Gabriele Dziuba (b.Germany 1951), a pupil of Herman Jünger; and Therese Hilbert, (b.Germany 1948), another of Jünger's pupils.

figuration and meaning

Just as it is tempting but wrong to characterize north-west European jewelry as 'abstract', it is wrong to over-generalize about North American jewelry and see it as wholly concerned with figuration and narrative. There are several notable American artists, including Lisa Gralnick, Mary Lee Hu (b.USA 1943), Marjorie Schick (b.USA 1941) and Helen Shirk (b.USA 1942), who confound that proposition through the quality of their abstract compositions. Nevertheless, one of the strengths of North American jewelry during our period has been its narrative and figurative jewelry – unsurprising given that America is an image-drenched society, and has been since the 1930s. The key narrative jewelers in the USA grew up with billboards and Disney.

There has been, in the work of J. Fred Woell (b.USA 1934), Ron Ho (b.Hawaii 1937), Don Tompkins (b.USA, 1933–82) and his sister Merrily Tompkins, Ken Cory, and Les LePere (b.USA 1946) in his collaboration with Cory as the Pencil Brothers, or Richard Mawdsley, a richness of storytelling and commentary, and an emotional inter-action with day-to-day American culture. Some of the work is deliberately vulgar – not coolly ironic, but an upswell of belly laughs. The content of new American jewelry, including and especially that of Woell and Don

Tompkins, was both personal and public: public in that by incorporating photographs and pieces of advertising or pieces of found manufactured objects, as in Woell's brooch *Come Alive, You're in the Pepsi Generation*, 1966, (discussed in Chapter 4), the content could be a shared experience.

To state that a section of American jewelry is a form of new folk art is, in some company, to consign the work to the second division. But in the jewelry of Don Tompkins, Merrily Tompkins, Woell and Cory there is an approach to contemporary culture that does not exist in Europe, and that is as conceptually interesting as it is emotionally affecting.

For example, between 1971 and 1973 Don Tompkins produced a series of commemorative 'medals', pendants celebrating events in American history or culture, or satirizing heroes or icons. Tompkins and his friends, such as Ken Cory, made intelligent folk art, not irony, not postmodernism, not punk. In 1972 Tompkins produced a medal called *Nixon*; it includes a photograph of a Kent State University student grieving over the deaths of students shot by the National Guard and a figure of Mickey Mouse with his hands raised, mocking Nixon's characteristic gesture of victory. Another medal marks the death of

Janis Joplin, a pearl tear rolling from her eye. Others commemorate different kinds of heroes and heroines – Minnesota Fats, the famous snooker player; Jackson Pollock, who was the James Dean of American art, several artists having paid homage to him in their work.

The medals or pendants are seriously meant. That does not mean that they are ponderous but that they are sincere. They are an expression, his expression, of what he felt was important; they are not making a statement about art. This kind of sincerity, this desire to make a full-blooded response to what is going on in society is like an act of charity. Tompkins made his art about people whom he applauded (and a few whom he did not), and did it for the sake of what he felt, not for its contribution to the art movement.

Moreover, the notion of wanting to honour your heroes through your art is also a generous idea. It is far removed from the selfconscious manoeuvrings that we expect of those seeking success in the 'art' world. The literalness of the work, with its mixture of strong images and words, puts it into the context of American graphics and into the context of popular culture generally: Tompkins's work is like powerful but simple song lyrics that scan and rhyme and talk about everyday emotions.

The use of newspaper, magazine or home photographs of famous people, friends or families, is quite widespread in American jewelry throughout our period, although not all American artists who began their careers with figurative imagery have continued with it. Eleanor Moty (b.USA 1945), a former student of Stanley Lechtzin, is an example. Since the 1980s she has produced jewelry whose starting-point is the geometry of quartz crystals, but in the late 1960s and early 1970s she helped to pioneer techniques in photofabrication. In 1971, in *Crafts Horizon*, she published an influential article about her technology which she had adopted and adapted from industry. She explained:

The excitement of photofabrication is that the process continues to allow new discoveries. Recently I discovered that a photo image can dictate the form of the metal if the metal itself is initially raised or chased in areas to conform to the image applied afterwards. It is also feasible to photograph the finished object or some part of the object, such as a stone, and apply this image to repeat the form....Patterns that would require intricate piercing techniques can be produced through photofabrication by etching completely through the metal.

The pioneering work of Moty's had significance because it linked technology of the mass production of imagery – the camera – with the fine craft of one-off jewelry production.

In America, however, one strand of figurative art has developed in the new jewelry movement that may not survive into the next century because of the way the moral landscape has changed what is culturally permissible. And that strand concerns the type of work that brings together ideas and images from more than one culture. Figurative jewelry can offend, not because the artist intends an offence, but because certain attitudes towards the making of art are acceptable no longer. This is especially the case with multiculturalism.

William Harper (b.USA 1944), active throughout the 1970s, became especially prominent in the early 1980s with a collection of enamelled jewelry called *Saints, Martyrs and Savages*. Writing in the catalogue to his exhibition at the Kennedy Galleries in New York, 1982, Harper explained that these works were about religion and brought together iconographic images from two religious cultural groups – the Songye tribes of the Congo and medieval Catholicism. Regarding the nature of religious and supernatural ornament he asks:

...At what point does the hope for supernatural protection stop, and the desire for individual adornment begin? Does the contemporary man who wears the large shiny cross or gold/turquoise mezuzah do so to demonstrate his religious beliefs, or to add sex appeal, hence religious motifs as 'disco jewelry'? He is probably doing both. Is he dissimilar from the 'savage' New Guinea tribesmen who lavishly paint their bodies and adorn them further with fresh flora and exotic feathers in order to participate in religious festivals? We might view this as barbarian, as savage. How might they view St Sebastian?

Such questions and the work produced by Harper as a result of his questions are undoubtedly interesting. In the 1990s, however, Harper has found himself under some criticism for his sources of influence. Since the 1980s, the cultural landscape has been changed for jewelry as for all other activities in the West by debates arising from political correctness and multiculturalism.

With the rapid increase in the numbers of people practising art and craft of various kinds, including figurative jewelry, coupled with the use of museums as resources for information and reinforced by back-packing travel and cheap cameras, 'other cultures' became available to artists. But the question that is now asked is what, exactly, has become available? How accessible is other people's art? How well do we understand it? If we do not understand it, should we use it?

The problem has been set out in an article discussing the appreciation of African art, both historical and contemporary in *The Economist*, December 24 1994:

Any well-educated Westerner knows that an owl symbolizes wisdom and an ostrich stupidity; that Apollo personifies beauty, Narcissus vanity and Hercules strength; that a man, a lion, an ox and an eagle represent the evangelists who wrote the first four books of the New Testament. Equivalent knowledge of Africa is more complicated and elusive...

Appropriation of other people's cultures is a live issue for jewelers who take 'other' images and use them to create their own meanings. The issue here is twofold. First, such activity can be described as a form of exploitation. Using other people's imagery to one's own ends, which may not be in harmony with that culture, can be regarded as a dubious activity. After all, multinational corporations, including Disney, spend large amounts of money and employ teams of lawyers to protect the use of their logos and visual identities, while the family estates of famous, and not-so-famous artists, police the use of their artworks with vigour. So why do we not accord the same protection to other cultures?

Secondly, the appropriation of the imagery of other cultures can be a path to creating kitsch – at least that was what the American critic Clement Greenberg thought when he wrote his famous essay 'Avant Garde and Kitsch'.

The precondition for kitsch, a condition without which kitsch would be impossible, is the availability close at hand of a fully matured cultural tradition, whose discoveries, acquisitions, and perfected self-consciousness kitsch can exploit for its own ends. It borrows from it devices, tricks, stratagems, rules of thumb, themes, converts them into a system, and discards the rest.

When he wrote this in 1939, the notion of a culture close at hand was very different. Today, in a sense, all cultures are close at hand because travel and the media make them so: all cultures are candidates for kitsch. The process of taking themes and rules of thumb from other traditions is exactly what happens in most cases where Westerners, including the politically and culturally aware, use the art of other cultures to kickstart their own. It is doubtful whether multiculturalism can ever be as honest and as pure as liberal protagonists would wish; the only way to understand a culture is to be born in it.

With multiculturalism, metalsmithing and jewelry, like all the arts, has to watch its behaviour. It is noticeable how the very language used by metalsmiths (as with everyone) is obliged to change in the face of new attitudes of cultural and political awareness. Politically correct manners would not now allow Olaf Skoogfors to say. 'I have been interested in the strength/vitality of barbaric, primitive and peasant design…' Had Skoogfors not died so young, he might now have adopted the sense, as well as the sensibility, of informed multiculturalism, although one person's 'appropriation' may be another's homage or, to put it another way, 'I quote, you borrow, he appropriates.'

The appropriation of images within one's own culture is sometimes less contentious, although, as Chapter 4 discusses, there are examples, such as the Christian cross, whose non-religious or sceptical use in art can cause considerable offence. What is especially interesting, particularly bearing in mind Margaret West's phrase 'pourer-in of meaning', is how a piece of jewelry, with political comment as a part of its intent, can go on accruing meaning far beyond the artist's dreams.

Otto Künzli (b.Switzerland 1948) has created at least one such object; it is not illustrated in this book, but it is hoped that the following description makes the point clear. Among a number of pieces he began producing in the 1980s that were comments on the United States was a brooch called *M-16* – it is interesting that Europeans so freely make reference in their art to the excesses of the USA, but American artists do not seem to return the compliment. The *M-16* brooch consists of a piece of fabric from the American flag sandwiched between two discs of stainless steel. The flag can be seen through the hole piercing the steel discs. The hole is 5.56 mm wide – the calibre of the M-16 assault rifle used by the US Army in Vietnam.

Such a piece of work is undoubtedly clever and intellectually elegant. There are many American families for whom this brooch can raise the most complex and subtle issues because they will know, through the participation in the war of their sons, brothers, husbands and fathers, that the M-16 was a military scandal. The original version of this weapon was, apparently, superb but, allegedly, the Army Ordnance Corps insisted on modifications that turned it into a liability – it kept jamming. According to the American journalist James Fallows, writing in *The National Defense* in 1981, 'American troops in Vietnam were equipped with a rifle their superiors knew would fail when put to the test.' Soldiers started writing home complaining about the gun, and questions were raised in Congress. Many American soldiers lost their lives, it has been suggested, because this rifle jammed too often.

For anyone then who knows about this background, the M-16 brooch means something entirely different from that which a European liberal observer, hostile to the United States but ignorant of the M-16 scandal, might infer. Certainly it adds another dimension to the brooch's general metaphorical content, which is that Vietnam was a self-inflicted wound.

It does, however, add substance to the proposition by Klaus Ottman (curator of exhibitions at the Zilkha Gallery, Connecticut) writing in 1992, that Künzli is less concerned with meaning than with how meaning is produced. Ottman argues that Künzli's work (or anyone's for that matter) requires the participation of others. It would not even matter if Künzli himself was unaware of the history of the M-16. The object will gain meaning by eventually making contact with those who know of its history. This is one of the most powerful aspects of art jewelry. Given its durability, the art object will go on acquiring and shedding meaning. Sometimes the congruence of object and owner/wearer will be intensely powerful, at other times it will be meaningless.

The question of how meaning is produced in jewelry is a vexed one, but it is fundamental to any activity that claims its status as art. One of the most important definitions of art in Western culture is that art conveys meanings and stimulates emotion alongside or instead of other functions, such as being decorative. Jewelers as artists may be pourers-in of meaning, but meaning is a public, not a private affair, and the challenge that artist jewelers have always to consider (although they may choose to ignore it, and some do) is to what degree they think other people can understand their work. Many jewelers, like many other artists, are happy to leave the individual viewer or purchaser to decide on the meaning, worth or value of the work they produce. Others consider that such relativism is the last bolthole of the scoundrel, and try hard to fix their metaphors and symbolism firmly in the images they use and the titles with which they name their work.

Yet, however hard we try to fix meanings in our work, our efforts are provisional. History will interpret whatever we claim to be doing or saying. Moreover, the work shown here is too recent for an overview of its historical context. We are aware that our judgments are speculative, and what follows is a series of well-intended observations.

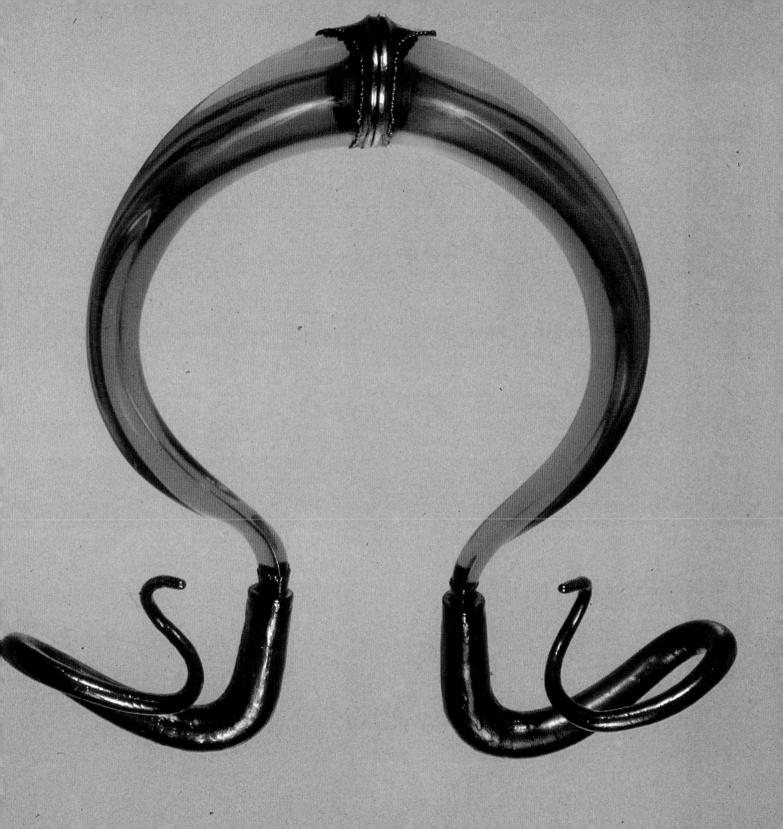

Previous page
Stanley Lechtzin
American

Torque. 1971
Silver, polyester resin;
electroformed
23.5 x 24.5 x 5.7 cm

Stanley Lechtzin
American

Brooch. 1969
Gold-plated silver, mica,
baroque pearls; electroformed
10.5 x 9.5 x 5 cm

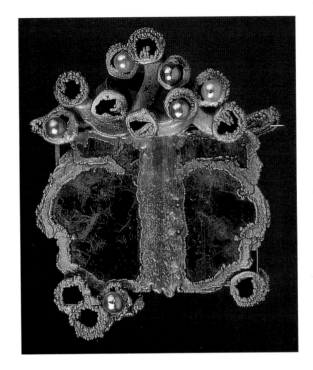

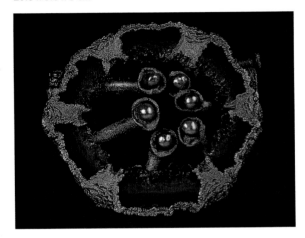

Brooch. 1967
Gold-plated silver, amethyst,
blue baroque pearls;
electroformed
9 x 11 x 2.5 cm

Brooch. 1967
14k gold, quartz,
baroque pearls; electroformed
8.4 x 7.4 x 3.5 cm

Stanley Lechtzin
American

Brooch. *c.*1967
Gold-plated silver, quartz,
watermelon tourmalines;
electroformed
10 x 13 x 5 cm

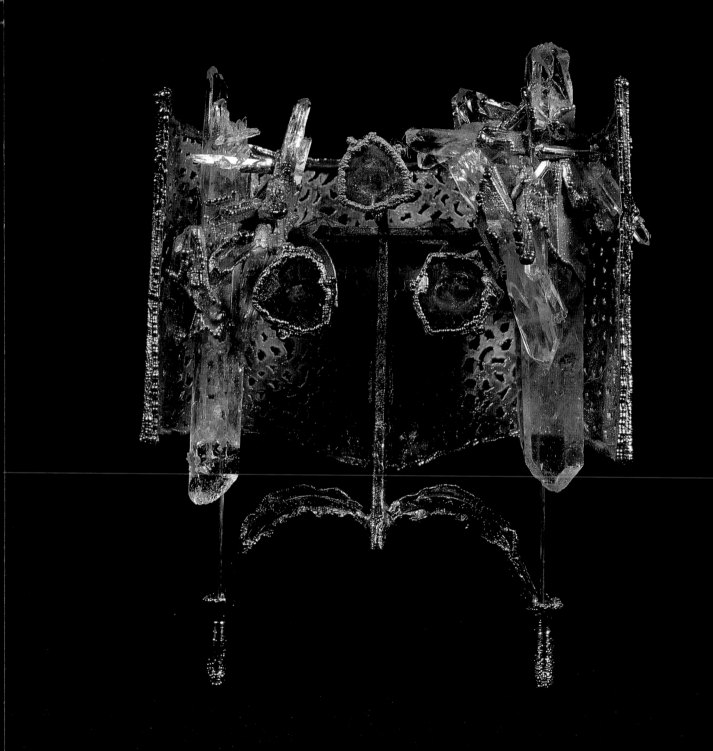

Olaf Skoogfors
American

Brooch. 1966
Gold-plated silver,
round pearls, Biwa pearls; cast
5 x 5.2 cm

Brooch. 1973
Gold-plated silver,
blue baroque pearl
6.5 x 5.8 cm

Brooch. 1970
Gold-plated silver, ivory
9.4 x 5.7 cm

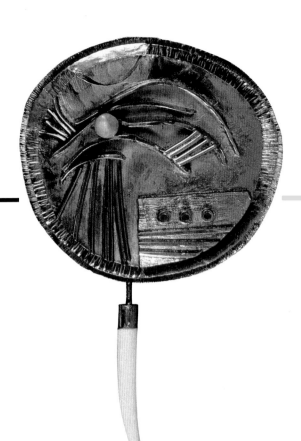

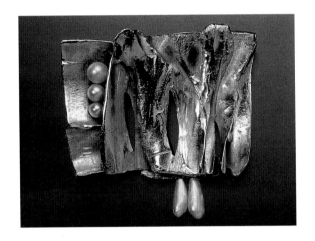

Olaf Skoogfors
American

Dimsdale Machine
Brooch. 1969
Gold-plated silver, moonstone
5.2 x 5.7 cm
Collection Matthew J.W. Drutt, USA

Pendant, detail. 1972
Silver, brass, copper, ivory
24 x 14.5 cm

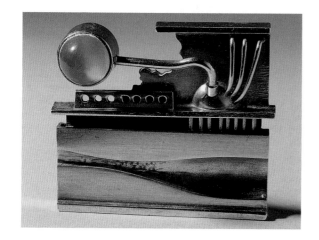

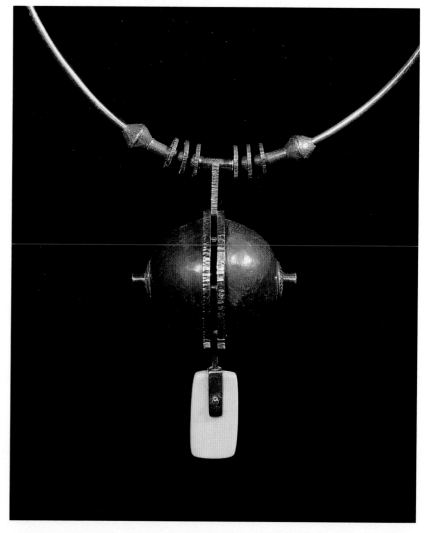

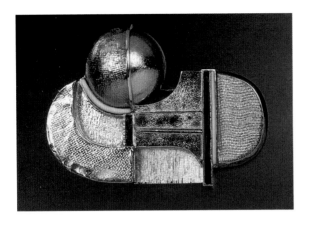

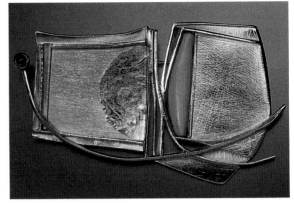

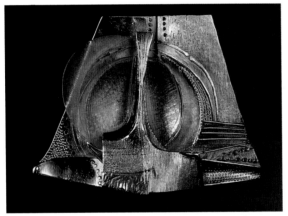

Toni Goessler-Snyder
German, active USA

Brooch. 1974
18, 24k gold, silver,
amine-catalysed resin, ivory
5.1 x 7.3 cm

Brooch/pendant. 1974
Gold, silver, Lucite
7 x 9.1 cm

Brooch/pendant, 1975
24k gold, silver,
amine-catalysed resin
6.4 x 7 cm

Brooch/pendant. 1979
Silver, 24k gold, ivory,
pink tourmaline
8.9 x 5 cm

Toni Goessler-Snyder
German, active USA

Bracelet, 1975
24k gold leaf, Lucite
4.2 x 8 x 6 cm

Albert Paley
American

Fibula
Brooch. 1969
Gold, silver, pearls,
labradorite
15.7 x 9 cm

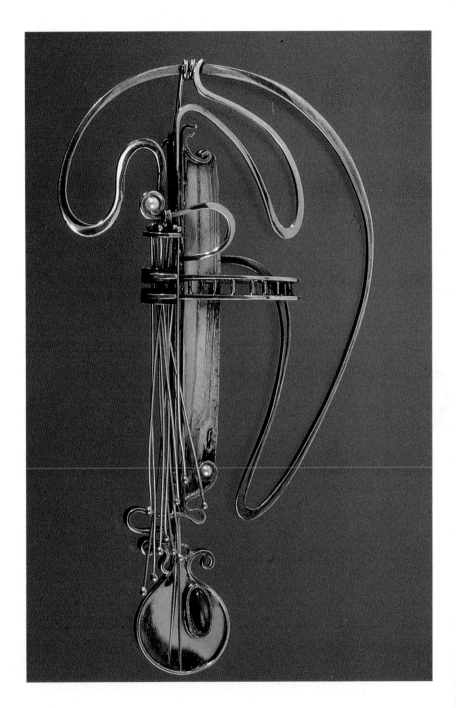

Albert Paley
American

Double Fibula
Brooch. 1968
Gold, silver, bronze, pearls,
moonstones, labradorite
13.7 x 15 cm

Albert Paley
American

Brooch. 1971
Gold, silver,
Delrin, tourmalines,
synthetic sapphires
21.5 x 15.5 cm

Eleanor Moty
American

Cameo
Brooch. 1970
Silver, 14k gold, copper,
agate; photo-electroplated,
electroformed
6.8 x 10.3 cm

Box Bracelet
1969
14k gold, silver,
phantom quartz
7 x 6 x 7 cm

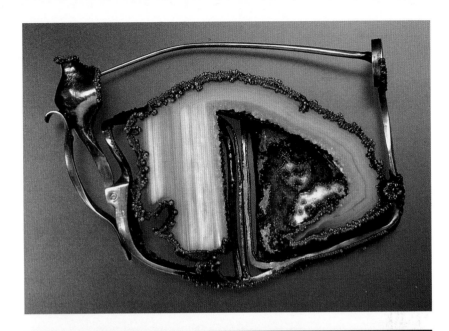

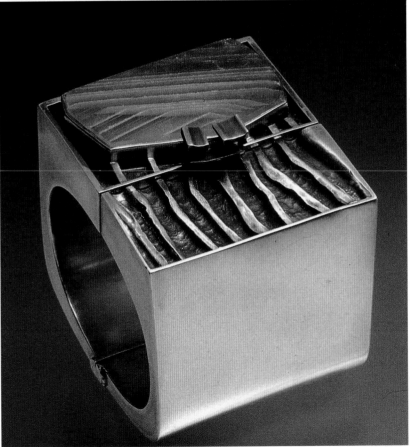

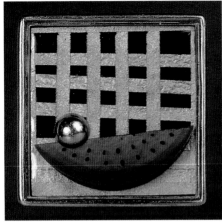

Robin Quigley
American

Brooch. 1982
Silver, 14k gold, tourmaline, carnelian
5.5 x 5.3 cm

Watermelon Pin #2
1977
Silver, gold, gold leaf, epoxy resin
4.7 x 4.7 cm

Fringe Bracelet
1983
Pewter, copper, brass alloys
10.5 x 8.5 cm, fringe 3.8 cm

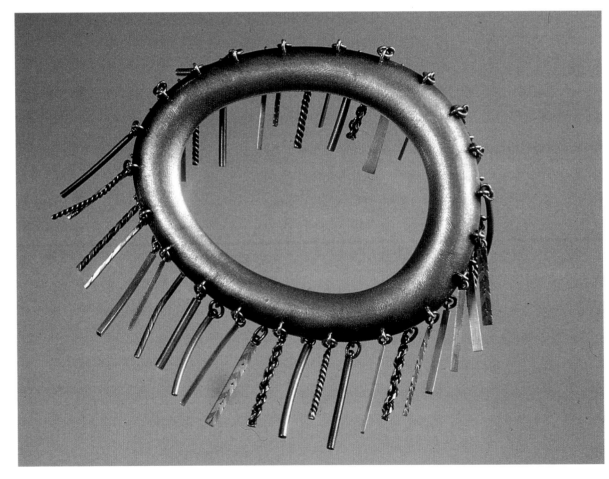

Robin Quigley
American

Triangular Pin/Pendant #1
1978
14k gold, silver, acrylic,
epoxy resin, gold leaf
Neckpiece 19 cm
Pin 6.2 x 7.5 x 2 cm

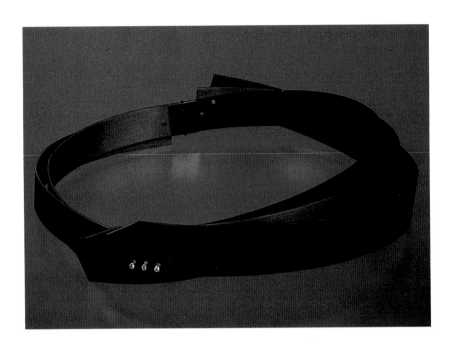

David Tisdale
American

Necklace. 1981
Anodized aluminium,
silver, diamonds
12 x 17.5 cm

Suzan Rezac
Swiss, active USA

Bracelet. 1983
Silver, 18k gold, nickel silver,
copper, shakudo
14 dia x 2.4 cm

Suzan Rezac
Swiss, active USA

Brooch. 1983
Silver, 18k gold
5.3 dia x 0.9 cm

Necklace. 1981
Gold-plated and silver-plated
brass, steel, pewter,
soapstone
48 x 2.3 cm

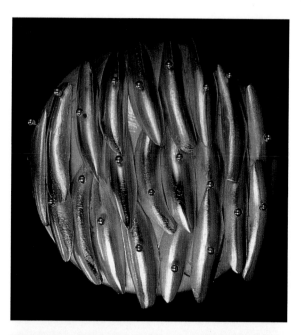

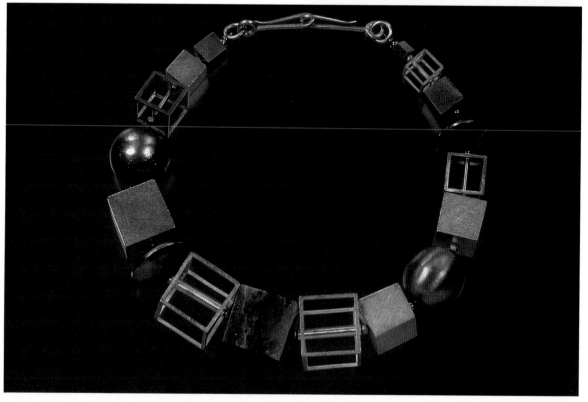

Walter Kelley Morris
American

Flasher
Brooch. 1975-76
Acrylic, silver,
copper, agate
17 x 8 x 3.5 cm

Amy Buckingham-Flammang
American

Brooch. 1973
Gold-plated bronze, Lexan
7.4 x 9.1 cm

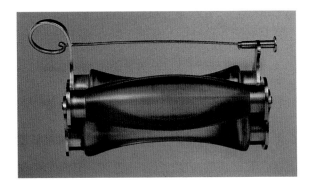

Richard H. Reinhardt
American

Torque. 1980
Silver
19 dia x 3.5 cm

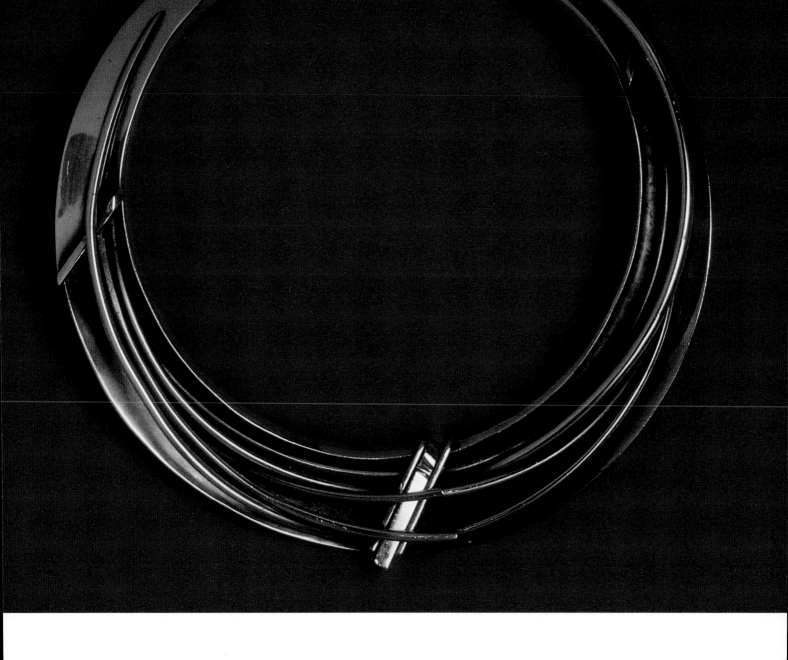

Frans van Nieuwenborg/Martijn Wegman
Dutch

Closed Neck-Pipe
Neckpiece. 1972
Aluminium, elastic, leather case;
multiple edition
16 cm dia

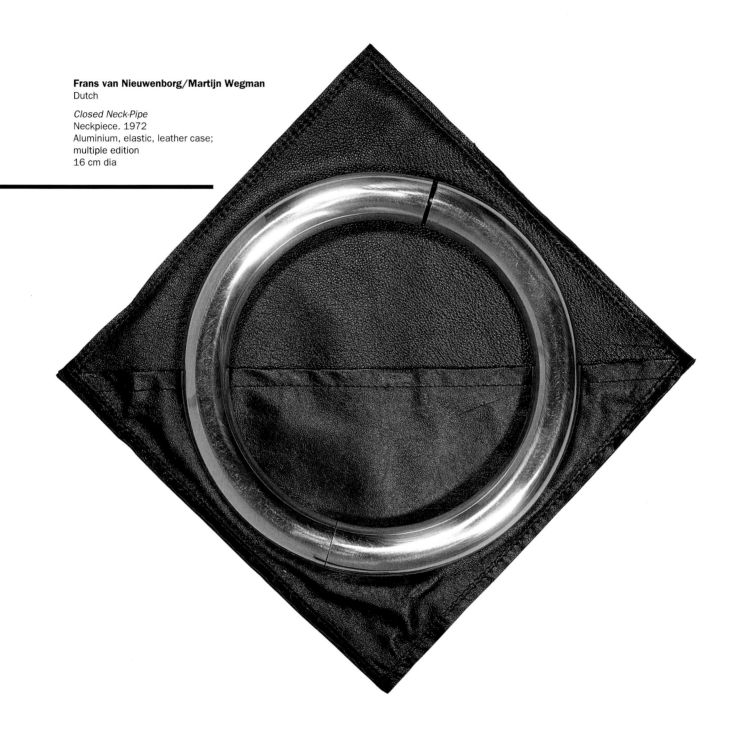

Gary S. Griffin
American

Neckpiece. 1976
Aluminium, brass,
acrylic, plastic, nylon
39 x 23.4 cm

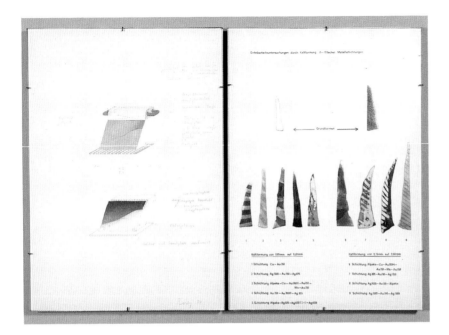

Claus Bury
German

Brooch. 1974
Silver, brass, copper,
gold alloys
5.7 x 8.5 cm

Two studies for brooch
Watercolour, pen and ink
Metal research for brooch,
Degussa Factory, Germany
Brooch on mount
1974

Claus Bury
German

Ring. 1972
Gold, acrylic
4.7 x 3.1 cm

Brooch. 1977
Silver, gold,
copper alloys
5 x 4.5 cm

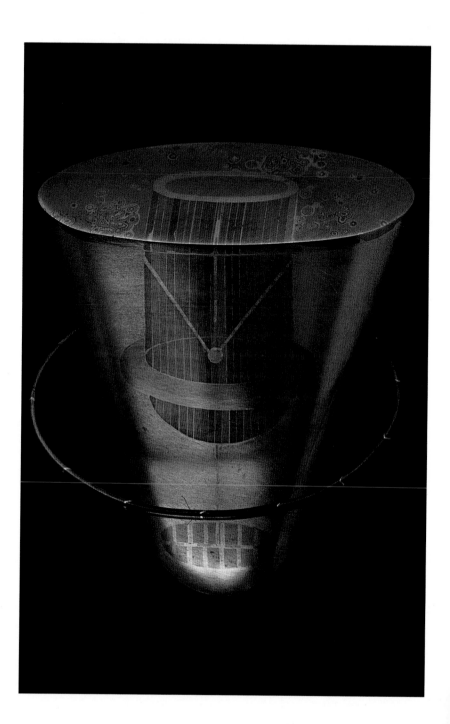

Max Fröhlich
Swiss

Belt Buckle. 1979-80
Silver; Ashanti-cast
5.7 x 5.5 cm

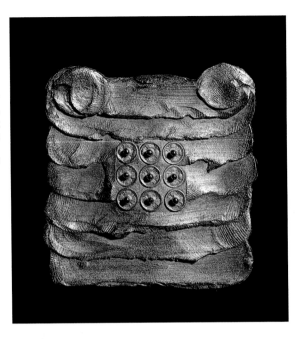

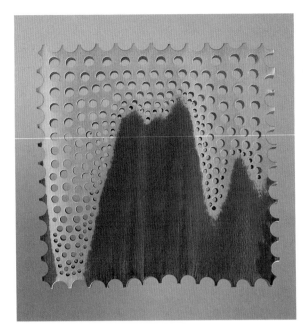

Pavel Opočenský
Czech, active USA 1982-90

Brooch. 1989-90
ColorCore
8.4 x 8.4 x 1.3 cm

Max Fröhlich
Swiss

Bijou Barbare
Bracelet and Ring. 1984
Silver alloy
Bracelet 7.6 dia x 3.8 cm
Ring 3.4 x 3.4 x 3 cm

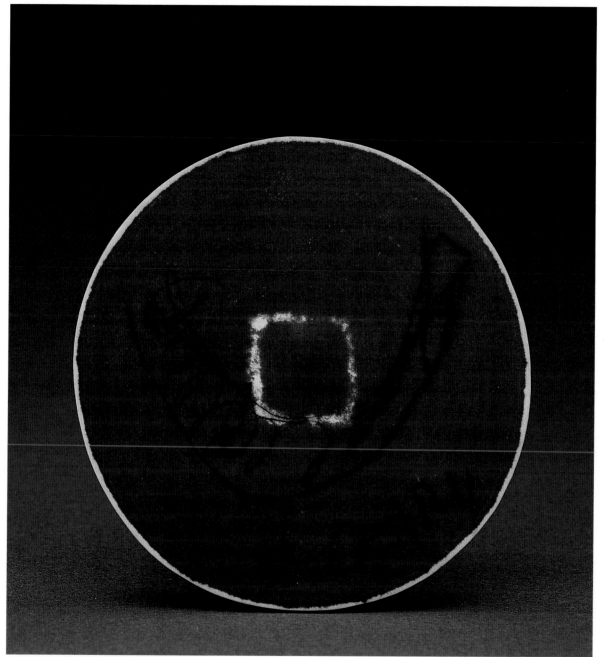

Pavel Opočenský
Czech, active USA 1982-90

Brooch. 1990
ColorCore; ink drawing by
Frank Gehry
10.2 cm dia

Helen Shirk
American

Bracelet. 1982
Silver, titanium
7 dia x 2.8 cm

Brooch. 1982
Silver, gold, titanium
8.5 x 3.2 x 1.5 cm

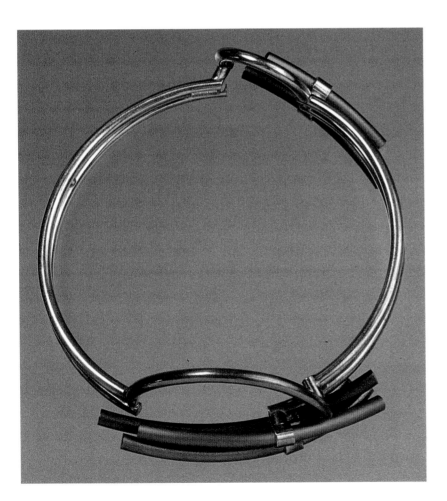

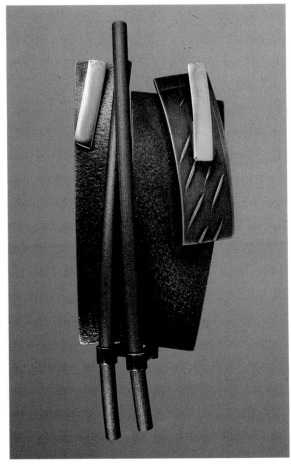

Helen Shirk
American

Brooch. 1981
Silver, titanium
10 cm x 3.8

Brooch. 1978
Sterling silver, onyx
17.8 x 5.1 cm

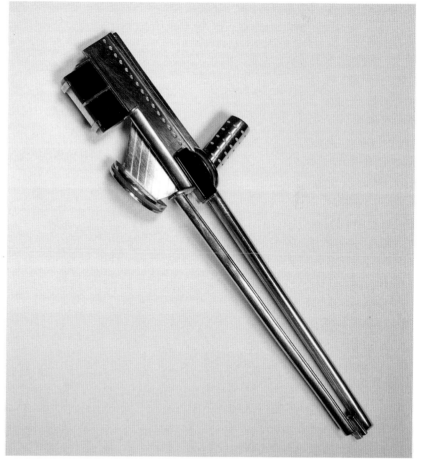

Hans Appenzeller
Dutch

Bracelets *#1, #2* and *#3. c.*1981
#1 Corian, rubber; limited edition.
#2 and *#3* Corian; limited edition
10 dia x 3 cm, 10.5 dia x 3.4 cm,
10 dia x 2 cm

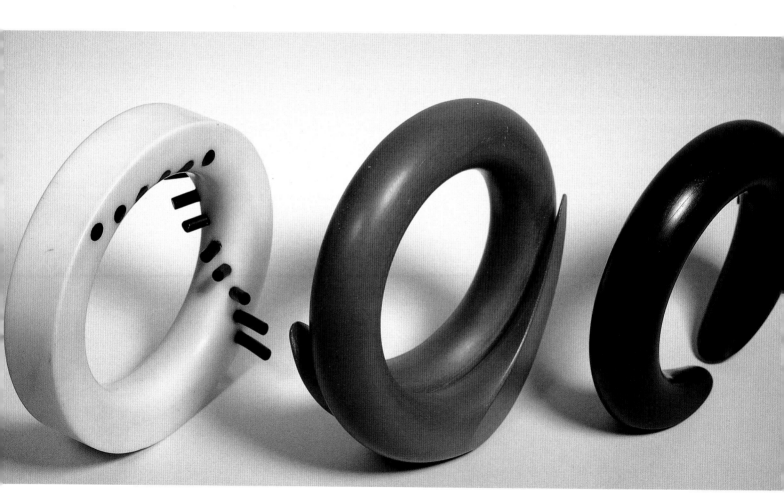

Peter Blodgett
American

Bracelet. 1976
Black plated nickel silver,
silver-plated brass, acrylic
6.7 x 6.8 x 5.2 cm

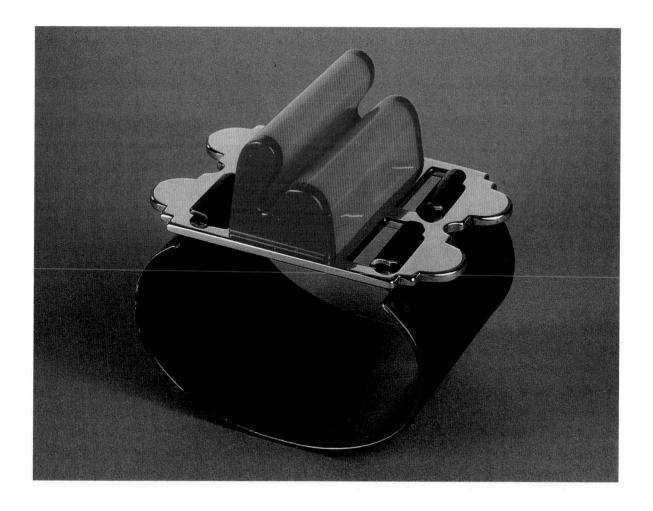

Joke van Ommen
Dutch, active USA

Pin. 1980
Titanium, silver
6 cm dia

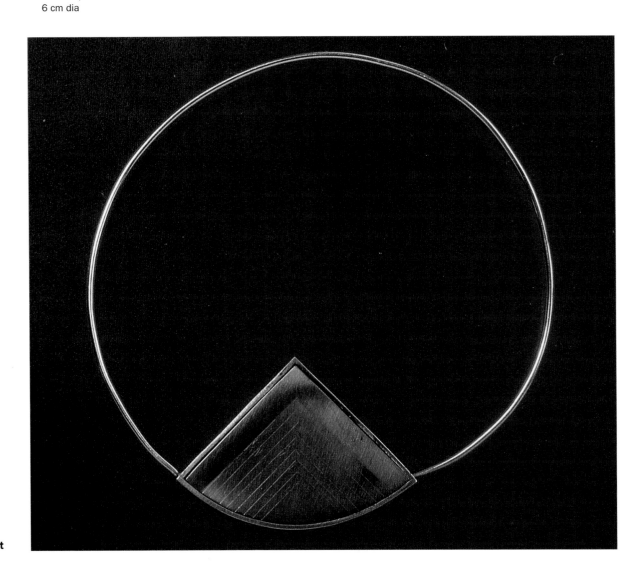

Emmy van Leersum
Dutch

Bracelet. 1982
Steel, paint, limited edition
11 dia x 8 cm

Bracelet. 1974
Stainless steel
6 dia x 6.5 cm

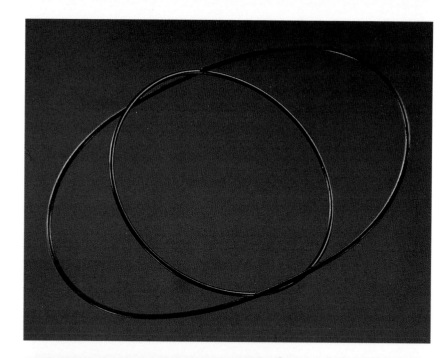

Earl Pardon
American

Brooches #1353 and #1365. *c.*1988
#1353 sterling silver, 14k gold, enamel, amethyst
#1365 sterling silver, 14k gold, enamel, mother-of-pearl,
amethyst, peridot
1.3 x 13.3 cm, 4.5 x 5.7 cm

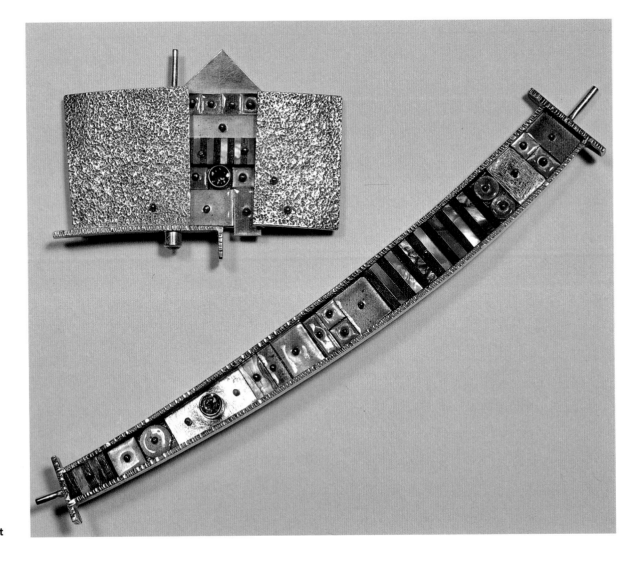

Edward de Large
British, active USA/England

Brooch. 1982
Silver, titanium; electro-coloured
5.7 x 5.7 cm

Edward de Large
British, active USA/England

Brooch. 1982
Silver, titanium;
electro-coloured
5.7 x 5.7 cm

Overleaf
Ron Ho
American

Dog Stars
Pendant, detail. 1985
African gold weight,
bronze Afghan fragment,
sterling silver,
1930 reproduction of
pre-Columbian dog beads
25.4 x 15.2 x 2.5 cm

2 scale, form and content

2 scale, form and content

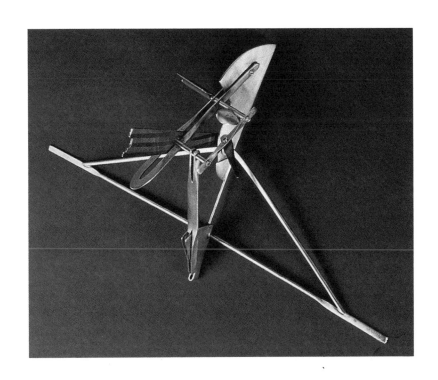

2 scale, form and content

2 scale, form and content

Previous page
Deganit Schocken
Israeli

Brooch. 1987
Silver, copper
10 x 15.5 x 4 cm
Private collection

We write in this chapter of jewelry and form rather than sculpture because there is no agreement among jewelry artists that jewelry is 'sculpture'. Indeed, the word 'sculpture', like 'skill' or 'craft' or 'statement', is a word guaranteed to provoke an argument among jewelers. For whatever reason, we in the West are not inclined to regard objects below a certain size as sculptures, but as ornaments, prototypes or models. There is no conspiracy about this. It is not that the key curators or critics in the art world have decided, out of prejudice against jewelry (or ceramics for that matter), to pull rank by saying that only objects of a certain size can be regarded as sculpture; practically everyone views small artefacts in a different way from things that are large. They are different and more modest, intimate, domestic.

This would cause jewelers no problem except for the fact that the term 'sculpture', like art, has an honorific value which ornament does not. It is so tempting for ambitious jewelry artists to take the word 'sculpture' and apply it to their work, and thereby borrow its status. But this issue over status is a trivial matter compared with the direct, aesthetic consequences of size and scale. The size of an object has a direct effect upon its aesthetic ordering

and detailing. A large sculpture is not an inflated small sculpture. The design process of a large sculpture can involve the making of small models, but these small models are conceived in terms of their future large-scale development.

Jamie Bennett (b.USA 1948) wrote in a foreword to an exhibition catalogue *Other Voices*, 1991: 'To understand what is full scale when the object is the size of an earring is to understand jewelry. On the other hand to realize a form in a sculptural context, is a totally different sensibility.' The phrase 'totally different' is, perhaps, an exaggeration. Artists such as Anton Cepka , David Watkins and Bruno Martinazzi, for example, work in both small and large scale, and to deny that their large works are sculpture or that there are substantial links between the jewelry and the sculptures produced by them would seem perverse. Nevertheless, the point Bennett is making emphasizes the question of scale and its defining effects upon the aesthetic decisions involved.

Jamie Bennett's point about 'the sculptural context' is important. Most sculptors think of a setting for their work. It might be a city square, the foyer of a large building, or the interior of a home. Whatever the location, the conventional sculptor is working in the conventional three-dimensional world. The jeweler creates objects for the conventional world, but the convention for objects the size of jewelry is governed by the genre of 'ornament'. What is the difference between an ornament and a sculpture? Is it more than mere convention or semantics? The convention is strong and it is ingrained into the 'tradition' of post-war fine art. Robert Morris (b.1931), the well-known American sculptor, wrote in 1967, 'The size range of useless three-dimensional things is a continuum between the monument and the ornament.'

That term 'continuum' is a warning: some artists might reasonably argue that they are on the continuum at the point where their work is neither ornament nor sculpture but both ornament and sculpture. This is an uncomfortable position because, on the whole, the world likes its definitions tidily logical: either, or, but not both. To be either, or, *and* both may account for the difficulties that people such as art critics, gallery curators and museum directors have with evaluating modern jewelry.

One of those who is at an interesting point on this continuum is Marjorie Schick. She says, 'My work is a sculptural statement which is complete when off the figure,

yet it is constructed and exists because of the human body. I am intrigued by the idea that the human body is capable of carrying large objects both physically and visually.' Her work falls, broadly, into two categories: there are the volumetric papier-mâché pieces and the rather older series of 'stick' constructions. She complicates her position on the continuum still further by adding, 'I refer to the linear constructions as three-dimensional drawings to wear and to the newer works, consisting primarily of planes, as paintings to wear.'

Bennett says that working at the size of an earring is different from working on the scale associated with sculpture. It is true that what works in terms of proportion – whether volumetrically or as planes – in one range of sizes, does not work when merely scaled up to enter another range of sizes. This is where proportion becomes the important issue.

Certain rules of proportion, such as the golden section, seem to hold at most sizes. Giampaolo Babetto (b.Italy 1947) is a jeweler who uses classical rules of proportion to guide the design of his work. He says, 'Supposing a piece is, say, 12cm long, the height should be, say, 3cm. The measures are always in relation to each other, they are not created by chance....I discovered others had used this system, Palladio, for example, in his architecture.'

Many designers, jewelers included, find that, if they are good at creating well-proportioned compositions, the measurements embedded in their designs correspond naturally to golden section proportions. It appears that the ratio 5:8 is one that most human beings, at least in the West, tend to like. Renaissance artists developed the golden section into a science of aesthetics, although like all sciences of aesthetics it palls if followed too rigidly.

But it is not only the relatively straightforward relationship of different sized parts of the forms that are important in achieving the right sense of scale within a piece of jewelry. Other aspects matter as much, if not more, such as giving materials the right scale of texture or finish. Methods of construction have their effect upon the grain and proportion of objects. Hence Bennett is probably right when he yokes *his* rejection of jewelry as sculpture to an insistence on the differences between the making processes of jewelry and the making processes of conventionally sized sculpture.

Bennett also argues about the importance of specific kinds of artistic space:

I see painting and sculpture primarily existing in ideal space (autonomous), that it is not dependent or related to the specific space in which it exists in order to be understood (although there is specific 'site-related' sculpture); whereas jewelry exists primarily in concrete space, it is understood as it relates to the body or to wearing, either conceptually or physically.

Yet some jewelers in effect square the circle between 'ideal' and 'concrete' space without becoming sculptors and by keeping faith with the function of wearability. Wendy Ramshaw (b.UK 1939) is one such example. She has worked in most materials but has always worked with gold and silver. She has also produced art for public places, including fast-food restaurants, designed batch-produced jewelry for the British Museum in London to sell, and worked with non-jewelry companies, such as the famous British ceramics firm Wedgwood.

She is particularly well known for her sets of rings. She had introduced this idea into her work in 1967. The sets were made up of many rings, from two to as many as twenty, with the idea that the wearer could choose to wear some or all of the rings, some with stones and others not. Although the ring-sets were presented as groups of works, some potential buyers wanted one or two rings rather than the set, not recognizing that the 'the group' was 'the object', so she began exhibiting each group of rings on Perspex stands. By 1970 the stands themselves had become more elaborate, and people used them as a means of displaying the rings when they were not being worn.

The idea of putting rings on stands may seem trivial, but it caused a stir in the jewelry world because it was simple, direct and imaginative. It solved the problem of displaying rings in the round – and rings are almost never seen fully in the round, not even when they are being worn – and it also opened the way to new ideas for the combination of rings. The directness of Wendy Ramshaw's invention for the viewing of jewelry as an art off the body has not been bettered.

A rather different challenge from Jamie Bennett's argument is provided by the work of Deganit Schocken (b.Israel 1947) who thinks in terms of her jewelry as small sculptures and as small 'linear machines', and, at the same time, says that the way they are worn is also very important. The near-mechanical movements she introduces into some of her works allow you to play with them – extending or reconfiguring them. She said: '…Movement plays an important part, a movement which gives the brooch a life of its own even when not being worn on a piece of clothing as a brooch but when being held in one's hands as a play object or when being exhibited as a miniature sculpture.' It is not jewelry as such that seems to excite her so much as working on a small scale.

Deganit Schocken's education is in large-scale design. She trained as an architect and takes an active interest in her husband's architectural practice. Several of her works have a great deal in common with the paintings and drawings of Zaha Hadid (b.Iraq 1950). Hadid is an architect, most of whose works are on paper. Neither woman knows the other, neither is affected by the work of the other, but the linear, planar and spatial geometries are remarkably similar, although Hadid's aesthetic provenance seems less to do with the Bauhaus and more to do with Russian Constructivism and Suprematism. Both these 'architects' reject bulk. In Hadid's proposal for an opera house in Wales (United Kingdom) – a project which stands some chance of being built – she describes her design as being light and extended and 'like a necklace'.

However, architecture, purely by virtue of its size, is an ostentatious art, and Schocken, who values a combination of smallness, finesse and robustness in her work, also craves secrecy. Hadid does not. Schocken views her work as 'theoretical buildings', much as Hadid's work is often 'theoretical architecture'. Schocken seldom wears her work in public, but she will wear it in private – her work is a little like a private cult.

Architecture is a source of influence for many jewelers interested in the dynamics of form and space. Michael Becker (b.Germany 1958) said in an exhibition catalogue that his collection of brooches in the late 1980s was the result of his interest in classically orientated architecture of both the Renaissance and modern periods. He says, 'The analyses of particular buildings was my point of departure for designing groups of related objects. I developed spatial, three-dimensional brooches based on two-dimensional forms, rhythmical units and principles of arrangement.' And the importance of the technology of jewelry contributing to the scale of the finished work is further underlined by Becker when he explains, 'As a rule the surfaces of the brooches were filed, or if the scored lines should remain visible, sand-papered. I always left the metal surfaces mat in order to give the pieces plasticity.'

When we want to draw attention to an artefact that we believe will not be marginalized by changing fashion, or that we believe has stood 'the test of time', we are happy to use the word 'timeless'. It is a pity that no similar word in English exists for objects that are 'sizeless', for that would describe some of the works in this book, including those by Francesco Pavan (b.Italy 1937). Pavan produces small works in gold and silver that are 'architectural' and absolutely independent of size because their internal proportions and the scale of the textures render them 'sizeless'. They are not miniature versions of anything. They would not change if they were enlarged.

Anton Cepka works on a similar range of scale. His jewelry is delicate, extremely well crafted, and his designs incorporate images from 20th-century technology: there are echoes in his small constructions of space stations, cranes and utilitarian structures such as electricity pylons. The aesthetic which disciplines these references is in part a consequence of Cepka's interest in the Scottish Arts and Crafts imagery as developed by the architect and designer Charles Rennie Mackintosh, and also of his interest in the Russian Constructivists. There is a strong sense, for example, of the Tatlin tower aesthetic in Cepka's pieces.

The visual ideas in Cepka's work are as large as the utilitarian structures to which he makes reference. In other words, he has interpreted the spatial and architectural aspects of these structures and organized them in such a way that they retain the essence of the source material, but are by no means a simple reduction of scale. The proportions, even though they are millimetres and centimetres wide, are such that these literally small and wafer-thin structures have the idea of 'bigness' about them. In Slovakia he is known also for creating large-scale, outdoor structures, including mobiles that catch the wind. These large works may be described as liberating the interests he pursues in his jewelry.

Liberating one's interests through jewelry is what drives some artists to change the size as well as the content of their work. Lisa Gralnick is an example. Although she began by working precious materials she became internationally known during the 1980s for her large, bulky, black acrylic jewelry that was at first reminiscent of ominous objects such as missiles or submarines, although these gave way to objects that were more analogous to everyday industrially designed products or parts of products. Each of these works, because its volume as much as anything else was 'sculptural'. Submarines, missiles, automobile parts and the like are in themselves sculptural, and it is inevitable that works of art that are analogous to them share the same characteristics. Around 1989 she returned to working in gold, and, in particular, began a series of pendants and neckpieces that were based on spools, pulleys and cranks. These were the *Anti-Gravity* neckpieces, and she explained the differences between the acrylic works and the mechanical pieces in an interview in *Metalsmith* magazine in the Summer of 1992:

My black acrylic work was reminiscent of mechanical devices…at the same time I was experimenting with kinetic devices using rubber bands and coat hanger wire and eventually the frozen visual allusion of these black pieces seemed insubstantial and ultimately motivated by a direct, more visceral involvement with an industrial aesthetic.

And so she began producing works that explored the physics of mechanics. 'I have attempted in my pieces to employ simple types of movement or functions that are significant only to the degree to which they invite participation and establish themselves as a bridge: accessible, celebrating, often poetic.'

As far as the content of Lisa Gralnick's work is concerned there is an irony in that the simple mechanisms that she employs metaphorically in her 1990s jewelry are, in a sense, more nostalgic than her acrylic works. For it is the case that much 'mechanical' movement in modern machines is no longer mechanical but electronic. Indeed, Gralnick's acrylic objects of the 1980s, with their mute inexplicability, are the typical black boxes of late 20th-century industrial design which hide the way they work. Because of the microchip, the world no longer works in a way that is as explanatory as clockwork. Nevertheless, it is appropriate that a craftsperson who, after all, battles with the physics of the natural world should herself use physics as a subject. In pursuit of this interest, she has produced objects that, although purposeless, are of the same size as genuinely useful machines. Her art is about the wonder of mechanical principles and the world of cause and effect.

Lisa Gralnick is not alone in her interest in physics, finesse and preciousness as both form and content for jewelry. The development of kinetic jewelry in 1965 by the artist Friedrich Becker who has explained:

My work has consisted of pieces of jewelry which take up, amplify and transform the chance of movements of the wearer into new and differentiated configurations of movement. This is achieved by the use of moving parts, of centric and eccentric, vertical and horizontal bearings, of balances and impulse balls of platinum.

A similar question of scale – and a parallel question of content to that contained in Lisa Gralnick's work – is raised by Eva Eisler. As an adult, Eisler has worked in the USA. The content of her jewelry has certain parallels with that of Gralnick in that she too is dealing with technology. But Eisler's work suggests a sustained ambivalence towards technology. One may be awed by the forms in which technology appears but wary, perhaps fearful, of what that technology can do. One of the ambivalences in a crafted statement about technology is rooted in the very fact that the work is crafted: craft is in the hands and the control of one person, technology is distributed among many people, none of whom has complete control over the outcome. There is a powerful metaphor in jewelry artists making statements by hand about technology and the machine.

The architectural element to Eisler's work seems especially important because once more it demonstrates the irrelevancy of the debate over whether a piece of 'jewelry' can be sculptural or architectonic or not. Her work is very large within itself. You could most easily use these constructions as models for buildings, and, at the enlarged scale of buildings, the tension and harmony of Eisler's spaces and forms would still work. But the obvious advantage, so obvious that we often forget to state it, of exploring architectural concerns in jewelry is that the observer can see the composition of the forms and lines and the interaction of volumes and spaces which are present in the best of modernist architecture, but can seldom be wholly appreciated except from the air. Jewelry does not often reveal an aspect of contemporary visual culture to us. Eisler's work capitalizes on the perspective of small size to reveal the nature of the large-scale aesthetics that dominate our built culture but which is so often not revealed to us simply because we are so small and our buildings are so large.

The connection between jewelry and architecture is one of the constant strands in the development of the new jewelry. Quite apart from the shared subject matter of formalist design and construction, there is a connection in the relationship between design and making. Architectonic jewelry is less dependent upon discoveries through making than some other approaches to jewelry. Obviously the quality of making, the connoisseurship of practical experience revealed in the making or manufacture of a piece of work – whether by Bury, Eisler, Schocken or Cepka – is important, but to a great extent the design process can be separated from the making, as in architecture.

But, above all, what connects a certain approach to metalsmithing with the contemporary technology of architecture is the concept and practice of fabrication. Modern buildings are not built, they are assembled from large prefabricated parts. And fabrication, and the design aesthetic it encourages, is a part of metalsmithing's own history.

The Constructivist aesthetic – the assembling of planes and line in space (as distinct from working solid form) – has been an inspiration to several jewelers who have wanted to include in their work the architectural aspect of using space as well three-dimensionality. One such person is Helen Shirk. The twenty-five-year career of Helen Shirk has fallen into three parts. The work of the first ten years consists of carefully assembled three-dimensional abstract constructions. To some extent her architectonic works of the 1970s seem to anticipate the deconstructionist experiments in architecture of the 1980s. However, in the 1980s, Helen Shirk began producing holloware vessels which, she says, freed her because vessels do not get worn and do not need to function. Shirk was therefore able to follow her ideas even more freely than she had been able to do with her brooches.

In the 1990s her work, using precious metals, consists of compilations of fragments that echo both her deepened

interest in natural forms and the foundations of the abstract, architectonic composition she developed in the 1970s. The constructivist/deconstructivist approach enables jewelers to break the limitations of the small scale without having to build large objects – this is a 'sizelessness' that is elusive.

Some artists have taken the sizelessness inherent in the constructive approach to design and interpreted it in their work by inventing innovative constructional techniques. For example, Liv Blåvarp (b.Norway 1956) employs simple tools to shape the wood she uses into discrete elements; these are then assembled into flexible jewelry. Her forms are carefully worked out from the beginning, the spontaneity comes with their embellishment. She progresses through three stages: making a sketch; shaping a series of wooden elements; colouring and 'glazing' these shapes with layers of colour. The shapes are then strung on flexible thread. The results are a combination of lightweight, hard-surface but soft forms. One may also see in the shapes she creates, and the compositions into which they are combined, hints of Nordic decoration and carving, but these are generalized rather than specific.

Only a few jewelers appear to want to create complex figurative worlds within the scale of ornament. There are good reasons for this, not the least of which is the problem that the creation of miniature tableaux or narratives in which literal and straighforwardly figurative elements dominate means that one is flirting with 'dinkiness': one can end up producing toys. A very few men and women have braved these risks and perhaps the best known of those to have done so is Richard Mawdsley. Here we see the thirty-year career of a man producing elaborate figurative objects in the round, some of which are to be worn. These are no airy artefacts; they give the appearance of solidity, and they have no connection with the Constructivist aesthetic that characterizes the work of Schocken or Cepka. Nowhere in Europe in this period (1960–95) is anyone daring to make anything similar – at least not in professional art jewelry. There may be many individuals like Mawdsley producing complex figurative works in metal but, if so, they are hidden from the art world, lost in the deeply unfashionable (and uncharted) waters of the amateur or hobbyist enthusiast (as so much alternative painting, sculpture, wood carving and crafts probably are hidden). For our purposes in our period Mawdsley is unique.

Mawdsley is greatly skilled, and has a fantastical imagination; he is the creator of miniature worlds. He traces some of the interests that shape his work to time spent as a child on his grandfather's farm where he was engrossed in the machinery, including a pre-World War II harvester. But the content of Mawdsley's work is more literal than, say, Cepka's, which, as we saw is also influenced by an interest in engineering. The content of a Cepka work encourages an emotional response – a vaguely optimistic mixture of nostalgia and futurism: Mawdsley is telling a story in detail.

Take the *The Pequod* pendant (1972) as an example. Mawdsley says:

The Pequod pendant is the last piece in which I made realistic machine parts and the first work in which I attempted to depict other objects realistically using construction technology. This led to the still life pieces which were primarily influenced by the realist painting movement [the photo-realist painting, especially strong in the USA at that time].

But a strong inspiration for making *The Pequod* pendant was found by Mawdsley in the history of metalsmithing itself and especially the manufacture of Renaissance pendants. The particular subject is taken from the novel *Moby*

Dick, a romance of the sea, by Herman Melville. The *Pequod* is the ship in which Captain Ahab and a strange collection of sailors are in pursuit of the cunning and ferocious whale Moby Dick. In the end the whale wins, breaking Ahab's neck and sinking the *Pequod*. Mawdsley says that he had no conscious agenda but it was made when there was 'deep concern morally over the Vietnam war and at the subconscious level the imagery might relate'. A literal interpretation could be that Captain Ahab and his ship represent the United States of America and its allies seeking and failing to destroy the cunning Vietcong.

From a 'sculptural' point of view these objects and others, such as the internationally famous *Feast* bracelet of 1974, are interesting in so far as they are complex objects that work in the round. There is for many of us a fascination, not often admitted in contemporary art circles, for the 'model-maker's' world. The re-creation of tiny worlds, whether they be dolls' houses, model engines or aircraft, is beguiling. Whether this is rooted in a desire to revive the pleasures of childhood (or toyhood), or a more sinister subconscious desire for control, is hard to discover. But a pleasure in the making of small worlds appears to be a widespread human emotion and it is one that jewelry is well placed to serve.

Moreover, Mawdsley's works revive a 'traditional' approach to sculpture inasmuch as they have a clear subject matter relating to their titles. Of particular relevance here, however, are the aspects of construction and scale.

Mawdsley is not interested in surface decoration but in built structures. In an issue of *Perspective* magazine, published by Southern Illinois University at Carbondale where he teaches, Mawdsley explains that he creates works that are 'one of a kind and structural'. He is also concerned to keep the sense of 'preciousness' in the work. It is this, together with the fact that his work has

consistently displayed the sort of attention to detail that we more frequently associate with model makers, that causes Mawdsley's work to create a deep ambivalence in the minds of some contemporary artists and observers. For even if it is to be worn or to be displayed as ornament, it seems unusually large and also unusually clamorous in its claims upon our pictorial imagination. Yet, as 'sculpture', it coincides with very few of the expectations possessed by the contemporary observer of sculpture. After all, in an age which over thirty years has seen the rise of installation art via such phenomena as discard art and Arte Povera, then the very idea that preciousness is a quality worth pursuing in sculpture is subversive.

Figuration on the small scale can be immensely powerful because it can be most unexpected. *Bull Bracelet* by Petra Hartman (b.Netherlands 1960) is an example. It was made to coincide with the 'Expo 92' in Seville, an exhibition which marked Spain's recognition in the European Community and the wider world as a country of contemporary culture and of democratic values. Some people, however, are uneasy with elements of Spanish culture, not least its tradition of bull-fighting. Whether one reads the *Bull Bracelet* as a satire, a comment or just as a piece of decoration, its power as an object comes from the wholly unexpected use of such a massive object as a bull's head as a piece of decoration to be worn on the wrist. The play-off between reality and image, especially the play-off between expectations of size, is full of energy – appropriately so considering the subject matter.

And yet sometimes an image that is the 'right' size can be equally striking, especially when it relates to the human anatomy. Martinazzi's *Aquila* (a brooch based on his 1989 'eye of the eagle' design for Cepka's Ring of Honour) is an excellent example: its vividness is a consequence of its being the 'right' size for an eye. Making it smaller or larger would turn it into a safer object; seen at human size it is more watchful, more appraising, more judgmental.

Within contemporary European figurative jewelry the most unusual 'small worlds' are the Surreal or 'theatre of the absurd' content of the work by the German artist, Manfred Bischoff.

Bischoff is regarded by some as one of the most important jewelry artists to have emerged in the 1980s; he is attractive to those who are sympathetic to metaphysics or who have the capacity to accept such concepts as 'the soul'. And those with such a disposition find that his strange figures and his 'theatre of the absurd' compositions convey a rawness of feeling that they can either recognize in themselves or at least respond to as observers.

Bischoff's figures are usually small, fluid and have the nakedness of new-born rabbits; they also exhibit a liveliness that appears as frantic and directionless as does the activity of a colony of ants, termites, bees or any other animal that is quite 'other' from ourselves. His figures are surrounded by objects that are familiar but that appear senseless because of the unusual or Surreal combinations in which Bischoff places them. And, in this context, it is useful to recall Kiff Slemmons's counsel about the desirability of achieving a definitive rather than an arbitrary image. To some extent, Bischoff wants the uncertainty of what we feel when confronted by arbitrary events to be a part of our response to his work. In his discussions with the Dutch critic Gert Staal and Helen W. Drutt English, it appears that one of the ideas important to Bischoff is that of the difficulty of finding one's place in life.

Apparently Bischoff is not concerned whether or not others can follow him or even whether they should, 'My jewelry has no purpose other than to be there, to exist.' He may be a little disingenuous, however, because he does carefully title his work, and these titles are a way of focusing the viewer's mind on ideas that he wants us to realize. For example, one piece produced in 1992 called *Workingman Hero*, with a skull and a human hand coming out of a wheelbarrow, could be interpreted in a number of ways. According to Bischoff, it is an exposition of the physicality of sex, sexual power, life and optimism – a skull is a sign of life in the Bischoff lexicon of visual images. How so? Because, and this is illustrative of Bischoff's philosophical technique of coming at both questions and facts from behind, if we were to find a skull on the moon, then this might be evidence that at one time a living thing had been on the moon. 'Dead' relics are therefore evidence of life. Other recurring images in Bischoff's work include that of the house, which for him is a universal symbol of 'the mother'.

Bischoff's intriguing and oblique handling of meaning is at the opposite end of the scale from J. Fred Woell, or Don and Merrily Tompkins; between them lies the whole spectrum of symbolic figuration and narration that has evolved within the new jewelry.

One of the aesthetic attributes that fine art has appeared to deal with less and less as the century has progressed is a sense of preciousness. This is significant because in the world of large objects – sculptures, buildings and structures – the one quality that is most often missing is that of acute refinement, of real preciousness. What we tend to find in the world of large objects is a workmanship that is just adequate or good enough. What jewelry brings, albeit on its small scale, to qualities that are sculptural or spatial, is the further quality of preciousness. Yet it is possible that 'preciousness' is one of the most confusing qualities for contemporary artists and art observers. It is doubly confusing in jewelry because there are some materials that are described as precious and others that are not. Essentially what we need to do is to draw a distinction between preciousness defined in terms of monetary value, and preciousness as an aesthetic value. For example, a natural pearl is worth a lot of money and therefore it is precious; but the pearl-like surface you find on the interior of some sea shells is precious in the sense of its delicate colouring, finesse and detailing though it is not worth much financially.

However, there is a complication. One of the reasons why some materials are valuable in money terms is because they are also beautiful – a cut diamond is precious in two senses – aesthetically and as a commodity. But the fact remains that it is in the artist's gift to make financially modest materials into artefacts of beauty, and that one category of beauty is described by the word precious, and entails qualities such as refinement, elegance, smallness, fastidiousness, excellence in complex craftsmanship and also notions of intimacy and particularity.

Another fact, however, relating to materials that are valuable and which we are in the habit of calling precious, such as gold, silver and gemstones, is this: these materials are not 'naturally' precious to us, not even in the monetary sense, for they have to be made precious by the expertise of craftspeople. Gold or silver ore, gemstones and the like do not look much in their natural state. Their preciousness is given to them by the work of industry, craftspeople, artists and designers.

Eugene Michael Pijanowski (b.USA 1938) and Hiroko Sato Pijanowski (b.Japan 1942) have made some of the most beautiful jewelry using paper (and in so doing have perfectly exemplified the thesis of 'the precious' as a quality in jewelry, one that can be separated from monetary value). They provided us with the following statement about their work:

Man is the only creature whose consciousness forces him to confront issues of mortality and the ephemeral and precious nature of life. Through our work we try to reflect, communicate and comment upon these universal themes…in 1984 we began to work with Japanese papercord, or *mizuhiki*, a traditional material developed over two hundred and fifty years ago, Papercord's strength, in spite of its fragility and its threadlike form, are metaphors for life.

The bright metallic colours of these papercord pieces, traditionally associated with Japanese rituals of celebration, also create an illusion similar to the one under which we live a large part of our lives. These colours, combined with exaggerated size and subtly erotic, contemporary forms, create a sense of drama and excitement. The contrasts between this organic material and its artificial metallic colour, and between the traditional applications of papercord and these abstract designs, comment on the evolution of man's position in the universe. We are part of the natural world, and of an historic and cultural world of our own making.

Lisa Gralnick, discussed above, adds a further twist to these ruminations with the following observation (from 'Artists' Statements' included in *Exhibitions in Print* to be published in 1995 by *Metalsmith*):

Sometime in the late 1980s, the German sculptor and installation artist, Reinhard Mucha declared, 'There are no neutral materials,' and, unknowingly, spoke directly to an issue that is of particular interest to the contemporary jeweler and goldsmith. I have, in fact, become obsessed with this notion, and have discovered that the non-neutrality of materials can inherently suggest the non-neutrality of other things, including language, producing, in a manner of speaking, a second or third generation metaphor…

However, the reason why there are no neutral materials is because it is people who make materials what they are: they choose materials for specific properties because they need these properties for particular uses; they learn that certain materials can be worked upon to produce effects that they, and others, gain much pleasure from. Jewelers, of all craftspeople, with the exception of woodworkers, know how much they must bring to a material to make it precious, and also what a range of choices they have over the way a material is used or how it looks. In this sense the preciousness of jewelry is a part of its content.

One of the less obvious aspects about contemporary attitudes towards preciousness is touched upon by Claire Dinsmore (b.USA 1961) in correspondence. She notes that the very concepts that one associates with preciousness (other than financial ones) have been unfashionable for long periods during the history covered by this book. She says: 'I…still cling to Kant's dictum, still tout taboo words such as beauty, quality, sublime…'

Dinsmore has more reason than many to be interested in the multi-layered concept of preciousness, particularly when it is reflected that it is the artist or craftsperson who adds the preciousness to the material and to the work. What if, overnight as it were, this ability is taken away from the craftsperson? She used to produce very precise work; now she does not. This is how she writes of the new direction in her work:

The initial changes were due to physical disabilities acquired as a result of the removal of a large brain tumour. I am right-handed and lost the fine motor movements in my right hand and arm. My work in the past was very architectonic with very clean lines, many right angles and small, fine details. After the tumour I could no longer work like this without spending over half the time on a piece cleaning up and mending my mistakes; the work which I had so greatly loved was now an immense and hazardous chore.

It was the perceptive advice of a colleague, Gary Griffin, that she should accept her condition because 'it's your truth and that's where the art is' that helped her change her work. It has changed from a demonstration of the value of human ability and prowess to an exploration of added value of a more elusive kind. 'The concepts behind the work are now much more spiritual and inward; about feeling and mood. The chief inspiration behind my new work is Mark Rothko.'

Rothko's art, which many people find moving or even 'spiritual', is of a kind that jewelry artists rarely aspire to because it explores preciousness – of feeling in depth – both on the grand scale (long series of large, colour saturated paintings) and in an expressionistic manner. It is not easy to find an analogy in jewelry for either approach. The challenge Dinsmore has accepted (for it was in truth thrust upon her) is a significant one. It is a much more ambitious goal than merely questioning the conventions which shape jewelry; she is seeking to take jewelry into the high game, exploring the 'spiritual' aspect of preciousness, something that most contemporary artists dare not consider.

Certain assumptions are often made, however, regarding the relationship between notions of 'the spiritual' and other qualities such as 'liveliness' and methods of working. We noted in the last chapter the views of Albert Paley, namely that:

In order that the metal will 'record the raw energy of its own formation' he recommends punching instead of drilling out a hole. The metal is thus dislocated rather than removed, and a swelling remains to document the action. Looking at examples in Paley's metalwork, one sees how details like the punched rivet convey animation, while a drilled version would appear mechanical and, in consequence, lifeless.

There is, however, a need to take such distinctions with a pinch of scepticism: it is too easy to polarize methods of working in such a way that one process suggests life and soul, the other not. It is far from true that all mechanical objects or machined designs look lifeless – whatever that really means. Language is something of a trap here. Words like 'punched' automatically convey energy and suggest (erroneously) the human gesture (machines do punching as well). But a number of metalsmiths have seen the liveliness and the sensuousness that is possible in machined designs. Friedrich Knupper (Germany 1947–87) was one of them. But again, in his work, what brings the designs to 'life', is an understanding of scale and proportion and especially the contribution that repetitive elements within a design can make to the musical look of a work. And objects can have the look of music about them because the parallel is there in the rhythms set up in the distribution, organization and the spacing and visual weight of the details and the relationship to the parts.

In the light of this chapter's concern with scale, form and preciousness it is interesting to consider Peter Chang (b.UK 1944) – an artist who does not limit himself to one scale, and who is also a good example of the artist bringing preciousness to a material, for he works a lot with discarded plastics.

The major components of Chang's career are his graphic design and sculpture training, supplemented by his employment as a young man making reproduction antiques, which fostered his prodigious skills as a versatile maker and developed his understanding of three-dimensional form. Chang's bracelets are large, they are sculptures with holes in them through which you can put your hand.

Chang's aesthetic is neither English nor European. Observers of his work relate his art to the fact that he was a student in Liverpool, one of the cities in England that flourished as post-war centres for pop music, art and literature. Liverpool's art school where Chang trained, was one of the engines of the pop art culture of Britain in the early 1960s and through to the mid-1970s. A depressed city with a colourful past as a port, Liverpool's contribution to contemporary art has been to mock conventional good taste with vivid and energetic imagery. Chang's work in jewelry in the 1980s may be related to this development in British art in his use of bright colour and bold forms. But, to an English person, Chang's aesthetic is closer to that of modern China or to Hong Kong. Why should this be? Chang's father was a Chinese merchant seaman and there is a Chinese community in Liverpool, but Chang had also grown up with an English mother and an English education, and English art schools are not noted for their interest in China or Oriental art.

Chang's jewelry developed through the 1980s (his 1970s were a mixture of experiments in sculpture and furniture). The forms are large, the colours vibrant, but the works are light and comfortable to wear, as well as robust. They also have an immaculate finish. Chang's refinement is extraordinary. He is a master craftsman, and we see this elusive quality of 'preciousness' being brought into play. It is a fine example of the principle that it is human intelligence which makes materials precious – recycled acrylics from waste products in Chang's case.

Chang has returned to furniture in the mid-1990s. It is a change of scale but a retention of utility. Furniture shares with some jewelry, such as bracelets or pendants, the fact that it is functional, but the functions are so general that they do not have a strong deterministic effect upon the design (almost any form can be used to serve as a table or chair just as almost any form can be worn in some way).

Chang's tables are like his bracelets – they have elaborate acrylic surfaces, they are highly coloured and they employ a geometry which, though organic, is not natural.

This is the kind of organic geometry that we are familiar with from computer renderings of fractal patterns. Fractals are meant to be the mathematics of the natural world but, mediated through the software and hardware of computer technology, they are given a definite, late 20th-century technological style. The content of Chang's work is at one with its scale: it is an ambivalent mixture of nature and technology, and a balance between refinement and vulgarity; it is work most expressive of late 20th-century urban, consumerist living. And even its cultural ambivalence – its living fusion of East and West – speaks loudly of the late 20th century.

Thomas Gentille (b.USA, 1936) is on record as saying 'Beauty is a quality I am always seeking'. Beauty is not the same as preciousness but it is a part of it. And Gentille is an artist who has sought preciousness, often, as is the craftsman-artist's responsibility, in materials that look unpromising. Gentille says, 'I was the first jeweler in America to work with what has become known as "alternative materials", and I began this exploration in 1957 and I have never moved from that direction.'

Gentille's work is all wearable but over the years shows a variety of form and also of dimension. He states that all artists are craftsmen; not all craftsmen are artists. This statement might be contested, since many artists strongly disavow any interest in the craft of their work, some, indeed, delegating it to others. Nevertheless, at the heart of Gentille's work there is an attention to detail – a refusal to subscribe to the idea of the best being the enemy of the good. Yet he subscribes to the modernist theology that all skill is subservient to the 'idea of the work'. Equally, his is an art which belongs to the category of 'art for art's sake' – it is not about social commentary, nor is it about design – for design implies service to someone else. Gentille insists, 'My responsibilities are the same as a painter or a sculptor, in that I have no responsibilities, except to myself and the work. I have no ambition except to do each work, if possible, better than the last.'

In a sense, and using the term 'precious' in a more general way, such an heroic and independent view of art is in itself precious. It distinguishes and separates 'the artist' from almost all other kinds of person and activity, for it acknowledges no responsibility to any one other than the artist and the art.

The artist Onno Boekhoudt (b.Netherlands 1944) was especially interesting to new jewelers in the early 1980s because he produced collections of small objects with titles such as *Rings with objects* and *Armband with objects* in which the small, minimalist 'things' in silver or copper or lead give a sculptural identity to the ring or the bracelet in question while the ring or the bracelet confer an aspect of preciousness.

Boekhoudt's work also raised another aspect central to Mawdsley, and to jewelry generally. The objects in his collections were small lumps or sections or slivers of unworked metals. This in itself reinforces the point that there are no innately precious materials. All materials from lead to gold, from granite chips to diamonds, become precious only through being worked by men and women.

In the visual arts the pendulum swings between rejection and acceptance of preciousness with long, slow arcs. It has been vilified by Puritans as ungodly, but also accepted by Christian Epicureans as a necessary ingredient for the glory of God. In more recent times, preciousness in art is rejected because of its apparent lack of seriousness. Sculpture which is precious is sculpture that goes against the grain of post-World War II convention.

Preciousness – most usually ascribed to a limited range of metals and gems – is to some extent a quality of smallness. (A sculpture is seldom described as precious – rather as important). Almost any small thing that you care to value, including a choice pebble from a beach, becomes precious because it can be held carefully in the hand, and because, being small, it can easily be lost and thus requires you to pay more attention to its 'safety' than something large. This inevitable correlation between smallness and preciousness (the obverse of the other inevitable correlation – smallness and triviality) means that jewelry as sculpture is an idea that already looks suspect in the eyes of those for whom preciousness has no place in sculpture. But the prejudice against preciousness and against preciousness in sculpture is a temporary convention; in other centuries the reverse has held – and will, in all probability, hold again.

Previous page
Peter Chang
British

Bracelet. 1992
Acrylic, polyester,
PVC found objects
19.7 dia x 4.4 cm

Peter Chang
British

Bracelet. 1992
Acrylic, polyester
14.6 dia x 6.4 cm

Bracelet. 1991
Acrylic, gold leaf,
polyester
16.5 dia x 6.4 cm

Peter Chang
British

Brooch. 1991
Acrylic, polyester
15.5 x 8.5 cm

Manfred Bischoff
German

Il Mio Casa
Brooch, front and back. 1986
Gold, silver, coral, ivory
9.5 x 5.2 cm

Workingman Hero
Brooch. 1989
Gold, silver, coral
9.5 x 7.6 cm
Collection Edna S. Beron, USA

Manfred Bischoff
German

Brooch. *c.*1982
Sheet metal, paint
8.9 x 12 cm

Kraft-Versus-Host-Reaction
Brooch. 1986
Gold, silver,
coral
12.5 cm

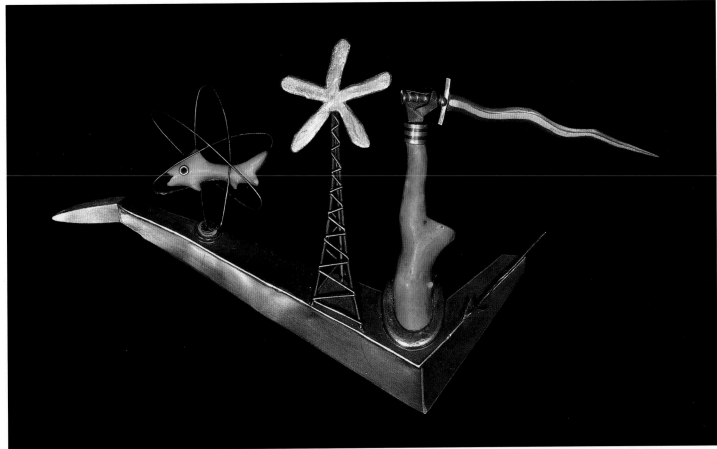

Richard Mawdsley
American

Camera
Pendant, detail. 1971
Silver, amethyst, pearl
Overall 36 x 6.5 cm
Pendant 11.4 x 6.6 cm

The Pequod
Pendant, detail. 1972
Silver, green onyx, carnelian
Overall 35 x 7.5 cm
Pendant 11.8 x 7.7 cm

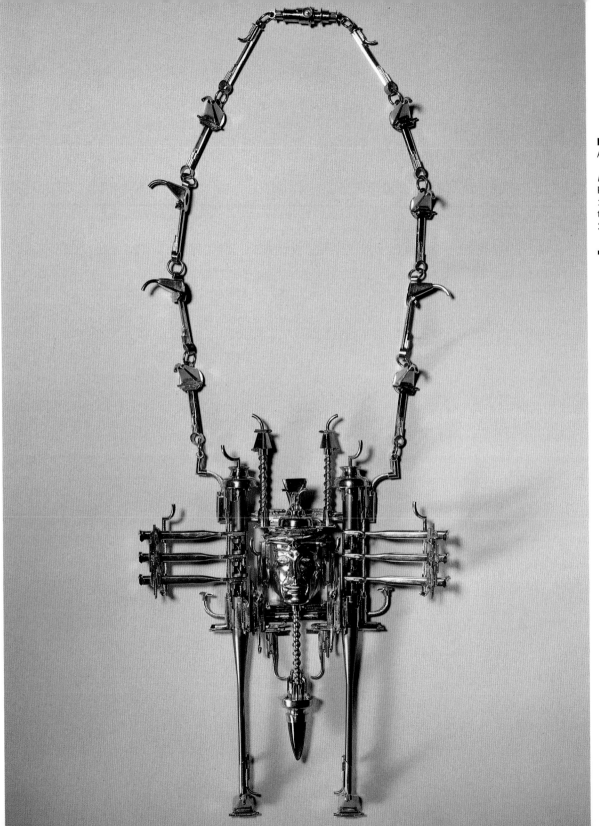

Richard Mawdsley
American

Headdress #5
Pendant. 1984
18k gold, titanium,
tantalum, garnet
26.7 x 12 x 2 cm

Petra Hartman
Dutch

Bull Bracelet; Expo.'92 Seville
1992
Papier mâché, found objects
20.3 dia x 6.4 cm

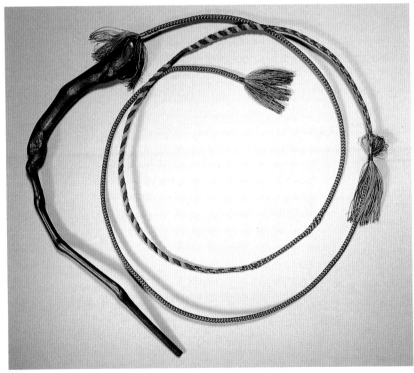

Sima Farjadi
British, active France

Necklace. 1992
Textile, found wood object
21.6 cm dia

Liv Blåvarp
Norwegian

Neckpiece. 1993
Birchwood, paint
27.9 x 5.7 cm

Wendy Ramshaw
British

Ring Set with stand (8 rings). 1972
14k gold, amethyst, carnelian, moonstone, acrylic, enamel
Stand: acrylic
Overall 11.3 x 2.5 cm
Ring Set with stand (6 rings). 1976
Silver, amethyst, peridot, serpentine, acrylic. Stand: acrylic
Overall 16.3 x 2.5 cm

Ring Set with stand and base (9 rings). 1977
18k yellow gold, garnets, pink sapphires, rubies, brass
Stand: gold plated brass, resin
Overall 17 x 11.5 cm

Wendy Ramshaw
British

Orbit
Neckpiece. 1988
Nickel alloy, resin inlay
28 cm dia

Breon O'Casey
British

Bracelets. 1993
Gold, silver
6.4 dia x 2.5 cm
Private collection, USA

Bracelet. 1986
Gold, silver
8.3 dia x 6.4 cm

Necklace. *c.*1982-83
Stones, silk thread
23 dia x 2.8 cm

Breon O'Casey
British

Necklace. *c.*1982
Silver, velvet cord
33.2 dia x 3.8 cm

Necklace. 1982
Granite, silver, silk thread
22.5 dia x 2.7 cm

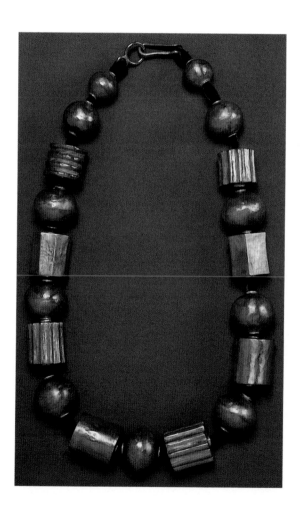

Francesco Pavan
Italian

Brooch. 1988
Gold, silver, alpaca
6.4 x 7.6 cm

Brooch. 1988
Gold, silver, alpaca
5.7 x 5.1 cm

Thomas Gentille
American

Square in Circle
Brooch. *c.*1982
Bronze
7 dia x 1.3 cm

Brooch. 1991
Eggshell inlay, over wood
6.7 x 5.7 x 2.2 cm

Anton Cepka
Slovak

Brooch. *c.*1963-64
Silver
7 x 13.3 x 0.6 cm

Anton Cepka
Slovak

Brooch. *c.*1975
Metal, slate, plastic, glass
6.4 x 13.3 cm

Sound
Brooch. *c.*1980
Silver
2.5 x 10.2 x 0.6 cm

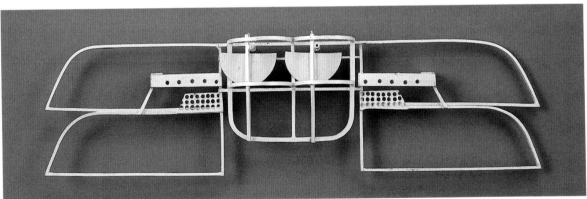

Friedrich Knupper
German

Brooch. 1985
Steel, paint
12.1 x 4.4 cm

Brooch. 1985
Steel, paint
15.2 x 1.3 cm

Brooch. 1985
Steel, paint
20.3 x 6.4 cm

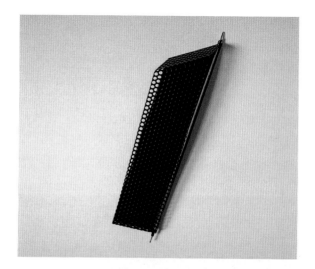

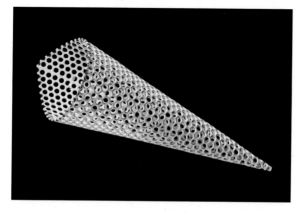

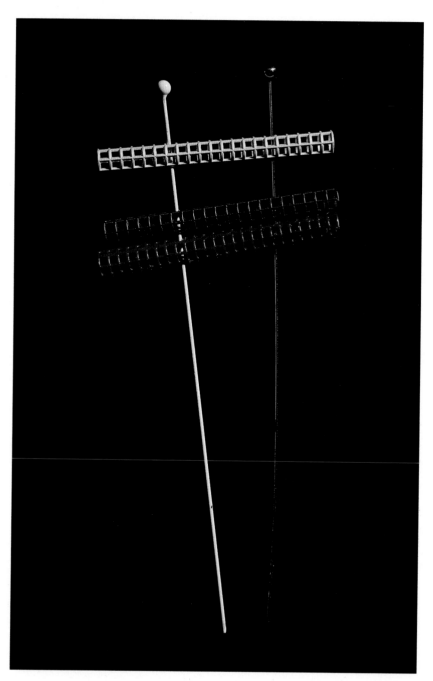

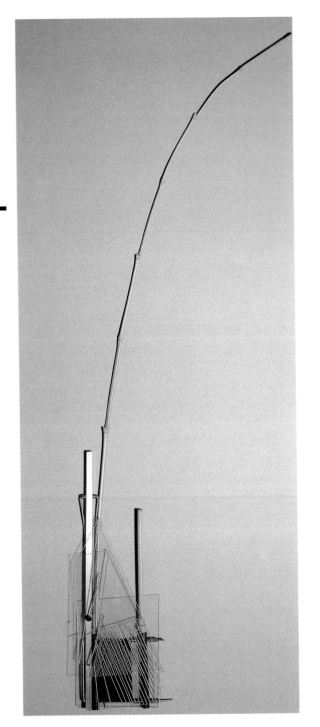

Marta Breis
Spanish

Brooch. 1989
Plastic, metal, bamboo
50 x 7 cm

Brooch. 1989
Plastic, metal, bamboo
21.6 x 14 cm

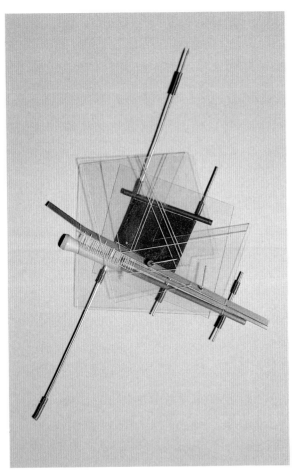

Hiroko Sato Pijanowski
Japanese, active USA

Eugene Pijanowski
American

Neckpiece. 1987
Gold-coloured paper cord (*mizuhiki*)
30.5 x 58.4 x 30.5 cm

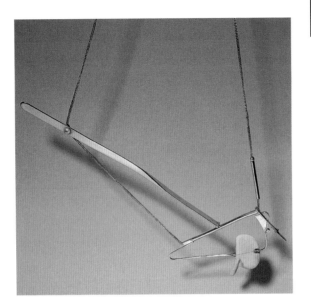

Deganit Schocken
Israeli

Necklace, detail
1984
14k gold, silver,
porcelain, pearl
16.8 x 6 x 1.2 cm

Brooch. *c.*1993
Silver, silk
3.5 x 11 x 1.8 cm

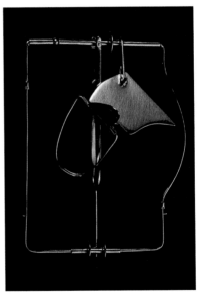

Brooch. 1982
Silver, gold, nylon
7.9 x 5 cm

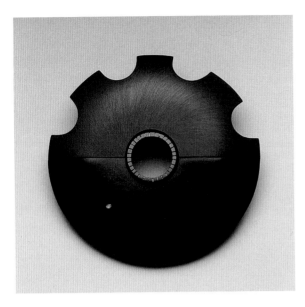

Lisa Gralnick
American

Brooch. *c.*1989
Acrylic, gold
8.3 cm dia

Anti-Gravity Neckpiece #6
1992
Sterling silver, 18k gold
Length 1.37 m (extended)
Central piece 6.4 cm dia

Eva Eisler
Czech, active USA

Brooch, 1990
Silver
10 x 7.5 x 2 cm

Bruno Martinazzi
Italian

Berkeley
Brooch. 1967
20k gold
3.8 x 2.9 x 1.3 cm

Mito/Logos
Brooch. 1989
20k gold
3.8 x 7.4 x 2 cm
Boardman Family Collection, USA

Overleaf
Bruno Martinazzi
Italian

Aquila
Brooch. 1990
20k gold, marble
2.9 x 3.2 x 1.3 cm

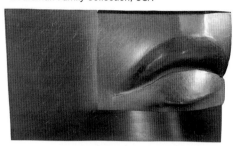

Daniel Jocz
American

(left) *Iceberg*
Ring. 1991-92
Sterling silver, 14k gold
(right) *Zuk Series*
Ring. 1991-92
Sterling silver, 14k gold
1.6 dia x 1.3 x 5.1 cm

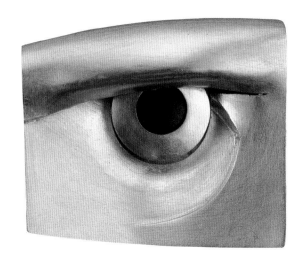

3 the body and jewelry

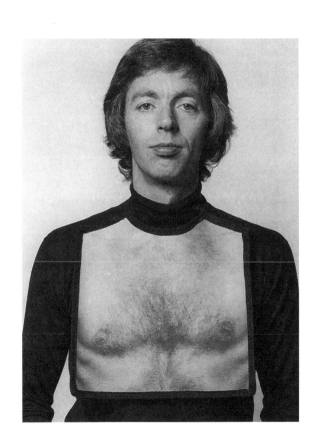

3 the body and jewelry

3 the body and jewelry

Previous page
Gijs Bakker
Dutch

Bib. 1976
Photograph on linen
Life size
Portrait: Gijs Bakker
Collection of the artist

One of the most striking and minimalist images in the last thirty years of art jewelry was created by Gijs Bakker – it is a mark left by a wire band pulled tight around an upper arm. The band is taken off, the imprint in the flesh remains. It is a clever image – conceptual and fetishistic. It is a fine demonstration of that commonplace of contemporary art-production artspeak – 'mark making'. Of course, without the photograph, this particular piece of mark making would have been lost to us. Photography wields an immensely powerful influence over artists and especially those who work in jewelry, because it is the way in which their work is communicated to the world and to posterity in an ideal position on an ideal body.

Some artists and designers, notably Gijs Bakker, have produced work which uses the photograph as an integral part of the jewelry. Sometimes this jewelry is easily wearable, sometimes it is wearable only in the sense that it is best seen worn in a photograph. A good example is provided by Gijs Bakker's flower pieces, such as *Dew Drop*, in which a huge photograph of a rose (with a dew drop) is laminated between plastic and worn as a neckpiece. Although this is a real object, and Bakker has produced many such real objects, it is for most of us a 'virtual' object, a theoretical object in that it works ideally as a photograph in a book or in a magazine. For most people it is not a functional piece of jewelry and many more people will enjoy it vicariously than would want to wear it for themselves.

The photograph is now the most common of visual artefacts in the Western world, and all image making has become subordinated to the power of the photographer. Much high or fine art is mediated through photography. A great many people know the works of the European masters of the Renaissance only through reprographic and photographic images. Bakker uses these images as material for his jewelry, see, for example, his works such as *Botticelli Project* or *Adam*.

Another well-known piece by Bakker is *The Tongue*. In some cultures (such as that of the Marai) the protruding tongue is a gesture of power, and in this brooch the balancing of a cut diamond on the tongue gives that gesture some style and irony. It is a gift for a deconstructionist literary critic. In Western culture the tongue is used to poke fun at something, and Bakker is well known for trying to prick what he regards as the pretentions of 'precious' jewelry.

In his recent book *The Body*, (Thames and Hudson, 1994) – a collection of photographic images of the human body, ranging from medico-scientific imagery via side-show freaks to erotica – William A. Ewing writes:

…Darker themes characterize much late-twentieth-century photography of the naked figure. This is partly in reaction to what are perceived as particularly troubled times for the body, and partly because nudity has become such a commonplace motif in popular culture and so ubiquitous in advertising that serious photographers believe that some shock therapy is needed in order to reclaim the body for art.

This comment, especially the notion of reclaiming the body for art, is interesting from the art-jewelry perspective, for it might be argued that jewelers have used the body to reclaim jewelry as art. That is to say, not content with using the humdrum idea that people wear jewelry, art jewelers have used the body in photography as a near-inanimate sculpture upon which their own art may work.

On the whole, the photograph of the body and new jewelry have been less concerned with the probing of fears and feelings and more with formal abstraction and fragmentation, for, and this is consistent with one of the many pertinent observations made by Ewing about 20th-century photography and the body, both art jewelers and photographers share an interest in the abstraction of the human body. In art jewelry this has frequently meant the isolating of a part of the body by means of an artefact, whilst, as Ewing points out, the marked difference between art photography of the 19th century and that of the 20th is in the 20th-century preoccupation with the fragmenting of the figure to achieve abstract compositions. Time and again the jewelry catalogues of the last thirty years show that the abstractionist ambitions of the art jeweler and the photographer coincide.

Examples of this are found in the work of Emmy van Leersum, David Watkins and Marjorie Schick. Framing the head or the torso (Van Leersum, Gijs Bakker, David Watkins), or building around the head with large light constructions objects (Marjorie Schick), or draping parts of the body with objects that are half jewelry, half clothing (Lam de Wolf, b.Netherlands 1949, Caroline Broadhead), are all stratagems for making the human sculpture work in terms of form and volume. The body is treated like a still life.

It is surprising, however, given the central role that photography has in Western capitalist societies as a means of selling things, that relatively few catalogues of new jewelry have been successful in selling the idea of new jewelry as ornament that can reasonably and pleasurably worn by the person in the street. For, as the photographs in this book will reveal, most new jewelry is not shocking, and most of it can be worn with physical and psychological comfort.

One publication managed to be both inventive and propagandist in its use of new jewelry and photography: the catalogue for the *Europea Joieria Contemporania* exhibition, Barcelona, 1987. This catalogue used colour-portrait photography to model a variety of new jewelry made from everything from gold to candy-bar and chewing-gum wrappers. The photography is clever, artful, contrived, but also kind and humane. A variety of lived-in faces of both sexes are portrayed with some young, some middle-aged, some beautiful, some ordinary-looking people. All the portraits are of famous Spanish artists: writers, painters, actors, actresses and dancers, and, because one photographer has been in control, the whole catalogue has a powerful unity. But its essential humanity lies in the fact that the photographer has for once provided the viewer with credible living human beings, not models. It breaks away from the body as an object, and emphasizes individuality and personality. And to see pictures of people who look as if they have walked in off Main Street, wearing non-Main Street jewelry in a relaxed way, is significant advertising for the new art. *Europea Joieria Contemporania* was a break with the hermetic status of art jewelry for art jewelry's sake.

Another landmark publication was Galerie Ra's book published in 1986 to celebrate ten years of the gallery's existence. Black-and-white portrait photographs of each artist (one posing naked) is pictured with his or her work in a tableau. This beautifully designed catalogue is also humane, but for quite the opposite reason from that of *Europea Joieria Contemporania*, for in the Ra book we have a fascinating folio of artistic vanity.

The advantages of photography notwithstanding, many art jewelers want people to wear their work in real life. This means making work that it is possible to wear. Wearability is a design problem and there are several functional aspects such as the nature of the clasps, weight and durability. It also means making work that is possible to wear psychologically. There is a range of values that is still important to the 'ordinary but visually informed buyer', expressed in a vocabulary that may make art critics shudder but which have its place in the purpose of jewelry, such as: pretty, charming, attractive, it suits you, it really matches that dress/suit/blouse/shirt/your complexion/personality, that's really you and I wouldn't be seen dead wearing that.

body objects, bodies as objects

body objects, bodies as objects

The careers of most jewelry artists develop quite slowly, and, although experiments with 'the body' and 'art' have been well established and publicly documented since the early part of the century, each individual appears to take her or his own route to a discovery of the body. Johanna Dahm is an example of the individualistic, evolutionary approach.

Johanna Dahm (formerly Hess-Dahm, b.Switzerland 1947) is a professor in the Fachhochschule für Gestaltung in Pforzheim. She has had a variety of commissions, including commercial design projects: she designed the badges for all the employees of the airline SWISSAIR, as well as the 'Wings' and hat badges of the pilots. She had a Bauhaus-inspired vocational training at the Schule für Gestaltung, Zurich and she is a former pupil of Max Fröhlich.

As her work developed during the 1970s she began exploring the connection between jewelry and clothing. She took part in a textile and metals symposium held in Zurich in 1980, after which she began intensifying her search for a unity of form, function and visual effect by developing a series of pin-brooches which could dip in and out of the fabric. During the early 1980s Dahm produced a variety of brooches in non-precious materials and often with the goal of serial/batch production in mind. This goal was not always realized, although certain categories of brooch designed by her were produced in large numbers: these included the 'pierce through' brooch, the 'fabric edge' brooch and the 'stick' brooch.

In 1986 and 1987 she began experimenting with light, working in workshops with other artists and students. There were workshops at, for example, the International Summer Academy in Salzburg in 1986 and in the Fachhochschule in Dusseldorf in 1987. She and a group of students would experiment first by projecting a random collection of slides on to someone. Then, by making small stencils and putting these into slide frames and projecting on to the body, it was possible to create shapes on the body. There are eight ways of projecting each slide. One student coined a descriptive expression for this process: 'Jewelry out of the socket'. Such work is a good example of the concept mentioned earlier of fragmenting the body and thereby abstracting it.

Such work is communal: one person has to operate the projector, one has to stand in the light, and, inevitably, someone must take the photographs. This performance-based, non-material orientated, non-craft-founded and communally approached work is of considerable interest educationally, and runs counter to some of the conventions of jewelry making. According to Dahm, the creative anxieties occasioned by this approach include the difficulty of separating oneself from an exclusively individual way of working, and coping with the fear of allowing oneself be influenced by others or of being copied.

One of the advantages of the 'light works' approach, however, is its economy of effort and its respect for the model – the person in the light is not really inconvenienced or imposed upon physically. Moreover, with the exception of Gijs Bakker's 'mark making in the flesh', the use of projected light is about as free of the burden of the innate value or preciousness of the material as you can get. On the other hand it is static, it is fixed-point 'jewelry' and consequently contradicts one of the central characteristics of jewelry art – its portability.

However, in Dahm's work of the 1990s, she has capitalized with élan upon her interest and expertise in light by creating a series of three-dimensional brooches which are like long, shallow, open vessels which capture, contain and reflect light. Dahm's work shows how experimentation on the edge of the design avant-garde can also produce innovative mainstream jewelry.

Such continuity of development is prized by many jewelers including Gijs Bakker and David Watkins. Gijs Bakker declared in correspondence with us that, 'I am not concerned with changes in my own work. I continue with developments in the work which are connected both to the new and the old'. He suggests that:

Probably I am the only one to see a straight line between the clothing suggestions Emmy [van Leersum] and I made in the sixties (especially the 'open breast case') and the *Waterman* brooch which is part of Helen Drutt's collection. Someone once noticed that my jewelry always refers to my own work. I believe this to be true.

More than many designers of jewelry (and Bakker is arguably a designer first and foremost), Bakker can claim innovation in his work. His use of the photograph has been both contemporary and witty. He has made breastplates which show a photograph of the male chest or female breasts, and he has made several series of large neckpieces from photographs of flowers laminated in plastic. He created the *Waterman* brooch, which features a photograph of a beautiful naked man pouring water down his back. The idea for this work was conceived when Helen Drutt commissioned Bakker to recycle a family ring encrusted with diamonds.

Such an image is typical of Bakker's approach: it is an ingenious piece of assemblage in the way the diamonds have been made to represent the reflections of light sparkling on water. And, pondering this, we might consider how the history of 20th-century art is punctuated with examples of 'clever' transformations of found objects – Picasso, of course, being a master of this art. Looking at *Waterman,* anyone who is visually and artistically aware can continue the list.

Bakker designs for industry and is well known as a furniture and product designer. He wants the freedom to slip between disciplines, and he says, writing at the end of 1994, 'Why should one make jewelry? It puzzles me why there should be only one way a designer can deal with the human body – jewelry – when we can make fashion, theatre…' And there are strong elements of fashion and theatre in his work. Bakker believes that what is noticeable about Dutch jewelry in the last thirty years, and has become more significant during the 1980s in Netherlands generally, is the fact that the Dutch have no specific crafts culture as in the USA or Britain. He says, 'This means there is no sealed-off domain for the crafts. They have to compete with industrial design on the same stage.'

This is a vitally important aspect of Dutch design culture. In some countries, the USA and Britain in particular, there is a concern about the recreation of aesthetic quality in industrial design. From time to time it is argued that in order to bring finesse or humanity, or simply a variation of texture to commercial design, there needs to be some input into industrial design and manufacture by 'the crafts'. Such arguments always amount to wishful thinking because artists-craftspeople have put themselves into ghettos and have lost credibility with commercial and industrial designers, who argue, with good reason, that the art for art's sake approach of contemporary craft is not appropriate to design, which must cope with the modern disciplines of manufacture that are utterly unlike those of a modern workshop. In societies like the Netherlands, however, where there is a continuum between all kinds of design – as Bakker's career demonstrates – there is a constant movement up and down the scale of production with ideas that can be explored in one-offs, and also expressed in long production runs when or if the demand exists. The 'craft' aesthetic is integrated with the aesthetic of design and the design aesthetic is integrated with art – this is the unifying message of Gijs Bakker's work. Gert Staal has said of Bakker that he is the jewelry designer who dislikes jewelry and the industrial designer with a deep-rooted mistrust of industry.

Similarly, David Watkins, Professor of the Gold and Metalsmithing Department at the Royal College of Art, London, has worked steadily as an artist-jeweller of 'the body'. The links between Watkins's work and the body have always been strong, but also oblique rather than literal. In 1976, ten years into his career as an artist, he began producing wire body 'cages'. Constructed from thin steel rod and even thinner gold wire, they framed the body three-dimensionally, sectioning it off on all 'four sides'. These are related to the body but did not describe it; they fitted a body but they are not particular to any single body.

Watkins has sometimes said that sculpture is the anchor of his work (he trained as a sculptor), but the body, even in his big sculptures, appears to be the constant theme. Sometimes the cross-referencing between a brooch and a sculpture is close. In 1978, he produced a jewelry series whose structure was that of a ladder, and this form also appeared in 1981 as a site-specific sculpture called *Nimbus*. It is a large ladder-like sculpture that floats over the tomb of St Thomas Cantilupe in Hereford Cathedral. The site specific is the body of the saint.

In the early years of making jewelry (late 1960s to around 1973) Watkins says, 'I drew directly on the forms of my earlier sculpture, but gradually moved towards objects and proposals which were more closely dependent on the body. The miniaturized sculpture approach – rings where the shank or finger essentially formed a platform for a sculptural event, and brooches which were more or less framed relief constructions – ran out in 1973.

In 1973 he began producing large, rigid, wearable objects in coloured acrylic and then monochrome acrylic and gold. In appearance these objects were functionally ambiguous, and also expressed the mass, contour and attitude of the body. He began working in steel and produced the bodywork pieces mentioned above and also rigid square 'neckpieces'.

With these and also simple bangles of the period, the wearer could 'forget' that she or he was wearing them. The polished steel would, most often, be inlaid at regular intervals with gold. The square geometry is an obvious contrast to anyone's body, but the diameter of the steel is small, the square has finesse in its bulk, lightness in its weight, and so the geometry, though it opposes the body, is also comfortable with it. It exists as a sculpture when off the body – and when on it – although the content changes. It demonstrates a view of the definition of preciousness: it uses gold with commonplace steel and shows how the conjunction is precious.

Later works by Watkins, in the 1980s, include quite complex neckpieces in coloured neoprene-covered steel. The constant theme of the body remains as a tension between wearability and the seeming non-wearability of the shapes in non-Euclidean geometry. The earlier fragmentation and abstraction of the body has been retained as a compositional element in the jewelry but it no longer appears as the central preoccupation as it did in the body-cage-photographic studies of the 1970s.

The sensuousness of the object is important to Watkins. Although he is researching the applications of computer technology and numerically controlled milling machines, as he has, at intervals throughout the 1970s and 1980s, he is concerned that the quality of the object should be itself full of 'meaning'. Therefore he would reject, as some might not, the idea that 'virtual objects' – jewelry designed on screen and published on screen, say through the Internet or on CD-ROM disk – are sufficient. They do not have the final, all-important sensuousness.

He also believes that the wearing of an object can transform or complete it, and that one designs a piece of work to be worn. This means one thinks about the specific viewpoints that might be important. As he says, this can lead you to realizing that the back of a neckpiece is as important or more important than the front. For, although the wearer thinks in terms of what she or he sees in the mirror, the designer or artist will know that the work, like the wearer, is seen in the round and in movement. It therefore becomes legitimate, if subversive of expectations, to play up the back of a necklace rather than the front.

Another aspect of David Watkins's work is the use of paper, a material that both he and his wife, Wendy Ramshaw have used to great effect, exploiting its usefulness as a wearable material. As far as we know, they were the first to produce and market paper jewelry intended for serious use in a wide and popular market. Their work was a success and made fashion headlines everywhere. Mary Quant's Bazaar, Biba, Palisades – all the style-creating shops of 'swinging London' took it up. Not surprisingly, the complete Ramshaw/Watkins collection of original work from the mid-1960s – the prototypes, colourways, artwork and publicity – has gone into the archives of London's Victoria and Albert Museum.

In the late 1980s, after twenty years of exploring jewelry in several media, they returned to paper. Throughout the 1980s both Watkins and Ramshaw made serious art jewelry using paper, paper pulp, cut paper, folded paper and paper with real gold leaf on the surface. Ramshaw combined paper with precious metals, such as 18 carat gold, while Watkins combined lightweight paper with steel and gold leaf. Flexibility in materials has always intrigued them, and pliability is a part of paper's appeal, as well as its low cost.

In 1989 they designed a book of paper jewelry which the customer would buy, taking out a page at a time to make up into a piece of jewelry. Unfortunately the costs of producing the book to the standards demanded means that this project has still to go into production.

Sensuousness is an essential part of jewelry, and it is an element that has been fully explored by Scandinavian artists such as the Norwegian, Tone Vigeland (b.1938). Her metalwork is constructed in a way that suggests textiles, although the fabrication techniques are those of a metalsmith. Vigeland's works are simple but very subtle, taking in the light slowly like a gently undulating sea of oil. They also have a silken, fluid quality in the hand, and they move with languor when they are worn. Much of the quality of her work is due to the way it flexes and moves on the body. What also counts, however, are the visual rhythms of the strips of metal and their junctions – and again, thinking back to the previous chapter, it is the artist's facility for scale and proportion that gives a design life, as well as the more literal aspects of the way a piece moves mechanically. These qualities are the result of the intense detail that characterizes her work: she has the ability to create a design that is monumental in its effect but delicate in its particularities, the result of the careful hammering and processing by hand of hundreds of separate parts that are joined together. One is aware both of the overall form – the mass – and the detail.

Knitted and woven metal and acrylics have provided another means of experimenting with sensuousness because these forms of construction allow inventive ways of framing parts of the body and enclosing it. One of the pioneers of knitted metals has been Arline Fisch (b.USA 1931) who, in 1975 published an influential book called *Textile Techniques in Metal for Jewelers*. It was in 1970, during her third visit to Denmark, that she began to study textile structures with a view to translating them into metal. A close study in the Viking Museum in Roskilde fed her ideas about woven structures. As well as pursuing experiments in the technology herself, she subsequently led graduate classes at San Diego State University in which students explored weaving, plaiting, knitting, crochet, knotting and lace-making in sterling and fine silver, copper, brass and resin-coated metals.

Fisch, wittingly or not, had anticipated a new interest among applied scientists, designers and engineers in using woven three dimensional-forms for industrial design and engineering. By the end of the 1980s there was much interest in weaving three-dimensional forms in carbon fibre because of the excellent strength-to-weight ratios this form of manufacture offers – and which Fisch exploits in her own work.

Fisch's purpose is decoration through the partial or whole enclosure of the human body, and she has dissolved the distinction between ornament and dress. Apart from her importance as a teacher, Fisch's contribution to modern jewelry is threefold: she has contributed a rich vein of craft ideas through the development of woven structures; she has demonstrated a means of making jewelry volumetric and decorative without compromising the function of wearability.

Mary Lee Hu is another jeweler who is famous for her use of textile techniques in metal. She studied at Cranbrook. She told Katherine M. Davidson in an unpublished interview in 1982, 'I chose to investigate macramé. I did it in wire and I really liked the result – especially the play of light on the many wires, and the masses of repeated texture which built up the forms.' Her work is refined, and has, over the years, incorporated ideas that she has found interesting in Taiwanese, Chinese and Tibetan art. And her work has contributed to modern jewelry some much needed luxury of form, although, as she said back in 1982, 'I had rather the pieces be precious because of what I have done to them rather because of their intrinsic value.'

In Europe one of the most famous woven images in new jewelry, one that works best as a photograph, is a nylon monofilament neckpiece called *Veil* produced by Caroline Broadhead in 1983. It can be worn as thickish ruff around the neck but it can also be pulled up to encompass the entire head, sitting upon the shoulders like a wobbling, shimmering cylinder of light. It can be worn as a veil because the wearer can see through it but it is at its most poetic when carefully lit and photographed (as it was by David Ward in 1983).

One goldsmith has taken the idea of wearability to an extreme, and in so doing has given it a literalness which can be discomforting. Gerd Rothmann (b.Germany 1941) has for some years produced silver and gold pieces that fit their owners perfectly, at least until age or weight take their toll, because he makes casts of bits of the body and then produces silver or gold ornaments to fit. So he has produced pieces for navels, noses, the heels of feet, nipples on breasts and pieces for ears. There is no doubt about the physical comfort – the works fit as snugly as a prosthesis. But that is where the edginess begins: who before Rothmann had thought of jewelry in terms of it being a prosthesis? There are certain precedents where a real prosthesis has been made in terms of an ornament: the famous 16th-century astronomer Tycho Brahe lost the tip of his nose in a sword fight with a Danish nobleman. In order to conceal this disfigurement he had prosthetic nose-tip made from gold and silver.

Rothmann has also made use of the body parts in other, ingenious ways. One of his most famous works is the *Schmuck einer Tänzerin* (Jewelry of a Dancer) necklace which at first sight looks like a necklace of small gold discs, but on closer inspection is revealed to be gold pressings of nipples (a dancer's). Some people revel in such audaciousness and find it amusing, others dismiss it as a form of tasteless clowning. Rothmann's work can be quite controversial or even irritating. His wittiest piece may well be *Kaugummikette* (Chewing-gum Necklace) in which he strings together several gold-plated nuggets cast from lumps of chewed gum. It undoubtedly raises the question of what exactly he is able to cast next, and provides the notion of jewelry as an intimate art with a new degree of accuracy.

Rothmann's work is also an interesting play on the notion of identity: one becomes one with one's ornament, as one might with one's artificial eye/dental bridge/artificial hand/arm/leg. A prosthesis is the artificial replacement of something missing on the body. Do people wear jewelry as a form of prosthetic therapy to make up for something they feel is missing about themselves or to enhance a feature of which they are proud?

Rothmann's comments on his own work both support and contradict the ornament as prosthesis interpretation. He says:

I like to watch people wear my jewelry, how they handle it, identify with it, how the piece becomes a part of the person....A diamond necklace, a gipsy's gold teeth, a tattoo, or an expensive Rolex interests me. Decoration, a planned improvement of appearance, doesn't....Imagining a ring on a finger, on a hand, on a person, is different from an actual ring on a finger, on a hand, on a person.

Bruno Martinazzi's use of body fragments is an interesting foil to Rothmann's. Martinazzi does not cast his pieces, he fabricates them; they are metaphors for his own responses to personal and political concerns. *Aquila* repeats his design for the Golden Ring of Honour, presented to Anton Cepka in 1990, in which he uses the powerful eye of an eagle to symbolize Cepka's keen vision.

jewelry and the craft aesthetic

ｊｅｗｅｌｒｙ　ａｎｄ　ｔｈｅ　ｃｒａｆｔ　ａｅｓｔｈｅｔｉｃ

Much of the work produced by the metalsmiths of the last thirty-five years combines modernity with a sense of well-being: that is to say, its design reflects a consensus among the American and north-west European middle class that good taste is clean, uncluttered, forward looking, optimistic, non-subversive and yet demonstrably different from the styles favoured by their mothers and fathers. Consensus always promotes well-being. In this category, we could include, among other North American artists, Toni Goessler-Snyder (b.Germany, active USA, 1942–82), Rena Koopman (b.USA 1945) and Louis Mueller (b.USA 1943), and from north-west Europe, Hermann Jünger, Robert Smit, and Philip Sajet (b.Netherlands 1953).

They are among the many jewelers who were not interested in denying themselves the use of materials such as gold and silver and precious stones, and among them are people sceptical about the new jewelry's new orthodoxies in which words such as 'experiment', 'research' and 'innovation' dominated. One Dutch goldsmith who has produced some outstandingly beautiful jewelry in a modern idiom is Robert Smit. His work has more in common with German goldsmiths (Smit did a part of his training at Pforzheim, one of the centres of German craft metal-

smithing) and also with the Italian movement in contemporary jewelry as represented by figures such as Giampaolo Babetto and Francesco Pavan.

In the mid-1980s an intense public debate between Smit and Bakker occurred. According to Godert van Colvnjon writing in the catalogue *Robert Smit – Beyond Reach* (1987), 'The display of Robert Smit's jewelry at the *Concerning Amsterdam* exhibition in 1986 at the Stedelijk Museum in Amsterdam caused quite a stir within the circle of Dutch modern jewelry designers.' Gijs Bakker had apparently dismissed it as 'old-fashioned "schmuck" which rehabilitates the jewel as a status symbol and as an object for investment.' Smit later replied, in a written statement and in public debate, and with regard to the experimentation of the 1960s and 1970s, 'Jewelry's specific function was completely disregarded.... The fundamental error at the root of this dreadful development is the notion that one can employ design principles in approaching the possibilities, ambitions, and intentions of the visual arts.'

It is not clear what is really at the heart of this debate, but it is probable that what differentiates art from design for some people, including Smit, is the argument (cited in Chapter 1) of Francesco de Bartolomeis, namely that an artist is someone who is thinking and changing his work throughout its manufacture. Design is the reverse of this: in a design you specify all that is to be done before you make it.

Among the possibilities of the visual arts that Smit could have had in mind is the attempt to create objects which express meaning in a metaphorical or allusive way that remains complex and open to further interpretation by an observer or user. For example, Elizabeth Garrison (b.USA 1952), who gave up making jewelry and now concentrates on painting, wrote that her jewelry was based on intuitive symbolism. The source of this symbolism was her dreams. She wrote:

The medium of jewelry is particularly well suited for the depiction of dream imagery because of its inherent personal, intimate and magical quality. Sometimes I create pieces about a specific dream and sometimes about an image which is contained in many dreams. I am always interested in communicating the feeling of the night and the mystery and strangeness of it.

For several important jewelry artists the Western concept of design as an activity separate from craft has never really been relevant. The work of Miyé Matsukata, (b.Japan, 1922–81), is an illustration. As an article by Robert J. Cardinale in *Metalsmith*, Spring 1986, explains, her career illustrates the multicultural fluidity that characterizes the evolution of the new jewelry, particularly as it has developed in the USA.

As the daughter of an influential, political and artistic family in Japan, Matsukata received a Japanese 'arts and craft' education, which included Japanese flower-arranging and dress-making. She was taught at the American School in Tokyo, and from there went on to higher education in the United States. She spent four years at Boston Museum of Fine Arts School, studying the craft of holloware and jewelry. In 1950 she visited Scandinavia where she worked in the metalsmithing studio of Baron Erik von Fleming at the Atelier Borgila.

Returning to the USA, her career developed throughout the 1950s as a general 'jobbing' metalsmith, working mainly in sterling silver. She is quoted as saying, 'For the first decade and a half of my career I made almost anything...'

In the 1960s she began including non-valuable materials in her work. A grant in 1966 enabled her to travel to the Middle East and Greece, where Egyptian gold work excited her imagination, and gold subsequently became an important part of her work. According to her biographers, Matsukata 'had an infatuation with stone'; and she caught the textures of the skin of stones in her gold work:

She admits conscious inspiration from her visits to the pyramids of Egypt, the amphitheatre at Epidaurus, the Mycenae grave sites, the Göreme valley in Turkey and Machu Picchu in Peru. Not only did she use a variety of chasing tools to achieve the texture of stone, but also she often literally lifted the quality of surface from the stone itself as the thin sheets of gold accurately registered a varied surface.

Matsukata herself is recorded by Cardinale as referring to her work as 'painting-sculptures'. She also employed techniques such as enamelling, and, following a period of study with Arline Fisch in the mid 1970s, she produced work involving the crocheting of metal. She introduced into jewelry other elements, especially in her necklaces, such as water pearls, pieces of silk cloth, and ancient glass or stone beads.

There are many approaches to the incorporation of other elements into jewelry. Undoubtedly one of the most influential artists in Northwest American jewelry as far as assemblage is concerned has been Ramona Solberg. Like

Alexander Calder, she pioneered found-object jewelry, and because she is a great world traveller her jewelry combines objects from all kinds of places and cultures. Such an approach puts the emphasis upon design and composition rather than hand craftsmanship; it is the intelligence of ideas-association rather than the craft of metals that her work demonstrates. Solberg has been a highly influential teacher, and so too has Robert Ebendorf (b.USA 1938), another American artist who has used the assemblage approach consistently throughout his career to much purpose. His first solo exhibition in 1967 consisted, not of jewelry as such, but of wall-mounted pieces using garbage as part of their worked material. Ebendorf, however, has capitalized upon the conceptual core that is implicit in assemblage and has used texts as a part of his imagery.

Another approach is the incorporation of 'other objects' by allusion rather than by embodying them physically in the work. Herman Jünger is arguably in this latter category. Although their work is dissimilar physically, there is a shared aesthetic flavour in Matsukata and Jünger's earlier work. This may be because Jünger has always maintained that his work owes little to other jewelers and a great deal to a German painter called Julius Bissier. In an interview in 1984 he explained that Bissier had a fluidity that he wanted in his own work and also an Oriental feel for composition.

Jünger's watercolour drawings for his jewelry are interesting in this respect. It is also relatively unusual for a studio jeweler to use drawing as an important part of his work. His drawing is fluid and flows with a rhythm punctuated by sharp emphases, and is just like his handwriting. Gretchen Raber, also a goldsmith, has said, 'Jünger's adventure is in drawing. His exploration and intellectualism is in calligraphic notation.' This drawing is the source of spontaneity that characterizes Jünger's work. And although Jünger's watercolours can never be mistaken for Oriental paintings, there is that sense that the watercolour depicts the ideal world, the ideal object – seen, not definitively, but in the hints, nuances, nudges and ambiguities. The viewer makes his or her contribution to fill in the missing information and, in so doing, creates the perfect world. Old buildings gradually acquire an analogous ambiguity which allows each viewer to make them perfect. The ambiguity in Jünger's jewelry allows others to make them perfect. In a discussion with Lisa Spiros and Gretchen Raber, both goldsmiths who studied in Germany (see *Metalsmith,* Fall 1990), he said his objective was the quality found in ancient work. He thought that the particular characteristic of the old pieces that attracted him was that they were not perfect. He said, '…And whilst some jewelry needs an unbelievable amount of precision to exist, i.e. that of Friedrich Becker, there is another category of jewelry that starts to live because it doesn't have this perfection – what makes one piece live makes another die.'

The appeal of old objects rests partly in their ambiguity – they may be incomplete, we may not know what they are or what they are used for – and so the viewer can supply the missing ingredients and make them 'perfect'. Perhaps this is why old objects provide so much inspiration to new jewelers. Additionally, as Paul Derrez has remarked, the sense of history, the presence of old craftsmanship (past technology) and the sense that these are works that others, now dead, have valued and loved, provide the 'perfection' that Jünger is speaking of here. Jünger has explained also that the shapes and images that he uses have an affinity with ritual devices or tools that are anything up to five thousand years old.

In the late 1980s, Jünger produced a series of necklaces which allowed the owner to configure the components in whatever pattern she or he desired. The basic necklace is gold wire on to which can be threaded objects whose shapes are taken from Euclidean geometry, made in agate, rock crystal, bloodstone, silver or gold. The colour, texture, light-refracting qualities of each piece allows a variety of subtle composition. Moreover, when the piece is not worn, it is disassembled and packaged in a box for open display – each box looking like a highly aesthetizised kit of parts.

Some of the younger German jewelers have shown a similar interest (albeit differently explored) to Jünger's in expanding outwards from abstraction to explore the middle ground between abstraction and nature. Georg Dobler is a particular case. From the late 1970s onwards and through the 1980s, his light, airy, three-dimensional wire constructions are, like the colours he uses, influenced by his reading of Johannes Itten's book on the Bauhaus foundation course. This famous piece of art school pedagogy from this century's most influential art school, the German Bauhaus, is a series of exercises in linear construction, tonal values and pictorial composition – a mixture of science and nature.

For a while, from the late 1970s and through the 1980s, Dobler drew mostly on the 'recipes' of line that Itten taught in which diagonals are veered off against horizontals and verticals. However, Dobler also produced freer works of a more obviously organic form, such as flattish, pancakes of papier mâché in saturated red that resemble the surface of the moon. One of the most notable aspects of Itten's *Foundation Course* is its mixture of ideas about abstraction, representation, form and feeling and nature. Gradually all these elements are finding their way into Dobler's work. So, alongside the geometry, he is now introducing brooches which feature twigs cast and placed in compositions with diagonal pieces of smoothly planed wood. The content is obvious: it includes nature versus man over nature, Euclidean geometry against fractal geometry, a visual pun on the Bauhaus teaching and even, if you wish, a little playfulness with the work of De Stijl and Mondrian. After all, one of the most famous developments in 20th-century art is Mondrian's transition from drawing trees naturalistically, to drawing angular trees, to drawing and painting grids: from nature to abstraction. This development was often offered to art students in north-west Europe in the 1960s and 1970s as a classic example of the power of the idea that art was 'science', that it was a research proceeding from one phase to the next. Dobler's development in jewelry can be viewed as playing against each other the ideas that Mondrian apparently went through in sequence. And, indeed, one of the features of modern jewelry is that for some artists, such as Dobler, a part of the content is a selfconscious awareness of this century's history of fine art.

This sense of a continuity with contemporary art history is an important element in the work of the British jeweler, Breon O'Casey (b.UK 1928). O'Casey has lived and worked for many years in Cornwall, first in St Ives, at the southernmost tip of Britain, and then outside Mousehole. St Ives is a artists' colony. It was the home of the pioneer studio craft potter Bernard Leach, and later it was the place where the painter Ben Nicholson and the sculptor Barbara Hepworth established their studios. However, these distinguished artists did not discover St Ives. It had been a popular artists' community since the early 20th century: it had good light, sea, sand and cheap accommodation – it also had a rail link with London.

Leach, however, was the pivot of the art-crafts community, and his eminence helped to establish 'the crafts' as a respectable subject for interest and debate among other artists. St Ives was and, to some extent, remains, a community of artists where artists and crafts-people talk and exhibit together. When Breon O'Casey set up his studio there, the town was still, as he explained to the British poet Christopher Reid, a place where there was 'something in the air' which sustained creative endeavour. Reid writes, 'Breon O'Casey remembers how poverty and lack of supplied entertainment drew artists together in pubs…where ideas were expounded and exchanged in an atmosphere that uniquely combined camaraderie and disputatiousness.'

O'Casey is a painter, weaver and printmaker as well as a jeweler, studied under Fernand Léger and had a part-time job as an assistant to Barbara Hepworth, helping her to carve her marble and file her bronze, and assisted her with the bronze *Single form* (1962–63) that now stands outside the United Nations building in New York.

He happily admitted to Christopher Reid that he was a copycat. Not for him the disingenuous claims made by some artists never to have been influenced by anyone. He has taken ideas from Alexander Calder as well as the pre-Columbian metalwork of Peru. He chooses materials because he likes them, not because they are either valuable or ideologically favoured. Thus he uses gold and silver, but not diamonds; he carves granite (the local rock) and uses other non-precious materials such as carnelian or lapis lazuli. His work is subtle in colour and texture, but it has the colours, the light, the atmosphere and the textures of Cornwall. For, strange as it may seem, his work, though intended for wearing and the pleasure of ornament, is akin to a landscape art. It it derives from the place. This sense of being rooted in a geographical locality is quite rare in contemporary jewelry.

on what can be worn _____
on what can be worn

The sceptical critic of new jewelry, if asked, 'What can be worn?', might be tempted to reply, 'Anything.' After all, there is nothing left that one can think of that has not been proposed as jewelry – if not in public then you can be fairly sure in private. But jewelers themselves, in so far as they are designing for other jewelers or competing with other artists, do not believe that anything goes. If it did, the game would hold no interest. Instead what we see is a really startling series of invented objects. Just compare the variety of the following: Jamie Bennett (whose lucid comments about the nature of sculpture in the previous chapter are contextualized by the fact that he is a 'painter' in terms of the enamelled work illustrated in this chapter), Susan Hamlet, (b.USA 1954), Maria Hees (b.Netherlands 1948), Fritz Maierhofer (b.Austria 1941), Louis Mueller, Ramón Puig Cuyàs (b.Spain 1953), and Janna Syvänoja (b.Finland 1960).

All the work that these artists have produced is wearable. After all, as jewelers know, wearability is not such a difficult design function to fulfil. Most materials are acceptable, and size is a matter of what you can persuade your clients to wear. Only weight is the real issue and there are many solutions to that problem. Thus the artist (or designer) is more or less free to do what he or she wants.

The body is so obliging: there are blank walls – the torso – and plenty of hooks and ledges, fingers, wrists, upper and lower arms, ears, necks, hair, ankles and so on.

What remains important, however, is the inner coherence of the design itself. None of the works attributable to the variety of artists listed is arbitrarily conceived or created. For each object you can discern a critical, aesthetically motivated intelligence – one can infer the judgements and decisions retrospectively by looking at the works, noting the relationships of scale in form, volume and texture, how colour has been used, which of the 20th-century orthodoxies on design and decoration a piece tends towards, and so forth.

The result is a cornucopia of images and forms that shows more variety than has been achieved in the worlds of museum, gallery or publicly sited sculpture. Within this variety, almost all the criteria that anyone might wish to list as necessary to the creation of *good* art is present: some work shows great craft knowledge, some is conceptually clever, some of it shows concept and craft working together, some of it explores ornamentation, some of it rejects ornament, some of it seizes upon contemporary imagery, and other work is classically orientated. All that is holding it together as a body of work is the body. Someone must wear it but, as wearability itself is not a strict taskmaster, the degree to which the body itself is acknowledged as providing both artistic constraints and a subject matter is left up to the individual artist.

And the body is where the 'art' of the jeweler resides. It is frequently only when a piece of jewelry is worn – not posed for a photograph – but used, moving with its wearer, becoming part of the wearer's appearance, that the work can be judged. Jewelry becomes linked with the wearers' identity, with their view of themselves and with how others view them. The bodies that we see in the street or in the office or on the beach are people. The way they move and display themselves is not only a matter of biology and physics, but also of psychology. If the work is relatively conventional, there will be those whose conventions and tastes coincide with the jeweler's. But for artists pursuing the extremes there are some interesting choices. The body can be seen as a soft machine for displaying the art in a photograph, or it can be ignored entirely if the the goal is a gallery-wall or a showcase. But to pursue the extreme and to want that extreme worn by a person takes a different sort of imagination. It requires an understanding of the psychology of wearing unconventional objects. This understanding is probably quite rare. Perhaps the best 'extreme' jewelry is that conceived for a specific person.

Wearability is not, in new jewelry, a function of market research, but a function of imagination. New jewelry may be interesting to look at, but no contemporary jeweler is likely to be bothered by mass appeal. There would be no point. That aspect of wearability is solved more easily and economically by industry. New jewelry is a product of the culture of individualism: there are shared values, but they tend to be shared between individuals within minorities rather than in crowds. This has been the *raison d'être* of the last thirty-five years of craft or craft-like production of unique objects in an age of mass manufacture.

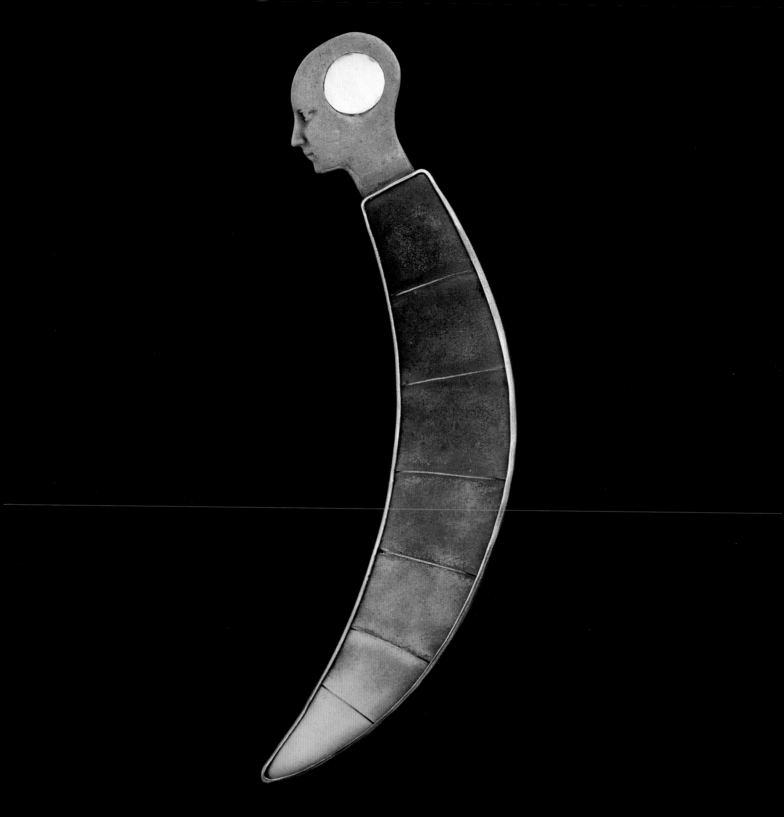

Previous page
Elizabeth Garrison
American

Moon #4
Brooch, 1987
Silver, copper, found
object, enamel,
mother-of-pearl
7.6 x 5.1 x 2 cm

Stuart M. Buehler
American

Nine Grains
Necklace. 1982
Cow bone, beads,
string, paint
Length 35.6 cm

Falko Marx
German

Brooch. 1988
Sapphires, diamonds,
sardine can
3.8 x 6.6 cm

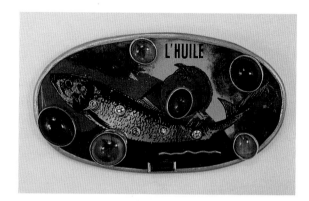

Elizabeth Garrison
American

Brooch. 1982
Silver, bronze, copper,
mother-of-pearl,
cloisonné enamel,
5.4 x 7.3 x 0.8 cm

Elizabeth Garrison
American

The Swimmer of Dreams
Brooch. 1988
Fine and sterling silver,
cloisonné enamel
2.5 x 9.5 cm

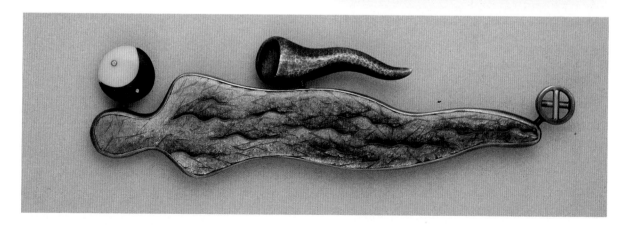

William Harper
American

Pagan Baby #11: Green Scarab
Brooch. 1978
14, 24k gold, silver, bronze, scarab shell, pearls,
bone, glass, cloisonné enamel, fine gold, fine silver
10 x 3.5 x 1.5 cm

Pagan Baby #6: The Scarab
Brooch. 1977
14, 18, 24k gold, silver, scarab shell,
pearl, cloisonné enamel
8.5 x 4.5 x 1.3 cm

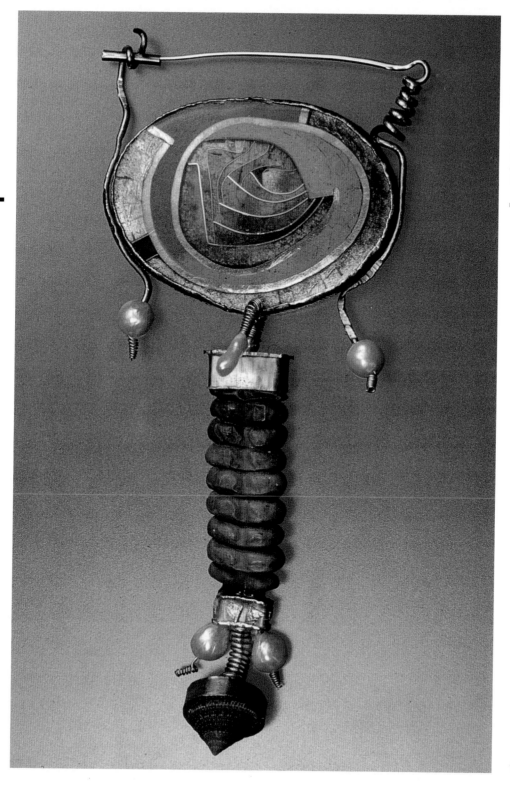

William Harper
American

Pagan Baby #3: The Serpent
Brooch. 1977
14, 18k gold, silver, pearls,
snake rattler, shell,
cloisonné enamel, copper
16.8 x 7.2 x 2.5 cm

Fritz Maierhofer
Austrian

Crumblestone Farm
Brooch. 1976
Aluminium, Plexiglas,
photograph;
edition 9/20
8.1 x 5.5 cm

Michael Becker
German

Barcelona
Brooch. 1988
Gold, haematite
2.5 x 5.7 cm

Fritz Maierhofer
Austrian

Brooch. 1977
Gold, gold alloy, silver
6 dia x 1 cm

Hermann Jünger
German

*Necklace with Four
Pendants #40*
1992
Gold, lapis lazuli,
pyrite, wood
Box 14.5 x 14.5 cm

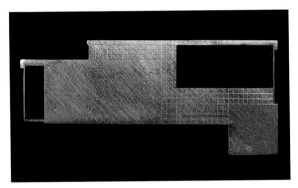

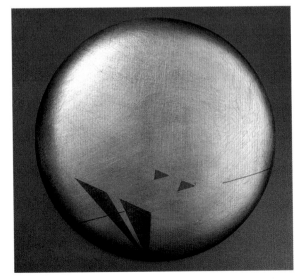

Louis Mueller
American

Brooch. 1985
24k gold-plated silver,
jade, rose quartz, crystal
5.7 x 5.7 x 1 cm

Brooch. 1985
24k gold-plated silver, onyx
5.7 x 5.7 x 1 cm

 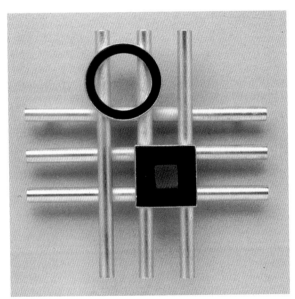

Susan Hamlet
American

Shim Bracelet #1
Bracelet. 1983
Stainless steel, plastic, rubber, silver
9.5 dia x 1.3 cm

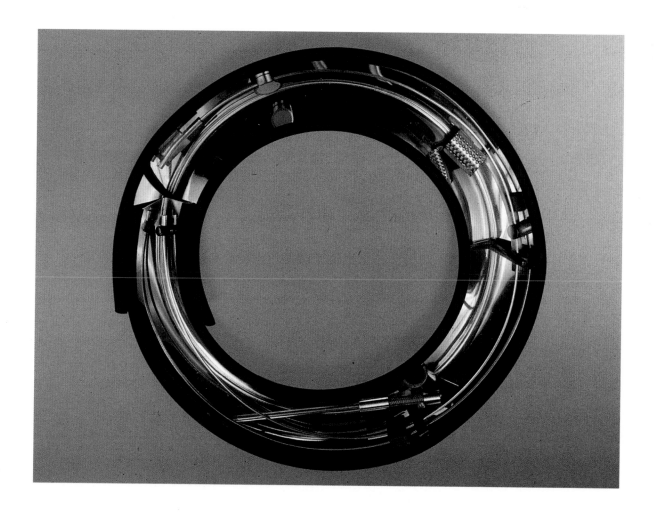

Debra Rapoport
American

Pendant. 1981-82
Found object, epoxy resin,
paint, commercial chain
8 x 7.2 cm

William Harper
American

Barbarian Bracelet #1
1980
Gold, silver, cloisonné enamel,
copper, sterling silver,
24k gilt; electroformed
15.4 dia x 2.7 cm

Tone Vigeland
Norwegian

Neckpiece. 1989
Silver
31.5 x 31.5 cm

Tone Vigeland
Norwegian

Neckpiece. 1981
Steel, silver,
14, 18k gold
30 x 18 cm

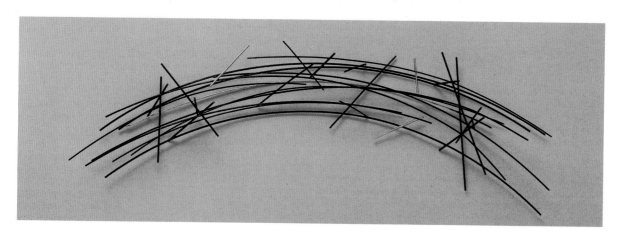

Georg Dobler
German

Brooch. 1985
Steel wire,
acrylic lacquer, gold
20.3 x 3.2 x 2.5 cm

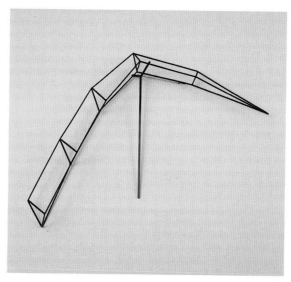

Georg Dobler
German

Salvadore
Brooch. 1985
Steel wire,
acrylic lacquer
20.3 x 12.7 cm

Tone Vigeland
Norwegian

Necklace. 1981
Steel, 14k gold,
mother-of-pearl
20 cm dia

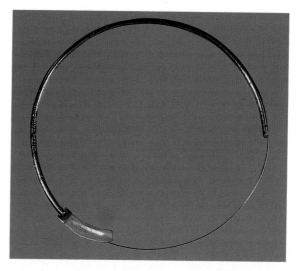

Gijs Bakker
Dutch

Botticelli Project
Three Neckpieces. 1990
PVC laminated
photographs, mirror,
gilded brass
Each 30.5 cm dia

Gijs Bakker
Dutch

Bouquet
Brooch. 1988
PVC laminated
photograph,
yellow sapphires
10 x 8.4 cm

Anna Heindl
Austrian

Brooch. 1989
Silver, glass
3.2 x 10.2 cm

Gijs Bakker
Dutch

Dewdrop
Neckpiece. 1982
PVC laminated photograph;
limited edition, #23
Portrait: Emmy van Leersum,
1982
49 x 51 cm

Daniel Kruger
South African, active Germany

Necklace. *c.*1987-88
Gold and glass
24 cm dia
Private collection, USA

Gijs Bakker
Dutch

The Tongue
Brooch. 1989
PVC laminated
photograph, diamond
11 x 8.4 cm

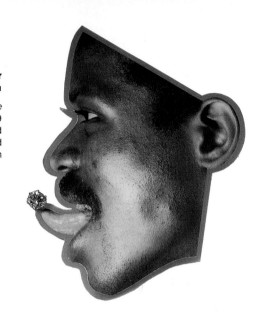

Gijs Bakker
Dutch

Waterman
Brooch. 1991
PVC laminated photograph,
diamonds; commission
15.2 x 7.6 cm

Stephan Seyffert
German

Herz
Bracelet. 1992
Silver, rhodonite
10 x 9 x 7 cm
Collection of the artist

Stephan Seyffert
German

Für Muttern
Brooch. *c.*1992
Silver, zircon
Length 9 cm

Arline Fisch
American

Necklace. 1986
Fine silver, 18k gold;
spool knit
25.4 x 2.5 cm

Birgit Laken
Dutch

Spiral
Brooch. 1990
Silver
12.7 x 11.4 cm

Spiral
Brooch. 1990
Steel, gold, silver
15.2 x 14.6 cm

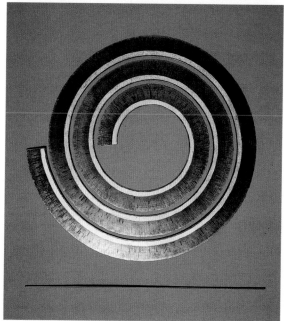

Miyé Matsukata
Japanese

Ring. 1974
18k white and 24k yellow gold,
heart-of-watermelon tourmaline
3 x 2 x 3.2 cm

Louis Mueller
American

Brooch. 1983
Oxidized silver, gold
4.5 x 6 cm

Joan Fraerman Binkley
American

Necklace. 1983
Porcelain, gold, silver lustre glazes
50 dia x 5 cm

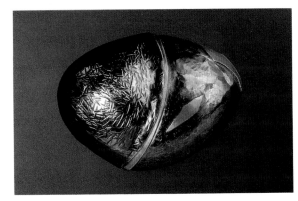

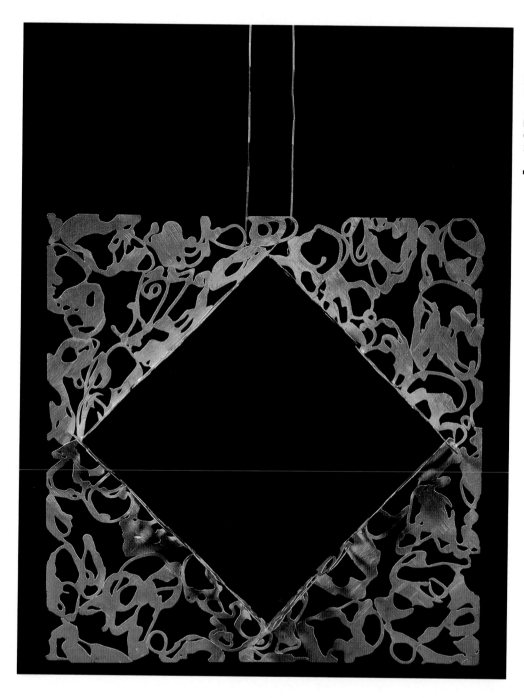

Robert Smit
Dutch

Square
Pendant. 1989
Gold
15.2 x 15.2 cm

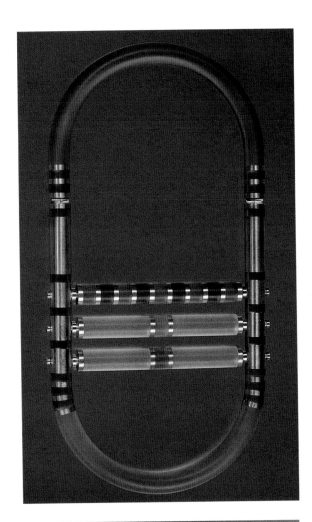

David Watkins
British

Neckpiece. 1974
Acrylic, silver
26.7 x 13.8 x 1.3 cm

Bracelet, 1981
Gold, acrylic
8 cm dia

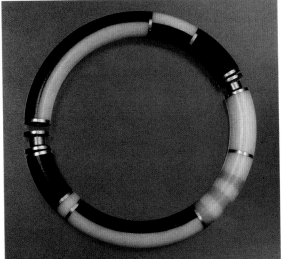

David Watkins
British

Voyager
Neckpiece. 1984-85
Neoprene-coated steel,
wood; 5 sections;
limited edition
34.9 x 30.5 cm

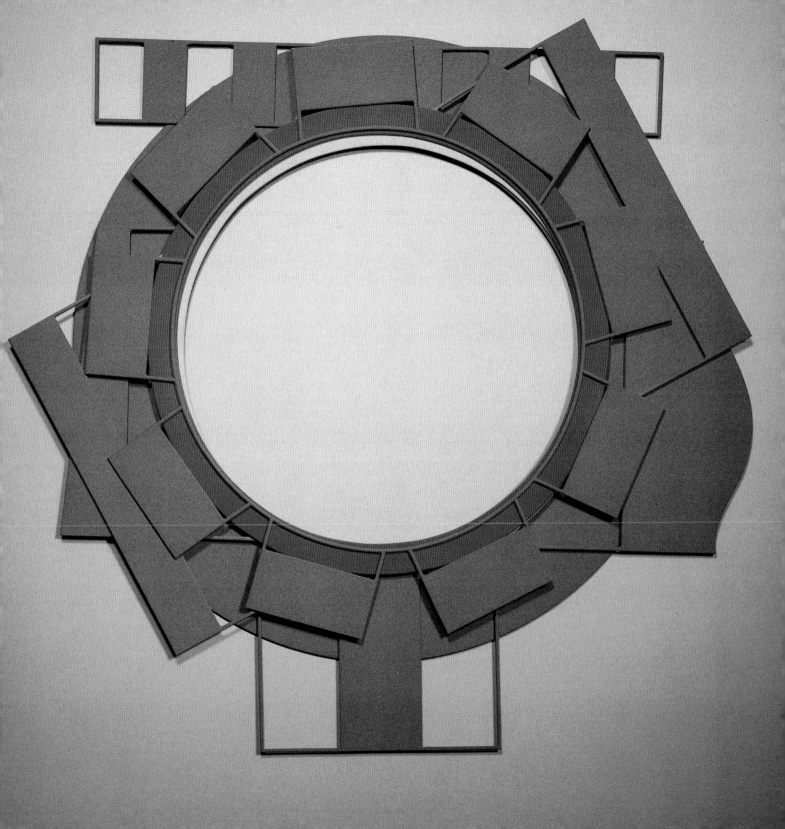

Maria Hees
Dutch

Brooch. 1983
Plastic
5 x 5 x 1.5 cm

Bracelets, 1983
Plastic
10 cm dia

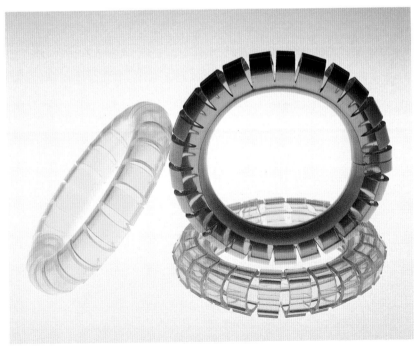

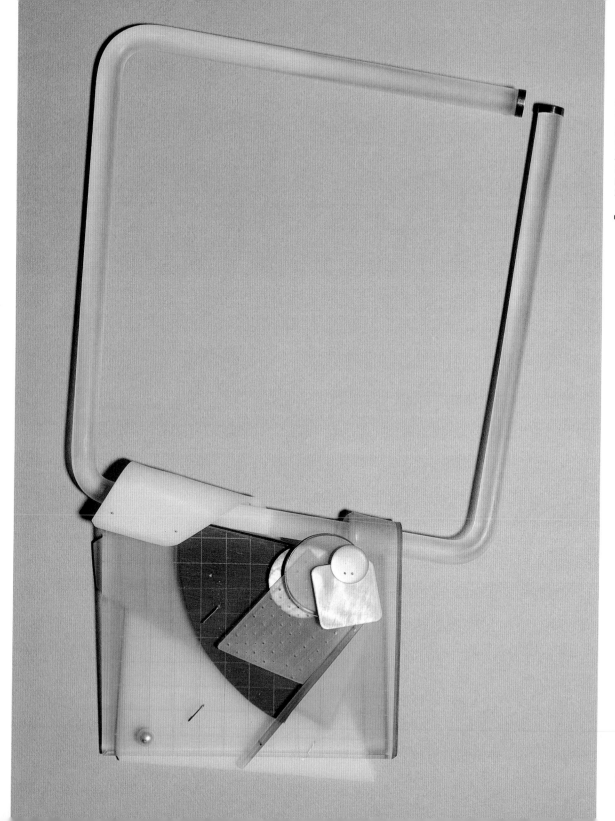

Alice H. Klein
American

Haru
Neckpiece. 1984
Acrylic, gold-filled wire,
sterling silver, mother-of-
pearl, cultured pearl
21.5 x 33 x 1.8 cm

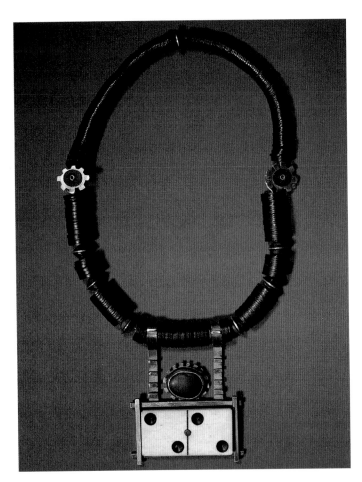

Ramona Solberg
American

Pendant. 1994
Silver, agate,
domino, shell
28.5 x 15.5 cm

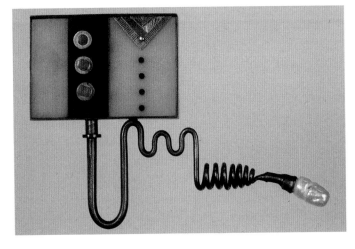

Robert Ebendorf
American

Brooch. 1974
Silver, Plexiglas, gold-plated
bronze, baroque pearl
9.5 x 6.5 cm

Esther Knobel
Israeli

Necklace, 1983
Tin, plastic,
paint, elastic
33 cm

Ramón Puig Cuyàs
Spanish

Mermaid
Brooch, 1989
Silver, acrylic paint
15.2 x 5.7 cm

L'ambraçada
Brooch. 1989
Silver, steel, acrylic,
acrylic paint
10 x 10 cm

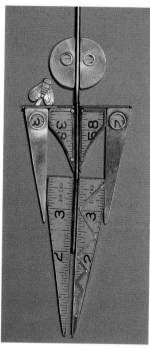

Kiff Slemmons
American

Zig Zag
Pendant, 1994
Silver, wooden ruler
Length 44.5 cm
Pendant 17.8 x 6.4 x 1.9 cm

Ramón Puig Cuyàs
Spanish

Brooch. *c.*1981
Silver, steel, PVC
5.1 x 7.6 cm

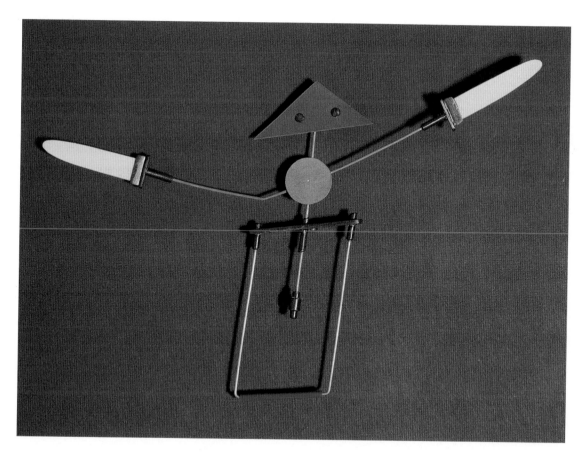

Jamie Bennett
American

Palermo
Brooch, 1985
Enamel, copper, sterling silver
11.1 x 3 cm

Blue Petrossa #4
Brooch, 1992
Enamel, gold, copper; electroformed
13.5 x 1.5 x 1.2 cm
Collection Donna Schneier, USA

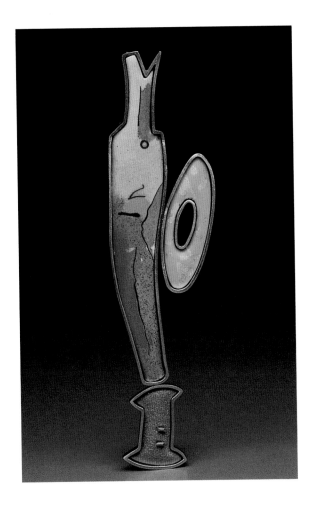

Jamie Bennett
American

Rocaille #13
Brooch. 1992
Enamel, copper,
22, 14k gold; electroformed
12.7 x 5.1 x 1.3 cm

Janna Syvänoja
Finnish

Brooch. 1992
Fishnet, wire;
edition, 1/3
12 cm

Sieglinde Karl
Australia

Necklace. 1990
Natural pods,
thread
25 x 30 cm

Janna Syvänoja
Finnish

Necklace. 1994
Book paper, metal;
edition, 2/3
36 cm dia

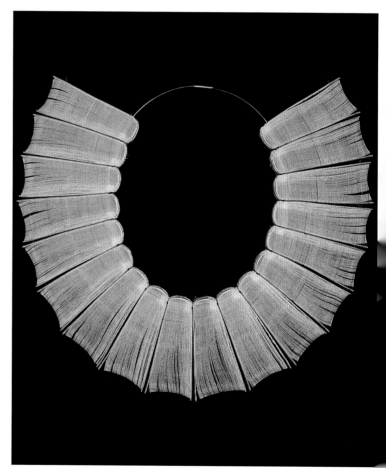

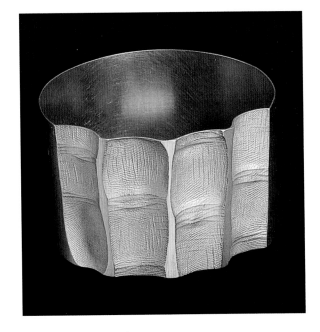

Gerd Rothmann
German

Schmuck einer Tänzerin
Neckpiece. 1986
Gold-plated silver;
edition, 2/5
22 dia. Each disk 4.7 cm
Collection Helen Bershad, USA

Othmar Zschaler
Swiss

Oval Relief
Ring. 1994
Gold
3.5 x 3 x 2.5 cm

Gerd Rothmann
German

Golden Nose of Helen Drutt
1994
Gold
Life size

Gerd Rothmann
German

Four Finger Bracelet
1992
18k gold
6.8 x 4.3 cm
Collection Inge Asenbaum,
Austria

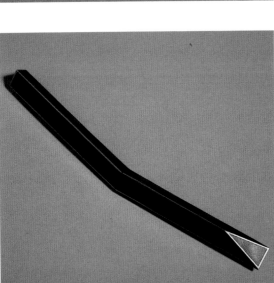

Giampaolo Babetto
Italian

Brooch. 1982
18k gold,
epoxy resin
1.3 x 12 cm

Brooch. 1984
Nickel silver,
epoxy resin
17 x 1.2 x 1 cm

Paul Derrez
Dutch

Neckpiece. 1983
Plastic, steel;
limited edition
38 dia x 10 cm

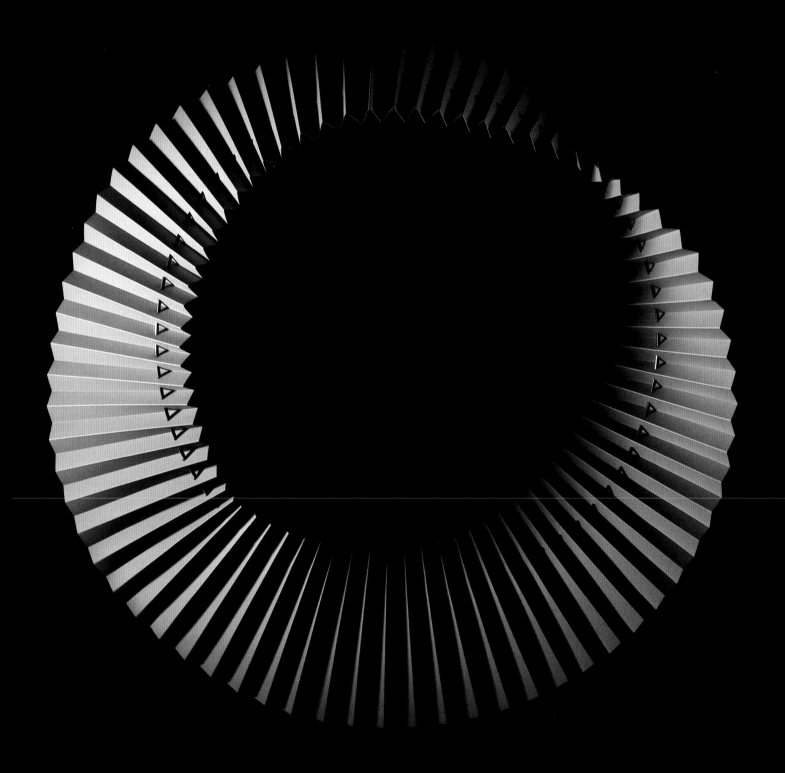

Debra Rapoport
American

Hat Pin with Rose Bud
1993
Cloth, netting, latex rosebud, paint, wire
28.6 x 10.8 x 13.2 cm

Warwick Freeman
New Zealander

Necklace. 1989
Paua shell, lava stone, paint
Length 120.7 cm

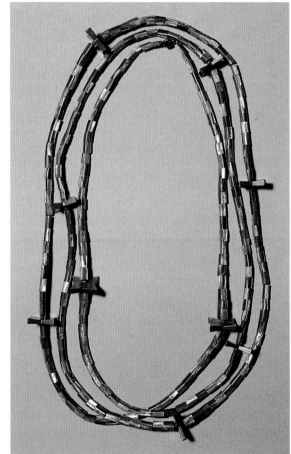

Lam de Wolf
Dutch

Neckpiece. 1983
Silk, paint;
commission
35.6 dia x 7.6 cm

_____

Overleaf
Johanna Dahm
Swiss

Bewegte Linie
(Moving Line)
Box with Pins. 1983
Pins: anodized
aluminium, steel wire
Box: wood, paint;
edition, 19/25
Pins 17 cm
Box 36 x 36 cm

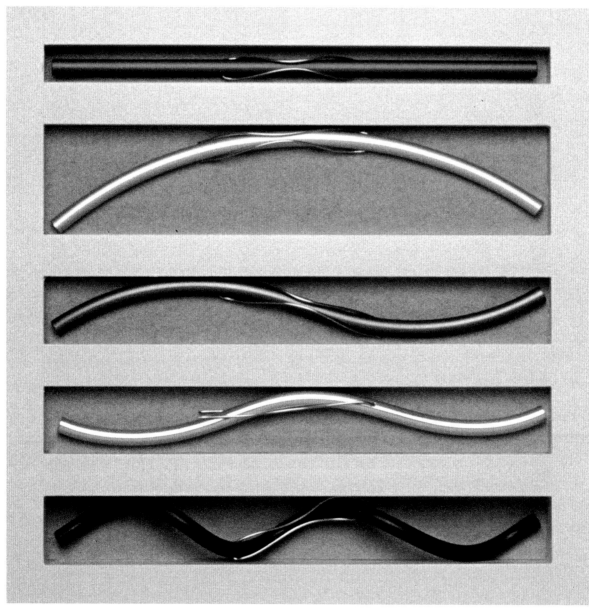

4 jewelry and identity

4 jewelry and identity

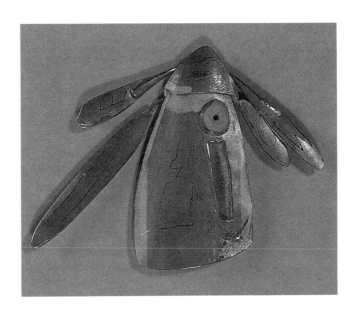

4 jewelry and identity

4 jewelry and identity

Previous page
Manfred Bischoff
German

Home
Brooch. 1988
Gold, silver, coral
6.4 x 8.9 cm
Collection Helen Bershad,
USA

The work discussed in this chapter falls, more or less, into three types. First, there is jewelry which is broadly 'political' or at least social in its commentary, such as that produced by Pierre Cavalan (b.France 1954, active Australia), Otto Künzli and Bernhard Schobinger (b.Switzerland 1946). Second, there is jewelry which has elements of private ritual about it such as that created by Margaret West or Carlier Makigawa (b.Australia 1952). Third, there is work that might be described as a form of private/public comment.

Examples here could include Bruce Metcalf (b.USA 1949), Kim Overstreet and Robin Kranitzky, and, of course, Manfred Bischoff, whose work is discussed and illustrated in Chapter 2. Bischoff's delicate narratives combining private and public symbols share a resonance with some of the work that is described in this chapter, though Bischoff's jewelry incorporates a less explicit, a less 'public', mental imagery. It is not suggestive of scenes or images from other, publicly known media, such as film or fairy-story illustration.

This chapter concentrates on a few artists at the expense of the many because this is the most efficient, least fragmented method of raising more general questions. All the work that is discussed is linked by the interest that its makers implicitly demonstrate in the notion of individual or institutional identity – a sense of identity, that is, which it is understood as related to the things, ideas and behaviour that we value. It is identity in terms of a moral being, rather than simply a matter of what class or culture one sees when one looks in the mirror. The questions that are raised, albeit obliquely in some cases, are, 'What do we value, what do we desire and what do we fear?'

Perhaps none of the work makes an unequivocally clear statement on its own. Visual art is an art of fragments – they have to be fitted in with other pieces of culture – texts, discussions, popular culture and whatever debates about moral and aesthetic value are dominant. Jewelry art, especially of the kind shown in this chapter, is particularly fragmentary. Although each object is complete in itself, its meaning is generally partial; you have to know a lot more about the context and the culture that brought it into being. Such information has to be learned, either through knowledge about the art culture in general in order to 'pick up the references', or by information offered by the artist, or the artist's nominated spokespeople, in the catalogues, seminars and lectures that most frequently provide a supporting context for exhibitions of the work under discussion in this chapter.

Some of the work shown here also raises questions about the nature of art jewelry itself. Is there such a thing as a art jewelry which is political? Is controversial jewelry merely playing about with public and private manners – no more consequential than poking out a tongue at the television screen whenever a political leader whom one dislikes appears? Or, to take another facet of art jewelry, is it possible for artists to 'invent' art that is ritualistic? Why would we want such art? Can individuals invent rituals for other people to understand? Or, to put all these questions into a single locket case, is there substance to the following assertion of Beverly Penn in *Metalsmith,* Spring 1993: 'Artists can address the complicated relationships that exist on a personal as well as a socio-economic level.' The job of this introduction is to put a little flesh on some of these issues before enlarging on the work of particular artists.

Many artists, whatever their preferred medium or discipline, want to use their art to make social comment. This is no new development. One of the histories of art is the history of art used for religious, political and moral comment. This is not just a history of painting, sculpture and building, but also of calligraphy and illumination, ceramics and, in particular, metalwork and jewelry.

In the past, in Western or European cultures, moral themes, sometimes quite abstract, used a complex shared visual language based upon, among other ingredients, classical and Judaeo-Christian ideas and symbols. (Other countries, other cultures, clearly have their mature, publicly understood art, allegories, oral or written histories, technologies and sciences). In the 20th century, much of this inherited visual vocabulary has been jettisoned and replaced by an imagery that is taken directly from the prevailing culture of our time: industrial design, advertising, film and consumerism. It is significant just how many times in how many art forms, including art jewelry, that the Coca Cola motif or bottle appears (as with Bernhard Schobinger), not to mention the USA's most famous fictional character, Mickey Mouse (Don Tompkins and Rebecca Batal, b. USA 1967).

The imagery may be new but the impulse to make comment, to 'say something', is not. The themes are broadly the old ones: fear of moral chaos, fear of disease, fear of authority, fear, if you will, of 'the devil', although the devil is in modern guise: he, she or it is a Freudian mélange, a masculine hegemony, a feeling of alienation or a physical disease. In addition, there are the traditional themes of 'time passing' and the poignancy of memory which, for example, Margaret West tackles. Some of the artistic strategies for commenting on the particularities of these fears are also familiar to us, especially the use of caricature and visual satire.

The motives for wanting to produce 'art with a subject' are probably and usually mixed. First, artists need a subject matter – they need to have 'a something' about which they can make their work. Most artists want a theoretical, social or moral foundation for their work. Secondly, making social comment is a way of exploring what one thinks of a subject or a situation. Thirdly, making social comment as art is often a form of therapy that is of particular benefit to the artist concerned.

This last point is rather important. The word therapy, derived from the Greek 'therapia', means healing. And it is significant that jewelry, and the 'new' arts, such as performance work and installation art, often have a lot to do with the subjects that directly affect the body and which, particularly in some cases, takes their cue from the artist's own body. For example, William Harper has produced jewelry that relates to his being subject to migraine. In the wider world of art generally, there has been a spate of art works dealing with sickness, and many women artists, inspired by the success of the AIDS campaign, have used their art to draw attention to such diseases as cancer of the breast.

More and more art undertaken in the West appears to be conducted in the spirit of healing. This does not, of course, guarantee its success as art, although it does, as will be discussed later, throw into contention several of the traditional criteria for evaluating what art is good and what bad. It throws the discussions about quality into moral confusion as well as contention by wrong-footing the critic: how can you be critical of someone in pain? On the other hand should one be manipulated into accepting or glossing over uninteresting or incomprehensible 'art' simply because the person who produced it deserves sympathy for his or her physical or mental pain? Surely not?

And it remains the case that, outside hospitals and old persons' homes, the concept of 'healing' art has not – for understandable reasons – found a sympathetic critical audience. Healing art, like 'defiantly personal art', can appear to be a retreat from competition and debate into a cosiness that is protected by a cordon sanitaire of political correctness. On the other hand, 'critical audiences' are not the same as 'real' audiences – critics are the minority – for many people it may be that an artist's healing art speaks to them because they too share that pain. Perhaps Harper's migraine jewelry finds an audience with those who are migraine sufferers. People appear to search out those who share similar adversities and perhaps jewelry is as good a conduit for this as any other media.

Some quite simple images involving contemporary jewelry are surprisingly effective in raising questions about abstract themes, such as 'aggression'. For example, a poster image advertising a London exhibition called *What is Jewelry* (Crafts Council, London 1994–95), showed an artist, Maria Hanson, holding and wearing a white metal truncheon on a stainless steel cord. The truncheon is a weapon and it is also phallic. The artist herself, slight but muscular, white and shaven-headed and with an inscrutable expression on her face, adds to the narrative of the work. She is quoted in the exhibition display as saying:

I wear this piece to evoke comment and contemplation that questions boundaries. As one of a series requiring the body for its context it rejects purely decorative accessory values. It is not 'nice' or 'pretty'. Its visual and tactile language triggers many other responses. Is it a sexual statement? It is bold, even aggressive, yet for myself sensually soothing.

Such a subject matter, which shifts the emphasis away from the 'body beautiful' as an object upon which to hang beautiful work and on to 'the body in crisis', raises interesting social and aesthetic problems for jewelry artists. For the truth is that the general thrust of jewelry art since the World War II, especially that of the avant-gardes of radical jewelry, new jewelry and so forth, has been the tacit acceptance that jewelry art should be promoted by beautiful people, and that the art itself, whether experimental or populist, has generally been quite tasteful. For all its radicalism, jewelry, as an art has been centred upon ideas about 'looking good'.

Exhibition catalogues do not generally feature ordinary, still less ugly, people wearing art jewelry. The thirty-five-year history after World War II of the avant-garde of art jewelry, like the much longer history of the avant-garde approach to dress and fashion (that runs from Schiaparelli to Vivienne Westwood) is at best the history of putting the rough, the awkward and the oppositional upon beautiful bodies in order that the art may make use of the body as a foil – and also so that the body may use the art as *its* foil. This conformist approach is partly accounted for by the fact that all exhibitions and their accompanying catalogues are, necessarily, promotional and one rarely finds a critical assessment of a living artist in that artist's catalogue.

Presentation is important for jewelry focusing on social issues, because one of the judgments made by critics is that jewelry can be narcissistic – like fashion. And like fashion, like most performance-based art, beautiful, or at least very attractive, models or performers are preferred to present the work to the public.

It may be an unavoidable problem. After all, if jewelers use ugly people then they are guilty of the exploitation of the odd and the freakish – a charge that was brought against the photographer Diane Arbus and served, for a time, to undermine the reputation of one of the century's most exciting, innovative and revealing photographers. And ordinary people, although they may be the subject or target of the artist's intent, are generally regarded as too uninteresting to make art with. And there, after all, is the rub: what counts more for the socially committed jewelry artist, the social comment or the art? It is not a question answered easily by saying 'both'.

Among the issues confronting social comment in art jewelry are where and when to wear it, and what it means to want to wear it. Obviously answers to such questions depend upon the nature of the jewelry and upon the definition of what jewelry is. For example, is the AIDS ribbon a piece of jewelry?

Being jewelry is not the main purpose of the ribbon but one suspects that some people wear it as such, since it is a tasteful red, and suitably discreet in design – a modernist version of the more familiar, and in Europe at any rate, widespread Flanders poppy design which is worn in remembrance of the dead of the two World Wars.

Neither item is jewelry as such. That is to say, their primary purpose is to function as signs establishing camaraderie with others, indications of social belonging rather than comment, although there are circumstances and places where, rightly or wrongly, the wearing of the AIDS ribbon will be provocative. It is important that such signs should look 'nice', however, and indeed they sit well on much that is acceptable as formal, academic or business dress. The AIDs ribbon did not start by being well-designed; it evolved into good design as it evolved into a 'status' symbol for the politically correct, the chic and the media stars to wear. It was important that those with taste (including most artists) as well as those without taste would want to wear it.

Some types of body ornament are almost generally unacceptable throughout government, corporate business and professional institutions everywhere in the West and Western-style countries and cultures: notably tattooing and body piercing. It does not matter what the content of such work is, the very act of wearing it will reduce the status of the wearer in the eyes of the authority concerned. Tattoos and body piercing are read as signs of nuisance, aggression, criminality and rebellion. Some acts of rebellion are important only in so far as the wearer and his or her fellow-travellers know of the act. Among the possibilities for body piercing, such acts as the piercing of genitalia are believed to be on a rapid increase, but who is to know? However, within the sexually or socially active group in which body piercing or tattooing is taken seriously as an aesthetic activity, such body adornment is quite public. It seen as a means of strengthening one's sense of identity within the group as well declaring that one belongs to the group. No art seems to thrive without an audience.

Among the many stupidities of authoritarian regimes is their lack of awareness regarding the investment of meaning into otherwise trivial acts. Singapore is an example. It bans beards and long hair and the chewing of gum in the streets. It thus gives these (surely?) unimportant matters a political dimension. A radical jeweler in Singapore need do no more than chew gum and then, in its malleable sticky state, turn it into an artefact and stick it on his or her lapel in order to make a 'political comment'. Making such 'trivial' political comment requires courage: in Singapore one risks a fine and time in the cells.

But making moral gestures through wearing unconventional or provocative art can also be self-congratulatory, especially in the West. Some jewelers understand the power of Narcissus and they recognize that their clients are obsessed with the reflection in the mirror. The narcissistic element extends also not only to the things we wear but to the things with which we surround ourselves. Why do people buy art? Perhaps to define themselves in their own and others' eyes through status objects. Perhaps this is the idea at the heart of Otto Künzli's necklace which has the fragment of the picture frame hanging on a chain. It is a clever piece given the connotations of the frame and the way it is used by artists and photographers to present pictures and images of ourselves.

Künzli has made an unusual impact in art jewelry. Künzli's work, although 'provocative', is inherently stylish, and calculated to tantalize rather than upset the intelligent, professional middle classes who take an interest in 'contemporary art'. In fact the 'models' appearing in photographs wearing Künzli's work are often drawn from these very classes. Yet what he has made them wear has played cleverly upon the 'what do I look like, what do I value' theme.

Much of his work in the mid-to-late 1970s is reductivist, minimalist, extremely tasteful modern jewelry, a considerable number of the pieces being brooches in precious metal. These really are the inheritance of Max Fröhlich, one of his teachers, and they exist as the end of one chapter and the beginning of another in Künzli's career. In the early 1980s, though keeping his simple forms of circles, triangles, and rectangles, Künzli progressed to more performance-like work which needed the presentation of a model in a gallery or a model in a photograph to articulate the idea. The polystyrene pieces – cubes, sticks and blocks – are covered in decorative wallpaper, and are frequently very amusing. There is something intelligently silly in seeing a well-fed, middle-class professional man or woman wearing a large wallpapered cube as if it were any common brooch. The silliness lies in the unconventional nature of the artefact, the intelligence in asking, 'But why should this be unconventional, why should it be silly?' The kind willingness of the subjects to make slight clowns of themselves, the recognition that such people have the inner confidence to do so, leads us to wonder where self-confidence ends and self-love begins.

Some critics believe that Künzli's work is too stylish, too well-edited in its wit, but one can argue that Künzli's target is the well-off, well-educated, discreetly charming upper-middle-classes, and that the way to sow seeds of unease is through the very stylishness that they expect and accept as the norm. Unlike Bernard Schobinger, another Swiss-born jeweler who seeks to get beneath the skin of the middle-classes, Künzli does not so much use his ideological fists as set barbs at the end of what seem at first sight to be compliments.

It is credible to argue that Künzli's work is wholly in tune with one of the truths of European, if not Western culture generally, which is that the most popular and effective art is found in the chic presentations of design through advertising and the design itself – be it motor cars, boxes of chocolates or CD-players. Künzli thinks in the style that seduces most of us. His design-orientated, advertising-orientated approach misleads critics, who think that art, in order to be oppositional ought to look oppositional. They should perhaps remember Hamlet's remark about his mother, the line most likely to be the motto adopted by any advertising agency, 'Smile, and smile, and be a villain.'

poetic truths

One of the most obvious features of contemporary Western or Western-style culture is that it owes its content to a belief in science and rationality. This is our inheritance from the 18th century, and it is immensely valuable. Through reasoning, logic and the belief (justified or not) in 'objectivity', we give ourselves the power to do many things and, moreover, correct things we get wrong. Reasoning is a tool for exposing our own error. But artists, and some philosophers, and now some rationalists (including scientists, especially those from the biological disciplines) point out that there are different kinds of rationality and that one of the most mistaken things we can do is always to divorce what we think of as 'pure' reason from our affective desires and emotions. In other words, there is more than one model of rationality, or, to put it more simply still, there may be meaning in the notion of 'poetic truth'.

This is why individual artists, such as Margaret West are interesting. With a mixture of poetry, jewelry and installation art, she wants to make people aware of ideas and feelings that if put in more concrete, monological forms would simply disappear.

She says, 'I think a lot of my work in the 1980s…was made with one of the intentions being to look at possible interactions between the body and the object....The objects I have made have not always been jewelry but frequently have been informed by some of the concerns of jewelry.'

The following observations are taken from West's catalogue called *Interstices* which accompanied an exhibition in Canberra of the same name. Consider first a work called *Eight Stones with Steel* (1985) which consists of rounded but abraded river stones threaded on to a length of steel cable. One may wear the assemblage around one's neck, but one can weight one side more heavily than the other: one can weigh a heavier stone against several lighter ones, or balance both sides evenly – like an old-fashioned pair of scales. One can feel the different weights by holding them in one's hands or allowing them to dangle around the neck. The cable will cut into the flesh a little.

The essayist for the catalogue, Julie Ewington, says 'In effect, the stones…have a ceremonial function – to measure the stature and weight (worth) of each person who wears them, bringing them into balance.' Of another series of works by West, using caskets (the size of jewelry boxes) that are lined with lead, Ewington writes:

It's a question of scale: one must lean forward to inspect the contents....The caskets treasure disparate things, like children's little boxes filled with snatches of days marked by their brilliant clarity of perception, with captured memories and also with insistent, but almost forgotten, emotions.

The contents include birds' feathers, red sand and tokens with modern runic markings. That is to say, many of the marks refer to, or actually are, scientific signs and symbols which are mysterious to the layperson but mean something to the initiated. This is an interesting comment on the status of science in our society. For most people a belief in science is almost on a par with a belief in religion since most people do not understand the language of science.

The emotion of nostalgia is one of the strongest emotions, and one that seems particularly widespread among the citizens of modern, industrial cultures. Whether or not the cause of this nostalgia is the speed or violence of change, coupled with the sense of time passing – a sense which deepens morbidly the older one gets – a surprising amount of contemporary installation art deals with the traces of memory, and the ephemeral nature of lived experience. One of the terrors of losing one's memory is to be trapped in the present. Rituals have long been used by all kinds of societies as a means of maintaining memories and hence identity – without memories there is no identity of self, institution, culture or country.

Memory, identity and ritual are subjects in West's work. However, it is worth noting two aspects. First, although such art is a break with conventional jewelry and sculpture, it is one example among many of a notable 20th-century theme in art connected with privacy, secrecy and the poetry of poignancy. Thus West's casket works can be seen in the context of the artwork-in-a-box 'movement'. This is a movement with some key figures, such as Joseph Cornell and Marcel Duchamp, with roots in the avant-garde movements of Dada and Surrealism. Art historian Alexandra Noble describes the box movement as follows:

The fascination that artists have shown for this form is, to some extent, inseparable from the histories of assemblage and collage, for art in boxes is a hybrid genre combining painting, printmaking, photography, collage, sculpture and assemblage to create new modes of expression. It is with assemblage, where the constituent elements are not carved, modelled or drawn, but taken from pre-existing manufactured or found materials and objects, that the box most readily adapts itself: three-dimensional configurations often need a structure which acts as container, boundary and protection.

Box art finds a counterpart in jewelry. Not only is jewelry often presented (and kept) in boxes, but certain forms of jewelry such as the brooch-form are analogous to box art. Several artists, notably Overstreet and Kranitsky, Betsy King (b.USA 1953) and J.Fred Woell in his early work, use the hybrid process of different kinds of making and assemblage, and use the brooch-form as a 'container' to provide a framework or bounded area within which fluid compositions can take place. These artists produce very different work, however: the box art comparison is offered as a loose analogy to show how some art jewelry connects with other elements in the art world.

The gallery or museum space in which work is displayed has been described as box art (a gallery is a box). West says of exhibiting in a gallery:

I do not agree with those who claim that work is dead within the gallery or museum. For me, the potential is an important part of the work. And the particular potential of the gallery is to provide the space, the opportunity – even to coerce – the viewer to take up at least a part of that potential, cerebrally, if not physically.

She points out that the viewer of jewelry in a gallery may put herself or himself in a complex relationship with the work: 'They may place themselves as both wearer and viewer.'

Some of her work is politically motivated. A piece called *Detail* consisted of hundreds of small black medals (the waste discs created by stamping out the holes of steel washers) hung on black ribbons and pinned row upon row upon row, refers to the wastage in war of children and of other 'unimportant' people.

Another Australian, Carlier Makigawa, provides an example of the artist jeweler whose work has a role as a generator of private reverie. Her works have an architectural content and a metaphorical content: they are about protection, security and preciousness. Makigawa has produced a series of constructions which are cages containing an organic form. This is a simple but effective visual metaphor that would suggest something to most human beings – or so one imagines. The idea of protection and also the idea of being kept out are capable of literary, psychological and practical interpretations. The ideas gain their force by being jewelry-sized – the size you can hold or wear – they also gain from not being literal. One may reflect on the value of this by considering the all too literal public sculptures that have been popular this century, especially in Scandinavia, of the ensemble of mother and father and child, which also projects the idea of protection, but does so in a way that allows in too much sentimentality. Perhaps popular culture – too many B films, too many television soaps, too many 'True Life' stories in magazines – have killed off, for the time being, the literal representation of a range of human affections and emotions.

Another artist whose work is as complex as Margaret West's is that of Bernhard Schobinger. In some ways Schobinger's work seems more outgoing than West's in so far as it has on occasions appeared to make a direct comment upon issues in the world. For example, there is his *Holiday in Cambodia* bracelet which is a band of skulls in the form of a bracelet, itself the colour and texture of bone (the work is further discussed below). However, without wanting to intrude with amateur psychology, but merely comparing what he has done with what he has said about himself, we may infer that his work is as much the product of a quarrel with himself, his background and even his father as it is with the rest of the world.

With Schobinger, as with a number of the jewelers in this book, we may be seeing the fruits of the discreet rage of a disaffected middle-class individual. Indeed, in conversation, he has said that he accepted the view that middle-class conservatism breeds 'anarchists'.

Schobinger says that when he was a child he saw an elaborate silver, glass and enamelled reliquary in a Swiss Baroque church and, 'I knew I wanted to make something like this.' His father, a wealthy merchant who died when Schobinger was twelve, wanted his son to follow him in commerce, and arranged his education accordingly. As the only child of elderly parents (his mother gave birth to him when she was forty-three, his father was in his sixties) and as a pupil in a strict Catholic monks' school which discouraged art, the conditions for encouraging Bernhard's rebellion are obvious.

His subsequent work is not all anti-authoritarian; it has gone through phases. He produced some quite conventional jewelry in a modernist, rational style of Ulm-like calm and proportion, as well as the pieces made from broken and found objects, including shards of Coca Cola bottles and other detritus. This 'rubbish' is often chosen by Schobinger because of its associations for him: the Coca Cola shards, for example, were picked out of the gutter in the artists' quarter in Maritzplatz, West Berlin, where Schobinger was temporarily staying and working; they are juxtaposed with 19th-century hand-cut crystal beads. Another necklace joins amethyst with stone engraved with the image of barbed wire, and linked with iron. Now in his forties, Schobinger says that after a period of rebellion he is calmer, and has found harmony in his work.

Switzerland, that rich, middle-class and secretive nation, has been home to several 'subversive' artists in this century. Zurich in 1916 has been described as the birthplace of Dada. There is no direct lineage between Schobinger and the Dadaists, but Dada sets an important precedent for the type of work that Schobinger and others have done. Dada, so often described as only nihilistic and anti-rational, and remarked upon more for its attack upon artistic conventions than upon other more substantial targets, might, viewed in a different light, appear as very reasonable response to a most unreasonable world. After all, World War I, which nurtured Dada, was conducted in the spirit of a series of rational acts and yet, even at the time, was perceived by many people as being itself an act of the most extraordinary collective 'non sense' and nihilism. Dada, with its deliberately absurd art and performances, was both as pointless and as reasonable as the rest of the modern world.

Dada might be regarded as an extension of the 18th and 19th-century Romantic movement, and we know that, in some of the Romantic movement's excesses, artists lovingly embraced decay, corruption and ruined bodies, ruined nature and ruined objects. Much of Schobinger's work is about rubbish, dirt, rebellion and the potential of broken things. Indeed, some of his earlier experiments when he was twenty-four flirted with elements that in retrospect seem almost self-destructive. In a letter to Helen W. Drutt English in 1994, he describes experiments in 1968 with mercury: 'I experimented with this metal. At that time, I simply filled in long PVC tubes, which one could wind around the neck and arm....I was under medical treatment, since by mistake I swallowed a large quantity of mercury which I wanted to suck into a tube. I have survived it.' He also experimented with Bostich-clips which are shot by a kind of 'gun' as a fixing mechanism for joining materials together. He had himself anaesthetized while a surgeon shot these clips into his ears. Schobinger said he did this 'out of sheer curiosity as to whether the surgeon really would do something like that. He did do it. In return, for one year, I had to fight against infections until I removed the clips.'

Such behaviour can be given an even more modern art-history gloss than that of 19th-century Romanticism: there is a history of 'self-destructive' or 'flirting with death' behaviour in male body and performance art dating from the early 1960s with Yves Klein's photograph of himself leaping from a wall into a street, and including work in the early 1970s by an American artist called Chris Burden who, in 1971, stood in a gallery and asked someone to shoot him. The bullet grazed his arm; surprisingly the resultant wound and the bandage applied to it has not yet been claimed for the annals of the new jewelry. Performances by Burden in subsequent years included having himself nailed to the roof of a Volkswagen car. In this behaviour he was bested in 1991 by a poet turned performance artist called Bob Flanagan who nailed his penis to a board. Flanagan, a man ill with cystic fibrosis and an incurable lung disease, was engaged in a public art about the private aspect of pain.

Schobinger did not pursue his own bodily experimentation, but deflected his curiosity about pain into the creation of visual metaphors – the more usual route of the artist. Many times Schobinger's jewelry uses the form of the sharp shard and the broken fragment – it is a true crown-of-thorns imagery – but it only suggests rather than inflicts bodily pain.

One of the most important aspects of Schobinger's work, especially in the way it developed during the 1980s with its emphasis upon fragmentation and found and natural objects, concerns his collaboration with his wife Annelies Štrba. She is an eminent photographer. The books they have produced are fascinating, once more showing the contemporary importance of the photograph as the contributor to art-jewelry's meaning. There is a book of black and white photographs of their daughter wearing a collection of sixty-two pieces produced by Schobinger between 1984 and 1987. There are bracelets with long thin barbs, necklaces of indiarubbers or pieces of handsaw, contrasted with bracelets and necklaces of the utmost linear delicacy. The collection shows two aspects of Schobinger's work: his interest in the metaphors of antagonism and provocation, and his natural tendency to give style to things, to make them chic. This effect of chic antagonism is intensified by the black and white photography of a young woman whose expression of bruised intelligence and scepticism is a look that we have are accustomed to from the heroines of a hundred European art movies. Most assuredly, some people will wonder at this imagery of the young woman as victim, and it would be interesting to see what reaction the pictures would provoke in a politically correct, morally alert North American conference on, say, sexism and art.

This is art that is half in love with the idea of suffering; it is deeply romantic. The model is posed to suggest the idea of the emotional and the visionary. Schobinger's jewelry reveals his romantic interest in nature (Romanticism itself being linked with a heightened appreciation of the beauties of nature), and all in all we see an art that is provocative, sweet-natured and sexually charged.

Schobinger's most overtly political piece of jewelry is his *Holiday In Cambodia* bracelet. Cambodia, now Kampuchea, was bombed in the early 1970s by the USA. The Khmer Rouge, a left-wing group of insurgents originally led by French-educated Marxists, but expanded and militarized during the late 1960s and early 1970s, took over the country in 1975. The Khmer Rouge government, led by Pol Pot, forced the city population to move into the countryside – it was an attempt to reject and reverse Western-style culture. It is believed that three million people were murdered by the Khmer Rouge between 1975 and 1978.

Schobinger's bracelet can obviously be read in a number of ways. It is a memorial to yet another 20th-century genocide, and is a reminder of similar atrocities in Europe and elsewhere. The poignancy in turning a representation of human skulls into an ornament arises from the legacy of the belief that human remains from the German death camps, including skin and hair, were turned into ornaments. Yet the idea of wearing a bracelet that refers metaphorically to an act of human slaughter is necessarily in questionable taste. It is from this ambiguity that the work may be said to draw some of its power.

The art gains justification if it is regarded as a comment on the way we – necessarily – live comfortably, side by side, with the knowledge of horror every day. This is not the book for a description of past horrors – whether in Germany, South Africa, Vietnam or the former USSR. But we might note that the continuing relevance of a work such as Schobinger's *Holiday in Cambodia* bracelet lies in its reminder that we live with the knowledge of savagery and with its products. In Britain, for example, there is a big market for garden furniture made in China because it is so astonishingly cheap. It is cheap because it is made by prison labour; Chinese prisons are not noted for their humanity. The irony of wearing a bracelet that refers to savagery is merely artistically poignant compared with the actual, dare we say, immorality of reading an improving book while sitting on a summer evening on a garden bench made by Chinese prisoners.

The combination of the catastrophic with the comfortable is an old artistic device, and it is at the root of Schobinger's *Cambodia* bracelet – but it remains effective. And because it is a bracelet and therefore an intimate object, it might also be argued that it is a piece of art for private reverie and enlightenment. The individual sometimes needs to pay an act of private homage to others. Private art – such as the war poem – can be a conduit for such homage, and, arguably, Schobinger's bracelet acts in a similar way.

It is a testimony to the power of Schobinger's work that it is one of the very few bodies of work that tends to arouse really passionate moral and aesthetic opinions in other jewelers. Paul Derrez has remarked of Schobinger's work:

I felt it was morbid, aggressive, neurotic and at the same time brilliant. I see jewelry (and the making of it) as a very optimistic, joyful thing. Although I think Schobinger is an important artist, his lack of humour, irony and self-reflection makes his work unbearable, destructive and decadent.

Other people disagree with this assessment, and draw comparisons between Schobinger and the German artist Joseph Beuys, who confronted political and 'spiritual' values through his art.

Various claims of a more social and psychological rather than political kind are made on behalf of Bruce Metcalf's work. His approach uses a raw caricature and expressionist representation: his work is like a bitterly humorous cartoon nightmare. By far the most uncomfortable of his images, for this writer at any rate, are those foetus-like figures which also seem reptilian and also adult. It is an image that combines viciousness with vulnerability, and is, I suppose, as good a visual metaphor as any for work that reflects the angst of contemporary Western society. There is some ambiguity in the work in so far as Metcalf hints that he takes angst seriously, but not that seriously. It is, after all, a condition of free-floating guilt or remorse that is something of a luxury that one can afford only if one is comfortable enough to have time to indulge in it. The moral seriousness with which some people treat their angst is, in its way, narcissistic, and Metcalf seems to be aware of this, and incorporates this awareness in his work. That is why the humour is there.

Metcalf wishes to argue, both in his writing and in his art, for a balanced view of humanity. He wrote, in 1991, 'I propose to strike a balance; to produce images of the self that accept the moral and social flaws we all acknowledge, but also suggest that strength, courage, persistence, integrity and an insistence on responsibiity for our own actions can recover dignity in our lives.' Having established his moral agenda, he then explains his practice:

My strategy is to employ a double-negative. The figures are distorted, with inflated heads and shrivelled bodies. Their hands and legs are attenuated and ineffective. Some are scarred, several are covered with thorns. They occupy perilous positions: crushed between two rocks; dancing on the edge of an axe; threatened by a falling bundle of missiles. But at the same time, they are ultimately too silly to be credible. I eschew high art conventions....Instead, each figure is rendered with cartoon usages, which imply a humorous condition. In fact, I find the images funny.

private comments

J.Fred Woell is a very important figure in North American jewelry. In his later work he has used himself – or rather his feelings, his private emotional and psychological pain – as his subject matter, although his earlier work made substantial use of the American popular culture. He is among the first jewelers to use assemblage (in the 1960s), and his work is an illustration of the point raised earlier in this chapter that some art jewelry belongs to the box-art movement. Assemblage art was given a post-war boost by an important exhibition held in 1961 at the Museum of Modern Art, New York.

A characteristic early work by J. Fred Woell is his brooch *Come Alive, You're in the Pepsi Generation,* 1966, made of copper, silver, steel, camera lens and photograph. As a practitioner of assemblage, Woell brought to the art a gentleness and a fondness for the material he found and used. He saw found objects not only as interesting forms and designs but as mementos of events, as carriers of meaning from one generation to the next. He says, 'My work is partly satire and tries to mimic…with such things as campaign badges, fan-club buttons, awards, medals, etc. It also provides me with a tool to express my thoughts and reactions about the conditions and situations that exist.'

His involvement with discard art and assemblage began as a reaction to an exhibition of Scandinavian silver jewelry that he saw in New York in 1965.

I returned home in disgust! Why should the material that a work of Art be made of determine its saleability? I went back to the studio and promptly began making jewelry out of junk, found objects, anything that crossed my path. I began making jewelry that commented on our way of life and upon what Americans seemed to hold as being valuable; I began to discuss the American Dream.

The result was an exhibition in 1966 in the Museum of Contemporary Crafts in New York. In the years 1968–71 he had three solo shows; at this time he was creating sculptural miniatures cast from plastic toys. He set up the metals programme at the University of Wisconsin, Whitewater, then, with Jamie Bennett, reorganized the course for the Program in Artisanry at the University of Boston, and established the metal programme at Swain School of Design in Massachusetts.

In the 1980s his personal circumstances altered so radically that, looking back, he says, 'The 1980s for me were about pain. Emotional pain. Everything I did during the first half of the '80s was about facing my mortality…lots of major emotional and physical upheaval led to work that became a metaphor of everything I was experiencing.' He made a series of works for an exhibition, *Back To Square One,* due to be held in 1984, but which had to be cancelled. It was of work that was like jewelry, but not jewelry: a series of wallpanels, 20 cm square, each dealing with a personal issue relating to the breakup of his marriage, the loss of a house he had been building for ten years, his teaching job and his studio. The work for this exhibition, even though it never took place, is an example of the way in which art is a healing process for the artist. This is from Woell's statement, written in 1983:

This show is about pain.... This show is about recognizing pain as a part of the celebration of life and its importance in understanding our humanity. It's my attempt to understand its importance to my personal growth and learn to discipline myself to deal with it creatively.

Woell relates work to experience: art as healing can be quite different from social comment. Obviously so, because art as healing allows the practitioner no distance, no ironic detachment. The grand theme (genocide, Vietnam) is easier to deal with than personal illness or torment because the personal illness or torment occupies the same space as the artist: it is in the artist's body and mind in a way that a concern for another – unless it is someone very close like a child or a spouse – never is.

Woell says, 'I've never really thought of myself as an artist or jeweler. I make things (objects). Some of them you can wear.' He takes pains to ensure that wearable objects are wearable (they will not break, fall off the body or cut the wearer with sharp edges). He continues:

On the other hand, I do not make jewelry that is about personal adornment in the usual or traditional sense. My need to use the body as an exhibition area or personal platform for my social political ideas remains constant. I don't make jewelry to glorify or make the wearer more attractive or sexually exciting.

Woell thus raises one of the oddest aspects of the 'artist jeweler', which is the notion of making private statements about the artist's identity via some one else's body – 'the body as an exhibition area or personal platform'. Now it is notable that, when Woell was most in need of art as therapy, he did not make objects to wear, he made objects that were like jewelry but not jewelry – intimate but not requiring involvement with anyone else.

Many people might wish to say the same of the work produced by Kim Overstreet and Robin Kranitzky. The small worlds that these two women create are a continuation of the box-art genre discussed above. Indeed, one of their brooches is shaped as a box – a coffin. Some of the 'boxes' that Overstreet and Kranitzky's works suggest are the traditional theatre stages with a proscenium arch. This is true of the brooch called *Threshold.* It has a number of allusions: to fairy tales, to theatre stage sets, to the sets for animated films, to children's book illustrations. *Threshold* is typical of their work in so far as it suggests a scene in a narrative – and the narrative appears to be continuing because the scene is caught in mid action – rain is suggested, the movement of wind in a curtain, a bird caught in movement. Traditionally grim imagery (traditional in fairy-story illustrations) menaces beauty: for example, a cameo brooch is held in the claw-like fingers of a pair of leafless trees. The title *Threshold* allows viewers to interpret the scene any way they want, but there is an element of possible terror.

This is a private art in that its full range of meanings is not accessible unless disclosed to the viewer by the two artists in conversation or by an accompanying text. On the other hand, the allusive nature of the work is grounded in imagery that many millions recognize: the imagery of the savage fairy tale. Yet there is no violence in the work: all is suggestion. And it may mean nothing. It may be a form of kitsch masquerading as something serious (so much art is just that).

This work, though clearly engaging, is not a comment on anything, more an object of unease – of private unease in a private reverie. Yet the connection with fairy tales and the violence that these contain can, by allusion, connect the viewer to real-life nightmares. The image of the threshold is a potent one in Western culture. It is present in the traditional story of the woodcutter's children in the forest who find a path to a gingerbread cottage inhabited by a murderer waiting to put the children in the oven. The 20th-century reality is the single railway track passing through pretty green fields somewhere in Poland and disappearing into the woods and then passing through a gateway into horror. Such a reading may have nothing at all to do with the artists' intentions, but ambiguous works are particularly vulnerable to the re-interpretations of the viewer. The viewer becomes the author, the artist – indeed, this possibility is the big idea of post-modern European literary criticism – one that has been happily embraced by artists and critics in the visual arts.

Extreme ambiguity can be a powerful weapon in the artist's armoury. Peter Tully (b.Australia, 1947–92), produced some enigmatic brooches – his wrapped figures and aircraft are very intriguing. All wrapped objects are. In Tully's case the objects have been made to appear as though they could have been animate as well as inanimate objects: the bodies of people as well as the bodies of aircraft.

public imagery

Sometimes apparently straightforward, highly recognizable images turn out to be slippery. For example, Rebecca Batal produced a pendant showing a plastic Mickey Mouse crucified on a cross. Everyone in the West has heard of and seen pictures of Mickey Mouse. Mickey Mouse is a symbol of all kinds of things: the brilliance of animation as a high art (the studios of Disney have been one of the great repositories of academic draughtsmanship and representational skills), the power of American culture in its inventiveness, marketing and ability to create a popular entertainment, the happiness of childhood, the ruthlessness of corporate identity (you mess around with Mickey's image and you take on the might of the Disney Corporation), and it is also an image of kitsch. The Christian cross has too many meanings to unpack, although it also runs the gamut of association from high art to kitsch.

Nailing Mickey to the Cross means what? That for many people in North America Mickey Mouse is more important to them than Jesus Christ? It is an interesting thought, although in the context of the USA, which in the 1990s appears to be generating a mass movement in fundamentalist Christianity, the notion that Mickey is more important to millions than Christ is debatable.

However, some people might wish that Mickey was more important than Christ, or one might say that the techniques that market the happy land of Mickey are exactly those used so successfully by North American Christian fundamentalists to market Christ.

Or one might argue that the Batal piece is just a work of easy montage, a sleight of hand, and an example of ersatz intellectualism. The bringing together of two such powerful and contradictory images may be seen as a stroke of genius or as an easy victory. It is a dangerous combination, less because of the risk of offending people's sensibilities and more because it can be a generator of facile thinking. Perhaps the piece is 'suggesting' one or both of the following: Mickey Mouse means more to many Americans than Jesus Christ; Mickey Mouse does less harm than Jesus Christ. Are these thoughts genuinely insightful? How do we know that Mickey Mouse means more to many Americans than Jesus Christ? And if we do know that he does, then does that mean either that many Americans have no serious values, or that many Americans have consciously decided that Mickey Mouse does less harm than Jesus Christ and therefore have a very sophisticated code of values? Perhaps these questions are an example of second-rate sophistry, or perhaps Rebecca Batal's work is a powerful piece of work because it makes you think. Or perhaps we should concede that Mickey Mouse is also Mickey Muse.

An equally straightforward piece of imagery with almost as slippery a meaning is provided by Ruudt Peters (b.Holland 1950) with his architectural jewelry. We are presented with classical architectural ornament, one of the three Greek orders of pillar. Classicism is an immensely powerful, extremely large body of culture, covering and still informing many Western ideas about science, morals, architecture, the design and nature of cities and democracy itself. But while we can say that an image taken from a classical building is a trigger for all manner of thoughts about the meaning of classicism, we cannot claim that the image itself is a bearer of any but a very general form of meaning. If the image is taken from a particular building and we know its place, history and current use, then the particularity of meaning is increased. However, the artist is dependent on the the viewer, and, more importantly, on how much history that viewer knows, or even on whether that viewer cares at all about the cultures that classicism informs.

At one time, perhaps as late as the 1950s, a certain kind of artist or critic or intellectual who was writing, painting, opining or observing to an audience of 'educated' men and women, could count on a more extensive knowledge of classical literature, philosophy, art and architecture than she or he dare expect today. At one time classicism was a 'shared symbolic order'. Today it is a shared historical backdrop, largely ignored.

Ruudt Peters said in correspondence: 'I try to combine my personal feelings with a historical perspective. I used the Architectural language and meaning of a building to express my personal feeling about certain places. Out of this I created the series of works with holes. The hole represents *nothing.*' This he describes as a framework around nothingness. This could be interpreted as a very negative view on culture, but apparently not, 'You can look through them [the holes] to see the body behind the brooch. And the opening often raises a question. Again and again jewelry provides the starting point between two people.'

Peters has also said, in an interview with Anna Frayling, published in *Art Aurea*, that, 'It's not a matter of trying to figure out how to make art, but rather a matter of trying to figure out what one is trying to say. That's one of the weaknesses of the jewelry scene – everyone is trying to be an artist.'

But perhaps the bigger weakness is the hopelessness of everyone trying to create their own public languages about their private feelings. We are approaching the stage where images are meaningless without an interview with their creator. Indeed, whatever claims are made for jewelry as an art that expresses a relationship between personal experience and public understanding, it has to be admitted that in this area of jewelry, as in so much art, the images need their words.

One of the clearest essays written on the subject is E.H.Gombrich's 'Image and Word in Twentieth-Century Art' (*Topics of Our Time,* Phaidon, 1991). His subject is painting, and his particular interest is the relationship of the image and its title. Gombrich observes that the vital distinction between images and words is that words can distinguish between universals and particulars. The title becomes crucial when the artist feels she or needs to offer the viewer instructions or, almost as frequently in our period, when the artist wants to confuse us further and throws us something that is either gnomic or tantalizing but not explicit. As an example of an instruction, Gombrich cites James McNeill Whistler's famous portrait of his mother. The title of which is *Arrangement in Grey and Black*: *Portrait of the Artist's Mother, 1871.* As Gombrich puts it, the painter wanted the viewer to pay attention to the sensory qualities of colour and composition before going straight to a consideration of the painting as a likeness of an old lady (unless you knew Whistler's mother you are hardly likely to be interested in how close a likeness it was of her).

Some titles and their images go hand in glove. Perhaps the most successful example in this chapter is Ken Cory's *Squash Blossom* – a necklace of light bulbs and bullet shells and other found objects. This arrangement of modern artefacts, echoing all our flower garlands, lovers' daisy chains and victors' laurels, is given deeper meaning with its title. It 'quotes' the classic Navajo necklace, with its squash-blossom beads and crescent-shaped pendant, whose design had been borrowed from the silver bridle-ornaments of the Spanish, borrowed in their turn from Moorish ornaments. Cory was a clever, witty man, very serious about jewelry and metalsmithing, and a formidable educator, but also a person who wore his seriousness with a light touch. In the summer of 1993, the Washington State Arts Commission asked a select group of jewelry artists to submit slides and an Artist's Statement. Included in his statement was the following paragraph: 'I think that we have in recent years, forgotten the primary function of jewelry which is, of course, to communicate with folks from other planets in other solar systems. Anyone wearing one of my badges will have nothing to fear when we are invaded from outer space.'

Titles, even gnomic ones, trigger a debate between the object or image and the viewer – hence the tangents explored above with *Threshold* by Overstreet and Kranitzky. Sometimes a title exists to reinforce what is, in fact, represented by the image. An example of this is provided by the work of Betsy King. A brooch of hers called *Bound To Be Back* (1992) with a comic-strip picture of Superman in flying mode, bound in a silver frame and a steel cord, does gain from its title – a comic strip might show Superman in a situation from which he cannot possibly escape (but he always does), and Superman always returns, and so the title *Bound To Be Back* is a pun. But even without the title, the image of Superman is so well known that most Westerners would be able to draw some inferences of their own. The background to this piece concerns the fact that in the early 1990s the syndicate that owns the copyright to Superman were going to kill him off. Some people felt sad and even outraged that an icon of popular American culture could be eliminated. Others, like Betsy King, responded with the traditional reaction: he was bound to be back, he always came back, and, suffice it to say, he's still around.

Yet possibly one of the most affecting pieces of jewelry by Betsy King is one that appears more personal than the clever *Bound to be Back*. In *Raised on Promises,* a group of young children, one of whom is the artist, are dancing in a circle – probably playing Ring-a-ring o'roses. The picture is torn apart by a lightning bolt. As a picture of childhood as another country where many of us were happy for a while, this brooch is simply eloquent. We only return to this other country when we lose ourselves – perhaps in work, almost certainly in laughter. The most dangerous route to take back to the happiness of childhood is nostagia, not least because it also causes us to forget that even children (especially children) have fears.

One point worth noting in passing is that many, many artists have picked up on the fact that the photographs of ordinary people, provided they are of the same culture as ourselves, are extraordinarily affecting. Photographs engage our interest in strangers in a way that strangers in

real life seldom do. Photographs of people from cultures very different from our own do not to excite our sympathetic interest so readily. They tend to remain strangers or objects rather than subjects of curiosity. Yet any old photograph from our own culture is immediately seized upon as in some way belonging to our own memory.

Laurie Hall provides interesting titles to her works which, if not wholly explicit, contain useful hints. Here is a selection of them: *Clap Hands, Here Comes Charlie* (1979); *Help, Help, House on Fire* (1984); *Puzzled Solution* (1985); *The Conversation* (1985); or *Rule of Thumb* (1985). A piece called *No 2, Please* (*c.*1988-89) reflects her experience as a dedicated secondary school teacher, and the title refers to the grade of pencil requested by children in her art classes. This is a small piece of autobiography, and it would be pleasant to think that she did this piece, out of pleasure, just for herself, because she is happy in her work both as an artist and as a teacher.

A good example of the crucial role a title can play in making the viewer attend to an object in one way rather than other is provided by Joyce J. Scott (b.USA 1948). Consider her piece *The Sneak*. It makes you wonder who the sneak might be among this assembly of phantasmagoric figures, and what secret has been divulged. Scott's technique, like Judy Onofrio's (b.USA 1939), is a form of beadwork called peyote stitch. Onofrio's bracelets incorporate glass balls. Scott uses glass beads and found objects; her choice of peyote stitch evolved out of her interest in sewing and quilt-making, and it enables her to work in three dimensions. The figures in this piece do not look naturalistic, but horror-cartoon in a recognizably American style. The figures, some more dream-like or hallucinatory than others, are all linked together. They are bound by what? Family ties, guilt, the secret? The title *The Sneak* inclines us to the idea that all the figures are bound by the secret, presumably connected with violence. Is it sexual abuse within the family? Rape? Murder? It can be read as any of these things but, most effectively, it can be read – because of the medium, the composition, the neurotic images and the title – as a generalized representation of guilt and treachery. It is given a twist of nastiness by the cartoon-like character of the work. In fact *The Sneak* is about murder. When the piece is worn, the murderer sits on your shoulder looking at you, about to run off behind your back.

Joyce Scott, the subject of a lengthy profile in *Ornament*, Summer 1992, told writer Karen Searle, that she was a migrant worker for the arts, constantly on the road doing performance art. And in addition to being a performance artist and jeweler, she produces quilts. As a black woman artist, it is unsurprising, although by no means inevitable, that the subject matter of her art tends to race, violence and prejudice. A lot of her work is laced with satire.

In the light of the discussion about jewelry, the body and beauty in Chapter 3, it is interesting to note that Joyce Scott, described in the article as 'always aware of how she is viewed as a large woman', said to Searle:

People are not satisfied with themselves. They keep trying to change the external self in the hope that it will make the internal self more acceptable.…The issues become more complex for people of colour who don't fit our culture's acceptable role models.…I come in, a fat black woman with gappy teeth and wild hair, my outfits, my humour – in many senses, I am the stereotype that African-Americans have tried to debunk since the 1960s.

Scott's narrative jewelry tells urgent stories with a twist of anger. This anger which is in her work and which one sees, albeit of a different kind, in Schobinger's work, is quite unusual in art jewelry.

It is rare to find jewelry with content in which the titles could be redundant, but the work of Pierre Cavalan, such as his piece *Order of Darwin,* is one of them. Pierre Cavalan assembles found objects and junk material into complex 'medals', badges and fake insignia of office: he is parodying the jewelry with which men and women – especially men – adorn themselves as part of the ritual of belonging to an institution. He is especially interested in recent but now dead or dying imagery, such as the medals of old wars or former imperial or colonial institutions. France, Britain, Germany, Holland and Portugal are all former empire builders with a rich history of elaborately decorated buildings, ceremonial objects, quaintly dressed ceremonial processions and layer upon layer of old societies and royal colleges each with their insignia and ceremonial clutter.

Robert Nelson, one of Cavalan's essayists, explains that Cavalan takes the ingredients of institutional adornment and accentuates them – he plays up the wreathing, or the crowns, the elaborate frames and the centring devices. Nelson argues that Cavalan not only subverts the notion of authority, he also celebrates some basic and potent popular affection for ornament that runs deep in our society.

Nelson writes:

The old men who used to wear a badge declaring their allegiance to the Masonic club are neither championed nor reviled; their invention of ornament, on the other hand, is acknowledged and exploited; their devotion to a redundant tradition perhaps seen as quaint and ridiculous…but the notion of ornamental tradition is strongly recommended to the senses and mind. One must bring ceremony to life.

One of the points made by Cavalan's jewelry is actually in opposition to the concept of the defiantly personal: it is the concept of energetic belonging. Old men and their ridiculous ceremonies are, at least, sharing a communal life with a language both verbal and visual that reinforces the pleasures (and pains) of being an insider. Refreshingly, perhaps, Cavalan's work is not just for insiders (as some new jewelry is) for, with a little effort and the reinforcement of his explicit titles, his work is open to the intelligent many rather than the artfully informed few.

Medals are their own titles, their own labels, they signify to other people that we are distinguished (or believe ourselves to be distinguished). Labelling oneself is assumed to be one of the functions of personal adornment, but Deganit Schocken, earlier discussed in Chapter 2, took this idea a stage further when she attended a conference about jewelry and produced a series of conference labels. Most of us are familiar with (some of us always mildly uncomfortable about) these plastic tags announcing our name and profession. These tags with their plastic or cheap metal clasps are usually thrown away, but Schocken did the most surprising thing, she made the clasps out of precious metals and in the form of detailed heads. This completely altered the value of the tag. Arguably it is an idea that recalls the American artist Jasper Johns's casting of beer cans in bronze, but that was such a ponderous statement about Art with a capital A; Schocken's idea is capricious, stylish and optimistic, pleasant partly because it is such a positive interpretation of the theme of identity.

ideas and game rules

ideas and game rules

Titles are really only the tip of the textual iceberg. It is arguable that all the visual arts are gradually becoming shaped by ideas that are rooted in post-modern literary theory and that these ideas are beginning to contribute to the way artists regard the relationship between their work and the texts that surround their work, such as titles, artists' statements and catalogue essays. One certainly sees evidence that people who write about the arts, including jewelry, are taking some of their own ideas from post-modern literary theory.

One of the most influential theorists on culture generally has been the French philosopher Jacques Derrida, and it was he, or one of his followers, who is credited with coining the phrase, 'There is nothing outside the text.' Derrida and his followers are also credited with promoting an approach to the world in which everything in it, including the objects we make, can be read as texts.

The idea that nothing is outside the text can become taken literally in such a way that everything is subject to a literary interpretation. And everything means everything. One can supply a literary view of any object – it does not have to be a text. You can read an object whether it be a pot, a bridge, a nut and bolt, or piece of jewelry. Reading objects as if they were a text is one thing, but not the whole thing; objects are there also to be seen and to be used; objects are there because they are made. Objects therefore, while they can be read, are not to be confused with texts.

Indeed, thinking of an object as just another kind of written or philosophical text is filled with several contradictions. For one thing, and this is obvious, an artefact composed of words is a different kind of artefact, a different kind of thinking, from one built in plastic, gold or steel. It would be convenient for writers if this were not so, and perhaps one of the problems for some critics is that they do too readily treat other objects, such as jewelry, as if they were like the written texts they feel familiar with. To treat a necklace as though it were a poem or a piece of discursive philosophy is a mistake.

Arguably, it is even more of a mistake if the artist herself or himself begins to treat objects as though they were to be read as texts. Then all kinds of confusions set in. Some jewelry artists, in common with other artists, refer to their works as statements. Some go further and say that this part of their work represents this idea, that part represents another. But the important test – for the artist as well as the critic – is to ask in what sense a work represents an idea.

There is all the difference in the world between saying that a thing represents an idea, as distinct from expressing it. What we generally expect of a visual artist is that their work, dependent though it may be upon a title to point us in the right direction, should express some aspect of the idea (or emotion) that is attributed to it. One might claim that a piece of narrative jewelry represents the innocence of childhood seared by the reali-zation of adulthood, that dreams are shattered, but the greater art is to express that emotion so that the poignancy of the idea is felt. It is the belief that Betsy King, succeeds in expressing an idea rather than merely stating it that has singled her out in this text. Anything can be said to represent something else, provided you supply the connection with a title or a text. The goal that should interest visual artists is representation in the sense of expression.

One of the differences between objects and texts is that objects can contribute a range of 'meanings' that are not capable of expression in words. The pleasure that one may have from even the simplest piece of worked metal may not be expressible in language. So much that makes art of value is tacit rather than explicit; if only the explicit is valued, then we downgrade the value of objects and object-making. For example, the curve of the line of a piece of jewelry, or the finish that a form is given, the precise nature of the way a surface interacts with light, are the result of a connoisseurship and tacit knowledge owned by an individual maker, and this knowledge is the reason why we value that maker's work. Such knowledge is not easily captured by any text, and is certainly not appreciated in the same way as one appreciates a text.

Yet, for obvious reasons, language is our medium for exploring ideas and shaping our values. Most of the important aspects of a culture – its morality, its politics, its science – are shaped in words. The visual artist may wish to participate in this shaping, and wants, increasingly, to share the same subject matter in his or her work as can be explored in other, discursive media. Most artists need a subject about which to make art, and most of the very interesting subjects are explicit rather than tacit. The artist, including the aspirant artist-jeweler, is therfore driven towards words, to the text. It is in the text that the contemporary artist finds her subject matter, and it is in the text rather than the object that the critic finds it so much easier to discover common ground with the artist.

More and more it seems as though the real objects of art are no longer objects *per se,* but exhibition catalogues, for it is in the catalogue essay that artist and critic jointly 'make' their most perfect creations.

Without a subject matter, the artist, whoever she or he is, whatever the medium, is in crisis. Wherever one looks in the period of new jewelry covered by this book, one will see that the most anxious part of the artist's work is centred upon the subject matter. The subject provides not only the meaning of the work but the motive for producing it. That may strike some artists as wrong. The motive for some artists is the sheer pleasure of making. But that pleasure turns to dust if there is no rationale or framework. Nothing is more horrible for any creative person than to have the desire to create, but with nothing upon which that creativity can be directed.

Thus we see artists dreaming up ideologies for themselves or inventing rules of procedures governing the design. They adopt firm sets of beliefs about what is or is not possible in jewelry. Even those who claim to be of the avant-garde are as ruthless in the rule-playing and their setting-up of game strategies as any other artist. They have to be. Without the rules, the art game cannot be pursued.

The adoption of moral content is a powerful strategy because it takes care of the other concern that many decent artists worry about: how can I justify enjoying my work? The addition of a moral point to that work necessarily makes them feel better. Sometimes the motivation is stronger than that. Sometimes it is a sense of outrage so strong that they want everything they do and say to articulate their sense of the outrage. Yet even the most politically charged art jewelry is primarily art for art's sake. A good novel is not judged by its ability to convert you to this or that moral philosophy, even though its plot and its characters may be dealing with moral issues (indeed, it's hard to think of any novel that does not in some way deal with morality). A good novel is judged in terms of its own, internal consistency and how well the characters are drawn and whether the novelist offers insights into the behaviour of the characters. The novel's subject matter provides motives, interest, a framework, and it might win prizes for doing this well, but not for whether it changes the world. Whereas if Amnesty International fails to change the world, then it is a failure.

This reasoning holds true with jewelry art: it would be disingenuous to argue that the role or purpose or effectiveness of any of the work discussed above lies in its power to convert or play the role of advocate or prosecutor: the subject matter's prime role is in its usefulness to activate the art.

After all, if the question, 'Mother, what did you do to stop the Vietnam war?' is answered with, 'I made jewelry about it,' then the child might reasonably think that Mother had made a category mistake. Yet if the jewelry that Mother made whilst others were yielding placards is good art, then we will all be grateful that she spent her time making jewelry with the war as its theme rather than tangling with the National Guard. Everything in art comes back to the quality of the art: bad art is not redeemed by the virtue of its intentions.

What remains fascinating is the sheer breadth of the content that artists feel able to tackle in their work. This is an especially interesting phenomenon in a century which has been characterized as the age of the specialist.

The following remarks from Peter Skubic offer a demonstration: 'My jewelry is like an internal portrait of myself. All my troubles, my feelings, my wishes, my aggression are in my work.' He says he chose to work in stainless steel because gold, although the classic material of jewelers, has been obtained with the expense of too much blood (another sense in which there are no neutral materials). Different jewelers possess different senses of proportion. Skubic said, 'I produced a print with the words: The BLACK HOLE IS THE INSIDE OF THE RING OF GOD.' He says this suggests the idea of jewelry so big that it wears him. 'And so you see,' he added, 'the dimension of jewelry is not a problem for me.' Skubic further consolidates his philosophical scaling-up of jewelry by stating, 'The Greek word Kosmos means jewelry, order and space. My philosophy is to find the relationship between these different meanings.'

And there we have it – jewelry: an art of small objects and large subjects.

Pierre Cavalan
French, active Australia

Pigs Might Fly
Brooch. 1992
Silver, imitation stones, found objects
21 x 13.3 cm

Order of Darwin
Brooch. 1992
Enamel, souvenir tacks, mixed media
15.2 x 7 cm

Previous page
Judy Onofrio
American

*Hear No Evil, See No Evil,
Speak No Evil*
Brooch. 1990
Costume jewelry
fragments, found objects
11 x 8 cm

Pierre Cavalan
French, active Australia

Air Neckpiece
1993
Enamel, souvenir tacks,
mixed media
39 x 23 cm

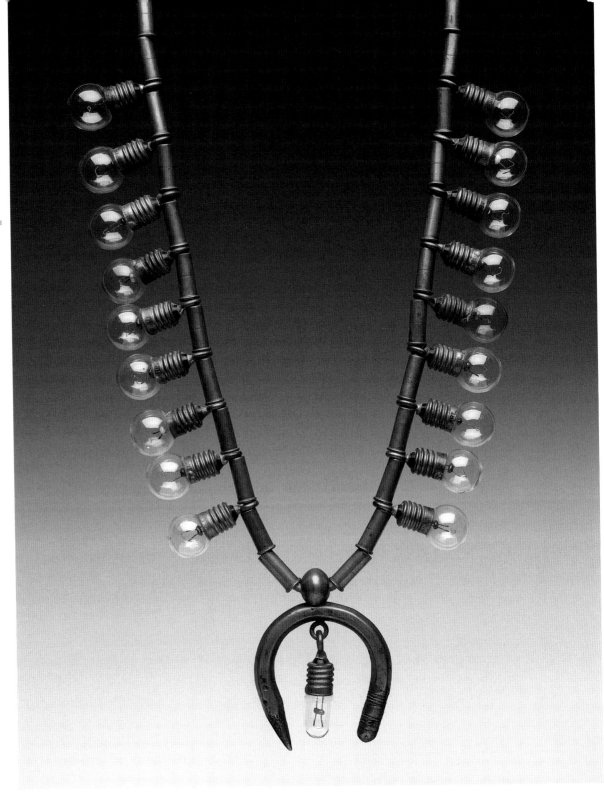

Ken Cory
American

Squash Blossom Necklace
1974
Light bulbs, bullet shells,
bronze cast pencil, brass
bead, leather thong
40.6 x 5.1 x 1.3 cm
Collection Merrily
Tompkins, USA

Laurie Hall
American

No.2 Please
Necklace. 1988
Brass, pencil, wood
Length 81 cm

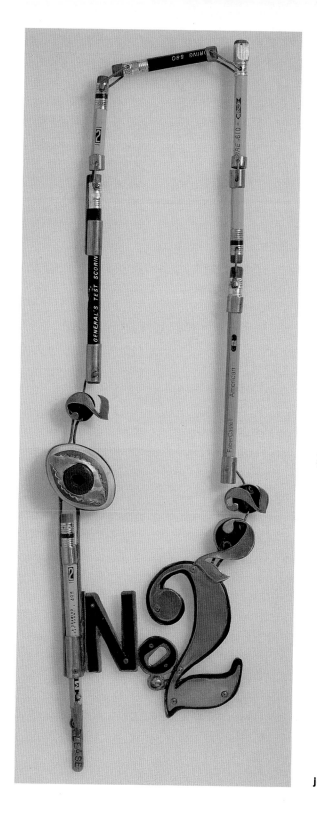

Betsy King
American

Bound To Be Back
Brooch. 1992
Sterling silver, Plexiglas
paper, brass
3.8 x 12.7 x 1.3 cm

Hat Pin
1990
Brass, pearl, silver, glass,
postcard fragments, liquid
29.2 x 2.5 cm

Don Tompkins
American

Minnesota Fats
Medal, detail. 1971
Sterling silver,
pearl, photograph,
Plexiglas, flocking
7.6 x 16.5 cm

Betsy King
American

Trouble in Paradise
Brooch. 1989
Silver, brass, photograph,
copper, Plexiglas, plastic
8.3 x 8.3 cm

Betsy King
American

Raised on Promises
Brooch. 1990
Copper, silver, etched
brass, photograph
8.9 x 12.1 cm

Robin Kranitzky/Kim Overstreet
American

Threshold
Brooch. 1991
Mixed media
9.2 x 6.3 x 2 cm

Sustain
Brooch. 1992
Mixed media
7.6 x 5.7 x 3.5 cm

Robin Kranitzky/Kim Overstreet
American

Pressures of Life
Brooch. 1989
Mixed media
8.9 x 6.4

All for You
Brooch. 1990
Mixed media
7.6 x 7 x 2.3 cm

J. Fred Woell
American

Love Object
Brooch. 1968
Steel, glass, gold leaf, screws,
copper, silver, photograph, mirror
6.5 x 1.2 cm

Training Fetish
Brooch. 1971
Brass; edition 2/50
3.5 x 5 cm

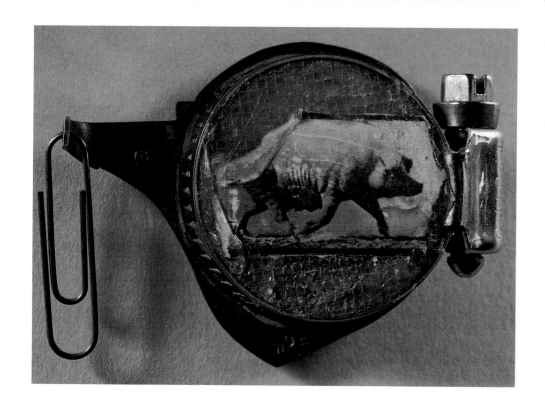

J. Fred Woell
American

Class of '78
Brooch. 1978
Found object, brass, paper clip,
photograph, steel, silicone rubber
5.1 x 6.4 x 0.9 cm

West of Jersey
Neckpiece. 1986
Brass, silver, copper, leather
7 x 11 cm

Carlier Makigawa
Australian

Burning Building
Brooch. 1989
Stainless steel, papier mâché, lacquer, gold leaf, fine silver
11.5 x 5 x 2.5 cm

Brooch. 1993
Silver, monel, 18k gold
12.7 x 5.1 x 3.2 cm

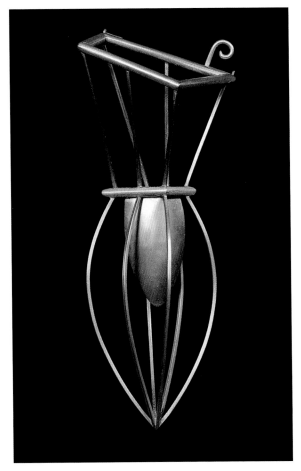

Peter Tully
Australian

Set of Three Brooches. 1990-91
Mixed media
7.6 x 5.5 cm, 7.6 x 5.6 cm, 8.4 x 3.8 cm

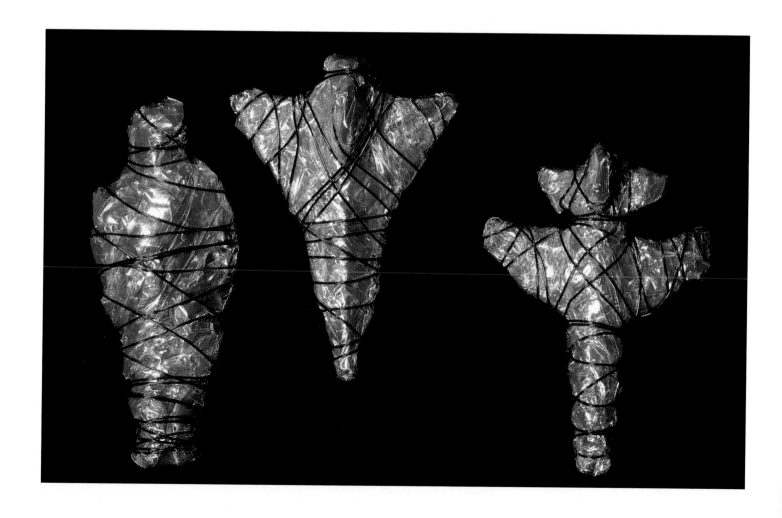

Bruce Metcalf
American

Wood Neckpiece #7
1992
Maple, cherry, oak, walnut,
pine, rosewood, cork,
glass eye, plastic, teeth,
tagua nut, brass, cord,
23k gold leaf, paints,
pigments
35.6 x 25.4 cm

Bruce Metcalf
American

Self Portrait with Structure and Straitjacket
Brooch. 1976
Brass, copper, acrylic, Delrin, enamel, Plexiglas
18.5 x 8.3 x 2 cm

Don't Go Out at Night
Brooch on pedestal. 1977
Silver, Plexiglas, brass, pen and ink, paint,
commercial chain
Overall 20.8 x 10 x 5.9 cm
Brooch 10.5 x 10 x 2.8 cm

Peter Skubic
Yugoslav, active Germany/Austria

Peeping Tom
Brooch. 1993
Wood, plastic, mirror, photograph, paint
7.6 x 6.1 x 4.4 cm

Balance
Hat Pin. 1989-90
Steel, rubber, stone
33 x 14 cm

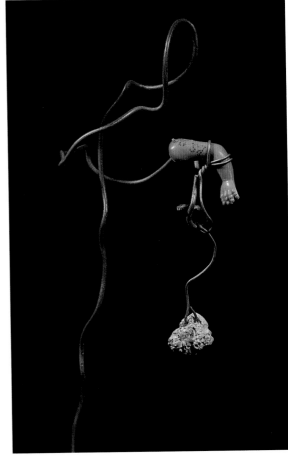

Joyce Scott
American

The Sneak
Necklace. 1989
Beads, thread
14 x 34.3 x 27.9 cm

Rebecca Batal
American

Chopin
Neckpiece, detail. 1989
Crystal beads, haematite,
plaster, found objects
Length 37 cm
Pendant 6 x 2.8 cm

Mickey Mouse Crucifix
Neckpiece, detail. 1989
Plastic, wood, steel wire
Length 50.8 cm
Pendant 7.5 x 5.5 x 3.5 cm

Bernhard Schobinger
Swiss

Necklace. 1994
Tin, rock crystal, iron,
gold, found objects
Length 33 cm
Rock crystal 11.4 x 5.1 cm
Collection of the artist

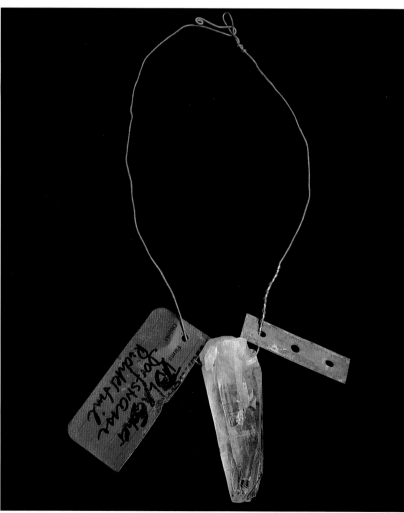

Bernhard Schobinger
Swiss

Scherbew von Moritzplatz, Berlin
Necklace. 1983-84
Antique crystal beads,
Coca Cola bottle shards
Length 25.4 cm

Bernhard Schobinger
Swiss

Ring. 1991
Brass, carborundum
3.2 dia x 7 cm

Garden of Paradise
Bracelet. 1990
Gold
6.5 dia x 9 cm
Private collection

Holiday in Cambodia
Bracelet. 1990
Silver
7.5 dia x 8 cm
Private collection, Switzerland

Bernhard Schobinger
Swiss

Edelstein mit Stacheldraht
(Jewel with Barbed Wire)
Necklace. *c.*1990
Copper, rock, amethyst, rose
quartz crystal, haematite
57.8 x 7 cm

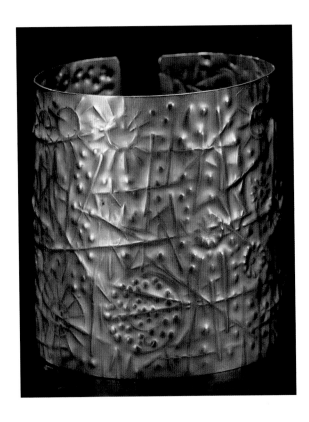

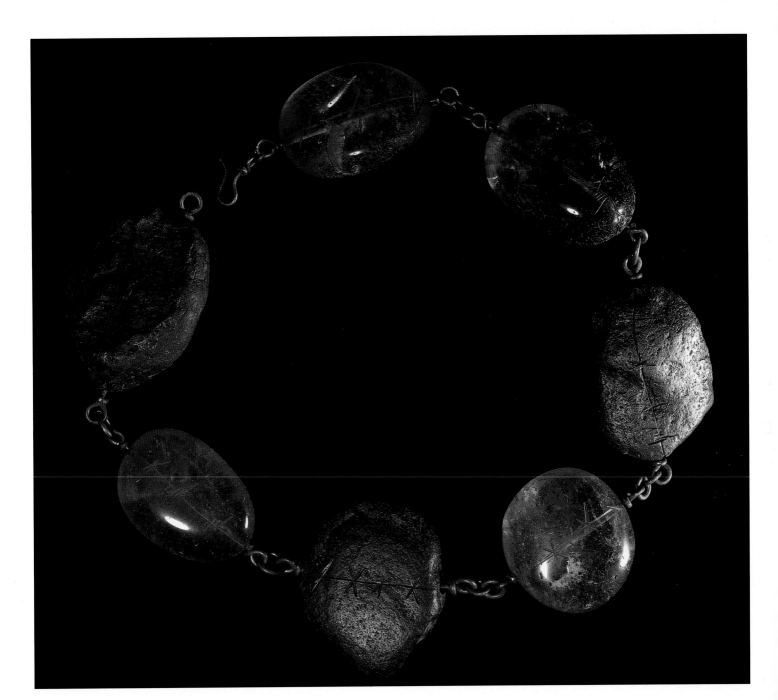

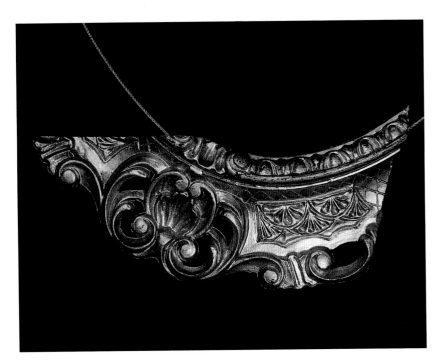

Otto Künzli
Swiss, active Germany

Fragment Necklace,
detail. 1986
PVC, gold leaf, steel
9 x 23 cm

Brooch. 1982
Wood, wallpaper, steel
8.3 x 11.3 x 0.9 cm

Ruudt Peters
Dutch

Pin and Bracelet. 1983
Acrylic, wire,
laminated photograph
Pin 24.7 x 5.3 x 0.2 cm
Bracelet 16.7 x 13 x 0.2 cm

Overleaf
Margaret West
Australian

Neckpiece, detail
1985
Stone, monel
Length 114 cm

information

biographies of the artists

biographies of the artists

Note

* = Exhibitions of the Helen
Williams Drutt Collection, listed
under a short form of the titles
given by the exhibiting bodies:
A Moveable Feast 1964-1994,
Museum voor Moderne Kunst,
Ostend, 1995; Stedelijk Museum,
Amsterdam, 1994/1995

Schmuck Unserer Zeit 1964-1994,
Museum Bellerive, Zurich, 1994

*Contemporary Jewelry 1964-1993:
Selected Works, HWD Collection*,
The Arkansas Arts Center, Little
Rock, AK, 1993

*Korun Kieli (The Language of
Jewelry) 1964-1992*, Röhsska
Konstslöjdmuseet, Gothenburg,
1992/1993; Taideteollisuusmuseo,
Helsinki, 1992

Modern Jewelry 1964-84,
Philadelphia Museum of Art, PA,
1986/1987; Cleveland Institute of
Art, OH, 1986; Honolulu
Academy of Arts, HI, 1986;
Montreal Musée des Arts
Décoratifs, 1984/1985

SNAG = Society of North
American Goldsmiths

SOFA = Sculpture, Objects,
Functional Art – International
Art Fair

NCFA = National Collection
of Fine Arts, Smithsonian
Institution, Washington, DC,
renamed in 1985 as
NMAA = National Museum
of American Art

Museum of Contemporary Crafts
in New York renamed in 1979 as
American Craft Museum

Hans Appenzeller

Born: April 21, 1949,
Amsterdam,
The Netherlands

Education:
1966-70 Gerrit Rietveld Academie,
Amsterdam

Selected Exhibitions:
1994 *A Moveable Feast**,
Amsterdam; *Schmuck
Unserer Zeit**, Zurich
1993 *Voorzien: Benno Premsela Applied Art Collection*, Stedelijk
Museum, Amsterdam
1992-93 *Korun Kieli**, Gothenburg; Helsinki
1986 *Sieraad 1986, Draagteken?* Museum Het Kruithuis,
's-Hertogenbosch, The Netherlands
1985 *New Tradition*, British Crafts Centre, London
1984-87 *Modern Jewelry**, Philadelphia, PA; Cleveland, OH; Honolulu,
HI; Montreal
1982 *Visies op Sieraden 1965-1982*, Stedelijk Museum, Amsterdam
1979 *56 Bracelets, 17 Rings, 2 Necklaces*, Gemeentelijke van
Reekummuseum, Apeldoorn, The Netherlands
Mode-Kleding-Mode, Stedelijk Museum, Amsterdam
1976 *Hans Appenzeller/Jans Aarntzen*, Stedelijk Museum, Amsterdam
1973 *Jewelry as Sculpture as Jewelry*, Institute of Contemporary Art,
Boston, MA

Related Professional Experience:
1983 Established Hans Appenzeller, Inc., New York (closed 1991)
1981 Corian-Collection presented with Jan Aarntzen, Hans
Appenzeller, Inc., Amsterdam
1977– Established second location Hans Appenzeller, Inc.,
Amsterdam
1975-77 Established first location Hans Appenzeller, Inc., Amsterdam

1972 First thematic collection of work presented, Hans Appenzeller,
Inc., Amsterdam; annual collections followed
1970-77 Faculty, Academie voor Beeldende Vorming, Amersfoort,
The Netherlands
1969-75 Co-founder/Director with Lous Martin, Galerie Sieraad,
Amsterdam

Selected Public Collections:
Museum Het Kruithuis, 's-Hertogenbosch, The Netherlands; Stedelijk
Museum, Amsterdam

Klaus Arck

Born: March 22, 1956, Bonn, Germany

Education:
1981-87 Fachhochschule, Cologne
1974-76 Goldschmiedeschule, Pforzheim, Germany

Related Professional Experience:
1982– Establishes independent atelier, Cologne

Selected Exhibitions:
1994 *A Moveable Feast**, Amsterdam; *Schmuck Unserer Zeit**, Zurich
Köln Gold, Museum für Angewante Kunst, Cologne
1992 *Der Stamm des Tannenbaumes ist das Herz des Schmuckes*,
Kunstraum Daxer, Munich
1991 *Formes des Metropoles – Nouveaux Designs en Europe*, Centre
Georges Pompidou, Paris
Neues Europäisches Design, Kunstmuseum Dusseldorf im
Ehrenhof
1989 *Ornamenta I*, Schmuckmuseum, Pforzheim, Germany

1988	Design: Interior architecture of Cafe Rathenau, Cologne
1987	*Contemporary European Jewellery*, Seu Central de la Caixa de Pensions, Barcelona
	Solo Exhibition, Galerie VO, Washington, DC
1986	Design: Interior architecture, Bar Königswasser; Cologne
1984	*Contemporary Jewellery: The Americas, Australia, Europe and Japan*, The National Museum of Modern Art, Kyoto; Tokyo
	Solo Exhibition, Galerie V & V, Vienna
	Design for Scupture Entrance, Schloss Morsbroich, Museum für Moderne Kunst, Leverkusen
1983	*Contemporary Jewellery*, Goethe Institute, Tokyo
	Solo Exhibition, Galerie CUBO, Lugano

Giampaolo Babetto

Born: March 24, 1947, Padua, Italy

Education:
1966-68 Accademia di Belle Arti, Venice
1963-66 Istituto d'Arte Pietro Selvatico, Padua

Selected Awards:
1991 Gold Medal, State of Bavaria
1985 Herbert Hoffmann Prize, *Form Formel Formalismus*, Internationale Handwerksmesse, Munich
1983 Grand Prix, Japan Jewellery Designers Association, Tokyo
1975 Herbert Hoffmann Prize, *Form und Qualität*, Internationale Handwerksmesse, Munich

Selected Exhibitions:
1994-95 *Giampaolo Babetto: Ritratti*, Museum für Konkrete Kunst, Ingolstadt, Germany; Neue Galerie der Stadt Linz, Austria; Museu Textil i d'Indumetària, Barcelona
1994 *In Touch*, Maihaugen, Lillehammer, Norway
A Moveable Feast*, Amsterdam; Zurich
Schmuck und Gerät, Deutsches Goldschmiedehaus, Hanau, Germany (travelled)
1993 *13 Goldschmiede: von Amsterdam bis Tokyo*, Bayerische Akademie der Schönen Künste, Munich
The Art of Jewellery, Setagaya Art Museum, Tokyo
Contemporary Jewelry*, Little Rock, AK
Facet I, Kunsthal, Rotterdam
Schmuck: Die Sammlung der Danner-Stiftung, Galerie für angewandte Kunst, Munich
Solo Exhibition, Museum für Kunst und Gewerbe, Hamburg
Voorzien: Benno Premsela Applied Art Collection, Stedelijk Museum, Amsterdam

1992-93	*Korun Kieli**, Gothenburg; Helsinki
1992	*Solo Exhibitions*, Musée d'Art Moderne et d'Art Contemporain, Nice; Kunstverein, Dusseldorf
	Triennale du Bijou, Musée des Arts Décoratifs, Paris
1991	*Europäisches Kunsthandwerk*, Haus de Wirtschaft, Stuttgart
1990	*Triennale du Bijou*, Musée du Luxembourg, Paris
1989	*Infinite Riches*, Museum of Fine Arts, St Petersburg, FL, USA
	Ornamenta 1, Schmuckmuseum, Pforzheim, Germany
	Perth International Crafts Triennial, Art Gallery of Western Australia, Perth
	Solo Exhibition, Provinciaal Museum Voor Modern Kunst, Ostend
1988	*Biennale Svizzera del Gioiello d'Arte Contemporaneo*, Villa Malpensata, Lugano, Switzerland
	Tragezeichen, Museum Schloss Morsbroich, Leverkusen, Germany
1987	*Joieria Europea Contemporània*, Fundació Caixa de Pensions, Barcelona
	Schmuck, Zeichen am Körper, Francisco Carolinum Museum, Linz, Austria
1986	*Nove Artisti Orafi di Scuola Padovana*, Museo Civico Eremitani, Padua (travelled)
1985	*25 Jahre Galerie Nouvelles Images*, Haags Gemeentemuseum, The Hague
1985,84,83,82,75,67	
	Internationale Schmuckschau, Internationale Handwerksmesse, Munich
1984-87	*Modern Jewelry**, Philadelphia, PA; Cleveland, OH; Honolulu, HI; Montreal
1984	*Contemporary Jewellery: The Americas, Australia, Europe and Japan*, National Museum of Modern Art, Kyoto; Tokyo
	Jewelry International, American Craft Museum II, New York
1983	*Dieci Orafi Padovani*, Schmuckmuseum, Pforzheim, Germany (travelled)
	International Jewellery Art Exhibition, 5th Tokyo Triennial, Isetan Art Museum, Tokyo
1982	*Schmuck '82 – Tendenzen*, Schmuckmuseum, Pforzheim, Germany
1980	*Schmuck International 1900-1980*, Künstlerhaus, Vienna
1977	*Solo Exhibition*, Stedelijk Museum, Amsterdam (travelled)

Related Professional Experience:
1985 Professor, Fachhochschule, Dusseldorf
1979-80,83
Visiting Lecturer, Gerrit Rietveld Academie, Amsterdam
1969-83 Lecturer, Istituto d'Arte Pietro Selvatico, Padua

Selected Public Collections:
Art Gallery of Western Australia, Perth; Danner-Stiftung Collection, Munich; Kunstgewerbemuseum, Berlin; Musée d'Art Moderne et d'Art Contemporain, Nice; Musée des Arts Décoratifs, Paris; Museum für Konkrete Kunst, Ingolstadt, Germany; Museum für Kunst und Gewerbe, Hamburg; Nordenfjeldske Kunstindustrimuseum, Trondheim, Norway; Schmuckmuseum, Pforzheim, Germany; Victoria and Albert Museum, London

Gijs Bakker

Born: February 20, 1942, Amersfoort, The Netherlands

Education:
1962   Konstfack Skolan, Stockholm
1958-62   Gerrit Rietveld Academie

Selected Awards:
1995   Prince Bernhard Foundation Award for Applied
       Arts and Architecture
1988   Françoise van den Bosch Prize, Amsterdam
1983   Architecture Award, Foundation 'De Fantasie',
       Almere, The Netherlands

Selected Public Collections:
Boymans-van Beuningen
Museum, Rotterdam;
Centraal Museum, Utrecht;
Cooper-Hewitt, National
Museum of Design,
Smithsonian Institution,
New York; Denver Museum
of Art, CO; Gemeentelijke
van Reekummuseum,
Apeldoorn, The
Netherlands; Montreal
Musée des Arts Décoratifs,
Quebec; Museum
Het Kruithuis,
's-Hertogenbosch, The
Netherlands; National
Museum of Modern Art,
Kyoto; Nordenfjeldske
Kunstindustrimuseum,
Trondheim, Norway; Power
House Museum, Sydney;
Rijksdienst Beeldende
Kunst, The Hague;
Schmuckmuseum,
Pforzheim, Germany;
Stedelijk Museum,
Amsterdam;
Taideteollisuusmuseo,
Helsinki

Selected Exhibitions:
1994   *Gijs Bakker: Holes Project*, Galerie Spektrum, Munich; Galerie Ra,
       Amsterdam; Salone Internazionale d'Arredo, Marijke Studio:
       Padua, Milan; SOFA, Helen Drutt: Philadelphia; Chicago
       A Moveable Feast*, Amsterdam; *Schmuck Unserer Zeit**, Zurich
1993   *Contemporary Jewelry**, Little Rock, AK
       Subjects, Design Forum, Helsinki
       Voorzien: Benno Premsela Applied Art Collection, Stedelijk
       Museum, Amsterdam
1992-93   *Korun Kieli**, Gothenburg; Helsinki
1991   *Art in the Street*, Groningen, The Netherlands
1990-91   *Fremd. Körper aus der Sammlung Teunen*, Willhelm-Hack
          Museum, Ludwigshafen, Rhein, Germany
1990   *L'Arte della Gioia*, Pedrocchi, Padua
       News from the Netherlands, Fundacao Calouste Gulbenkian,
       Lisbon (travelled)
1989   *An Art Collection of Combs*, organized by Galerie Marzee,
       Nimwegen, The Netherlands (travelled)
       Gijs Bakker, vormgever, Centraal Museum, Utrecht, The
       Netherlands; Helen Drutt Gallery, New York
       Infinite Riches, Museum of Fine Arts, St Petersburg, FL, USA
       Jewelry: Means: Meaning, University of Tennessee, Knoxville
       Ornamenta 1, Schmuckmuseum, Pforzheim, Germany
1987   *Joieria Europea Contemporània*, Fundació Caixa de Pensions,
       Barcelona
1986   *Jewellery Images*, VES 10th anniversary exhibition, Stedelijk
       Museum, Amsterdam (travelled)
       Sieraad 1986, Draagteken?, Museum Het Kruithuis,
       's-Hertogenbosch, The Netherlands
       Sieraad Vorm en Idee, Gemeentelijke van Reekummuseum,
       Apeldoorn, The Netherlands
       Six Dutch Jewelry Designers, Kunstformen, Salzburg
1985   *New Tradition*, British Crafts Centre, London
       Nya Smycken, Nya Material, Kulturhuset, Stockholm
1984-87   *Modern Jewelry**, Philadelphia, PA; Cleveland, OH; Honolulu
          HI; Montreal
1984   *Contemporary Jewellery: The Americas, Australia, Europe and
       Japan*, National Museum of Modern Art, Kyoto; Tokyo

1984   *Jewelry International*, American Craft Museum II, New York
       Jewellery Redefined, British Crafts Centre, London
       Visies op Sieraden 1965-1982, Stedelijk Museum, Amsterdam
1980   *Schmuck International 1900-1980*, Künstlerhaus, Vienna
1979   *56 Bracelets, 17 Rings, 2 Necklaces*, Gemeentelijke van
       Reekummuseum, Apeldoorn, The Netherlands
1978   *The Industrial Art of Gijs Bakker*, Crafts Advisory Committee
       Gallery, London

Selected Projects:
1993   Design for Cor Unum Ceramics,
       's-Hertogenbosch, The Netherlands
       Street Lighting, Arnhem Shopping Center, The Netherlands
1992   Fan, Dutch Telecom, World Expo, Seville
1991   Street Furniture for Verwo
1989   Environmental Design for the centre of Oostburg, The Netherlands

Related Professional Experience:
1992–   Design Consultant, Cor Unam Ceramics,
        's-Hertogenbosch, The Netherlands
1987–   Senior Lecturer, Academie voor Industriële Vormgeving,
        Eindhoven, The Netherlands

Rebecca Batal

Born: June 26, 1967, Methuen, MA, USA

Education:
1989   BFA, Rhode Island School of Design, Providence
1985   Phillips Academy, Andover, MA

Selected Exhibitions:
1994   *A Moveable Feast**, Amsterdam; *Schmuck Unserer Zeit** Zurich
1993   *The Body Adorned*, University of Texas, El Paso
1992-93   *Korun Kieli**, Gothenburg; Helsinki
1992   *Rebecca Batal: Sieraden*, Galerie Carin Delcourt van Krimpen,
       Rotterdam
       Rebecca Batal/Martina Windels, Jewelerswerk Galerie,
       Washington, DC
1991   *Beauty is a Story*, Museum Het Kruithuis,
       's-Hertogenbosch, The Netherlands
1990   *American Dreams, American Extremes*, Museum Het Kruithuis,
       's-Hertogenbosch, The Netherlands
       Schmuckszene '90, Internationale Handwerksmesse, Munich
1989   *Invitational Group Exhibitions*, Helen Drutt Gallery,
       Philadelphia, PA; Jewelerswerk Galerie, Washington, DC;
       Rezac Gallery, Chicago, IL
1986   *Group Exhibition*, Woods Gerry Gallery, Rhode Island School
       of Design, Providence

Selected Public Collections:
Museum Het Kruithuis, 's-Hertogenbosch, The Netherlands

Frank Bauer

Born: May 25, 1942,
Hanover, Germany

Education:
1969   Hochschule für
        Bildenden Künste,
        Hamburg
1967   Artschool, Kassel,
        Germany
1962   Apprenticeship, Carl van
        Dornick and Reinhard
        Rischke, Hildesheim,
        Germany
1959   Musik Konservatorium,
        Hanover

Selected Awards:
1991   Grant, Department for the Arts, South Australia
1989   Award of Merit in Art & Architecture, RAIA, South Australia
1978,75 Grants, Australian Crafts Board

Selected Exhibitions:
1992   *Body Decorated*, Ayers House, Alice Springs, NT, Australia
        Recent Acquisitions, Art Gallery of South Australia, Adelaide
1991   *Contemporary Australian Hollowware*, travelled through
        Australia and Europe
        Lighting Exhibition, Jam Factory, Adelaide
1990   *Solo Exhibition*, BMG Fine Art, Adelaide
1989   *Australian Art Collection*, Australian National Gallery,
        Canberra
1988   *Australian Decorative Arts 1788-1988*, Australian National
        Gallery, Canberra
        A Child's View, Australian National Gallery, Canberra
        Contemporary Jewellery: The Australian Experience,
        Contemporary Jewellery Gallery, Sydney
        A Freehand, Power House Museum, Sydney
1985   *Solo Exhibitions*, Galerie am Graben, Vienna; Victoria and
        Albert Museum, London
1983   *Solo Exhibition*, Galerie Marzee, Nimwegen, The Netherlands
1982   *Australian Contemporary Jewellery*, Goldsmiths' Hall, London
        (travelled)
        Jewellery Redefined, British Crafts Centre, London
        The Maker's Eye, Crafts Council Gallery, London
        Solo Exhibition, Galerie Spektrum, Munich
1982,77 *Schmuck – Tendenzen*, Schmuckmuseum, Pforzheim, Germany
1981   *Frank Bauer/Elisabeth Holder*, Arnolfini Gallery, Bristol
1980   *5. Internationaler Wettbewerb – Armschmuck*,
        Schmuckmuseum, Pforzheim, Germany
        A Case for the Spectacular, Design Centre, London
        Objects to Human Scale, organized by the Australia Council
        (travelled)
        Solo Exhibition, Electrum Gallery, London

1977   *10 Australian Jewellers*, travelled through SE Asia
1976   *Frank Bauer: Jewellery and Objects*, Jam Factory, Adelaide
1975   *Australian Jewellery*, Art Gallery of South Australia, Adelaide
        (travelled)

Related Professional Experience:
1992   Received full patent for 'FB-Grid-Light System', a new low-
        voltage lighting system
1988–   Commissioned architectural installations throughout Australia
1984-89 Lecturer, South Australian School of Design, Adelaide

Selected Public Collections:
Art Gallery of South Australia, Adelaide; Art Gallery of Western
Australia, Perth; Australian National Gallery, Canberra; Bauhaus
Archives, Museum für Gestaltung, Berlin; Müncher Stadtmuseum,
Munich; National Gallery of Victoria, Melbourne; Power House
Museum, Sydney; Schmuckmuseum, Pforzheim, Germany; Victoria
and Albert Museum, London

Michael Becker

Born: January 10, 1958, Paderborn, Germany

Education:
1982-87 Fachhochschule für Kunst und Design, Cologne

Selected Awards:
1988   Herbert Hoffmann Prize, *Schmuckszene '88*, Internationale
        Handwerksmesse, Munich
1987   Förderpreis, *Schmuck 1987*, Haus der Kunst, Munich

Selected Exhibitions:
1994   *A Moveable Feast**, Amsterdam; *Schmuck Unserer Zeit**, Zurich
1993   *Contemporary Jewelry**, Little Rock, AK
        Facet I, Kunsthal, Rotterdam
        Schmuck: Die Sammlung der Danner-Stiftung, Galerie für
        angewandte Kunst, Munich
1992-93 *Korun Kieli**, Gothenburg; Helsinki
1990   *Solo Exhibition*, Helen Drutt Gallery, New York
        Solo Exhibition, Studio Ton Berends, The Hague
        Triennale du Bijou, Musée du Luxembourg, Paris
        Zeitgenössisches deutsches Kunsthandwerk, Museum für
        Kunsthandwerk, Frankfurt a.M.
1990,88 *Solo Exhibitions*, Galerie Louise Smit, Amsterdam
1988   *Schmuckszene '88*, Internationale Handwerksmesse, Munich
1987   *Schmuck, Zeichen am Körper*, Francisco Carolinum Museum,
        Linz, Austria
        Schmuck 1987, Haus der Kunst, Munich

Selected Public Collections:
Danner-Stiftung Collection, Munich

James (Jamie) Bennett

Born: October 6, 1948, Philadelphia, PA, USA

Education:
1974   MFA, State University of New York, New Paltz
1970   BFA, University of Georgia, Athens

Selected Awards:
1990   Fellowship, New York Foundation for the Arts
1988,79,73
        Fellowships, National Endowment for the Arts,
            Washington, DC
1984,80   Fellowships, Massachusetts Council on the Arts
            and Humanities

Selected Exhibitions:
1994   *In Touch*, Maihaugen, Lillehammer, Norway
        A Moveable Feast*, Amsterdam; *Schmuck Unserer Zeit**, Zurich
        Solo Exhibition, SOFA, Helen Drutt Gallery, Chicago, IL
        Working in Other Dimensions: Objects and Drawings II, The
            Arkansas Arts Center, Little Rock, AK
1993   *Contemporary Jewelry**, Little Rock, AK
        Facet I, Kunsthal, Rotterdam
        Sculptural Concerns, Contemporary Arts Center, Cincinnati,
            OH (travelled)
1992-93 *Korun Kieli**, Gothenburg, Helsinki
1992   *Design Visions*, Art Gallery of Western Australia, Perth
1991   *National Objects Invitational*, The Arkansas Arts Center, Little
            Rock, AK
1990   *The Primary and its Mannerisms*, University of the Arts,
            Philadelphia, PA
1989   *Craft Today: USA*, Musée des Arts Décoratifs, Paris (travelled)
        Ornamenta 1, Schmuckmuseum, Pforzheim, Germany
1988   *Color and Image: Recent American Enamels*, circulated by the
            Gallery Association of New York State
1987   *Masterworks/Enamel/87*, Taft Museum, Cincinnati, OH
1986   *Contemporary Arts: An Expanding View*, Monmouth Museum,
            Lincroft, NJ
        Craft Today: Poetry of the Physical, American Craft Museum,
            New York (travelled)
1985   *Masterworks of Contemporary American Jewelry*, Victoria and
            Albert Museum, London
1984-87 *Modern Jewelry**, Philadelphia, PA; Cleveland, OH; Honolulu,
            HI; Montreal
1984   *Contemporary Jewellery: The Americas, Australia, Europe and
            Japan*, National Museum of Modern Art, Kyoto; Tokyo
        Jewelry and Beyond: Metalwork by Members of SNAG, Mitchell
            Museum, Mount Vernon, IL
        Jewelry USA, American Craft Museum II, New York
1983   *Bennett-Coles-Keens-Lloyd*, Galveston Art Center, TX

1981   *Good as Gold*, Renwick Gallery, NCFA, Smithsonian
            Institution, Washington, DC (travelled)
1979   *SNAG – Gold- und Silberschmiedearbeiten*, Schmuckmuseum,
            Pforzheim, Germany (travelled)
1977   *The Metalsmith: SNAG Exhibition*, Phoenix Museum of
            Art, AZ
1974   *The Goldsmith*, Renwick Gallery, NCFA, Smithsonian
            Institution, Washington, DC

Related Professional Experience:
1985–   Professor, State University of New York, New Paltz
1985-89 Board of Directors, Society of North American Goldsmiths,
            St Paul, MN

Selected Public Collections:
American Craft Museum, New York; Arkansas Arts Center, Decorative
Arts Museum, Little Rock, AK; Art Gallery of Western Australia, Perth;
Fuller Museum of Art, Brockton, MA; Kunstindustrimuseet, Oslo;
McCabe, Grodon, P.C., Boston, MA; Renwick Gallery, NMAA,
Smithsonian Institution, Washington, DC; Nordenfjeldske
Kunstindustrimuseum, Trondheim, Norway; Royal College
of Art, London

Joan Fraerman Binkley

Born: December 4, 1927, Chicago, IL, USA

Education:
1950   BA, Roosevelt University, Chicago, IL

Selected Awards:
1968   First Prize, Evanston Art Fair, IL

Selected Exhibitions:
1994   *A Moveable Feast**, Amsterdam; *Schmuck Unserer Zeit**, Zurich
1993   *Ahead of Fashion: Hats of the 20th Century*, Philadelphia
            Museum of Art, PA
1992-93 *Korun Kieli**, Gothenburg; Helsinki
1987   *Afshar/Binkley/Drendel/Morreale*, Hyde Park Art Center,
            Chicago, IL
1986   *Contemporary Arts: An Expanding View*, Monmouth Museum,
            Lincroft, NJ
        Neckpieces and Wearable Textiles, Craft Alliance, St Louis, MO
1984-87 *Modern Jewelry**, Philadelphia, PA; Cleveland, OH; Honolulu,
            HI; Montreal
1984,80 *Solo Exhibitions*, Helen Drutt Gallery, Philadelphia, PA
1982   *Solo Exhibition*, Linda Einfeld Gallery, Chicago, IL
1981   *Good as Gold*, Renwick Gallery, NCFA, Smithsonian
            Institution, Washington, DC (travelled)
        Solo Exhibition, C. Corcoran Gallery, Muskegon, MI
        Solo Exhibition, Octagon Gallery, Evanston Art Center, IL

1977	*Solo Exhibition*, Suburban Fine Arts Center, Highland Park, IL
1971	*Solo Exhibition*, Edward Sherbyn Gallery, Chicago, IL
1970	*Two Woman Show*, Chicago Public Library, IL

Related Professional Experience:
Maintains independent studio in Lake Bluff, IL

Selected Public Collections:
Springfield Art Museum, IL

Manfred Bischoff

Born: November 7, 1947, Schömberg/Calw, Germany

Education:
1977-82 Akademie der Bildenden Künste, Munich
1972-77 Fachhochschule für Gestaltung, Pforzheim, Germany

Selected Awards:
1992 Françoise van den Bosch Prize, Amsterdam
1987 Prize, Bayerische Akademie der Schönen Künste, Munich
1983 Scholarship for Study in Florence, Deutscher Akademischer Austauschdienst, Bonn
1982 Prize for Young Artists, State of Bavaria

Selected Exhibitions:
1994 *A Moveable Feast**, Amsterdam; *Schmuck Unserer Zeit**, Zurich
 Solo Exhibition, SOFA, Helen Drutt: Philadelphia; Chicago, IL
1993 *Contemporary Jewelry**, Little Rock, AK
 Facet I, Kunsthal, Rotterdam
 Schmuck: Die Sammlung der Danner-Stiftung, Galerie für angewandte Kunst, Munich
 üb ersetzen, Solo Exhibition, Museum Het Kruithuis, 's-Hertogenbosch, The Netherlands
1992-93 *Korun Kieli**, Gothenburg; Helsinki
1992 *Joies Indissenyables*, Escola Massana, Barcelona
 Kunstrai 92, Galerie Louise Smit, Amsterdam
 Sieraden, Centrum Beeldende Kunst, Groningen, The Netherlands
 Triennale du Bijou, Musée des Arts Décoratifs, Paris
1991 *Beauty is a Story*, Museum Het Kruithuis, 's-Hertogenbosch, The Netherlands

1990	*Schmuckszene '90*, Internationale Handwerksmesse, Munich
1989	*British Jewellery – German Jewellery*, Crafts Council Gallery, London (travelled)
	Infinite Riches, Museum of Fine Arts, St Petersburg, FL, USA
	Ornamenta 1, Schmuckmuseum, Pforzheim, Germany
	Solo Exhibition, Helen Drutt Gallery, New York
1989,87	*Solo Exhibitions*, Galerie Louise Smit, Amsterdam
1988	*Tragezeichen*, Museum Schloss Morsbroich, Leverkusen, Germany
1987	*Joieria Europea Contemporània*, Fundació Caixa de Pensions, Barcelona
	Schmuck, Zeichen am Körper, Francisco Carolinum Museum, Linz, Austria
	Solo Exhibition, V & V Galerie, Vienna
1985	*Schmuck: Manfred Bischoff/Werner Buttner*, Galerie Cada, Munich
1984	*Cross Currents: Jewellery from Australia, Britain, Germany and Holland*, Power House Museum, Sydney (travelled)
	Jewelry International, American Craft Museum II, New York
1983	*Manfred Bischoff/Gabi Dziuba*, Galerie Cada, Munich
1982	*Zeitgenössische Schmuckkunst aus der Bundesrepublik Deutschland*, Goethe Institute, Hong Kong (travelled internationally)
1981	*Schmuck*, Studio f, Ulm, Germany
1980	*8 Orafi*, Galerie Albrecht, Bozen, Italy
	Schmuck International 1900-1980, Künstlerhaus, Vienna

Selected Public Collections:
Danner-Stiftung Collection, Munich; Museum Het Kruithuis, 's-Hertogenbosch, The Netherlands; Power House Museum, Sydney; Schmuckmuseum, Pforzheim, Germany; Stedelijk Museum, Amsterdam

Liv Blåvarp

Born: April 19, 1956, Furnes, Norway

Education:
1983-84 Royal College of Art, London
1979-83 National College of Art, Craft and Design, Oslo

Selected Awards:
1990 Kulturpris, Foreningen Norsk Forms, Norway
1989 Kunsthåndverkprisen, Norway
 Kunstnerpris, Den Norske Hypotekforenings, Norway

Selected Exhibitions:
1996,88 *Solo Exhibitions*, Kunstnerforbundet, Oslo
1994 *In Touch*, Maihaugen, Lillehammer, Norway
A Moveable Feast*, Amsterdam
Nordiska Profiler, Kunstindustrimuseet, Stockholm (travelled)
1993 *Rotter*, Maihaugen, Lillehammer, Norway
1993,91,90,89,88,87,85,84,83,82
Norske Kunsthåndverkeres årsutstilling, Oslo
1991 *Solo Exhibition*, Galleri Ram, Oslo
1990 *Nord Form 90*, Malmö, Sweden
Norwegian Wood, travelled through Great Britain
Triennale du Bijou, Musée du Luxembourg, Paris
1989 *Alle ting er tre*, Kunstindustrimuseet, Oslo
An Art Collection of Combs, organized by Galerie Marzee, Nimwegen, The Netherlands (travelled)
1988 *Firework of Vanity*, Kunstindustrimuseet, Oslo
Norska Smycken, Röhsska Konstslöjdmuseet, Gothenburg, Sweden
1987 *Scandinavian Craft Today*, Yurakucho Art Forum, Tokyo (travelled)
Schmuckszene '87, Internationale Handwerksmesse, Munich
1986 *Designs for the Body*, American Scandinavian Foundation Gallery, New York (travelled)
1985 *Nya Smycken, Nya Material*, Kulturhuset, Stockholm

Selected Public Collections:
Cooper-Hewitt, National Museum of Design, Smithsonian Institution, New York; Epcot Center, Orlando, FL; Kunstindustrimuseet, Copenhagen; Kunstindustrimuseet, Oslo; Lillehammer City Hall, Norway; Nordenfjeldske Kunstindustrimuseum, Trondheim, Norway; Norsk Kulturråd, Norway; Röhsska Konstslöjdmuseet, Gothenburg, Sweden; Vestlandske Kunstindustrimuseet, Bergen, Norway

Peter Blodgett

Born: June 5, 1935, New York, USA

Education:
1973 MFA, Rhode Island School of Design, Providence
1966-67 Museum School of Fine Arts, Boston, MA
1960-66 Studied with Conte Carlo Alberto Petrucci, Rome
1960 BFA, Rhode Island School of Design, Providence

Selected Exhibitions:
1994 *A Moveable Feast**, Amsterdam; *Schmuck Unserer Zeit**, Zurich
1992-93 *Korun Kielt**, Gothenburg; Helsinki
1984-87 *Modern Jewelry**, Philadelphia, PA; Cleveland, OH; Honolulu, HI; Montreal
1980 *Contemporary Works by Master Craftsmen*, Museum of Fine Arts, Boston, MA
Technical Innovations in Metal and Clay, Rhode Island College, Providence
1977 *The Metalsmith: SNAG Exhibition*, Phoenix Museum of Art, AZ
1975 *Invitational Jewelry Exhibition*, Pensacola Junior College, FL
1974 *The Goldsmith*, Renwick Gallery, NCFA, Smithsonian Institution, Washington, DC
The Metalsmith, Phoenix Art Museum, Phoenix, AZ

Exhibited in following Selected Institutions
Brockton Art Centre, Boston, MA; Brown University, Providence, RI; Marlboro College, VT; Minnesota Museum of Art, WI; Museum of Art, Rhode Island College, Providence; Rhode Island School of Design, Providence; School of the Museum of Fine Art, Boston; Southern Vermont Art Centre, Manchester, VT

Related Professional Experience:
1989– Established, pb Design, Trinity, TB, NF, Canada
Founder/Director, Northern Light Studios, Ltd., Kee, NF, Canada
1974-85 Faculty, School of the Museum of Fine Arts, Boston
1973-85 Established, Peter Blodgett, Ltd. (Freelance & Consulting), Providence, RI
Design Consultant (Selected):
Coro, Inc., Providence, RI; Miller-Burrows Inc., New York; Monet Corporation, New York; Osiris Ltd., Providence, RI; Reed & Barton, Inc., Taunton, MA

Marta Breis

Born: March 2, 1953, Barcelona, Spain

Education:
1972-75 University of Barcelona
1975-80 Escola Massana, Barcelona

Selected Awards:
1987 Gold Medal, *Jablonec '87 – International Exhibition of Jewelry VIII*, Muzeum skla a bizuterie, Jablonec nad Nisou, Czechoslovakia

Selected Exhibitions:

1994   *A Moveable Feast**, Amsterdam; *Schmuck Unserer Zeit**, Zurich

1993   *Contemporary Jewelry**, Little Rock, AK

1992-93   *Korun Kieli**, Gothenburg; Helsinki

1989   *An Art Collection of Combs*, organized by Galerie Marzee, Nimwegen, The Netherlands (travelled)

1987   *Jabonlec '87 – International Exhibition of Jewelry VIII*, Muzeum skla a bizuterie, Jablonec nad Nisou, Czechoslovakia

       Joieria Europea Contemporània, Fundació Caixa de Pensions, Barcelona

1984-87   *Modern Jewelry**, Philadelphia, PA; Cleveland, OH; Honolulu, HI; Montreal

1984   *Contemporary Jewellery: The Americas, Australia, Europe and Japan*, National Museum of Modern Art, Kyoto; Tokyo

1984   *Jewelry International*, American Craft Museum II, New York

1982   *Schmuck, 82 – Tendenzen* , Schmuckmuseum, Pforzheim, Germany

Related Professional Experience:

1987-94   Manager, Galeria Espai Positura, Barcelona

Caroline Broadhead

Born: June 28, 1950, Leeds, England

Education:

1969-72   Central School of Art and Design, London

1968-69   Leicester School of Art, England

Selected Awards:

1991   London Dance and Performance Award with Rosemary Lee for *Stranded*, South Bank Centre, London

1989   Grant, British Council, London

1982   Bursary, British Crafts Council, London

Selected Exhibitions:

1994   *A Moveable Feast**, Amsterdam

1993   *On the Edge*, Crafts Council Gallery, London (travelled)

       Visions of Craft, Crafts Council Gallery, London

       Voorzien: Benno Premsela Applied Art Collection, Stedelijk Museum, Amsterdam

1992-93   *Korun Kieli**, Gothenburg; Helsinki

1992   *Arts and Crafts to the Avant Garde*, South Bank Centre, London

1992   *Crafts in Performance*, Crafts Council Gallery, London

1990   *Three Ways of Seeing*, Crafts Council Gallery, London

1989   *Jewelry: Means: Meaning*, University of Tennessee, Knoxville (travelled)

1988   *Contemporary British Crafts*, National Museum of Modern Art, Kyoto; Tokyo

1987   *Joieria Europea Contemporània*, Fundació Caixa de Pensions, Barcelona

1986   *British Design*, Künstlerhaus, Vienna

       Sieraad 1986, Draagteken?, Museum Het Kruithuis, 's-Hertogenbosch, The Netherlands

       Solo Exhibition, Norwich Castle Museum, Norfolk

1985   *Body Works and Wearable Sculpture*, Visual Arts Center of Alaska, Anchorage

       Contemporary Jewelry Redefined, Pittsburgh Center for the Arts, PA

       New Tradition, British Crafts Centre, London

       Nya Smycken, Nya Material, Kulturhuset, Stockholm

1984-87   *Modern Jewelry**, Philadelphia, PA; Cleveland, OH; Honolulu, HI; Montreal

1984   *Contemporary Jewellery: The Americas, Australia, Europe and Japan*, National Museum of Modern Art, Kyoto; Tokyo

       Cross Currents: Jewellery from Australia, Britain, Germany and Holland, Power House Museum, Sydney (travelled)

       Jewelry International, American Craft Museum II, New York

1983   *The Jewellery Project*, Crafts Council Gallery, London

       New Departures in British Jewellery, American Craft Museum, New York

1982   *Jewellery Redefined*, British Crafts Centre, London

       Visies op Sieraden 1965-1982, Stedelijk Museum, Amsterdam

1980   *Schmuck International 1900-1980*, Künstlerhaus, Vienna

1979   *Michael Brennand-Wood/Caroline Broadhead*, Crafts Council Gallery, London (travelled)

1978   *British Jewellers on Tour in Holland*, Gemeentelijke van Reekummuseum, Apeldoorn, The Netherlands (travelled)

       Loot & Superloot, Minneapolis Institute of Art, MN

Related Professional Experience:

1987–   Middlesex Polytechnic, London

1978-87   Brighton Polytechnic, England

Selected Public Collections:

Bristol City Art Gallery, England; British Crafts Council, London; Cleveland County Museum, Middlesbrough, England; East Midlands Arts, Loughborough, England; Gemeentelijke van Reekummuseum, Apeldoorn, The Netherlands; Israel Museum, Jerusalem; Kostuummuseum, The Hague; Manchester Royal Exchange Education Collection, England; National Museum of Modern Art, Kyoto; North West Arts Association, Manchester; Norwich Castle Museum, Norfolk, England; Stedelijk Museum, Amsterdam; West Midlands Arts, Stafford, England; Worshipful Company of Goldsmiths, London

Amy Buckingham-Flammang

Born: June 24, 1943, Kansas City, MO, USA

Education:
1972   MFA, Tyler School of Art, Temple University, Elkins Park, PA
1967-68 University of Kansas, Lawrence
1966-67 Craft Student League, New York
1965   BA, Mills College, Oakland, CA

Selected Awards:
1973   Honorable Mention, National Copper Competition, USA
      Juror's Award, *Kansas Designer-Craftsmen*, Lawrence Kansas
1973,72 Honorable Mention, National Sterling Silver Competition, New York

Selected Exhibitions:
1994   *A Moveable Feast**, Amsterdam; *Schmuck Unserer Zeit**, Zurich
1993   *A Common Thread: Year of the American Craft*, travelled through Nevada
1992-93 *Korun Kieli**, Gothenburg; Helsinki
1992   *Retrospective*, Northeastern Nevada Museum, Elko
1984-87 *Modern Jewelry**, Philadelphia, PA; Cleveland, OH; Honolulu, HI; Montreal
1976   *2nd Annual Jewelry Invitational*, Central Washington State College, Ellensburg
      8 Contemporary Metalsmiths, Bradley University, Peoria, IL
      National Metalwork and Jewelry Exhibition, Eastern Washington University, Cheny
1975   *National Metals Invitational*, Humboldt State University, Arcata, CA
      Solo Exhibition, Western Illinois University, Macomb
1974   *Baroque '74*, Museum of Contemporary Crafts, New York
      National Invitational Exhibition in Contemporary Jewellery, Georgia State University, Atlanta
      A Touch of Gold, Philadelphia Museum of Art, PA
1973   *Kansas Designer-Craftsmen*, Lawrence, Kansas
1972   *Metal +72*, State University of New York, Brockport

Related Professional Experience:
1984–   Adjunct Professor, Northern Nevada Community College, Elko
1974-75 Assistant Professor, Western Illinois University, Macomb
1970-74 Instructor, Philadelphia College of Art, PA

Selected Public Collections:
Northeastern Nevada Museum, Elko; Tyler School of Art, Temple University, Elkins Park, PA

Stuart M. Buehler

Born: June 5, 1945, Fremont, CA, USA

Education:
1983   Humboldt State University, Arcata, CA
1963-65 American River Junior College, Sacramento, CA

Selected Awards:
1983   Humboldt Arts Council Award/Honorable Mention, *Northern California Crafts*, Humboldt Cultural Center, Eureka, CA
1979   Merit Award, *California Crafts XI*, Crocker Art Museum, Sacramento, CA

Selected Exhibitions:
1994   *Jewels and Gems: Collecting California Jewelry*, Oakland Museum, CA
      A Moveable Feast*, Amsterdam; *Schmuck Unserer Zeit**, Zurich
1993,92 *Solo Exhibitions*, Susan Cummins Gallery, Mill Valley, CA
1992   *Dreams and Shields*, Salt Lake Art Center, UT
      The Edge of Childhood, Heckscher Museum, Huntington, NY
      Of Magic, Power and Memory, Bellevue Art Museum, WA
1992-85 *Solo Exhibitions*, Jamison/Thomas Gallery, Portland, OR
1991   *Vocations*, Humboldt Cultural Center, Eureka, CA
1989   *First Impressions, Northwest Monoprints*, Seattle Art Museum, WA
1987   *The Ubiquitous Bead*, Bellevue Art Museum, WA
1984   *West Coast Works on Paper*, Humboldt State University, Arcata, CA
1983   *Boneworks*, John Michael Kohler Art Center, Sheboygen, WI
      California Crafts XIII, Crocker Art Museum, Sacramento, CA
      Northern California Crafts, Humboldt Cultural Center, Eureka, CA
      Stuart Buehler/John O'Brien: Prints, Paintings and Sculpture, Humboldt State University, Arcata, CA
1982,79 *Solo Exhibitions*, Humboldt State University, Arcata, CA
1981   *Good as Gold*, Renwick Gallery, NCFA, Smithsonian Institution, Washington, DC (travelled)

Related Professional Experience:
1990   Ramboy Records: Designed CD cover

Selected Public Collections:
Crocker Art Museum, Sacramento, CA; Renwick Gallery, NMAA, Smithsonian Institution, Washington, DC; Oakland Museum, CA; Portland Art Museum, OR

Claus Bury

Born: March 29, 1946, Meerholz/Gelnhausen, Germany

Education:
1965-69 Kunst und Werkschule, Pforzheim, Germany
1962-65 Staatlichen Zeichenakademie, Hanau, Germany

Selected Awards:
1991 Municipal Sculptor, Hanau, Germany
1990 Grant, Am Seestern Sculpture Park, Dusseldorf
      Grant, Schloss Philippsruhe Sculpture Park, Hanau, Germany
1986 August-Seeling Förderpreis, Duisburg, Germany
      Kunstfonds e.V. Grant, Bonn
1985 Grant, Casa Baldi, Olevano Romano, Italy
1979 Visiting Artist, Goethe Institute, Sydney
1976 Fellowship, Kulturkreis im Bundesverband der Deutschen
      Industrie, Cologne

Selected Exhibitions/Commissioned Site-Sculptures:
1994 *A Moveable Feast**, Amsterdam; *Schmuck Unserer Zeit**, Zurich
1993 *13 Goldschmiede: Von Amsterdam bis Tokyo*, Bayerische
      Akademie der Schönen Künste, Munich
      Contemporary Jewelry*, Little Rock, AK
      Gold oder Leben!, Akademie der Bildenden Künste, Munich
1992-93 *Korun Kieli**, Gothenburg; Helsinki
1990 *Solo Exhibition*, Helen Drutt Gallery, New York
1989 *Claus Bury: Im Goldenen Schnitt*, Art Frankfurt, Germany
      Der Augenblick, Kunstverein Springhornhof Neuenkirchen,
      Germany
      Stadtportal Nürnberg, Germanisches Nationalmuseum,
      Nuremberg, Germany
1988 *Berlin-Denkmal oder Denkmodell? Architecktonische Entwürfe
      für den Aufbruch in das 21 Jahrhundert*, Staatliche
      Kunsthalle, Berlin
      Haus des Hasselbacher Reiters, Hasselbach, Germany
1986 *Mercator*, Wilhelm Lehmbruck Museum, Duisburg, Germany
1984-87 *Modern Jewelry**, Philadelphia, PA; Cleveland, OH; Honolulu,
      HI; Montreal
1984 *Fibonaccis Tempel*, Museum Ludwig, Cologne
1983 *Bridge Project*, Madison Square Park, New York
1982 *Two Elevated Walkways*, Moore College of Art,
      Philadelphia, PA
1981 *Concave-Convex-Construction*, Brown University,
      Providence, RI
1980 *Wind Sculpture*, Barrington, RI
1979 *Solo Exhibition*, Art of Man Gallery, Sydney
      Solo Exhibition, National Gallery of Victoria, Melbourne
      Wave Sculpture, Goethe Institute, Sydney
1978 *3 Konzepte – 3 Goldschmiede: Bury/Jünger/Rothmann*,
      Hessisches Landesmuseum, Darmstadt, Germany
1977 *Ars Viva*, Kunsthalle, Nuremberg, Germany
      Solo Exhibition, Landesmuseum, Oldenburg, Germany
1977,73,70
      Schmuck – Tendenzen, Schmuckmuseum, Pforzheim, Germany

1976 *10 Goldschmiede*, Galerie Albertstrasse, Graz, Austria
      Ars Viva, Wilhelm Lehmbruck Museum, Duisburg, Germany
1975 *Jewellery in Europe*, Scottish Arts Council Gallery, Edinburgh
      (travelled)
1974 *18 Orfèvres d'Aujourd'hui*, Musée des Arts Décoratifs, Lausanne
      Claus Bury, Schmuck-Objekte-Zeichnungen, Schmuckmuseum,
      Pforzheim, Germany
      Solo Exhibition, Deutsches Goldschmiedehaus, Hanau,
      Germany
1973 *Aspects of Jewellery*, Aberdeen Art Gallery and Museum,
      Scotland
1971 *Gold+Silber Schmuck+Gerät*, Norishalle, Nuremberg, Germany

Selected Public Collections:
Artothek Berlin, Berlin; Deutsches Goldschmiedehaus, Hanau, Germany;
Germanisches Nationalmuseum, Nuremberg, Germany; KPMG Peat
Marwick, New York; Kunstgewerbemuseum, Berlin; Kunsthalle,
Nuremberg, Germany; Landesmuseum, Oldenburg, Germany;
The Metropolitan Museum of Art, New York; Museum Ludwig, Cologne;
National Gallery of Victoria, Melbourne; Schmuckmuseum, Pforzheim,
Germany; Victoria and Albert Museum, London; Wilhelm Lehmbruck
Museum, Duisburg, Germany

Pierre Cavalan

Born: February 16, 1954, Paris, France

Education:
1977-79 National School of Jewellery, Paris

Selected Awards:
1994 National Contemporary Jewellery Award, Sydney
1993 Alice Craft Acquisition Award, Alice Springs, NT, Australia
1992 West Australia Neckworks Award
1991 Elected, Chair for Jewellers and Metalsmiths Group of Australia NSW Inc.
 Project Grant, Australia Council

Selected Exhbitions:
1994 *Family Diversity and Tradition*, Jakarta Museum, Indonesia
 A Moveable Feast*, Amsterdam; *Schmuck Unserer Zeit**, Zurich
 Pins and Needles: Identity of Meaning, University of Tasmania, Launceston, Australia
 Solo Exhibition, Jam Factory, Adelaide
1993 *2nd Australian Jewellery Biennial*, Jam Factory, Adelaide, SA
 Contemporary Jewelry*, Little Rock, AK
 Ornament, National Gallery of Victoria, Melbourne
 Schmuckszene '93, Internationale Handwerksmesse, Munich
 Solo Exhibition, Ben Grady Gallery, Canberra
1992-93 *Korun Kieli**, Gothenburg; Helsinki
1992 *Australian Crafts: New Works*, Power House Museum, Sydney
 Desire, Blaxland Gallery, Sydney
 Neckworks, Fremantle Art Centre, Perth
 Solo Exhibition, Alliance Francaise de Sydney, Sydney
 Solo Exhibition, Despard Gallery, Hobart, TAS, Australia
 Wearable Glass, Jam Factory, Adelaide, SA
1991 *1st Australian Contemporary Jewellery Biennial*, Jam Factory, Adelaide (travelled)
 Art of the Metropolis, Australian National Gallery, Canberra
 Body in Question, University of Tasmania, Launceston, Australia
 Solo Exhibitions, Punch Gallery, Sydney, University of Sydney
1990 *Darwin Craft Acquisition*, Northern Territory Museum of Arts and Sciences, Darwin
1984 *Artists for Nuclear Disarmament*, Sydney Town Hall, Sydney

Selected Public Collections:
Art Gallery of South Australia, Adelaide; Artbank, Sydney; Australian National Gallery, Canberra; Coventry Collection, Sydney; Craft Council of Northern Territory, Alice Springs, Australia; Griffith Regional Gallery, NSW; Northern Territory Museum of Arts and Sciences, Darwin; Power House Museum, Sydney

Anton Cepka

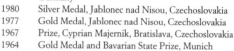

Born: January 17, 1936, Sulekovo, Czechoslovakia

Education:
1957-63 Academy of Applied Arts, Prague, Czechoslovakia
1953-57 School of Arts and Crafts, Bratislava, Czechoslovakia

Selected Awards:
1990 Recipient, Golden Ring of Honour, Association for Goldsmiths' Art, Deutsches Goldschmiedehaus, Hanau, Germany
1980 Silver Medal, Jablonec nad Nisou, Czechoslovakia
1977 Gold Medal, Jablonec nad Nisou, Czechoslovakia
1967 Prize, Cyprian Majernik, Bratislava, Czechoslovakia
1964 Gold Medal and Bavarian State Prize, Munich

Selected Exhibitions:
1994 *A Moveable Feast**, Amsterdam; *Schmuck Unserer Zeit**, Zurich
 Schmuck und Gerät, Deutsches Goldschmiedehaus, Hanau, Germany (travelled)
1993 *13 Goldschmiede: Von Amsterdam bis Tokyo*, Bayerische Akademie der Schönen Künste, Munich
 Contemporary Jewelry*, Little Rock, AK
 Facet I, Kunsthal, Rotterdam
1992-93 *Korun Kieli**, Gothenburg; Helsinki
1992 *Joies Indissenyables*, Escola Massana, Barcelona
1990 *Schmuckszene '90*, Internationale Handwerksmesse, Munich
1989 *Perth International Crafts Triennial*, Art Gallery of Western Australia, Perth
1988 *Anton Cepka – Vratislav Novák*, Schmuckmuseum, Pforzheim, Germany; Deutsches Goldschmiedehaus, Hanau, Germany
1987 *Contemporary Slovak Glass and Jewelry*, National Galerie, Bratislava, Czechoslovakia
 Czechoslovak Exhibition of Applied Arts and Design, Warsaw; Moscow
 Joieria Europea Contemporània, Fundació Caixa de Pensions, Barcelona
 Schmuck, Zeichen am Körper, Francisco Carolinum Museum, Linz, Austria
 Schmuck in Bewegung, Bewegung in Schmuck, Deutsches Goldschmiedehaus, Hanau, Germany
1986 *Novák/Cepka/Pràsil*, Galerie am Graben, Vienna (travelled)
1986,82,76,71,68,66
 Slovak Exhibitions of Applied Art and Industrial Design, Bratislava, Czechoslovakia

1986,76	*International Jewellery Art Exhibition*, Tokyo Triennials
1984	*Contemporary Jewellery: The Americas, Australia, Europe and Japan*, National Museum of Modern Art, Kyoto; Tokyo
1983,82	*Material Schmuck und Gerät*, Internationale Handwerksmesse, Munich
1982,77,73,70	
	Schmuck – Tendenzen, Schmuckmuseum, Pforzheim, Germany
1980	*Schmuck International 1900-1980*, Künstlerhaus, Vienna
1979	*Cepka/Cepková/Svitana*, Ostslowakische Museum, Kosice, Czechoslovakia
1978	*Anton Cepka/Vàclav Cigler*, Galerie am Graben, Vienna
	Contemporary Czechoslovakian Jewelry, Jablonec nad Nisou, Czechoslovakia
1978,71	*Solo Exhibitions*, National Galerie, Bratislava, Czechoslovakia
1977	*International Jewelry Exhibition*, Jablonec nad Nisou, Czechoslovakia
1976	*Aurea '76 Biennale dell'Arteorafa*, §Florence
1975	*Jewellery in Europe*, Scottish Arts Council Gallery, Edinburgh (travelled)
1971	*Gold+Silber Schmuck+Gerät*, Norishalle, Nuremberg, Germany
1968	*International Jewelry Exhibition*, Muzeum skla a bizuterie, Jablonec nad Nisou, Czechoslovakia
1967	*Expo '67*, Montreal

Related Professional Experience:
Current Professor, Academy of Fine Arts, Bratislava, Slovakia

Selected Public Collections:
Deutsches Goldschmiedehaus, Hanau, Germany; Umeleckoprumyslove Muzeum, Prague, Czech Republic; Muzeum skla a bizuterie, Jablonec nad Nisou, Czech Republic; National Galerie, Bratislava, Slovakia; National Gallery of Victoria, Melbourne; Ostslowakische Museum, Kosice, Slovakia; Regionalgalerie, Trencin, Slovakia. Schmuckmuseum, Pforzheim, Germany

Peter Chang

Born: December 1, 1944, London

Education:
1968-70 Slade School of Fine Art, University College, London
1962-66 Liverpool College of Art, England

Selected Awards:
1994	Bursary, Scottish Arts Council
1991	1st prize, *Merseycraft '91*, Walker Art Gallery, Liverpool,
1989	1st prize, *Scottish Gold*, Scottish Gallery, Edinburgh

Selected Exhibitions:
1994	*Kunstoff Schmuck Kunst 1923-1993*, Museum of Applied Arts, Budapest
	Solo Exhibition, Showhouse, Visionfest, Liverpool
	A Moveable Feast*, Amsterdam; *Schmuck Unserer Zeit**, Zurich
	Solo Exhibition, Galerie Biro, Munich
1994-90,88	
	Schmuckszene, Internationale Handwerksmesse, Munich
1993	*Contemporary Jewelry**, Little Rock, AK
	Facet I, Kunsthal, Rotterdam
	Kunstoff Schmuck Kunst 1923-1993, Galerie Brio, Munich
	Solo Exhibition, David Gill Gallery, London
1992-93	*Korun Kieli**, Gothenburg; Helsinki
1992	*British Council Inaugural Exhibition*, Prague
	Contemporary Scottish Jewellery, Hipotesi, Barcelona
	Interplays '92, Expozicia Suhry, Bratislava, Slovakia
	Solo Exhibition, Helen Drutt Gallery, Philadelphia, PA
	Triennale du Bijou, Musée des Arts Décoratifs, Paris
1991	*Merseycraft '91*, Walker Art Gallery, Liverpool
1990	*Classical Plastics*, Scottish Gallery, Edinburgh
	Great British Design, Mitsukoshi Museum, Tokyo
1989	*Ornamenta 1*, Schmuckmuseum, Pforzheim, Germany
	Scottish Gold, Scottish Gallery, Edinburgh
	Wealth of a Nation, National Museums of Scotland, Edinburgh
1988	*London/Amsterdam*, Crafts Council Gallery, London (travelled)
1987	*Biennale du Bijou Contemporain*, Hotel du Sens, Paris
	Gems II, The Williamson Art Gallery, Birkenhead, England
1986	*Gems*, The Prescott Museum, Prescott, (travelled)

Related Professional Experience:
1984-87	Fashion Accessory Designer, Bloomingdale's, New York; Mary Williams Knitwear Collection, Commonwealth Institute, London; Olympia, London; Port Sunlight, Merseyside, England; Rifat Osbek Collection, Mansion House, London; Victoria and Albert Museum, London

Selected Public Collections:
Aberdeen Museum, Scotland; British Crafts Council, London; British Council Collection, Prague, Czech Republic; Castle Museum, Nottingham, England; Kelvingrove Museum and Art Gallery, Glasgow; Lancashire Museum, Preston, England; Montreal Musée des Arts Décoratifs, Quebec; National Museums of Scotland, Edinburgh; Scottish Crafts Collections, Edinburgh; Shipley Collection, Shipley Art Gallery, Gateshead, England; Society for Contemporary Art, London; Taideteollisuusmuseo, Helsinki; Victoria and Albert Museum, London

Sharon Church

Born: October 15, 1948, Richland, WA, USA

Education:
1973   MFA, School for American Craftsmen, Rochester
        Institute of Technology, NY
1970   BS, Skidmore College, Saratoga Springs, NY

Selected Awards:
1978   Fellowship, National Endowment for the Arts,
        Washington, DC

Selected Exhibitions:
1990   *Contemporary American Craft*, Philadelphia Museum of
        Art, PA
1989   *The Craft Enigma*, University of the Arts, Philadelphia, PA
        Skidmore 1989: Five Goldsmiths, Helen Drutt Gallery,
        Philadelphia, PA
1986   *Craft Today: Poetry of the Physical*, American Craft Museum,
        New York (travelled)
1985   *Form Formel Formalismus*, Internationale Handwerksmesse,
        Munich
1984   *American Jewelry Now*, organized by the American Craft
        Museum, New York (travelled)
        Jewelry USA, American Craft Museum II, New York
1974   *Metal '74*, State University of New York, Brockport

Related Professional Experience:
1979–   Associate Professor, University of the Arts, Philadelphia, PA

Selected Public Collections:
Delaware Art Museum, Wilmington

Ken Cory

Born: December 5, 1943, Kirkland, WA, USA
Died: January 16, 1994, Ellensburg, WA ,USA

Education:
1969   MFA, Washington State University, Pullman
1967   BFA, California College of Arts and Crafts, Oakland

Selected Exhibitions:
1993   *Documents Northwest, The Poncho Series: Six Jewelers*, Seattle
        Art Museum, WA
1987   *The Eloquent Object*, Philbrook Museum of Art, Tulsa, OK
        (travelled)
1986   *Pencil Brothers Twenty Year Retrospective* (Ken Cory/Les
        LePere), Cheney Cowles Museum, Spokane, WA (travelled)
1980   *Robert L. Pfannebecker Collection*, Moore College of Art,
        Philadelphia, PA
1979   *International Jewellery Art Exhibition*, 4th Tokyo Triennial,
        Ginza Mikimoto Hall, Tokyo
1978   *Modern American Jewelry Exhibition*, Mikimoto and Co., Ltd.
        Gallery, Tokyo
1976   *2nd Annual Jewelry Invitational*, Central Washington State
        College, Ellensburg
1974   *American Metalsmiths*, DeCordova Museum, Lincoln, MA
        Metal '74, State University of New York, Brockport
1971   *Jewellery '71*, Art Gallery of Ontario, Toronto
1970   *Goldsmith '70: SNAG Inaugural Exhibition*, Minnesota Museum
        of Art, St Paul (travelled)
        Solo Exhibition, Museum of Contemporary Crafts, New York
1969   *Objects: USA*, National Collection of Fine Arts, Smithsonian
        Institution, Washington, DC (travelled)
        Young Americans 1969, Museum of Contemporary Crafts,
        New York
1968   *Objects Are?...*, Museum of Contemporary Crafts, New York

Related Professional Experience:
1972-94 Professor, Central Washington University, Ellensburg
1969-86 Collaborated with Leslie LePere as Art Team, 1969-71, and
         as Pencil Brothers, 1972-86

Selected Public Collections:
American Craft Museum, New York; University of Georgia, Athens,
Georgia; Washington State University, Pullman, Washington

Pencil Brothers: Les LePere (left) and Ken Cory (right)

Selected Public Collections:
Badisches Landesmuseum, Karlsruhe, Germany;
Boymans-van Beuningen Museum, Rotterdam;
Bundesamt für Kultur, Berne; Haags
Gemeentemuseum, The Hague; Musée de
l'horlogerie et de l'émaillerie, Geneva; Musée
des Arts Décoratifs, Lausanne; Museum für
angewandte Kunst, Cologne; Museum für
Gestaltung, Zurich; National Museum of
Modern Art, Kyoto; Nordenfjeldske
Kunstindustrimuseum, Trondheim, Norway;
Röhsska Konstslöjdmuseet, Gothenburg;
Sammlung C. Vögele, Pfaffikon, Switzerland;
Stedelijk Museum, Amsterdam;
Württembergisches Landesmuseum,
Stuttgart

Johanna Dahm
(formerly Johanna Hess-Dahm)

Born: September 16, 1947, Basle, Switzerland

Education:
1967-72 Kunstgewerbeschule, Zurich

Selected Awards:
1984,82,73
        Eidgenössisches Stipendium für Angewandte Kunst, Swiss Federal
           Government
1983   Werkbeitrag, Canton of Zurich
1978   Leistungspreis, Kunstgewerbeschule, Zurich

Selected Exhibitions:
1994   *A Moveable Feast**, Amsterdam; *Schmuck Unserer Zeit**, Zurich
        Solo Exhibition, Galerie Michele Zeller, Berne
1992-93 *Korun Kieli**, Gothenburg; Helsinki
1992   *Triennale du Bijou*, Musée des Arts Décoratifs du Louvre, Paris
1990-91 *Fremd. Körper aus der Sammlung Teunen*, Wilhelm-Hack Museum, Ludwigshafen,
           Rhein, Germany
1989   *An Art Collection of Combs*, organized by Galerie Marzee, Nimwegen,
           The Netherlands (travelled)
        Jewelry: Means: Meaning, University of Tennessee, Knoxville (travelled)
1987   *Joieria Europea Contemporània*, Fundació Caixa de Pensions, Barcelona
        Schmuck, Zeichen am Körper, Francisco Carolinum Museum, Linz, Austria
1987,81 *Solo Exhibitons,* Museum Bellerive, Zurich
1986   *International Contemporary Art Fair*, London
        Sieraad 1986, Draagteken?, Museum Het Kruithuis, 's-Hertogenbosch,
           The Netherlands
        Solo Exhibition, Galerie Ra, Amsterdam
1986,83 *International Jewellery Art Exhibition*, Tokyo Triennials
1985   *Form Formel Formalismus*, Internationale Handwerksmesse, Munich
        New Tradition, British Crafts Centre, London
        Nya Smycken, Nya Material, Kulturhuset, Stockholm
1984-87 *Modern Jewelry**, Philadelphia, PA; Cleveland, OH; Honolulu, HI;
           Montreal
1984   *Contemporary Jewellery: The Americas, Australia, Europe and Japan*, National
           Museum of Modern Art, Kyoto; Tokyo
        Jewelry International, American Craft Museum II, New York
        Four Swiss Artists, Röhsska Konstslöjdmuseet, Gothenburg, Sweden
1983   *The Jewellery Project*, Crafts Council Gallery, London
1982   *Jewellery Redefined*, British Crafts Centre, London
        Visies op Sieraden 1965-1982, Stedelijk Museum, Amsterdam
1973   *Jewelry as Sculpture as Jewelry*, Institute of Contemporary Art, Boston, MA

Related Professional Experience:
1990–   Professor, Fachhochschule für Gestaltung, Pforzheim,
         Germany
1976–   Maintains independent studio, Zurich

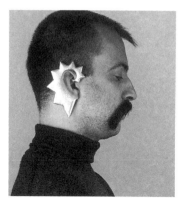

Paul Derrez

Born: February 20, 1950, Sittard, The Netherlands

Education:
1972-75 Schoonhoven Gold and Silversmith College,
The Netherlands
1968-70 Akademie voor Industriële Vormgeving,
Eindhoven, The Netherlands

Selected Awards:
1990 Honorary Member, National Association of
Heads of Three-Dimensional Design, UK
1986 Fine Works Prize, *International Jewellery Art
Exhibition*, Yurakucho Art Forum, Tokyo
1980 Françoise van den Bosch Prize, Amsterdam

Selected Exhibitions:
1994 *A Moveable Feast**, Amsterdam; *Schmuck Unserer Zeit**, Zurich
1993 *Contemporary Jewelry**, Little Rock, AK
Subjects, Design Forum, Helsinki
1992-93 *Korun Kieli**, Gothenburg; Helsinki
1992 *Sieraad en sieraad*, Kritzraedthuis, Sittard, The Netherlands
1990 *Amphoria*, Gallery Jocelyne Gobeil, Montreal
Hedendaagse Sieraadkunst 1990, travelled through Benelux
L'Arte della Gioia, Pedrocchi, Padua
News from the Netherlands, Fundacao Calouste Gulbenkian,
Lisbon (travelled)
Point of View: Dutch Contemporary Jewelry and Design,
travelled through the USA
Triennale du Bijou, Musée du Luxembourg, Paris
1989 *Jewelry: Means: Meaning*, University of Tennessee, Knoxville,
TN (travelled)
Kunstobject als onderscheiding II, Galerie Het Kapelhuis,
Amersfoort, The Netherlands
1989,82,81,80,78
VES, Stedelijk Museum, Amsterdam
1987 *Joieria Europea Contemporània*, Fundació Caixa de Pensions,
Barcelona
Kunstobject als onderscheiding, Galerie Het Kapelhuis,
Amersfoort, The Netherlands
1986 *International Jewellery Art Exhibition*, 6th Tokyo Triennial,
Yurakucho Art Forum, Tokyo
Jewellery Images, VES 10th anniversary exhibition, Stedelijk
Museum, Amsterdam (travelled)
1985 *Body Works and Wearable Sculpture*, Visual Arts Center of
Alaska, Anchorage
Contemporary Jewelry Redefined, Pittsburgh Center for the
Arts, PA
New Tradition, British Crafts Centre, London
Nya Smycken, Nya Material, Kulturhuset, Stockholm
Paul Derrez, 10 jaar sieraden, Kritzraedthuis, Sittard, The
Netherlands
1984-87 *Modern Jewelry**, Philadelphia, PA; Cleveland, OH; Honolulu,
HI; Montreal

1984 *Contemporary Jewellery: The Americas, Australia, Europe and
Japan*, National Museum of Modern Art, Kyoto; Tokyo
*Cross Currents: Jewellery from Australia, Britain, Germany and
Holland*, Power House Museum, Sydney (travelled)
Jewelry International, American Craft Museum II, New York
1983 *The Jewellery Project*, Crafts Council Gallery, London
1982 *Schmuck '82 – Tendenzen*, Schmuckmuseum, Pforzheim,
Germany
Visies op Sieraden 1965-1982, Stedelijk Museum, Amsterdam
1980 *Kunststof*, Galerie Het Kapelhuis, Amersfoort, The Netherlands
Schmuck International 1900-1980, Künstlerhaus, Vienna
1975 *Sieraad '75*, Galerie Het Kapelhuis, Amersfoort, The Netherlands

Related Professional Experience:
1992– Chairman, Foundation Françoise van den Bosch, Amsterdam
1979-81 Chairman, Dutch Society of Goldsmiths and Jewellery
Designers (VES)
1976– Founder, Director, Galerie Ra, Amsterdam

Selected Public Collections:
Centraal Museum, Utrecht; Cleveland County Museum, Middlesbrough,
England; Dutch National Service for the Arts, The Hague; Gemeentelijke
van Reekummuseum, Apeldoorn, The Netherlands; Gemeentemuseum,
Arnhem, The Netherlands; Jewish Historical Museum, Amsterdam;
Kostuummuseum, The Hague; Museum Het Kruithuis,
's-Hertogenbosch, The Netherlands; National Museum of Modern Art,
Kyoto; Nordenfjeldske Kunstindustrimuseum, Trondheim, Norway;
Power House Museum, Sydney; Rijksdienst Beeldende Kunst,
The Hague; Stedelijk Museum, Amsterdam

Claire Dinsmore

Born: October 16, 1961, Princeton, New Jersey, USA

Education:
1981-85 Parsons School of Design, New York
1982 Parsons School of Design, Summer School in Japan, Tokyo,
Kyoto and Bizen

Selected Awards:
1988 Grant, Empire State Crafts Alliance, Saratoga Springs, NY
1983 Scholarship, Tiffany & Co., New York
1982-85 Merit Awards for Outstanding Achievement, Parsons School
of Design, New York

Selected Exhibitions:
1994 *A Moveable Feast**, Amsterdam; *Schmuck Unserer Zeit**, Zurich
1993 Scuptural Concerns: Contemporary American Metalworking.
Fort Wayne Museum of Art, Indiana (travelled)
1991 *Metals Expressions II*, Appalachian Center for Crafts,
Smithville, TN

1988   *Young Americans*, American Craft Museum, New York (travelled)
1987-91 *Collect New York!*, Empire State Crafts Alliance Benefit
        Auction, New York
1987   *Simply Silver* & *The Spring Earring Put On*, Tony Papp Gallery,
        New York
1985   *Emerging Talent*, Quadrum Gallery, Chestnut Hill, MA
1984   *Holiday Show*, Automation House, New York

Related Professional Experience:
1989-90 Instructor, Parsons School of Design, New York
1986   Assistant Instructor, Parsons School of Design, New York

Selected Public Collections:
American Craft Museum, New York

Georg Dobler

Born: April 6, 1952, Bayreuth, Germany

Education:
1969-71 Berufsfachschule für Goldschmiede, Pforzheim, Germany

Selected Awards:
1993   Herbert Hoffman Prize, Schmuckszene '93, Munich
1986   Anerkennung, Benvenuto-Cellini-Wettbewerb,
1984   Preis für das gestaltende Handwerk, Landes Berlin
1980,75 Gold Medal, Benvenuto-Cellini-Wettbewerb,

Selected Exhibitions:
1994   *A Moveable Feast**, Amsterdam; *Schmuck Unserer Zeit**, Zurich
        Op Art: Eyeglasses by Jewelers, Oregon School of Arts and
        Crafts, Portland (travelled)
1993   *Contemporary Jewelry**, Little Rock, AK
        Schmuck: Die Sammlung der Danner-Stiftung, Galerie für
        angewandte Kunst, Munich

1993   *Subjects*, Design Forum, Helsinki
        The Art of Jewellery, Japan Jewellery Designer Associates, Inc.,
        Tokyo, Osaka
1992-93 *Korun Kieli**, Gothenburg; Helsinki
1992   *Schmuckszene '92*, Internationale Handwerksmesse, Munich
1991   *Europaisches Kunsthandwerk 1991*, Stuttgart
        15 Jahre Galerie RA, Amsterdam
        10 Jahrerie, Werkstattgalerie Berlin
1990   *Triennale du Bijou*, Musée de Luxembourg, Paris
        Zeitgenossisches Deutsches Kunsthandwerk, 90/91, Triennale,
        Museum fur Kunsthandwerk, Frankfurt
1989   *Infinite Riches*, Museum of Fine Arts, St Petersburg, FL, USA
        Jewelry: Means: Meaning, Ewing Gallery of Art and
        Architecture, University of Tennessee, Knoxville (travelled)
        Ornamenta 1, Schmuckmuseum, Pforzheim.
        Perth International Crafts Triennial, Art Gallery of Western
        Australia, Perth
        *Zeitgenössische Schmuckkunst aus der Bundesrepublik
        Deutschland*, Instituts für Auslandsbeziehungen, Stuttgart
1987   *7 Goldschmiede, 50 Schmuckstucke*; Kunstgewerbemuseum,
        Berlin; Galerie am Graben, Wien
        Joieria Europea Contemporània, Fundació Caixa de Pensions,
        Barcelona
1986   *Contemporary Arts: An Expanding View*, Monmouth Museum,
        Lincroft, NJ
1985   *Attitudes*, International Cultureel Centrum, Antwerp, Belgium
        (travelled)
        Contemporary Jewelry Redefined, Pittsburgh Center for the
        Arts, PA
        Nya Smycken, Nya Material, Kulturhuset, Stockholm
1985,83 *Internationale Schmuckschau*, Internationale Handwerksmesse,
        Munich
1984-87 *Modern Jewelry**, Philadelphia, PA; Cleveland, OH; Honolulu,
        HI; Montreal
1984   *Contemporary Jewellery: The Americas, Australia, Europe and
        Japan*, National Museum of Modern Art, Kyoto; Tokyo
        Jewelry International, American Craft Museum II, New York
        Metalforum '84, Taideteollisuusmuseo, Helsinki
        Solo Exhibition, Museum Het Kruithuis,
        's-Hertogenbosch, The Netherlands
        Zeitgenössische deutsche Goldschmiedekunst, Goethe Institute,
        Tokyo (travelled)
1983   *International Jewellery Art Exhibition*, 5th Tokyo Triennial,
        Isetan Art Museum, Tokyo
        The Jewellery Project, Crafts Council Gallery, London
1982   *Jewellery Redefined*, British Crafts Centre, London
        Schmuck '82 – Tendenzen, Schmuckmuseum, Pforzheim,
        Germany

Selected Public Collections:
Art Gallery of Western Australia, Perth; Danner-Stiftung Collection,
Munich; Israel Art Museum, Jerusalem; Kunstgewerbemuseum, Berlin;
Museum für angewandte Kunst, Vienna; National Museum of Modern
Art, Kyoto; Schmuckmuseum, Pforzheim, Germany; Stadtmuseum,
Munich; Stedelijk Museum, Amsterdam; Taideteollisuusmuseo, Helsinki

Selected Public Collections:
American Craft Museum, New York; The Arkansas Arts Center, Decorative Arts Museum, Little Rock, AK; Art Gallery of Western Australia, Perth; Art Institute of Chicago, IL; The Brooklyn Museum, NY; Cleveland Museum of Art, OH; Cooper-Hewitt, National Museum of; Design, Smithsonian Institution, New York; Kunstindustrimuseet, Oslo; The Metropolitan Museum of Art, New York; Montreal Musée des Arts Décoratifs, Quebec; Museum of Fine Arts, Boston; Renwick Gallery, NMAA, Smithsonian Institution, Washington, DC; National Museum of Modern Art, Seoul, Korea; Nordenfjeldske Kunstindustrimuseum, Trondheim, Norway; Schmuckmuseum, Pforzheim, Germany; Victoria and Albert Museum, London; Yale University Art Gallery, New Haven, CT

Robert William Ebendorf

Born: September 30, 1938, Topeka, KS, USA

Education:
1963 MFA, University of Kansas, Lawrence
1958 BFA, University of Kansas, Lawrence

Selected Awards:
1994 Elected, College of Fellows, American Crafts Council
1984 Award, Surface and Ornament Competition II, Formica Corporation, New York
1970 Grant, National Endowment for the Arts, Washington, DC
1966 Grant, Louis Comfort Tiffany Foundation

Selected Exhibitions:
1994 *A Moveable Feast**, Amsterdam; *Schmuck Unserer Zeit**, Zurich
    The Object Redux, Charles A. Wustum Museum of Fine Arts, Racine, WI
    Recycle, Reuse, Recreate, sponsored by United States Information Agency, travelled through Africa and USA
    Robert Ebendorf: Humble Beginnings – Elegant Ends, Virginia Center for the Craft Arts, Richmond
1993 *From Our Vault to the Studio*, Charles A. Wustum Museum of Fine Arts, Racine, WI
1992-93 *Korun Kieli**, Gothenburg; Helsinki
1992 *Design Visions*, Art Gallery of Western Australia, Perth
    Of Magic, Power and Memory, Bellevue Art Museum, WA
1989 *Craft Today: USA*, Musée des Arts Décoratifs, Paris (travelled)
    Ornamenta 1, Schmuckmuseum, Pforzheim, Germany
    Robert Ebendorf: Retrospective Exhibition, State University of New York, New Paltz
1988 *The Founding Masters: SNAG Exhibition*, Skidmore College, Saratoga Springs, NY
1987 *The Eloquent Object*, Philbrook Museum of Art, Tulsa, OK (travelled)
    Modern Jewelry: New Design, Cleto Munari Collection, Vicenza, Italy
1986 *Craft Today: Poetry of the Physical*, American Craft Museum, New York (travelled)
    Form Beyond Function, Mitchell Museum, Mt Vernon, IL
    Surface and Ornament, Contemporary Arts Center, Cincinnati, OH
1985 *6. Internationaler Wettbewerb – Schmuck für Kopf und Haar*, Schmuckmuseum, Pforzheim, Germany
    1962-1985 Works by Robert Ebendorf, Nordenfjeldske Kunstindustrimuseum, Trondheim, Norway
    Masterworks of Contemporary American Jewelry, Victoria and Albert Museum, London
1984-87 *Modern Jewelry**, Philadelphia, PA; Cleveland, OH; Honolulu, HI; Montreal
1984 *Contemporary Jewellery: The Americas, Australia, Europe and Japan*, National Museum of Modern Art, Kyoto; Tokyo
    Jewelry and Beyond: Metalwork by Members of SNAG, Mitchell Museum, Mount Vernon, IL
    Jewelry USA, American Craft Museum II, New York
1983 *International Jewellery Art Exhibition*, 5th Tokyo Triennial, Isetan Art Museum, Tokyo
1981 *Good as Gold*, Renwick Gallery, NCFA, Smithsonian Institution, Washington, DC (travelled)
1979 *SNAG – Gold- und Silberschmiedearbeiten*, Schmuckmuseum, Pforzheim, Germany (travelled)
1977 *The Metalsmith: SNAG Exhibition*, Phoenix Museum of Art, AZ
1974 *The Goldsmith*, Renwick Gallery, NCFA, Smithsonian Institution, Washington, DC
1970 *Goldsmith '70: SNAG Inaugural Exhibition*, Minnesota Museum of Art, St Paul (travelled)
1965 *American Jewelry Today*, Everhart Museum, Scranton, PA
    Art of Personal Adornment, Museum of Contemporary Crafts, New York

Related Professional Experience:
1971-89 Professor, State University of New York, New Paltz
1989– Maintains independent studio

Eva Eisler

Born: July 27, 1952, Prague, Czechoslovakia

Education:
1983   Parsons School of Design, New York
1971-73   School of Graphic Design, Prague
1967-71   School of Building Technology and Architecture, Prague

Selected Awards:
1993   Fellowship, New York Foundation for the Arts

Selected Exhibitions:
1994   *A Moveable Feast**, Amsterdam; *Schmuck Unserer Zeit**, Zurich
          Space for Jewelry, Manes, Prague, Czech Republic
1993   *Contemporary Jewelry**, Little Rock, AK
1992   *Design Visions*, Art Gallery of Western Australia, Perth
          Off the Wall, American Craft Museum, New York
          Solo Exhibition, Columbia University, New York
          Takenobu Igarashi/Eva Eisler, Igarashi Studio, Tokyo
1991   *Matter anti Matter*, Galerie Marzee, Nimwegen, The Netherlands (travelled)
1990   *Desenhos e Jolas*, Artefacto 3, Lisbon
          Jewelries/Epiphanies, Artists Foundation Gallery, Boston, MA
1989   *Contemporary Crafts: Concept in Flux*, Museum of Fine Arts, St Petersburg, FL, USA
          East Meets West in Design, Javits Center, New York (travelled)
          Infinite Riches, Museum of Fine Arts, St Petersburg, FL, USA
          National Jewelry Invitational Exhibition, Drake University, Des Moines, IA
          Ornamenta 1, Schmuckmuseum, Pforzheim, Germany
          Schmuckszene '89, Internationale Handwerksmesse, Munich
1988   *Work in Progress*, Helen Drutt Gallery, New York
1987   *Solo Exhibition*, Gallery of Modern Art, Los Angeles, CA
1986   *Contemporary Arts: An Expanding View*, Monmouth Museum, Lincroft, NJ
1985   *Barbara Rockefeller Jewelry Exhibition*, Automation House, New York
          Contemporary Jewelry Redefined, Pittsburgh Center for the Arts, PA

Related Professional Experience:
1989-92   Guest Lecturer, Parsons School of Design, New York; Escola Massana, Barcelona; Rhode Island School of Design, Providence
1987-90   Faculty, Parsons School of Design, New York

Selected Public Collections:
American Craft Museum, New York; The Brooklyn Museum, New York; Charles A; Wustum Museum of Fine Arts, Racine, WI; Cooper-Hewitt, National Museum of Design, Smithsonian Institution, New York

Gry Eide

Born: May 30, 1956, Bergen, Norway

Education:
1985   Diploma, National College of Art, Craft and Design, Oslo
1979   Apprenticeship, David-Andersen a.s., Oslo

Selected Awards:
1987   National Travelling and Education Grant for Artists, Norway
1984   First Prize, Tique Design Competition, Oslo, Norway

Selected Exhibitions:
1994   *A Moveable Feast**, Amsterdam; *Schmuck Unserer Zeit**, Zurich
1993   *Contemporary Jewelry**, Little Rock, AK
1992-93   *Korun Kieli**, Gothenburg; Helsinki
1989   *Solo Exhibition*, Galerie RA, Amsterdam
          Ornamenta 1, Schmuckmuseum, Pforzheim, Germany
1988   *Norwegian Jewellery*, 19 artists exhibited: in Japan: Marui Imai Department Store, Sapporo; Takashimaya Department Store, Yokohama; Mikimoto Hall, Ginza, Tokyo; Seibu Department Store, Oskak; also Electrum Gallery, London; Scottish Gallery, Edinburgh; Stadtmuseum, Dusseldorf
1987   *Biennale du Bijou Contemporain*, Hotel du Sens, Paris
          Made in Norway, Galerie Trits Sieraden, Delft (travelled through the Netherlands)
1986   *Designs for the Body*, American Scandinavian Foundation Gallery, New York (travelled)
          Summer Exhibition, Kunstnerforbundet, Oslo

Related Professional Experience:
1985–   Maintains independent studio
1987   Member, Board of Norwegian Craftspeople Distribution and Information Center
1979-81   Goldsmith, David-Andersen a.s., Oslo

Selected Public Collections:
Kunstindustrimuseet, Oslo, Nordenfjeldske Kunstindustrimuseum, Trondheim; Norwegian Council of Culture; Vestlandske Kunstindustrimuseet, Bergen, Norway

Sima Farjadi

Born: August 14, 1951, Tehran, Iran
1991 takes British citizenship

Education:
1993   Member, French Ordre Des Architectes
1990   Member, Architects Registration Council of
        the United Kingdom (ARCUK)
        Royal Institute of British Architects (RIBA),
        Part III
        Studied *Kumi Hi Mo*, Japanese weaving technique
        with Catharine Martin, London
1979   Diploma, Architectural Association School of
        Architecture, London (AA)

Private Commissions:
1994   Wins international architectural competition for Headstart,
        Moorestown, NJ; collaboration with Homa Fardjadi
1993   Proposal, design of Greek Orthodox Chapel, Paris
        Proposal, interior design of Office of Minister of Education,
        Paris
1991   *Urban Public Spaces*, Heinz Gallery, London
1988   Proposal, Patrons Club, Royal Festival Hall, London (with
        Conran Design Group)
1986   Extension and alteration of Georgian House, Camden Town,
        London
        Interior design, external facade and working drawing of BDP
        Advertising office, Baker Street, London (with Fletcher
        Priest Architects)
1985   Renovation and extension of house and photographic studio,
        Hampstead, London (with Brian Muller Architects)

Related Professional Experience:
1989-90   Faculty, PNL and Canterbury Institute of Art, London
1988-89   Faculty, School of Architecture, Cambridge University,
        England
1984-87   Faculty, AA Intermediate School, Design Unit, London

Arline M. Fisch

Born: August 21, 1931, Brooklyn, NY, USA

Education:
1954   MA, University of Illinois, Urbana-Champaign
1952   BS, Skidmore College, Saratoga Springs, NY

Selected Awards:
1989   Fulbright Fellowship, Montevideo, Uruguay
1986   Distinguished Alumni Achievement Award, Skidmore College,
        Saratoga Springs, NY
1985   'Living Treasure of California', California State Assembly
1982   Fulbright Fellowship, Vienna
1981,79,76,74
        Fellowships, National Endowment for the Arts, Washington, DC
1966,56   Fulbright Fellowships, Denmark

Selected Exhibitions:
1994   *A Moveable Feast**, Amsterdam; *Schmuck Unserer Zeit**, Zurich
1993   *Ahead of Fashion: Hats of the 20th Century*, Philadelphia
        Museum of Art, PA
        Contemporary Jewelry*, Little Rock, AK
        Silver/Wood/Clay/Gold, San Diego Museum of Art, CA
        Visuelle Spiele, Internationale Handwerksmesse, Munich
1992-93   *Korun Kieli**, Gothenburg; Helsinki
1992   *American Crafts: The National Collection*, Renwick Gallery,
        NMAA, Smithsonian Institution, Washington, DC
        Borne with a Silver Spoon, National Ornamental Metal Museum,
        Memphis, TN
        Design Visions, Art Gallery of Western Australia, Perth
        Silver Jubilee Exhibition, John Michael Kohler Arts Center,
        Sheboygan, WI
1991   *Schmuckszene '91*, Internationale Handwerksmesse, Munich
1989   *Craft Today: USA*, Musée des Arts Décoratifs, Paris
        (travelled)
        Infinite Riches, Museum of Fine Arts, St Petersburg, FL, USA
        Ornamenta 1, Schmuckmuseum, Pforzheim, Germany
        Solo Exhibition, Museum of Fine Arts, Montevideo,
        Uruguay
1988   *The Founding Masters: SNAG Exhibition*, Skidmore College,
        Saratoga Springs, NY
        Hong-ik Metalcrafts Association Annual Exhibition, Walker Hill
        Art Center Museum, Seoul, Korea
        Solo Exhibition, De Saaisset Museum, Santa Clara, CA
1986   *Craft Today: Poetry of the Physical*, American Craft Museum,
        New York (travelled)
1985   *California Crafts XIV*, Crocker Art Museum, Sacramento, CA
        New Tradition, British Craft Centre, London
        New Visions, Traditional Materials, Carnegie Institute Museum
        of Art, Pittsburgh, PA
1984-87   *Modern Jewelry**, Philadelphia, PA; Cleveland, OH; Honolulu
        HI; Montreal

1984	*Contemporary Jewellery: The Americas, Australia, Europe and Japan*, National Museum of Modern Art, Kyoto, Tokyo
	Jewelry and Beyond: Metalwork by Members of SNAG, Mitchell Museum, Mount Vernon, IL
	Jewelry USA, American Craft Museum II, New York
1982	*Solo Exhibition*, Museum für angewandte Kunst, Vienna
1981	*Good as Gold*, Renwick Gallery, NCFA, Smithsonian Institution, Washington, DC (travelled)
	Old Traditions – New Directions, Textile Museum, Washington, DC
1980	*Schmuck International* 1900-1980, Künstlerhaus, Vienna
1979	*SNAG – Gold- und Silberschmiedearbeiten*, Schmuckmuseum, Pforzheim, Germany (travelled)
1978	*Craft, Art and Religion*, The Vatican Museum, Vatican City
1977	*The Metalsmith: SNAG Exhibition*, Phoenix Museum of Art, AZ
1977,73	*Schmuck – Tendenzen*, Schmuckmuseum, Pforzheim, Germany
1974	*1st World Crafts Exhibition*, Ontario Science Center, Toronto
	The Goldsmith, Renwick Gallery, NCFA, Smithsonian Institution, Washington, DC
1971	*Jewellery '71*, Art Gallery of Ontario, Toronto
	Solo Exhibition, Goldsmiths' Hall, London
1970	*Goldsmith '70: SNAG Inaugural Exhibition*, Minnesota Museum of Art, St Paul (travelled)
1969	*Objects: USA*, National Collection of Fine Arts, Smithsonian Institution, Washington, DC (travelled)
1968	*Solo Exhibition*, Museum of Contemporary Crafts, New York

Related Professional Experience:
1961– Professor, San Diego State University, CA

Selected Public Collections:
American Craft Museum, New York; Art Gallery of Western Australia, Perth; Charles A. Wustum Museum of Fine Arts, Racine, WI; Detroit Institute of the Arts, MI; Kunstindustrimuseet, Copenhagen; Kunstindustrimuseet, Oslo; Minnesota Museum of Art, St Paul; Museum of Fine Arts, Boston, MA; National Museum of Modern Art, Kyoto; Nordenfjeldske Kunstindustrimuseum, Trondheim, Norway; Oakland Museum, CA; Renwick Gallery, NMAA, Smithsonian Institution, Washington, DC; Royal Scottish Museum, Edinburgh; Schmuckmuseum, Pforzheim, Germany; The Vatican Museum, Vatican City; Victoria and Albert Museum, London; Worshipful Company of Goldsmiths, London

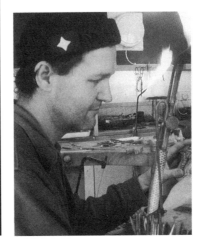

Warwick Freeman

Born: January 5, 1953, Nelson, New Zealand

Education:
1972   Started making jewellery, self-taught, Perth

Selected Awards:
1989,86,82
       Grants, Arts Council of New Zealand

Selected Exhibitions:
1994	*A Moveable Feast**, Amsterdam; *Schmuck Unserer Zeit**, Zurich
1994,92	*Solo Exhibition* , Crawford Gallery, Sydney
1993	*Contemporary Jewelry**, Little Rock, AK
1992-93	*Korun Kieli**, Gothenburg; Helsinki
1990	*Solo Exhibition*, Galerie Ra, Amsterdam
1989	*Solo Exhibition*, Contemporary Jewellery Gallery, Sydney
1988	*Bone – Stone – Shell: New Jewellery, New Zealand*, sponsored by New Zealand Ministry of Foreign Affairs and Craft Council of New Zealand (travelled)
1986	*Solo Exhibition*, Contemporary Jewellery Gallery, Sydney

Related Professional Experience:
1984	Founder, Details Group, Contemporary Jewelers Bone and stone carvers
1978–	Jeweler/Partner, Fingers, Auckland
1973-75	Established jewelry workshop, Nelson, New Zealand (with Ray Mitchell)

Selected Public Collections:
Auckland Museum, New Zealand; Australian National Gallery, Canberra; Carrington Polytechnic, Auckland; Danner-Stiftung Collection, Munich; Dowse Art Museum, Lower Hutt, New Zealand; Power House Museum, Sydney; Sarjeant Gallery, Wanganui, New Zealand

Jem Freyaldenhoven

Born: August 23, 1948, Jonesboro, AR, USA
Died: March 3, 1986, Pontiac, Michigan

Education:
1971-73 MFA, Tyler School of Art, Elkins Park
Temple University, Philadelphia
1966-70 BFA, Memphis Academy of Art, Tennessee

Selected Exhibitions:
(Complete information not available)
1979 *Solo Exhibition,* Helen Drutt Gallery, Philadelphia, PA
1976 *Jewelry '76,* Georgia State University, Atlanta, GA
1974 *American Metalsmith*, De Cordova Museum, Lincoln, MA
Metal '74, State University College at Brockport, NY
National Invitational Exhibition in Contemporary Jewelry,
Georgia State University, Atlanta, GA
1971-86 Works included in exhibitions organized by:
American Embassy, Bucharest, Roumania; Corcoran
Gallery of Art, Washington, DC; High Museum of Art,
Atlanta, GA; Lowe Art Gallery, University of Miami,
Coral Gables, FL; Memphis Academy of Art,(now
Memphis College of Art), Memphis, TN; Memphis Brooks
Museum of Art, Memphis, TN; Museum of Contemporary
Crafts (now ACM), New York Tyler School of Art, Temple
University, Elkins Park, PA

Selected Public Collections:
The Arkansas Arts Center, Decorative Arts Museum, Little Rock, AK;
Tyler School of Art, Temple University; Elkins Park, PA

Tribute:
Memphis College of Art: Endowed Jem Freyaldenhoven Memorial
Scholarship to be given annually

Donald Friedlich

Born: October 25, 1954, Montclair, NJ, USA

Education:
1979-82 BFA, Rhode Island School of Design, Providence
1978-79 Apprentice, Timothy Grannis, Underhill, VT
1975-79 University of Vermont, Burlington

Selected Awards:
1985 Young Alumnus Achievement Award, Rhode Island School of
Design, Providence
1984 Distinguished Member, Society of North American Goldsmiths,
St Paul, MN
The Jose Hess Inc. Award for Excellence in Jewelry,
Philadelphia Craft Show, PA

Selected Exhibitions:
1993 *10 American Jewelers*, Perimeter Gallery, Chicago, IL
The Body Adorned, University of Texas, El Paso
1992-93 *Korun Kieli*,* Gothenburg; Helsinki
1992 *A Decade of Craft, Recent Acquisitions, Part II*, American Craft
Museum, New York
1989 *Craft Today: USA*, Musée des Arts Décoratifs, Paris (travelled)
1987 *Craft as Content*, University of Akron, OH
1986 *Body Adornment*, Wichita Art Museum, KS
Craft Today: Poetry of the Physical, American Craft Museum,
New York (travelled)
International Jewellery Art Exhibition, 6th Tokyo Triennial,
Yurakucho Art Forum, Tokyo
1985 *Affordable Frills*, Renwick Gallery, NMAA, Smithsonian
Institution, Washington, DC
1984 *American Jewelry Now*, organized by the American Craft
Museum, New York, NY (travelled)
Contemporary Metals USA, Downey Museum of Art, CA
Group Exhibition, Hudson River Museum, Yonkers, NY
Jewelry USA, American Craft Museum II, New York
1983 *Selections from the Washington Craft Show*, Renwick Gallery,
NCFA, Smithsonian Institution, Washington, DC

Max Fröhlich

Born: December 16, 1908,
Ennenda, Kt. Glarus,
Switzerland

Education:
1925-28 Kunstgewerbeschule,
Zurich
1924-25 Ecole des Beaux Arts,
Geneva

Selected Awards:
1966 State Prize, *Form und Qualität*, Internationale
Handwerksmesse, Munich
1965 Recipient, Golden Ring of Honour, Association for Goldsmiths'
Art (created by Soren Georg Jensen '63), Deutsches
Goldschmiedehaus, Hanau, Germany

Selected Exhibitions:
1994 *A Moveable Feast*,* Amsterdam; *Schmuck Unserer Zeit**, Zurich
Schmuck und Gerät, Deutsches Goldschmiedehaus, Hanau,
Germany (travelled)

1993   *Contemporary Jewelry**, Little Rock, AK
        Schmuckszene '93, Internationale Handwerksmesse, Munich
1992-93 *Korun Kieli**, Gothenburg; Helsinki
1988   *Max Fröhlich: Silverware and Jewelry 1982-1988*, (80th birthday)
            Helen Drutt Gallery, New York
1984-87 *Modern Jewelry**, Philadelphia, PA; Cleveland, OH; Honolulu,
            HI; Montreal
1984   *Jewelry International*, American Craft Museum II, New York
1983   *Max Fröhlich, Retrospective Exhibition*, Kunstgewerbemuseum,
            Zurich
1982   *Solo Exhibition*, Galerie am Graben, Vienna
1981   *Solo Exhibition*, Society of North American Goldsmiths,
            University of Missouri, Kansas City
1980   *Schmuck International 1900-1980*, Künstlerhaus, Vienna
1979   *International Jewellery Art Exhibition*, 4th Tokyo Triennial,
            Ginza Mikimoto Hall, Tokyo
        Solo Exhibition, Galerie Florimont, Lausanne
1975   *Solo Exhibition*, Galerie für Goldschmiedekunst, Ulm, Germany
1973   *Schmuck '73 – Tendenzen*, Schmuckmuseum, Pforzheim,
            Germany
1972   *Solo Exhibition*, Galerie Atrium, Reinach,
1971   *Schmuck – Objekte*, Museum Bellerive, Zurich
        Solo Exhibition, Ingrid Hansen, Zurich
1967   *Solo Exhibition*, Galerie Objet, Zurich
1966   *Form und Qualität*, Internationale Handwerksmesse, Munich

Related Professional Experience:
1972–   Maintains independent studio, Zurich
1954-72 Dean, Kunstgewerbeschule, Zurich
1945-72 Chairman, Metal Department, Kunstgewerbeschule, Zurich
1935-45 Lecturer, Kunstgewerbeschule, Zurich
1934-45 Maintained atelier/studio, Zurich

Selected Public Collections:
Heimatwerk, Zurich; Kunstgewerbemuseum, Zurich; Schmuckmuseum,
Pforzheim, Germany

Elizabeth Garrison

Born: 1952, Elmira, NY, USA

Education:
1978-80 MS, Florida State University, Tallahassee
1976-78 Mansfield State College, PA
1970-73 BFA, Ringling School of Art and Design, Sarasota, FL

Selected Awards:
1981   Fellowship, National Endowment for the Arts, Washington, DC
1980   Fellowship, Florida State University, Tallahassee

Selected Exhibitions:
1994   *A Moveable Feast**, Amsterdam; *Schmuck Unserer Zeit**, Zurich

1993   *Contemporary Jewelry**, Little Rock, AK
1992-93 *Korun Kieli**, Gothenburg; Helsinki
1990   *American Dreams, American Extremes*, Museum Het Kruithuis,
            's-Hertogenbosch, The Netherlands
1989   *Infinite Riches*, Museum of Fine Arts, St Petersburg, FL, USA
1988   *Color and Image: Recent American Enamels*, circulated by the
            Gallery Association of New York State
1986   *Contemporary Arts: An Expanding View*, Monmouth Museum,
            Lincroft, NJ, Squibb Gallery, Princeton, NJ
        *Contemporary Crafts: A Concept in Flux, The Society for Art in
            Crafts*, Pittsburgh, PA
        Solo Exhibition, Helen Drutt Gallery, Philadelphia, PA
1984-87 *Modern Jewelry**, Philadelphia, PA; Cleveland, OH; Honolulu,
            HI; Montreal
1984   *Jewelry USA*, American Craft Museum II, New York
1983   *Jewelry Design: New York State Artists*, Cornell University,
            Ithaca, NY
1982   *Enamels '82*, George Washington University, Washington, DC
        Solo Exhibition, Mansfield University, PA
1981   *5th National Invitational Crafts Exhibition*, Skidmore College,
            Saratoga Springs, NY
        The Animal Image, Renwick Gallery, NCFA, Smithsonian
            Institution, Washington, DC
        Good as Gold, Renwick Gallery, NCFA, Smithsonian
            Institution, Washington, DC (travelled)
        National Crafts '81, Greenville County Museum of Art, SC
1980   *Young Americans: Metal*, American Craft Museum, New York
            (travelled)

Related Professional Experience:
1981-94 Maintained independent metal studio until 1994.

Selected Public Collections:
Honolulu Academy of Arts, Hawaii; Kunstgewerbemuseum, Berlin;
Museum Het Kruthaus, The Netherlands

Thomas Gentille

Born: August 11, 1936,
Mansfield, OH, USA

Education:
1954-58 Cleveland Institute of Art, OH

Selected Awards:
1990,88 Sorrel, Formica Corporation,
New York
1987 Colortiers, Formica Corporation,
USA
1985,86 Unlimited Materials Grant,
Formica Corporation, USA
1984 First Prize, *Ornament*,
International Jewelry Exhibition

Selected Exhibitions:
1994 *In Touch*, Maihaugen,
Lillehammer, Norway
A Moveable Feast*, Amsterdam;
Schmuck Unserer Zeit*, Zurich
1993 *Contemporary Jewelry**, Little Rock, AK
1992-93 *Korun Kieli**, Gothenburg, Helsinki
1992 *Design Visions*, Art Gallery of Western Australia, Perth
1991 *Americky Sperk*, Umeleckoprumyslove Muzeum, Prague
Solo Exhibition, Helen Drutt Gallery, New York
1990 *American Dreams, American Extremes*, Museum Het Kruithuis,
's-Hertogenbosch, The Netherlands
Jewelries/Epiphanies, Artists Foundation Gallery, Boston, MA
1989 *Infinite Riches*, Museum of Fine Arts, St Petersburg, FL, USA
Ornamenta 1, Schmuckmuseum, Pforzheim, Germany
Schmuckszene '89, Internationale Handwerksmesse, Munich
1987 *Wally Gilbert/Thomas Gentille*, Victoria and Albert Museum,
London
1983 *Solo Exhibition*, Fundacao Calouste Gulbenkian, Lisbon,
1981 *Good as Gold*, Renwick Gallery, NCFA, Smithsonian
Institution, Washington, DC (travelled)
*c.*1968 *Solo Exhibition*, Asheville Museum of Fine Arts, NC

Related Professional Experience:
1989-93 Faculty, Parsons School of Design, New York
1978-89 Director, Jewelry Department, 92 Street Y, New York
1987 Artist-in-Residence, Center for Creative Studies, Detroit, MI
(first Artist-in-Residence)

Selected Public Collections:
American Craft Museum, New York; Cooper-Hewitt, National Museum
of Design, Smithsonian Institution, New York; Philadelphia Museum of
Art, Philadelphia, PA; Victoria and Albert Museum, London

Toni Goessler-Snyder

Born: November 19, 1942, Heidenheim, Germany
Died: June 10, 1982, Philadelphia, PA, USA

Education:
1965-67 Apprentice for Richard Boss, Pforzheim, Germany
Kunst-und Werkschule, Pforzheim
1965-68 Fachhochschule für Gestaltung, Pforzheim
1963-65 Goldschmiedeschule, Pforzheim

Selected Exhibitions:
1994 *A Moveable Feast**, Amsterdam; *Schmuck Unserer Zeit**, Zurich
1993 *Contemporary Jewelry**, Little Rock, AK
1992-93 *Korun Kieli**, Gothenburg; Helsinki
1989 *Infinite Riches*, Museum of Fine Arts, St Petersburg, FL, USA
1986 *Contemporary Arts: An Expanding View*, Monmouth Museum,
Lincroft, NJ
1984-87 *Modern Jewelry**, Montreal, Canada; Honolulu, HI; Cleveland,
OH; Philadelphia, PA
1984 *Jewelry and Beyond: Metalwork by Members of SNAG*, Mitchell
Museum, Mount Vernon, IL
1979 *SNAG – Gold- und Silberschmiedearbeiten*, Schmuckmuseum,
Pforzheim, Germany (travelled)
Solo Exhibition, Helen Drutt Gallery, Philadelphia, PA
1976 *Exhibition of Liturgical Arts*, Philadelphia Civic Center, PA
1974 *American Metalsmiths*, DeCordova Museum, Lincoln, MA
The Collector, Museum of Contemporary Crafts, New York
Fiber, Clay, Metal, Philadelphia 'Y' Arts Council, PA
The Goldsmith, Renwick Gallery, NCFA, Smithsonian
Institution, Washington, DC
Metalsmith Art, John Michael Kohler Arts Center, Sheboygan, WI
Opals, organized by Kenneth Helfand, Australia (travelled)
A Touch of Gold, Philadelphia Museum of Art, PA
1973 *Technology and the Artist-Craftsman*, The Octagon, Ames, IA
1972 Commission, Institute of Contemporary Art, Philadelphia, PA
1970 *Craftsmen '70*, Philadelphia Civic Center, PA

Lisa Gralnick

Born: September 27, 1956,
New York, USA

Education:
1980   MFA, State University
        of New York, New Paltz
1977   BFA, Kent State
        University, OH

Selected Awards:
1993   Grant, Louis Comfort
        Tiffany Foundation
1992,88 Fellowships, National
        Endowment for the Arts,
        Washington, DC
1991,87 Fellowships, New York Foundation for the Arts
1990   Grant, Empire State Crafts Alliance, Saratoga Springs, NY

Selected Exhibitions:
1994   *A Moveable Feast**, Amsterdam; *Schmuck Unserer Zeit**, Zurich
1993   *Contemporary Jewelry**, Little Rock, AK
1992-93 *Korun Kieli**, Gothenburg; Helsinki
1992   *A Decade of Craft, Recent Acquisitions, Part II*, American Craft
        Museum, New York
        Design Visions, Art Gallery of Western Australia, Perth
        In The Vicinity, Johnstown Art Museum, PA
        More Than One: Contemporary Studio Production, American
        Craft Museum, New York
        Schmuckszene '92, Internationale Handwerksmesse, Munich
1990   *Building a Permanent Collection: A Perspective on the 1980s*,
        American Craft Museum, New York
        Jewelries/Epiphanies, Artists Foundation Gallery, Boston, MA
1989   *American Enamels: A View From the West*, Aoki Metal Gallery,
        Tokyo
        Craft Today: USA, Musée des Arts Décoratifs, Paris (travelled)
        National Metals Invitational, Drake University, Des Moines, IA
        National Metals Invitational, University of Texas, El Paso
        Ornamenta 1, Schmuckmuseum, Pforzheim, Germany
1988   *Alumni and Stonington Enamelists, 1969-1988*, Kent State
        University, OH
        Solo Exhibition, Galerie Ra, Amsterdam
1986   *The Wichita National*, The Wichita Art Association, KS
1982   *Jewellery Redefined*, British Crafts Centre, London
1979   *Enamelists and Their Students*, Case Western Reserve
        University, Cleveland, OH
        Metal, Memphis Academy of Fine Art, TN

Related Professional Experience:
1991—   Faculty, Parsons School of Design, New York

Selected Public Collections:
American Craft Museum, New York; Museum of Fine Arts, Boston, MA;
Schenectady Museum, NY; Stedelijk Museum, Amsterdam

Gary S. Griffin

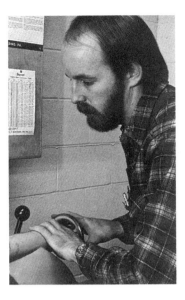

Born: June 18, 1945, Wichita Falls, TX, USA

Education:
1974   MFA, Tyler School of Art, Temple University,
        Elkins Park, PA
1968   BA, California State University, Long Beach, CA

Selected Awards:
1977,76 Fellowships, National Endowment for the Arts,
        Washington, DC

Selected Exhibitions:
1994   *A Moveable Feast**, Amsterdam; *Schmuck Unserer
        Zeit**, Zurich
1993   *Sculptural Concerns: Contemporary American
        Metalsmithing*, The Contemporary Arts Center,
        Cincinnati
1990-93 *Art That Works: The Decorative Arts of the
        Eighties*, Crafted in America, Mint Museum,
        Charlotte, North Carolina
1993   *Contemporary Jewelry**, Little Rock, AK
1992-93 *Korun Kieli**, Gothenburg; Helsinki
1988   *Masters of American MetalSmithing*, National Ornamental
        Museum
1987   *The Eloquent Object*, Philbrook Museum of Art, Tulsa, OK
        (travelled)
1986   *Craft Today: Poetry of the Physical*, American Craft Museum,
        New York (travelled)
1985   *Gary S. Griffin: Recent Works in Steel*, Cranbrook Academy
        of Art Museum, Bloomfield Hills, MI
        Metals: New Directions, One Mellon Bank Center,
        Pittsburgh, PA
1984-87 *Modern Jewelry**, Philadelphia, PA; Cleveland, OH; Honolulu,
        HI; Montreal
1984   *Contemporary Jewellery: The Americas, Australia, Europe and
        Japan*, National Museum of Modern Art, Kyoto; Tokyo
        Jewelry and Beyond: Metalwork by Members of SNAG, Mitchell
        Museum, Mount Vernon, IL
1980   *Robert L. Pfannebecker Collection*, Moore College of Art,
        Philadelphia, PA
1979   *SNAG – Gold- und Silberschmiedearbeiten*, Schmuckmuseum,
        Pforzheim, Germany (travelled)
1976   *Jewelry '76*, Georgia State University, Atlanta
1974   *Metal '74*, State University of New York, Brockport
        A Touch of Gold, Philadelphia Museum of Art, PA

Commissions:
Currently developing gates
for Cranbrook Educational
Community.

Related Professional Experience:
1984—   Artist-in-Residence/Head of Metalsmithing, Cranbrook
        Academy of Art, Bloomfield Hills, MI

Selected Public Collections:
Georgia State University, Atlanta; Tyler School of Art, Temple University,
Philadelphia; Cranbrook Academy of Art, Bloomfiel Hills, MI

Laurie J. Hall

Born: May 30, 1944, Portland, OR, USA

Education:
1976 MAT, University of Washington, Seattle
1966 BA, Willamette University, Salem, OR

Selected Public Collections:
King County Arts Collection, Seattle, WA; Washington State Arts Commission, WA

Selected Exhibitions:
1994 *I Wood If I Could*, MIA Gallery, Seattle, WA
A Moveable Feast*, Amsterdam; *Schmuck Unserer Zeit**, Zurich
Op Art: Eyeglasses by Jewelers, Oregon School of Arts and Crafts, Portland (travelled)
1993 *Screams with Laughter*, 1993 Seattle Arts Festival, WA (travelled)
1992 *Brilliant Stories: American Narrative Jewelry*, USIS Exhibition Hall, Amman, Jordan (travelled)
Just Plane Screwy, Charles A. Wustum Museum of Fine Arts, Racine, WI
Of Magic, Power and Memory, Bellevue Art Museum, WA
1991 *Artists at Work*, Cheney Cowles Museum, Spokane, WA (travelled)
1990 *New Generation Metal*, Oregon School of Arts and Crafts, Portland, OR
United States Metal/ Northwest Metal, Cheney Cowles Museum, Spokane, WA
1989 *Eloquent Resolutions: Jewelry by and for Women*, National Ornamental Metal Museum, Memphis, TN
Washington Crafts – Then and Now, Tacoma Art Museum, WA
1987 *The Ubiquitous Bead*, Bellevue Art Museum, WA
1985 *Contemporary Jewelry Redefined*, Pittsburgh Center for the Arts, PA
Lost and Found: Ho/Hall/Slemmons/Solberg, Traver-Sutton Gallery, Seattle, WA
1984 *American Jewelry Now*, organized by the American Craft Museum, New York (travelled)
Jewelry USA, American Craft Museum II, New York
1981 *Good as Gold*, Renwick Gallery, NCFA, Smithsonian Institution, Washington, DC (travelled)
Washington Craft Forms: Creators and Collectors, State Capitol Museum, Olympia, WA
1980 *Solo Exhibition*, Gail Chase Gallery, Bellevue, WA
1976 *Northwest Designer Craftsmen*, Bellevue Art Museum, WA
1973 *Body Craft Show*, Portland Art Museum, OR

Related Professional Experience:
1992 Faculty, Chair, Art Department, Mercer Island Public Schools, WA
1968-92 Chair, Art Department, The Bush School, Seattle, WA

Susan H. Hamlet

Born: May 12, 1954, Evanston, IL, USA

Education:
1976 BA, Mount Holyoke College, South Hadley, MA
1978 MFA, Rochester Institute of Technology, NY

Selected Awards:
1988,79 Fellowships, National Endowment for the Arts, Washington, DC

Selected Exhibitions:
1994 *A Moveable Feast**, Amsterdam; *Schmuck Unserer Zeit**, Zurich
National Metals Invitational, University of Akron, OH
1993 *Sculptural Concerns*, Contemporary Arts Center, Cincinnati, OH (travelled)
1992 *Borne with a Silver Spoon*, National Ornamental Metal Museum, Memphis, TN
A Decade of Craft, Recent Acquisitions, Part II, American Craft Museum, New York
Design Visions, Art Gallery of Western Australia, Perth
1990 *Jewelries/Epiphanies*, Artists Foundation Gallery, Boston, MA
1989 *Craft Today USA*, American Craft Museum, New York; Musée des Arts Décoratifs, Paris (travelled)
1987 *Solo Exhibition*, The Wichita Art Association, KS
1986 *Craft Today: Poetry of the Physical*, American Craft Museum, New York (travelled)
Contemporary Arts: An Expanding View, Monmouth Museum, Lincroft, NJ
Machine as Metaphor, Purdue University, West Lafayette, IN
1985 *Contemporary Jewelry Redefined*, Pittsburgh Center for the Arts, PA
Nya Smycken, Nya Material, Kulturhuset, Stockholm
1984 *American Jewelry Now*, organized by the American Craft Museum, New York, NY (travelled)
Celebration '84, Art Gallery at Harbourfront, Toronto (travelled)
Contemporary Jewellery: The Americas, Australia, Europe and Japan, National Museum of Modern Art, Kyoto; Tokyo
Jewelry USA, American Craft Museum II, New York
Multiplicity in Clay, Fiber and Metal, Skidmore College, Saratoga Springs, NY
1983 *Ferrous Finery*, National Ornamental Metal Museum, Memphis, TN
Group Exhibition, Iowa State University, Ames
1982 *Young Americans: Award Winners*, American Craft Museum, New York

1981   *Metalsmith '81*, University of Kansas, Lawrence
1980   *Young Americans: Metal*, American Craft Museum, New York
          (travelled)

Related Professional Experience:
1992–   Associate Professor, University of Massachusetts,
          Dartmouth, MA

Selected Public Collections:
American Craft Museum, New York; The Arkansas Arts Center,
Decorative Arts Museum, Little Rock, AK; AT&T, Dallas; National
Museum of Modern Art, Kyoto; The Wichita Art Association Inc., KS

William Harper

Born: June 17, 1944, Bucyrus, OH, USA

Education:
1967   Cleveland Institute of Art, OH
1967   MS, Case Western Reserve University, Cleveland, OH
1966   BS, Case Western Reserve University, Cleveland, OH

Selected Awards:
1985,80   Fellowships, Florida Arts Council
1980,79   Grants, National Endowment for the Arts, Washington, DC
1978   Fellowship, National Endowment for the Arts, Washington, DC

Selected Exhibitions:
1994   *A Moveable Feast**, Amsterdam; *Schmuck Unserer Zeit**, Zurich
          Solo Exhibition, Peter Joseph Gallery, New York
1993   *Contemporary Crafts and the Saxe Collection*, Toledo Museum
          of Art, OH (travelled)
          Contemporary Jewelry*, Little Rock, AK
          Facet I, Kunsthal, Rotterdam
          William Harper: Mythmaker and Shaman, Images Friedman
          Gallery, Louisville, KY
1992-93   *Korun Kieli**, Gothenburg; Helsinki
1992   *Of Magic, Power and Memory*, Bellevue Art Museum, WA
1991   *William Harper: Talismans for Our Time*, Art Space,
          Atlanta, GA
1990   *Collecting for the Future*, Victoria and Albert Museum, London
1989   *Infinite Riches*, Museum of Fine Arts, St Petersburg, FL, USA
          Structure and Surface: Beads in Contemporary American Art,
          John Michael Kohler Arts Center, Sheboygan, WI
          William Harper: Artist as Alchemist, Orlando Museum of Art,
          FL (travelled)
1988   *Color and Image: Recent American Enamels*, circulated by the
          Gallery Association of New York State
          Extraordinarily Fashionable, Columbia Museum of Art, SC

1988   *Hong-ik Metalcrafts Association Annual Exhibition*, Walker Hill
          Art Center Museum, Seoul, Korea
1987   *The Eloquent Object*, Philbrook Museum of Art, Tulsa, OK
          (travelled)
          Masterworks/Enamel/87, Taft Museum, Cincinnati, OH
1986   *Craft Today: Poetry of the Physical*, American Craft Museum,
          New York (travelled)
1985   *Masterworks of Contemporary American Jewelry*, Victoria and
          Albert Museum, London
          New Visions, Traditional Materials, Carnegie Institute Museum
          of Art, Pittsburgh, PA
1984-87   *Modern Jewelry**, Philadelphia, PA; Cleveland, OH; Honolulu,
          HI; Montreal
1984   *Jewelry USA*, American Craft Museum II, New York
1982   *Solo Exhibition*, Phoenix Art Museum, AZ
1981   *Solo Exhibition*, Kennedy Galleries, New York
1980   *Email – Schmuck und Gerät in Geschichte und Gegenwart*,
          Schmuckmuseum, Pforzheim, Germany (travelled)
          Robert L. Pfannebecker Collection, Moore College of Art,
          Philadelphia, PA
          Solo Exhibition, Florida State University, Tallahassee
1979   *SNAG – Gold- und Silberschmiedearbeiten*, Schmuckmuseum,
          Pforzheim, Germany (travelled)
1978   *Rattlesnakes*, Goldsmiths' Hall, London
1977   *The Metalsmith: SNAG Exhibition*, Phoenix Museum of
          Art, AZ
          Solo Exhibition, Renwick Gallery, NCFA, Smithsonian
          Institution, Washington, DC
1974   *The Goldsmith*, Renwick Gallery, NCFA, Smithsonian
          Institution, Washington, DC

Selected Public Collections:
American Craft Museum, New York; The Arkansas Arts Center,
Decorative Arts Museum, Little Rock, AK; Butler Institute of American
Art, Youngstown, OH; Cleveland Museum of Art, OH; Columbus
Museum of Fine Art, OH; Cooper-Hewitt, National Museum of Design,
Smithsonian Institution, New York; The Massillon Museum, OH;
Metropolitan Museum of Art, New York; Minnesota Museum of Art,
St Paul; Mint Museum of Art, Charlotte, NC; Museum of Fine Arts,
Boston; Nordenfjeldske
Kunstindustrimuseum,
Trondheim, Norway;
Patrick J Lannan Foundation,
FL; Philadelphia Museum of
Art, PA; Renwick Gallery,
NMAA, Smithsonian
Institution, Washington, DC;
Schmuckmuseum, Pforzheim,
Germany; Texas Tech
University Museum, Lubbock;
The Vatican Museum, Vatican
City; Victoria and Albert
Museum, London; Yale
University Art Gallery, New
Haven, CT

Petra Hartman

Born: 1960, The Hague, The Netherlands

Education:
1979-83   Academie voor Beeldende Kunsten, Arnhem

Selected Exhibitions:
1994   *A Moveable Feast**, Amsterdam; *Schmuck Unserer Zeit**, Zurich
1990   *Schrag*, Rheinisches, Landesmuseum, Bonn, Germany;
          Gemeente Museum, Arnhem; Centro de Arte Moderna,
          Gulbenkian Foundation, Lisbon
1989   *Nederlandse Toegepaste Kunst*, Groningen
1988   *Solo Exhibition*, Galerie Ra, Amsterdam
1986   *Solo Exhibition*, Galerie de Hollandse Spoorweg, Nimwegen
          Oberhemden Projekt, Galerie Coumans, Utrecht und Centraal
          Museum, Utrecht

Maria Hees

Born: September 19, 1948, Bergeijk, The Netherlands

Education:
          Arnhem Art Academy, The Netherlands

Selected Exhibitions:
1994   *A Moveable Feast**, Amsterdam; *Schmuck Unserer Zeit**, Zurich
          Op Art: Eyeglasses by Jewelers, Oregon School of Arts and
          Crafts, Portland (travelled)
1992-93   *Korun Kieli**, Gothenburg; Helsinki
1990   *News from the Netherlands*, Fundacao Calouste Gulbenkian,
          Lisbon (travelled)
1989   *An Art Collection of Combs*, organized by Galerie Marzee,
          Nimwegen, The Netherlands (travelled)
1986   *Sieraad 1986, Draagteken?*, Museum Het Kruithuis,
          's-Hertogenbosch, The Netherlands
          European Crafts Today, Tokyo, Osaka
1985   *New Tradition*, British Crafts Centre, London
          Vormgevers in Beweging, Haags Gemeentemuseum, The Hague
1984-87   *Modern Jewelry**, Philadelphia, PA; Cleveland, OH; Honolulu,
          HI; Montreal
1984   *Object and Image*, Museum Het Kruithuis,
          's-Hertogenbosch, The Netherlands
          Ontwerpen in Kleine Oplagen, Galerie Het Kapelhuis,
          Amersfoort, The Netherlands
          Kleding/Mode, Gemeentelijke van Reekummuseum, Apeldoorn,
          The Netherlands
1980-84   *Design from the Netherlands* (travelled through Germany)

Selected Public Collections:
Gemeentemuseum, Arnhem,
The Netherlands; Israel
Museum, Jerusalem;
Museum für Kunsthandwerk,
Frankfurt a.M., Germany;
Rijksdienst Beeldende Kunst,
The Hague; Stedelijk
Museum, Amsterdam

Anna Heindl

Born: February 13, 1950,
          Perg, Austria

Education:
1975-76   Akademie der Bildenden
          Künste, Munich
1970   Hochschule für
          angewandte Kunst,
          Vienna

Selected Awards:
(dates not available)
          Dr-Theodor-Körner-Preis, Austria
          Kunstförderungspreis, Vienna

Selected Exhibitions:
1994   *A Moveable Feast**, Amsterdam; *Schmuck Unserer Zeit**, Zurich
1993   *The Art of Jewellery*, Setagaya Art Museum, Tokyo
          Solo Exhibition, Galerie Farel, Aigle, Switzerland
          Solo Exhibition, Galerie Menotti, Baden,
          Solo Exhibition, Galerie Wassermann, Munich
          The Wedding Collection, Galerie Vandelieuhove, Ghent
1993,91   *Solo Exhibitions*, Galerie Louise Smit, Amsterdam
1992-93   *Korun Kieli**, Gothenburg; Helsinki
1992   *Anna Heindl: Ears and Tears*, Galerie V & V, Vienna (travelled)
          Solo Exhibition, New Jewels Kunstgalerij, Knokke, Belgium
          Triennale du Bijou, Musée des Arts Décoratifs, Paris
1991   *Beauty is a Story*, Museum Het Kruithuis,
          's-Hertogenbosch, The Netherlands
          Solo Exhibition, Galerie Friederike Glück, Stuttgart, Germany
1990   *Gioelli e Legature: Artisti del XX Secolo*, Biblioteca Trivulziana,
          Milan
          Triennale du Bijou, Musée du Luxembourg, Paris
1990,86   *Solo Exhibitions*, Neue Galerie am Landesmuseum Joanneum,
          Graz, Austria
1989   *Ornamenta 1*, Schmuckmuseum, Pforzheim, Germany
          Perth International Crafts Triennial, Art Gallery of Western
          Australia, Perth
          Rahmen und Ornament: Schmuck Anna Heindl, Galerie
          Zaunschirm, Zurich (travelled)
1988   *Austrian Artists*, Museum für angewandte Kunst, Vienna
1987   *Biennale du Bijou Contemporain*, Hotel du Sens, Paris
          Schmuck, Zeichen am Körper, Francisco Carolinum Museum,
          Linz, Austria
          Solo Exhibition, Galerie Krinzinger, Vienna
1986,83,78
          Solo Exhibitions, Galerie am Graben, Vienna
1984   *Schmuck, zeitgenössische Kunst aus Österreich*, Ateneo San
          Basso, Venice

1984 *Austrian Artists*, Museum für angewandte Kunst, Vienna
1983 *International Jewellery Art Exhibition*, 5th Tokyo Triennial,
    Isetan Art Museum, Tokyo
    Material Schmuck und Gerät, Internationale Handwerksmesse,
    Munich
1982 *Schmuck '82 – Tendenzen*, Schmuckmuseum, Pforzheim,
    Germany
1980 *Schmuck International 1900-1980*, Künstlerhaus, Vienna
1979 *Keramik – Schmuck – Tapisserie*, Hanover; Gmunden; Galerie
    Kapelhuis, Amersfoort
1978 *Schmuck – Tischgerät aus Österreich 1904/08 - 1973/77*, Galerie
    am Graben, Vienna

Selected Public Collections:
Art Gallery of Western Australia, Perth; Museum für angewandte Kunst,
Vienna; Museum Het Kruithuis, 's-Hertogenbosch, The Netherlands;
Sammlung Hochschule für angewandte Kunst, Vienna; Schmuckmuseum,
Pforzheim, Germany

Therese Hilbert

Born: July 19, 1948,
            Zurich, Switzerland

Education:
1972-78 Akademie der
        Bildenden Künste,
        Munich
1964-69 Kunstgewerbeschule,
        Zurich, Switzerland

Selected Awards:
1986 Prize, Art Council, Munich
1985 Prize of the Prinz Luitpold, Stiftung, Munich
1975 Leistungspreis der Kunstgewerbeschule, Zurich,
1974 Herbert Hoffmann Prize, *Internationale Schmuckschau*,
     Internationale Handwerksmesse, Munich

Selected Exhibitions:
1994 *A Moveable Feast**, Amsterdam; *Schmuck Unserer Zeit**,
     Zurich
     Zeitgenössisches Kunsthandwerk, Museum für Kunsthandwerk,
     Frankfurt a.M., Germany
1993 *Contemporary Jewelry**, Little Rock, AK
     Müncher Goldschmiede, Müncher Stadtmuseum, Munich

1993 *Schmuck: Die Sammlung der Danner-Stiftung*, Galerie für
     angewandte Kunst, Munich
1992-93 *Korun Kieli**, Gothenburg; Helsinki
1992 *Solo Exhibition*, Galerie Slavik, Vienna
     Solo Exhibition, Galerie Michele Zeller, Berne
1991 *Neoteric Jewelry*, Snug Harbor Cultural Center, Staten
     Island, NY
1989 *British Jewellery – German Jewellery*, Crafts Council Gallery,
     London (travelled)
     Perth International Crafts Triennial, Art Gallery of Western
     Australia, Perth
     *Zeitgenössische Schmuckkunst aus der Bundesrepublik
     Deutschland*, Instituts für Auslandsbeziehungen, Stuttgart
1987 *Joieria Europea Contemporània*, Fundació Caixa de Pensions,
     Barcelona
1985 *Attitudes*, International Cultureel Centrum, Antwerp, Belgium
     (travelled)
     Bijou Frontal, Museum für Gestaltung, Basle
     Solo Exhibition, Galerie V & V, Vienna
1984-87 *Modern Jewelry**, Philadelphia, PA; Cleveland, OH; Honolulu,
     HI; Montreal
1984 *Contemporary Jewellery: The Americas, Australia, Europe and
     Japan*, National Museum of Modern Art, Kyoto; Tokyo
     *Cross Currents: Jewellery from Australia, Britain, Germany and
     Holland*, Power House Museum, Sydney (travelled)
     Jewelry International, American Craft Museum II, New York
     Razionale e fantastico nel decoro del corpo, M. Vallanzasca
     Bianchi, Padua
     Zeitgenössische deutsche Goldschmiedekunst, Goethe Institute,
     Tokyo (travelled)
1983 *International Jewellery Art Exhibition*, 5th Tokyo Triennial,
     Isetan Art Museum, Tokyo
1982 *Jewellery Redefined*, British Crafts Centre, London
     Solo Exhibition, Galerie Ra, Amsterdam
     Visies op Sieraden 1965-1982, Stedelijk Museum, Amsterdam
1981 *Körper-Schmuck-Zeichen-Raum*, Kunstgewerbemuseum, Zurich
1980 *Schmuck International 1900-1980*, Künstlerhaus, Vienna
     Solo Exhibition, Deutsches Goldschmiedehaus, Hanau,
     Germany
1979 *Körper-Schmuck-Zeichen-Raum*, Kestner-Gesellschaft, Hanover
     Körper-Zeichen, Städtische Galerie im Lenbachhaus, Munich
     Therese Hilbert – Otto Künzli, Schmuckmuseum, Pforzheim,
     Germany
1978 *Der Ring*, Deutsches Goldschmiedehaus, Hanau, Germany
1977 *Schmuck '77 – Tendenzen*, Schmuckmuseum, Pforzheim,
     Germany
1973-77 *Internationale Schmuckschau*, Internationale Handwerksmesse,
     Munich

Selected Public Collections:
Danner-Stiftung Collection, Munich; Deutsches Goldschmiedehaus,
Hanau, Germany; Hiko Mizuno Collection, Tokyo ; Israel Museum,
Jerusalem; Müncher Stadtmuseum, Munich; Power House Museum,
Sydney; Schmuckmuseum, Pforzheim, Germany; Schweizerische
Eidgenossenschaft, Berne; Stedelijk Museum, Amsterdam

Yasuki Hiramatsu

Born: April 30, 1926, Osaka Prefecture, Japan

Education:
1952   Tokyo National University of Fine Arts and Music, Tokyo

Selected Awards:
1994   Recipient, Golden Ring of Honour, Association for Goldsmiths' Art, Deutsches Goldschmiedehaus, Hanau, Germany
1991   Award of Excellence, Japanese Government Ministry of Education
1990   Creator, present for Japanese Emperor's mother to give to Empress on occasion of inauguration
1972   Prize, *King George VI and Queen Elizabeth Stakes*, Ascot, England
1970   Prize, *'70 Japan New Craft Exhibition*, Tokyo
1969   Gold Prize, 3rd Craft Center, Japan
1952-57   Prizes, Living Industrial Arts Institute, Japan

Selected Exhibitions:
1994   Schmuck and Gerat, Deutsches Goldschmiedehaus, Hanau Germany (travelled)
1994-93   *Yasuki Hiramatsu Retirement Exhibition*, Tokyo National University of Fine Arts and Music, Tokyo
1993   *13 Goldschmiede: Von Amsterdam bis Tokyo*, Bayerische Akademie der Schönen Künste, Munich
       Ahead of Fashion: Hats of the 20th Century, Philadelphia Museum of Art, PA
       Gold oder Leben!, Akademie der Bildenden Künste, Munich
       Voorzien: Benno Premsela Applied Art Collection, Stedelijk Museum, Amsterdam
1991   *Schmuckszene '91*, Internationale Handwerksmesse, Munich
1990   *Triennale du Bijou*, Musée du Luxembourg, Paris
1989   *Ornamenta 1*, Schmuckmuseum, Pforzheim, Germany
1987   *Schmuck, Zeichen am Körper*, Francisco Carolinum Museum, Linz, Austria
1986,83,79,76
       International Jewellery Art Exhibition, Tokyo Triennials
1985   *Nya Smycken, Nya Material*, Kulturhuset, Stockholm, Sweden
1985,82   *Internationale Schmuckschau*, Internationale Handwerksmesse, Munich
1984   *Contemporary Jewellery: The Americas, Australia, Europe and Japan*, National Museum of Modern Art, Kyoto; Tokyo
       Jewelry International, American Craft Museum II, New York
1982   *Scandinavia and Japan Craft and Design*, Ishikawa Prefectural Industrial Design Exhibition Hall, Kanazawa, Japan
1982,77,73,70,67
       Schmuck – Tendenzen, Schmuckmuseum, Pforzheim, Germany
1980   *Japan Style*, Victoria and Albert Museum, London
       Schmuck International 1900-1980, Künstlerhaus, Vienna
1977   *Masterpieces of Contemporary Japanese Crafts*, Inaugural Exhibition, Craft Gallery, National Museum of Modern Art, Tokyo
       Solo Exhibition, Galerie am Graben, Vienna

1976   *Aurea '76 Biennale dell'Arteorafa*, Florence
1972   *Bird's Eye View of Modern Craft*, National Museum of Modern Art, Kyoto, Japan
1971   *Gold+Silber Schmuck+Gerät*, Norishalle, Nuremberg, Germany
1968-70   *International Jewellery Biennale*, Carrara, Italy
1966   *International Goldschmiedekunst*, Aalen, Germany
1964-72   *Form und Qualität, Internationale Handwerksmesse*, Munich (exhibited 6 times)
1964-88   *Japan Jewellery Exhibitions*, Tokyo

Related Professional Experience:
–1994   Professor, National University of Fine Arts and Music, Tokyo
       Member, Japan Craft Design Association
       Director, Japan Jewellery Designers Association

Selected Public Collections:
Imperial Household Agency, Tokyo; National Museum of Modern Art, Tokyo; Royal College of Art, London; Schmuckmuseum, Pforzheim, Germany; Tokyo National Museum of Fine Arts and Music, Tokyo; Victoria and Albert Museum, London

Ron Ho

Born: November 1, 1936, Honolulu, Hawaii, USA

Education:
1968   MAT, University of Washington, Seattle
1958   BA, Pacific Lutheran University, Tacoma, WA

Selected Awards:
1990   100 Outstanding Alumni, Pacific Lutheran University, Tacoma, WA
       Outstanding Achievement in the Arts, Bellevue Arts Commission, WA
       Pacific Regional Elementary Art Educator of the Year, National Art Education Association
1989   Washington State Elementary Art Educator of the Year, Washington Art Education Association
1988   Asian Art of the Year, Wing Luke Asian Art Museum, Seattle, WA

Selected Exhibitions:
1995   *Becoming Chinese: Jewelry Art by Ron Ho*, Honolulu Academy of Arts, HI
1994   *A Moveable Feast*, Amsterdam
       Two Friends: Ramona Solberg/Ron Ho, Facèrè Jewelry Art, Seattle, WA

1993	*Screams with Laughter*, 1993 Seattle Arts Festival, WA (travelled)
1992	*Brilliant Stories: American Narrative Jewelry*, USIS Exhibition Hall, Amman, Jordan (travelled)
	Of Magic, Power and Memory, Bellevue Art Museum, WA
1991	*Artists at Work*, Cheney Cowles Museum, Spokane, WA (travelled)
1990	*Artworks for AIDS*, Seattle Center, WA
	Contemporary Tomfoolery, Facèré Jewelry Art, Seattle
1988	*Solo Exhibition*, Wing Luke Asian Art Museum, Seattle
1987	*The Ubiquitous Bead*, Bellevue Art Museum, WA
1986	*10/40*, Bellevue Art Museum, WA
1985	*Lost and Found: Ho/Hall/Slemmons/Solberg*, Traver-Sutton Gallery, Seattle
1984	*Remains to be Seen*, John Michael Kohler Arts Center, Sheboygan, WI
	Washington Crafts 1984, Bellevue Art Museum, WA
1981	*Good as Gold*, Renwick Gallery, NCFA, Smithsonian Institution, Washington, DC (travelled)
	Washington Crafts Forms: Creators and Collectors, State Capitol Museum, Olympia, WA
1980	*Made in America*, Wing Lake Asian Art Museum, Seattle
1980,73,72	
	Governor's Invitational of Washington, State Capitol Museum, Olympia, WA
1978	*Crafts Biennial*, Tacoma Art Museum, WA
1976,75	*Solo Exhibitions*, Henry Gallery, Seattle
1975	*Ho/Lew/Sekimachi/Solberg*, Northwest Craft Center, Seattle
1974	*Body Craft*, Portland Art Museum, OR
1971	*Spokane Crafts Invitational*, Cheney Cowles Museum, Spokane, WA

Related Professional Experience:

1992–	Maintains independent studio, Seattle
1991–	Instructor, Seattle University
1960-92	Faculty, Bellevue School District, WA

Mary Lee Hu

Born: April 13, 1943, Lakewood, OH, USA

Education:

1967	MFA, Southern Illinois University, Carbondale
1965	BFA, Cranbrook Academy of Art, Bloomfield Hills, MI

Selected Awards:

1992,84,76	
	Fellowships, National Endowment for the Arts, Washington, DC
1988	Alumni Achievement Award, Southern Illinois University-Carbondale Alumni Association

Selected Exhibitions:

1994	*Contemporary Metalsmithing: Behind and Beyond the Bench*, Craft Alliance, St Louis, MO
	A Moveable Feast*, Amsterdam; *Schmuck Unserer Zeit**, Zurich
1993	*Documents Northwest, The Poncho Series: Six Jewelers*, Seattle Art Museum, Seattle
	Metal '93 Invitational: Master Metalsmiths and Proteges, State University of New York, Brockport
	Ohio Metals: A Legacy, Miami University Art Museum, Oxford, OH
1992-93	*Korun Kieli**, Gothenburg; Helsinki
1992	*Design Visions*, Art Gallery of Western Australia, Perth
	Repair Days Reunion, National Ornamental Metal Museum, Memphis, TN
1991	*US Metal/NW Metal*, Cheney Cowles Museum, Spokane, WA
1989	*Artfest Jewelry Exhibition*, Cheney Cowles Museum, Spokane, WA
	Craft Today: USA, Musée des Arts Décoratifs, Paris (travelled)
	Infinite Riches, Museum of Fine Arts, St Petersburg, FL, USA
1988	*Hong-ik Metalcrafts Association Annual Exhibition*, Walker Hill Art Center Museum, Seoul, Korea
1987	*The Eloquent Object*, Philbrook Museum of Art, Tulsa, OK (travelled)
1986	*Craft Today: Poetry of the Physical*, American Craft Museum, New York (travelled)
1985	*Masterworks of Contemporary American Jewelry*, Victoria and Albert Museum, London
1984	*American Jewelry Now*, organized by the American Craft Museum, New York (travelled)
	Jewelry and Beyond: Metalwork by Members of SNAG, Mitchell Museum, Mount Vernon, IL
	Jewelry USA, American Craft Museum II, New York
	Multiplicity in Clay, Fiber and Metal, Skidmore College, Saratoga Springs, NY
1981	*Good as Gold*, Renwick Gallery, NCFA, Smithsonian Institution, Washington, DC (travelled)
1979	*SNAG – Gold- und Silberschmiedearbeiten*, Schmuckmuseum, Pforzheim, Germany (travelled)
1978	*Rattlesnakes*, Goldsmiths' Hall, London
1977	*The Metalsmith: SNAG Exhibition*, Phoenix Museum of Art, AZ
1974	*American Metalsmiths*, DeCordova Museum, Lincoln, MA
	The Goldsmith, Renwick Gallery, NCFA, Smithsonian Institution, Washington, DC
	Metal '74, State University of New York, Brockport
1970	*Goldsmith '70: SNAG Inaugural Exhibition*, Minnesota Museum of Art, St Paul (travelled)
1969	*Young Americans 1969*, Museum of Contemporary Crafts, New York
1965	*American Jewelry Today*, Everhart Museum, Scranton, PA

Related Professional Experience:

1980–	Professor of Art, University of Washington, Seattle

Selected Public Collections:
American Craft Museum, New York; Art Institute of Chicago, IL; Columbus Museum of Fine Arts, OH; Illinois State University, Normal, IL; Renwick Gallery, NMAA, Smithsonian Institution, Washington, DC; University of Indiana Art Gallery, Bloomington; Victoria and Albert Museum, London; Worshipful Company of Goldsmiths, London; Yale University Art Gallery, New Haven, CT

Daniel Jocz

Born: January 3, 1943,
Beloit, WI, USA

Education:
1969   MFA, University of
        Massachusetts, Amherst
1966   BFA, Philadelphia College
        of Art, PA

Selected Awards:
1994   Jurors Award,
            Brooch: The Subject,
            Tempe Arts Center, AZ
1989,85   Patricia Jellinek Hallowell Prize for Outstanding Jeweler in
            Massachusetts
1985   Fellowship, Massachusetts Council on the Arts and Humanities

Selected Exhibitions:
1994   *Brooch: The Subject*, Tempe Arts Center, AZ
        Contemporary Metalsmithing: Behind and Beyond the Bench,
            Craft Alliance, St Louis, MO
1993   *Sculptural Concerns: Contemporary American Metal Working*,
            Fort Wayne Museum of Art, IN (travelled)
        Horizons Faculty, Hudson River Museum, Yonkers, NY
1992   *Schmuckszene '92*, Internationale Handwerksmesse, Munich
1991   *Americky Sperk*, Umeleckoprumyslove Muzeum, Prague
        Faculty Show, Museum School of Fine Arts, Boston, MA
1990   *Jewelries/Epiphanies*, Artists Foundation's Gallery at City Place,
            Boston, MA
1989   *The Decade of the Eighties*, Western Carolina University,
            Cullowhee, NC
1988   *Amulett & Talisman*, Stadtischen Museum, Schwäbisch
            Gmünd, Germany (travelled)
        Crafts 22, Pennsylvania State University, State College
1988,86 *The Wichita Nationals*, The Wichita Art Association, KS
1985   *Contemporary Metals USA*, Downey Museum of Art, CA
        Crafts National, State University College at Buffalo, NY
1984   *Jewelry USA*, American Craft Museum II, New York
1975   *Solo Exhibition*, Westminster College, New Wilmington, PA

Related Professional Experience:
1992–   Instructor, Elder Hostel, Horizons School, Milta, Mexico
1991–   Instructor, Elder Hostel, Horizons School, Williamsburg, MA
1986   Visiting Artist/Professor, Summer Session, Western Carolina
            University, Cullowhee, NC

Selected Public Collections:
American Craft Museum, New York; University of Massachusetts, Amherst

Sculpture Commissions:
Boston Properties, Boston, MA; Sprague Associates, Boston, MA; Strouse
Greenberg & Co., Philadelphia, PA; University of Massachusetts Student
Union, Amherst

Kazuhiro Itoh

Born: 1948, Insel Shikoku, Japan

Education:
1971-73 Akademie der Bildenden Künste, Munich
1968-71 Tama Art University, Tokyo

Selected Exhibitions:
1993   *Shiyoku no Utsuwa*, Gallery Isogaya, Tokyo
        Subjects, Design Forum, Helsinki, Finland
1992   *Contemporary Japanese Jewellery*, Electrum Gallery, London
        Maborogi, Kita Kamakura Museum, Japan
1991   *Group Exhibition*, Gallery IF, Tokyo
        Group Exhibition, Jewelerswerk Galerie, Washington, DC
1986   *Itoh/Kruger/Mattar/Pasquale*, Galerie Mattar, Cologne
1985   *Contemporary Jewelry Redefined*, Pittsburgh Center for the
            Arts, PA
        Nya Smycken, Nya Material, Kulturhuset, Stockholm
        Group Exhibition, Galerie Cardillac, Kahlsruhe, Germany
1984   *Jewelry International*, American Craft Museum II, New York
1984,82 *Internationale Schmuckschau*, Internationale Handwerksmesse,
            Munich
1983   *Ringe*, Galerie Mattar, Cologne
        Solo Exhibition, Tokyo
1982   *Sieben Japaner*, Galerie Mattar, Cologne
1981   *The Ring from Antiquity to the 20th Century*, Electrum Gallery,
            London
1980   *Schmuck International 1900-1980*, Künstlerhaus, Vienna
1979   Exhibited, Artwear, New York
1977   *Cloth and Stone*, Electrum Gallery, London
        Schmuck '77 – Tendenzen, Schmuckmuseum, Pforzheim,
            Germany

Selected Public Collections:
National Museum of Modern Art, Tokyo; Royal Scottish Museum,
Edinburgh; Schmuckmuseum, Pforzheim, Germany

Hermann Jünger

Born: June 6, 1928, Hanau, Germany

Education:
1953-56 Akademie der Bildenden Künste, Munich
1947-49 Staatlichen Zeichenakademie, Hanau, Germany

Selected Awards:
1968 Recipient, Golden Ring of Honour, Association for Goldsmiths' Art, Deutsches Goldschmiedehaus, Hanau, Germany
1966,63 Preis des Internationalen Kunsthandwerks, Stuttgart

Selected Exhibitions:
1995 *Uta Feiler, Rolf Lindner, Hermann Jünger*, Galerie am Fischmarkt, Erfurt, Germany
1994 *A Moveable Feast**, Amsterdam; *Schmuck Unserer Zeit**, Zurich
Schmuck und Gerät, Deutsches Goldschmiedehaus, Hanau, Germany (travelled)
Solo Exhibition, Galeria Contacto Directo, Lisbon
Group Exhibition, Kent State University, OH; Canadian Clay and Glass Museum, Toronto
1993 *Contemporary Jewelry**, Little Rock, AK
Drei Generationen, Museum für Angewandte Kunst, Munich
Goldschmiede Silberschmiede: Drei Generationen: die Neue Sammlung, Galerie für angewandte Kunst, Munich
Münchner Goldschmiede: Schmuck und Gerät 1993, Münchner Stadtmuseum, Munich
Schmuck: Die Sammlung der Danner-Stiftung, Galerie für angewandte Kunst, Munich
1990 *Solo Exhibitions*, Galerie IF, Tokyo; *Jeweler's Werk*, Washington, DC
1989 *Hermann Jünger*, Schmuckmuseum, Pforzheim, Germany
Perth International Crafts Triennial, Art Gallery of Western Australia, Perth
Zeitgenössische Schmuckkunst aus der Bundesrepublik Deutschland, Instituts für Auslandsbeziehungen, Stuttgart
1988 *Hermann Jünger: Schmuck nach 1945*, Germanisches Nationalmuseum, Nuremberg, Germany (travelled)
1987 *Solo Exhibition*, Galerie am Graben, Vienna
Zeitgenössisches deutsches und finnisches Kunsthandwerk, Museum für Kunsthandwerk, Frankfurt a.M.,
1984 *Jewelry International*, American Craft Museum II, New York
Zeitgenössische deutsche Goldschmiedekunst, Goethe Institute, Tokyo (travelled)
1983,79,70
International Jewellery Art Exhibition, Tokyo Triennials
1982 *Solo Exhibition*, State University of New York, New Paltz
1981 *Hermann Jünger: Goldschmiede Arbeiten*, Galerie am Graben, Vienna (travelled)
1980 *Email – Schmuck und Gerät in Geschichte und Gegenwart*, Schmuckmuseum, Pforzheim, Germany (travelled)
Schmuck International 1900-1980, Künstlerhaus, Vienna
1979 *Körper-Schmuck-Zeichen-Raum*, Kestner-Gesellschaft, Hanover
Körper-Zeichen, Städtische Galerie im Lenbachhaus, Munich
1978 *3 Konzepte – 3 Goldschmiede: Bury/Jünger/Rothmann*, Hessisches Landesmuseum, Darmstadt, Germany
1977,73 *Schmuck – Tendenzen*, Schmuckmuseum, Pforzheim, Germany
1975 *Jewellery in Europe*, Scottish Arts Council Gallery, Edinburgh (travelled)
1974 *18 Orfèvres d'Aujourd'hui*, Musée des Arts Décoratifs, Lausanne
1971 *Gold+Silber Schmuck+Gerät*, Norishalle, Nuremberg, Germany
1969 *Solo Exhibition*, Deutsches Goldschmiedehaus, Hanau, Germany
1967 *metal: germany*, Museum of Contemporary Crafts, New York
1965 *Novas Igrejas na Alemanha*, Rio de Janeiro, Brazil
1964 *Internationale Austellung: Schmuck Jewellery Bijoux*, Hessisches Landesmuseum, Darmstadt, Germany
1958 *Schmuck und Gerät von 1800 bis heute*, Deutsches Goldschmiedehaus, Hanau, Germany

Selected Public Collections:
Art Gallery of Western Australia, Perth;
Danner-Stiftung Collection, Munich; Museum
für Kunst und Gewerbe, Hamburg; Museum
für Kunsthandwerk, Frankfurt a.M.;
Schmuckmuseum, Pforzheim, Germany;
Victoria and Albert Museum, London

Sieglinde Karl
(formerly Sieglinde Brennan)

Born: September 24, 1943, Lahr, Germany

Education:
1974-78 Middlesex Polytechnic, London

Selected Awards:
1992 Project Grant. Multi-Artform Panel, Arts Tasmania
      National Contemporary Jewellery Award: Griffith Regional Art
      Gallery, NSW
1991 Grant: site-specific installation. Waverly Flora Park,
      Hobart; Tasmania Arts Council
1990 Project Grant. Visual Arts & Crafts Board, Australia Council
1988 Transience, Place Memories' Exhibition Grant – Visual Arts
      & Crafts Board of Australia Council
1987 Craftsperson-in-Residence, Tasmanian State Institute of
      Technology, Launceston
1978-79 New Craftsperson Grant, Crafts Council of Great Britain

Selected Exhibitions/Site-Specific Works:
1995,94,91
      Site-specific transitory 'offerings', Tasmania, Lord Howe Island;
      Northumberland, UK
      *Crossing Borders: History, Culture and Identity in Australian
      Contemporary Textile Art* (travelling USA)
1994 *reveal/conceal*, Artspace, Adelaide Festival Centre
1993 *Griffith Sons & Daughters Exhibition,*10th birthday exhibition,
      Griffith Regional Art Gallery, NSW
1992 *Schmuckszene 92*, Internationalen Handwerksmesse, Munich
      Unfamiliar Territory, Adelaide Biennial of Australian Art, Art
      Gallery of South Australia, Adelaide
      First Australian Contemporary Jewellery Biennial, Canberra
      School of Art
      National Contemporary Jewellery Award, Griffith Regional Art
      Gallery, NSW

1992 *20 Years of Art Funding*, Australia Council, Parliament House,
      Canberra
1991 *20th Anniversary Exhibition*, Electrum Gallery, London
      Contemporary Jewellery & Metalwork: 1977-91, Queen Victoria
      Museum & Art Gallery, Launceston, Tasmania
      Precious & the Body, University of Tasmania Gallery,
      Launceston
1991 *First Australian Contemporary Jewellery Biennial*, Jam Factory,
      Adelaide; Queen Victoria Museum, Launceston;
      Powerhouse Museum, Sydney
1990 *Australian Contemporary Jewellery*, Pacific Nations Tour
1990-91 *Australian Fashion: The Contemporary Art*, Marimura Art
      Museum, Marajuku, Japan
1989 *Australian Fashion: The Contemporary Art*, Victoria and Albert
      Museum, London; Powerhouse Museum, Sydney
1988-87 *Solo Exhibition: Tasmania Marks & Relics*, Devonport Art
      Gallery, Tasmania
      Australian Decorative Arts – 1788-1988, Australian National
      Gallery, Canberra
1986 *Solo Exhibition: Australian Impressions*, Electrum Gallery,
      London
1985 *Inaugural Exhibition*, Contemporary Jewellery Gallery,
      Sydney
1984 *Cross Currents*, Powerhouse Museum, Sydney (travelled)
1983 *Australian Decorative Arts: The Past Ten Years*, Australian
      National Gallery, Canberra
1982 *Enamels Today*, Goldsmiths Hall, London
1981 *10th Anniversary*, Electrum Gallery, London
1980 *Loot 80*, Goldsmiths Hall, London

Public Collections:
Art Gallery of Western Australia, Perth; Australian National Gallery,
Canberra; Box Hill Town Hall Collection, Melbourne, Victoria;
Orange Civic Centre Gallery, Orange, NSW; Powerhouse Museum,
Sydney; Queen Victoria Museum and Art Gallery, Launceston, Tasmania

Betsy King

Born: June 1, 1953, Washington, DC, USA

Education:
1982 Gemological Institute of America, Richmond, VA
1975 BFA, Virginia Commonwealth Institute of America,
      Richmond

Selected Awards:

1991,85 Fellowship Grants, New Jersey State Council on the Arts, Trenton

1989 Merit Award, Ringling Museum of Art, Sarasota, FL

1978 Fellowship Grant, Virginia Museum of Fine Arts, Richmond

Selected Exhibitions:

1994 *A Moveable Feast**, Amsterdam; *Schmuck Unserer Zeit**, Zurich

1993 *Contemporary Jewelry**, Little Rock, AK
New Jersey State Council – Art Fellowship Exhibition, Stedman Art Gallery, Camden, NJ

1992-93 *Korun Kieli**, Gothenburg; Helsinki

1992 *Brilliant Stories: American Narrative Jewelry*, USIS Exhibition Hall, Amman, Jordan (travelled)
New Jersey Art Annual, New Jersey State Museum, Trenton

1991 *Featured Artists – September*, Del Mano Gallery, Pasadena, CA
Jewelry Woman Exhibition, Susan Cummins Gallery, Mill Valley, CA

1990 *American Dreams, American Extremes*, Museum Het Kruithuis, 's-Hertogenbosch, The Netherlands
New Jersey Designer Craftsmen: 40 Years, The Newark Museum, NJ
Schmuckszene '90, Internationale Handwerksmesse, Munich

1990,88 *New Jersey Arts Annuals*, Noyes Museum, Oceanville, NJ

1988 *Artists Liaison Exhibition*, Evanston Art Center, IL

1987 *Metalvision*, New Jersey State Museum, Trenton

1986 *In Recognition of Excellence 1971-1986*, Montclair Art Museum, NJ

1984 *American Politics and the Presidency*, Renwick Gallery, NCFA, Smithsonian Institution, Washington, DC
Jewelry USA, American Craft Museum II, New York

1982 *Southeast '82 Craft Competition*, LeMoyne Center for the Visual Arts, Tallahassee, FL

1981 *Metalsmith '81*, University of Kansas, Lawrence

1980 *Copper 2: The Second Brass and Bronze Exhibition*, University of Arizona, Tucson

1980,77,76 *Virginia Craftsmen 80, 77, 76*, Virginia Museum of Fine Arts, Richmond

Related Professional Experience:

1975-91 Craftsmen Jeweler/Designer/Setter/Engraver/Supervisor, Best Products Company, Inc., Cherry Hill, NJ

Selected Public Collections:

Museum Het Kruithuis, 's-Hertogenbosch, The Netherlands

Alice H. Klein

Born: April 3, 1956, Waukesha, WI, USA

Education:

1980 MFA, Tyler School of Art, Temple University, Elkins Park, PA

1978 BFA, University of Wisconsin, Milwaukee

Selected Awards:

1986 Fellowship Grant, Wisconsin Arts Board, Madison

Selected Exhibitions:

1994 *A Moveable Feast**, Amsterdam; *Schmuck Unserer Zeit**, Zurich

1993 *Contemporary Jewelry**, Little Rock, AK

1992-93 *Korun Kieli**, Gothenburg; Helsinki

1992 *A Decade of Craft, Recent Acquisitions, Part II*, American Craft Museum, New York

1989 *Craft Today: USA*, Musée des Arts Décoratifs, Paris (travelled)

1986 *All That Glitters: Personal Ornaments*, Milwaukee Art Museum, WI
Contemporary Arts: An Expanding View, Monmouth Museum, Lincroft, NJ
Craft Today: Poetry of the Physical, American Craft Museum, New York (travelled)

1985 *Contemporary Jewelry Redefined*, Pittsburgh Center for the Arts, PA

1984-87 *Modern Jewelry**, Philadelphia, PA; Cleveland, OH; Honolulu HI; Montreal

1984 *Celebration '84*, Art Gallery at Harbourfront, Toronto, Canada (travelled)
Contemporary Jewellery: The Americas, Australia, Europe and Japan, National Museum of Modern Art, Kyoto; Tokyo
Golden Years: Tyler's 50th Anniversary, Tyler School of Art, Elkins Park, PA

1982 *22 Contemporary Artists*, University of Pennsylvania, Philadelphia
Patterns, Museum of Contemporary Crafts, New York

1981 *Good as Gold*, Renwick Gallery, NCFA, Smithsonian Institution, Washington, DC (travelled)

1980 *Young Americans: Metal*, American Craft Museum, New York

Related Professional Experience:

1993– Maintains studio, TKO Designs, Clarksville, DE

Selected Public Collections:

American Craft Museum, New York; Cooper-Hewitt, National Museum of Design, Smithsonian Institution, New York; Milwaukee Art Museum, WI; Tyler School of Art, Temple University, Elkins Park, PA

Esther Knobel

Born: January 14, 1949, Poland

Education:
1975-77   Royal College of Art, London
1970-74   Bezalel Academy of Art and Design, Jerusalem

Awards:
1994   Françoise van den Bosch Prize, Amsterdam
1993   Grant, American Israeli Foundation,
1986   Alix De Rothschild Foundation Prize for Jewellery

Selected Exhibitions:
1994   *Esther Knobel: Sketches in Raw Material*, Galerie Ra,
      Amsterdam
      Local Goddesses, David Tower Museum, Jerusalem
      A Moveable Feast*, Amsterdam; *Schmuck Unserer Zeit**, Zurich
1993   *Contemporary Jewelry**, Little Rock, AK
      Holography in Jewellery Design, Museum für angewandte
         Kunst, Cologne
      Tekens en Ketens, Gemeentemuseum, Arnhem, The Netherlands
      Voorzien: Benno Premsela Applied Art Collection, Stedelijk
         Museum, Amsterdam
1992-93 *Korun Kieli**, Gothenburg; Helsinki
1992   *Triennale du Bijou*, Musée des Arts Décoratifs, Paris
1991   *Arsenale*, Museum für Kunsthandwerk, Frankfurt a.M. (travelled)
      Jehi or, Jewish Museum, Frankfurt a.M.
1989   *Jewellery and Objects from Israel*, Museum für angewandte
         Kunst, Cologne
      Jewelry: Means: Meaning, University of Tennessee, Knoxville
         (travelled)
      Perth International Crafts Triennial, Art Gallery of Western
         Australia, Perth
1987   *Joieria Europea Contemporània*, Fundació Caixa de Pensions,
         Barcelona
      Schmuck, Zeichen am Körper, Francisco Carolinum Museum,
         Linz, Austria
1985   *Body Works and Wearable Sculpture*, Visual Arts Center of
         Alaska, Anchorage
      Contemporary Jewelry Redefined, Pittsburgh Center for the Arts, PA
      New Tradition, British Crafts Centre, London
      Nya Smycken, Nya Material, Kulturhuset, Stockholm
      Vrije Vormgeving 1900-1984, Museum Fodor, Amsterdam
1984-87 *Modern Jewelry**, Philadelphia, PA; Cleveland, OH; Honolulu,
         HI; Montreal
1984   *Contemporary Jewellery: The Americas, Australia, Europe and
         Japan*, National Museum of Modern Art, Kyoto; Tokyo
      *Cross Currents: Jewellery from Australia, Britain, Germany and
         Holland*, Power House Museum, Sydney (travelled)
      Jewelry International, American Craft Museum II, New York

1983   *The Jewellery Project*, Crafts Council Gallery, London
1983,82 Material Schmuck und Gerät, Internationale Handwerksmesse,
         Munich
1982   *The Maker's Eye*, Crafts Council Gallery, London
      Schmuck '82 – Tendenzen, Schmuckmuseum, Pforzheim,
         Germany
      Visies op Sieraden 1965-1982, Stedelijk Museum, Amsterdam
1980   *Fancy Goods: Ralph Turner's Collection of Popular Jewellery*
         (travelled UK)
      Schmuck International 1900-1980, Künstlerhaus, Vienna
1979   *Sieraden in Singer*, Singer Museum, Laren, The Netherlands

Related Professional Experience:
1985-91 Faculty, Bezalel Academy of Art and Design, Jerusalem

Selected Public Collections:
Art Gallery of Western Australia, Perth; Cleveland County Museum,
Middlesborough, England; Israel Museum, Jerusalem; Museum für
angewandte Kunst, Vienna; Museum Het Kruithuis, 's-Hertogenbosch,
The Netherlands; National Museum of Modern Art, Kyoto; National
Museum of Modern Art, Tokyo; Stedelijk Museum, Amsterdam

Friedrich Knupper

Born: April 4, 1947,
         Hamburg, Germany
Died: December 9, 1987,
         Berlin

Education:
1963-66   Goldschmiedeaus-
         bildung, Hamburg

Selected Awards:
1987   Landespreis, Berlin
1986   Auszeichnung, Schmuck und Edelsteinpreis, Idar-Oberstein,
         Germany
1973   Auszeichnung, Landespreis, Berlin

Selected Exhibitions:
1994   *A Moveable Feast**, Amsterdam; *Schmuck Unserer Zeit**,
      Zurich
1993   *Contemporary Jewelry**, Little Rock, AK
1992-93 *Korun Kieli**, Gothenburg; Helsinki
1990   *Friedrich Knupper: Schmuck und Objekte*, Germanisches
         Nationalmuseum, Nuremberg, (travelled)
1988   *Schmuck Berlin-West*, Deutsches Goldschmiedehaus, Hanau

1987 *7 Goldschmiede 50 Schmuckstücke*, Kunstgewerbemuseum,
      Berlin
      Joieria Europea Contemporània, Fundació Caixa de Pensions,
      Barcelona
      Schmuckszene '87, Internationale Handwerksmesse, Munich
      Solo Exhibition, Galerie Orfèvre, Dusseldorf
      Solo Exhibition, Galerie V & V, Vienna
      Solo Exhibition, VO Galerie, Washington, DC
      Zeitgenössisches deutsches und finnisches Kunsthandwerk,
      Museum für Kunsthandwerk, Frankfurt a.M., (travelled)
1986 *International Jewellery Art Exhibition*, 6th Tokyo Triennial,
      Yurakucho Art Forum, Tokyo
      Solo Exhibition, Die Werkstattgalerie, Berlin
1985,83 *Internationale Schmuckschau*, Internationale Handwerksmesse,
      Munich
1984 *Zeitgenössisches deutsches Kunsthandwerk,* Museum für
      Kunsthandwerk, Frankfurt a.M., (travelled)
1978,76,74
      Der Ring, Deutsches Goldschmiedehaus, Hanau, Germany

Related Professional Experience:
1974 Establishes workshop, Berlin. Closes on death in 1987
1973 Gastsemester, Hochschule der Künste, Berlin
1971 Meisterprüfung in Berlin

Selected Public Collections:
Kunstgewerbemuseum, Berlin; Museum für Kunst und Gewerbe,
Hamburg; Museum für Kunsthandwerk, Frankfurt a.M

Rena Koopman

Born: December 29, 1945, Harrisburg, PA, USA

Education:
1972 University of Wisconsin, Milwaukee
1967 Cornell University, Ithaca, NY
      BA, Vassar College, Poughkeepsie, NY

Selected Exhibitions:
1994 *A Moveable Feast**, Amsterdam; *Schmuck Unserer Zeit**, Zurich
1992-93 *Korun Kieli**, Gothenburg; Helsinki
1992 *Metamorphoses: Convertible Jewelry*, Atrium Gallery, New York
1991 *Gold*, Helen Drutt Gallery, Philadelphia, PA
1990 *Solo Exhibition*, Clark Gallery, Lincoln, MA
1988 *Solo Exhibition*, Helen Drutt Gallery, New York
1986 *Contemporary Arts: An Expanding View*, Monmouth Museum
      of Art, Lincroft, NJ
      Contemporary Crafts: A Concept in Flux, Society for Art in
      Crafts, Pittsburgh, PA
1984-87 *Modern Jewelry**, Philadelphia, PA; Cleveland, OH; Honolulu,
      HI; Montreal

1982 *Schmuck '82 – Tendenzen*, Schmuckmuseum, Pforzheim,
      Germany
1979 *Clay, Metal, Fiber Invitational*, Southeastern Massachusetts
      University, North Dartmouth
1978-90 *Solo Exhibitions*, Clark Gallery, Lincoln, MA
1977 *Jewelry as Sculpture as Jewelry*, La Jolla Museum, CA
1975 *American Images II*, Goethe Institute, Boston, MA
      Metalforms, Brockton Art Center, MA
1973 *Crafts '73 Invitational*, Attleboro Museum, MA

Related Professional Experience:
      Maintains independent studio, MA
1986 Seminar Instructor, Wellesley College, MA
1977 Metalsmithing Instructor, Haystack Mountain School,
      DeerIsle, ME

Robin Kranitzky and Kim Overstreet

Kranitzky
Born: November 10, 1956, Richmond, VA, USA
Overstreet
Born: January 29, 1955, Christiansburg, VA, USA

Education:
Kranitzky
1975-79 BFA, Virginia Commonwealth University,
      Richmond
Overstreet
1974-76 Virginia Western Community College,
      Richmond

Robin Kranitzky (left) and Kim Overstreet (right)

Selected Awards:
1993 Best in Show '93, Philadelphia Craft Show, PA
1991 Award for Excellence, Washington Craft Show, Washington, DC

Selected Exhibitions:
1994 *Desire in Time, Time as Intimacy*, University of Wisconsin,
      Milwaukee
      A Moveable Feast*, Amsterdam; *Schmuck Unserer Zeit**, Zurich
      Solo Exhibition, SOFA, Helen Drutt Gallery, Philadelphia, PA;
      Chicago, IL
1993 *Contemporary Jewelry**, Little Rock, AK
1992-93 *Korun Kieli**, Gothenburg; Helsinki
1992 *Brilliant Stories: American Narrative Jewelry*, USIS Exhibition
      Hall, Amman, Jordan (travelled)
      Many Mansions, The Art of Shelter, San Fransico
      Craft and Folk Art Museum, CA
      Dream House, Peninsula Fine Arts Center, Newport News, VA
      Of Magic, Power and Memory, Bellevue Art Museum, WA

1991   *Beauty is a Story*, Museum Het Kruithuis,
       's-Hertogenbosch, The Netherlands
1990   *American Dreams, American Extremes*, Museum Het Kruithuis,
       's-Hertogenbosch, The Netherlands

Selected Public Collections:
Montreal Musée des Arts Décoratifs, Quebec; Museum Het Kruithuis,
's-Hertogenbosch, The Netherlands; Renwick Gallery, NMAA,
Smithsonian Institution, Washington, DC

Daniel Kruger

Born: 1951, Capetown,
          South Africa

Education:
1974-80 Akademie der Bildenden
        Künste, Munich
1973-74 Michaelis School of
        Fine Art, University
        of Capetown
1971-72 University of
        Stellenbosch,
        South Africa

Selected Exhibitions:
1994   *Daniel Kruger*, Museum Het Kruithaus, 's-Hertengebosch,
      The Netherlands
1993   *Müncher Goldschmiede*, Müncher Stadtmuseum, Munich
      Schmuck: Die Sammlung der Danner-Stiftung, Galerie für
        angewandte Kunst, Munich
1992   *Triennale du Bijou*, Musée des Arts Décoratifs, Paris
1991   *Beauty is a Story*, Museum Het Kruithuis, 's-Hertogenbosch,
      The Netherlands
1989   *Michael Becker/Daniel Kruger*, Galerie für Modernen Schmuck,
      Frankfurt a.M.
      Perth International Crafts Triennial, Art Gallery of Western
        Australia, Perth
      Zeitgenössische Schmuckkunst aus der Bundesrepublik
        Deutschland, Instituts für Auslandsbeziehungen, Stuttgart
1985,83,82,77,76,75
      Internationale Schmuckschau, Internationale Handwerksmesse,
        Munich
1984   *Cross Currents: Jewellery from Australia, Britain, Germany and*
        Holland, Power House Museum, Sydney (travelled)
      Daniel Kruger, Schmuckmuseum, Pforzheim, Germany (travelled)
1983   *Solo Exhibition*, Galerie Mattar, Cologne
      Solo Exhibition, Die Werkstattgalerie, Berlin
1983,79 *International Jewellery Art Exhibition*, Tokyo Triennials
1982,77 *Schmuck – Tendenzen*, Schmuckmuseum, Pforzheim, Germany

1981   *Körper-Schmuck-Zeichen-Raum*, Kunstgewerbemuseum, Zurich
      Solo Exhibition, Museum Het Kruithuis, 's-Hertogenbosch
1980   *Schmuck International 1900-1980*, Künstlerhaus, Vienna
1979   *Körper-Schmuck-Zeichen-Raum*, Kestner-Gesellschaft, Hanover
      Körper-Zeichen, Städtische Galerie im Lenbachhaus, Munich
      Sieraden in Singer, Singer Museum, Laren, The Netherlands
1978   *Der Ring*, Deutsches Goldschmiedehaus, Hanau, Germany

Selected Public Collections:
Boymans-van Beuningen Museum, Rotterdam; Danner-Stiftung
Collection, Munich; Instituts für Auslandsbeziehungen, Stuttgart;
Museum Het Kruithuis, 's-Hertogenbosch, The Netherlands; Powehouse
Museum, Sydney; Schmuckmuseum, Pforzheim, Germany

Otto Künzli

Born: July 22, 1948, Zurich, Switzerland

Education:
1972-78 Akademie der Bildenden Künste, Munich
1965-70 Schule für Gestaltung, Zurich

Selected Awards:
1992   Honorary Fellow, Bezalel Academy, Jerusalem
1990   Françoise van den Bosch Prize, Amsterdam

Selected Exhibitions:
1994   *A Moveable Feast**, Amsterdam; *Schmuck Unserer Zeit**, Zurich
      A New Century in European Design, Tokyo Metropolitan Teien
        Art Museum, Tokyo (travelled)
1993   *Contemporary Jewelry**, Little Rock, AK
      Goldschmiede Silberschmiede: Drei Generationen, Galerie für
        angewandte Kunst, Munich
      Müncher Goldschmiede, Müncher Stadtmuseum, Munich
      Schmuck: Die Sammlung der Danner-Stiftung, Galerie für
        angewandte Kunst, Munich
      Voorzien: Benno Premsela Applied Art Collection, Stedelijk
        Museum, Amsterdam
1992-93 *Korun Kieli**, Gothenburg; Helsinki
1992   *Das dritte Auge*, Museum Bellerive, Zurich
      Joies Indissenyables, Escola Massana, Barcelona
      Solo Exhibition, Museum Bellerive, Zurich
      The Third Eye, Kelvingrove Museum and Art Gallery, Glasgow,
        Scotland
1991   *Naakte Schoonheid*, Museum van Hedendaagse Kunst, Antwerp
      Solo Exhibition, Stedelijk Museum, Amsterdam
1990-91 *Fremd. Körper aus der Sammlung Teunen*, Wilhelm-Hack
        Museum, Ludwigshafen, Rhein, Germany
      Solo Exhibition, Museum Fodor, Amsterdam
1989   *symboliek in het moderne en antieke sieraad*, Allard Pierson
        Museum, Amsterdam
      Zeitgenössische Schmuckkunst aus der Bundesrepublik
        Deutschland, Instituts für Auslandsbeziehungen, Stuttgart

1987 *Joieria Europea Contemporània*, Fundació Caixa de Pensions, Barcelona
1986 *Sieraad Vorm en Idee*, Gemeentelijke van Reekummuseum, Apeldoorn, The Netherlands
1985 *Attitudes*, International Cultureel Centrum, Antwerp, Belgium (travelled)
Body Works and Wearable Sculpture, Visual Arts Center of Alaska, Anchorage
New Tradition, British Crafts Centre, London
1984-87 *Modern Jewelry**, Philadelphia, PA; Cleveland, OH; Honolulu, HI; Montreal
1984 *Contemporary Jewellery: The Americas, Australia, Europe and Japan*, National Museum of Modern Art, Kyoto; Tokyo
Cross Currents: Jewellery from Australia, Britain, Germany and Holland, Power House Museum, Sydney (travelled)
Jewelry International, American Craft Museum II, New York
1984 *The Jewellery Project*, Crafts Council Gallery, London
Kollektion Künzli '83, Deutsches Tapetenmuseum, Kassel, Germany
Körperkultur, Landesmuseum, Oldenburg, Germany
1983,79 *International Jewellery Art Exhibition*, Tokyo Triennials
1982 *Jewellery Redefined*, British Crafts Centre, London
Visies op Sieraden 1965-1982, Stedelijk Museum, Amsterdam
1981 *Körper-Schmuck-Zeichen-Raum*, Kunstgewerbemuseum, Zurich
1980 *Schmuck International 1900-1980*, Künstlerhaus, Vienna
Solo Exhibition, Deutsches Goldschmiedehaus, Hanau, Germany
1979 *Therese Hilbert – Otto Künzli*, Schmuckmuseum, Pforzheim,
1975 *Jewellery in Europe*, Scottish Arts Council Gallery, Edinburgh (travelled)
1973 *Schmuck '73 – Tendenzen*, Schmuckmuseum, Pforzheim, Germany

Related Professional Experience:
1991– Professor, Akademie der Bildenden Künste, Munich

Selected Public Collections:
Australian National Gallery, Canberra; Cleveland County Museum, Middlesborough, England; Danner-Stiftung Collection, Munich; Detroit Institute of the Arts, MI; Deutsches Goldschmiedehaus, Hanau, Germany; Deutsches Tapetenmuseum, Kassel, Germany; Gemeentelijke van Reekummuseum, Apeldoorn, The Netherlands; Israel Museum, Jerusalem; Müncher Stadtmuseum, Munich; Museum Het Kruithuis, 's-Hertogenbosch, The Netherlands; National Gallery of Victoria, Melbourne; National Museum of Modern Art, Kyoto; Nordenfjeldske Kunstindustrimuseum, Trondheim, Norway; Power House Museum, Sydney; Schmuckmuseum, Pforzheim, Germany; Stedelijk Museum, Amsterdam; Victoria and Albert Museum, London

Birgit Laken

Born: November 13, 1948, Leiden, The Netherlands

Education:
1972-76 Gerrit Rietveld Academie, Amsterdam
1967-72 Koninklijke Academie van Beeldende Kunsten, The Hague

Selected Exhibitions:
1995 *Solo Exhibition*, Galerie D19, Chemnitz, Germany
Group Exhibition, Studio Ton Berends, The Hague; Djakarta Bandung, Indonesia
1994 *A Moveable Feast**, Amsterdam; *Schmuck Unserer Zeit**, Zurich
Solo Exhibition, Artefacto 3, Lisbon
Group Exhibition, Museum für Kunst und Gewerbe, Hamburg
Solo Exhibition, Schmuckforum, Zurich
1993 *Contemporary Jewelry**, Little Rock, AK
Tekens en Ketens, Gemeentemuseum, Arnhem, The Netherlands
Solo Exhibition, Frans Halsmuseum, Haarlem, The Netherlands
1992-93 *Korun Kieli**, Gothenburg; Helsinki
1992 *Group Exhibition*, Fremantle Art Centre, Perth, Western Australia
Solo Exhibition, Jewelers'werk, Washington, DC
Triennale du Bijou, Musée des Arts Décoratifs, Paris
1991 *Jewel as Object, Object as Jewel*, Librye Zwolle, The Netherlands
Solo Exhibition, Die Werkstattgalerie, Berlin
Solo Exhibition, Gemeentelijke van Reekummuseum, Apeldoorn, The Netherlands
Group Exhibition, Studio Ton Berends, The Hague
1990 *News from the Netherlands*, Fundacao Calouste Gulbenkian, Lisbon, Portugal (travelled)
Solo Exhibition, Galerie Ra, Amsterdam
Solo Exhibition, Galerie Trits, Delft
1989 *An Art Collection of Combs*, organized by Galerie Marzee, Nimwegen, The Netherlands (travelled)
Kopf und Kragen, Frankfurter Herbstmesse, Frankfurt a.M.
Ornamenta 1, Schmuckmuseum, Pforzheim, Germany
A Tribute for Joke, Jewelerswerk Galerie, Washington, DC
1988,85,81 *VES*, Stedelijk Museum, Amsterdam
1987 *Biennale du Bijou Contemporain*, Hotel du Sens, Paris
Holland in Vorm, Gemeentemuseum, Arnhem, The Netherlands
1986 *Jewellery Images*, VES 10th anniversary exhibition, Stedelijk Museum, Amsterdam (travelled)
1985 *16 Dutch Jewellery Designers*, Nordenfjeldske Kunstindustrimuseum, Trondheim, Norway
25 Jahre Galerie Nouvelles Images, Haags Gemeentemuseum, The Hague
Attitudes, International Cultureel Centrum, Antwerp (travelled)

1985	*Nya Smycken, Nya Material*, Kulturhuset, Stockholm
1984	*Contemporary Jewellery: The Americas, Australia, Europe and Japan*, National Museum of Modern Art, Kyoto; Tokyo
1982	*Schmuck '82 – Tendenzen*, Schmuckmuseum, Pforzheim, Germany
1982,80	*Internationale Schmuckschau*, Internationale Handwerksmesse, Munich
1981	*Zeitgenössisches deutsches und niederländisches Kunsthandwerk*, Museum für Kunsthandwerk, Frankfurt a.M.

Related Professional Experience:

1984-86	Academie van Beeldende Kunsten, Kampen, The Netherlands
1979-80	Faculty, Academie voor Beeldende Vorming, Amersfoort, The Netherlands

Selected Public Collections:
Boymans-van Beuningen Museum, Rotterdam; Centraal Museum, Utrecht; Cleveland County Museum, Middlesbrough, England; Cooper-Hewitt, National Museum of Design, Smithsonian Institution, New York; Frans Halsmuseum, Haarlem, The Netherlands; Gemeentelijke van Reekummuseum, Apeldoorn, The Netherlands; Gemeentemuseum, Arnhem, The Netherlands; Haggs Gemeentemuseum, The Hague; Kunstindustrimuseet, Oslo; Musée de l'horlogerie et de l'émaillerie, Geneva; Museum für Kunst und Gewerbe, Hamburg; Museum für Kunsthandwerk, Frankfurt a.M.; Nordenfjeldske Kunstindustrimuseum, Trondheim, Norway; Schmuckmuseum, Pforzheim, Germany

Edward De Large

Born: May 15, 1949, Lincoln, England

Education:

1972-75	MA Royal College of Art, London
1966-71	DIP. AD, Grimsby and Camberwell Schools of Art

Selected Awards:

1984	Bavarian State Prize, Internationale Schmuckshau, Munich.
1983	Freeman of the Worshipful Company of Goldsmiths, London,
1979	UK-USA Bicentennial Arts Fellowship: National Endowment for the Arts and the British Council

Selected Exhibitions:

1994	*A Moveable Feast**, Amsterdam; *Schmuck Unserer Zeit**, Zurich
1993	*Contemporary Jewelry**, Little Rock, AK
1992-93	*Korun Kieli**, Gothenburg; Helsinki
1984	*National Invitational Metals Show*, University of Alabama, Birmingham
	25th Anniversary International Jewelry Exhibition, Handwerkskammer fur Oberbayern, Munich

1983	*American Metalwork*, Kyoto Municipal Museum of Traditional Industry, Kyoto
	Internationale Schmuckschau, Handwerkskammer fur Oberbayern, Munich
1982	*Color and Form*, Tyler School of Art, Temple University, Philadelphia, PA
	Contemporary Metals Invitational, University of Texas, El Paso
	Edward de Large: Recent Work, Helen Drutt Gallery, Philadelphia, PA
	Edward de Large: New Jewellery, Oxford Gallery, Oxford, UK
1981	*Tenth Anniversary Exhibition*, Electrum Gallery, London,
	Good as Gold: Alternative Materials in American Jewelry, Smithsonian Institution Traveling Exhibition, Washington, DC
	Collectors' Choice, St Louis Art Museum, St Louis, MO
1980	*401 1/2 Workshops 1970-1980*, Commonwealth Institute, London
	Marietta College Crafts National, Marietta, OH
1979	*New Faces*, Crafts Council, London
1978	*Objects*, Victoria and Albert Museum Collection, London
1977	*Loot*, Goldsmith's Hall, London
	Jubilee Jewelry, Victoria and Albert Museum, London
	Tendenzen, Schmuckmuseum, Pforzheim, Germany

Selected Public Collections:
Crafts Council of Great Britain; Gemeentelijks, Van Reekumgalerie, Apeldoorn, The Netherlands; Goldsmiths' Hall, London; Kyoto Municipal Museum of Traditional Industry, Japan; National Gallery of Victoria, Melbourne; Schmuckmuseum, Pforzheim, Germany; Victoria and Albert Museum, London

Rebekah Laskin

Born: April 1, 1955, New York, NY, USA

Education:

1982	BFA, State University of New York, New Paltz

Selected Awards:

1984	Honorable Mention, *Ornament* Magazine, Jewelry International Competition
1982	Jurors' Award for Excellence, *Enamels '82*, National Enamelist Guild, USA

Selected Exhibitions:

1994	*A Moveable Feast**, Amsterdam; *Schmuck Unserer Zeit**, Zurich
1993	*10 American Jewelers*, Perimeter Gallery, Chicago, IL
	Contemporary Metal: Form and Narrative, University of Illinois, Urbana-Champaign
	Enamelrama, University of West Florida, Pensacola
1992-93	*Korun Kieli**, Gothenburg; Helsinki

1991	*Solo Exhibition*, Helen Drutt Gallery, New York
1990	*L'Art de L'Email*, Bienalle Internationale de Limoges, Limoges, France
1989	*Beyond Craft: A Celebration of Creativity*, School of Visual Arts, New York
	Clay, Fiber and Metal, Skidmore College, Saratoga Springs, NY
	National Jewelry Invitational, Drake University, Des Moines, IA
	Rebekah Laskin – New Enamel Jewelry, VO Galerie, Washington, DC
	Schmuckszene '89, Internationale Handwerksmesse, Munich
1988	*Color and Image: Recent American Enamels*, circulated by the Gallery Association of New York State
1987	*American Enamels: A View from the West*, Aoki Metal Gallery, Tokyo
	Craft as Content: National Metals Invitational, University of Akron, OH
	Masterworks/Enamel/87, Taft Museum, Cincinnati, OH
1986	*Contemporary Arts: An Expanding View*, The Monmouth Museum, Lincroft, NJ
	Craft Today: Poetry of the Physical, American Craft Museum, New York (travelled)
	New Jewelry, Virginia Museum of Fine Arts, Richmond (travelled)
1985	*Jewelry 85*, Nordenfjeldske Kunstindustrimuseum, Trondheim, Norway
	Rebekah Laskin: Enamelist, The Wichita Art Association, KS
1984-87	*Modern Jewelry**, Philadelphia, PA; Cleveland, OH; Honolulu, HI; Montreal
1984	*American Jewelry Now*, organized by the American Craft Museum, New York (travelled)
	Jewelry USA, American Craft Museum II, New York
1983	*Metals Invitational*, Montana State University, Bozeman
1982	*Enamels '82*, George Washington University, Washington, DC
1981	*Good as Gold*, Renwick Gallery, NCFA, Smithsonian Institution, Washington, DC (travelled)

Related Professional Experience:

1991–	Jewelry Instructor, Fashion Institute of Technology, New York
1990–	Faculty, Parson's School of Design, New York
1981-82	Artist-in-Residence, Oregon School of Arts and Crafts, Portland

Selected Public Collections:
Art Institute of Chicago, IL; Charles A; Wustum Museum of Fine Arts, Racine, WI; Cooper-Hewitt, National Museum of Design, Smithsonian Institution, New York; Kunstindustrimuseet, Oslo; Nordenfjeldske Kunstindustrimuseum, Trondheim, Norway

Stanley Lechtzin

Born: June 9, 1936, Detroit, MI, USA

Education:

| 1962 | MFA, Cranbrook Academy of Art, Bloomfield Hills, MI |
| 1960 | BFA, Wayne State University, Detroit, MI |

Selected Awards:

1994	Arts Achievement Award, Wayne State University, Detroit, MI
1992	Elected, College of Fellows, American Crafts Council
1984	Hazelett Memorial Award for Excellence in the Arts in Pennsylvania, PA, Council for the Arts
1984,76	Fellowships, National Endowment for the Arts, Washington, DC

Selected Exhibitions:

1994	*A Moveable Feast**, Amsterdam; *Schmuck Unserer Zeit**, Zurich
1993	*Contemporary Jewelry**, Little Rock, AK
	Lifetime Achievements: The ACC College of Fellows in Metal, National Ornamental Metal Museum, Memphis, TN
1992-93	*Korun Kieli**, Gothenburg; Helsinki
1990	*American Dreams, American Extremes*, Museum Het Kruithuis, 's-Hertogenbosch, The Netherlands
	Contemporary American Craft, Philadelphia Museum of Art, PA
1989	*Artful Objects: Recent American Crafts*, Fort Wayne Museum of Art, IN
	Infinite Riches, Museum of Fine Arts, St Petersburg, FL, USA
	Ornamenta 1, Schmuckmuseum, Pforzheim, Germany
1988	*The Founding Masters: SNAG Exhibition*, Skidmore College, Saratoga Springs, NY
1987	*Body Adornment*, Renwick Gallery, NMAA, Smithsonian Institution, Washington, DC
	The Eloquent Object, Philbrook Museum of Art, Tulsa, OK (travelled)
1986	*Craft Today: Poetry of the Physical*, American Craft Museum, New York (travelled)
1985	*Masterworks of Contemporary American Jewelry*, Victoria and Albert Museum, London
1984-87	*Modern Jewelry**, Philadelphia, PA; Cleveland, OH; Honolulu, HI; Montreal
1983,79	*International Jewellery Art Exhibition*, Tokyo Triennials
1981	*Good as Gold*, Renwick Gallery, NCFA, Smithsonian Institution, Washington, DC (travelled)
1980	*Robert L. Pfannebecker Collection*, Moore College of Art, Philadelphia, PA
1974	*The Goldsmith*, Renwick Gallery, NCFA, Smithsonian Institution, Washington, DC
1973	*Solo Exhibition*, Goldsmiths' Hall, London
1971	*Gold+Silber Schmuck+Gerät*, Norishalle, Nuremberg
	Jewellery '71, Art Gallery of Ontario, Toronto
1970	*Goldsmith '70: SNAG Inaugural Exhibition*, Minnesota Museum of Art, St Paul (travelled)
1969	*Objects: USA*, National Collection of Fine Arts, Smithsonian Institution, Washington, DC (travelled)

1968	*The American Contemporary Jewelry Exhibition*, Odakyu Department Store, Tokyo
	Olaf Skoogfors/Stanley Lechtzin, William Penn Memorial Museum, Harrisburg, PA
1965	*Solo Exhibition*, Museum of Contemporary Crafts, New York
1961	*International Exhibition of Modern Jewellery: 1890-1961*, Goldsmiths' Hall, London

Related Professional Experience:

1962– Professor, Tyler School of Art, Temple University, Elkins Park, PA

Selected Public Collections:

American Craft Museum, New York; The Arkansas Arts Center, Decorative Arts Museum, Little Rock, AK; Cooper-Hewitt, National Museum of Design, Smithsonian Institution, New York; Cranbrook Academy of Art, Bloomfield Hills, MI; Detroit Institute of the Arts, MI; Minnesota Museum of Art, St Paul, MN; Philadelphia Museum of Art, PA; Renwick Gallery, NMAA, Smithsonian Institution, Washington, DC; Temple University, Philadelphia, PA; Tokyo University of Fine Arts and Music, Tokyo; Schmuckmuseum, Pforzheim, Germany; Yale University Art Gallery, New Haven, CT; Worshipful Company of Goldsmiths, London

Emmy van Leersum

Born: April 16, 1930, Hilversum, The Netherlands
Died: November 2, 1984, Amersfoort, The Netherlands

Education:
1962-63 Konstfack Skolen, Stockholm
1958-62 Instituut voor Kunstnijveerheidsonderwijs, Amsterdam, (later renamed Gerrit Rietveld Academie)

Selected Exhibitions:
1994	*A Moveable Feast**, Amsterdam; *Schmuck Unserer Zeit**, Zurich
1993	*Broken Lines: Emmy van Leersum, 1930-1984*, Museum Het Kruithuis, 's-Hertogenbosch, The Netherlands (travelled)
	Contemporary Jewelry*, Little Rock, Ak
	Voorzien: Benno Premsela Applied Art Collection, Stedelijk Museum, Amsterdam
1992-93	*Korun Kieli**, Gothenburg; Helsinki
1989	*Ornamenta 1*, Schmuckmuseum, Pforzheim, Germany
1987	*Concepts Comments Process: Dutch Jewellery 1967-1987*, Rijksdienst Beeldende Kunst, Amsterdam (travelled)
	Holland in Vorm, Gemeentemuseum, Arnhem, The Netherlands
1986	*Sieraad 1986, Draagteken?*, Museum Het Kruithuis, 's-Hertogenbosch, The Netherlands
1985	*Body Works and Wearable Sculpture*, Visual Arts Center of Alaska, Anchorage
	Contemporary Jewelry Redefined, Pittsburgh Center for the Arts, PA

1985	*New Tradition*, British Crafts Centre, London
1984-87	*Modern Jewelry**, Philadelphia, PA; Cleveland, OH; Honolulu, HI; Montreal
1984	*Cross Currents: Jewellery from Australia, Britain, Germany and Holland*, Power House Museum, Sydney (travelled)
	Jewelry International, American Craft Museum II, New York
	Solo Exhibition, Galerie Atkut, Krefeld, Germany
1983	*The Jewellery Project*, Crafts Council Gallery, London
	Sieren en Versieren, Gemeentelijk van Reekummuseum, Apeldoorn, The Netherlands
1982	*Jewellery Redefined*, British Crafts Centre, London
	Solo Exhibition, Galerie Ra, Amsterdam
	Visies op Sieraden 1965-1982, Stedelijk Museum, Amsterdam
1981	*Solo Exhibition*, Galerie Hermanns, Munich
1979	*56 Bracelets, 17 Rings, 2 Necklaces*, Gemeentelijke van Reekummuseum, Apeldoorn, The Netherlands
	Emmy van Leersum, Solo Exhibition, Stedelijk Museum, Amsterdam (travelled)
1975	*Jewellery in Europe*, Scottish Arts Council Gallery, Edinburgh (travelled)
1973	Aspects of Jewellery, Aberdeen Art Gallery and Museum
1971	*Schmuck - Objekte*, Museum Bellerive, Zurich
1969	*Objects to Wear*, Van Abbemuseum, Eindhoven, The Netherlands

Selected Public Collections:

Centraal Museum, Utrecht; Museum Het Kruithaus, The Netherlands; Kostuummuseum, The Hague; Nederlands Dans Theater, The Hague; Powerhouse Museum, Sydney; Stedelijk Museum, Amsterdam; Victoria and Albert Museum, London

Fritz Maierhofer

Born: February 2, 1941, Vienna, Austria

Education:
1966 Master's examination with Anton Heldwein

Selected Awards:
1976	Grant, Ministeriums für Unterricht und Kunst, Pforzheim
1972	Förderungpreis des Wiener Kunstfonds, Vienna
	Prize, *4. Internationaler Wettbewerb – Ansteckschmuck*, Schmuckmuseum, Pforzheim, Germany

Selected Exhibitions:
1994	*A Moveable Feast**, Amsterdam; *Schmuck Unserer Zeit**, Zurich
1993	*Contemporary Jewelry**, Little Rock, AK
	Solo exhibition, New Jewels Kunstgalerij, Knokke, Belgium
1992-93	*Korun Kieli**, Gothenburg; Helsinki

1992	*Solo Exhibition*, Künstlerhaus, Vienna
1991	*Austrian Designs and Architecture*, Art Institute of Chicago, IL
1989	*Perth International Crafts Triennial*, Art Gallery of Western Australia, Perth
1988	*Group Exhibition*, Victoria and Albert Museum, London
1987	*Joieria Europea Contemporània*, Fundació Caixa de Pensions, Barcelona
1985	*Nya Smycken, Nya Material*, Kulturhuset, Stockholm,
1984-87	*Modern Jewelry**, Philadelphia, PA; Cleveland, OH; Honolulu, HI; Montreal
1984	*Jewelry International*, American Craft Museum II, New York
	Schmuck, zeitgenössische Kunst aus Österreich, Ateneo San Basso, Venice
1982,79	*Solo Exhibitions*, Galerie am Graben, Vienna
1982,77,73	
	Schmuck – Tendenzen, Schmuckmuseum, Pforzheim, Germany
1980	*Email – Schmuck und Gerät in Geschichte und Gegenwart*, Schmuckmuseum, Pforzheim, Germany (travelled)
	Schmuck International 1900-1980, Künstlerhaus, Vienna
1979,76,73	
	International Jewellery Art Exhibition, Tokyo Triennials
1978	*Schmuck – Tischgerät aus Österreich 1904/08–1973/77*, Galerie am Graben, Vienna
1975	*Jewellery in Europe*, Scottish Arts Council Gallery, Edinburgh (travelled)
1973	*Aspects of Jewellery*, Aberdeen Art Gallery and Museum, Scotland
	Jewelry as Sculpture as Jewelry, Institute of Contemporary Art, Boston, MA
1972	*4. Internationaler Wettbewerb – Ansteckschmuck*, Schmuckmuseum, Pforzheim, Germany

Selected Public Collections:
Art Gallery of Western Australia, Perth; Museum für angewandte Kunst, Vienna; National Museums of Scotland, Edinburgh ; Schmuckmuseum, Pforzheim, Germany; Victoria and Albert Museum, London; Worshipful Company of Goldsmiths, London

Carlier Makigawa

Born: September 9, 1952, Perth, Western Australia

Education:
1985-87	MFA, Royal Melbourne Institute of Technology, Victoria, Australia
1978-80	BA, Western Australian Institute of Technology, Perth

Awards:
1992	Award, Victoria Health National Craft, Melbourne
1982	Acquisitive Award, Diamond Valley Art Awards, Victoria, Australia

Selected Exhibitions:
1994	*Australian Contemporary Craft*, travelled through South America
	A Moveable Feast*, Amsterdam; *Schmuck Unserer Zeit**, Zurich
1993	*The Art of Jewellery*, Setagaya Art Museum, Tokyo
	Australia Gold, travelled through SE Asia
	Contemporary Jewelry*, Little Rock, AK
	Solo Exhibition, Helen Drutt Gallery, Philadelphia
1992-93	*Korun Kieli**, Gothenburg; Helsinki
1992	*Vic Health National Craft Award*, National Gallery of Victoria, Melbourne, Australia
199	*First Australian Contemporary Jewellery Biennial*, Jam Factory, Adelaide, South Australia (travelled)
	Twenty Years, Electrum Gallery, London, UK
1989	*Ornamenta 1*, Schmuckmuseum, Pforzheim, Germany
	Perth International Crafts Triennial, Art Gallery of Western Australia, Perth
1987	*Four Australian Jewellers*, National Gallery of Victoria, Melbourne (travelled)
1986	*Four Contemporary Australian Jewellers*, Woolongong City Art Gallery, NSW, Australia
	Sixth Toyko Triennial-International Jewellery Exhibition Yurakucho Art Forum, Tokyo
	Ten Years Ra, Gallerie Ra, Amsterdam
1986,83	*International Jewellery Art Exhibition*, Tokyo Triennials
1985	*Contemporary Jewellery Redefined*, Pittsburgh Center for the Arts, PA
	Impulse and Form, Art Gallery of Western Australia, Perth
	Nya Smycken, Nya Material, Kulturhuset, Stockholm
1984	*Contemporary Jewellery: The Americas, Australia, Europe and Japan*, National Museum of Modern Art, Kyoto; Tokyo
	Cross Currents: Jewellery from Australia, Britain, Germany and Holland, Power House Museum, Sydney (travelled)
	Jewelry International, American Craft Museum II, New York
1982	*Australian Contemporary Jewellery*, travelled through Europe
	Jewellery Redefined, British Crafts Centre, London

Related Professional Experience:
1985-88	Lecturer, Royal Melbourne Institute of Technology, Victoria, Australia

Selected Public Collections:
Art Gallery of Queensland, Brisbane; Art Gallery of South Australia, Adelaide; Art Gallery of Western Australia, Perth; Australian National Gallery, Canberra; Cooper-Hewitt, National Museum of Design, Smithsonian Institution; Montreal Museum of Decorative Arts; National Gallery of Victoria, Melbourne; National Museum of Modern Art, Kyoto; Power House Museum, Sydney; Queen Victoria Museum and Art Gallery, Launceston, Tasmania

Bruno Martinazzi

Born: December 10, 1923, Turin, Italy

Education:
1970   Ph.D., University of Turin
1953-54 Art Institutes of Turin, Florence and Rome
1947   University of Turin

Selected Awards:
1987   Recipient: Golden Ring of Honour, Association for Goldsmiths'
        Art, Deutsches Goldschmiedehaus, Hanau, Germany
1976   Herbert Hoffmann Prize, *Internationale Schmuckschau*,
        Internationale Handwerksmesse, Munich
1972   Prize, *4. Internationaler Wettbewerb – Ansteckschmuck*,
        Schmuckmuseum, Pforzheim, Germany
1965   Bavarian State Prize, Munich
1961   Acquisition Award, International Exhibition of Modern
        Jewellery, Goldsmiths' Hall, London

Selected Exhibitions:
1994   *A Moveable Feast**, Amsterdam; *Schmuck Unserer Zeit**, Zurich
        Schmuck und Gerät, Deutsches Goldschmiedehaus, Hanau,
        Germany (travelled)
1993   *13 Goldschmiede: Von Amsterdam bis Tokyo*, Bayerische
        Akademie der Schönen Künste, Munich
        Contemporary Jewelry*, Little Rock, AK
        Schmuck: Die Sammlung der Danner-Stiftung, Galerie für
        angewandte Kunst, Munich
1992-93 *Korun Kieli**, Gothenburg; Helsinki
1992   *Sieraden*, Centrum Beeldende Kunst, Groningen,
        The Netherlands
1990   *Ehrenringträger*, Gesellschaft für Goldschmiede Kunst,
        Hamburg
        Solo Exhibition, Helen Drutt Gallery, New York
1989   *Infinite Riches*, Museum of Fine Arts, St Petersburg, FL, USA

1989   *Ornamenta 1*, Schmuckmuseum, Pforzheim, Germany
1987   *Solo Exhibition*, Helen Drutt Gallery, Philadelphia, PA
1986   *Arte Moderna a Torino*, Fondazione de Fornaris, Turin
1985   *Martinazzi: Contro le Guerre*, Basilica di Santa Maria
        all'Imprunetta, Florence (travelled)
1984   *Contemporary Jewellery: The Americas, Australia, Europe
        and Japan*, National Museum of Modern Art, Kyoto;
        Tokyo
        Jewelry International, American Craft Museum II,
        New York
        Martinazzi: Sculture e Disegni, Museo Diocesano, Venice
1983,79,76,73,70
        International Jewellery Art Exhibition, Tokyo Triennials
1982,77,73,70
        Schmuck – Tendenzen, Schmuckmuseum, Pforzheim,
        Germany
1982,75 *Solo Exhibitions*, Galleria Gian Enzo Sperone, Rome
1981   *Martinazzi*, Museo di Torre Pellice, Turin
        Triennale Internazionale: Marmo, Lavoro, Scultura, Carrara,
        Italy
1980   *Schmuck International 1900-1980*, Künstlerhaus, Vienna
        Tin Symposium, Hochschule für angewandte Kunst, Vienna
1978   *Martinazzi*, Galerie am Graben, Vienna
1976   *Internationale Schmuckschau*, Internationale Handwerksmesse,
        Munich
1975   *Jewellery in Europe*, Scottish Arts Council Gallery, Edinburgh
        (travelled)
1974   *18 Orfévres d'Aujourd'hui*, Musée des Arts Décoratifs,
        Lausanne
1973   *21 Premio del Fiorino*, Florence
1972   *4. Internationaler Wettbewerb – Ansteckschmuck*,
        Schmuckmuseum, Pforzheim, Germany
1971   *Gold+Silber Schmuck+Gerät*, Norishalle, Nuremberg
1968   *International Jewelry Exhibition*, Muzeum skla a bizuterie,
        Jablonec nad Nisou, Czechoslovakia
1966   *Art in Jewelry*, Finch Museum, New York
1964   *Solo Exhibition*, Galleria Il Punto, Turin (travelled)
1961   *International Exhibition of Modern Jewellery: 1890-1961*,
        Goldsmiths' Hall, London

Related Professional Experience:
1977-82 Professor, Academy of Fine Arts, Turin

Selected Public Collections:
Centro Direzionale Fiat, Turin; Danner-Stiftung Collection, Munich;
Fondazione de Fornaris, Turin; Museo d'Arte Moderna, Turin; Museum
des 20.Jahrhunderts, Vienna; Muzeum skla a bizuterie, Jablonec nad
Nisou, Czech Republic; Schmuckmuseum, Pforzheim, Germany;
Worshipful Company of Goldsmiths, London

Falko Marx

Born: 1941, Cologne, Germany

Selected Exhibitions:
1994   *A Moveable Feast**, Amsterdam; *Schmuck Unserer Zeit**, Zurich
1993   *Contemporary Jewelry**, Little Rock, AK
        Facet I, Kunsthal, Rotterdam
1993,90 *Schmuckszene*, Internationale Handwerksmesse, Munich
1992-93 *Korun Kieli**, Gothenburg; Helsinki
1989   *Infinite Riches*, Museum of Fine Arts, St Petersburg, FL, USA
        Ornamenta 1, Schmuckmuseum, Pforzheim, Germany
        Solo Exhibition, Helen Drutt Gallery, New York
        Strange Attractors: The Spectacle of Chaos, Susan Rezac Gallery,
          Chicago, IL
1988   *Tragezeichen*, Museum Schloss Morsbroich, Leverkusen,
        Germany
1987   *Solo Exhibition*, Galerie Louise Smit, Amsterdam
1986   *Group Exhibition*, Archaeologisches Museum, Nicosia,
        Cyprus
1985   *Attitudes*, International Cultureel Centrum, Antwerp
        (travelled)
1980   *Schmuck International 1900-1980*, Künstlerhaus, Vienna
1977   *Group Exhibition,* Bonner Kunstverein, Bonn
1975   *Group Exhibition,* Kölnischer Kunstverein, Cologne

Related Professional Experience:
1979–   Maintains independent studio

Miyé Matsukata

Born: January 27, 1922, Tokyo, Japan
         Immigrated to the US, 1940
Died: February 16, 1981, Boston, MA

Education:
*c.*1946-49 Studied with Joseph Sharock,
          Museum School of Fine Arts, Boston, MA
1940-44   Principia College, Elsah, IL

Selected Awards:
1966   Travel Grant – Middle East/Greece, Museum of Fine Arts,
        Boston, MA

Selected Exhibitions:
1994   *A Moveable Feast**, Amsterdam; *Schmuck Unserer Zeit**, Zurich
1993   *Contemporary Jewelry**, Little Rock, AK
1992-93 *Korun Kieli**, Gothenburg; Helsinki
1988   *The Founding Masters: SNAG Exhibition*, Skidmore College,
        Saratoga Springs, NY
1984-87 *Modern Jewelry**, Philadelphia, PA; Cleveland, OH; Honolulu,
        HI; Montreal
1984   *Jewelry and Beyond: Metalwork by Members of SNAG*, Mitchell
        Museum, Mount Vernon, IL
1977   *The Metalsmith: SNAG Exhibition*, Phoenix Museum of Art, AZ
1974   *American Metalsmiths*, DeCordova Museum, Lincoln, MA
        The Goldsmith, Renwick Gallery, NCFA, Smithsonian
        Institution, Washington, DC
1973   *The Art of Enamels*, State University of New York, New Paltz
        Jewelry as Sculpture as Jewelry, Institute of Contemporary Art,
        Boston, MA
1972   *Jewelry and Holloware Invitational*, Iowa State University, Ames
1970   *Goldsmith '70: SNAG Inaugural Exhibition*, Minnesota Museum
        of Art, St Paul (travelled)
1968   *The American Contemporary Jewelry Exhibition*, Odakyu
        Department Store, Tokyo
1966   *Craftsmen USA 66*, Museum of Contemporary Crafts,
        New York (travelled)

Related Professional Experience:
1963-65 Chairman, Ceramic Art Association, Boston, MA
1960   Sole proprietor, Atelier Janiyè, Boston, MA
*c.*1950   One of three to establish Atelier Janiyè, Boston, MA

Selected Public Collections:
American Craft Museum, New York; Museum of Fine Arts, Boston, MA

Richard Mawdsley

Born: July 11, 1945, Winfield, KS, USA

Education:
1969 MFA, University of Kansas, Lawrence
1967 BSE, Kansas State Teachers College, Emporia

Selected Awards:
1994,78 Fellowships, National Endowment for the Arts,
        Washington, DC
1987-89 President, Society of North American Goldsmiths,
        St Paul, MN
1987 Artist Fellowship, Illinois Arts Council

Selected Exhibitions:
1994 *Contemporary Metalsmithing: Behind and Beyond the Bench*,
     Craft Alliance, St Louis, MO
     A Moveable Feast*, Amsterdam; *Schmuck Unserer Zeit**, Zurich
1993 *Contemporary Jewelry**, Little Rock, AK
     Contemporary Metal: Form and Narrative, University of Illinois,
     Urbana-Champaign
     National Objects Invitational, The Arkansas Arts Center, Little
     Rock, AK
1992-93 *Korun Kieli**, Gothenburg; Helsinki
1992 *American Crafts: The National Collection*, Renwick Gallery,
     NMAA, Smithsonian Institution, Washington, DC
     Of Magic, Power and Memory, Bellevue Art Museum, WA
     Revolving Techniques: Thrown, Blown, Spun, and Turned,
     John A. Michener Museum, Doylestown, PA
1991 *Collecting American Decorative Arts and Sculpture*, Museum of
     Fine Arts, Boston, MA
1990 *Explorations: The Aesthetic of Excess*, American Craft Museum,
     New York
1989 *Infinite Riches*, Museum of Fine Arts, St Petersburg, FL, USA
     Silver: New Forms of Expression I, Fortunoff, New York
1988 *Fakes, Forgeries and Frauds*, National Ornamental Metal
     Museum, Memphis, TN
     Hong-ik Metalcrafts Association Annual Exhibition, Walker Hill
     Art Center Museum, Seoul, Korea
1987 *The Eloquent Object*, Philbrook Museum of Art, Tulsa, OK
     (travelled)
     Solo Exhibition, National Ornamental Metal Museum,
     Memphis, TN
1985 *Masterworks of Contemporary American Jewelry*, Victoria and
     Albert Museum, London
     New Visions, Traditional Materials, Carnegie Institute Museum
     of Art, Pittsburgh, PA
1984-87 *Modern Jewelry**, Philadelphia, PA; Cleveland, OH; Honolulu,
     HI; Montreal
1984 *Jewelry and Beyond: Metalwork by Members of SNAG*, Mitchell
     Museum, Mount Vernon, IL
     Jewelry USA, American Craft Museum II, New York
1981 *The Animal Image*, Renwick Gallery, NCFA, Smithsonian
     Institution, Washington, DC

1980 *Robert L. Pfannebecker Collection*, Moore College of Art,
     Philadelphia, PA
1979 *SNAG – Gold- und Silberschmiedearbeiten*, Schmuckmuseum,
     Pforzheim, Germany (travelled)
     Solo Exhibition, Columbia College, Chicago, IL
1978 *Craft, Art and Religion*, The Vatican Museum, Vatican City
     Modern American Jewelry Exhibition, Mikimoto and Co., Ltd.
     Gallery, Tokyo
1977 *The Metalsmith: SNAG Exhibition*, Phoenix Museum of
     Art, AZ
1974 *Baroque '74*, Museum of Contemporary Crafts, New York
     An Exhibition of Eight American Metalsmiths and Jewellers,
     Richard DeMarco Gallery, Edinburgh
     The Goldsmith, Renwick Gallery, NCFA, Smithsonian
     Institution, Washington, DC
     Metal '74, State University of New York, Brockport
1972 *The Contemporary American Silversmith and Goldsmith*,
     Fairtree Gallery, New York
1970 *Goldsmith '70: SNAG Inaugural Exhibition*, Minnesota Museum
     of Art, St Paul (travelled)

Related Professional Experience:
1981– Professor, Southern Illinois University, Carbondale

Selected Public Collections:
American Craft Museum, New York; Evansville Museum of Arts and
Sciences, IN; Illinois State University, Normal; Minnesota Museum of
Art, St Paul; Museum of Fine Arts, Boston, MA; Renwick Gallery,
NMAA, Smithsonian Institution, Washington, DC; National Ornamental
Metal Museum, Memphis, TN; Texas Tech University Museum,
Lubbock; Yale University Art Gallery, New Haven, CT

Bruce Metcalf

Born: September 30, 1949, Amherst, MA, USA

Education:
1977   MFA, Tyler School of Art, Temple University, Elkins Park, PA
1973-74 State University of New York, New Paltz
1972-73 Montana State University, Bozeman
1972   BFA, Syracuse University, NY

Selected Awards:
1992,77 Fellowships, National Endowment for the Arts,
              Washington, DC
1990   Fulbright Fellowship, Seoul, Korea
1989,83 Creative Activity Grant, Kent State University
1988,84,83
              Fellowships, Ohio Arts Council
1980   Fellowship, Massachusetts Council on the Arts and Humanities

Selected Exhibitions:
1994   *In Touch*, Maihaugen, Lillehammer, Norway
              A Moveable Feast*, Amsterdam; *Schmuck Unserer Zeit**, Zurich
1993   *The Art of Jewellery*, Setagaya Art Museum, Tokyo
              Contemporary Jewelry*, Little Rock, AK
              Facet I, Kunsthal, Rotterdam
              Sculptural Concerns, Contemporary Arts Center, Cincinnati,
                OH (travelled)
              Solo Exhibition, Perimeter Gallery, Chicago, IL
1992-93 *Korun Kieli**, Gothenburg; Helsinki
1992   *Brilliant Stories: American Narrative Jewelry*, USIS Exhibition
                Hall, Amman, Jordan (travelled)
              Silver, John Michael Kohler Arts Center, Sheboygan, WI
              Solo Exhibition, Contacto Directo Galeria, Lisbon
              Solo Exhibition, Susan Cummins Gallery, Mill Valley, CA
1991   *Arsenale*, Museum für Kunsthandwerk, Frankfurt a.M.,
                (travelled)
1990   *American Dreams, American Extremes*, Museum Het Kruithuis,
                's-Hertogenbosch, The Netherlands
1989   *An Art Collection of Combs*, organized by Galerie Marzee,
                Nimwegen, The Netherlands (travelled)
              Jewelry:Means:Meaning, University of Tennessee, Knoxville
                (travelled)
              Ornamenta 1, Schmuckmuseum, Pforzheim, Germany
1988   *Goldsmithing: New Concepts and Ancient Traditions in Jewelry*,
                Louisiana State University, Baton Rouge
1987   *National Metals Invitational 1987*, Pasadena City College, CA
1986   *Craft Today: Poetry of the Physical*, American Craft Museum,
                New York (travelled)
              Mainstreams in Metal, Galveston Arts Center, TX
1985   *Metals: New Directions*, One Mellon Bank Center, Pittsburgh, PA
              Solo Exhibition, Indiana University, Bloomington
1984-87 *Modern Jewelry**, Philadelphia, PA; Cleveland, OH; Honolulu,
                HI; Montreal
1984   *Jewelry and Beyond: Metalwork by Members of SNAG*, Mitchell
                Museum, Mount Vernon, IL

1984   *Jewelry USA*, American Craft Museum II, New York
              Solo Exhibitions, DBR Gallery, Cleveland, OH; Massachusetts
                College of Art, Boston
1983   *Solo Exhibitions*, Akron Art Museum, OH; John Michael
                Kohler Arts Center, Sheboygan, WI
1982   *Young Americans: Award Winners*, American Craft Museum,
                New York
1981   *Good as Gold*, Renwick Gallery, NCFA, Smithsonian
                Institution, Washington, DC (travelled)
1980   *Robert L. Pfannebecker Collection*, Moore College of Art,
                Philadelphia, PA
              Young Americans: Metal, American Craft Museum, New York

Related Professional Experience:
1981-91 Faculty, Kent State University, OH
1980–   Contributing Editor, *Metalsmith* magazine

Selected Public Collections:
American Craft Museum, New York; Arizona State University Print
Collection; Cranbrook Academy of Art, Bloomfield Hills, MI; Illinois
State University, Normal; Montreal Musée des Arts Décoratifs, Quebec;
Philadelphia Museum of Art, PA; Tyler School of Art, Temple University,
Philadelphia, PA; University of Northern Iowa Gallery, Cedar Falls

Walter Kelley Morris

Born: February 12, 1945, Bellingham, WA, USA

Education:
1976   MFA, Tyler School of Art, Temple University, Elkins Park, PA
1973   BFA, University of Washington, Seattle
1970   Everett Community College, WA

Selected Awards:
1976,75 Fellowships, Tyler School of Art, Temple University, Elkins
                Park, PA
1974   Honor Award, Friends of the Crafts, Seattle, WA
1973   Award for Study, Northwest Craft Center, Seattle, WA

Selected Exhibitions:
1994   *A Moveable Feast**, Amsterdam; *Schmuck Unserer Zeit**, Zurich
1992-93 *Korun Kieli**, Gothenburg; Helsinki
1984-87 *Modern Jewelry**, Philadelphia, PA; Cleveland, OH; Honolulu,
                HI; Montreal
1979   *SNAG – Gold- und Silberschmiedearbeiten*, Schmuckmuseum,
                Pforzheim, Germany (travelled)
1978   *Art Metal Exhibition*, Boise State University, ID
              National Spoon and Ashtray Show, Sangre de Christo Art
                Center, Pueblo, CO
              Regional Metals Exhibition, University of Wisconsin, River Falls
1977   *American Art 1977*, Helen Drutt Gallery, Philadelphia, PA

1977   *The Metalsmith: SNAG Exhibition*, Phoenix Museum of
        Art, AZ
        Third Profile of U.S. Jewelry, Texas Tech University, Lubbock
1976   *Pennsylvania Bicentennial Exhibition,* Pennsylvania State
        University, State College
        Sterling Silver Design Competition, Lever House, New York
1975   *9th Biennial Exhibition*, 2nd Crossing Gallery, Valley City
        College, Valley City, ND
        Lake Superior International Crafts Exhibition, Tweed Museum
        of Art, Duluth, MN
        Miniature World and Delicate Object, Fairtree Gallery,
        New York

Selected Public Collections:
Tyler School of Art, Temple University, Elkins Park, PA

Eleanor H. Moty

Born: November 10, 1945,
              Glen Ellyn, IL, USA

Education:
1971   MFA, Tyler School of
        Art, Temple University,
        Elkins Park, PA
1968   BFA, University of
        Illinois, Urbana

Selected Awards:
1992,89,85,83
        Graduate School Research Grants, University of Wisconsin,
        Madison
1988,75 Fellowships, National Endowment for the Arts,
        Washington, DC
1981   First Prize Medal, *Contemporary Crafts of the Americas*,
        Colorado State University, Fort Collins
1980   H. I. Rommes Fellowship, University of Wisconsin, Madison
1974   Purchase Award, *National Invitational Exhibition in
        Contemporary Jewellery*, Georgia State University, Atlanta
1973   Metals Award, *Technology and the Artist-Craftsman*,
        The Octagon, Ames, IA

Selected Exhibitions:
1994   *A Moveable Feast**, Amsterdam; *Schmuck Unserer Zeit**, Zurich
1993   *10 American Jewelers*, Perimeter Gallery, Chicago, IL
        Contemporary Jewelry*, Little Rock, AK

1993   *Sculptural Concerns*, Contemporary Arts Center, Cincinnati,
        OH (travelled)
1992-93 *Korun Kieli**, Gothenburg; Helsinki
1992   *Metal & Fiber USA Invitational*, Craft Alliance, St Louis, MO
1991   *Copper III*, Old Pueblo Museum, Tucson, AZ
        National Objects Invitational, The Arkansas Arts Center, Little
        Rock, AK
1990   *Silver: New Forms of Expression II*, Fortunoff, New York
        (travelled)
1989   *Artful Objects: Recent American Crafts*, Fort Wayne Museum of
        Art, IN
        Craft Today: USA, Musée des Arts Décoratifs, Paris (travelled)
1988   *Hong-ik Metalcrafts Association Annual Exhibition*, Walker Hill
        Art Center Museum, Seoul, Korea
1986   *All That Glitters: Personal Ornaments*, Milwaukee Art
        Museum, WI
        Craft Today: Poetry of the Physical, American Craft Museum,
        New York (travelled)
1984-87 *Modern Jewelry**, Philadelphia, PA; Cleveland, OH; Honolulu,
        HI; Montreal
1984   *10th Biennial National Invitational Craft Exhibition*, Illinois
        State University, Normal
        *Contemporary Jewellery: The Americas, Australia, Europe and
        Japan*, National Museum of Modern Art, Kyoto; Tokyo
        Jewelry and Beyond: Metalwork by Members of SNAG, Mitchell
        Museum, Mount Vernon, IL
        Jewelry USA, American Craft Museum II, New York
1983   *Craft as an Art Form*, John Michael Kohler Arts Center,
        Sheboygan, WI
1982   *National Metals Invitational*, University of Texas, El Paso
1981   *Solo Exhibition*, Birmingham Museum of Art, AL
        Moty2 – New Perspectives, John Michael Kohler Arts Center,
        Sheboygan, WI
1980   *Robert L. Pfannebecker Collection*, Moore College of Art,
        Philadelphia, PA
1979   *SNAG – Gold- und Silberschmiedearbeiten*, Schmuckmuseum,
        Pforzheim, Germany (travelled)
1978   *Landscape – New Views*, Herbert F. Johnson Museum of Art,
        Ithaca, NY
1977   *Contemporary Jewelry Exhibition*, Design Center, Manila, The
        Philippines
        The Metalsmith: SNAG Exhibition, Phoenix Museum of
        Art, AZ
1976   *American Crafts 1976 – An Aesthetic View*, Museum of
        Contemporary Art, Chicago
        American Metalsmiths Exhibition, American Embassy,
        Bucharest, Romania
        International Jewellery Art Exhibition, 3rd Tokyo Triennial,
        Seibu Gallery, Tokyo
1975   *Precious Metals*, University of Miami, Coral Gables, FL
        Uncommon Smiths of America, Eastern Michigan University,
        Ypsilanti
1974   *Baroque '74*, Museum of Contemporary Crafts, New York
        The Goldsmith, Renwick Gallery, NCFA, Smithsonian
        Institution, Washington, DC

1974	*An Invitational Exhibition of Work by Eight American Metalsmiths and Jewelers*, Aberdeen Art Gallery and Museum, Scotland (travelled)
	A Touch of Gold, Philadelphia Museum of Art, PA
1973	*Technology and the Artist-Craftsman*, The Octagon, Ames, IA
1972	*Zlataraa Cleje Invitational Jewelry Exhibition*, Yugoslavia
1972,70	*Form und Qualität*, Internationale Handwerksmesse, Munich
1971	*Jewellery '71*, Art Gallery of Ontario, Toronto, Canada
1970	*Goldsmith '70: SNAG Inaugural Exhibition*, Minnesota Museum of Art, St Paul (travelled)
1969	*Young Americans 1969*, Museum of Contemporary Crafts, New York

Related Professional Experience:
1981–   Professor, University of Wisconsin, Madison
1975-81 Associate and Assistant Professor, University of Wisconsin, Madsion

Selected Public Collections:
Birmingham Museum of Art, AL; Charles A. Wustum Museum of Fine Arts, Racine, WI; Georgia State University, Atlanta; Minnesota Museum of Art, St Paul; Patrick J. Lannan Foundation, Palm Beach, FL; Tyler School of Art, Temple University, Elkins Park, PA

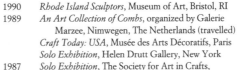

Louis Mueller

Born: June 15, 1943, Paterson, NJ, USA

Education:
1971   MFA, Rhode Island School of Design, Providence
1969   BFA, Rochester Institute of Technology, New York

Selected Awards:
1990,88 Fellowships, Rhode Island State Council on the Arts
1985   Fellowship, New York Foundation for the Arts
1985   Development Grant,Rhode Island School of Design, Providence
1983   Mellon Travel Study Grant
1978   Ford Foundation Grant, Museum of Fine Art, Boston, MA

Selected Exhibitions:
1995	*Solo Exhibition,* Carin Delcourt van Krimpen Gallery, Amsterdam
1994	*A Moveable Feast**, Amsterdam; *Schmuck Unserer Zeit**, Zurich
1993	*Contemporary Jewelry**, Little Rock, AK
	Louis Mueller/Benjamin Moore, Grover/Thurston Gallery, Seattle, WA
1992-93	*Korun Kieli**, Gothenburg; Helsinki
1991	*Outdoor Sculpture Festival*, Snug Harbor Cultural Center, Staten Island, NY

1990	*Rhode Island Sculptors*, Museum of Art, Bristol, RI
1989	*An Art Collection of Combs*, organized by Galerie Marzee, Nimwegen, The Netherlands (travelled)
	Craft Today: USA, Musée des Arts Décoratifs, Paris
	Solo Exhibition, Helen Drutt Gallery, New York
1987	*Solo Exhibition*, The Society for Art in Crafts, Pittsburgh, PA
1987-82	Five *Solo Exhibitions*, Helen Drutt Gallery, Philadelphia, PA
1986	*Contemporary Arts: An Expanding View*, Monmouth Museum, Lincroft, NJ
	Craft Today: Poetry of the Physical, American Craft Museum, New York
1985	*Urban Light*, New York Center for Design, New York
1984-87	*Modern Jewelry**, Philadelphia, PA; Cleveland, OH; Honolulu, HI; Montreal
1984	*Design in the Service of Tea*, Cooper-Hewitt Museum, New York
	The Extension of the Hand, General Foods Collection Gallery, Rye, NY
1983	*International Jewellery Art Exhibition*, 5th Tokyo Triennial, Isetan Art Museum, Tokyo
1982	*Solo Exhibition*, North Dakota Museum of Art, Grand Forks
1981,78,74	
	Solo Exhibitions, Rhode Island School of Design, Providence
1977	*The Metalsmith: SNAG Exhibition*, Phoenix Museum of Art, AZ
1975	*First Artist's Soap Box Derby*, San Francisco Museum of Modern Art, CA
	Forms in Metal, Museum of Art, Finch College, New York
1974	*The Goldsmith*, Renwick Gallery, NCFA, Smithsonian Institution, Washington, DC
	Joan Miró Drawing Exhibition, Joan Miró Museum, Barcelona,
1969	*Young Americans 1969*, Museum of Contemporary Crafts, New York

Selected Commissions:
1992	Lighting, Port of Seattle, WA (with Benjamin Moore)
1988	Fence and Gate Panels for three parks, Phoenix Arts Commission, AZ
1986	Mermaid Loving Cup, Philadelphia Maritime Museum, PA
	Three Bronze Sculptures, Hyatt Hotel, Scottsdale, AZ
1985	Bronze Medal for Philadelphia Craft Show Award, Philadelphia Museum of Art, PA
	Bronze Sculpture, Locust Club of Philadelphia, PA
	Sculpture, Braceland Brothers, Inc., Philadelphia, PA

Related Professional Experience:
1977   Faculty, Rhode Island School of Design, Providence

Selected Public Collections:
American Craft Museum, New York; First Capital Corporation, New York; General Foods, Ryebrook, NY; Rhode Island School of Design, Museum of Art, Providence

Erico Nagai

Born: February 11, 1947, Tokyo, Japan

Education:
1968-77 Akademie der Bildenden Künste, Munich
1967 Kunstgewerbeschule, Basle

Selected Awards:
1986,85,82
  City Art Prize, Munich
1985,76 Herbert Hoffmann Prize, *Form Formel Formalismus*,
  Internationale Handwerksmesse, Munich
1976 Bavarian State Prize, Munich

Selected Exhibitions:
1993 *Müncher Goldschmiede: Schmuck und Gerät 1993*, Müncher
  Stadtmuseum, Munich
  Schmuck: Die Sammlung der Danner-Stiftung, Galerie für
  angewandte Kunst, Munich
  Solo Exhibition, Gallery Lichtblick, Aachen, Germany
1993,90 *Solo Exhibitions*, Galerie für Modernen Schmuck, Frankfurt a.M.
1992 *Solo Exhibition*, New Jewels Kunstgalerij, Knokke, Belgium
1992,86,84
  Solo Exhibitions, Gallery Fred Jahn, Munich
1989 *Ornamenta 1*, Schmuckmuseum, Pforzheim, Germany
  Perth International Crafts Triennial, Art Gallery of Western
  Australia, Perth
1988 *Solo Exhibition*, Gallery Atrium, Basle
1987 *Jahesgabe,* Kestner Geuschaft, Hanover
1985 *25 Jahre Galerie Nouvelles Images*, Haags Gemeentemuseum,
  The Hague
1985,84,83,82,79,78,77,76,75
  Internationale Schmuckschau, Internationale Handwerksmesse,
  Munich
1984 *Contemporary Jewellery: The Americas, Australia, Europe and
  Japan*, National Museum of Modern Art, Kyoto; Tokyo
  Zeitgenössische deutsche Goldschmiedekunst, Goethe Institute,
  Tokyo (travelled)
1983 *Zeitgenössischer Schmuck aus Japan*, Schmuckmuseum,
  Pforzheim, Germany (travelled)
1983,79 *International Jewellery Art Exhibition*, Tokyo Triennials
1982,77 *Schmuck – Tendenzen*, Schmuckmuseum, Pforzheim, Germany
1981 *Körper-Schmuck-Zeichen-Raum*, Kunstgewerbemuseum, Zurich
1980 *Jahresgabe 1980/81*, Kestner-Gesellschaft, Hanover
  Schmuck International 1900-1980, Künstlerhaus, Vienna
1979 *Körper-Schmuck-Zeichen-Raum*, Kestner-Gesellschaft, Hanover
  Körper-Zeichen, Städtische Galerie im Lenbachhaus, Munich

Related Professional Experience:
1991 Visiting Faculty, Fachhochschule für Gestaltung, Pforzheim
1991 Visiting Faculty, Hiko Mizuno Jewelry College, Tokyo

Selected Public Collections:
Danner-Stiftung Collection, Munich; Schmuckmuseum, Pforzheim

Frans van Nieuwenborg and Martijn Wegman

Frans van Nieuwenborg

Van Nieuwenborg
Born: November 9, 1941,
  Venlo, The Netherlands
Wegman
Born: November 4, 1955, The Hague

Education:
Van Nieuwenborg
1958-63 Akademie voor Industriële Vormgeving,
  Eindhoven, The Netherlands
Wegman
1973-78 Gerrit Rietveld Academie, Amsterdam

Selected Awards:
Van Nieuwenborg
1993 Design Prize, City of Rotterdam
1992 IF Product Award, Industrie Forum Design, Hanover
1975 Grant, Amsterdam Foundation for the Arts
Van Nieuwenborg and Wegman
1986 Emmy van Leersum Award, Amsterdam Foundation for the Arts

Selected Exhibitions:
1994 *A Moveable Feast**, Amsterdam; *Schmuck Unserer Zeit**, Zurich
1993 *Contemporary Jewelry**, Little Rock, AK
1992-93 *Korun Kieli**, Gothenburg; Helsinki
1986 *Sieraad 1986, Draagteken?* Museum Het Kruithuis,
  's-Hertogenbosch, The Netherlands
  Serie Sieraad, Stedelijk Museum, Amsterdam
1985 *Contemporary Jewelry Redefined*, Pittsburgh Center for the Arts, PA
  New Tradition, British Crafts Centre, London
  Vrije Vormgeving 1900-1984, Museum Fodor, Amsterdam
1984-87 *Modern Jewelry**, Philadelphia, PA; Cleveland, OH; Honolulu,
  HI; Montreal
1984 *Contemporary Jewellery: The Americas, Europe, Australia and
  Japan*, National Museum of Modern Art, Kyoto; Tokyo
1980 *Schmuck International 1900-1980*, Künstlerhaus, Vienna
1979 *56 Bracelets, 17 Rings, 2 Necklaces*, Gemeentelijke van
  Reekummuseum, Apeldoorn, The Netherlands

Related Professional Experience:
Van Nieuwenborg
1986 Founded Buro for Industrial Design, The Netherlands
1985 Lecturer, Gerrit Rietveld Academie, Amsterdam
1973 Co-founded VES, association of jewellery designers, Amsterdam
Wegman
1990 Initiated Wegman Industrial Design, Leiden

Selected Public Collections:
Boymans-van Beuningen Museum, Rotterdam; Gemeentemuseum,
Arnhem; Kostuummuseum, The Hague; Museum of Modern Art,
New York; Rijksdienst Beeldende Kunst, The Hague; Stedelijk Museum,
Amsterdam; University Museum of Mexico City, Mexico

Breon O'Casey

Born: April 30, 1928,
London, England

Education:
1954 Studied with Fernand
Léger, Paris
1950-53 Anglo-French Art
Centre, London; met
and befriended Oskar
Kokoschka

Selected Exhibitions:
1994 *A Moveable Feast**, Amsterdam; *Schmuck Unserer Zeit**, Zurich
Solo Exhibition, Cornwall Craft Association, England
1993 *Contemporary Jewelry**, Little Rock, AK
Solo Exhibition, The Taylor Galleries, Dublin
1993,91,89,86,84,83
Solo Exhibitions, Helen Drutt Gallery, Philadelphia
1992-93 *Korun Kieli**, Gothenburg; Helsinki
1992 *Schmuckszene '92*, Internationale Handwerksmesse, Munich
1990 *Solo Exhibition*, The Collier/Campbell Shop, London
1989 *Infinite Riches*, Museum of Fine Arts, St Petersburg, FL
Solo Exhibition, Helen Drutt Gallery, New York
1988 *Craft Classics*, Craft Council Gallery, London
Decorative Arts Award Exhibition, Sotheby's, London
Solo Exhibition, The Scottish Gallery, Edinburgh
Solo Exhibition, The Taylor Galleries, Dublin
1987,85 *Solo Exhibition*, The Oxford Gallery, Oxford, UK
1986 *Contemporary Arts: An Expanding View*, Monmouth Museum,
Lincroft, NJ
1985 *Solo Exhibition*, Eltville Castle Gallery, Germany
Solo Exhibition, Victoria and Albert Museum Craft Shop,
London
1984-87 *Modern Jewelry**, Philadelphia, PA; Cleveland, OH; Honolulu,
HI; Montreal
1984 *Jewelry International*, American Craft Museum II,
New York
Solo Exhibition, British Crafts Centre, London
1982 *Solo Exhibition*, Prescote Gallery, Banbury, England

Related Professional Experience:
1962-65 Studio Apprentice, Barbara Hepworth, Cornwall, England
1960-62 Studio Apprentice, Dennis Mitchell, Cornwall, England
*c.*1960 Maintains independent studio for jewelry and painting,
Cornwall, England

Selected Public Collections:
Arts Council Collection, London, England; Arts Council of Southern
Ireland; British Crafts Council, London; Cooper-Hewitt, National
Museum of Design, Smithsonian Institution, New York; Craft Council,
England; Dartington Hall, Devonshire, England; Granada TV, London;
Leeds Museum and Art Gallery, England; Arts Council of Northern
Ireland, Belfast; Plymouth Museum and Art Gallery, England;
Schmuckmuseum, Pforzheim, Germany; Trinity College, Dublin;
Victoria and Albert Museum, London; Worshipful Company of
Goldsmiths, London

Joke van Ommen

Born: August 28, 1948, Amsterdam, The Netherlands
Died: October 23, 1988, Accokeek, MD, USA

Education:
1976-77 Hochschule für angewandte Kunst, Vienna
1975-76 Private student, Erika Leitner, Vienna
1967-74 University of Amsterdam

Selected Exhibitions:
1994 *A Moveable Feast**, Amsterdam; *Schmuck Unserer Zeit**, Zurich
1993 *Contemporary Jewelry**, Little Rock, AK
1992-93 *Korun Kieli**, Gothenburg; Helsinki
1985 *Body Works and Wearable Sculpture*, Visual Arts Center of
Alaska, Anchorage
1984-87 *Modern Jewelry**, Philadelphia, PA; Cleveland, OH; Honolulu,
HI; Montreal
1984 *Jewelry USA*, American Craft Museum II, New York
1981 *Good as Gold*, Renwick Gallery, NCFA, Smithsonian
Institution, Washington, DC (travelled)
Solo Exhibition, Fendrick Gallery, Washington, DC
Solo Exhibition, Helen Drutt Gallery, Philadelphia, PA
1980 *Group Exhibition*, Gallery Alto, Rotterdam
Group Exhibition, Stedelijk Museum, Amsterdam
Schmuck International, 1900-1980, Künstlerhaus, Vienna
Solo Exhibition, Gallery Cosa, Delft, The Netherlands
1979 *Solo Exhibition*, Galerie Het Kapelhuis, Amersfoort,
The Netherlands
Solo Exhibition, Galerie Nouvelles Images, The Hague
1977 *Kunstwerk-Schmuckwerk*, Vienna
Körperschmuck, Solo Exhibition, Gallery Roser, Vienna

Related Professional Experience:
1984-88 Established VO Galerie, Washington, DC (with Jan Maddox),
after her death, renamed Jewelers'werk Galerie
1975-76 Faculty, Kabulonga Girls School, Zambia
1974-76 Curator, Art Centre Foundation, Zambia

Selected Public Collections:
Art Council, City of Amsterdam ; Centraal Museum, Utrecht,
The Netherlands; Kostuummuseum, The Hague

Judy Onofrio

Born: November 21, 1939,
New London, CT, USA

Education:
1957   Sullins College, Bristol, VA

Selected Awards:
1994   Fellowship in the Visual Arts, McKnight Foundation,
        Minneapolis, MN
1993   Career Opportunity Grant, Minnesota State Arts Board,
        St Paul, MN
        Fellowship, National Endowment for the Arts, Washington, DC
1978   Fellowship, Minnesota State Arts Board, St Paul, MN

Selected Exhibitions:
1994   *A Moveable Feast**, Amsterdam; *Schmuck Unserer Zeit**, Zurich
1993   *Contemporary Jewelry**, Little Rock, AK
        Judyland: The Art of Judy Onofrio, Minneapolis Institute of
        Arts, MN (travelled)
1992-93 *Korun Kieli**, Gothenburg; Helsinki
1992   *Brilliant Stories: American Narrative Jewelry*, USIS Exhibition
        Hall, Amman, Jordan (travelled)
1990   *American Dreams, American Extremes*, Museum Het Kruithuis,
        's-Hertogenbosch, The Netherlands
1989   *2-D, 3-D*, Minneapolis Institute of Arts, MN
        Judy Onofrio/William Weege, Peter M. David Gallery,
        Minneapolis, MN
1988   *Altered Planes*, Rochester Art Center, MN
1984   *Judy Onofrio/Lee Bjorklund*, Minneapolis Institute of Arts, MN
1982   *Clay on Walls*, Rochester Art Center, MN
1979   *Famous Finger Hall of Fame*, Pennsylvania State University,
        University Park
        National Invitational: Women Artists, Springfield Art Museum, IL
1977   *Birthday Celebration Invitational*, John Michael Kohler Art
        Center, Sheboygan, WI
1974   *Solo Exhibition*, Illinois State University, Normal
1972   *Solo Exhibition*, University of Wisconsin, River Falls

Selected Public Collections:
The Arkansas Art Center, Decorative Arts Museum, Little Rock, AK;
Cooper-Hewitt, National Museum of Design, Smithsonian Institution,
New York; Greenville County Museum, Greenville, NC; Museum
Bellerive, Zurich; Museum Het Kruithuis, 's-Hertogenbosch, The
Netherlands; Philadelphia Museum of Art, Philadelphia, PA;
North Dakota Museum of Art, Grand Forks; Rochester Community
College, MN; University of Minnesota, Minneapolis;
Taipeteollisuusmuseo, Helsinki

Pavel Opočenský

Born: August 7, 1954,
Karlovy Vary,
Czechoslovakia

Education:
1973-74 School for Jewelry
        and Metals, Turnov,
        Czechoslovakia
1971-72 School for Jewelry
        Design, Jablonec nad
        Nisou, Czechoslovakia

Selected Awards:
1990   Grant, Empire State Craft Alliance, Saratoga Springs, NY
        Grant, Pollack-Krasner Foundation, New York
1986   Fellowship, New York Foundation for the Arts
1985   First Prize, *Art Quest '85*, California State University,
        Long Beach

Selected Exhibitions and Commissions:
1994   *A Moveable Feast**, Amsterdam; *Schmuck Unserer Zeit**, Zurich
1993   *Contemporary Crafts and the Saxe Collection*, Toledo Museum
        of Art, OH (travelled)
        Contemporary Jewelry*, Little Rock, AK
1992-93 *Korun Kieli**, Gothenburg; Helsinki
1992   *A Decade of Craft, Recent Acquisitions, Part II*, American Craft
        Museum, New York
        Design Visions, Art Gallery of Western Australia, Perth
1991   *Matter/Anti-Matter*, Galerie Marzee, Nimwegen, The
        Netherlands (travelled)
1990   *American Dreams, American Extremes*, Museum Het Kruithuis,
        's-Hertogenbosch, The Netherlands
        Jewelries/Epiphanies, Artists Foundation Gallery, Boston, MA
        (travelled to Prague)
        Desenhos e Jolas, Artefacto 3, Lisbon
1989   *Craft Today: USA*, Musée des Arts Décoratifs, Paris (travelled)
        Infinite Riches, Museum of Fine Arts, St Petersburg, FL, USA
        Schmuck 1989, Haus der Kunst, Munich
1989,88 *Solo Exhibitions*, OK Harris Works of Art, New York
1988   *Solo Exhibitions*, Artwear, New York; Susan Cummins Gallery,
        Mill Valley, CA
1987   *Grand Prix des Metiers d'Art New York*, Montreal, Canada
1986-87 *Modern Jewelry**, Philadelphia, PA
1986   *Contemporary Arts: An Expanding View*, Monmouth Museum,
        Lincroft, NJ
        Craft Today: Poetry of the Physical, American Craft Museum,
        New York (travelled)
        Jewelry, Perry Ellis Fall Collection
        Lexena National, Lexena Park, Lexena, KS
        Solo Exhibition, Helen Drutt Gallery, Philadelphia, PA
1985   *6. Internationaler Wettbewerb – Schmuck für Kopf und Haar*,
        Schmuckmuseum, Pforzheim, Germany
        Art Quest '85, California State University, Long Beach, CA

1985   *Contemporary Jewelry Redefined*, Pittsburgh Center for the
        Arts, PA
1983   *Doppel Form*, Ivory Museum, Erbach, Germany
1977   *Solo Exhibition*, Theatre Rubin, Prague, Czechoslovakia

Related Professional Experience:
1982   Maintains independent studio, Prague

Selected Public Collections:
American Craft Museum, New York; Moravská Galerie, Brno, Czech
Republic; Muzeum Ceskeho Raje, Turnov, Czech Republic; Museum für
Kunsthandwerk, Frankfurt a.M.; National Galerie, Bratislava, Slovakia;
Turnovshé Museum, Turnov, Czech Republic; Umeleckoprumyslove
Muzeum, Prague

Albert Paley

Born: March 28, 1944,
            Philadelphia, PA, USA

Education:
1969   MFA, Tyler School of
        Art, Temple University,
        Elkins Park, PA
1966   BFA, Tyler School of
        Art, Temple University,
        Elkins Park, PA

Selected Awards:
1991,84,79,76
        Fellowships, National Endowment for the Arts, Washington, DC
1989   Honorary Doctorate, University of Rochester, NY
1979,76,75
        Master Craftsman Apprentice Grants, National Endowment
        for the Arts, Washington, DC

Selected Exhibitions:
1994   *A Moveable Feast**, Amsterdam; *Schmuck Unserer Zeit**, Zurich
        Sculpture and Drawings, The Temple Gallery, Philadelphia, PA
        Sculpture Installation, Mitchell Cohen Statehouse,
        Camden, NJ
1993   *Contemporary Jewelry**, Little Rock, AK
1992-93 *Korun Kieli**, Gothenburg; Helsinki
1992   *Albert Paley: Studies for the 'Portal Gates'*, Renwick Gallery,
        NMAA, Smithsonian Institution, Washington, DC
        Design Visions, Art Gallery of Western Australia, Perth
        Solo Exhibition, University of the Arts, Philadelphia, PA

1992   *Treasures: Jewelry & Other Metalwork from the Permanent
        Collection*, American Craft Museum, New York
1991   *Albert Paley: Sculptural Adornment*, Renwick Gallery, NMAA,
        Smithsonian Institution, Washington, DC
1989   *Craft Today: USA*, Musée des Arts Décoratifs, Paris
        (travelled)
        Solo Exhibition, National Museum of Wales, Cardiff
1987   *The Eloquent Object*, Philbrook Museum of Art, Tulsa, OK
        (travelled)
1986   *Contemporary Arts: An Expanding View*, Monmouth Museum
        of Art, Lincroft, NJ
        Craft Today: Poetry of the Physical, American Craft Museum,
        New York
1985   *Albert Paley: The Art of Metal*, Birmingham Museum of Art, AL
        (travelled)
1984-87 *Modern Jewelry**, Philadelphia, PA; Cleveland, OH; Honolulu,
        HI; Montreal
1983   *The New Decorativeness in Architecture and Design*, Hudson
        River Museum, Yonkers, NY
        Towards a New Iron Age, Victoria and Albert Museum, London
        (travelled)
1980   *The Metalwork of Albert Paley*, John Michael Kohler Arts
        Center, Sheboygan, WI (travelled)
1979   *SNAG – Gold- und Silberschmiedearbeiten*, Schmuckmuseum,
        Pforzheim, Germany (travelled)
1978   *Craft, Art and Religion*, The Vatican Museum, Vatican City
1975   *Precious Metals*, University of Miami, Coral Gables, FL
1974   *Baroque '74*, Museum of Contemporary Crafts, New York
        The Goldsmith, Renwick Gallery, NCFA, Smithsonian
        Institution, Washington, DC
1971   *Jewellery '71*, Art Gallery of Ontario, Toronto
1970   *Goldsmith '70: SNAG Inaugural Exhibition*, Minnesota Museum
        of Art, St Paul, MN (travelled)
        Schmuck '70 – Tendenzen, Schmuckmuseum, Pforzheim,
        Germany
1965   *American Jewelry Today*, Everhart Museum, Scranton, PA

Related Professional Experience:
1984–   Artist-in-Residence, Rochester Institute of Technology, NY
1972-84 Professor, State University of New York, Brockport

Selected Public Collections:
Art Gallery of Western Australia, Perth; Birmingham Museum of Art,
AL; Columbus Museum of Fine Art, OH; Cooper-Hewitt, National
Museum of Design, Smithsonian Institution, New York; Delaware Art
Museum, Wilmington; Detroit Institute of the Arts, MI; High Museum
of Art, Atlanta, GA; Hunter Museum of Art, Chattanooga, TN;
Metropolitan Museum of Art, New York; Minnesota Museum of Art,
St Paul; Museum of Fine Arts, Boston, MA; Museum of Fine Arts,
Houston, TX; Newark Museum, NJ; Philadelphia Museum of Art, PA;
Springfield Museum of Art, MA; Renwick Gallery, NMAA, Smithsonian
Institution, Washington, DC; Strong Museum, Rochester, NY; University
of Rochester, NY; Victoria and Albert Museum, London; Virginia
Museum of Fine Arts, Richmond; The White House, Washington, DC;
Yale University Art Gallery, New Haven, CT

Anthony (Tony) Papp

Born: September 26, 1961,
New York, NY, USA
Died: June 1, 1991, New York, NY

Education:
1985   BFA, Parsons School
of Design, New York
1983   Studied under Deborah Aguado

Selected Awards:
1988   Award, *Young Americans*,
American Craft Museum,
New York

Selected Exhibitions:
1994   *A Moveable Feast**, Amsterdam; *Schmuck Unserer Zeit**, Zurich
1992-93   *Korun Kieli**, Gothenburg; Helsinki
1989   *Solo Exhibition*, Helen Drutt Gallery, Philadelphia, PA
1988   *Young Americans*, American Craft Museum, New York
1987   *Christmas Show*, Elaine Potter Gallery, San Francisco, CA
Jewelry by Tony Papp, Restivo Spring Collection, New York
Jewelry to Object, Tony Papp Gallery, New York
Simply Silver, Tony Papp Gallery, Trump Tower, New York
The Singular Brooch, Sculpture-to Wear, Los Angeles, CA
A Stone's Throw, Sculpture-to Wear, Los Angeles, CA
1986   *Fine Art Jewelry in America*, Cross Creek Gallery, Malibu, CA
Mary Ann Restivo Resort Show, New York
Studies in Marriage of Metals, Solo Exhibition, Neil Isman
Gallery, New York
1985   *Emerging Talent*, Artwear, New York

Related Professional Experience:
1988-89   Faculty, Parsons School of Design, New York

Earl Pardon

Born: September 6, 1926, Memphis, TN, USA
Died: May 1, 1991, Boston, MA, USA

Education:
1959   MFA, Syracuse University, NY
1951   BFA, Memphis Academy of Art, TN

Selected Awards:
1955   Award, *American Jewelry and Related Objects*, Huntington
Galleries, Huntington, WV

1952   Award in Metal, *Young Americans*, American Craftsmen's
Council, New York
First Prize, *7th National Decorative Arts Exhibition*, Wichita Art
Association, KS
1948   Scholarship, *4th National Silversmiths Conference*, sponsored by
Handy and Harman

Selected Exhibitions:
1994   *A Moveable Feast**, Amsterdam; *Schmuck Unserer Zeit**,
Zurich
1993   *Contemporary Crafts and the Saxe Collection*, Toledo Museum
of Art, OH (travelled)
Contemporary Jewelry*, Little Rock, AK
1992-93   *Korun Kieli**, Gothenburg; Helsinki
1992   *A Tribute to Earl Pardon*, Connell Gallery, Atlanta, GA
1991   *Design 1935-1965: What Modern Was*, Montreal Musée des Arts
Décoratifs (travelled)
1989   *Artful Objects: Recent American Crafts*, Fort Wayne Museum
of Art, IN
Skidmore 1989: Five Goldsmiths, Helen Drutt Gallery,
Philadelphia, PA
1985   *Masterworks of Contemporary American Jewelry*, Victoria and
Albert Museum, London
1984   *Structure and Ornament, American Modernist Jewelry 1940-1960*,
FIFTY/50 Gallery, New York
1981   *Enamels 50/80*, Brookfield Craft Center Gallery, CT
(travelled)
1980   *Earl Pardon: Retrospective Exhibition*, Skidmore College,
Saratoga Springs, NY
1961   *Imperial Exhibition*, organized by the American Craftsmen's
Council, New York
1959   *Enamels*, Museum of Contemporary Crafts, New York
1956   *Craftsmanship in a Changing World*, Museum of Contemporary
Crafts, New York
1954   *Eight Top Silversmiths*, Philadelphia Art Alliance, PA
Fiber, Clay and Metal, St Paul Gallery and School of Art, MI
1952   *Young Americans*, American Craftsmen's Council,
New York

Related Professional Experience:
1968-77   Chair, Department of Art, Skidmore College, Saratoga
Springs, NY
1954-55   Assistant Director of Design, Towle Silversmiths,
Newburyport, MA
1951-89   Professor, Skidmore College, Saratoga Springs, NY

Selected Public Collections:
American Craft Museum, New York; The Arkansas Arts Center,
Decorative Arts Museum, Little Rock, AK; Charles A. Wustum
Museum of Fine Arts, Racine, WI; Huntington Museum of Art, WV;
Memphis College of Art, TN; The Metropolitan Museum of Art,
New York; Montreal Musée des Arts Décoratifs, Quebec; Museum of
Fine Arts, Boston, MA; Renwick Gallery, NMAA, Smithsonian
Institution, Washington, DC; St Paul Gallery and School of Art, MI;
Towle Silversmiths Museum, Newburyport, MA

Francesco Pavan

Born: October 13, 1937,
Padua, Italy

Education:
1949-55 Istituto d'Arte *Pietro Selvatico*,
Padua

Selected Awards:
1989   Herbert Hoffmann Prize, *Schmuckszene '89*, Internationale
Handwerksmesse, Munich
1986   Prize, *International Jewellery Art Exhibition*, Yurakucho Art
Forum, Tokyo
1985   Herbert Hoffmann Prize, *Form Formel Formalismus*,
Internationale Handwerksmesse, Munich
1973   Herbert Hoffmann Prize, *Form und Qualität*, Internationale
Handwerksmesse, Munich
1968   Gold Medal, *Form und Qualität*, Internationale
Handwerksmesse, Munich

Selected Exhibitions:
1994   *A Moveable Feast**, Amsterdam; *Schmuck Unserer Zeit**, Zurich
Solo Exhibition, Galerie Marzee, Nimwegen, The Netherlands
1993   *13 Goldschmiede: Von Amsterdam bis Tokyo*, Bayerische
Akademie der Schönen Künste, Munich
Contemporary Jewelry*, Little Rock, AK
1992-93 *Korun Kieli**, Gothenburg; Helsinki
1992   *Triennale du Bijou*, Musée des Arts Décoratifs, Paris
Sieraden, Centrum Beeldende Kunst, Groningen, The Netherlands
1990   *Gioelli e Legature: Artisti del XX Secolo*, Biblioteca Trivulziana,
Milan
1989   *Infinite Riches*, Museum of Fine Arts, St Petersburg, FL, USA
Ornamenta 1, Schmuckmuseum, Pforzheim, Germany
Perth International Crafts Triennial, Art Gallery of Western
Australia, Perth
Schmuckszene '89, Internationale Handwerksmesse, Munich
1988   *Solo Exhibition*, Helen Drutt Gallery, New York
Solo Exhibition, Galerie Louise Smit, Amsterdam
Tragezeichen, Museum Schloß Morsbroich, Leverkusen, Germany
1986   *Goldschmuck aus Italien: Pinton und Pavan*, Galerie Cada,
Munich
International Jewellery Art Exhibition, 6th Tokyo Triennial,
Yurakucho Art Forum, Tokyo
Nove Artisti Orafi di Scuola Padovana, Museo Civico Eremitani,
Padua, (travelled)
1985   *25 Jahre Galerie Nouvelles Images*, Haags Gemeentemuseum,
The Hague
1985,73,68
Internationale Schmuckschau, Internationale Handwerksmesse,
Munich
1984   *Jewelry International*, American Craft Museum II, New York

1983   *Dieci Orafi Padovani*, Schmuckmuseum, Pforzheim, Germany
(travelled)
1980   *Schmuck International 1900-1980*, Künstlerhaus, Vienna
5. Internationaler Wettbewerb – Armschmuck,
Schmuckmuseum, Pforzheim, Germany
1977,73 *Schmuck – Tendenzen*, Schmuckmuseum, Pforzheim, Germany
1972   *Solo Exhibition*, Boymans-van Beuningen Museum, Rotterdam
1971   *Gold+Silber Schmuck+Gerät*, Norishalle, Nuremberg
1965   *1. Internationaler Wettbewerb – Ohrschmuck in Gold*,
Schmuckmuseum, Pforzheim, Germany

Related Professional Experience:
1961   Faculty, Istituto d'Arte *Pietro Selvatico*, Padua

Selected Public Collections:
Danner-Stiftung Collection, Munich; Schmuckmuseum, Pforzheim,
Germany

Ruudt Peters

Born: August 17, 1950, Naaldwijk, The Netherlands

Education:
1970-74 Gerrit Rietveld Academie, Amsterdam

Selected Awards:
1995,89 Scholarship, The Netherlands Foundation for Fine
Arts, Design and Architecture
1989   Scholarship, Fonds voor de Beeldende Kunsten,
Amsterdam
1987   Scholarship, Ministerie van WVC Rijswijk,
The Netherlands

Selected Exhibitions:
1994   *A Moveable Feast**, Amsterdam; *Schmuck Unserer Zeit**,
Zurich
Op Art: Eyeglasses by Jewelers, Oregon School of Arts and
Crafts, Portland (travelled)
1994,92,91
Solo Exhibitions, Galerie Spektrum, Munich
1993   *Contemporary Jewelry**, Little Rock, AK
Designprijs, Kunsthal, Rotterdam
Tekens en Ketens, Gemeentemuseum, Arnhem, The Netherlands
Voorzien: Benno Premsela Applied Art Collection, Stedelijk
Museum, Amsterdam
1992-93 *Korun Kieli**, Gothenburg; Helsinki
1992   *Maestri di Gioia*, Marijke Studio, Padua
Triennale du Bijou, Musée des Arts Décoratifs, Paris
1992,91,89,86
Solo Exhibitions, Galerie Marzee, Nimwegen, The Netherlands
1991   *Solo Exhibition*, Gemeentelijke van Reekummuseum,
Apeldoorn, The Netherlands

1991   *Solo Exhibition*, Galerie Sophie Lachaert, Ghent
1991,89 *Solo Exhibitions*, Galerie V & V, Vienna
1990   *L'Arte della Gioia*, Pedrocchi, Padua
        News from the Netherlands, Fundacao Calouste Gulbenkian,
            Lisbon (travelled)
        Schmuckszene '90, Internationale Handwerksmesse, Munich
        Solo Exhibition, Galerie für Modernen Schmuck, Frankfurt a.M.
        Triennale du Bijou, Musée du Luxembourg, Paris
1989   *An Art Collection of Combs*, organized by Galerie Marzee,
            Nimwegen, The Netherlands (travelled)
        Ornamenta 1, Schmuckmuseum, Pforzheim, Germany
        symboliek in het moderne en antieke sieraad, Allard Pierson
            Museum, Amsterdam
1989,87 *Kunstobject als onderscheiding*, Galerie Het Kapelhuis,
            Amersfoort, The Netherlands
1987   *Holland in Vorm*, Gemeentemuseum, Arnhem, The Netherlands
1985   *New Tradition*, British Crafts Centre, London
1984-87 *Modern Jewelry**, Philadelphia, PA; Cleveland, OH; Honolulu,
            HI; Montreal
1984   *Solo Exhibition*, Aspects, London
1983   *The Jewellery Project*, Crafts Council Gallery, London
        Solo Exhibition, Galerie Nouvelles Images, The Hague
        Solo Exhibition, Galerie Ra, Amsterdam
1982   *Visies op Sieraden 1965-1982*, Stedelijk Museum, Amsterdam

Related Professional Experience:
1990   Coordinator, Jewelry Department, Gerrit Rietveld Academie,
            Amsterdam

Selected Public Collections:
Boymans-van Beuningen Museum, Rotterdam; Cleveland County
Museum, Middlesbrough, England; Danner Stiftung, Munich;
Gemeentemuseum, Arnhem, The Netherlands; Gemeentemuseum,
Tilburg, The Netherlands; Museum für angewandte Kunst, Hamburg;
Museum für angewandte Kunst, Vienna; Musée des Arts Decoratifs,
Montreal; Provincie Overijssel, The Netherlands; Rijksdienst Beeldende
Kunst, The Hague; Schmuckmuseum, Pforzheim, Germany; Stedelijk
Museum, Amsterdam

Eugene Michael Pijanowski

Born: 1938, Detroit, MI, USA

Education:
1967-69 MFA, Cranbrook Academy of Art, Bloomfield Hills, MI
1965-67 MA, Wayne State University, Detroit, MI
1959-64 BFA, Wayne State University, Detroit, MI

Selected Awards:
1987   Herbert Hoffmann Prize, *Schmuckszene '87*, Internationale
            Handwerksmesse, Munich
1985   Fulbright Fellowship, Vienna
1978,75 Grants, National Endowment for the Arts, Washington, DC

Selected Exhibitions:
1994   *A Moveable Feast**, Amsterdam; *Schmuck Unserer Zeit**, Zurich
1993   *Contemporary Jewelry**, Little Rock, AK
        Facet I, Kunsthal, Rotterdam
        Schmuck: Die Sammlung der Danner-Stiftung, Galerie für
            angewandte Kunst, Munich
        Sculptural Concerns, Contemporary Arts Center, Cincinnati,
            OH (travelled)
1992-93 *Korun Kieli**, Gothenburg; Helsinki:
1992   *Design Visions*, Art Gallery of Western Australia, Perth
1989   *An Art Collection of Combs*, organized by Galerie Marzee,
            Nimwegen, The Netherlands (travelled)
        Craft Today: USA, Musée des Arts Décoratifs, Paris (travelled)
        Infinite Riches, Museum of Fine Arts, St Petersburg, FL, USA
        Ornamenta 1, Schmuckmuseum, Pforzheim, Germany
1987   *Schmuckszene '87*, Internationale Handwerksmesse, Munich
1986   *Craft Today: Poetry of the Physical*, American Craft Museum,
            New York (travelled)
        Form Beyond Function, Mitchell Museum, Mt. Vernon, IL
1986,83,79
        International Jewellery Art Exhibition, Tokyo Triennials
1984-87 *Modern Jewelry**, Philadelphia PA; Cleveland, OH; Honolulu,
            HI; Montreal
1984   *American Jewelry Now*, organized by the American Craft
            Museum, New York (travelled)
        *Contemporary Jewellery: The Americas, Australia, Europe and
            Japan*, National Museum of Modern Art, Kyoto; Tokyo
        Jewelry and Beyond: Metalwork by Members of SNAG, Mitchell
            Museum, Mount Vernon, IL
        Multiplicity in Clay, Fiber and Metal, Skidmore College,
            Saratoga Springs, NY
1981   *Good as Gold*, Renwick Gallery, NCFA, Smithsonian
            Institution, Washington, DC (travelled)

1980   *Robert L. Pfannebecker Collection*, Moore College of Art, Philadelphia, PA

1979   *SNAG – Gold- und Silberschmiedearbeiten*, Schmuckmuseum, Pforzheim, Germany (travelled)

1977   *Copper Brass Bronze Exhibition*, University of Arizona Museum of Art, Tucson

           The Metalsmith: SNAG Exhibition, Phoenix Museum of Art, AZ

1975   *Forms in Metal: 275 Years of Metalsmithing in America*, Museum of Contemporary Crafts, New York (travelled)

1974   *The Goldsmith*, Renwick Gallery, NCFA, Smithsonian Institution, Washington, DC

1965   *American Jewelry Today*, Everhart Museum, Scranton, PA

Related Professional Experience:

1991–   Professor, University of Michigan, Ann Arbor

1986–   Associate Dean, School of Art, University of Michigan, Ann Arbor

1981-85   Faculty, University of Michigan, Ann Arbor

Selected Public Collections:

American Craft Museum, New York; Art Gallery of Western Australia, Perth; Cranbrook Academy of Art, Bloomfield Hills, MI; Danner-Stiftung Collection, Munich; Georgia State University, Atlanta; Inge Asenbaum Collection, Vienna; Museum für angewandte Kunst, Vienna; National Museum of Modern Art, Kyoto; Texas Tech University, Lubbock; Wichita Art Museum, KS; Worshipful Company of Goldsmiths, London

---

Hiroko Sato Pijanowski

Born   January 1, 1942, Tokyo, Japan

Education:

1966-68   MFA, Cranbrook Academy of Art, Bloomfield Hills, MI

1960-64   BA, Rikkyo University (St. Paul's), Tokyo

Selected Awards:

1988   Grant, Michigan Council of the Arts, Detroit

1987   Herbert Hoffmann Prize, Schmuckszene '87, Internationale Handwerksmesse, Munich

1982   Grant, The Japan Foundation

1978,76,75

           Grants, National Endowment for the Arts, Washington, DC

Selected Exhibitions:

1994   *A Moveable Feast** Amsterdam; *Schmuck Unserer Zeit**, Zurich

1993   *Contemporary Jewelry**, Little Rock, AK

           Facet I, Kunsthal, Rotterdam

           Schmuck: Die Sammlung der Danner-Stiftung, Galerie für angewandte Kunst, Munich

           Sculptural Concerns, Contemporary Arts Center, Cincinnati, OH (travelled)

1992-93   *Korun Kieli**, Gothenburg; Helsinki

1992   *Design Visions*, Art Gallery of Western Australia, Perth

1990   *Triennale du Bijou*, Musée du Luxembourg, Paris

1989   *An Art Collection of Combs*, organized by Galerie Marzee, Nimwegen, The Netherlands (travelled)

           Craft Today: USA, Musée des Arts Décoratifs, Paris (travelled)

           Infinite Riches, Museum of Fine Arts, St Petersburg, FL, USA

           Ornamenta 1, Schmuckmuseum, Pforzheim, Germany

1987   *Craft as Content: National Metals Invitational*, University of Akron, OH

           Schmuckszene '87, Internationale Handwerksmesse, Munich

1986   *Craft Today: Poetry of the Physical*, American Craft Museum, New York (travelled)

           Form Beyond Function, Mitchell Museum, Mt Vernon, IL

1986,79   *International Jewellery Art Exhibition*, Tokyo Triennials

1984-87   *Modern Jewelry**, Philadelphia, PA; Cleveland, OH; Honolulu, HI; Montreal

1984   *American Jewelry Now*, organized by the American Craft Museum, New York (travelled)

           Contemporary Jewellery: The Americas, Australia, Europe and Japan, National Museum of Modern Art, Kyoto; Tokyo

           Jewelry and Beyond: Metalwork by Members of SNAG, Mitchell Museum, Mount Vernon, IL

           Multiplicity in Clay, Fiber and Metal, Skidmore College, Saratoga Springs, NY

1981   *Good as Gold*, Renwick Gallery, NCFA, Smithsonian Institution, Washington, DC (travelled)

1980   *Robert L. Pfannebecker Collection*, Moore College of Art, Philadelphia, PA

           Schmuck International 1900-1980, Künstlerhaus, Vienna

1979   *SNAG – Gold- und Silberschmiedearbeiten*, Schmuckmuseum, Pforzheim, Germany (travelled)

1978   *Art in Crafts: Works in Fiber, Clay and Metal by Women*, Bronx Museum, Bronx, NY

1977   *Copper Brass Bronze Exhibition*, University of Arizona Museum of Art, Tucson

           The Metalsmith: SNAG Exhibition, Phoenix Museum of Art, AZ

1975   *Forms in Metal: 275 Years of Metalsmithing in America*, Museum of Contemporary Crafts, New York (travelled)

1974   *The Goldsmith*, Renwick Gallery, NCFA, Smithsonian Institution, Washington, DC

Related Professional Experience:

1986–   Professor, University of Michigan, Ann Arbor

1978-85   Faculty, University of Michigan, Ann Arbor

Selected Public Collections:

American Craft Museum, New York; Art Gallery of Western Australia, Perth; Cranbrook Academy of Art, Bloomfield Hills, MI; Crocker Art Museum, Sacramento, CA; Danner-Stiftung Collection, Munich; Morikami Museum, Delray Beach, FL; Museum für angewandte Kunst, Vienna; National Museum of Modern Art, Kyoto, Japan; Nordenfjeldske Kunstindustrimuseum, Trondheim, Norway; Texas Tech University, Lubbock; Worshipful Company of Goldsmiths, London

Ramón Puig Cuyàs

Born: June 10, 1953, Mataró, Spain

Education:
1969-74 Escola Massana, Barcelona

Selected Awards:
1994 Herbert Hoffmann Prize, *Schmuckszene '94*, Internationale Handwerksmesse, Munich
1984 Herbert Hoffmann Prize, *Schmuck und Gerät*, Internationale Handwerksmesse, Munich
1981 Herbert Hoffmann Prize, *Internationale Schmuckschau*, Internationale Handwerksmesse,Munich

Selected Exhibitions:
1994 *In Touch*, Maihaugen, Lillehammer, Norway
A Moveable Feast*, Amsterdam; *Schmuck Unserer Zeit**, Zurich
1994,92 *Schmuckszene*, Internationale Handwerksmesse, Munich
1993 *The Art of Jewellery*, Setagaya Art Museum, Tokyo
Contemporary Crafts and the Saxe Collection, Toledo Museum of Art, OH (travelled)
Contemporary Jewelry*, Little Rock, AK
Facet I, Kunsthal, Rotterdam
Schmuck: Die Sammlung der Danner-Stiftung, Galerie für angewandte Kunst, Munich
Subjects, Design Forum, Helsinki
1992 *Design aus Spanien*, Museum für angewandte Kunst, Cologne
Triennale du Bijou, Musée des Arts Décoratifs, Paris
1989 *Jewelry: Means: Meaning*, University of Tennessee, Knoxville (travelled)
1987 *Joieria Europea Contemporània*, Fundació Caixa de Pensions, Barcelona,
Schmuck, Zeichen am Körper, Francisco Carolinum Museum, Linz, Austria
1986,83 *International Jewellery Art Exhibition*, Tokyo Triennials
1985 *Contemporary Jewelry Redefined*, Pittsburgh Center for the Arts, PA
Joies de Catalunya, Schmuckmuseum, Pforzheim, Germany
1985,84,81 *Internationale Schmuckschau*, Internationale Handwerksmesse, Munich
1984 *Contemporary Jewellery: The Americas, Australia, Europe and Japan*, National Museum of Modern Art, Kyoto; Tokyo
Jewelry International, American Craft Museum II, New York
1977 *Solo Exhibition*, Escola Massana, Barcelona

Related Professional Experience:
1977– Faculty, Escola Massana, Barcelona

Selected Public Collections:
Cooper-Hewitt, National Museum of Design, Smithsonian Institution, New York; Danner-Stiftung Collection, Munich; Kunstindustrimuseet, Copenhagen; Montreal Musée des Arts Décoratifs, Quebec; Museum für Kunst und Gewerbe, Hamburg; Nordenfjeldske Kunstindustrimuseum, Trondheim, Norway; Schmuckmuseum, Pforzheim, Germany

Robin Quigley

Born: October 11, 1947, New York, NY, USA

Education:
1976 MFA, Rhode Island School of Design, Providence
1974 BFA, Tyler School of Art, Temple University, Elkins Park, PA

Selected Awards:
1987,79 Fellowships, National Endowment for the Arts, Washington, DC

Selected Exhibitions:
1994 *A Moveable Feast**, Amsterdam; *Schmuck Unserer Zeit**, Zurich
1993 *Contemporary Jewelry**, Little Rock, AK
1992-93 *Korun Kieli**, Gothenburg; Helsinki
1992 *Design Visions*, Art Gallery of Western Australia, Perth
1989 *Craft Today: USA*, Musée des Arts Décoratifs, Paris (travelled)
1986 *Contemporary Arts: An Expanding View*, Monmouth Museum, Lincroft, NJ
Craft Today: Poetry of the Physical, American Craft Museum, New York (travelled)
1984-87 *Modern Jewelry**, Philadelphia, PA; Cleveland, OH; Honolulu, HI; Montreal
1985 *National Crafts Invitational*, Kent State University, OH
New Visions, Traditional Materials, Carnegie Institute Museum of Art, Pittsburgh, PA
Nya Smycken, Nya Material, Kulturhuset, Stockholm
1985,81,78 *Solo Exhibitions*, Helen Drutt Gallery, Philadelphia, PA
1984 *American Jewelry Now*, organized by the American Craft Museum, New York (travelled)
Jewelry USA, American Craft Museum II, New York
Multiplicity in Clay, Fiber and Metal, Skidmore College, Saratoga Springs, NY
1983 *International Jewellery Art Exhibition*, 5th Tokyo Triennial, Isetan Art Museum, Tokyo
1982 *Patterns*, Museum of Contemporary Crafts, New York
Production: Art/Craft/Design, Philadelphia College of Art, PA
1981 *Good as Gold*, Renwick Gallery, NCFA, Smithsonian Institution, Washington, DC (travelled)
1980 *Robert L. Pfannebecker Collection*, Moore College of Art, Philadelphia, PA
Schmuck International 1900-1980, Künstlerhaus, Vienna
1978 *Modern American Jewelry Exhibition*, Mikimoto and Co., Ltd. Gallery, Tokyo
Young Americans, Museum of Contemporary Crafts, New York
1974 *The Goldsmith*, Renwick Gallery, NCFA, Smithsonian Institution, Washington, DC

Related Professional Experience:
current   Faculty Assistant Professor, Rhode Island School of Design, Providence

---

Wendy Ramshaw

Born: May 26, 1939, Sunderland, England

Education:
1969   Central School of Art and Design, London
1960-61   ATD, Reading University, England
1956-60   NDD, Newcastle-upon-Tyne College of Art and Industrial Design, England

Selected Awards:
1993   OBE (Officer of the Order of the British Empire)
     Travelling Fellowship, Winston Churchill Memorial Trust
1984   Research Grant, Crafts Council, London
1975   Award, De Beers Competition, *Diamonds International*,
1972   Award, Council of Industrial Design, London

Selected Exhibitions:
1994   *Exhibition of Platinum Jewellery*, Worshipful Company of Goldsmiths, London
     A Moveable Feast*, Amsterdam; *Schmuck Unserer Zeit**, Zurich
1993   *Contemporary Jewelry**, Little Rock, AK
     David Watkins/Wendy Ramshaw, Musée d'Art Moderne et d'Art Contemporain, Nice
1992-93   *Korun Kieli**, Gothenburg; Helsinki
1992   *British Goldsmiths of Today*, Worshipful Company of Goldsmiths, London
     Triennale du Bijou, Musée des Arts Décoratifs, Paris
1991   *Exhibition of Platinum Jewellery*, Goldsmiths' Hall, London
1990   *Collecting for the Future*, Victoria and Albert Museum, London
     Triennale du Bijou, Musée du Luxembourg, Paris
     Wendy Ramshaw: From Paper to Gold, Royal Festival Hall, London
1989   *British Jewellery – German Jewellery*, Crafts Council Gallery, London (travelled)
     David Watkins: Xingu – Wendy Ramshaw: Picasso's Ladies, Scottish Gallery, Edinburgh (travelled)
     Jewelry: Means: Meaning, University of Tennessee, Knoxville (travelled)
     Ornamenta 1, Schmuckmuseum, Pforzheim, Germany
     Perth International Crafts Triennial, Art Gallery of Western Australia, Perth
1987   *Biennale du Bijou Contemporain*, Hotel du Sens, Paris
     Joieria Europea Contemporània, Fundació Caixa de Pensions, Barcelona
     Wendy Ramshaw – David Watkins: Schmuck – Jewellery, Schmuckmuseum, Pforzheim, Germany (travelled)

1986   *Contemporary Arts: An Expanding View*, Monmouth Museum, Lincroft, NJ
1985   *Body Works and Wearable Sculpture*, Visual Arts Center of Alaska, Anchorage
     New Tradition, British Crafts Centre, London
1984-87   *Modern Jewelry**, Philadelphia, PA; Cleveland, OH; Honolulu; Montreal
1984   *Contemporary Jewellery: The Americas, Australia, Europe and Japan*, National Museum of Modern Art, Kyoto; Tokyo
     Jewelry International, American Craft Museum II, New York
1983   *International Jewellery Art Exhibition*, 5th Tokyo Triennial, Isetan Art Museum, Tokyo
1982   *Jewellery Redefined*, British Crafts Centre, London
     Wendy Ramshaw, Victoria and Albert Museum, London
1982,73   *Schmuck – Tendenzen*, Schmuckmuseum, Pforzheim, Germany
1981   *50 Years of Design*, Design Centre, London
     Solo Exhibition, Jam Factory, Adelaide, South Australia
1980   *Email – Schmuck und Gerät in Geschichte und Gegenwart*, Schmuckmuseum, Pforzheim, Germany (travelled)
     Schmuck International 1900-1980, Künstlerhaus, Vienna
1978   *Solo Exhibition*, National Gallery of Victoria, Melbourne, Australia
1977   *Masterpiece: A Jubilee Exhibition of Crafts 1977*, British Crafts Centre, London
1975   *Jewellery in Europe*, Scottish Arts Council Gallery, Edinburgh (travelled)
1974   *In Praise of Hands*, Ontario Science Center, Toronto
1973   *Aspects of Jewellery*, Aberdeen Art Gallery and Museum, Scotland
     The Observer Jewellery Exhibition, National Museum of Wales, Cardiff (travelled)
     Wendy Ramshaw/David Watkins, Goldsmiths' Hall, London; AIA Gallery, Philadelphia, USA
1971   *Gold+Silber Schmuck+Gerät*, Norishalle, Nuremberg

Related Professional Experience:
1978   Artist-in-Residence, Western Australian Institute of Technology, Perth

Selected Public Collections:
Australian National Gallery, Canberra; Birmingham City Art Gallery and Museum, England; Contemporary Arts Society, London; Corning Museum of Glass, Corning, New York; Fonds National d'Art Contemporain, Paris; Kunstindustrimuseet, Oslo; Musée des Arts Décoratifs, Paris; Museum of Modern Art, Kyoto, Japan; National Gallery of Victoria, Melbourne, Australia; National Museum of Modern Art, Kyoto, Japan; National Museum of Wales, Cardiff; Philadelphia Museum of Art, PA; Royal Scottish Museum, Edinburgh; Schmuckmuseum, Pforzheim, Germany; Stedelijk Museum, Amsterdam; Victoria and Albert Museum, London; Worshipful Company of Goldsmiths, London

Debra Rapoport

Born: July 6, 1945,
New York, NY, USA

Education:
1969   MFA, University of California,
        Berkeley
1967   BFA, Carnegie Mellon University,
        Pittsburgh, PA

Selected Public Collections:
Boonshaft, Inc., New York;
Costume Institute, The
Metropolitan Museum of
Art, New York; Deutsch
Foundation, Belmont-sur-
Lausanne, Switzerland;
Musée des Beaux-Arts,
Lausanne

Selected Awards:
1976   Grant, National Endowment for the Arts, Washington, DC

Selected Exhibitions:
1994   *A Moveable Feast**, Amsterdam; *Schmuck Unserer Zeit**, Zurich
        Turning a Corner/Playing with an Open Heart, University of
        California, Davis
1993   *Ahead of Fashion: Hats of the 20th Century*, Philadelphia
        Museum of Art, PA
1992-93 *Korun Kieli**, Gothenburg; Helsinki
1991   *Fans*, Galerie Philharmonie, Liège
        Passion de fleurs et de vegeteaux, Musée des arts Décoratifs,
        Lausanne
1988   *Dreamworlds: Eight Artists from Australia and the United States*,
        San Diego State University, CA
1986   *Contemporary Arts: An Expanding View*, Monmouth Museum,
        Lincroft, NJ
        Craft Today: Poetry of the Physical, American Craft Museum,
        New York (travelled)
        Lam de Wolf/Debra Rapoport, Galerie Maya Behn, Zurich
        Legends in Fiber, Octagon Gallery for the Arts, Ames, IA
1985   *Architecture of Textiles*, University of California, Davis
        Contemporary Jewelry Redefined, Pittsburgh Center for the
        Arts, PA
        Interior Garden I, Helen Drutt Gallery, Philadelphia, PA
1984-87 *Modern Jewelry**, Philadelphia, PA; Cleveland, OH; Honolulu,
        HI; Montreal
1984   *American Jewelry Now*, organized by the American Craft
        Museum, New York (travelled)
        Jewelry USA, American Craft Museum II, New York
1983   *Paper: A New Artistic Language*, Musée des arts Décoratifs,
        Lausanne
        Solo Exhibition, Neil Isman Gallery, New York
1981   *Good as Gold*, Renwick Gallery, NCFA, Smithsonian
        Institution, Washington, DC (travelled)
1971   *The Metal Experience*, Oakland Museum, CA

Related Professional Experience:
1993–   Co-owner, A Tropical Fiber Paper Company, New York
1983–   In Situ Presentations, Floral Design Company, New York

Richard H. Reinhardt

Born: September 8, 1921, Philadelphia, PA, USA

Education:
1986   Doctor of Fine Arts, Honorus Causa, Philadelphia College
        of Art, PA
1948-49 Independent Study with Baron Eric Flemming, Court
        Silversmith to King of Sweden
1947   BAA, Philadelphia Museum School of Industrial Art, PA

Selected Awards:
1980   J.E. Caldwell, Inc., Philadelphia, PA
1975   Silver Star Award, Philadelphia College of Art, PA
1948   Handy and Harmon Award, National Silversmithing
        Competition,Providence, RI
1947   Alumni Award, Philadelphia College of Art, PA
1942,41 Art Education Prize, Philadelphia College of Art, PA

Selected Exhibitions:
1994   *A Moveable Feast**, Amsterdam; *Schmuck Unserer Zeit**, Zurich
1993   *Contemporary Jewelry**, Little Rock, AK
        Daley/Vaskys/Reinhardt, University of the Arts,
        Philadelphia, PA
1992-93 *Korun Kieli**, Gothenburg; Helsinki
1986   *Gold II Invitational*, Quadrum Gallery, Chestnut Hill, MA
1985   *Worked in Gold*, Quadrum Gallery, Chestnut Hill, MA
1984-87 *Modern Jewelry**, Philadelphia, PA; Cleveland, OH; Honolulu,
        HI; Montreal
1984   *Multiplicity in Clay, Fiber and Metal*, Skidmore College,
        Saratoga Springs, NY
        Solo Exhibition, Swan Gallery, Philadelphia, PA
1983   *Affects/Effects*, Philadelphia College of Art, PA
1983,80 *Solo Exhibitions*, Helen Drutt Gallery, Philadelphia, PA
1982   *Group Exhibition*, Philadelphia Art Alliance, PA
1978   *Wayne Bates/William Daley/Richard Reinhardt*, Helen Drutt
        Gallery, Philadelphia, PA

1950	*Richard Reinhardt/Virginia Cute* Philadelphia Art Alliance, PA
1949	*Handy and Harmon Workshop Exhibition,* The Metropolitan Museum of Art, New York
	University of Rochester, New York
	Detroit Institute of the Arts, MI
1948	*Richard Reinhardt/Virginia Cute,* Philadelphia Art Alliance, PA

Selected Commissions:

1984	*Academic Mace, President's Medallion,* Philadelphia College of Art, PA
1982	*Chafing Dish,* Pennsbury Manor, Morrisville, PA
1964,60,58	
	Offering Plates, Messiah Lutheran Church, Newtown Square, PA
1960	*Procession Cross,* Immanuel Lutheran Church, Philadelphia, PA
1958	*Board Room Table,* Magee Hospital, Philadelphia, PA
1957	*Board Room Table,* Lavino Shipping Co., Philadelphia, PA
1956	*Conference Tables,* E.I. Dupont De Nemours, Wilmington, DE
1950	*Trophy,* National Rifle Association, Washington, DC
1949	*Chalice,* Lutheran Mission Church, Corpus Christi, TX
	Flagon, St Aidian's Episcopal Church, Philadelphia, PA
	Large Pitcher, Huntington Valley Hunt Club, PA

Related Professional Experience:

1947-86	Faculty/Administration, Philadelphia College of Art, PA
1963-65	Co-founder/President, Industrial Design Educators Association, New York
1955–	Maintains independent studio, Newtown Square, PA

Selected Public Collections:
Philadelphia Museum of Art, PA; Renwick Gallery, NMAA, Smithsonian Institution, Washington, DC

Suzan Rezac

Born: June 27, 1958, Vrchlaby, Czechoslovakia

Education:

1983	MFA, Rhode Island School of Design, Providence
1981	BFA, Rhode Island School of Design, Providence

Selected Awards:

1984	Fellowship, National Endowment for the Arts, Washington, DC
1982	Honorable Mention, *Ornament* Magazine, Jewelry Competition Herbert Hoffmann Prize, *Material Schmuck und Gerät,* Internationale Handwerksmesse, Munich

Selected Exhibitions:

1994	*A Moveable Feast*,* Amsterdam; *Schmuck Unserer Zeit*,* Zurich
1993	*Contemporary Jewelry*,* Little Rock, AK

1992-93	*Korun Kieli*,* Gothenburg; Helsinki
1989	*Craft Today: USA,* Musée des Arts Décoratifs, Paris (travelled)
	Structure and Surface: Beads in Contemporary American Art, John Michael Kohler Arts Center, Sheboygan, WI
1986	*Contemporary Arts: An Expanding View,* Monmouth Museum, Lincroft, NJ
	Craft Today: Poetry of the Physical, American Craft Museum, New York (travelled)
1985	*Forty Four Alumni,* Museum of Art, Rhode Island School of Design, Providence
1984-87	*Modern Jewelry*,* Philadelphia, PA; Cleveland, OH; Honolulu, HI; Montreal
1984	*Jewelry International,* American Craft Museum II, New York
	Solo Exhibition, Helen Drutt Gallery, Philadelphia, PA
1983	*International Jewellery Art Exhibition,* 5th Tokyo Triennial, Isetan Art Museum, Tokyo
	Solo Exhibition, Musée de l'horlogerie et de l'emaillerie, Geneva, Switzerland
1983,82	*Material Schmuck und Gerät,* Internationale Handwerksmesse, Munich
1982	*Solo Exhibition,* Woods Gerry Gallery, Rhode Island School of Design, Providence

Selected Public Collections:
Museum of Art, Rhode Island School of Design, Providence, RI

Gerd Rothmann

Born: January 21, 1941, Frankfurt a.M., Germany

Education:
1961-64 Staatlichen Zeichenakademie, Hanau, Germany

Selected Awards:
1990 *Danner Preis '90,* Danner-Stiftung, Munich

Selected Exhibitions:

1994	*A Moveable Feast*,* Amsterdam; *Schmuck Unserer Zeit*,* Zurich
	Solo Exhibition, Galerie Fred Jahn, Munich
1993	*Contemporary Jewelry*,* Little Rock, AK
	Münchner Goldschmiede, Müncher Stadtmuseum, Munich
	Schmuck: Die Sammlung der Danner-Stiftung, Galerie für angewandte Kunst, Munich
	Schmuckmassnahmen, Deutsches Goldschmiedehaus, Hanau, Germany
1992-93	*Korun Kieli*,* Gothenburg; Helsinki
1992	*Neotoric Jewellery (Virgin),* Snug Harbor Cultural Center, Staten Island, NY
1991	*Europäisches Kunsthandwerk,* Haus de Wirtschaft, Stuttgart, Germany

1990   *Signatüren*, Stadtischen Museum, Schwäbisch Gmünd, Germany
1989   *Jewelry Means Meaning*, University of Tennessee, Knoxville
        (travelled)
        Perth International Crafts Triennial, Art Gallery of Western
        Australia, Perth
        *Zeitgenössische Schmuckkunst aus der Bundesrepublik
        Deutschland*, Instituts für Auslandsbeziehungen, Stuttgart
1989,85 *Solo Exhibitions*, Galerie Spektrum, Munich
1987   *Joieria Europea Contemporània*, Fundació Caixa de Pensions,
        Barcelona
        Körpersensationen, Vienna; Galerie Spektrum, Munich
1985   *New Tradition*, British Crafts Centre, London
1984-87 *Modern Jewelry**, Philadelphia, PA; Cleveland, OH; Honolulu,
        HI; Montreal
1984   *Contemporary Jewellery: The Americas, Australia, Europe and
        Japan*, National Museum of American Art, Tokyo; Kyoto
1983   *Körperkultur*, Galerie am Graben, Vienna
1982   *Body Prints*, Solo Exhibition, Electrum Gallery, London
        *Zeitgenossische Schmuckkunst aus der Bundesrepublik
        Deutschland*, Goethe Institute, Hong Kong
1981   *Körper-Schmuck-Zeichen-Raum*, Kunstgewerbemuseum, Zurich
1978   *3 Konzepte – 3 Goldschmiede: Bury/Jünger/Rothmann*,
        Hessisches Landesmuseum, Darmstadt, Germany
1976   *Solo Exhibition*, Landesmuseum, Oldenburg, Germany
1975   *Jewellery in Europe*, Scottish Arts Council Gallery, Edinburgh
        (travelled)
1973   Aspects of Jewellery, Aberdeen Art Gallery and Museum,
        Schmuck '73 – Tendenzen, Schmuckmuseum, Pforzheim, Germany

Selected Public Collections:
Danner-Stiftung Collection, Munich; Deutsches Goldschmiedehaus,
Hanau, Germany; Landesmuseum, Oldenburg, Germany; Müncher
Stadtmuseum, Munich; Museum für angewandte Kunst, Vienna; Museum
für Kunst und Gewerbe, Hamburg; Museum of Modern Art, New York;
National Museum of Modern Art, Tokyo; Schmuckmuseum, Pforzheim;
Stedelijk Museum, Amsterdam; Victoria and Albert Museum, London

1992   *Sieraden*, Centrum Beeldende Kunst, Groningen, The Netherlands
        Triennale du Bijou, Musée des Arts Décoratifs, Paris
1991   *Arsenale*, Museum für Kunsthandwerk, Frankfurt a.M.,
        Beauty is a Story, Museum Het Kruithuis, 's-Hertogenbosch,
        The Netherlands
        Europäisches Kunsthandwerk, Haus de Wirtschaft, Stuttgart
        Neoteric Jewelry, Snug Harbor Cultural Center, Staten Island, NY
1990   *Kunst Rai*, Galerie Marzee, Amsterdam
        L'Arte della Gioia, Pedrocchi, Padua
        Triennale du Bijou, Musée du Luxembourg, Paris
1989   *Ornamenta 1*, Schmuckmuseum, Pforzheim, Germany
        symboliek in het moderne en antieke sieraad, Allard Pierson
        Museum, Amsterdam
1988,87,86
        Solo Exhibitions, Galerie Louise Smit, Amsterdam
1987   *Holland in Vorm*, Gemeentemuseum, Arnhem, The Netherlands
        Schmuckszene '87, Internationale Handwerksmesse, Munich
1985   *6 Dutch Jewellery Designers*, Nordenfjeldske
        Kunstindustrimuseum, Trondheim, Norway

Selected Public Collections:
Gemeentelijke van Reekummuseum, Apeldoorn, The Netherlands;
Gemeentemuseum, Arnhem, The Netherlands; Museum Het Kruithuis,
's-Hertogenbosch, The Netherlands; Stedelijk Museum, Amsterdam

Philip Sajet

Born: October 15, 1953, Amsterdam, The Netherlands

Education:
1977-81 Gerrit Rietveld Academie, Amsterdam

Selected Exhibitions:
1994   *Philip Sajet: Elf Colliers*, Stedelijk Museum, Amsterdam
1994,93,91
        Solo Exhibitions, Galerie Carin Delcourt van Krimpen, Rotterdam
1993   *Facet I*, Kunsthal, Rotterdam
        Les Grandes Epoques de la Bague, Musée d'Art Moderne et
        d'Art Contemporain, Nice

Marjorie Schick

Born: August 29, 1941, Taylorville, IL, USA

Education:
1966   MFA, Indiana University, Bloomington
1963   BS, University of Wisconsin, Madison

Selected Awards:
1990   Distinguished Alumni Award, Indiana University School of
        Fine Arts, Bloomington
1985   Fellowship award in Crafts, Mid-America Arts
        Alliance/National Endowment for the Arts

1983   Prize, *International Jewellery Art Exhibition*, Isetan Art
Museum, Tokyo

Selected Exhibitions:
1994   *Individual Objects*, Montana State University, Bozeman
*KPMG Peat Marwick Collection of American Craft: A Gift to the
Renwick*, Renwick Gallery, NMAA, Smithsonian
Institution, Washington, DC
A Moveable Feast*, Amsterdam; *Schmuck Unserer Zeit**, Zurich
1993   *Ahead of Fashion: Hats of the 20th Century*, Philadelphia
Museum of Art, PA
The Art of Jewelry, Setagaya Art Museum, Tokyo
The Body Adorned, University of Texas, El Paso
Contemporary Jewelry*, Little Rock, AK
Contemporary Metal: Form and Narrative, University of Illinois,
Urbana-Champaign
Subjects, Design Forum, Helsinki
1992-93 *Korun Kieli**, Gothenburg; Helsinki
1992   *Design Visions*, Art Gallery of Western Australia, Perth
1990   *Building a Permanent Collection: A Perspective on the 1980's*,
American Craft Museum, New York
A Retrospective, Indiana University, Bloomington
1989   *Craft Today: USA*, Musée des Arts Décoratifs, Paris (travelled)
Jewelry: Means: Meaning, University of Tennessee, Knoxville
(travelled)
Ornamenta 1, Schmuckmuseum, Pforzheim, Germany
Solo Exhibition, Nordenfjeldske Kunstindustrimuseum,
Trondheim, Norway
1988   *Dreamworlds: Eight Artists from Australia and the United States*,
San Diego State University, CA
Hong-ik Metalcrafts Association Annual Exhibition, Walker Hill
Art Center Museum, Seoul, Korea
1987   *Bodyworks*, Solo Exhibition, University of Oklahoma, Norman
The Eloquent Object, Philbrook Museum of Art, Tulsa, OK
(travelled)
Schmuckszene '87, Internationale Handwerksmesse, Munich
1986   *Craft Today: Poetry of the Physical*, American Craft Museum,
New York (travelled)
Sieraad Vorm en Idee, Gemeentelijke van Reekummuseum,
Apeldoorn, The Netherlands
1986,83 *International Jewellery Art Exhibition*, Tokyo Triennials
1985   *6. Internationaler Wettbewerb – Schmuck für Kopf und Haar*,
Schmuckmuseum, Pforzheim, Germany
New Tradition, British Crafts Centre, London
Nya Smycken, Nya Material, Kulturhuset, Stockholm
1985,84 *Internationale Schmuckschau*, Internationale Handwerksmesse,
Munich
1984-87 *Modern Jewelry**, Philadelphia, PA; Cleveland, OH; Honolulu,
HI; Montreal
1984   *Celebration '84*, Art Gallery at Harbourfront, Toronto, Canada
(travelled)
*Contemporary Jewellery: The Americas, Australia, Europe and
Japan*, National Museum of Modern Art, Kyoto; Tokyo
Jewelry and Beyond: Metalwork by Members of SNAG, Mitchell
Museum, Mount Vernon, IL

1984   *Jewelry USA*, American Craft Museum II, New York
1983   *10 Jewelers*, Gemeentelijke van Reekummuseum, Apeldoorn,
The Netherlands
1982   *Jewellery Redefined*, British Crafts Centre, London
1970   *Goldsmith '70: SNAG Inaugural Exhibition*, Minnesota Museum
of Art, St Paul (travelled)
1967   *American Jewelry Today*, Everhart Museum, Scranton, PA

Related Professional Experience:
1967–   Professor, Pittsburg State University, KS

Selected Public Collections:
American Craft Museum, New York; Cleveland County Museum,
Middlesborough, England; Gemeentelijke van Reekummuseum,
Apeldoorn, The Netherlands; Indiana University Fine Arts Museum,
Bloomington; John Michael Kohler Art Center, Sheboygan, WI;
Kunstindustrimuseet, Oslo; National Museum of Contemporary Art,
Seoul, South Korea; National Museum of Modern Art, Kyoto;
Nordenfjeldske Kunstindustrimuseum, Trondheim, Norway; Renwick
Gallery, NMAA, Smithsonian Institution, Washington, DC

Bernhard Schobinger

Born: January 18, 1946, Zurich, Switzerland

Education:
1968–   Maintains independent studio, Richterswil, Switzerland
1963-67 Goldsmith, E. Kundig & Co., Zurich
1962-63 Kunstgewerbeschule, Zurich

Selected Awards:
1972   Deutscher Schmuck und Edelsteinpreis, Oberstein, Germany
1971   Eidgenossisches Stipendium fur angewandte Kunst
1970,69 International De Beers Diamond Award, New York

Selected Exhibitions:
1994   *A Moveable Feast**, Amsterdam; *Schmuck Unserer Zeit**, Zurich
1993   *Contemporary Jewelry**, Little Rock, AK
Facet I, Kunsthal, Rotterdam
1992-93 *Korun Kieli**, Gothenburg; Helsinki
1991   *Group Exhibition*, Grassimuseum, Leipzig
Neotoric Jewellery, Snugharbor, Cultural Center, New York
City, NY
1990   *Solo Exhibition*, Galerie Ziegler, Zurich
Zeitgenössisches deutsches Kunsthandwerk, C. Voegele, Museum
für Kunsthandwerk, Frankfurt a.M.
1989   *An Art Collection of Combs*, organized by Galerie Marzee,
Nimwegen, The Netherlands (travelled)
Jewelry: Means: Meaning, University of Tennessee, Knoxville
(travelled)

| 1988 | *Tragezeichen*, Museum Schloss Morsbroich, Leverkusen, Germany |

1988   *Tragezeichen*, Museum Schloss Morsbroich, Leverkusen, Germany
1987   *Joieria Europea Contemporània*, Fundació Caixa de Pensions, Barcelona
1985   *Grossformate*, Peter Noser Galerie, Zurich
        Vorschau/Ruckschau, Peter Noser Galerie, Zurich
1984   *Contemporary Jewellery: The Americas, Australia, Europe and Japan*, National Museum of Modern Art, Kyoto, Tokyo
1983,79 *Triennial International Jewellery Arts*, Tokyo
1982   *Solo Exhibition*, Electrum Gallery, London
        Swiss Avantgarde, Galerie Nouvelles Images, The Hague
1981   *Solo Exhibition*, Kunsthaus Aarau
1978   *Solo Exhibition*, Museum Bellerive, Zurich
1973   *International Jewellery Art Exhibition*, 2nd Tokyo Triennial, Seibu Gallery, Tokyo

Selected Public Collections:
Grassimuseum, Leipzig, Germany; Wurttembergisches, Landesmuseum, Stuttgart; Sammlung C. Vögele, Pfaffikon, Switzerland; Stedelijk Museum, Amsterdam

Deganit Schocken

Born: November 21, 1947, Kibbutz Amir, Israel

Education:
1977-79 Middlesex Polytechnic, Hornsey School of Art, London
1974-76 Sir John Cass School of Art, London
1968-73 Bezalel Academy of Art and Design, Jerusalem

Selected Awards:
1990   Commendation, *Using Gold and Silver*, Stadtischen Museum, Schwäbisch Gmünd, Germany
1979   Commendation, De Beers Competition, *Diamonds Tomorrow*, London

Selected Exhibitions:
1994   *Tel Aviv in the tracks of the Bauhaus*, Ha Haretz, Tel Aviv
1994   *Israeli Contemporary Crafts*, National Museum of Modern Art, Kyoto
        Local Goddesses, The Museum of the History of Jerusalem, Israel
        A Moveable Feast*, Amsterdam; *Schmuck Unserer Zeit**, Zurich
1993   *Contemporary Jewelry**, Little Rock, AK
1992-93 *Korun Kieli**, Gothenburg; Helsinki
1992   *Stone – Touch – Jewelry*, Oppenheimer Diamond Museum, Ramat Gan, Israel
        Triennale du Bijou, Musée des Arts Décoratifs, Paris
1991   *Twentieth Anniversary*, Electrum Gallery, London
1990   *Schmuckszene '90*, Internationale Handwerksmesse, Munich
        Triennale du Bijou, Musée du Luxembourg, Paris

1990   *Signaturen: Using Gold and Silver*, Stadtischen Museum, Schwäbisch Gmünd, Germany
1988   *Amulett & Talisman*, Stadtischen Museum, Schwäbisch Gmünd, Germany (travelled)
        Bezalel Graduates, Israel Museum, Jerusalem
1987   *Schmuck in Bewegung, Bewegung in Schmuck*, Deutsches Goldschmiedehaus, Hanau, Germany
1986   *Contemporary Arts: An Expanding View*, Monmouth Museum of Art, Lincroft, NJ
1985   *6. Internationaler Wettbewerb – Schmuck für Kopf und Haar*, Schmuckmuseum, Pforzheim, Germany
1984-87 *Modern Jewelry**, Philadelphia, PA; Cleveland, OH; Honolulu, HI; Montreal
1984   *Jewelry International*, American Craft Museum II, New York
1983   *International Jewellery Art Exhibition*, 5th Tokyo Triennial, Isetan Art Museum, Tokyo
1976   *Bezalel 70+*, Tel Aviv Museum of Art, Israel (travelled)

Related Professional Experience:
1991–   Instructor, Bloomfield College of Art and Design, Haifa
1985-89 Instructor, Bezalel Academy of Art and Design, Jerusalem

Selected Public Collections:
The Brooklyn Museum, New York; Israel Museum, Jerusalem; Nordenfjeldske Kunstindustrimuseum, Trondheim, Norway

Joyce J. Scott

Born: November 15, 1948, Baltimore, MD, USA

Education:
1971   MFA, Instituto Allende, San Miguel de Allende, Guanajuato, Mexico
1966-70 BFA, Maryland Institute College of Art, Baltimore

Selected Awards:
1994   Visual Studies Workshop, Rochester, NY
1992   Art Matters Inc., New York
1990   National Printmaking Fellowship, Rutgers Center for Innovative Printmaking, New Brunswick, NJ
1988   Fellowship, National Endowment for the Arts, Washington, DC

Selected Exhibitions:
1994   *Bad Girls*, New Museum of Contemporary Art, New York
        Hard Choices, Solo Exhibition and Site-Specific Installation, Laumeier Sculpture Park, St Louis, MO
        A Moveable Feast*, Amsterdam; *Schmuck Unserer Zeit**, Zurich
        World Glass Now '94, Hokkaido Museum of Modern Art, Sapporo, Japan
1993   *Ahead of Fashion: Hats of the 20th Century*, Philadelphia Museum of Art, PA

Related Professional Experience:
1992   Artist-in-Residence, Pilchuk Glass School, Seattle, WA
1990   Artist-in-Residence/Distinguished Visiting Professor, University
        of Delaware, Newark
1987   Artist-in-Residence, The Mid-Atlantic Consortium Grant,
        Pyramid Atlantic, Tacoma Park, MD

Selected Public Collections:
American Craft Museum, New York; The Baltimore Museum of
Art, MD; The Bannecker-Douglass Museum, Annapolis, MD;
The Mint Museum of Art, Charlotte, NC; Museum Het Kruithuis,
's-Hertogenbosch, The Netherlands; Pennsylvania Convention Center,
Philadelphia; Philbrook Museum of Art, Tulsa, OK

1993   *American Quilt Festival 4*, Museum of American Folk Art,
            New York
            Connected Passages, Afro-American Historical and Cultural
            Museum, Philadelphia, PA
            Subservice Crafts, Massachusetts Institute of Technology,
            Cambridge
            Uncommon Beauty in Common Objects, National Afro-
            American Museum and Cultural Center, Wilberforce, OH
            (travelled)
            USA-Today: In Fibre Art, Nederlands Textielmuseum, Tilburg,
            The Netherlands
1992-93   *Korun Kieli**, Gothenburg; Helsinki
1992   *Accounts Southeast: Joyce J. Scott*, Southeastern Center for
            Contemporary Art, Winston-Salem, NC
            Brilliant Stories: American Narrative Jewelry, USIS Exhibition
            Hall, Amman, Jordan (travelled)
            The New Narrative: Contemporary Fiber Art, North Carolina
            State University, Raleigh
            Of Power, Magic, and Memory, Bellevue Art Museum, WA
            Present Tense, University of Wisconsin, Milwaukee
            Solo Exhibition, Brooklyn College, NY
            Solo Exhibition, Drew University, Madison, NJ
1991   *Beauty is a Story*, Museum Het Kruithuis,
            's-Hertogenbosch, The Netherlands
            I Con Nobody/Iconography, Solo Exhibition, The Corcoran
            Gallery of Art, Washington, DC
            Places with a Past: New Site Specific Art in Charleston, Spoleto
            Festival USA, Charleston, SC
1990   *American Dreams, American Extremes*, Museum Het Kruithuis,
            's-Hertogenbosch, The Netherlands
            Explorations: The Aesthetic of Excess, American Craft Museum,
            New York
            Southern Black Aesthetic, Southeastern Center for
            Contemporary Art, Winston-Salem, NC (travelled)
1989   *Craft Today: USA*, Musée des Arts Décoratifs, Paris (travelled)
            Structure and Surface: Beads in Contemporary American Art,
            John Michael Kohler Arts Center, Sheboygan, WI
1987   *The Eloquent Object*, Philbrook Museum of Art, Tulsa, OK
            (travelled)

Heikki Seppä

Born: August, 3, 1927,
              Vijpuri, Finland

Education:
1960-61   Cranbrook Academy
          of Art, Bloomfield Hills,
          MI
1941-45   Golsmith School of
          Helsinki, Finland
          Central School of
          Industrial Art of
          Finland, Helsinki

Selected Awards:
1992   Gold Medal for Professional Loyalty, Finland
1987   Elected, College of Fellows, American Crafts Council
1964   Master Status, Ministry of Education, Finland

Selected Exhibitions:
1994   *A Moveable Feast**, Amsterdam; *Schmuck Unserer Zeit**, Zurich
1993   *Lifetime Achievements: The ACC College of Fellows in Metal*,
            National Ornamental Metal Museum, Memphis, TN
1992-93   *Korun Kieli**, Gothenburg; Helsinki
1989   *Infinite Riches*, Museum of Fine Arts, St Petersburg, FL, USA
1988   *The Founding Masters: SNAG Exhibition*, Skidmore College,
            Saratoga Springs, NY
1984-87   *Modern Jewelry**, Philadelphia PA; Cleveland, OH; Hawaii, HI;
            Montreal
1984   *Jewelry and Beyond: Metalwork by Members of SNAG*, Mitchell
            Museum, Mount Vernon, IL
            Precious Objects, Worcester Crafts Center, MA
1979   *Contemporary Silversmiths*, Museum of Fine Arts,
            St Petersburg, FL, USA
            SNAG – Gold- und Silberschmiedearbeiten, Schmuckmuseum,
            Pforzheim, Germany (travelled)

1978 *Rattlesnakes*, Goldsmiths' Hall, London
1977 *The Metalsmith: SNAG Exhibition*, Phoenix Museum of
Art, AZ
1975 *Precious Metals*, University of Miami, Coral Gables, FL
1974 *American Metalsmiths*, DeCordova Museum, Lincoln, MA
The Goldsmith, Renwick Gallery, NCFA, Smithsonian
Institution, Washington, DC
1971 *Jewellery '71*, Art Gallery of Ontario, Toronto
1970 *Goldsmith '70: SNAG Inaugural Exhibition*, Minnesota Museum
of Art, St Paul (travelled)
1965 *American Jewelry Today*, Everhart Museum, Scranton, PA
1964 *Jewelry '64: An International Exhibition*, State University
College, Plattsburg, NY

Related Professional Experience:
1965-92 Professor, Washington University, St Louis, MO

Selected Public Collections:
City Art Museum, St Louis, MO; Cranbrook Academy of Art, Bloomfield
Hills, MI; Evansville Museum of Arts and Sciences, IL; Kent State
University, OH; St Louis Art Museum, MO; Texas Tech University,
Lubbock; University of Illinois, Normal; University of Texas, El Paso;
Washington University, St Louis, MO

Stephan Seyffert

Born: August 6, 1960, Kaiserslautern, Germany

Education:
1992–   Establishes independent atelier, Karlsruhe
1990-91   Akademie der Bildenden Kunste, Karlsruhe
1985-89   Fachhochschule für Gestaltung, Pforzheim, Germany

Selected Exhibitions:
1994 *A Moveable Feast**, Amsterdam
waar heb je al die tijd GEZETEN, Verzameled Werk, Ghent
Clean a way, Akademie der Schonen Kunste, Institute, Berlin
Solo Exhibition, Verzamelt Werk, Ghent
1993 *Gold ist gut, Kuchen ist besser*, Kunsthesser, Nuremberg
Das Magazin, Gesellschaft der Freunde junger Kunst Institute,
Baden-Baden
Solo Exhibition, Werkstattgalerie, Berlin
1992-93 *Solo Exhibition*, Galerie Ra, Amsterdam
1992 *Group Exhibition*, Werkstattgalerie, Berlin
Solo Exhibition, Schmuckgalerie Cardillac, Karlsruhe
1991 *Installation*, Orgelfabrik, Karlsruhe
1989 *Group Exhibition*, Galerie Mattar, Cologne
1988 *Group Exhibition*, Galerie GU, Barcelona
1987 *Group Exhibition*, Gallerie Cebra, Dusseldorf

Miriam Sharlin

Born: June 17, 1952,
Hackensack, NJ, USA

Education:
1976   BFA, State University of
New York, New Paltz
1971-72   Bennington College, VT

Selected Awards:
1982   Herbert Hoffmann
Prize, *Material Schmuck
und Gerät*, Internationale
Handwerksmesse,
Munich

Selected Exhibitions:
1994 *Schmuck Unserer Zeit**, Zurich
1992-93 *Korun Kieli**, Gothenburg; Helsinki
1985 *Attitudes*, International Cultureel Centrum, Antwerp
(travelled)
Miriam Sharlin/Deganit Schocken, Galerie in der Hofstatt,
Marbourg, Germany
New Visions, Traditional Materials, Carnegie Institute Museum
of Art, Pittsburgh, PA
1985,82,79,78,77
Internationale Schmuckschau, Internationale Handwerksmesse,
Munich
1984-87 *Modern Jewelry**, Philadelphia, PA; Cleveland, OH; Honolulu,
HI; Montreal
1984 *Jewelry International*, American Craft Museum II, New York
Solo Exhibition, Die Werkstattgalerie, Berlin
Solo Exhibition, Galerie Britta Heberle, Frankfurt a.M.
1983 *Solo Exhibition*, Museum of Art, Rhode Island School of
Design, Providence
1982 *Die Kette*, Deutsches Goldschmiedehaus, Hanau, Germany
Schmuck '82 – Tendenzen, Schmuckmuseum, Pforzheim,
Germany
1981 *Elisabeth Holder/Miriam Sharlin*, Electrum Gallery, London
Solo Exhibition, Concepts, Carmel, CA
1981,77 *Solo Exhibitions*, Galerie Orfevre, Dusseldorf
1980 *Schmuck International 1900-1980*, Künstlerhaus, Vienna
1979 *Solo Exhibition*, Helen Drutt Gallery, Philadelphia, PA
1975 *Metals Invitational, 1975 AD*, State University of New York,
New Paltz (travelled)

Selected Public Collections:
Schmuckmuseum, Pforzheim, Germany

Helen Shirk

Born: January 25, 1942, Kenmore, NY, USA

Education:
1969 MFA, Indiana University, Bloomington
1963-64 Kunsthaandvaerkerskolen, Copenhagen
1963 BS, Skidmore College, Saratoga Springs, NY

Selected Awards:
1988,78 Fellowships, National Endowment for the Arts, Washington, DC
1982 First Prize, *Ornament* Magazine, Jewelry Competition
1963 Fulbright Fellowship, Copenhagen

Selected Exhibitions:
1994 *Contemporary Metalsmithing: Behind and Beyond the Bench*, Craft Alliance, St Louis, MI
Jewels and Gems: Collecting California Jewelry, Oakland Museum, CA
A Moveable Feast*, Amsterdam; *Schmuck Unserer Zeit**, Zurich
1993 *Contemporary Jewelry**, Little Rock, AK
Contemporary Metal: Form and Narrative, University of Illinois, Urbana-Champaign
Metal '93 Invitational, State University of New York, Brockport
Sculptural Concerns, Contemporary Arts Center, Cincinnati, OH (travelled)
1992-93 *Korun Kieli**, Gothenburg; Helsinki
1992 *Design Visions*, Art Gallery of Western Australia, Perth
1990 *California Metal Forms '90*, California Crafts Museum, San Francisco
Progressive Metals, Monterey Peninsula Museum of Art, Monterey, CA
1989 *Craft Today: USA*, Musée des Arts Décoratifs, Paris (travelled)
Helen Shirk: Twenty Years, National Ornamental Metal Museum, Memphis, TN
Skidmore 1989: Five Goldsmiths, Helen Drutt Gallery, Philadelphia, PA
1988 *By Hammer and Hand: Four Contemporary Silversmiths and Metalworkers*, Los Angeles County Museum, Los Angeles, CA
1986 *Contemporary Arts: An Expanding View*, Monmouth Museum, Lincroft, NJ
Craft Today: Poetry of the Physical, American Craft Museum, New York (travelled)
1985 *New Visions, Traditional Materials*, Carnegie Institute Museum of Art, Pittsburgh, PA
1984-87 *Modern Jewelry**, Philadelphia, PA; Cleveland, OH; Honolulu, HI; Montreal
1984 *Contemporary Jewellery: The Americas, Australia, Europe and Japan*, National Museum of Modern Art, Kyoto; Tokyo
The Great West Jewelry/Metal Exhibition, Northern Arizona University, Flagstaff
Jewelry USA, American Craft Museum II, New York
1984 *Multiplicity in Clay, Fiber and Metal*, Skidmore College, Saratoga Springs, NY
Schmuck und Gerät, Internationale Handwerksmesse, Munich
1982 *Schmuck '82 – Tendenzen*, Schmuckmuseum, Pforzheim, Germany
1981 *Good as Gold*, Renwick Gallery, NCFA, Smithsonian Institution, Washington, DC (travelled)
Helen Shirk: Metal Forms and Jewelry, Grossmont College, El Cajon, CA
Two Decades of Metal, San Diego State University, CA
1980 *5. Internationaler Wettbewerb-Armschmuck*, Schmuckmuseum, Pforzheim, Germany
Progressions IV: Helen Shirk and Bea Wax, California Crafts Museum, CA
Robert L. Pfannebecker Collection, Moore College of Art, Philadelphia, PA
1979 *SNAG – Gold- und Silberschmiedearbeiten*, Schmuckmuseum, Pforzheim, Germany (travelled)
1977 *The Metalsmith: SNAG Exhibition*, Phoenix Museum of Art, AZ
1974 *The Goldsmith*, Renwick Gallery, NCFA, Smithsonian Institution, Washington, DC
1970 *Goldsmith '70: SNAG Inaugural Exhibition*, Minnesota Museum of Art, St Paul (travelled)
1967 *American Jewelry Today*, Everhart Museum, Scranton, PA
1962 *Young Americans*, Museum of Contemporary Crafts, New York

Related Professional Experience:
1975– Professor, San Diego State University, CA

Selected Public Collections:
American Craft Museum, New York; Carnegie Institute, Museum of Art, Pittsburgh, PA; The Contemporary Museum, Honolulu, HI; Indianapolis Museum of Art, IN; Memphis Brooks Museum of Art, Memphis, TN; Minnesota Museum of Art, St Paul; National Museum of Modern Art, Kyoto; Oakland Museum, CA; Philadelphia Museum of Art, PA; Renwick Gallery, NMAA, Smithsonian Institution, Washington, DC; Schmuckmuseum, Pforzheim, Germany

---

Olaf Skoogfors

Born: June 27, 1930, Bredsjo, Sweden; Gustav Olaf Jansson
1934 anglicized surname Jansson to Johnson
1945 changed surname Johnson to Skoogfors (meaning 'forest stream')
Died: December 20, 1975, Philadelphia, PA, USA

Education:
1955-57 School for American Craftsmen, Rochester Institute of Technology, NY
1949-53 Philadelphia Museum School of Art, PA

Selected Awards:
1967 Grant, Louis Comfort Tiffany Foundation
1965 Good Design Award, American Jewelry Today, Everhart Museum, Scranton, PA

Olaf Skoogfors

Selected Exhibitions:

1994   *A Moveable Feast**, Amsterdam; *Schmuck Unserer Zeit**, Zurich
1993   *Contemporary Jewelry**, Little Rock, AK
1992-93 *Korun Kieli**, Gothenburg; Helsinki
1989   *Infinite Riches*, Museum of Fine Arts, St Petersburg, FL, USA
1988   *The Founding Masters: SNAG Exhibition*, Skidmore College, Saratoga Springs, NY
1986   *Contemporary Arts: An Expanding View*, Monmouth Museum, Lincroft, NJ
1984-87 *Modern Jewelry**, Philadelphia, PA; Cleveland, OH; Honolulu, HI; Montreal
1980   *Robert L. Pfannebecker Collection*, Moore College of Art, Philadelphia, PA
1979   *Olaf Skoogfors: 20th-Century Goldsmith, 1930-1975*, Philadelphia College of Art, PA; Renwick Gallery, NCFA, Smithsonian Institution, Washington, DC
1978   *Contemporary Jewelry from the Permanent Collection*, Museum of Contemporary Crafts, New York
1977   *Memorial Exhibition*, University of Washington, Seattle
1976   *American Metal Work 1976*, University of Nebraska, Lincoln
        Four Goldsmiths, Pennsylvania State University, University Park
        Philadelphia: Three Centuries of American Art, Philadelphia Museum of Art, PA
1975   *4th Invitational Contemporary Crafts Exhibit*, Skidmore College, Saratoga Springs, NY
        Precious Metals, University of Miami, Coral Gables, FL
        Solo Exhibition, Helen Drutt Gallery, Philadelphia, PA
1974   *American Metalsmiths*, DeCordova Museum, Lincoln, MA
        Masterworks of the '70's: Jewelers, Weavers, Albright-Knox Art Gallery, Buffalo, NY
        Metal '74, State University of New York, Brockport
        A Touch of Gold, Philadelphia Museum of Art, PA
1973,70 *International Jewellery Art Exhibition*, Tokyo Triennials
1972   *International Invitational Jewelry Exhibition*, Zlatarna-Celje, Yugoslavia
1971   *Gold+Silber Schmuck+Gerät*, Norishalle, Nuremberg
        Jewellery '71, Art Gallery of Ontario, Toronto
        Schmuck – Objekte, Museum Bellerive, Zurich
1970   *Goldsmith '70: SNAG Inaugural Exhibition*, Minnesota Museum of Art, St Paul (travelled)
1970,67 *Schmuck – Tendenzen*, Schmuckmuseum, Pforzheim, Germany
1969   *Objects: USA*, National Collection of Fine Arts, Smithsonian Institution, Washington, DC (travelled)
1969,66,65
        Form und Qualität, Internationale Handwerksmesse, Munich
1968   *The American Contemporary Jewelry Exhibition*, Odakyu Department Store, Tokyo
        Objects Are...?, Museum of Contemporary Crafts, New York
        Olaf Skoogfors/Stanley Lechtzin, William Penn Memorial Museum, Harrisburg, PA
        Solo Exhibition, Museum of Contemporary Crafts, New York
1965   *American Jewelry Today*, Everhart Museum, Scranton, PA

1962   *Fibre/Clay/Metal*, St Paul Arts Center, St Paul, MN
1960   *Solo Exhibition*, Philadelphia Art Alliance, PA
1957   *American Jewelry and Related Objects*, University of Rochester, NY (travelled)

Related Professional Experience:

1970   Founding Member, Society of North American Goldsmiths, St Paul, MN
1969   Member/Delegate/Vice President, United States Committee, World Crafts Council
1967-74 Founding Member/Past President, Philadelphia Council of Professional Craftsmen, PA
1966-75 Faculty, Philadelphia College of Art, PA
1959-75 Professor, Philadelphia Museum College of Art, PA

Selected Public Collections:

American Craft Museum, New York; Cooper-Hewitt National Museum of Design, Smithsonian Institution, New York; Delaware Museum of Art, Wilmington; Georgia State University, Atlanta; Minnesota Museum of Art, St Paul; Musée des Arts Décoratifs, Montreal; Renwick Gallery, NMAA, Smithsonian Institution, Washington, DC; Philadelphia Museum of Art, PA; Schmuckmuseum, Pforzheim, Germany; Yale University Mueum, New Haven, CN

Peter Skubic

Born: August 11, 1935, Gornji-Milanovac, Yugoslavia

Education:
1954-58 Akademie für angewandte Kunst, Vienna
1952-54 Fachschule für Metallkunstgewerbe, Steyr, Austria

Selected Awards:
1978   Preis der Stadt Wien, Austria
1977   Dr-Theodor-Körner-Preis, Austria
1976   Goldene Ehrenmedaille, Künstlerhaus, Vienna
1973   Förderpreis, Zentralsparkasse der Gemeinde, Vienna

Selected Exhibitions:
1994   *A Moveable Feast**, Amsterdam; *Schmuck Unserer Zeit**, Zurich
        Kolngold, Museum fur Angewandte Kunst, Cologne
1993   *Facet I*, Kunsthal, Rotterdam
        Subjects, Design Forum, Helsinki
1992   *Joies Indissenyables*, Escola Massana, Barcelona
1991   *Capitales Europeannes du Nouveau Design*, Centre George Pompidou, Paris

1990   *Haarsträubend*, Museum für angewandte Kunst, Cologne
        Solo Exhibition, Contacto Directo Galeria, Lisbon
        Triennale du Bijou, Musée du Luxembourg, Paris
1989   *An Art Collection of Combs*, organized by Galerie Marzee,
        Nimwegen, The Netherlands (travelled)
        Design in Köln, Kölnisches Stadtmuseum, Cologne
        Hommage à Sepp Schmölzer, Kunstverein für Kärnten,
        Klagenfurt, Germany
        Jewelry: Means: Meaning, University of Tennessee, Knoxville
        (travelled)
        Perth International Crafts Triennial, Art Gallery of Western
        Australia, Perth
1989,87 *Solo Exhibitions*, Galerie Louise Smit, Amsterdam
1989,85 *Solo Exhibitions*, Galerie Spektrum, Munich
1988   *Tragezeichen*, Museum Schloss Morsbroich, Leverkusen,
        Germany
1987   *Biennale du Bijou Contemporain*, Hotel du Sens, Paris
        Joieria Europea Contemporània, Fundació Caixa de Pensions,
        Barcelona
        Schmuck, Zeichen am Körper, Francisco Carolinum Museum,
        Linz, Austria
        Schmuck in Bewegung, Bewegung in Schmuck, Deutsches
        Goldschmiedehaus, Hanau, Germany
1986   *Solo Exhibition*, VO Galerie, Washington, DC
1986,83,79
        International Jewellery Art Exhibition, Tokyo Triennials
1985   *Form Formel Formalismus*, Internationale Handwerksmesse,
        Munich
        Solo Exhibition, Galerie am Graben, Vienna
1984   *Contemporary Jewellery: The Americas, Australia, Europe and
        Japan*, National Museum of Modern Art, Kyoto; Tokyo
        Schmuck, zeitgenössische Kunst aus Österreich, Ateneo San
        Basso, Venice
1983   *Peter Skubic und Studenten der Schmuckklasse an der Kölner
        Werkschule*, Kölnischer Kunstverein, Cologne,
1982,73 *Schmuck – Tendenzen*, Schmuckmuseum, Pforzheim, Germany
1981   *Email International*, Kunstverein, Coburg, Germany
        Subjekt-Objekt, Künstlerhaus, Klagenfurt, Germany
1980   *Schmuck International 1900-1980*, Künstlerhaus, Vienna
1978   *Der Ring*, Deutsches Goldschmiedehaus, Hanau, Germany

Related Professional Experience:
1980–   Lecturer, Hochschule für künstlerische und industrielle
        Gestaltung, Linz, Austria
1979-83 Faculty, Dept. of Art and Design, Fachschule, Cologne

Selected Public Collections:
Badisches Landesmuseum, Karlsruhe, Germany; Boymans-van
Beuningen Museum, Rotterdam; Bundesministerium für Unterricht
und Kunst, Vienna; Kunstgewerbemuseum, Berlin; Müncher
Stadtmuseum, Munich; Museum des 20.Jahrhunderts, Vienna;
Museum für angewandte Kunst, Vienna; National Museum of Modern
Art, Kyoto; Neue Galerie, Museum für moderne Kunst, Linz, Austria;
Neue Galerie, Sammlung Ludwig, Aachen; Oberösterreichisches
Landesmuseum, Linz, Austria

Kiff Slemmons

Born: October 18, 1944, Maxton, NC, USA

Education:
1963-68 BA, University of Iowa, Iowa City
1963   Sorbonne, Paris

Selected Awards:
1990   Grant, *Art and Autobiography: Ten Artists*, Washington State
        Arts Commission

Selected Exhibitions:
1995   *Schmuckszene '95*, Internationale Handwerksmesse, Munich
1994   *A Moveable Feast**, Amsterdam
1993   *The Body Adorned*, University of Texas, El Paso
        Documents Northwest, The Poncho Series: Six Jewelers, Seattle
        Art Museum, WA
        Material Vision: Image and Object, Eastern Illinois University,
        Charleston, SC
        Personal Views in Jewelry and Metalsmithing, Mackenthaler
        Cultural Center, Fullerton, CA
        Tales & Traditions: Storytelling in 20th Century American Crafts,
        Craft Alliance, St Louis, MO (travelled)
1993,92,89
        Solo Exhibitions, Susan Cummins Gallery, Mill Valley, CA
1992   *Brilliant Stories: American Narrative Jewelry*, USIS Exhibition
        Hall, Amman, Jordan (travelled)
        Historical References, SOFA, Susan Cummins Gallery, Chicago, IL
        Of Magic, Power, and Memory, Bellevue Art Museum, WA
1991   *Masterworks: Northwest Craft*, Bellevue Art Museum, WA
1991,90 *Solo Exhibitions*, MIA Gallery, Seattle, WA
1989   *Hands of the Heroes, Solo Exhibition*, Garth Clark Gallery,
        New York
1988   *Eight Contemporary Jewelers*, Jacksonville Art Museum, FL
1987   *Group Exhibition*, Cleveland Museum of Contemporary Art, OH
1985   *Lost and Found: Ho/Hall/Slemmons/Solberg*, Traver-Sutton
        Gallery, Seattle, WA
1975   *Solo Exhibition*, Whatcom Museum of History and Art,
        Bellingham, WA

**Related Professional
Experience:**
1970–   Maintains
        independent studio

Robert Smit

Born: March 29, 1941, Delft, The Netherlands

Education:
1963-66 Staatliche Kunst und Werkschule, Pforzheim, Germany
1954-57 Technische School, Delft

Selected Awards:
1967   Goldmedaille Handwerksmesse, Bayerischen Staatspreis, Munich

Robert Smit

Selected Exhibitions:

1994 *A Moveable Feast**, Amsterdam; *Schmuck Unserer Zeit**, Zurich
Solo Exhibition, Musée d'Art Moderne et d'Art
Contemporain, Nice

1994,92,89,87
Solo Exhibitions, Galerie Louise Smit, Amsterdam

1993 *13 Goldschmiede: Von Amsterdam bis Tokyo*, Bayerische
Akademie der Schönen Künste, Munich
Contemporary Jewelry*, Little Rock, AK
Facet I, Kunsthal, Rotterdam
Schmuck: Die Sammlung der Danner-Stiftung, Galerie für
angewandte Kunst, Munich

1993,92 *Solo Exhibitions*, Galerie Spektrum, Munich

1992-93 *Korun Kielt**, Gothenburg; Helsinki

1992 *Triennale du Bijou*, Musée des Arts Décoratifs, Paris

1991 *Artfair 'Lineart'* Ghent

1991 *Europäisches Kunsthandwerk*, Haus de Wirtschaft, Stuttgart
Linea Recta, Centraal Museum, Utrecht
Solo Exhibition, Studio Ton Berends, The Hague

1990 *L'Arte della Gioia*, Pedrocchi, Padua
Solo Exhibition, Helen Drutt Gallery, New York
Triennale du Bijou, Musée du Luxembourg, Paris

1989 *Infinite Riches*, Museum of Fine Arts, St Petersburg, FL, USA
KunstRai '89: 32 Portraits, Photography in Art, Amsterdam
KunstRai '89, Galerie Louise Smit, Amsterdam
Perth International Crafts Triennial, Art Gallery of Western Australia, Perth

1988 *Solo Exhibition*, Helen Drutt Gallery, Philadelphia, PA
Tragezeichen, Museum Schloss Morsbroich, Leverkusen, Germany

1987 *Beyond Reach*, Solo Exhibition, Stedelijk Museum 'Het Prinsenhof', Delft (travelled)
Holland in Vorm, Gemeentemuseum, Arnhem, The Netherlands
Schmuck, Zeichen am Körper, Francisco Carolinum Museum, Linz, Austria

1985 *Aspekten van Nederlandse Tekenkunst*, Stedelijk Museum 'Den Lakenhal', Leiden,
The Netherlands
Group Exhibition, Allen Memorial Art Museum, Oberlin, OH
Ornamentum Humanum, Solo Exhibition, Galerie Ra, Amsterdam
Wat Amsterdam betreft, Stedelijk Museum, Amsterdam

1984 *Solo Exhibition*, Stedelijk Museum, Amsterdam

1984,82,81
Solo Exhibitions, Galerie Orez Mobiel, The Hague

1983 *Tekeningen*, Nederlandse Kunststichting, Amsterdam (travelled)

1982 *Moment Bild*, Kestner-Gesellschaft, Hanover

1981 *Instant Fotografie*, Stedelijk Museum, Amsterdam

1980 *The Critic Sees*, Museum Fodor, Amsterdam

1978 *Towards the Liberation of Drawings 1 through 10*, (series of 10 exhibitions), Galerie Orez Mobiel,
The Hague

1977 *Solo Exhibition*, Galerie Waalkens, Finsterwolde, The Netherlands

1975 *Jewellery in Europe*, Scottish Arts Council Gallery, Edinburgh (travelled)

1973 *De Volle Maan*, Solo Exhibition, Stedelijk Museum 'Het Prinsenhof', Delft

1971 *Solo Exhibition*, Galerie Tietz-Odenwalt, Hamburg

Selected Public Collections:
Centraal Museum, Utrecht; Danner-Stiftung Collection, Munich; Gemeentelijke van Reekummuseum,
Apeldoorn, The Netherlands; Gemeentemuseum, Arnhem; Haags Gemeentemuseum, The Hague; Museum
Het Kruithuis, 's-Hertogenbosch, The Netherlands; Rijksdienst Beeldende Kunst, The Hague;
Schmuckmuseum, Pforzheim; Stedelijk Museum, Amsterdam; Stedelijk Museum 'Het Prinsenhof', Delft

Ramona Solberg

Born: May 10, 1921,
Watertown, SD, USA

Education:
1957 MFA, University of
Washington, Seattle
1951 BA, University of
Washington, Seattle

Selected Awards:
1987 Washington State
Governor's Award

Selected Exhibitions:

1994 *Two Friends: Ramona Solberg/Ron Ho*, Facèré Jewelry Art,
Seattle, WA

1993 *Documents Northwest, The Poncho Series: Six Jewelers*, Seattle
Art Museum, WA
Lifetime Achievements: The ACC College of Fellows in Metal,
National Ornamental Metal Museum, Memphis, TN
Screams with Laughter, 1993 Seattle Arts Festival, WA (travelled)

1992 *Of Magic Power and Memory*, Bellevue Art Museum, WA

1990 *Solo Exhibition*, Facèré Jewelry Art, Seattle, WA

1989 *Washington Crafts - Then and Now*, Tacoma Art Museum, WA

1987 *The Ubiquitous Bead*, Bellevue Art Museum, WA

1985 *Lost and Found: Hall/Ho/Slemmons/Solberg*, Traver-Sutton
Gallery, Seattle, WA

1981 *Good as Gold*, Renwick Gallery, NCFA, Smithsonian
Institution, Washington, DC (travelled)

1976 *Solo Exhibition*, Anchorage Museum of History and Art, Alaska

1974 *American Metalsmiths*, De Cordova Museum, Lincoln, MA

1972 *Solo Exhibition*, Boise State College, ID

1969 *Objects: USA*, National Collection of Fine Arts, Smithsonian
Institution, Washington, DC (travelled)

Related Professional Experience:
1967-83 Professor of Art, University of Washington, Seattle
1956-67 Professor of Art, Central Washington University, Ellensburg

Selected Public Collections:
American Craft Museum, New York; Jacksonville Art Museum, FL; King
County Arts Commission, Seattle, WA; Renwick Gallery, NMAA,
Smithsonian Institution, Washington, DC

Eric Spiller

Born: 1946, Staffordshire, England

Education:
1969-72 Royal College of Art, London
1966-69 Central School of Art and Design, London

Selected Exhibitions:

1994	*A Moveable Feast**, Amsterdam; *Schmuck Unserer Zeit**, Zurich
1993	*Schmuck: Die Sammlung der Danner-Stiftung*, Galerie für angewandte Kunst, Munich
1992-93	*Korun Kieli**, Gothenburg; Helsinki
1992	*Schmuckszene '92*, Internationale Handwerksmesse, Munich
1987	*Joieria Europea Contemporània*, Fundació Caixa de Pensions, Barcelona
1986	*10 Jaar Ra*, Galerie Ra, Amsterdam
1985	*Body Works and Wearable Sculpture*, Visual Arts Center of Alaska, Anchorage
	Nya Smycken, Nya Material, Kulturhuset, Stockholm
	New Tradition, British Crafts Centre, London
1984-87	*Modern Jewelry**, Philadelphia, PA; Cleveland, OH; Honolulu, HI; Montreal
1984	*Contemporary Jewellery: The Americas, Australia, Europe and Japan*, National Museum of Modern Art, Kyoto; Tokyo
	Body Works and Wearable Sculpture, Visual Arts Center of Alaska, Anchorage
	Jewelry International, American Craft Museum II, New York
1983	*The Jewellery Project*, Crafts Council Gallery, London
	New Departures in British Jewellery, American Craft Museum, New York
1982	*Jewellery Redefined*, British Crafts Centre, London
1980	*Armschmuck*, Schmuckmuseum, Pforzheim, Germany
1973	*Schmuck '73 – Tendenzen*, Schmuckmuseum, Pforzheim, Germany

Selected Public Collections:
Danner-Stiftung Collection, Munich

Vaughn Stubbs

Born: October 27, 1946, Reading, PA, USA

Education:
1981	Community College of Philadelphia, PA
1972	Pennsylvania Academy of the Fine Arts, Philadelphia, PA

Selected Awards:
1972	William A. Cresson Traveling Scholarship to Europe, Pennsylvania Academy of the Fine Arts, Philadelphia
1971	Experimental Painting Prize, Pennsylvania Academy of the Fine Arts, Philadelphia
1970	Cecelia Beaux Prize for Drawing, Pennsylvania Academy of the Fine Arts, Philadelphia

Selected Exhibitions and Commissions:
1994	*Gods, Myths, Legends, Icons*, Rowan College of New Jersey, Glassboro
	A Moveable Feast*, Amsterdam; *Schmuck Unserer Zeit**, Zurich
1992	*10 on 2: Art in City Hall*, Philadelphia, PA
	Legacy: Artist's Time Capsules 1992-2092, Rowan College of New Jersey, Glassboro

1991	*Mural*, Library for the Blind, Philadelphia, PA
1990	*American Dreams, American Extremes*, Museum Het Kruithuis, 's-Hertogenbosch, The Netherlands
	Philadelphia Art Now, Philadelphia Museum of Art, PA
1989	*Solo Exhibition*, Philadelphia Art Alliance, PA
1988	*Creativity*, Solo Exhibition, Side Bank Gallery, Brooklyn, NY
1987	*Faculty Art Exhibition*, Abington, Art Center, Jenkintown, PA
1986	*50 Friends*, Solo Exhibition, Painted Bride Art Center, Philadelphia, PA
1984	*Persistence of Memory*, Solo Exhibition, The Kling Gallery, Philadelphia, PA
1975	*Fellowship Exhibition: Pennsylvania Academy of the Fine Arts*, Woodmere Art Museum, Philadelphia, PA
1974	*Faculty Exhibition*, Philadelphia Museum of Art, PA
1973	*Fellowship Exhibition: Pennsylvania Academy of the Fine Arts*, Philadelphia Civic Center Museum, PA

Related Professional Experience:
1990–	Instructor, Institute of Contemporary Art, Philadelphia, PA
1974–	Instructor, Philadelphia Museum of Art, PA

Selected Public Collections:
Afro-American Historical and Cultural Museum, Philadelphia, PA; Duane, Morris & Heckscher, Inc., Philadelphia, PA

Janna Maria Kristiina Syvänoja

Born: March 3, 1960, Helsinki, Finland

Education:
1982-93 University of Industrial Arts, Helsinki

Selected Awards:
1993	Diploma, Information Management Center, City of Helsinki
	Finland Prize of Young Art, Ministry of Education, Helsinki,
1992,90	Scholarships, Cultural Foundation of Finland, Helsinki
1990	Zonta-Scholarship, Helsinki
1989	Diploma, *Finland Designs 7*, Taideteollisuusmuseo, Helsinki

Selected Exhibitions:
1994	*10 + 10*, Västerås Konstmuseum, Västerås, Sweden
	Kunsthandwerker aus Finland, Osnabrück, Germany
	Nordiska Profiler, Kunstindustrimuseet, Stockholm (travelled)
	A Moveable Feast*, Amsterdam; *Schmuck Unserer Zeit**, Zurich
1993	*Ingenuity and Creativity*, UNESCO House, Helsinki, Finland
	Paperipursi, Myllysaaren museo, Valkeakoski, Finland
	Paperista paperille/On Paper from Paper, Käsityömuseo, Lappeenranta, Finland
	Projects singuliers, Maison du Livre de l'image et du Son, Villourbanne, France
	Subjects, Design Forum, Helsinki
	Summer Exhibition, Design Center, Helsinki

Voorzien: Benno Premsela Applied Art Collection, Stedelijk
Museum, Amsterdam

1992 *Arbeitsgruppe Kunsthandwerk und Design*, Osnabrück, Germany
1992 *Contrasts and Connections: USA/Finland*, Galerie Handwerk,
Munich
Expo 92, Finnish Pavilion, Seville
Finland i dag, Stockholm
Incontri con l'arte, Milan
Kesä(t)yöt, Design Forum, Helsinki
Solo Exhibition, Cardillac Schmuckgalerie, Karlsruhe, Germany
Solo Exhibition, Galleria Kaj Forsblom, Helsinki
Triennale du Bijou, Musée des Arts Décoratifs, Paris
1991 *Arki*, Taideteollisuusmuseo, Helsinki
Configura 1: Triennale des Europäichen Kunsthandwerks,
Galerie am Fischmarkt, Erfurt, Germany
Finland Designs 8, Taideteollisuusmuseo, Helsinki
Garden of Form, Retretti, Punkaharju, Finland
Jewellery by Four Artists, Lahden taidemuseo, Lahti, Finland
Muodon tähdet, Merikaapelihalli, Helsinki
1990 *From Paper to Paper*, University of Industrial Arts, Helsinki
New Forms from Finland, Madrid, Barcelona, Bilbao, Spain
Nord Form 90, Form/Design Center, Malmö, Sweden;
Paperigalleria, Kuusankoski, Finland
Triennale du Bijou, Musée du Luxembourg, Paris
Schmuckszene '90, Internationale Handwerksmesse, Munich
Vuosikymmen – 80, Taideteollisuusmuseo, Helsinki
1989 *Finland Designs 7*, Taideteollisuusmuseo, Helsinki,
Utopia 2000, Grand Palais, Paris
The Youth Festival of Pyongyang, North Korea, Vanhan galleria,
Helsinki
1988 *Young Designers*, Amer Gallery, Helsinki
1985 *Proto*, Avatre, Helsinki

Related Professional Experience:
Maintains independent studio, Helsinki

Selected Public Collections:
Montreal Musée des Arts Décoratifs, Quebec; Röhskka
Konstslöjdmuseet, Gothenburg; Taideteollisuusmuseo, Helsinki

Olli Tamminen

Born: July 30, 1944, Kokkola, Finland

Education:
1962-66 University of Industrial Arts, Helsinki

Selected Awards:
1990   15-year Working Grant, Finnish State Grant, Visual Finland
Foundation, New York
1987   Scholarship, Finnish-Icelandic Cultural Foundation
1985   Scholarship, Finnish-Norwegian Cultural Foundation

1983   Honorary Award, *Finland Design 6*, Taideteollisuusmuseo,
Helsinki
1980,76,68
Scholarships, Cultural Foundation of Finland
1977   First Prize, Nuutajärvi Glass Works Competition, Finland

Selected Exhibitions:
1994   *A New Century in European Design*, Tokyo Metropolitan
Teien Art Museum, Tokyo (travelled)
Valon ja puun aika, Galleria Otso, Espoo, Finland
1993   *Solo Exhibition*, Artek, Helsinki
Subjects, Design Forum, Helsinki
1992   *Expo 92*, Finnish Pavilion, Seville
Triennale du Bijou, Musée des Arts Décoratifs, Paris
1991   *Configura 1: Triennale des Europäichen Kunsthandwerks*,
Galerie am Fischmarkt, Erfurt, Germany
Finnish Design, Israel Museum, Jerusalem
Garden of Form, Retretti, Punkaharju, Finland
Solo Exhibition, Suur-Helsingin Osuuspankki, Espoo, Finland
1991,88 *Espoo muotoilee*, Galleria Otso, Espoo, Finland
1990   *New Forms from Finland*, Madrid, Barcelona, Bilbao; Spain
Nord Form 90, Design Centre, Malmö, Sweden
Vuosikymmen, Taideteollisuusmuseo, Helsinki (travelled)
1989   *Jewellery Art 89*, Galleria 585, Helsinki
L'Éurope des Creatures, Grand Palais, Paris
1989,87,85,83,80
Finland Designs, Taideteollisuusmuseo, Helsinki
1988   *Finnish Design*, Royal Scottish Museum, Edinburgh
Kivi ja koru, Kemin Kivimuseo, Finland
The Language of Wood, Taideteollisuusmuseo, Helsinki
Paradisus terrestris, Taideteollisuusmuseo, Helsinki
Schmuckszene '88, Internationale Handwerksmesse, Munich
1987   *Scandinavian Craft Today*, Yurakucho Art Forum, Tokyo
(travelled)
Zeitgenössisches deutsches und finnisches Kunsthandwerk,
Museum für Kunsthandwerk, Frankfurt a.M. (travelled)
1985   *Crafts in Espoo*, Galleria Otso, Espoo, Finland
Solo Exhibition, Galleri Albin Upp, Oslo
1984   *Finsk Form*, Denmark, Norway, Germany, Iceland and
The Faroe Isles
Solo Exhibition, Galleria 585, Helsinki
1983   *Tanke och Object*, Stockholm
1982   *Finland Designs 4*, Norsk Arkitekturmuseum, Oslo (travelled)
Scandinavian and Japan Craft and Design, Ishikawa Prefectural
Industrial Design Exhibition Hall, Kanazawa, Japan
1981   *Finland Designs 2*, travelled through Asia
Finland Designs 3, Craft and Folk Art Museum, Los Angeles,
CA (travelled)
Metalli elää, Taideteollisuusmuseo, Helsinki
1978   *Métamorphoses Finlandaises*, Centre George Pompidou, Paris
1975   *100 Years of the Finnish Society of Crafts and Design*, Ateneum,
Helsinki
1973   *Arts and Crafts Exhibition*, Amos Andersonin Taidemuseo, Helsinki
1972   *En mä tiedä/I don't know*, Amos Andersonin Taidemuseo, Helsinki
1971   *Form und Qualität*, Internationale Handwerksmesse, Munich

1968   *Triennale di Milano*, Milan
1967   *New Jewellery*, Finnish Design Center, Helsinki

Related Professional Experience:
Maintains independent studio, Helsinki
1980-89   Director, Training Center, University of Industrial Arts, Helsinki
Professor, University of Industrial Arts, Helsinki

Selected Public Collections:
Kunstindustrimuseet, Oslo; Museum of Applied Arts, Budapest; Museum of Modern Art, New York; Suomen lasimuseo, Riihimäki, Finland; Taideteollisuusmuseo, Helsinki

---

David Tisdale

Born: April 15, 1956, San Diego, CA, USA

Education:
1981   MA, San Diego State University, CA .
1978   BS, University of California, Davis
1974-76   University of California, Berkeley

Selected Awards:
1988   Pantone Color Award, Pantone Color Institute,USA
1986   Arts America Grant – Indonesia/Singapore, United States Information Agency, State Department
        Best Designs, Industrial Design Publications Annual Design Review,
1985   Design Award, American Craft Museum, New York

Selected Exhibitions:
1994   *A Moveable Feast**, Amsterdam; *Schmuck Unserer Zeit**, Zurich
1993   *Contemporary Jewelry**, Little Rock, AK
1992-93   *Korun Kieli**, Gothenburg; Helsinki
1990   *Art That Works*, The Mint Museum of Art, Charlotte, NC (travelled)
1989   *Craft Today: USA*, Musée des Arts Décoratifs, Paris (travelled)
1988   *Design USA*, sponsored by US Information Agency, travelled through the USSR
1987   *Grand Prix des Métiers of Art*, Banque d'Epargue, Montreal (travelled)
1986   *Contemporary Arts: An Expanding View*, Monmouth Museum, Lincroft, NJ
        Craft Today: Poetry of the Physical, American Craft Museum, New York (travelled)
        Design in America, sponsored by US Information Agency, travelled through Eastern Europe
        Machine as Metaphor, Purdue University, West Lafayette, IN
1985   *Contemporary Jewelry Redefined*, Pittsburgh Center for the Arts, PA
        Contemporary Metals USA, Downey Museum of Art, CA
1984-87   *Modern Jewelry**, Philadelphia, PA Honolulu; Cleveland, OH; Montreal

1984   *Celebration '84*, Art Gallery at Harbourfront, Toronto, Canada (travelled)
        Jewelry USA, American Craft Museum II, New York
        Invitational, Southwest Texas State University
        Solo Exhibition, Helen Drutt Gallery, Philadelphia, PA
1983   *Art to Wear*, American Craft Museum, New York
        Contemporary Metalwork, Georgia State University, Atlanta
        Four American Jewelers, V & V Galerie, Vienna
1982   *The Belt Show*, Craft and Folk Art Museum, Los Angeles, CA
1981   *Good as Gold*, Renwick Gallery, NCFA, Smithsonian Institution, Washington, DC (travelled)
        Two Decades of Metal, San Diego State University, CA

Related Professional Experience:
1986–   President, David Tisdale Design, Inc., New York
1985-88   Faculty, New York University, New York
1982-88   Faculty, New School/Parsons School of Design, New York
1981-86   Independent studio, David Tisdale Jewelry Design, New York

Selected Public Collections:
American Craft Museum, New York; Cooper-Hewitt, National Museum of Design, Smithsonian Institution, New York; Montreal Musée des Arts Décoratifs, Quebec; Kunstgewerbemuseum , Berlin; Nordenfjeldske Kunstindustrimuseum, Trondheim, Norway; University of California, Davis; Virginia Museum of Fine Arts, Richmond; Yale University Art Gallery, New Haven, CT

Donald (Don) Tompkins

Born: November 1, 1933, Everett, Washington, USA
Died: March 23, 1982, Seattle, Washington, USA

Education:
1956-58   MFA University of Washington, Seattle
1963-66   Syracuse University, NY
1966-67   PhD Columbia University, New York
1954-56   BFA Everett Junior College

Selected Exhibitions:
1986   Tompkins/Tompkins, Sarah Spurgeon Gallery, Central Washington University, Ellensburg, WA
1975   *Symbolism and Imagery*, Central Washington State College, Ellensburg, WA
1973   Contemporary American Silversmith and Goldsmiths, Corcoran Gallery, Washington, DC
1972   *100 Craftsmen Celebrate 200 Years*, Fairtree Gallery, NYC; Xerox Gallery, Rochester, NY
1965   *American Jewelry Today*, Everhart Museum, Scranton, PA
1964   *Jewelry '64*, State University College, Plattsburg, NY

Related Professional Experience:
Faculty/Instructor, University of Washington, WA; Faculty, Everett Junior College, Everett, WA; Faculty/Lecturer, Syracuse University, Syracuse, NY; Faculty/Associate Professor of Art, Central Washington State College, Ellensburg, WA; Faculty/Assistant Professor of Art, Sculpture, Jewelry, New York University, NYC

Merrily Tompkins

Born: August 29, 1947, Everett, WA, USA

Education:
1967-69 Central Washington State College, Ellensburg
1966 University of Washington, Seattle

Selected Awards:
1979 Fellowship, National Endowment for the Arts, Washington, DC
1974 First Prize/metals, Tacoma Art Museum, WA

Selected Exhibitions:
1994 *Eyes on Public Art: Points of View*, Public Locations, Seattle, WA
1990 *'NW Women' Group Show*, MIA Gallery, Seattle, WA
1988-89 *Portraits: Here's Looking at You*, Anchorage Museum of History and Art, Anchorage, Alaska
1987 *Beautiful*, Tacoma Art Museum, WA
1987,85 *Solo Exhibitions*, Linda Farris Gallery, Seattle
1986 *Figure: Narrative*, Whatcom Museum, Bellingham, WA
Tompkins/Tompkins, Central Washington State University, Ellensburg, WA
1985 *New York/Seattle*, Center of Contemporary Art, Seattle
1981 *Five From Seattle*, Portland Center for Contemporary Crafts, OR
Women on Women, John Michael Kohler Arts Center, Sheboygan, WI
1980 *Robert L. Pfannebecker Collection*, Moore College of Art, Philadelphia, PA
Solo Exhibition, Museum Art School, Portland, OR
1980,72 *Governor's Invitational of Washington Artists*, State Capitol Museum, Olympia, WA
1979 *The Unpainted Portrait*, John Michael Kohler Arts Center, Sheboygan, WI
1978 *Art in Crafts: Works in Fiber, Clay and Metal by Women*, Bronx Museum, NY
1977 *Beauty of the Beast: Animal Images in Contemporary Art*, John Michael Kohler Arts Center, Sheboygan, WI
1976 *2nd Annual Jewelry Invitational*, Central Washington State College, Ellensburg
1975 *Celebration of Crafts*, Honolulu Academy of the Arts, HI
Homage to the Bag, Museum of Contemporary Crafts, New York
Portable Containers, Museum of Man, San Diego, CA
Symbolism and Imagery, Central Washington State College, Ellensburg, WA
1973 *Bodycraft*, Portland Art Museum, OR
Fun and Fantasy, Buffalo Art Museum, NY
Solo Exhibition, University of Washington, Seattle
1972-73 *Contemporary American Silversmiths and Goldsmiths, Invitational*, Corcoran Gallery of Art, Washington, DC
1972,71 *Northwest Craftsmen Exhibition*, University of Washington, Seattle

Commissions:
1982 *Portrait of Nikola Testa*, sculpture, Seattle Arts Commission/City Lights, Seattle, WA

Selected Public Collections:
Seattle Portable Works Collection

Peter Tully

Born: December 17, 1947, Melbourne, Victoria, Australia
Died: August 10, 1992, Sydney, Australia

Education:
1979 New School, New School for Social Research, New York
1975 Diploma, Randwick Technical College, Sydney

Selected Exhibitions:
1994 *A Moveable Feast**, Amsterdam; *Schmuck Unserer Zeit**, Zurich
1992,90 *Solo Exhibitions*, Barry Stern Galleries, Sydney
1991 *Urban Debris*, Australian National Gallery, Canberra
1989 *Fashion – The Contemporary Art*, Power House Museum, Sydney (travelled)
Silly Putty Park, folk art installation with Ron Smith, Festival Centre, Adelaide
1988 *Australian Decorative Arts 1788-1988*, Australian National Gallery, Canberra
Contemporary Jewellery: The Australian Experience, Contemporary Jewellery Gallery, Sydney
Summer Waves, Crafts Council of New South Wales, Sydney
1987 *A Decade of Craft*, organized by the Art Gallery of New South Wales (travelled)
Stormy Leather: Peter Tully, Gallery Gabrielle Pizzi, Melbourne
1986 *New Acquisitions*, Art Gallery of South Australia, Adelaide
Plastics, Leather and Rubber, Australian National Gallery, Canberra
1985 *Image Codes*, Australian Centre for Contemporary Arts, Melbourne
Makers Choice, Jam Factory, Adelaide
1984 *Australian Decorative Arts*, Australian National Gallery, Canberra
Contemporary Jewellery: The Americas, Australia, Europe and Japan, National Museum of Modern Art, Kyoto; Tokyo
1982 *Australian Art of the Last Ten Years*, Australian National Gallery, Canberra
Australian Contemporary Jewellery, Goldsmiths' Hall, London (travelled)
The Australian Experience, Crafts Council of New South Wales, Sydney
Australian Metalwork and Jewellery, National Gallery of Victoria, Melbourne

1980   *Objects to Human Scale*, organized by the Australia Council
        (travelled)
        Urban Tribalwear: Peter Tully, Gallery 321, New York
1977   *10 Australian Jewellers*, travelled through SE Asia

Selected Public Collections:
Art Gallery of Queensland, Brisbane; Art Gallery of South Australia,
Adelaide; Australian National Gallery, Canberra; Museum of Applied Art
and Sciences, Sydney; National Gallery of Victoria, Melbourne; Philip
Morris Collection, Canberra; Queen Victoria Museum and Art Gallery,
Launceston, Tasmania; Victorian State Craft Collection, Melbourne

Tone Vigeland

Born: August 6, 1938, Oslo, Norway

Education:
1957   Yrkesskol for Gullsmeder, Oslo
1955-57 Statens Handverk og Kunstindustriskole, Oslo

Awards:
1988   Prins Eugen Medaljen, HM King of Sweden
1987   Artist Prize, City of Oslo
1986   2nd Prize, *International Jewellery Art Exhibition*, Yurakucho
        Art Forum, Tokyo

Selected Exhibitions:
1995   *The Jewelry of Tone Vigeland*, Kunstindustrimuseet, Oslo,
        (American Federation of Arts, New York, will travel
        throughout the US 1996-97)
1994   *In Touch*, Maihaugen, Lillehammer, Norway
        A Moveable Feast*, Amsterdam; *Schmuck Unserer Zeit**, Zurich
        A New Century in European Design, Tokyo Metropolitan Teien
        Art Museum, Japan (travelled)
        Nordiska Profiler, Kunstindustrimuseet, Stockholm (travelled)
1993   *The Art of Jewellery*, Setagaya Art Museum, Tokyo
        Contemporary Jewelry*, Little Rock, AK
1993,89 *Solo Exhibitions*, Kunstnerforbundet, Oslo
1992-93 *Korun Kieli**, Gothenburg; Helsinki
1992   *Triennale du Bijou*, Musée des Arts Décoratifs, Paris
1989   *Ornamenta 1*, Schmuckmuseum, Pforzheim, Germany
1988   *Norska Smycken*, Röhsska Konstslöjdmuseet, Gothenburg,
        Sweden
1987   *Scandinavian Craft Today*, Yurakucho Art Forum, Tokyo
        (travelled)
        Schmuckszene '87, Internationale Handwerksmesse, Munich
1986   *Designs for the Body*, American Scandinavian Foundation
        Gallery, New York (travelled)
        International Jewellery Art Exhibition, 6th Tokyo Triennial,
        Yurakucho Art Forum, Tokyo
        Solo Exhibition, Kunstindustrimuseet, Oslo, Norway

1984-87 *Modern Jewelry**, Philadelphia, PA; Cleveland, OH; Honolulu,
        HI; Montreal
1984   *Contemporary Jewellery: The Americas, Australia, Europe and
        Japan*, National Museum of Modern Art, Kyoto; Tokyo
        Jewelry International, American Craft Museum II, New York
1977   *Scandinavian Crafts*, National Museum of Modern Art, Tokyo
1964   *Contemporary Scandinavian Jewelry*, Röhsska Konstlöjdmuseet,
        Gothenburg, Sweden
1964   *Modern Scandinavian Jewels: Denmark, Finland, Norway,
        Sweden*, Georg Jensen Inc., New York
1961   *International Exhibition of Modern Jewelry: 1890-1961*,
        Goldsmiths' Hall, London

Related Professional Experience:
1977   Visiting Teacher, Nova Scotia College of Art and Design,
        Halifax, Canada
1975   Faculty, National College of Art, Craft and Design, Oslo

Selected Public Collections:
Cooper-Hewitt, National Museum of Design, Smithsonian Institution,
New York; Kunstindustrimuseet, Copenhagen; Kunstindustrimuseet,
Oslo; Musée des Arts Décoratifs, Paris; Museum of Modern Art, New
York; National Museum of Modern Art, Tokyo; Nationalmuseum,
Stockholm; Nordenfjeldske Kunstindustrimuseum, Trondheim, Norway;
Nordnorsk Kunstmuseum, Tromso, Norway; Norsk Kulturråd; Oslo;
Kommunes Kunstsamlinger, Oslo; Royal Scottish Museum, Edinburgh;
Schmuckmuseum, Pforzheim, Germany; Värmlands Museum, Karlstad,
Germany; Vestlandske Kunstindustrimuseet, Bergen, Norway; Victoria
and Albert Museum, London

David Walker

Born: 1941, Manchester, England

Selected Awards:
1986   Acquisition Award, Diamond Valley Art Award, Victoria,
1983   Craft Award – Major Prize for Excellence, City of Perth
1962   Heywood Prize for Design, Royal Manchester Institution for the
        Advancement of Literature, Science and the Arts, England

Selected Exhibitions:
1994   *A Moveable Feast**, Amsterdam; *Schmuck Unserer Zeit**, Zurich
1991,84 *Solo Exhibitions*, Western Australian Institute of Technology, Perth
1990   *Argyle Contemporary Jewellery*, Crafts Council Gallery, Perth
        Schmuckszene '90, Internationale Handwerksmesse, Munich
1989   *Australian Crafts: The Urban Experience*, Art Gallery of
        Western Australia, Perth
        Body Language: David Walker, Contemporary Jewellery Gallery,
        Sydney
        Perth International Crafts Triennial, Art Gallery of Western
        Australia, Perth

1989   *Solo Exhibition*, University of Tasmania, Launceston
1988   *Contemporary Jewellery: The Australian Experience*,
        Contemporary Jewellery Gallery, Sydney
1986   *Flux*, Galerie Dusseldorf, Perth
1984   *Australian Decorative Arts*, Australian National Gallery,
        Canberra
        Body Rap '84, Art Gallery of Western Australia, Perth
        *Contemporary Jewellery: The Americas, Australia, Europe and
        Japan*, National Museum of Modern Art, Kyoto; Tokyo
        *Cross Currents: Jewellery from Australia, Britain, Germany and
        Holland*, Power House Museum, Sydney (travelled)
        Drawing on the Body: David Walker, Crafts Centre Gallery,
        Perth
        Solo Exhibition, Devise Gallery, Melbourne
        Solo Exhibition, Queen Victoria Museum and Art Gallery,
        Launceston, Tasmania
1983   *City of Perth Craft Awards Exhibition*, Art Gallery of Western
        Australia, Perth
        Western Australia Expo, Kobe, Japan
1982   *Australian Contemporary Jewellery*, Goldsmiths' Hall, London
        (travelled)
        Craftworks by Twelve Western Australians, Art Gallery of
        Western Australia, Perth
        Schmuck '82 – Tendenzen, Schmuckmuseum, Pforzheim,
        Germany
1981   *Australian Jewellery*, Museum of Applied Arts and Sciences,
        Sydney (travelled)
1980   *Jewellery from the West*, Melbourne State College, Victoria
        (travelled)
        Metal und Textil = ?, Kunstgewerbeschule, Zurich
        Objects to Human Scale, organized by the Australia Council
        (travelled)
1979   *Jewelry by David Walker*, Fremantle Art Centre, Perth
1972   *The History of Australian Book Design*, National Library
        of Australia (travelled)
        International Exhibition of Illustration and Book Design,
        Moravska Galerie, Brno, Czechoslovakia

Related Professional Experience:
Senior Lecturer/Co-ordinator, Jewellery and Three-
        Dimensional Design, Western Australian Institute
        of Technology, Perth
President, Crafts Council of Western Australia, Perth
Member, Board, Crafts Council of Australia, Sydney

Selected Public Collections:
Art Gallery of Western Australia, Perth; Australian National Gallery,
Canberra; Box Hill Regional Gallery, Victoria; Meat Market Craft
Collection, Melbourne ; Museum of Applied Arts and Sciences, Sydney;
National Gallery of Victoria, Melbourne; Power House Museum, Sydney;
Queen Victoria Museum and Art Gallery, Launceston, Tasmania;
Robert Holmes a Court Collection, Perth; Shire of Diamond Valley
Collection, Victoria; University of Queensland, Brisbane; Victorian
State Craft Collection, Melbourne; Western Australian Institute of
Technology, Perth

David Watkins

Born: November 14, 1940,
        Wolverhampton,
        England

Education:
1959-63 BA, University of
        Reading, England

Selected Awards:
1994   Project Artist, *Art for Architecture*, Royal Society of Arts, London
        Research Award, Royal College of Art, London
1992   Study Tour, Tokyo National University of Fine Arts and Music
1978   Travel Award, Australian Crafts Council
        Travel Award, Japan Foundation
1976   Bursary, Crafts Advisory Committee, London

Selected Exhibitions:
1994   *A Moveable Feast**, Amsterdam; *Schmuck Unserer Zeit**, Zurich
        A New Century in European Design, Tokyo Metropolitan Teien
        Art Museum, Japan (travelled)
1993   *Contemporary Jewelry**, Little Rock, AK
        David Watkins/Wendy Ramshaw, Musée d'Art Moderne et
        d'Art Contemporain, Nice
        Facet I, Kunsthal, Rotterdam
        Subjects, Design Forum, Helsinki
1992-93 *Korun Kieli**, Gothenburg; Helsinki
1992   *Triennale du Bijou*, Musée des Arts Décoratifs, Paris
1991   *Europäisches Kunsthandwerk*, Haus de Wirtschaft, Stuttgart
        Jewellery of the Twentieth Century, Museum für Kunst und
        Gewerbe, Hamburg (travelled)
1990   *Triennale du Bijou*, Musée du Luxembourg, Paris
1989   *British Jewellery – German Jewellery*, Crafts Council Gallery,
        London (travelled)
        David Watkins: Xingu – Wendy Ramshaw: Picasso's Ladies,
        Scottish Gallery, Edinburgh (travelled)
        Jewelry: Means: Meaning, University of Tennessee, Knoxville
        (travelled)
        Ornamenta 1, Schmuckmuseum, Pforzheim, Germany
        Perth International Crafts Triennial, Art Gallery of Western
        Australia, Perth
        Solo Exhibition, Contemporary Applied Arts, London
1988   *Contemporary British Crafts*, National Museum of Modern Art,
        Kyoto; Tokyo
1987   *Biennale du Bijou Contemporain*, Hotel du Sens, Paris
        Joieria Europea Contemporània, Fundació Caixa de Pensions,
        Barcelona

1987   *Schmuck, Zeichen am Körper*, Francisco Carolinum Museum,
        Linz, Austria
        Wendy Ramshaw – David Watkins: Schmuck – Jewellery,
        Schmuckmuseum, Pforzheim, Germany (travelled)
1986   *Contemporary Arts: An Expanding View*, Monmouth Museum,
        Lincroft, NJ
        David Watkins: Jewellery, Stedelijk Museum, Amsterdam
        David Watkins: Jewellery and Sculpture, City Art Gallery, Leeds
1985   *Body Works and Wearable Sculpture*, Visual Arts Center of
        Alaska, Anchorage
        Contemporary Jewelry Redefined, Pittsburgh Center for the
        Arts, PA
        David Watkins: Jewellery and Sculpture, Crafts Council Gallery,
        London (travelled)
        New Tradition, British Crafts Centre, London
1984-87 *Modern Jewelry**, Philadelphia, PA; Cleveland, OH; Honolulu,
        HI; Montreal
1984   *Contemporary Jewellery: The Americas, Australia, Europe and
        Japan*, National Museum of Modern Art, Kyoto; Tokyo
        *Cross Currents: Jewellery from Australia, Britain, Germany and
        Holland*, Power House Museum, Sydney (travelled)
        Jewelry International, American Craft Museum II, New York
1983   *International Jewellery Art Exhibition*, 5th Tokyo Triennial,
        Isetan Art Museum, Tokyo
        The Jewellery Project, Crafts Council Gallery, London
        New Departures in British Jewellery, American Craft Museum,
        New York
1982   *Towards a New Iron Age*, Victoria and Albert Museum, London
        (travelled)
        Visies op Sieraden 1965-1982, Stedelijk Museum, Amsterdam
1982,77 *Schmuck – Tendenzen*, Schmuckmuseum, Pforzheim
1980   *Schmuck International 1900-1980*, Künstlerhaus, Vienna
1978   *Solo Exhibition*, National Gallery of Victoria, Melbourne
1975   *Jewellery in Europe*, Scottish Arts Council Gallery, Edinburgh
        (travelled)
1973   *Wendy Ramshaw/David Watkins*, Goldsmiths' Hall, London
        A.I.A. Gallery, Philadelphia, PA,

Related Professional Experience:
1984–   Professor, Royal College of Art, London
1978   Artist-in-Residence, Western Australian Institute of
        Technology, Perth

Selected Public Collections:
Art Gallery of Western Australia, Perth; Australian National Gallery,
Canberra; Bristol City Art Gallery; British Crafts Council, London;
Contemporary Arts Society, London; Gemeentelijke van
Reekummuseum, Apeldoorn, The Netherlands; Kunstindustrimuseet,
Oslo; Museum für Kunst und Gewerbe, Hamburg; National Gallery of
Victoria, Melbourne; National Museum of Modern Art, Kyoto; National
Museum of Modern Art, Tokyo; Nordenfjeldske Kunstindustrimuseum,
Trondheim, Norway; Power House Museum, Sydney; Royal Scottish
Museum, Edinburgh; Schmuckmuseum, Pforzheim, Germany; Stedelijk
Museum, Amsterdam; Victoria and Albert Museum, London; Worshipful
Company of Goldsmiths, London

Claude Wesel

Born: 1942, Brussels, Belgium

Education:
1962-63 L'Cambre, School of Decorative Arts
1959-61 L'Abbaye de Maredsous

Selected Awards:
1985   First Prize, *National De Beers Competition*,
1984   First Prize, 'A Jewel for Him', *National De Beers Competition*
1983   Ambassador's First Prize, *Belgian Jewels Today*,
        Washington, DC
1982   Honorable Mention, *Belgian International Gold Corporation
        Competition*
1979   Second Prize, *Laureate of the National De Beers Competition*,
        Belgium

Selected Exhibitions:
1994   *A Moveable Feast**, Amsterdam; *Schmuck Unserer Zeit**, Zurich
1992-93 *Korun Kieli**, Gothenburg; Helsinki
1992   *Bijoux et Monnaies Insolites*, Museum, Cursius, Liège
        Group Exhibition: Nouveau Musee d'Art Plastic, Ghent
        Pari, Parure, Centre d'Art, Contemporain Wallonie-Bruxelles,
        Paris
        Bijoux Belges Contemporains, Maison de la Culture de Namur
1990   *Triennale European de Bijou*, Musee du Luxembourg, Paris
        Solo Exhibition: Galerie Harmagedon, Courtrai, Belgium
        Le Bijou Contemporain en BENELUX, Luxembourg
        Le Bijou Contemporain en Europe, Hamoir, Belgium
        10ème Biennale, L'Art de L'Email, Limoges, France
1989   *Bijou D'Aujourd'hui*, Kinshasa
1988   *L'Art de L'Email*, Biennale International, Limoges, France
1987   *Biennale de Bijoux Precieux et Semiprecieux*, Hotel de Sens,
        Paris
        Bruxelles, Jardin de l'Europe, Chateau Schewppes, Genval,
        Belgium
1986   *Solo Exhibition*, Galerie der Goldschmeide, Wiesbaden, RFA
1983   *Belgian Jewels Today*, Belgian Consulate, Washington, DC
1981   *Gold and Art*, Astoria Hotel; Brussels
1980   Group Exhibition, L'Atelier de B, Munsteiner, Oberstein,
        Austria
1979   Group Exhibition, Art Prospect Gallery, Brussels
1976   *Bijoux 200*, Credit Communal de Belgique, Brussels
1974   *Solo Exhibition*, Gallery Hof Ter Linde, Brussels
1973   *International Jewellery Art Exhibition, 2nd Tokyo Triennial*,
        Seibu Gallery, Tokyo

Related Professional Experience:
1989   Established Wesel Art Gallery in Waterloo, Belgium
1970–   Maintains independent studio

Selected Public Collections:
1989   Equinoxe par la Communaute française des Arts Plastiques
1982   Schmuckmuseum, Pforzheim, Germany

Margaret West

(formerly Margaret Jasulaitis)

Born: August 31, 1936,
Melbourne, Victoria,
Australia

Education:
1976   Graduate Diploma of Art,
Royal Melbourne Institute of
Technology, Victoria
1975   Diploma of Art, Royal
Melbourne Institute of Technology, Victoria

Selected Exhibitions:
1994   *A Moveable Feast**, Amsterdam; *Schmuck Unserer Zeit**, Zurich
1993   *The Art of Jewellery*, Setagaya Art Museum, Tokyo
        Contemporary Jewelry*, Little Rock, AK
        Four Elements, Blaxland Gallery, Sydney
1992   *Interstices: Works by Margaret West from 1981-1992*, Canberra
        School of Art Gallery (travelled)
1991   *1st Australian Contemporary Jewellery Biennial*, Jam Factory,
        Adelaide (travelled)
1989   *Perth International Crafts Triennial*, Art Gallery of Western
        Australia, Perth
1988   *Australian Decorative Arts 1788-1988*, Australian National
        Gallery, Canberra
1987   *4 Australian Jewellers*, National Gallery of Victoria, Melbourne
        (travelled)
        Schmuckszene '87, Internationale Handwerksmesse, Munich
1984   *Australian Decorative Arts: The Past Ten Years*, Australian
        National Gallery, Canberra
        Solo Exhibition, Queen Victoria Museum and Art Gallery,
        Launceston, Tasmania
1982   *Australian Contemporary Jewellery*, Goldsmiths' Hall, London
        travelled through Europe
1980   *Objects to Human Scale*, organized by the Australia Council
        (travelled)
1978   *Solo Exhibition*, Craft Centre, Melbourne
1977   *Schmuck '77 – Tendenzen*, Schmuckmuseum, Pforzheim, Germany

Related Professional Experience:
1989–   Faculty, Jewellery and Object Design, Sydney College of the Arts
1979–   Lecturer, Sydney College of the Arts, University of Sydney

Selected Public Collections:
Art Gallery of Queensland, Brisbane; Art Gallery of Western Australia,
Perth; Australia Council, Crafts Board, Sydney; Australian National
Gallery, Canberra; National Gallery of Victoria; Power House
Museum, Sydney; Queen Victoria Museum and Art Gallery,
Launceston, Tasmania; Robert Holmes a Court Collection, Perth;
Royal Melbourne Institute of Technology; Victorian Ministry for the
Arts, Melbourne

Peter De Wit

Born: 1952,
Leiden, The Netherlands

Education:
1976   Swedish Goldsmiths
        Master
1971-74   Fachhochschule für
        Gestaltung, Pforzheim,
        Germany

Selected Awards:
1987-90   Konstnärsnämdens Workstipend
1983   Estrid Ericsson Stipendium, Stockholm
        Honorable Mention, *Modischer Schmuck*, Idar-Oberstein,
        Germany
        Linköpings Stads Kulturstipend, Sweden
1979   Honorable Mention, *Diamonds Today*, Sweden
        Second Prize, *Edelstein Schmuckgestaltung*, Idar-Oberstein,
        Germany
1977   Second Prize, *Modeschmuck Wettbewerb*, Idar-Oberstein,
        Germany
1974   Silver Medal, *4th International Exhibition of Jewelry*, Muzeum
        skla a bizuterie, Jablonec nad Nisou, Czechoslovakia

Selected Exhibitions:
1994   *A Moveable Feast**, Amsterdam; *Schmuck Unserer Zeit**, Zurich
1993   *Contemporary Jewelry**, Little Rock, AK
        Silver till nytta och lust, Nationalmuseum, Stockholm
1992-93   *Korun Kieli**, Gothenburg; Helsinki
1992   *Triennale du Bijou*, Musée des Arts Décoratifs, Paris
        Smedjan flyttad till Storgatan 42, östergötlands Länsmuseet,
        Linköping, Sweden
1991   *NFS Vandringsutställning*, Tallin, Estland
        Solo Exhibition, Oskarshamns konsthall, Oskarshamn
        Schmuckszene '91, Internationale Handwerksmesse, Munich
1990   *NFS*, Röhsska Kunstindustrimuseet, Gothenburg
1989   *Infinite Riches*, Museum of Fine Arts, St Petersburg, FL, USA
1988   *Jubileums utställning*, NFS, Stockholm
1987   *Joieria Europea Contemporània*, Fundació Caixa de Pensions,
        Barcelona
        Konst Hant Verk, Västerås Konstmuseum, Västerås, Sweden
        Linköping konstnärer, östergötlands Länsmuseet, Linköping,
        Sweden
        Scandinavian Craft Today, Yurakucho Art Forum, Tokyo
        (travelled)
        Smycken, Maneten, Gothenburg
1986   *10 Smeder*, Matsuya Craft Gallery, Tokyo
1985   *16 Dutch Jewellery Designers*, Nordenfjeldske
        Kunstindustrimuseum, Trondheim, Norway
        Nya Smycken, Nya Material, Kulturhuset, Stockholm
        Solo Exhibition, Kristianstad Länsmuseum, Kristianstad, Sweden

1984   *Contemporary Jewellery: The Americas, Australia, Europe and Japan*, National Museum of Modern Art, Kyoto; *Tokyo Jewelry International*, American Craft Museum II, New York

1983   *International Jewellery Art Exhibition*, 5th Tokyo Triennial, Isetan Art Museum, Tokyo

1982   *Schmuck '82 – Tendenzen*, Schmuckmuseum, Pforzheim, Germany

1980   *Schmuck International 1900-1980*, Künstlerhaus, Vienna

1978   *Der Ring*, Deutsches Goldschmiedehaus, Hanau, Germany
        VES, Stedelijik Museum, Amsterdam

1977   *Fachhochschule für Gestaltung 100 Jahre*, Pforzheim, Germany

1976   *Margareth Sandstrom/Peter de Wit*, Konstforum, Norrköping, Sweden

1974   *4th International Exhibition of Jewelry*, Muzeum skla a bizuterie, Jablonec nad Nisou, Czechoslovakia

Related Professional Experience:

1974–   Maintained independent studio in Linköping, Sweden

Selected Public Collections:

Museum für angewandte Kunst, Vienna; Nationalmuseum, Stockholm; Nederlandse Kunstichting, Amsterdam ; Nordenfjeldske Kunstindustrimuseum, Trondheim, Norway; östergötlands Länsmuseet, Linköping, Sweden; Rijksdienst Beeldende Kunst, Amsterdam; Röhsska Kunstindustrimuseet, Gothenburg

---

J. Fred Woell

Born: February 4, 1934, Evergreen Park, IL, USA

Education:

1969-76   MFA, Cranbrook Academy of Art, Bloomfield Hills, MI
1960-62   MS, MFA, University of Wisconsin, Madison
1958-60   BFA, University of Illinois, Urbana-Champaign
1955-56   BA, University of Illinois, Urbana-Champaign

Selected Awards:

1993   Fellowship, National Endowment for the Arts, Washington, DC
1975   Fellowship, National Endowment for the Arts, Washington, DC
        Services to the Field, National Endowment for the Arts, Washington, DC

Selected Exhibitions:

1994   *A Moveable Feast**, Amsterdam; *Schmuck Unserer Zeit**, Zurich
1993   *Contemporary Jewelry**, Little Rock, AK
        Tales & Traditions: Storytelling in 20th Century American Crafts, Craft Alliance, St Louis, MO (travelled)
1992-93   *Korun Kieli**, Gothenburg; Helsinki
1992   *Born[e] with a Silver Spoon*, National Ornamental Metal Museum, Memphis, TN
        Brilliant Stories: American Narrative Jewelry, USIS Exhibition Hall, Amman, Jordan (travelled)

1990   *American Dreams, American Extremes*, Museum Het Kruithuis, 's-Hertogenbosch, The Netherlands
        Schmuckszene '90, Internationale Handwerksmesse, Munich

1988   *10*, Portland Museum of Art, ME

1987   *The Eloquent Object*, Philbrook Museum of Art, Tulsa, OK (travelled)

1986   *Craft Today: Poetry of the Physical*, American Craft Museum, New York (travelled)

1984-87   *Modern Jewelry**, Philadelphia, PA; Cleveland, OH; Honolulu, HI; Montreal

1984   *Politics and the President*, Renwick Gallery, NCFA, Smithsonian Institution, Washington, DC

1981   *Good as Gold*, Renwick Gallery, NCFA, Smithsonian Institution, Washington, DC (travelled)

1980   *Robert L. Pfannebecker Collection*, Moore College of Art, Philadelphia, PA

1977   *The Metalsmith: SNAG Exhibition*, Phoenix Museum of Art, AZ
        Schmuck '77 – Tendenzen, Schmuckmuseum, Pforzheim, Germany

1975   *Forms in Metal*, Museum of Contemporary Crafts, New York

1974   *American Metalsmiths*, DeCordova Museum, Lincoln, MA
        The Goldsmith, Renwick Gallery, NCFA, Smithsonian Institution, Washington, DC
        Metal '74, State University of New York, Brockport

1971   *Jewellery '71*, Art Gallery of Ontario, Toronto

1970   *Goldsmith '70: SNAG Inaugural Exhibition*, Minnesota Museum of Art, St Paul (travelled)

1969   *Objects: USA*, National Collection of Fine Arts, Smithsonian Institution, Washington, DC (travelled)

1968   *Objects Are...?*, Museum of Contemporary Crafts, New York

1967   *Jewelry by Fred Woell*, Museum of Contemporary Crafts, New York

1965   *The Art of Personal Adornment*, Museum of Contemporary Crafts, New York

1962   *Young Americans 1962*, Museum of Contemporary Crafts, New York

Related Professional Experience:

1989-93   Professor, State University of New York, New Paltz
1985-87   Professor, Swain School of Design, New Bedford, MA
1976-85   Professor, Program-In-Artisanry, Boston University, MA

Lam De Wolf

Born: February 12, 1949, Badhoevedrop, The Netherlands

Education:

1978-81   Gerrit Rietveld Academie, Amsterdam

Selected Exhibitions:

1994   *A Moveable Feast**, Amsterdam; *Schmuck Unserer Zeit**, Zurich

---

Selected Permanent Collections:

American Craft Museum, New York; The Contemporary Museum, Honolulu; Georgia State University, Atlanta; New York State University (SUNY), Plattsburgh; Renwick Gallery, NMAA, Smithsonian Institution, Washington, DC; Sheldon Memorial Art Gallery, Lincoln, Nebraska; University of Wisconsin, La Crosse; University of Wisconsin, Madison

Lam De Wolf

1994	*Niet Alleen Voor de Sier*, Keunstwurk, Leeuwarden, The Netherlands
1994-80	*Nine Solo Exhibitions*, Galerie Ra, Amsterdam
1993	*Ahead of Fashion: Hats of the 20th Century*, Philadelphia Museum of Art, PA
	The Art of Jewellery, Setagaya Art Museum, Tokyo
	Contemporary Jewelry*, Little Rock, AK
	Fascinatie Textyles 2, Museum Van Bommel-Van Dam, Venlo, The Netherlands
1992-93	*Korun Kieli**, Gothenburg; Helsinki
1992	*International Textile Biennial*, Musée des Arts Décoratifs, Lausanne
1991	*Solo Exhibition*, Textilemuseum, Toronto
1990	*Dutch Form*, Fundacao Calouste Gulbenkian Foundation, Lisbon
	News from the Netherlands, Fundacao Calouste Gulbenkian, Lisbon (travelled)
1989	*Jewelry: Means: Meaning*, University of Tennessee, Knoxville (travelled)
1989	*Ornamenta 1*, Schmuckmuseum, Pforzheim, Germany
	Solo Exhibition, Galerie Espai Positura, Barcelona
1988	*Solo Exhibition*, Arti et Amicitiae, Amsterdam
1987	*Joieria Europea Contemporània*, Fundació Caixa de Pensions, Barcelona
	Solo Exhibition, Helen Drutt Gallery, Philadelphia, PA
1986	*Jewellery Images*, VES 10th anniversary exhibition, Stedelijk Museum, Amsterdam (travelled)
	Lam De Wolf/Debra Rapoport, Galerie Maya Behn, Zurich,
	Sieraad 1986, Draagteken?, Museum Het Kruithuis, 's-Hertogenbosch, The Netherlands
1985	*Body Works and Wearable Sculpture*, Visual Arts Center of Alaska, Anchorage
	Contemporary Jewelry Redefined, Pittsburgh Center for the Arts, PA
	New Tradition, British Crafts Centre, London
	Nya Smycken, Nya Material, Kulturhuset, Stockholm
	Solo Exhibition, Galerie Spektrum, Munich
1984-87	*Modern Jewelry**, Philadelphia, PA; Cleveland, OH; Honolulu, HI; Montreal
1984	*Contemporary Jewellery: The Americas, Australia, Europe and Japan*, National Museum of Modern Art, Kyoto; Tokyo
	Cross Currents: Jewellery from Australia, Britain, Germany and Holland, Power House Museum, Sydney (travelled)
	Group Exhibition, Centraal Museum, Utrecht
	Jewelry International, American Craft Museum II, New York
	Object and Image, Museum Het Kruithuis, 's-Hertogenbosch, The Netherlands (travelled)
1983	*The Jewellery Project*, Crafts Council Gallery, London
1982	*Solo Exhibition*, British Crafts Centre, London
	Solo Exhibition, Galerie Het Kapelhuis, Amersfoort, The Netherlands
	Visies op Sieraden 1965-1982, Stedelijk Museum, Amsterdam

Related Professional Experience:

1985–	Instructor, Gerrit Rietveld Academie, Amsterdam

Selected Public Collections:

City of Amsterdam; Centraal Museum, Utrecht; Gemeentelijke van Reekummuseum, Apeldoorn, The Netherlands; Haags Gemeentemuseum, The Hague; Nederlands Textielmuseum, Tilburg, The Netherlands; NKS, Amsterdam ; Stedelijk Museum, Amsterdam

---

Othmar Zschaler

Born: 1930, Chur, Switzerland

Education:

1946-50	Apprenticeship as a goldsmith

Selected Awards:

1967	Bavarian State Prize
1957,58,59	
	Recipient: Confederate Grant for Practical Art

Related Professional Experience:

1960	Establishes and maintains atelier in Berne

Selected Exhibitions:

1984	*Contemporary Jewellery: The Americas, Australia, Europe and Japan*, National Museum of Modern Art, Kyoto; Tokyo
1984	*Jewelry International*, American Craft Museum II, New York
1981	*Schmuck 81*, Schweizer Heimatwerk, Zurich
1979,76,73,70	
	Schmuck – Tendenzen, Schmuckmuseum, Pforzheim, Germany
1978	*Schmuck 78*, Schweizer Heimatwerk, Zurich
1977	*Schmuck des 20. Jahrhunderts*, Jerusalem, Melbourne, Tokyo
1977,73,70	
	Schmuck – Tendenzen, Schmuckmuseum, Pforzheim, Germany
1977	*Glas – Holz – Metal*, Kunsthalle, Berne
1976	*Aurea Arte*, Palazzo Strozzi, Florence
1975	*Schmuck 75*, Werrt Galerie, Gottlieben
1974	*18 Orfèvres d'aujourd'hui*, Musée des Arts Décoratifs, Lausanne
1972	*Solo Exhibition*, Schmuckmuseum, Pforzheim, Germany
1971	*Gold+Silber, Schmuck+Gerat*, Norishalle, Nuremberg
1970	*2nd Biennale Internazionale del Gioiello d'Arte*, Carrara, Italy
1968	*Silberner Schmuck*, work from the Symposium Museum for Glass and Jewelry, Jablonec, Czechoslovakia
1967	*7 Schweizer Goldschmiede*, Nordiska Kompaniet, Stockholm
	Schmuck von Malern und Bildhauern, Hessisches Landesmuseum, Darmstadt
1964	*Internationale Ausstellung Schmuck*, Hessisches Landesmuseum, Darmstadt

Selected Public Collections:

Hessisches Landesmuseum, Darmstadt; Historisches Museum, Berne; Kantonales Gewerbrmuseum, Berne; Schmuckmuseum, Pforzheim, Germany; Schweizerisches Landesmuseum, Zurich; Traditionelles und Modernes Schweizer Kunsthandwerk Sammlung, Zurich

selected works 1963-94

selected works 1963-94

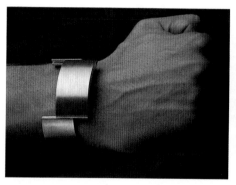

Hans Appenzeller

Armband. 1973
Aluminium; detachable
section
Private collection

Bracelet. 1976
PVC
Private collection

Klaus Arck

Brooch. 1987
Paper, wood

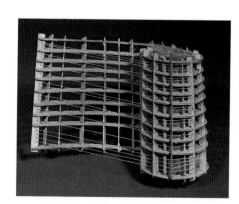

Giampaolo Babetto

Necklace. 1983
Gold
Collection Marijke
Vallanzasca, Italy

Necklace/Rings. 1983
Gold, epoxy resin
Private collection

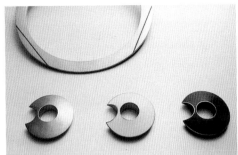

Gijs Bakker

5-Metre Necklace
1976
Gold wire

Comb. 1989-90
PVC laminated
photograph, gilded brass;
limited edition, #4

Holes Project
Bracelet. 1993
Gold
Collection of the artist

Adam
Neckpiece. 1982
PVC laminated
photograph, gilded brass;
limited edition

Moses
Brooch. 1987
PVC laminated
newspaper, gold

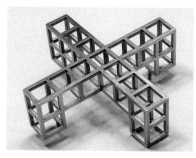

Frank Bauer

Palladium
(Age of Victoria)
Brooch. *c.*1980
Platinum
Private collection

Pendant. *c.*1981
Gold
Private collection

Jamie Bennett

Pattern Fragment
Brooch. 1978
Silver, enamel

Delta Neckpiece
1984
Enamel, silver,
black chrome
Collection Eleanor
and Samuel Rosenfeld,
USA

Priori #24
Brooch. 1990
Enamel, copper,
18k gold
Daphne Farago
Collection, USA

Ambage #11
Brooch. 1994
Enamel, copper, gold
Collection of the artist
Courtesy Helen Drutt

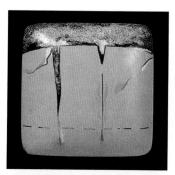

Joan Binkley

Neckpiece. 1981
Moroccan silver chain,
glazed ceramic
Private collection, USA

Headdress. 1993
Ceramic, mesh,
gold beads
Collection of the artist

 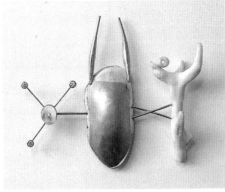

Manfred Bischoff

Taugenichts
Brooch. 1987
Silver, gold, enamel

Yo Metteur en Scène
Brooch. 1992
Gold, silver,
coral, diamond
Private collection, USA

Creator
Brooch. 1992
Gold, silver, coral,
Private collection, USA

Ring. 1994
Gold, coral, mirror
Boardman Family
Collection, USA

 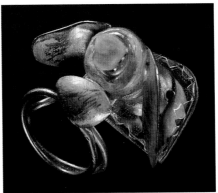

Liv Blåvarp

Neckpiece. 1992
Birch, dye, paint

Neckpiece. 1990
Indian rosewood,
satinwood.
Private collection,
Norway

Peter Blodgett

Brooch. *c.*1976
Sterling silver, ivory,
lapis lazuli
Private collection, USA

Neckpiece. *c.*1976
Silver
Private collection, USA

Marta Breis

Bracelet. 1983
Silver, steel,
thread

Necklace. 1983
Silver, copper,
steel, thread

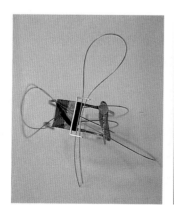
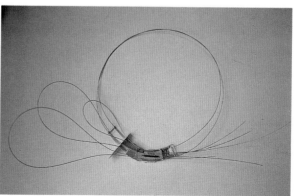

Caroline Broadhead

Armpiece. 1981
Wood hoop, nylon tufts
Private collection

Bracelets. 1980
Wood, nylon, silver
Private collection

Veil
Neckpiece. 1983
Nylon monofilament

Square Bracelets
1983
Cotton; cornered
Private collection

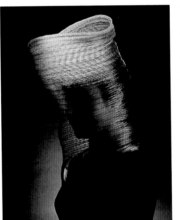

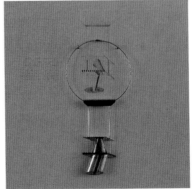

Claus Bury

Brooch. 1969
Arcylic
Collection Ida Boelen van
Gelder, The Netherlands

Pendant. 1976
Silver, gold, metal alloys;
mounted on drawing
Collection Metropolitan
Museum of Art, New York

Pierre Cavalan

*Star of the Grand Cross
of Sydney*
Brooch. 1994
Mixed media
Private collection,
Australia

*Knights Cross of Life
Saving*
Brooch. c.1993
Mixed media
Private collection,
Australia

 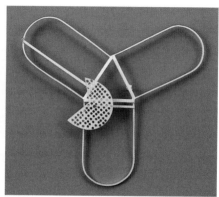

Anton Cepka

Brooch. 1964
Silver

Calibre
Brooch. c.1980
Silver

Peter Chang

Brick Bracelet
1989
Epoxy resin, inlaid

Bracelet. 1995
Acrylic, polyester,
PVC, lacquer
Collection Contemporary
Art Society, London

Brooch. 1992
Acrylic, polyester, lacquer
Collection Victoria and
Albert Museum, London

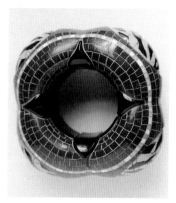  

Sharon Church

Long Chain
Neckpiece. 1986
Oxidized sterling silver,
onyx, diamonds,
silver ore
Boardman Family
Collection, USA

Neckpiece. 1989
Glass beads, oxidized
sterling silver
Daphne Farago
Collection, USA

Ken Cory

Hose
Brooch. 1968
Silver, plastic
Estate of Ken Cory

Broken Window
Brooch. 1972
Copper, silver, brass,
glass bead
Estate of Ken Cory

**Ken Cory/Les LePere:
Pencil Brothers**

Texas
Brooch. 1972
Copper, enamel, pencils,
carnelian, pencil drawing
Collection Leslie W.
LePere, USA

Ken Cory

Tent
Brooch. 1988
Sterling silver, 22k gold,
carnelian
Estate of Ken Cory

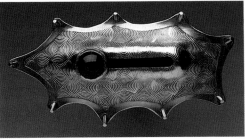

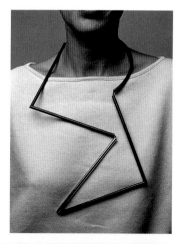

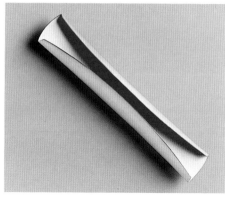

Johanna Dahm

Neckpiece. 1985
Chromed-plated brass,
rubber cord

Reflection
Pin. 1994
Oxidized silver,
acrylic colour

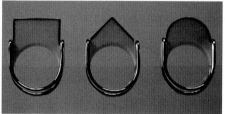

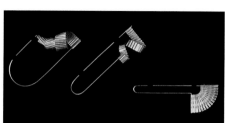

Paul Derrez

Rings. 1977
Gold, ivory
Collection of the artist
Courtesy Galerie Ra,
Amsterdam

Brooches. 1980
Silver
Collection of the artist
Courtesy Galerie Ra,
Amsterdam

Claire Dinsmore

Kokovo Series
Bracelet #1. 1987
Sterling silver,
anodized aluminium,
plated tubing, brass

Rietveld's Plumbing
Bracelet #4. c.1991
Sterling silver, Surel
Collection of the artist

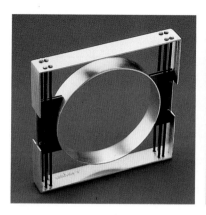

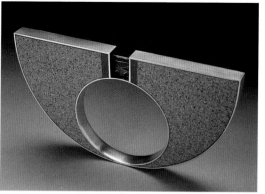

Georg Dobler

Neckpiece. 1985
Steel, acrylic
lacquer

Brooch. 1982
Silver, steel,
acrylic lacquer

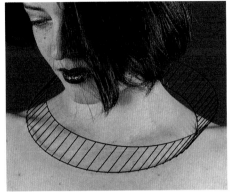

Brooch. 1987
Silver, steel wire,
acrylic lacquer
Collection of the artist
Courtesy Helen Drutt

Brooch. 1991
Silver
Private collection

Brooch. 1989
Steel, acrylic colour
Collection of the artist

Robert Ebendorf

Bracelet. 1987
Korean paper, ebony,
Formica, paint
Private collection

Cross Necklace
1993
Silver, iron, wire,
amber, carnelian,
found objects
Private collection

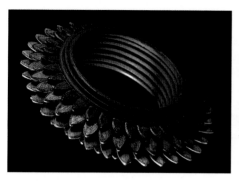
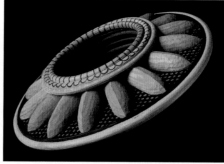

Gry Eide

Stave Church
Bracelet. 1989
Cane, wood, paint

Decorated Flower
Bracelet. 1989
Cane, wood, paint,
silver-foil, paper,
plastic

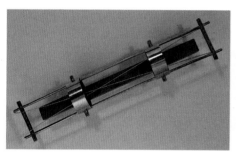

Eva Eisler

Brooch. 1988
Sterling silver,
steel wire, slate

Pin/Ring. 1994
Stainless steel
Collection of the artist

Arline Fisch

Halter and Skirt,
detail. 1968
Silver
Collection American Craft
Museum, New York

Collar. 1983
Copper wire; knitted

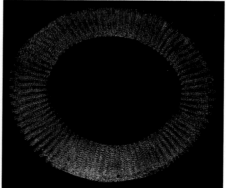

Jem Freyaldenhoven

Brooch. 1976
Peacock feather,
silver, acrylic
Collection Mr and Mrs
W.H. Freyaldenhoven,
USA

Brooch. *c.*1979
Silver, acrylic
Private collection

Brooch. *c.*1977-78
Silver, gold-plated
silver, acrylic
Private collection

Donald Friedlich

Erosion Series
Brooch. 1985
Ceramic tile, 18k gold

Erosion Series
Brooch. 1983
18k gold,
titanium, slate

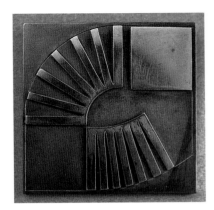 

Max Fröhlich

Brooch. 1985
Shibuichi on shakudo
Private collection

Brooch. 1986
Shibuichi on shakudo,
gold
Private collection

Elizabeth Garrison

Origin
Brooch. 1988
Silver, copper, 14k gold,
enamel, ivory

Volcano Dream #1
Brooch. 1985
Fine and sterling silver,
copper, cloisonné
enamel, found object
Private collection, USA

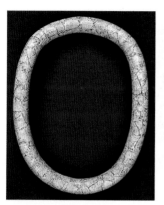

Thomas Gentille

Neckpiece. 1990
Eggshell inlay, wood
Collection of the artist
Courtesy Helen Drutt

Britannia
Armlet. 1987
Eggshell inlay, wood
Collection of the artist
Courtesy Helen Drutt

Armlet. 1991
Eggshell inlay, wood
Collection of the artist
Courtesy Helen Drutt

Toni Goessler-Snyder

Bracelet. 1979
24k gold, silver,
chalcedony, garnet

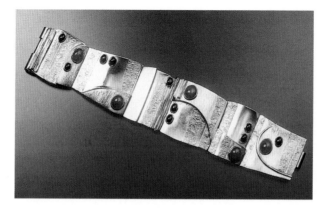

Lisa Gralnick

Brooch. *c.*1989
Acrylic

Brooch #6. 1990
18k gold
Private collection, USA

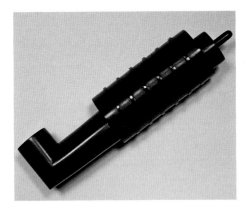 

Gary Griffin

Ring Set. 1972
Sterling silver, citrine
Collection of the artist

Plasma Sketch
Brooch. 1973
Acrylic, stainless
steel, copper
Collection of the artist

Laurie Hall

The Compleat Angler
Pin/Pendant/Compact,
details, open and closed.
1992
Compass paper,
bronze, sterling silver,
wood, rubber cord
Collection William Wall,
USA

 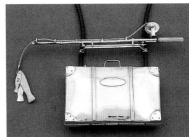

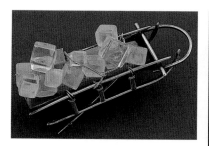

Laurie Hall

Sled
Brooch. 1992
Silver, copper, Plexiglas
Collection of the artist
Courtesy Helen Drutt

Rule of Thumb
Neckpiece. 1986
Mixed media
Collection Sandy and
Lou Grotta, USA

Stumped
Neckpiece. 1994
Wood, silver, compass
Courtesy Helen Drutt

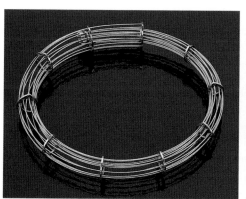

Susan Hamlet

Column Bracelet
1983
14k gold, stainless steel

Element of Escape
Brooch. 1992
Sterling silver
Collection Gail Brown,
USA

William Harper

Unrequited Valentine #3
Brooch. 1979
14k gold, silver,
baroque pearl, pearl,
cloisonné enamel,
copper

Rude Byzantine Saint
Brooch. 1991
Enamel, gold, pearl
Collection of the artist
Courtesy Peter Joseph
Gallery New York

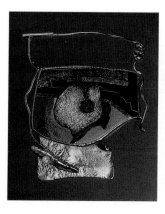

Therese Hilbert

Brooch. 1984
Brass
Private collection

Neckpiece, detail. 1983
Brass varnished black,
PVC, steel
Collection Sandy and
Lou Grotta, USA

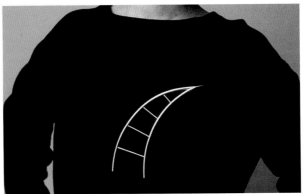

Ron Ho

Treasures of the Orient II
Neckpiece. 1979
Japanese ivory kamibuta,
Chinese jade button,
pearls, silver
Private collection, USA

Bering Sea
Neckpiece. 1985
North-west Coast
Indian harpoon tip,
Afghan beads,
mother-of-pearl, silver
Private collection, USA

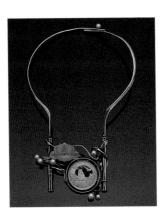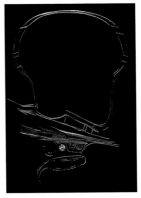

Mary Lee Hu

Choker #22. 1976
Fine and sterling silver
Private collection, USA

Choker #35. 1977
Fine and sterling silver,
24k gold, lacquered
copper electrical wire
Private collection, USA

Choker #41. 1978
Fine and sterling silver,
18k gold
Private collection, USA

Mary Lee Hu

Choker *#65*. 1981
Fine and sterling silver,
22k gold
Private collection, USA

Bracelet *#29*. 1984
Fine and sterling silver,
14k gold
Courtesy Telluride
Gallery, USA

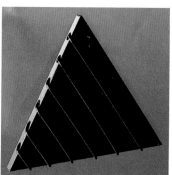

Kazuhiro Itoh

Brooch. 1979
Stone

Brooch. 1979
Stone

Brooch. 1982
Stone

Daniel Jocz

Caged Stone Series
Ring. 1991
Sterling silver,
14k gold, garnets
Collection of the artist

*Ceremonies of the
City: Shelter*
Ring. 1988
Sterling silver, 14k gold
Private collection, USA

Hermann Jünger

Brooch. 1964
Silver, gold, amethyst,
aquamarine, granite,
opal, sapphire, ruby,
turquoise, enamel
Collection Fran Waltraud
von Busse, Germany

Necklace/Pendant. 1967
Gold, silver, black opal,
turquoise, emerald
Collection Ida Boelen van
Gelder, The Netherlands

Brooch. 1978
Gold, silver
Collection Irene Dietzel

Brooch. 1984
Tombac, gold
Collection Museum für
Kunsthandwerk,
Frankfurt

Brooch. 1985
Tombac, gold
Private collection

Box with 9 Pendants.
1989
Silver, haematite,
chrysoprase,
chalcedony crystal
Private collection

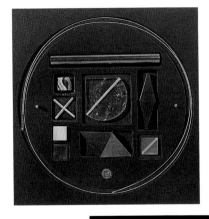

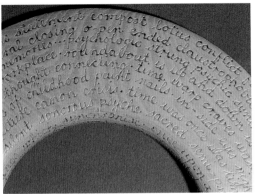

Sieglinde Karl

Bracelet. 1989
Wood, dye; words by
Hazel Smith

Bracelet, detail. 1989
Wood, dye; words by
Hazel Smith

Betsy King

Caught in a Trap
Brooch. 1988
Silver, Plexiglas,
brass, photograph

*Punch and Judy Fought
for a Pie*
Brooch. 1994
Postcard fragment,
copper, silver

Alice H. Klein

After Five
Necklace. 1982
Acrylic, silver, nickel
silver, cubic zirconia,
baroque pearl, gold
filled wire, staples

Luminescence
Necklace. 1983
Oxidized silver,
acrylic, gold

Esther Knobel

Neckpiece. 1983
Tin, paint, elastic
Private collection

Pendant. *c.*1981
Titanium, metal
Private collection

Rena Koopman

Earrings. 1990
Gold, shakudo
Private collection, USA

Brooch. 1992
Coloured golds,
shakudo
Private collection, USA

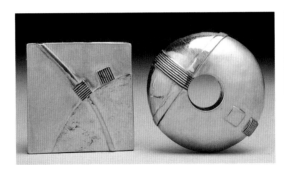

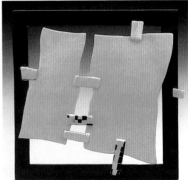

**Robin Kranitzky/
Kim Overstreet**

*Suppressed
Thoughts*
Brooch. 1990
Mixed media

Roots
Brooch. 1990
Mixed media

Notions
Brooch. 1990
Mixed media

Otto Künzli

Brooch. 1982
Wallpaper,
hardfoam, steel
Private collection

Brooch. 1982-83
Wallpaper,
hardfoam, steel
Private collection

Rebekah Laskin

Brooch. 1986
Sterling silver, copper,
enamel
Private collection, USA

Brooch. 1989
Sterling silver, copper
enamel

Stanley Lechtzin

Pendant *#85B*
1967
Diamond, citrine,
tourmaline, gold
Collection of the artist

Torque *#16-D*
1971
Silver, gilt,
polyester resin

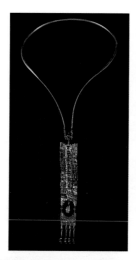

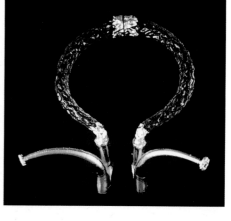

Brooch *#63-D*
1966
Silver, tourmaline,
crystal, pearl

Bracelet *#49F*
1994
CAD/CAM virtual acrylic,
anodized aluminium
Collection of the artist

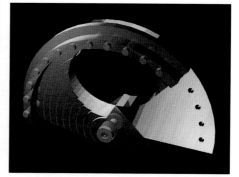

Emmy van Leersum

Dress with Neckpiece.
1966
Silver, acrylic
Rijks Collection,
The Netherlands

Bracelet. 1977
PVC laminated paper;
limited edition

Broken Lines Neckpiece
1980
Nylon; limited edition

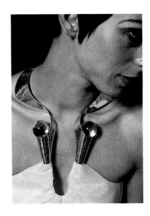

Fritz Maierhofer

Neckpiece. 1994
Silver, gold
Private collection

Brooch. 1991
Yellow, white gold,
amethyst, citrine,
rubellite, diamonds
Private collection

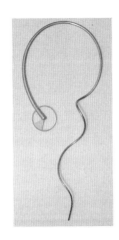
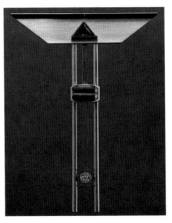

Carlier Makigawa

Brooches. 1985
Papier mâché, steel
Private collections

Rings, Objects and
Brooches. 1989
Marble, silver,
steel, papier mâché,
lacquer, gold leaf
Private collections

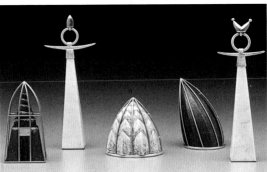

Bruno Martinazzi

Occhio
Brooch. 1971
White gold, lapis lazuli

Two Fingers
Bracelet. 1971
20k gold, 18k white gold
Collection Ida Boelen van
Gelden, The Netherlands

Angelo Rafaello
Brooch. 1987
White, yellow gold
Private collection, USA

Falko Marx

Brooch. 1988
Iron, gold, silver,
diamonds, pyrite
Private collection

Brooch. 1989
Antique ceramic
shard, diamond
Boardman Family
Collection, USA

Richard Mawdsley

Feast Bracelet
1974
Sterling silver, jade, pearls
Collection Renwick
Gallery, NMAA,
Smithsonian Institution,
Washington, DC

*Wonder Woman in her
Bicentennial Finery*
Pendant, detail. *c.*1976
Silver, pearls, jadite
Boardman Family
Collection, USA

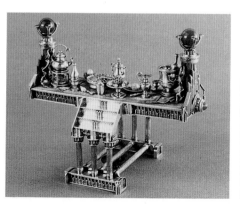

Bruce Metcalf

3 Naked Ladies
Brooch. 1975
Commercial white metal
castings, Plexiglas, silver,
stainless steel

Bagman
Brooch. 1987
Plexiglas, paint, silver

 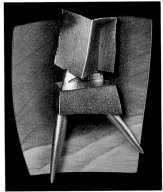

Walter Kelley Morris

Menlo Park Extra
Brooch. 1974
Silver, acrylic

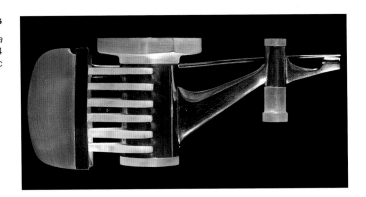

Eleanor Moty

Landscape Handbag
1973
Sterling silver, 14k gold,
brass, copper agate,
leather
Whereabouts unknown

*Tourmalinated Crystal
Brooch II*
1987
Silver, gold,
tourmalinated quartz

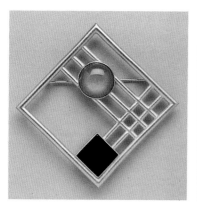

Louis Mueller

Brooch. 1983
Gold-plated silver,
onyx, moonstone

Pinocchio
Pendant. 1991
Silver, steel
Private collection

Pencil
Ring. 1994
Gold, enamel, haematite
Private collection

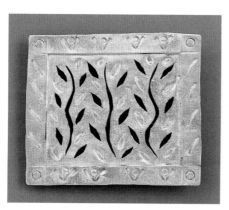

Breon O'Casey

Brooch. 1993
Silver

Necklace. 1993
Pebbles, gold,
silk cord

Joke van Ommen

Necklace. 1981
Brass
Estate of Joke
van Ommen

Kite Pin
1982
Anodized aluminium
Private collection

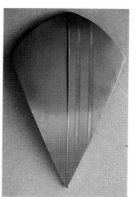

Judy Onofrio

Bracelets. 1993-94
Beads, glass,
peyote stitch

Reliquary with Brooch.
1989
Recycled costume
jewelry, found objects,
wood, paint
Private collection, USA

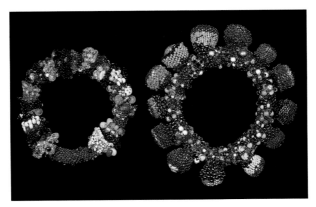

Pavel Opočenský

Brooch. 1986
Ivory, ebony
Private collection,
USA

Brooch. 1985
Ivory
Collection Edna S.
Beron, USA

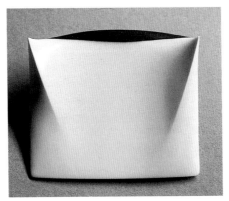

Albert Paley

Brooch. 1969
14k gold, silver,
freshwater and baroque
pearls

Brooch. 1971
Silver, gold, moonstone,
pearl, lens
Private collection, USA

Pendant. 1974
Silver, ivory, garnet
Private collection, USA

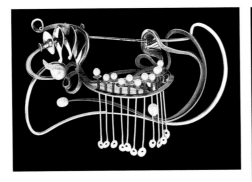
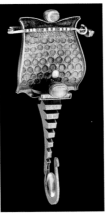

Tony Papp

Brooch. 1988
Silver

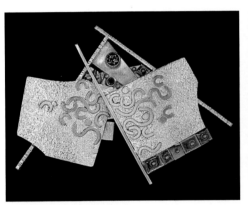

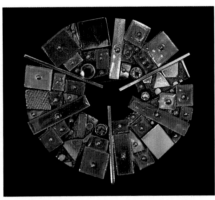

Earl Pardon

Brooch. *c.*1989
Enamel, gold, silver
Private collection, USA

Brooch. *c.*1989
Enamel, gold, silver
Private collection, USA

Francesco Pavan

Ring. 1987
Silver, gold, alpaca
Private collection

Vibrazione Cromatiche
Brooch. 1992
18k red, yellow,
green gold
Collection of the artist

Ruudt Peters

Passeo: Argus
Pendant, detail. 1993
Silver, optical lens
Collection of the artist
Courtesy Charon
Kransen, New York

Passeo: Aphrodite
Pendant, detail. 1993
Silver, coral beads
Collection of the artist
Courtesy Jewelers'werk,
Washington, DC

**Hiroko Sato Pijanowski/
Eugene Pijanowski**

Brooch. 1987
Paper, canvas,
(*mizuhiki*)
Private collection

Pendant
*c.*1985
Mixed media
Private collection

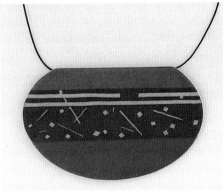

Ramón Puig Cuyàs

Arturus
Brooch. 1989
Silver, paint, acrylic
Private collection

Sonnentisch
Brooch. 1992
Silver, paint, alpaca
Private collection

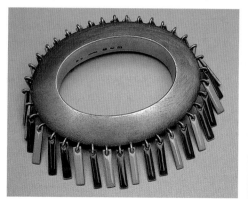

Robin Quigley

Fringe Bracelet
1983
Pewter, epoxy resin
Private collection

*Black and White
Dot Necklace*
1985
Pewter, epoxy resin
Collection Helen Bershad,
USA

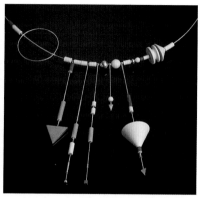

Wendy Ramshaw

Brooch. 1974
Gold, silver, ivory

Necklace with Open Circle
and Pendants. 1982
18k yellow gold with
Wedgwood parts
Private collection

Debra Rapoport

Cloth Amulets
Neckpiece. 1979
Fibre, paint, pins,
commercial chain

Pendant. 1979
Found object (detail of
Ford motor car), brass,
cord, commercial chain

Richard Reinhardt

Bracelet. 1979
Silver
Private collection, USA

Bracelet. 1983
Silver
Private collection, USA

Gerd Rothmann

Bracelet/Pendant.
1970-71
Steel, acrylic, paper;
limited edition, 2/30

Kaugummikette
Necklace. 1991
Gold-plated silver;
limited edition

Gold Finger
1992-93
Gold
Private collection

 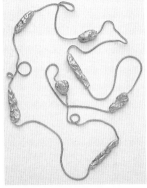 

 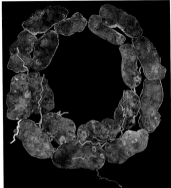

Philip Sajet

Ring. *c.*1988-89
White gold, semi-precious
stones, beads
Private collection

Thunder and Lightning
Neckpiece. 1993
Steel, gold
Collection Stedelijk
Museum, Amsterdam

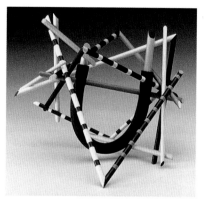

Marjorie Schick

Bracelet. 1985
Wood, paint, rubber

Spiral Necklace
1994
Papier mâché, cord,
wood, paint
Collection of the artist

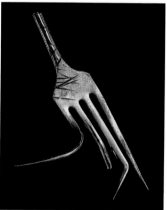

Bernhard Schobinger

Bottle Necklace
1990
Glass, cord
Private collection

Brooch. *c.*1988
Silver
Private collection

Deganit Schocken

Neckpiece. 1983
Gold, silver
Private collection

Brooch. 1987
Silver, copper
Collection of the artist
Courtesy Helen Drutt

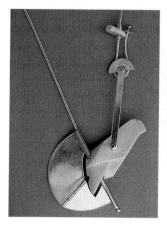
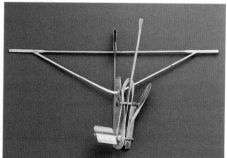

Joyce Scott

Suspense, Like on TV
Necklace. 1993
Beads, peyote stitch
Whereabouts unknown

Danger Done
Necklace. 1994
Glass beads, found
objects, peyote stitch

Miriam Sharlin

Brooch. 1979
18, 20, 24k gold,
silver, acid etched

Helen Shirk

Bracelet. 1980
Silver, 14k gold, onyx
Collection of the artist

Brooch. 1994
Sterling silver, 14k gold
Collection of the artist
Courtesy Helen Drutt

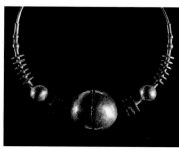

Olaf Skoogfors

Pendant. 1973
Gold-plated silver
Collection Ilene Weiss,
USA

Brooch. 1970
Gold-plated silver,
blue baroque pearl

Necklace. *c.*1970
Gold-plated; separate
elements

Peter Skubic

Cut-Ring. 1978
Yellow and white gold
Collection of the artist

Idol VI: Schmuckobjekt.
1986
Stainless steel, brass,
steel wire
Collection of the artist

Balance III
Series of Pins. *c.*1988-89
Mixed media
Collection of the artist

Brooch. 1994
Stainless steel, steel wire
Collection of the artist

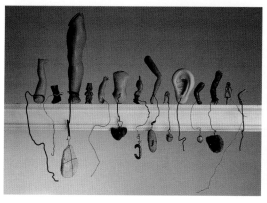

Kiff Slemmons

Hands of the Heroes:
William Carlos Williams
Brooch. 1989
Copper, silver, slate
Collection Emily Landau,
USA

Protection
Pendant. 1992
Brass, copper, silver,
pencils, mirror, nickel,
horsehair, leather
Collection Don and
Rita Newman, USA

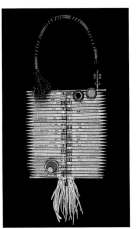

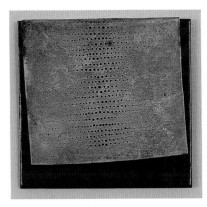

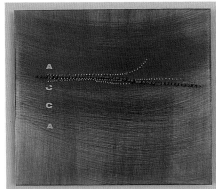

Robert Smit

Brooch. 1969
Silver, paint
Collection of the artist
Courtesy Louise Smit

Brooch. 1971
Gold, acrylic
Collection Ida Boelen van
Gelder, The Netherlands

Bello's Sister
Brooch. 1993
Gold, paint, pearls
Collection of the artist
Courtesy Helen Drutt

Bello, So Sad
Pendant. 1993
Gold, paint
Collection of the artist
Courtesy Helen Drutt

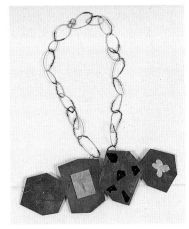

 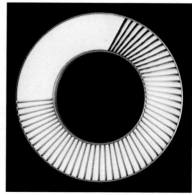

Eric Spiller

Brooch. 1979
Aluminium, acrylic,
synthetic material

Brooch. 1980
Aluminium, acrylic,
synthetic material

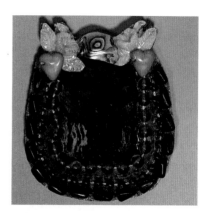

Vaughn Stubbs

Cherub Boys
Brooch. 1990
Mixed media,
found objects

Olli Tamminen

Pendant. 1990
Silver, steel, stones

Pendant. 1990
Silver, steel, stone
Collection of the artist

David Tisdale

Disc Bracelet. 1981
Aluminium

Bracelet. 1983
Aluminium, silver,
onyx, tiger's eye

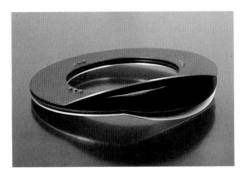

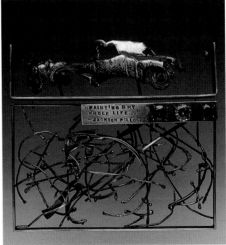

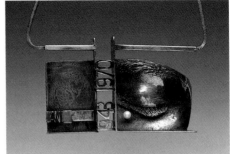

Don Tompkins

Nixon
Commemorative Medal
Pendant. 1972
Silver, photograph,
Plexiglas, synthetic stone
Collection Maryn
Tompkins, USA

Jackson Pollock
Commemorative Medal
Pendant. 1972
Silver, synthetic stones
Collection Merrily
Tompkins, USA

Hugh Hefner
Commemorative Medal
Pendant. 1971
Silver, found objects
Collection Maryn
Tompkins, USA

Janis Joplin
Commemorative Medal
Pendant. 1971
Silver, pearl
Collection Merrily
Tompkins, USA

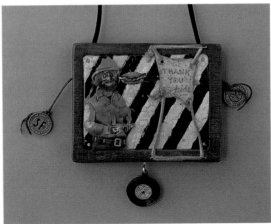

Merrily Tompkins

Slow Boat
(Portrait of Ken Cory)
Necklace. 1976
Wood, silver, brass,
enamel, copper,
found objects
Collection Merrily
Tompkins
Courtesy Estate of
Ken Cory

Thank You, Hide
Pendant. 1976
Enamel, wood, leather,
found objects

Snatch Purse
Waist Pendant. 1975
Leather, fur, enamel,
silver, velvet, satin
Collection Merrily
Tompkins
Courtesy Estate of
Ken Cory

No Pun Intended
Pendant. 1976
Enamel, wood, metal
Private collection, USA

Peter Tully

Australiana Necklace
1977
Found objects
Private collection,
Australia

Sundowner's Glasses
1982
Acrylic enamel
Private collection,
Australia

Tone Vigeland
Bracelet. 1976
Silver, gold
Collection
Kunstindustrimuseet,
Oslo

Necklace. 1981
Steel, silver, gold,
mother-of-pearl
Collection Cooper Hewitt
Museum of Design,
Smithsonian Institution,
New York

Necklace. 1983
Steel, silver, gold,
nickel-plated bronze
Collection of the artist

Bracelet. 1986
Silver
Collection Museum of
Modern Art, New York

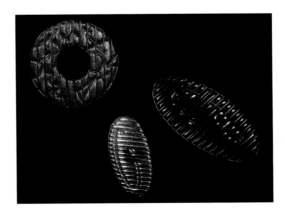

David Walker

Skin Series
(left to right):

Life Cycle
Brooch. 1989
Patinated copper,
stainless steel

Scar Tissue I
Brooch 1989
Silver, stainless steel

Twisting the Knife II
Brooch. 1989
Patinated copper,
stainless steel

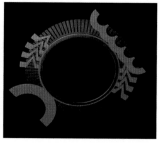

David Watkins

Wing-Wave 3
Neckpiece. 1983
Neoprene-coated steel,
wood

Jazzz
Neckpiece. 1986
Laser-cut ColorCore
Collection of the artist

Neckpiece. 1976
Steel, gold

Margaret West

Eight Stones with Steel
Necklace. 1985
Stone, steel, monel
Private collection

*Equation Disc with
Three Reflections*
1987
Granite, slate, steel

Detail
1991
Steel, ribbon, brass
Collection of the artist

Autumn Cantata
Brooch. 1993
Wood, lacquer
Collection of the artist

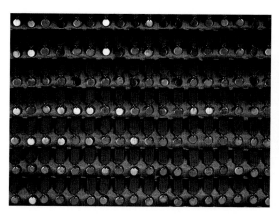
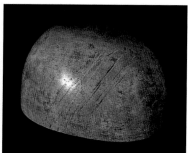

Peter de Wit

Necklace. 1983
Gold, quartz
Collection of the artist

Brooch. 1983
Gold, quartz
Private collection

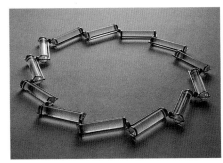

J. Fred Woell

*Come Alive, You're in the
Pepsi Generation*
Brooch. 1966
Copper, silver, steel,
camera lens, photograph
of Mia Farrow
Collection Kathleen
Woell, USA

*Cheap Shot. Pearl
Harbour, 7 Dec 1941*
Pendant. 1995
Mixed media
Collection of the artist

Lam de Wolf

Neckpiece. *c.*1984
Textile, paint
Private collection

Headdress. 1984
Textile, wood, paint
Private collection

chronology of selected exhibitions

chronology of selected exhibitions

Note:

This chronology concentrates on the exhibitions which have been organized by public museums and non-profit-making institutions. Where exhibition catalogues have been available, the list of participating artists has frequently been too long to include in full. The major solo exhibitions of the artists central to this book can be found in the previous section, 'Biographies of the Artists'. Exhibitions organized and sponsored by commercial galleries are too numerous to include here; the following list names some of those whose activities have made a highly important contribution to the development and documentation of contemporary jewelry:

Artwear, New York; Contemporary Jewellery Gallery, Sydney; Electrum Gallery, London; Galerie Biro, Munich; Galerie CADA, Munich; Galerie am Graben, Vienna; Galerie Marzee, Nimwegen; Galerie Mattar, Cologne; Galerie Ra, Amsterdam; Galerie Slavik, Vienna; Galerie Sofie Lachaert, Ghent; Galerie Spektrum, Munich; Galerie Ton Berends, The Hague; Helen Drutt, Philadelphia; Jocelyne Gobeil, Montreal; Louise Smit, Amsterdam; Marijke Studio, Padua; Michele Zeller, Berne; Schmuckforum, Zurich; The Scottish Gallery, Edinburgh; Susan Cummins Gallery, Mill Valley, CA; V & V Galerie, Vienna; VO Galerie/Jewelers'werk, Washington, DC; Werkstattgalerie, Berlin

1960

Europäisches Email, Internationale Ausstellung von Email am Schmuck, im Raum und am Bau, Deutsches Goldschmiedehaus, Hanau, Germany.

Golden Ring of Honour of the Association for Goldsmiths' Art (created by Walter Lochmuller '57), recipient: Bertel Gardberg, Deutsches Goldschmiedehaus, Hanau, Germany.

International Jewelry Exhibition, Nieman/Marcus, Dallas, Texas. Artists include: A. Pomodoro, G. Pomodoro and Bruno Martinazzi.

Sigurd Perrson: 7 x 7 Collection, Nordiska Kompaniet, Stockholm, Sweden.

1961

American Jewelry Today, First Biennial, Everhart Museum of Natural History, Science and Art, Scranton, PA, USA; discontinued 1967.

International Exhibition of Modern Jewellery: 1890–1961, Goldsmiths' Hall, London, England (Oct. 26– Dec. 2); organized by the Worshipful Co. of Goldsmiths in association with the Victoria and Albert Museum. Artists include: Arp, F. Becker, Brynner, Calder, Craver, Dalì, Ernst, Flöckinger, Fontana, Giacometti, Tuulikki Haivaoja, Kretsinger, Larsen, Lechtzin, Lewers, Lurcat, Martinazzi, J. P. Miller, P. Morton, E. R. Nele, De Patta, Persson, Pinton, Sottsass, Bülow Hübe, Vapaavuori, Vierthaler, T. Vigeland, Weiss-Weingart, Wirkkala.

1962

Dänisches Silber und Handwerk, Dänischen Wochen, Zurich, Switzerland (Jan. 26– Feb. 25).

Donald B Wright: Jewelry and Woodwork, Museum of Contemporary Crafts, New York (May 25– July 29).

Young Americans 1962, Museum of Contemporary Crafts, New York, USA (May 25 – Sept. 2), Jewelry artists include: Robert Ebendorf, Arline Fisch, Stanley Lechtzin, J. Fred Woell.

Modern British Jewellery, Worshipful Co. of Goldsmiths, London, England.

1963

Golden Ring of Honour of the Association for Goldsmiths' Art (created by Bertel Gardberg '60), recipient: Soren Georg Jensen, Deutsches Goldschmiedehaus, Hanau, Germany.

Jewelry '63: An International Exhibition, State University College, Plattsburg, New York, USA (April 17– May 7).

Jewelry and Holloware by Ronald Hayes Pearson, Museum of Contemporary Crafts, New York, USA (Jan. 25– March 10).

Mary Ann Scherr: Stainless Steel Jewelry, Museum of Contemporary Crafts, New York, USA (May 24– Sept. 8).

NFS (Föringen för Nutida Svenskt Silver/Swedish Society for Contemporary Silver) established Stockholm, Sweden.

1964

Contemporary Scandinavian Jewelry, Röhsska Konstlöjdmuseet, Gothenburg, Sweden; participating artist: Tone Vigeland.

Diamonds: International Awards, National Arts Club, New York, USA (Oct. 7– 9); Lowndes Lodge Gallery, London, England (Oct. 20–31).

First World Crafts Council Conference at Columbia University, New York, USA: Stanley Lechtzin delivers a paper on electroforming.

Internationale Ausstellung: Schmuck Jewellery Bijoux, Hessisches Landesmuseum, Darmstadt, Germany (Dec. 10, 1964– Feb. 14, 1965). Artists: Arp, Braque, I. Brynner, Clen-Murphy, Donald, Filhos, Flöckinger, Grima, Holmes, Jünger, R. King, Lurcat, Mercier, E. R. Nele, Penalba, Persson, A. Pomodoro, G. Pomodoro, S. Schmölzer, Thomas, Vieira, Zschaler.

Japan Jewellery Designers Association Inauguration party (June). *Modern Jewellery Design* exhibition, Maruzen, 19 founding members, (Sept.)

Jewelry '64: An International Exhibition, State University College, Plattsburg, NY, USA (April 15– May 8).

Judge: Earl Pardon. Artists include: Fike, Fisch, Lechtzin, Schick, Seppä, D. Tompkins, Woell.

Jewelry by Bruno Martinazzi, Galeria Il Punto, Turin, Italy (Nov.–Dec.), Musée de l'Athénée, Geneva, Switzerland (Dec.); Handwerkskammer für Oberbayern, Munich, Germany (Jan.– Feb. 1965); Goldsmiths' Hall, London, England (April– May 1965).

Jewelry by John Paul Miller, Museum of Contemporary Crafts, New York, USA (March 6– May 3).

Modern Scandinavian Jewels: Denmark, Finland, Norway, Sweden. Georg Jensen Inc., New York. Artists include: (Denmark) N. Ditzel, Von Fleming, S.G. Jensen, Koppel; (Finland) Gardberg, Saara Hopea, B. Weckström; (Norway) G. Prytz Korsmo, T. Vigeland; (Sweden) Bülow-Hübe, C. Johansson, Persson.

1965

1. Internationaler Wettbewerb des Schmuckmuseums Pforzheim-Ohrschmuck in Gold, Schmuckmuseum, Pforzheim, Germany; participating artist: Francesco Pavan.

American Jewelry Today, Everhart Museum, Scranton, PA (Nov. 1–30). Artists include: Ebendorf, Eikerman, Fenster, Fisch, B. Kington, Lee, Paley, E. M. Pijanowski, Roach, Schick, Seppä , Skoogfors.

The Art of Personal Adornment, Museum of Contemporary Crafts, New York, USA (Sept. 24– Nov. 7). Artists include: F. Becker, I. Brynner, Calder, Croft, Dehner, Ebendorf, Falkenstein, Fisch, Freund, Gentille, A. Giacometti, Kington, Loloma, Mafong, Packard, Pearson, Persson, A. Pomodoro, De Rivera, Roach, M. A. Scherr, Shannon, Surendorf, Torun, Winston, Woell, C. Zeisler.

Golden Ring of Honour of the Association for Goldsmiths' Art (created by Soren Georg Jensen '63), recipient: Max Fröhlich, Deutsches Goldschmiedehaus, Hanau, Germany.

Jewelry by Margaret de Patta, Museum of Contemporary Crafts, New York, USA (Jan. 29– March 21).

Novas Igrejas na Alemanha, Rio de Janeiro, Brazil; Hermann Jünger exhibits.

1966

'67 Japan Jewellery Exhibit, Hankyu Gallery, Tokyo, Japan (Nov.).

Art in Jewelry, Finch College Museum of Art, New York, USA (opened March 15). Artists: F. Becker, Braque, Dalì, P. Häiväoja, O. Landuyt, O. Lynggaard, Martinazzi, M. Ostier, G. Packard, Persson, Schmolzer, R. Yamada.

Atelier voor Sieraden established, Utrecht, The Netherlands; Founders: Gijs Bakker and Emmy van Leersum.

Craftsmen USA 66, Museum of Contemporary Crafts, New York, USA (June 3 – Sept. 11), toured USA.

Jewelry artists: Apodaca, I. Brynner, Ebendorf, Fenster, Fike, Golan, Jerry, Kington, Kriegman, Lechtzin, Marshall, Matsukata, J. P. Miller, Paley, Penington, R. C. Radakovich, S. Radakovich, Scherr, Skoogfors.

Friedrich Becker, Goldsmiths' Hall, London, England (Oct. 4–19).

Jewelry by Alice Shannon, Museum of Contemporary Crafts, New York, USA (April 1– May 22).

1967

'68 Japan Jewellery Exhibit, Hankyu Gallery, Tokyo, Japan (Nov.).

2. Internationaler Wettbewerb des Schmuckmuseums Pforzheim-Halsschmuck in Gold, Schmuckmuseum, Pforzheim, Germany.

Acquisitions: The David R. Campbell Memorial Collection, Museum of Contemporary Crafts, New York, USA (May 26– Sept. 10). Jewelry artists: Brynner, Craver, Kramer, Lechtzin, De Patta, Skoogfors, A. Smith, E. Wiener, Woell.

American Jewelry Today, Everhart Museum, Scranton, PA.

Expo '67, Australian Pavillion, Montreal, Canada. Jewelers exhibiting: Helge Larsen, Darani Lewers.

Jewelry series initiated by Gian Carlo Montebello, Milan (Gem Montebello Lab. Gem discontinued in 1973).

metal: germany, Museum of Contemporary Crafts, New York, USA (Jan. 20– March 5). Artists include: Jünger, Reiling, Seibert, Ullrich, Weiss-Weingart.

Schmuck '67 – Tendenzen, Schmuckmuseum, Pforzheim, Germany. Organized by Reinhold Reiling and Klaus Hallwass.

Sculpture to Wear, Exhibition, London, England

Schmuck Symposium, Haldenhof, Wissgoldingen, Germany. Initiated by Jo Stotz (d.1982), and held annually; continued by Judith Stotz.

Uudet korut (New Jewelry), Design Centre, Helsinki.

1968

The American Contemporary Jewelry Exhibition, sponsored by Yomiuri Shimbun, Odakyu Department Store, Tokyo, Japan (April 5–17). Artists: Lechtzin, Matsukata and Skoogfors.

Europäisches Silber handgearbeitet, Deutsches Goldschmiedehaus, Hanau, Germany.

Gerda Flöckinger, Crafts Centre of Great Britain, London, England.

Golden Ring of Honour of the Association for Goldsmiths' Art (created by Max Fröhlich '65), recipient: Hermann Jünger. Deutsches Goldschmiedehaus, Hanau, Germany.

International Jewellery Biennale, Carrara, Italy (Aug.)

Stříbny Šperk, Jablonec, CSSR, 1968, Symposium of Silver Jewelry; *International Invitational Exhibition*,

Symposium of Silver Jewelry, Czechoslovakia, 1968 with Cepka (seated extreme left, back row), Jünger, (seated centre, back row), Martinazzi (seated second right)

The American Contemporary Jewelry Exhibition, Tokyo, 1968: Skoogfors, Matsukata and Lechtzin (left to right)

Muzeum skla a bizuterie, Jablonec nad Nisou, Czechoslovakia. Artists include: Cepka, Jünger, E. Kodré-Defner, Martinazzi, Skubic, J. Symon.

1969

3. Internationaler Wettbewerb des Schmuckmuseums Pforzheim-Armschmuck, Schmuckmuseum, Pforzheim, Germany.

30 – An Invitational Jewelry Show, University of Texas, El Paso, USA.

Art Smith: Jewelry, Museum of Contemporary Crafts, New York, USA (Sept. 12– Oct. 12).

Brent Kington, Museum of Contemporary Crafts, New York, USA (April 19– June 15).

Galerie Sieraad established, Amsterdam, The Netherlands (closed 1975). Founders: Hans Appenzeller and Louis Martin. Devoted to the emergence of new ideas in jewelry; showed work by Nicolaas van Beek and Françoise van den Bosch.

Objects to Wear, Van Abbemuseum, Eindhoven, The Netherlands. Organized by Benno Premsela, toured USA; Gijs Bakker and Emmy van Leersum exhibited.

Objects: USA, Johnson Wax Collection of Contemporary American Crafts, National Collection of Fine Arts, Smithsonian Institution, Washington, DC, USA. Toured nationally and internationally. Jewelry artists: Apodaca, Brandt, I. Brynner, Cory, Craver, Eikerman, Engle, Fike, Fisch, Bailey Gieling, Griffiths, Jefferson, Jerry, Kreigman, Kretsinger, Lechtzin, Loloma, Martin, J. P. Miller, Peck, R. and S. Radakovich, Renk, Roach, Senungetuk, Shannon, Skoogfors, A. Smith, Solberg, L. Watson, Wiener, Winston, Woell.

Young Americans 1969, Museum of Contemporary Crafts, New York, USA (June 29– Oct. 12). Jewelry artists include: Cory, Hu, Moty, Mueller.

1970

1st International Jewellery Art Exhibit, Tokyo Triennial, Seibu Gallery, Tokyo, Japan (Feb.) Japanese and international artists including: Martinazzi, Pearson, Skoogfors.

Gold und Silberschmiedearbeiten Klasse H. Markl Akademie für Werkkunst und Mode Berlin, Deutsches Goldschmiedehaus, Hanau, Germany (May 24– June 14).

Goldsmith '70, Minnesota Museum of Art, St Paul, Minnesota, USA (March 26– May 17); inaugural exhibition organized by Society of North American Goldsmiths (SNAG), invitational and juried. Jurors: Stanley Lechtzin, John Prip. Coincides with first SNAG conference, to be held annually. Keynote speaker: Dr Harry Bober. Artists include: Christensen, Cory, Ebendorf, Eikerman, Fike, Fisch, Hu, Jerry, Kington, Ladousa, Laplantz, Lechtzin, Marshall, Matsukata, Matzdorf, Mawdsley, F. A. Miller, J. P. Miller, Morton, Moty, Paley, Pearson, Pine, Prip, Pujol, S. Radakovich, Schick, Seppä, Shirk, Skoogfors, Sublett, Vierthaler, B. Winston, Woell.

International Jewellery Biennale, Carrara, Italy (Aug.).

National Jewelry Competition, Texas Tech University, Lubbock, TX, USA (March 22 – April 19). Artists include: Mawdsley, Moty, O'Connor, Pearson, Pujol, Seppä, Shirk, Vierthaler, Woell.

Nicolaas van Beek, Stedelijk Museum, Amsterdam, The Netherlands.

Schmuck '70 – Tendenzen, Schmuckmuseum, Pforzheim, Germany. Second in series of biennials; assesses European and American jewelry; organized by Fritz Falk. Artists include: Bury, Cepka, Hiramatsu, Martinazzi, Paley, Skoogfors.

1971

Diamonds-International Awards, Plaza Hotel New York, USA. Toured internationally to Milan, Tokyo, Osaka, Sydney (Sept. – Nov.). Among award winners: Irena Brynner and Bernhard Schobinger.

Electrum Gallery established, London, England. Founder/Director: Barbara Cartlidge; Co–Director: Ralph Turner (leaves 1974). Committed to late 20th-century goldsmiths.

Gerda Flöckinger, Victoria and Albert Museum, London.

Gold+Silber Schmuck+Gerät: Von Albrecht Dürer bis zur Gegenwart, Norishalle, Nuremberg, Germany (March 19 – Aug. 22). Artists include: F. Becker, C. Bury, Cepka, Fröhlich, Hiramatsu, Jünger, E. and H. Kodré-Defner, Lechtzin, Rudiger-Lorenzen, Martinazzi, E. R. Nele, Pavan, Pinton, S. Persson, A. Pomodoro, Ramshaw, Rothmann, Von Skal, Skoogfors, Skubic, Smit, Symon, Zschaler.

Jewellery '71: An Exhibition of Contemporary Jewellery, Art Gallery of Ontario, Toronto, Canada (Nov. 6–

Dec. 5). Artists: Betteridge, Brynner, P. Bury, Calder, Chase-Riboud, N. Copley, Cory, C. Falkenstein, Fisch, Fontana, M. Golan, Kretsinger, Kriegman, Lechtzin, Lichtenstein, Moty, L. Nesbitt, Nevelson, Paley, L. B. Peck, G. Pellegrini, B. Pepper, Picasso, A. Pomodoro, G. Pomodoro, Scherr, Seppä, Skoogfors, A. Smith, Trova, T. Wada, J. Wines, Wirkala, Woell, J. Youngerman, Zelmanoff.

Mary Ann Scherr Retrospective, Akron Art Institute, Akron, OH, USA (Nov. 21, 1971– Jan. 2, 1972).

The Metal Experience, Oakland Museum Art Division, CA, USA (June 5– July 4). Artists include: J. Apodaca, E. Bielawski (MAG), Cory (juror), Gieling, La Plantz, LePere, M. Lewis, E. Lund, G. McLean, Pine (juror), Rapoport, Resnikoff (MAG), Utter, Van Duinwyk, L. Watson.

Ronald Hayes Pearson, Solo Exhibition, University of Rochester, NY, USA.

Schmuck-Objekte: Goldschmiede finden neue Formen, Museum Bellerive, Zurich, Switzerland (Sept. 24– Nov. 14). Artists: Augustin (Queenie), G. Bakker, Brynner, Coudenhove, Fisch, Fröhlich, Gasch, Immich, Krbálek, Lechtzin, Van Leersum, J. P. Miller, E. R. Nele, Prip, Skoogfors, Zelmanoff.

Sehen Erkennen Gestalten, Roemer Pelizaeus Museu, Hildesheim, Germany, celebration of Carl van Dornick's 60th birthday showing work by six former students.

1972

4. Internationaler Wettbewerb des Schmuckmuseums Pforzheim-Ansteckschmuck, Schmuckmuseum, Pforzheim, Germany. Participating artists: Fritz Maierhofer, Bruno Martinazzi.

1972 Jewelry Invitational Exhibition, Western New Mexico University, Silver City, NM (April 16 – May 5).

The Argyle Silversmiths Cooperative, established, by Wal van Heecskeren; The Argyle Arts Centre, The Rocks, Sydney, Australia.

The Contemporary American Silversmith and Goldsmith, Fairtree Gallery, New York, USA; Corcoran Gallery, Washington, DC, USA. Participating: Don Tompkins.

Der Goldschmied Othmar Zschaler, Schmuckmuseum, Pforzheim, Germany.

Galerie am Graben – Art of the Twentieth Century established, Nov. 1972, Vienna, Austria. Founder: Inge Asenbaum. Major commitment to contemporary jewelry; publishes extensively. Closes Sept. 1988.

Golden Ring of Honour of the Association for Goldsmiths' Art (created by Hermann Jünger '68), recipient: Friedrich Becker, Deutsches Goldschmiedehaus, Hanau, Germany.

Invitational Exhibition of Enamels, Memphis Academy of Arts, Memphis, TN, USA (Feb. 6–27). Artists include: Bates, Harper, E. Pardon, J. Schwarcz.

Jewelry and Holloware Invitational: 72, Iowa State University, Ames Iowa (Feb. 1–29). Artists: Eikerman, Fenster, Fisch, J. Fossee, M. Jerry, Kington, Lechtzin, Loloma, Mafong, Marshall, Matsukata, Matzdorf, Mawdsley, J. P. Miller, Norton, A. Pine, Schick, Senungetuk, Seppa, Shirk, Skoogfors, N. K. Thompson.

John Prip: Metal, Museum of Contemporary Crafts, New York, USA (April 14– May 26).

National Jewelry and Holloware Invitational: Twelve Metalsmiths and Recent Graduates, Northern Illinois University, Dekalb, IL, USA (Oct. 10–27). Jewelry artists include: Ebendorf, Eikerman, Fenster, Fike, Fisch, Kington, Lechtzin, Marshall, Matzdorf, Mazurkewicz, Moty, Paley, Shirk, Skoogfors.

Queensland Jewellery Workshop Group established, Brisbane, Australia. Initiated by Kit Shannon.

Jens-Rüdiger Lorenzen – Miniaturen und Objekte, Schmuckmuseum, Pforzheim, Germany.

Sieraad 1900–1972: Zonnehof Museum, Amersfoort, The Netherlands.

1973

The Art of Enamels, State University College, New Paltz, NY, USA (Sept. 10–30). Artists include: Harper, Kretsinger, J. Marshall, Matsukata, J. P. Miller.

Aspects of Jewellery, Aberdeen Art Gallery and Museum, Aberdeen, Scotland. Artists (35) include: M. Appleby, G. Bakker, C. Bury, Flöckinger, S. Heron, Van Leersum, Maierhofer, Ramshaw, Reiling, Rothmann, G. Treen, H. Zahn.

British Jewellery, Deutsches Goldschmiedehaus, Hanau, Germany.

De Volle Maan, Robert Smit Solo Exhibition, Stedelijk Musuem 'Het Prinsenhof', Delft, The Netherlands.

Ramshaw (right), with Watkins and Helen Drutt (on the left) and David Lundy of Mathey Bishop, Philadelphia, 1973

Gold, Metropolitan Museum of Art, New York, USA (April 14– Sept. 9); contemporary jewelry exhibited by A. Pomodoro and R. Lippold.

International Jewellery Art Exhibition, 2nd Tokyo Triennial, Seibu Gallery, Tokyo, Japan (Oct.).

Internationale Schmuckschau, Internationale Handwerksmesse, Munich, Germany.

Invitational Jewelry and Metal Exhibition, Virginia Commonwealth University, Richmond, VA, USA.

Jam Factory Workshops Incorporated, established by the South Australian Government (then called the South Australian Craft Authority).

Japan-Italy Exchange Show: *Japan Jewellery Art Exhibit*, Arezzo, Italy; *Italian Jewellery Exhibit*, Seibu Gallery, Tokyo, Japan.

Jewelry as Sculpture as Jewelry, Institute of Contemporary Art, Boston, MA, USA (Nov. 28 – Dec. 21). Artists: Appenzeller, Arman, Arp, Berrocal, F. van den Bosch, P. Bury, Calder, César, Chalem, P. Consagra, Craver, Croninger, Ernst, Fontana, Gonzalez, M. Herbst, Hess-Dahm, Lichtenstein, Maierhofer, Man Ray, Marisol, Matsukata, R. Matta, R. L. Morris, Nevelson, Nivola, Penalba, Pepper, Picasso, A. Pomodoro, G. Pomodoro, H. Richter.

The Observer Jewellery Exhibition, National Museum of Wales, Cardiff (Sept. 1– Oct. 27). Toured UK (London, Edinburgh and Bristol) until March 1974. Four established artists: J. Donald, G. Flöckinger, L. Osman, C. de Syllas; 16 emerging artists, including: S. Heron, C. Mannheim, E. Raft, W. Ramshaw, G. Treen.

Schmuck '73 – Tendenzen, Schmuckmuseum, Pforzheim, Germany (July 27 – Sept. 30). Organized by Fritz Falk. Artists include: S. Aguilar, U. Bahrs, F. Becker, C. Bury, Capdevila, Cepka, P. Degen, Fisch, A. Font, Fröhlich, M. Herbst, S. Heron, Hiramatsu, Jünger, S. Kasaly, Kodré-Defner, Künzli, Lorenzen, Maierhofer, Martinazzi, F. Müller, Pavan, O. Bent Petersen, A. Pomodoro, C. Rating, Reiling, Rothmann, Seibert-Philippen, G. Seibert, Ramshaw, Skubic, Souply, Spiller, Symon, G. Treen, Von Skal, Ullrich, T. Wada, Zschaler.

Stanley Lechtzin, Solo Exhibition, Goldsmiths' Hall, London, England.

Ting och bruksting, Kulturhuset, Stockholm, Sweden.

Wendy Ramshaw/David Watkins, Goldsmiths' Hall, London, England; American Institute of Architects Gallery, Philadelphia, PA, USA (their first exhibition in the USA).

1974

4th International Exhibition of Jewelry, Muzeum skla a bizuterie, Jablonec nad Nisou, Czechoslovakia; and Bratislava, Czechoslovakia.

8 American Metalsmiths, Sheffield Polytechnic, School of Art and Design, England; Edinburgh, Scotland.

18 Orfévres d'Aujourd'hui, Musée des Arts Décoratifs, Lausanne, Switzerland. Artists include: C. Bury, Jünger, Martinazzi.

American Metalsmiths: The Nancy Kurland Schmidt Memorial Exhibition, DeCordova Museum, Lincoln, MA (April 7– June 9). Artists include: Arentzen, Ebendorf, Eikerman, V. Ferrini, Fisch, Freyaldenhoven, N. Getty, Hu, Kington, Krentzin, Kriegman, Lechtzin, A. Lent, M. Lewis, Mafong, J. Marshall, Matsukata, Mawdsley, J. P. Miller, Pencil Bros. (Cory/Lepere), Pine, Scherr, Senungetuk, Seppa, Shirk, Skoogfors, Goessler-Snyder, Solberg, L. Watson, Woell.

BOE (Union of Rebellious Goldsmiths) founded, Amsterdam, The Netherlands, organized by Marion Herbst, Onno Boekhoudt, Karl Niehorster, Françoise van der Bosch, Berend Peter Hogenesch. Later known as VES. VES Exhibitions were held at Stedelijk Museum from 1978.

Charles Loloma, Museum of Contemporary Crafts, New York, USA (Jan.18 – March 17).

The Collector, American Craft Museum; (June 7– Sept. 2). First time selections from Helen Williams Drutt Collection exhibited.

The Goldsmith, Renwick Gallery, National Collection of Fine Arts, Smithsonian Institution, Washington, DC, USA (May 17– Aug. 18); Minnesota Museum of Art, St Paul, Minnesota, USA (Sept. 3– Dec. 29). Jurors: Arline Fisch, Lloyd Herman and William E. Woolfenden. Artists include: Bennett, Blodgett, N. Copley, Ebendorf, Eikerman, Fike, Fisch, Harper, Hu, Krentzin, Laplantz, Lechtzin, L. Leupp, M. Lewis, S. Lloyd, R. Long, G. McLean, Mafong and J. Riis, Matsukata, Mawdsley, Merritt, J. P. Miller, P. Morton, Mueller, W. Neumann, H. O'Connor, Paley, L. B. Peck, H. S. and E. M. Pijanowski, Alvin Pine, Quigley, S. Radakovich, G. Saunders, Seppä, Shirk, Goessler-Snyder, Hiroko Yamauchi Swornik, Woell.

In Praise of Hands, first contemporary world crafts exhibition, Ontario Science Center, Toronto, Canada. Organized by World Crafts Council for tenth anniversary: Arline Fisch, Stanley Lechtzin, Gijs Bakker, Wendy Ramshaw exhibited.

Inaugural Exhibition, Helen Drutt Gallery, Philadelphia, PA, USA; (Feb. 22). Artists: Buckingham, Pencil Brothers (Cory/LePere), Griffin, Lechtzin, A. Lent, M. Lewis, Moty, Paley, Skoogfors, Goessler-Snyder, Woell.

Internationale Schmuckschau, Internationale Handwerksmesse, Munich, Germany.

Schmuck und Stahl, International Symposium for Jewelry, Little Objects, Conceptions of Steel and High-Grade Steel (March–April), Vienna, Austria. Exhibitions follow in Austria: Kapfenberg, Ternitz, Leoben, Linz, Vienna; and Germany: Nuremberg, Pforzheim.

Van Leersum, Skubic, Bakker and Maierhofer (left to right) at the *Schmuck und Stahl* exhibition, Kapfenberg, Austria, 1974

Vail Symposium, Colorado, 1975 Woell, Pujol, Cory, Coulter, Pine, Watson, Cotter, Atterbury, O'Connor and Teleen (left to right)

Metal '74, Fine Arts Gallery, State University College Brockport, NY (Nov. 17– Dec. 20). Artists: Church, Ebendorf, Fenster, Fisch, Freyaldenhoven, Griffin, Harper, Hu, LaPlantz, Lechtzin, Marshall, Mawdsley, Moty, L. B. Peck, Pencil Brothers (Cory/LePere), Scherr, Sedman, Skoogfors, Van Dyke, Woell.

National Invitational Exhibition in Contemporary Jewellery, Georgia State University, Atlanta, GA. Artists include: Bennett, Buckingham, Ebendorf, Eikerman, Fenster, Fike, Fisch, Freyaldenhoven, Getty, Kington, LaPlantz, Lechtzin, Lund, Mafong, Markusen, Marshall, Matzdorf, Meyer, J. P. Miller, Moty, G. Noffke, Pencil Brothers (Cory/Lepere), H. S. and E. M. Pijanowski, Scherr, Seppä, Shirk, Skoogfors, Woell.

Tasmanian Metalcraft Group established in Hobart, Tasmania; as part of the Craft Association of Tasmania.

The Uncommon Smith, John Michael Kohler Arts Center, Sheboygan, WI, USA (June 23– Aug. 18).

1975

15 Jahre, Galerie Nouvelles Images, The Hague, The Netherlands. Artists: Giampaolo Babetto, Francesco Pavan.

Australian Jewellery, Art Gallery of South Australia, Adelaide (travelled). Artist: Frank Bauer.

Bijoux Finlandais, Musée des Beaux-Arts, Lyon, France (Oct. 15– Nov. 15).

Golden Ring of Honour of the Association for Goldsmiths' Art (created by Friedrich Becker '72), recipient: Mario Pinton, Deutsches Goldschmiedehaus, Hanau, Germany.

Invitational Jewelry Exhibition, Pensacola Junior College, Pensacola, FL, USA (March 4–21). Artists: Blodgett, Hu, Merritt, Paley, Shirk, Threadgill.

Jewellery in Europe, selected by Ralph Turner, The Scottish Arts Council Gallery, Edinburgh, Scotland (Dec. 20, 1975– Jan. 18, 1976), toured through Great Britain (Victoria and Albert Museum, London; Aberdeen; Glasgow; Bristol) until Aug. 1976. Artists: Aguilar, Bahrs, G. Bakker, F. Becker, C. Bury, Cepka, S. Heron, Jünger, Kasaly, Künzli, Van Leersum, Lorenzen, Maierhofer, Martinazzi, R. Morris, N. Muerrle, J. Plenderleith, D. Poston, Ramshaw, Rothmann, Von Skal, Smit, G. Treen, Watkins, Zahn.

L'Art de L'Email, Third International Biennial, Chapelle du Lycée Gay-Lussac, Limoges, France (July 8– Sept. 8). Participating: William Harper.

Metals Invitational, 1975 AD, College Art Gallery, State University of New York, New Paltz, NY, USA (Oct. 8–29), continued Feb. 1976.

National Metals Invitational, First Triennial (except 1983), Humboldt State University, Arcata, CA, USA. Each exhibition retitled, beginning 1983.

NFS Föringen för Nutida Svenskt Silver, Museum Bellerive, Zurich, Switzerland; travelled through Scandinavia until Aug. 1976.

Organic Jewellery, a touring exhibition compiled and sponsored by Leicestershire Museums and East Midlands Arts, England.

Precious Metals: The American Tradition in Gold and Silver, Lowe Art Museum, University of Miami, Coral Gables, FL (Nov. 20, 1975– Jan. 11, 1976). Artists include: Bennett, Ebendorf, Fisch, Getty, Harper, Hu, A. Lent, Matzdorf, Mawdsley, J. P. Miller, Moty, G. Noffke, Paley, H. S. and E. M. Pijanowski, Scherr, Seppä, Skoogfors, Threadgill.

Reprise, graduates of the Department of Metalsmithing of the Cranbrook Academy of Art, 1948–1975, Cranbrook Academy of Art Museum, Cranbrook

Academy of Art, Bloomfield Hills, MI, USA (Sept. 28– Nov. 9).

Second Annual National Exhibition in Contemporary Jewelry, (membership of the Society of North American Goldsmiths); Gallery of the Art Department, Georgia State University, Atlanta, GA, USA (April 8–18).

Symbolism and Imagery, 1975 Jewelry Invitational. Central Washington State College, Ellensburg, WA, USA. Artists: Lechtzin, Mawdsley, J. P. Miller, Pencil Brothers (Cory/LePere), D. Tompkins, M. Tompkins, L. Watson, Woell, Zelmanoff.

Vail Metals Symposium, Vail, Colorado, USA.

1976

Argentum established, Stockholm, Sweden. Founders: Gunnar Cyrén, Heinz Decker, Marika Dymling, B. Malin Gunnarsson, Carl Gustaf Jahnsson, Rolf Karlsson, Olle Ohlsson, Sigurd Persson, Karlheinz Sauer and Martin Öhman.

Bezalel 70+, Tel Aviv Museum of Art, Tel Aviv, Israel.

Contemporary Swedish Silver, Kunstindustrimuseet, Copenhagen, Denmark (Feb. 7–29). Toured through Scandinavia (Bergen, Trondheim, Stockholm) until Aug.

Gallery Ra established, Amsterdam, The Netherlands. Founder: Paul Derrez. Avant-garde artists exhibited, and gallery becomes forum for exchange.

Gerhard Rothmann: Goldschmiedearbeiten und Zeichnungen, Landesmuseum für Kunst, Oldenburg, Germany (April 6– May 2), travelled through Germany.

Hans Appenzeller/Jans Aarntzen, Stedelijk Museum, Amsterdam, The Netherlands.

Helga Zahn, a retrospective assessment, 1960–1976, Crafts Advisory Committee Gallery, London, England (April 14– June 12).

International Festival of Enamels, Laguna Beach Museum of Art, Laguna Beach, CA, USA. Jewelry artists: Harper, D. LaPlantz, J. Schwarcz, M. Seeler.

International Jewellery Art Exhibition, 3rd Tokyo Triennial, Seibu Gallery, Tokyo, Japan (Nov. 27– Dec. 19) Artists: Cepka, Hiramatsu, Jünger, Maierhofer, Martinazzi, Moty.

Internationale Schmuckschau, Internationale Handwerksmesse, Munich, Germany.

Jewelers, U.S.A., California State University, Fullerton, CA, USA (Feb. 27– March 25).

Jewelry: Then and Now, Evansville Museum of Arts and Sciences, IN, USA.

Jewelry '76, Third Annual National Exhibition in Contemporary Jewelry, Atlanta, GA, USA.

The Jewelry of Margaret de Patta: A Retrospective Exhibition, Oakland Museum, Oakland, CA, USA (Feb. 3– March 28).

Margareth Sandström/Peter de Wit, Konstforum, Norrköping, Sweden.

National Metalwork and Jewelry Exhibition, Eastern Washington University, Cheny, WA, USA: Amy Buckingham.

On Tour: 10 British Jewellers in Germany and Australia, Crafts Advisory Committee; British Council/Crafts Council; travelled throughout Germany and Australia until 1978).

Second Annual Jewelry Invitational, Central Washington State College, Ellensburg, Washington, DC, USA. Artists include: Buckingham, Cory, J. Cotter, L. Coulter, Ebendorf, N. Getty, Paley, N. K. Thompson and M. Tompkins.

1977

10 Australian Jewellers, South East Asian travelling exhibition. Participating artist: Peter Tully.

20th-Century Jewellery – from the collection of the Schmuckmuseum Pforzheim, Schmuckmuseum, Pforzheim (July 22 – Aug. 3). Artists include: Aguilar, Bahrs, F. Becker, Van den Bosch, C. Bury, Capdevila, Cepka, Demaret, Eshel-Gershuni, Flöckinger, Font, Fröhlich, A. Fruhauf, Hiramatsu, Jünger, Kasaly, Kodejs, Kodré-Defner, Kunzli, Lechtzin, Lorenzen, Maierhofer, L. Martin, Martinazzi, Muerrie, E. R. Nele, Persson, Pinton, A. Pomodoro, Ramshaw, Reiling, Rothmann, G. Seibert, Van Skal, Skoogfors, Slutzky, Smit, Symon, E. Treskow, Ullrich, Weiss-Weingart, Zahn, Zeitner, Zschaler.

Artwear Gallery established, New York, USA. Founder: Robert Lee Morris (closed 1993).

California Jewelry and Metalsmithing Exhibition, Fresno State University, Fresno, CA, USA.

Contemporary Jewelry Exhibition, Design Center, Manila, Philippines.

Copper Brass Bronze Exhibition, University of Arizona Museum of Art, Tucson, AZ, USA (April 3– May 15). Jurors: Robert Ebendorf, William Harper and Stephen Prokopoff.

Established and Emerging: an Exhibition of 25 artists working in vitreous enamel on metal, Chastain Arts and Crafts Center, Atlanta, GA, USA (May 22– June 18). Artists include: Jamie Bennett, William Harper.

Fachhochschule Düsseldorf, Fachbereich Design: Studienschwerpunkt Schmuck-Design, Deutsches Goldschmiedehaus, Hanau, Germany (April 2– May 8).

Fachhochschule für Gestaltung 100 Jahre, Pforzheim, Germany.

Giampaolo Babetto, Stedelijk Museum, Amsterdam, The Netherlands.

Internationale Schmuckschau, Internationale Handwerksmesse, Munich, Germany.

Jewelry as Sculpture as Jewelry, La Jolla Museum, La Jolla, CA, USA.

The Metalsmith, (SNAG Exhibition), Society of North American Goldsmiths Exhibition, Phoenix Museum of Art, Phoenix, AZ, USA (Jan. 14 – Feb. 20); Henry Gallery, University of Washington, Seattle, Washington, USA (June 23– July 31). Jurors: Jonathan Fairbanks, Ronald D. Hickman and Svetozar Radakovitch.

Metal Jewellery, a touring exhibition compiled by East Midlands Arts, England.

Mid American Metalcrafts '77: Jewelers and Metalsmiths of Kansas and Missouri, location (Nov. 1– Dec. 15).

Nine North Carolina Jewelers, Western Carolina University, Cullowhee, North Carolina, USA (April).

Ruth Nivola: Jewelry in Thread, Museum of Contemporary Crafts, New York, USA (April– June 19).

Van Leersum with Benno Premsela, Badhuis, Gorkum, The Netherlands, February 1977

Schmuck '77 – Tendenzen, Schmuckmuseum, Pforzheim, Germany (July 16– Sept. 11); organized by Fritz Falk. Artists: F. Bauer, F. Becker, C. Bury, B. Cartlidge, Cepka, B. Eshel-Gershuni, Fisch, Flöckinger, Hilbert, Hiramatsu, K. Itoh, Jünger, Kruger, H. Larsen, Maierhofer, Martinazzi, Nagai, E. R. Nele, Pavan, S. Persson, Pinton, Reiling, Ullrich, Watkins, E. Weiss-Weingart, M. West, Woell, Zschaler.

Third Profile of U.S. Jewelry, Texas Tech University, Lubbock, TX, USA.

Zunft Turm-Zunft Jungkunst, Schmuckmuseum, Pforzheim, Germany (Sept. 11– Oct. 9), toured through Germany until Feb. 1978. 43 artists participate, including: Reiling, H. Schafran and G. Seibert.

1978

3 Konzepte – 3 Goldschmiede: Bury/Jünger/Rothmann, Hessisches Landesmuseum, Darmstadt, Germany.

Arbeiten Seit 1948 + 1977–1978: Auswahl aus 2 Jahren, Bernhard Schobinger, Museum Bellerive, Zurich, Switzerland (Dec. 5, 1978– Feb. 4, 1979).

Bezalel Academy Jerusalem – Gold and Silversmithing Department, Schmuckmuseum, Pforzheim, Germany.

Contemporary Czechoslovakian Jewelry, Jablonec nad Nisou, Czechoslovakia.

Contemporary Jewelry from the Permanent Collection of the Museum of Contemporary Crafts, Museum of Contemporary Crafts, New York, USA (Jan. 28– April 2).

Der Ring, Deutsches Goldschmiedehaus, Hanau, Germany (Nov. 26, 1978 – Jan. 14, 1979); Schmuckmuseum, Pforzheim, Germany (Jan. 20 – Feb. 18, 1979). 400 artists participate.

Françoise van den Bosch, Solo Exhibition, Stedelijk Museum, Amsterdam, The Netherlands (Feb. 10– April 2), toured the Netherlands until April 1979.

Galerie for nutidig sflv-og guldsmedekunst established, Copenhagen, Denmark. Founders: Jan Lohmann and Peder Musse. Name changes to Galerie Metal in 1980.

Golden Ring of Honour of the Association for Goldsmiths' Art (created by Mario Pinton '75), recipient: Ebbe Weiss-Weingart. Deutsches Goldschmiedehaus, Hanau, Germany.

The Goldsmith/78, Minnesota Museum of Art, St Paul, MN, USA.

Grete Prytz Kittelsen: Emaljekunst og Design, Kunstindustrimuseet, Oslo, Norway.

Invitational Jewelry and Metalsmithing Exhibition, Arkansas State University, Jonesboro, AR, USA.

Jewellers and Metalsmiths Group of Australia (JMGA) formed as a national organization; held first national biennial conference in Melbourne and established newsletter *Lemel*.

Skoogfors, whose retrospective exhibition was held in 1979, is shown here (centre) shortly before his death in 1975

Hermann and Jo Jünger, Ebendorf, Rothmann and Kurt Matzdorf (left to right) at New Paltz, NY, USA, in 1979

L'Art de L'Email, Fourth International Biennial, Chapelle du Lycée Gay-Lussac, Limoges, France (July 12– Sept. 10).

Loloma, a retrospective view, The Heard Museum, Phoenix, Arizona, USA (Nov. 11, 1978–Jan. 12, 1979).

Loot & Superloot, organized by the Worshipful Company of Goldsmiths, London; Minneapolis Institute of Art, Minneapolis, Minnesota, USA (July 9–28). 393 artists participated.

Modern American Jewelry Exhibition, Mikimoto and Company, Ltd., Gallery, Tokyo, Japan. Participating artists: Ken Cory, Richard Mawdsley, Robin Quigley.

Rattlesnakes, (modern American jewelry), Goldsmiths' Hall, London, England (July 5–28).

Schmuck-Tischgerät aus Österreich 1904/08–1973/77, Galerie am Graben, Vienna. Anna Heindl, Fritz Maierhofer.

Silver in Silver City, 1978 Jewelry Invitational, Francis McCray Gallery, Western New Mexico University, Silver City, NM, USA (March 19– April 16).

SNAG: Jewelry and Metal Objects from the Society of North American Goldsmiths, Minnesota Museum of Art, St Paul, MN, USA.

1979

4th Tokyo Triennial, Japan Jewellery Exhibition, Tokyo Central Museum of Art, Tokyo, Japan (Oct. 16–21); International Jewellery Art Exhibition, Ginza Mikimoto Hall, Tokyo, Japan (Oct. 25– Nov. 2). Artists include: F. Becker, O. Boekhoudt, Cory, Fisch, Fröhlich, Yasuki Hiramatsu, S. Hopea-Untracht, Hu, Jünger, Kodejs, E. Kodré-Defner, Kruger, Künzli, Lechtzin, Lorenzen, Maierhofer, Martinazzi, Nagai, Persson, E. M. Pijanowski, Reiling, Rothmann, Schobinger, Shirk, P. Skubic, E. Souply, B. Weckström, Weiss-Weingart, Zschaler, S. P. Zilker.

56 Bracelets, 17 Rings, 2 Necklaces, Gemeentelijke van Reekummuseum, Apeldoorn, The Netherlands (March 31– April 29), travelled.

A Detailed Look: National Jewelry Invitational, University of Wisconsin, White Water, WI, USA.

Diamonds Today, Sweden; first competition organized by the goldsmith societies of all Scandinavian countries.

Edelstein Schmuckgestaltung, Idar-Oberstein, *Edelstein Schmuckgestaltung*, Idar-Oberstein, Germany.

Emmy van Leersum, Solo Exhibition, Stedelijk Museum, Amsterdam, The Netherlands (Nov. 23, 1979– Jan. 6, 1980), toured Europe (Graz, Austria, and The Hague, The Netherlands) until May 1980.

Internationale Schmuckschau, Internationale Handwerks-messe, Munich, Germany.

Körper–Schmuck–Zeichen–Raum, Kestnergesellschaft, Hanover, Germany; Kunstgewerbemuseum, Zurich.

Körper–Zeichen, Städtische Galerie im Lenbachhaus, Munich, Germany.

Metallplastik und Schmuck von Waltrud und Arthur Viehböck, Deutsches Goldschmiedehaus, Hanau, Germany (Oct. 12– Sept. 23).

Olaf Skoogfors, 20th-Century Goldsmith 1930–1975, Retrospective, Philadelphia College of Art, Philadelphia, USA (Jan. 22– Feb. 17) and Renwick Gallery, National Collection of Fine Arts, Smithsonian Institution, Washington, DC, USA (April 6– Aug. 19).

Schmuck '79 – Tendenzen, Schmuckmuseum, Pforzheim, Germany.

Sieraden in Singer, Singer Museum, Laren, The Netherlands. Artists include: Caroline Broadhead, Esther Knobel, Daniel Kruger.

SNAG – Gold- und Silberschmiedearbeiten der Society of North American Goldsmiths, Schmuckmuseum, Pforzheim, Germany (March 10 – April 16), toured Belgium, England, Finland, Germany, The Netherlands, Norway, until Feb. 1980.

1980

5. Internationaler Wettbewerb des Schmuckmuseums Pforzheim-Armschmuck, Schmuckmuseum, Pforzheim, Germany. Artists: Frank Bauer, Francesco Pavan, Helen Shirk.

1980/81 Year Exhibition, Kestnergesellschaft, Hanover, Germany.

Argentum, group exhibition, Historiska Museet, Stockholm, Sweden.

Copper 2: The Second Copper Brass and Bronze Exhibition, University of Arizona Museum of Art, Tucson, AZ, USA. (March 2 – April 6). Artists: Ebendorf, Fike, Fisch, Harper, Lechtzin, Mawdsley, Paley, Pearson, E. M. Pijanowski, H. S. Pijanowski, Prip, Seppä, Skoogfors.

David Poston, Solo Exhibition, British Crafts Centre, London, England; Sheffield City Polytechnic Gallery, England (1981).

Email-Schmuck und Gerät in Geschichte und Gegenwart, Schmuckmuseum, Pforzheim, Germany (Jan. 19– March 2). Toured Germany and Austria until Aug. 1981, in cooperation with Galerie am Graben.

Fancy Goods: Ralph Turner's Collection of Popular Jewellery, toured throughout the UK until 1981.

Flux, Fusion, Fireworks, exhibition sponsored by the Northwest Enamelists Guild, Contemporary Crafts Gallery, Portland, OR, USA (Sept. 25– Oct. 25).

Françoise van den Bosch Prize established, Amsterdam, The Netherlands. Awarded every two years. First Recipient: Paul Derrez.

Internationale Schmuckschau, Internationale Handwerks-messe, Munich, Germany. Participating: Birgit Laken.

The Metalwork of Albert Paley, John Michael Kohler Arts Center, Sheboygan, WI, USA (April 13 – June 1); Hunter Museum of Art, Chattanooga, TN, USA (Oct. 19 – Nov. 23).

Objects to Human Scale, Australian Modern Jewellery Exhibit, travelled throughout Japan, Philippines and

Hong Kong. Artists: Frank Bauer, Peter Tully, David Walker, Margaret West.

Pendants, Föreningen för Nutida Svenskt Silver, Stockholm, Sweden. Artists include: Lars Arby, Barve Dahlqvist, Theresia Hvorslev, Etsuko Minova, Kristian Nilsson.

Robert L. Pfannebecker Collection: A Selection of Contemporary American Crafts, Moore College of Art, Philadelphia, PA, USA (Oct. 17 – Nov. 20). Jewelry artists include: Cory, Griffin, Harper, Lechtzin, Mawdsley, Metcalf, Moty, H. Sato and E. M. Pijanowski, Quigley, Shirk, Skoogfors, Sublett, M. Tompkins, Woell, D. Wright.

Schmuck International 1900–1980, Künstlerhaus, Vienna, Austria (June 26 – Aug. 17). Artists: Appenzeller, Babetto, Bakker, Bennett, F. Becker, Bischoff, Boekhoudt, Broadhead, C. Bury, Cepka, Derrez, Ebendorf, Fisch, Flockinger, Frolich, Griffin, Herbst, Heron, Therese Hilbert, Hiramatsu, Knobel, Kruger, Kunzle, Jünger, van Leersum, Lorenzin, Martinazzi, Marx, Nagai, Pavan, E. M. Pijanowski, Pinton, Quigley, Ramshaw, Reiling, Rothman, Skubic, Watkins, F. van Wegman. Coincides with World Crafts Council Conference.

Second Annual Metalsmithing Invitational, Louisiana State University, Baton Rouge, LA, USA.

Southeastern Contemporary Metalsmiths, organized by the Mint Museum, Department of Art, Charlotte, NC, USA (Nov. 8– Dec. 31, 1981); Appalachian Center for the Crafts, Cookville, TN, USA (Sept. 15 – Oct. 29), toured museums of the south-east USA until Dec. 1981.

Susanna Heron: Bodywork Exhibition, Crafts Council Gallery, London, England (April 16 – May 31).

Young Americans: Metal, national competition, American Craft Museum, New York, USA (Jan. 18 – March 16).

Zeitgenössischer Schmuck aus Polen, Schmuckmuseum, Pforzheim, Germany (Sept. 20 – Nov. 2); in cooperation with Ars Polona, Warsaw. Toured Germany and France.

1981

10th Anniversary Exhibition, Electrum Gallery, London, England.

Australian Jewellery, Museum of Applied Arts and Sciences, Sydney, Australia (travelled). Participating: David Walker.

Contemporary Metals: Focus on Idea, Museum of Art, Washington State University, Pullman, Washington, USA (April 13– May 3).

Craft in Process: A Living Workshop, American Craft Museum, New York, USA (June 20–Aug. 30). Participating metal artist: Deborah Aguado.

Enamel, an international exhibition tour of Australia. Catalogue by Brisbane Civic Art Gallery and Museum.

Enamels 50/80, Brookfield Craft Center Gallery, Brookfield, CT, USA (July 12 – Aug. 30). Artists include: Martha Banyas, Earl Pardon.

Frank Bauer/Elizabeth Holder, Arnolfini Gallery, Bristol, England; Institute of Contemporary Art, London.

The Golden Thread – Textures in Gold, Deutschen Goldschmiedehaus, Hanau, and Stadtischen Museum, Schäbisch Gmünd, Germany; Focke Museum, Bremen, and Goud-en-Zilver Museum, Schoonhoven, The Netherlands. Participating artists: Mary Lee Hu, M. Sandstrom.

Good as Gold: Alternative Materials in American Jewelry, Smithsonian Institution Travelling Exhibitions Service (SITES), Renwick Gallery, National Collection of Fine Arts, Smithsonian Institution, Washington, DC, USA. Toured nationally. Curated by Lloyd Herman.

Internationale Schmuckschau, Internationale Handwerksmesse, Munich, Germany.

Körper-Schmuck-Zeichen-Raum, Kunstgewerbemuseum, Zurich, Switzerland. Artists: Therese Hilbert, Daniel Kruger, Otto Künzli, Erico Nagai.

Loot VII, Goldsmiths' Hall, London, England (Nov. 2– 21).

Metal 1981, State University of New York, Borckport, NY, USA.

Metalli elää (Metal Lives), Taideteollisuusmuseo, Helsinki, Finland. Artists include: Olli Tamminen.

Metalsmith '81, A National Exhibition of Juried and Invitational (SNAG), University of Kansas, Lawrence, KS, USA (June 5– July 5).

Opulent and Organic: The Jewelry of Merry Renk, California Crafts Museum, Palo Alto, CA, USA.

Sølv til Brug: Sølvsmeden Mogens Bjørn Andersen gennem 50 År, Kunstindustrimuseet, Oslo, Norway (Oct. 30– Dec. 6).

Torun Bülow-Hübe, Retrospective, Nordiska Kompaniet, Stockholm, Sweden.

Two Decades of Metal, San Diego State University, San Diego, CA, USA (Sept. 12– Oct. 10); Brigham Young University, Provo, UT, USA.

Werkstattgalerie established by Rosemarie Brodhag, Gündrum Wörn, Berlin, Germany.

1982

20 Years of Metal from Southern Illinois University at Carbondale, An Exhibition by L. Brent Kington and his Former Graduate Students, University Museum, Southern Illinois University at Carbondale (Aug. 22– Sept. 19); also National Ornamental Museum, USA.

Australian Contemporary Jewellery, Goldsmiths' Hall, London, travelled through Europe. Participating artists: F. Bauer, Carlier Makigawa, P. Tully, D. Walker, M. West.

Die Kette, Deutsches Goldschmiedehaus, Hanau, Germany (Oct. 23 – Nov. 28); Schmuckmuseum, Pforzheim, Germany.

Enamels '82, George Washington University, Washington, DC, USA (Oct. 20– Nov. 12). Jurors: Jamie Bennett, Constance Costigan and William Harper.

Françoise van den Bosch Prize: Second Recipient: Marion Herbst.

Galerie am Graben celebrates 10th anniversary. Publishes *Fritz Maierhofer* in honour of occasion.

Great Southwest Jewelry/Metals Symposium, University of Northern Arizona, Flagstaff, AZ, USA.

Hermann Jünger, Solo Exhibition, State University of New York, New Paltz, USA; delivers major lecture in United States.

Jewellery Redefined, First International Exhibition of Multi-Media Non-Precious Jewellery, British Crafts Centre, London, England (Oct. 1– Nov. 13). Artists: Bakker, Bauer, Broadhead, Dobler, Gralnick, Hess-Dahm, Hilbert, Künzli, Van Leersum, Makigawa, Ramshaw, Schick.

Material Schmuck und Gerät, Internationale Handwerksmesse, Munich, Germany. Artists: Babetto, Cepka, Hiramatsu, Itoh, Knobel, Kruger, Laken, Nagai, Poston, Rezac, Sharlin.

Max Frohlich, Galerie am Graben, Vienna, Austria (Sept 6– Oct 2); Kunstgewerbemuseum, Zurich, Switzerland; Museum fur Gestaltung (Jan.– Feb. 1983).

Metalsmithing at Cranbrook: The Five and One Half Decades, 1928–1982, Cranbrook Academy of Art Museum, Bloomfield Hills, MI, USA (May 14– Oct. 15).

National Metals Invitational, University of Texas, El Paso, TX, USA (Jan. 22– Feb. 21).

Pierre Degen: New Work, Crafts Council Gallery, London, England.

Reinhold Reiling, Goldschmied, Schmuckmuseum, Pforzheim, Germany.

The Recurring Theme: Susanna Heron, Gemeentelijke van Reeksmuseum, Apeldoorn, The Netherlands.

Schmuck '82 –Tendenzen, Schmuckmuseum, Pforzheim, Germany. Organized by Fritz Falk. Participating artists: Babetto, Bauer, Baines, J. Brakman, Cepka, B. Cesnik, De Wit, Dobler, D. Erikson, Heindl, Hiramatsu, Knobel, Koopman, Kruger, Laken, Maierhofer, Martinazzi, Nagai, Ramshaw, Shirk, Walker, Watkins.

Towards a New Iron Age, Victoria and Albert Museum, London, England (May 12 – July 10), travelled throughout USA until Sept. 1983.

Visies op Sieraden 1965–1982, Stedelijk Museum, Amsterdam; Gemeentemuseum, Arnhem, The Netherlands. Artists include: Appenzeller, Bakker, J. Brakman, Broadhead, Derrez, De Wolf, Hess-Dahm, Hilbert, Knobel, Künzli, Van Leersum, Peters, Watkins.

1983

10 fra Guldsmedehfiskolen, Kunstindustrimuseet, Copenhagen, Denmark (May 6 – June 4).

10 Jewelers, Gemeentelijke van Reekummuseum, Apeldoorn, The Netherlands; participating artist: Marjorie Schick.

Andreas Moritz: Silber- und Goldschmied 1901 bis 1983, Badisches Landesmuseum, Karlsruhe, Germany (April 16 – June 12).

Basler Goldschmiede Heute im Gewerbemuseum Basel, Museum für Gestaltung, Basle, Switzerland (Oct. 25– Nov. 20).

Dieci Orafi Padovani-moderne Goldschmiedekunst aus Italien, Schmuckmuseum, Pforzheim, Germany; Deutsches Goldschmiedehaus, Hanau, Germany; Diamanten Museum, Antwerp, Belgium; Museum Bellerive, Zurich, Switzerland.

Electronic Jewelry, Art Gallery, California State College, San Bernardino, CA, USA (Jan. 14– Feb. 24).

Ferrous Finery, National Ornamental Museum, Memphis, TN, USA (March 13– April 24).

Gallery 585 established, Helsinki, Finland.

Gallery Philippe Debray established, Riihimäki, Finland.

Hans Appenzeller, Inc., established New York, USA. (Closed 1991).

Hommage a la Main, Centre Culturel Suédois, Paris, France (Sept. 29 – Nov. 6). Jewelry artists: Torun Bülow-Hübe, A-C Conni Hultberg, Per Davik, Ulla Faleij, James Gaddenius, Birger Haglund, Michael Hamma, Horst Hild, Theresia Hvorslev, Hubert Hydman, Cecilia Johansson, Karl-Ingemar Johansson, Inga Lagervall-Ringbom, Suzanne Lindahl, Etsuko Minowa, Kristian Nilsson, Per Herman Nilsson, Ulla Helen Nilsson, Kerstin Öhlin-Lejonklou, Glenn Roll, Sigurd Persson, Margareth Sandström, Karlheinz Sauer.

International Jewellery Art Exhibition, 5th Tokyo Triennial, (Japan Jewellery Designers Association), Isetan Art Museum, Shinjuku, Tokyo, Japan (Feb. 11– 22); Nabio Gallery, Umeda, Osaka, Japan (March 10–30).

Invitational of American Jewelry, Kyoto Municipal Museum of Traditional Industry, Kyoto, Japan.

Japan Jewellery Designers Association-Zeitgenössischer Schmuck aus Japan, Schmuckmuseum, Pforzheim, Germany; Deutsches Goldschmiedehaus, Hanau, Germany; Gallery Handwerk, Munich; Kunstgewerbemuseum, Lausanne, Switzerland; Galerie am Graben, Vienna; travelled until 1984.

The Jewellery Project: New Departures in British and European Work, 1980–1983, Crafts Council Gallery, London, England (April 20– June 26); Harbourfront Gallery, Toronto, Canada. A collection made on behalf of Malcolm, Sue and Abigail Knapp, New York, by Susanna Heron and David Ward. Artists:

J. Brakman, Broadhead, S. Corke, Hess-Dahm, Degen, Derrez, Dobler, Dziuba, N. Fok, Herbst, H. Hermsen, S. Heron, Knobel, Künzli, van Leersum, J. Manheim, R. Park, R. Perry, R. Peters, A. Planteydt, A. de Rijk, Spiller, Watkins, J. Wehrens, L. de Wolf.

Jewelry Design: New York State Artists, Herbert F. Johnson Museum of Art, Cornell Univeristy, Ithaca, NY, USA.

Julia Mannheim: Wire Wear, Crafts Council, London, UK. (April 20– June 12, 1983).

Kollektion Künzli '83, Deutsches Tapetenmuseum Kassel, Germany.

Körperkultur, Landesmuseum, Oldenburg, Germany. Artists: Otto Künzli, Gerd Rothmann.

Material Schmuck und Gerät, Internationale Handwerksmesse, Munich, Germany.

Metal and Enamel Invitational, Robert Else Gallery, State University, Sacramento, CA, USA.

Modischer Schmuck, Idar-Oberstein, Germany.

Metallum Group, Röhsska Konstslöjdmuseet, Gothenburg, Sweden.

Metals and Enamels, Kyoto Municipal Museum of Traditional Industry, Kyoto, Japan.

New Departures in British Jewellery, American Craft Museum, New York, USA (April 14– June 5).

Nya Smycken: Kulturhuset, Stockholm, (July 7– Aug 28) Paul Derrez, Marion Herbst.

Paula Häiäjo, Solo Exhibition, Kludvin Galleria, Helsinki, Finland.

Peter Skubic und Studenten der Schmuckklasse an der Kölner Werkschule, Kölnischer Kunstverein, Cologne, Germany.

Svenskt silver idag, Nationalmuseum, Stockholm, Sweden (May 18 – Aug. 14), in honour of the 20-year jubilee of Nutida Svenskt Silvers.

Thomas Gentille Solo Exhibition, The Gulbenkian Museum, Lisbon, Portugal (April 28– June 1).

Vincent Ferrini: A Retrospective Exhibition, 1953–1983, Brockton Art Museum/Fuller Memorial, Brockton, MA, USA.

1984

10 Year Anniversary Exhibition of Norsk Kunsthåndverk Association, Kunstindustrimuseet, Oslo, Norway.

American Jewelry Now, organized by the American Craft Museum, New York, USA; toured Asia until 1987. Artists include: Bennett, Church, Ebendorf, Fisch, P. Flynn, D. Friedlich, Glowacki, L. Hall, S. Hamlet, V. Howe, Hu, Kington, Krentzin, LaPlantz, Laskin, Leupp, Loeber, R. J. Long, L. MacNeil, B. Mail, Metcalf, O'Hanrahan, H. S. and E. M. Pijanowski, Quigley, G. Raber, Rapoport, V. Reed, I. Ross, G. Saunders, Schick, B. J. Theide, R. Thiewes, L. Threadgill, Tisdale, J. van Ommen, B. Walter, I. M. Widiapradja, A. Young.

Contemporary Jewellery: The Americas, Australia, Europe and Japan, National Museum of Modern Art, Kyoto (Aug. 29– Oct. 7); National Museum of Modern Art, Tokyo, Japan (Oct. 25– Dec. 9). Artists: Babetto, Bakker, Bennett, J. Brakman, Broadhead, Cepka, Puig Cuyàs, Derrez, De Wit, L. de Wolf, Dobler, Ebendorf, Griffin, Hamlet, Hess-Dahm, Hilbert, Hiramatsu, A. Klein, Knobel, Künzli, Laken, Makigawa, Martinazzi, Moty, Nagai, Van Nieuwenborg, E. M. Pijanowski, H. S. Pijanowski, Poston, Ramshaw, Schick, Shirk, Skubic, Tully, T. Vigeland, Walker, Watkins.

Cross Currents: Jewellery from Australia, Britain, Germany and Holland, Power House Museum, Sydney, Australia. Travelled throughout Australia, New Zealand until 1986. Artists: Bakker, Bischoff, Boekhoudt, Brakman, Broadhead, Derrez, G. Dziuba, R. Gough, M. Herbst, Heron, Hilbert, Knobel, D. Kruger, Künzli, Van Leersum, Makigawa, Walker, Watkins, L. de Wolf.

Françoise van den Bosch Prize, Third Recipient: Pierre Degen.

Friedrich Becker, Goldschmied: Schmuck, Silbergerät, Kinetische Objekte 1951–1983, Kunstverein für die Rhinelande und Westfalen, Düsseldorf Grabbeplatz Kunsthalle, Germany (Feb. 10– April 1).

The Great West Jewelry/Metal Exhibition, Northern Arizona University, Flagstaff, AZ, USA.

Hermann Schafran: Arbeiten 1976–84, Städtische Kunsthalle, Mannheim, Germany (Nov. 24, 1984– Jan. 27, 1985).

Internationale Schmuckschau, Internationale Handwerksmesse, Munich, Germany. Artists: Babetto, Puig Cuyàs, Itoh, Nagai, Schick.

Jewelry and Beyond: Recent Metalwork by Distinguished Members of the Society of North American Goldsmiths, Mitchell Museum, Mount Vernon, IL, USA (April 21– May 20); Fashion Institute of Technology, New York, USA (June 7–17).

Jewelry International: Contemporary Trends, (May 25– Sept. 1); American Craft Museum II, New York, USA. Curated by Helen Drutt. Artists: Babetto, Bakker, Bischoff, Boekhoudt, Brakman, Breis, Broadhead, I. Dahan, De Large, Derrez, De Wit, L. de Wolf, Dobler, Evans, Fröhlich, Goudji, Hess-Dahm, Hilbert, Hiramatsu, Itoh, Jünger, Kasaly, Y. Kitamura, Knobel, Kodejs, Kodré-Defner, Künzli, C. Lewton-Brain, Lopez-Antei, Lorenzen, Maierhofer, Makigawa, Martinazzi, Mitsuyasu, B. O'Casey, Pavan, Puig Cuyàs, Ramshaw, Rezac, P. J. Ritchie, Schocken, Sharlin, Souply, Spiller, J. Symon, Van Leersum, T. Vigeland, Watkins, T. Zaremski, Zschaler.

Jewelry USA, American Craft Museum II, New York, USA (May 25– Sept. 1). Jurors: Sharon Church, Helen Drutt and John Paul Miller. Artists: Aguado, Bennett, Church, Colette, Craver, Ebendorf, S. Enterline, Fike,

Fisch, Foltz-Fox, Friedlich, Garrison, Hall, Hamlet, Harper, V. Howe, Hu, Jocz, B. King, B. Kington, Krentzin, Laplantz, Laskin, Lent, L. Leupp, Loeber, L. MacNeil, Mawdsley, Metcalf, J. P. Miller, Moty, H. O'Connor, B. O'Hanrahan, J. van Ommen, J. Parcher, Quigley, G. Klunder Raber, Rapoport, A. Revere, G. Saunders, Schick, S. Sherman, Shirk, C. Smith, C. Strieb, B. J. Theide, R. Thiewes, Tisdale, A. Young.

Marilynn Nicholson: Jeweller, Victoria and Albert Museum, London, England (Nov. 3, 1984 – Jan. 3, 1985).

Metaforum '84, Taideteollisussmuseo, Helsinki, Finland. 50 Finnish artists.

Metals, National Metals Invitational, Southwest Texas State University, San Marcos, TX, USA (Feb. 15– March 8).

Modern Jewelry, 1964–1984: The Helen Williams Drutt Collection, Chateau Dufresne, Montreal Museum of Decorative Arts, Montreal, Quebec, Canada (Nov. 15, 1984– Feb. 3, 1985).

Movements in Jewellery, Goldsmiths' Hall, London, England.

Musterbuch: Gerd Rothmann, Galerie Spektrum, Munich, Germany (May 2–30), toured Europe until April 1985.

NFS Föringen för Nutida Svenskt Silver, Kunst-industrimuseet, Oslo, Norway.

N.H.G.C.A. Metals Invitational, New Harmony Gallery of Contemporary Art, New Harmony, IN, USA (Nov. 18, 1984– Jan. 6, 1985).

Northern California Jewelers: Contemporary Metal Works, Redding Museum and Art Center, Redding, CA, USA (Feb. 29– March 25).

Patricia Meyerowitz, Victoria and Albert Museum, London, England (March 3– April 26).

Precious Objects, National Invitational Exhibition of Contemporary Metalwork, Worcester Crafts Center, Worcester, MA.

Schmuck Symposium, Erfurt, Germany, organized by Rolf Lindner, to be held every two years.

Schmuck, zeitgenössische Kunst aus Österreich, Biennale di Venezia 1984, Ateneo San Basso, Piazza San Marco, Venice, Italy (June 9– Aug. 19). Artists: Heindl, Kodré-Defner, H. Kodré, Kutschera, E. Leitner, Maierhofer, Gert Mosettig, M. Nisslmüller, Wolfgang Rahs, Skubic, Leonhard Stramitz, J. Symon.

Structure and Ornament, American Modernist Jewelry 1940–1960, FIFTY/50 Gallery, New York, USA (Nov. 29, 1984– Jan. 12, 1985).

VO Galerie established, Washington, DC. Founders: Joke van Ommen and Jan Maddox. Innovative European and American work exhibited. Renamed Jewelers'werk Galerie after death of Van Ommen in 1988. Director: Ellen Reiben (Sept).

Worn Issues?: Low Cost Jewellery Related to Environmental Issues in Australia, Jam Factory Gallery, Adelaide, Australia (Feb. 4–24).

Zeitgenössische deutsche Goldschmiedekunst, Goethe Institute, Tokyo, Japan; National Art Gallery, Wellington, New Zealand.

1985

6. Internationaler Wettbewerb des Schmuckmuseums Pforzheim-Schmuck für Kopf und Haar, Schmuck-museum, Pforzheim, Germany. Artists include: Robert Ebendorf, Pavel Opočenskỳ, Marjorie Schick, Deganit Schocken.

16 Dutch Jewellery Designers, Nordenfjeldske Kunst-industrimuseum, Trondheim, Norway (Nov. 14– Dec. 6).

25 Jahre Galerie Nouvelles Images, Haags Gemeente-museum, The Hague, The Netherlands; Den Galerie Werkstatt, Berlin, Germany.

1962–1985 Works by Robert Ebendorf, Nordenfjeldske Kunstindustrimuseum, Trondheim, Norway.

Alan Craxford: Jeweller, Victoria and Albert Museum, London, England (Jan. 12– March 7).

Attitudes, International Cultureel Centrum, Antwerp, Belgium (May 25– June 23). Toured through Europe until Sept. 1986. Participating artists: Georg Dobler, Therese Hilbert, Otto Künzli, Birgit Laken, Falko Marx, David Poston, Miriam Sharlin.

Bijou Frontal, Museum für Gestaltung, Basle, Switzerland.

Body Works and Wearable Sculpture, Visual Arts Center of Alaska, Anchorage, AK, USA (April 22– May 18); University of Alaska Museum, Fairbanks, AK, USA (May 24– July 7). Guest Curator: Marjorie Schick.

Chris Steenbergen: edelsmid, Museum Boymans-van Beuningen, Rotterdam, The Netherlands (Nov. 16, 1985– Jan. 5, 1986).

Contemporary Jewelry Redefined: Alternative Materials, Pittsburgh Center for the Arts, Pittsburgh, PA, USA (April 27 – May 26). Artists: Bakker, Broadhead, Derrez, L. de Wolf, Dobler, Eisler, Hall, Hamlet, A. Holdsworth, Itoh, A. Klein, Knobel, Makigawa, W. Manwaring, P. Niczewski, Opočenskỳ, Puig Cuyàs, Rapoport, Schick, Scott, Tisdale, Van Leersum, Van Nieuwenborg/Wegman, Watkins.

Contemporary Metals, USA, Downey Museum of Art, Downey, CA, USA.

David Watkins: Jewellery and Sculpture, Crafts Council Gallery, London, England, (Nov. 20, 1985 – Jan. 12, 1986); toured internationally until 1986, co-sponsored by Leeds City Art Galleries and Crafts Council.

Diamonds Today, Helsinki, Finland; competition organized by all Scandinavian goldsmith societies.

Enamels International 1985, competition, Long Beach Museum of Art, CA, USA; organized by Enamel Guild West.

Form Formel Formalismus: Schmuck 1985, Internationale Handwerksmesse, Munich, Germany (March 9–17).

Jacqueline Mina: Jewellery, 1973-1985, Victoria and Albert Museum, London, England (Sept. 7– Nov. 7).

Joies de Catalunya – 13 zeitgenössische Goldschmiede aus Barcelona, Schmuckmuseum, Pforzheim, Germany.

Masterworks of Contemporary American Jewelry: Sources and Concepts, Victoria and Albert Museum, London, England (May 11– June 27). Artists: Aguado, Bennett, Bertoia, Calder, Colette, Craver, Ebendorf, Fike, Harper, Hu, Lechtzin, J. Marshall, Mawdsley, J. P. Miller, Nevelson, Pardon, de Patta, S. Radakovich, A. Smith.

New Tradition: The Evolution of Jewellery 1966-1985, British Crafts Centre, London, England. Artists include: Appenzeller, Bakker, F. Becker, Boekhoudt, Brakman, Broadhead, Degen, Derrez, Fisch, Hees, Hermsen, Heron, Hess-Dahm, Holder, Honing, Knobel, Künzli, Van Leersum, Manheim, L. Martin, Van Nieuwenborg, Peters, A. Planteydt, Poston, Ramshaw, Rothman, Schick, Spiller, M. Staartjes, Watkins, M. Wegman, L. de Wolf, Zahn.

New Visions, Traditional Materials: Contemporary American Jewelry, Carnegie Institute, Museum of Art, Pittsburgh, PA, USA.

Nya Smycken, Nya Material, Kulturhuset, Stockholm, Sweden (Nov. 22, 1985– Feb. 9, 1986). Artists include: Bakker, Blåvarp, Brakman, Broadhead, Carlström, K. Chan, Derrez, Dobler, B. Eshlel Gershuni, Hamlet, Herbst, Hermsen, Hess-Dahm, Hiramatsu, Honing, Itoh, Kaminski, M. Kleppen, Knobel, Laken, Maierhofer, Makigawa, J. Manheim, Puig Cuyàs, Quigley, Spiller, De Wit, L. De Wolf, Wolters.

Reflections: A Tribute to Alma Eikerman, Master Craftsman, Retrospective of forty alumni metal-artists, Indiana University Art Museum, Bloomington, IN, USA (July 10– Oct. 6).

Roger Morris, Solo Exhibition, Crawford Gallery, St Andrews University, Scotland.

Silberschmiede, HWK Galerie, Düsseldorf, Germany, toured throughout Germany until 1986.

Variatinen in Metall und Porzellan: Gretchen Klunder Raber und Jolande Haas Goldberg, Schmuckmuseum, Pforzheim, Germany (Feb. 23–April 14); Deutsches Goldschmiedehaus, Hanau, Germany (April 28– June 2).

Vormgevers in Beweging, Haags Gemeentemuseum, The Hague, The Netherlands.

1986

4 Contemporary Australian Jewellers, Woolongong City Art Gallery, New South Wales, Australia.

10 Jaar Ra, Anniversary Exhibition of Galerie Ra, Amsterdam. First decade.

American Craft Today: Poetry of the Physical, American Craft Museum of Jewellery, New York, USA (Oct. 26, 1986– March 22, 1987), toured nationally until 1988. Artists: Aguado, Banyas, Bennett, Church, Colette, Ebendorf, Eikerman, Fisch, Friedlich, Hamlet, Harper, Hu, Klein, Laskin, Lechtzin, Leupp, Loeber, Loloma, MacNeil, Metcalf, J. P. Miller, Moty, Nivola, Opočenskỳ, H. S. and E. M. Pijanowski, G. Raber, Rapoport, V. Reed, Rezac, I. Ross, G. Saunders, Scherr, Schick, Thiewes, Threadgill, A. Young.

All That Glitters: Personal Ornaments, Milwaukee Art Museum, Milwaukee, WI, USA (July 19– Aug. 24).

Contemporary Arts: An Expanding View (II), Monmouth Museum, Lincroft, NJ, USA (March 9– June 15); Squibb Gallery, Princeton, NJ, USA (Oct. 1– Nov. 2). Participating jewelry artists: Bennett, Binkley, Dobler, Eisler, Fisch, Garrison, Goessler-Snyder, Hamlet, Harper, Klein, Koopman, Laskin, Mueller, O'Casey, Opočenskỳ, Quigley, Ramshaw, Rapoport, Rezac, Schick, Schocken, Shirk, Skoogfors, Tisdale, Watkins.

David Watkins: Jewellery, Stedelijk Museum, Amsterdam, The Netherlnds (April 25– June 14).

Designs for the Body: New Norwegian Jewelry, ASF (American Scandinavian Foundation) Gallery, New York, USA. Artists: Tove Becken, Millie Behrens, Liv Blåvarp, Christine Bongard, Gry Eide, Ingjerd Hanevold, Morten Kleppan, Ingrid Larsen, Laila Irene Olsen, Heidi Sand, Tone Vigeland, Ann-Rita B. Wold.

Françoise van den Bosch Prize, Fourth Recipient: Marijke de Goey.

Gioelli: Moda, Magia, Sentimento, Poldi Pezzoli Museum, Milan, Italy.

International Jewellery Art Exhibition, The 6th Tokyo Triennial, Yurakucho Art Forum, Tokyo, Japan. Artists: Cepka, Puig Cuyàs, Derrez, Friedlich, Hess-Dahm, Hiramatsu, Knupper, Makigawa, Pavan, E. M. Pijanowski, H. S. Pijanowski, Schick, Skubic, T. Vigeland.

Jewelry: Form and Idea, Gemeentelijke van Reekum-museum, Apeldoorn, The Netherlands.

Jewelry Images, 10th anniversary exhibition organized by VES (Society of Jewelry makers/designers), Stedelijk Musem, Amsterdam, The Netherlands, toured throughout The Netherlands, Germany and Scandinavia until 1987.

The Lunning Prize, travelled to all Scandinavian museums of Craft and Design. Jewelry artist recipients and exhibitors: Helga and Bent Exner, Torun Bulow-Hube, Jorgen and Nanna Ditzel, Bent Gabrielsen, Bertel Gardberg, Grete Prytz Kittelsen, Henning Koppel, Borge Rajalin and Bjorn Weckstrom.

Machine as Metaphor: Current Work by Contemporary Metalsmiths, Purdue Univeristy, West Lafayette, Indiana (Feb. 17– March 23). Participating jewelry artists: Cynthia Cetlin, Susan Ewing, Susan Hamlet, Richard Helzer, Richard Mawdsley, Joel Peterson, Jonathan Quick and David Tisdale.

Modern Jewelry, 1964–1986: The Helen Williams Drutt Collection, Honolulu Academy of Arts, Honolulu, HI (Jan. 22– March 9); Cleveland Institute of Art, Cleveland, OH (Sept. 5–30); Philadelphia Museum of Art, Philadelphia, PA (Nov. 2, 1986– Feb. 1, 1987).

Nove Artisti Orafi di Scuola Padovana: 14th Biennale Internazionale del Bronzetto e della Piccola Scultura, Museo Civico Eremitani, Padua, Italy. Artists: Babetto, Giorgio, Pasquale, Pavan, Piazza, Pinton, Piergiuliano, Visintin, Zorzi.

Pencil Brothers Twenty Year Retrospective (Ken Cory/Les LePere), Cheney Cowles Museum, Spokane, WA, USA (travelled).

Schmuck 1986, Haus der Kunst, Munich, Germany.

Serie Sieraad, Stedelijk Museum, Amsterdam, The Netherlands.

Sieraad 1986, Draagteken?, Museum Voor Hedendaagse Kunst, Het Kruithuis, 's-Hertogenbosch, The Netherlands (Jan. 11– Feb. 16). Artists: Appenzeller, Bakker, Van den Bosch, Brakman, Broadhead, Hees, Hess-Dahm, Herbst, Van Leersum and L. de Wolf.

Sieraad Vorm en Idee, Gemeentelijke van Reekum-museum, Apeldoorn, The Netherlands.

Six Dutch Jewelry Designers, Kunstformen, Salzburg, Austria.

1987

The 3rd Seoul Biennale, Society of Seoul Metalsmiths, Seoul, Korea (March 17–22).

4 Australian Jewellers, National Gallery of Victoria, Melbourne, Australia, toured internationally. Artists: Kate Durham, Rowena Gough, Carlier Makigawa and Margaret West.

7 Goldschmiede 50 Schmuckstücke, Kunstgewerbe-museum, Berlin.

Beyond Reach, Robert Smit Solo Exhibition, Stedelijk Museum 'Het Prinsenhof,' Delft, The Netherlands.

Biennale du Bijoux Contemporain, Hotel du Sens, Paris, France.

Body Adornment, Renwick Gallery, National Collection of Fine Arts, Smithsonian Institution, Washington, DC, USA.

Contemporary Metals USA III, Downey Museum of Art, Downey, CA, USA (Oct. 29– Dec. 18).

Concepts Comments Process: Dutch Jewellery 1967–1987/Concepts Commentaires Processus: Le Bijou Néerlandais 1967–87, Rijksdienst Beeldende Kunst, The Hague, The Netherlands; Art Gallery at Harbourfront, Toronto, Ontario, Canada; Centre Internationale de Sign et de Décoration, Montreal, Quebec, Canada.

Martinazzi receiving the Golden Ring of Honour in 1987 from its maker, Karl Gustav Hansen, the previous recipient

Craft as Content: National Metals Invitational, Emily Davis Gallery, School of Art, University of Akron, Akron, OH, USA (Oct. 29– Nov. 16).

The Eloquent Object: The Evolution of American Art in Craft Media Since 1945, Philbrook Museum of Art, Tulsa, Oklahoma; participating artists: Calder, Cory, Craver, V. Dozier, Ebendorf, Harper, Hu, S. Kramer, Lechtzin, Loloma, Mawdsley, J. P. Miller, Paley, De Patta, Schick, Scott, A. Smith, Woell.

Enamel International 2 Art Exhibition, Kunstoerlin Coburg, Germany (June 27– Aug. 30).

Golden Ring of Honour of the Association for Goldsmiths' Art (created by Karl Gustav Hansen '82), recipient: Bruno Martinazzi, Deutsches Goldschmiedehaus, Hanau, Germany.

Goldsmiths of Veneto, San Diego State University, San Diego, CA, USA.

International Exhibition of Jewelry, Muzeum skla a bizu-terie, Jablonec nad Nisou, Czechoslovakia.

Jede Gewünschte Gestalt–Bakelit & Co (Sammlung H. G. Klein) Stadtmuseum, Cologne, Germany.

Jewelry in Movement – Movement in Jewelry, Deutsches Goldschmiedehaus, Hanau, Germany.

John Prip: Master Metalsmith, Museum of Art, Rhode Island School of Design, Providence, RI, USA (Oct. 9– Dec. 20); American Craft Museum, New York, USA (Jan. 29– April 28, 1988).

Joieria Europea Contemporània, Fundació Caixa de Pensions, Barcelona, Spain (Feb.–March). Artists include: Arck, Babetto, Bakker, Bischoff, Boekhoudt, Breis, Broadhead, Cepka, Derrez, Dobler, Hermsen, Hess-Dahm, Hilbert, Hoke, Knupper, Knobel, Künzli, Lorenzen, Maierhofer, Nisslmüller, Novak, A. Planteydt, Puig Cuyàs, Ramshaw, Rothmann, Schobinger, Skubic, Spiller, Watkins, de Wit, L. de Wolf,

Konst Hant Verk, Västerås Konstmuseum, Västerås.
Masterworks/Enamel/87, Taft Museum, Cincinnati, OH, USA (July 23– Aug. 31).
Metallkonst 87, Röhsska Konstslöjdmuseet, Gothenburg, Sweden; Konstnärscentrum, Stockholm, Sweden.
New Norwegian Jewellery: supported by Norwegian Ministry of Foreign Affairs: travelled USA.
Roger Morris Retrospective Exhibition, The Scottish Gallery, Edinburgh, Scotland; Crawford Centre for the Arts, St Andrews, Scotland; Bankhead Museum, Halifax.
Saara Hopea-Untracht, Retrospective, Taideteollisuus-museo, Helsinki, Finland.
Schmuck 1987, Haus der Kunst, Munich, Germany.
Schmuck in Bewegung, Bewegung in Schmuck, Deutsches Goldschmiedehaus, Hanau, Germany. Artists: Anton Cepka, Deganit Schocken, Peter Skubic.
Schmuck, Zeichen am Körper, Francisco Carolinum Museum, Linz, Austria. Artists: Babetto, Becker, Bischoff, Cepka, Puig Cuyàs, Heindl, Hess-Dahm, Knobel, Skubic, Smit, Watkins.
Schmuckszene '87, Internationalen Handwerksmesse, Munich, Germany.
The Ubiquitous Bead, Bellevue Art Museum, Bellevue, WA, USA. Participating artists: Beuhler, Hall, Ho, Solberg.
Wally Gilbert/Thomas Gentille, Victoria and Albert Museum, London, England (June 17– Sept. 20).

1988

10, Portland Museum of Art, Portland, ME, USA.
1988 Japan Jewellery Exhibition, Shivuya Seibu, Tokyo, Japan (April 7–12); Hanshin Hyakkaten, Osaka, Japan (April 21–26).
Alumni and Stonington Enamelists, 1969–1988, Kent State University Student Center Gallery, Kent, OH, USA (Oct. 19– Nov. 19).
Amulett & Talisman: Friedrich Wilhelm Müller Wettbewerb 1988, Stadtischen Museum, Schwäbisch Gmünd, Germany im Prediger, (Nov. 27, 1988– Jan. 15, 1989); Goldschmiede- und Uhrmacherschule, Pforzheim, Germany (Feb. 16 – March 10, 1989); Deutsches Goldschmiedehaus, Hanau, Germany (April 2–30, 1989); Landesvertretung Baden-Württemberg, Bonn, Germany (May 10 – 24, 1989); Volksbank Freiburg (June 8– July 6, 1989).
Anton Cepka-Vratislav Novák, Schmuckmuseum, Pforzheim, Germany (Dec. 10, 1988– Feb. 5, 1989); Deutsches Goldschmiedehaus, Hanau, Germany (Feb. 26– March 27, 1989).
Bezalel Graduates, Israel Museum, Jerusalem, Israel.
Biennale Svizzera del Gioiello d'Arte Contemporaneo, Villa Malpensata, Lugano, Switzerland.
Bijoux d'Email 1988, Limoges Musée Municipale de L'Eveche, Limoges, France.

Gijs Bakker, Barbara Santos-Shaw and Peter Chang (left to right) at *Ornamenta I*, Pforzheim, 1989

Tone Vigeland receiving the Prins Eugen Medal from King Carl Gustaf of Sweden, Stockholm, 1988

Pavan, Marx, Skubic, (left), and Smit, Babetto, Bischoff, (right), together for the *Tragezeichen* exhibition at Leverkusen in 1988

Bone-Stone-Shell: New Jewellery, New Zealand, sponsored by New Zealand Ministry of Foreign Affairs and Craft Council of NZ; toured. Artists: Paul Annear, Hamish Campbell, Michael Couper, John Edgar, Warwick Freeman, Eléna Gee, David Hegglun, Paul Mason, Roy Mason, Jenny Pattrick, Alan Preston, Inia Taylor.
The Cleveland Enamelists: 1930–1955, Kent State University School Art Gallery, Kent, OH, USA (Oct. 12– Nov. 4). Jewelry: J.P. Miller, P. Studio, J. Puskas.

Color and Image: Recent American Enamels, circulated by the Gallery Association of New York State. Curator: Lloyd E. Herman. Jewelry artists: Banyas, Bennett, C. Braswell, H. W. Butt, Carter, Colette, J. Davidson, Garrison, K. R. Gough, Harper, Laskin, S. Willis.
Dreamworlds: Eight Artists from Australia and the United States, San Diego State University Art Museum, San Diego, CA, USA.

The Founding Masters, exhibition accompanied by conference of the Society of North American Goldsmiths, Skidmore College, Saratoga Springs, NY, USA (June 16– July 17). Artists: Ebendorf, Fenster, Fike, Fisch, Jerry, H. Kielman, Kington, Lechtzin, Matsukata, Matzdorf, R. F. McNeish, R. H. Pearson, Prip, Seppä, Skoogfors, H. G. Stacey. Also, O. Larson and P. Morton, Founding Masters, no work exhibited.

Françoise van den Bosch Prize, Fifth Recipient: Gijs Bakker.

Galerie Metal, 10 Year Anniversary Show, Copenhagen, Denmark.

Goldsmithing: New Concepts and Ancient Traditions in Jewelry, Louisiana State University, Baton Rouge, LA, USA (Feb. 5– March 4).

Hermann Jünger: Schmuck nach 1945, Germanisches Nationalmuseum, Nuremberg, Germany (June 26– Aug. 21), toured in Germany until April 9, 1989.

Hong-ik Metalcrafts Association Annual Exhibition, Walker Hill Art Center Museum, Seoul, Korea.

Jubileums utställning, Föringen för Nutida Svenskt Silver, Stockholm, Sweden.

London/Amsterdam, Crafts Council Gallery, London (July 13– Sept. 18) Galerie Ra/Galerie de Witte Voet, Amsterdam, (Oct. 15– Dec. 4).

Norska Smycken, Röhsska Konstlöjdmuseet, Gothenburg, Sweden. Participating artists: Liv Blåvarp, Tone Vigeland.

Olympian Effort: Korean Metalsmiths Today, Bowling Green State University, Ohio, (Feb. 1–19); Sun Gallery, Hayward, CA, USA (June 25– Aug. 13).

Otto und Gertrud Schamschula: Schmuck, Gerät, Objekte, 1954–1988, Museum für Kunsthandwerk, Frankfurt, Germany (May 19– July 17).

Schmuck-Ausstellung der DDR, Galerie am Fischmarkt, Erfurt, Germany (May 18– July 3).

Schmuck Berlin-West, Galerie Kunsthandwerk, Berlin, Germany (Sept. 6– Oct. 15); Deutsches Goldschmiedehaus, Hanau, Germany (Oct. 23– Nov. 20).

Schmuckszene '88, Internationale Handwerksmesse, Munich, Germany.

Tragezeichen: Schmuck von Giampaolo Babetto, Manfred Bischoff, Falko Marx, Manfred Nisslmüller, Francesco Pavan, Bernhard Schobinger, Peter Skubic and Robert Smit, Museum Morsbroich, Leverkusen, Germany.

1989

Alle ting er tre, Kunstindustrimuseet, Oslo, Norway. Participating artist: Liv Blåvarp.

An Art Collection of Combs, organized by Galerie Marzee, Nimwegen, The Netherlands, toured European museums (Boymans van Beuningen Museum, Rotterdam, The Netherlands; Museum Bellerive, Zurich, Switzerland; Museum für angewandte Kunst, Cologne, Germany).

British Jewellery – German Jewellery, Crafts Council Gallery, London, England (April 19– July 16), toured until 1990. Artists include: J. Adam, M. Bischoff, Cynthia Cousens, Flöckinger, Hilbert, E. Holder, J. Mina, Ramshaw, G. Stewart, Watkins.

Craft Today: USA, organized by the American Craft Museum, New York, USA, (USIA) – Arts America, Musée des Arts Décoratifs, Paris, France (May 24– Aug. 27); travelled in Europe until Jan. 1993. Jewelry artists: Aguado, Bennett, D. Chase, Ebendorf, Fisch, P. Flynn, Friedlich, Gralnick, Hu, A. Klein, Loeber, Loloma, Long, L. MacNeil, T. Mann, Moty, Opočenský, Paley, H. S. Pijanowski, Prip, Quigley, Raber, V. Reed, Rezac, G. Saunders, Schick, Scott, Shirk, B. J. Theide, Thiewes and Threadgill.

Eloquent Resolutions: Jewelry by and for Women, National Ornamental Metal Museum, Memphis, TN, USA.

Galerie Slavik established, Vienna. Director: Renata Slavik.

Gijs Bakker, vormgever: Solo voor een solist, Centraal Museum, Utrecht, The Netherlands (Sept. 22– Nov. 5); Helen Drutt Gallery, New York, USA (Dec. 7, 1989– Jan. 6, 1990).

Helen Shirk: Twenty Years, National Ornamental Museum, Memphis, TN, USA.

Hongik Metalcraft — 10 Years, Hyundai Art Center, Hongik, Korea (April 11-19).

Infinite Riches: Jewelry Through the Centuries, Museum of Fine Arts, St Petersburg, FL, USA (Feb. 19– April 30). Artists: Babetto, Bakker, Bischoff, De Wit, Dobler, Eisler, Fike, Fisch, Garrison, Gentille, Goessler-Snyder, Harper, Hu, Lechtzin, B. Mail, Martinazzi, Marx, Mawdsley, O'Casey, Opočenský, Pavan, E. M. Pijanowski, H. S. Pijanowski, Seppä, Skoogfors, Smit, Stark.

Jewellery and Objects from Israel, Museum für angewandte Kunst, Cologne, Germany.

Jewelry: Means: Meaning, University of Tennessee, Knoxville, USA; travelled throughout the US.

Ornamenta 1: Internationale Schmuckkunst, Schmuckmuseum, Pforzheim, Germany (Sept. 30– Nov. 19). Artists: Babetto, Bakker, Bennett, Bischoff, Chang, L. de Wolf, Ebendorf, Eisler, Fisch, Gentille, Gralnick, Heindl, Hiramatsu, B. Laken, Lechtzin, Van Leersum, Makigawa, Martinazzi, Marx, Metcalf, Nagai, Pavan, Peters, E. M. Pijanowski, H. S. Pijanowski, Ramshaw, Sajet, Schick, T. Vigeland, Watkins.

Perth International Crafts Triennial, Art Gallery of Western Australia, Perth, Australia (Oct. 14– Dec. 3). Jewelry artists include: Babetto, Cepka, Dobler, Heindl, Hilbert, Holder, Honing, Jünger, Knobel, D. Kruger, S. Lorraine, Maierhofer, Makigawa, J. Matthesius, Nagai, Pavan, Ramshaw, Rothmann, Skubic, Smit, Visintin, Walker, David Watkins, West, Zorzi.

Robert Ebendorf: Retrospective Exhibition, State University of New York, New Paltz, NY, USA (April 4–26).

Schmuckszene '89, Internationalen Handwerksmesse, Munich, Germany.

Structure and Surface: Beads in Contemporary American Art, John Michael Kohler Arts Center, Sheboygan, WI, USA (Dec. 4, 1988– Feb. 12, 1989; Renwick Gallery, National Collection of Fine Arts, Smithsonian Institution, Washington, DC, USA (July 27, 1990– Jan. 13, 1991). Participating jewelry artists: Ebendorf, Harper, Rezac.

William Harper: Artist as Alchemist, Orlando Museum of Art, Orlando, FL, USA (Nov. 4– Dec. 10), toured nationally and internationally until 1991.

Zeitgenössische Schmuckkunst aus der Bundesrepublik Deutschland, Instituts für Auslandsbeziehungen, Stuttgart, Germany. Artists: Arck, Baumgärtel, F. Becker, Bischoff, Dobler, G. Dziuba, Fraling, Hilbert, Jünger, Künzli, W. Krüger, D. Kruger, Lorenzen, Mattar, Rothmann, von Skal, J. Wehrens, N. Wolters.

1990

1990 Metals Invitational Exhibition, Haynes Fine Arts Gallery, Montana State University, Bozeman, MT, USA (Sept. 10– Oct. 19).

American Dreams, American Extremes: Jewelry from the United States, Museum Voor Hedendaagse Kunst, Het Kruithuis, 's-Hertogenbosch, The Netherlands (June); Provinciaal Museum Voor Modern Kunst, Ostend, Belgium. Artists: Batal, Garrison, Gentille, Iversen, King, Lechtzin, Metcalf, Onofrio, Opočenský, Overstreet and Kranitzky, Scott, Stubbs, Woell, Zwillinger.

Argyle Contemporary Jewellery, Crafts Council Gallery, Perth, Western Australia.

Arthur Smith: A Jeweler's Retrospective, Jamaica Arts Center, Jamaica, NY, USA (Feb. 1– March 24).

Bertel Gardberg: 50 Years of Art Handicraft, Linnoitusmuseo, Hanko, Finland; Amos Andersonin Taidemuseo, Helsinki, Finland.

Bolero, 32 Gold and Silversmiths, Nybro Pavillion, Stockholm, Sweden.

Ehrenringträger, Gesellschaft für Goldschmiedekunst, Hamburg, Germany.

Françoise van den Bosch Prize, Sixth Recipient: Otto Künzli.

Fremd-Körper aus der Sammlung Teunen, Wilhelm-Hack-Museum, Ludwigshafen, Germany. (Dec. 15, 1990– Feb. 13, 1991). Artists include: Bakker, Derrez, Künzli, Van Leersum, Van Nieuwenborg/Wegman, Rothmann.

Friedrich Knupper: Schmuck und Objekte, Germanisches Nationalmuseum, Nuremberg, Germany (Dec. 14, 1990– Feb. 17, 1991), toured throughout Germany until May 1992.

Gioelli e Legature: Artisti del XX Secolo, Biblioteca Trivulziana, Milan.

Golden Ring of Honour of the Association for Goldsmiths' Art (created by Bruno Martinazzi '87), recipient: Anton Cepka. Deutsches Goldschmiedehaus, Hanau, Germany.

Jewelries/Epiphanies, Artists Foundation's Gallery at CityPlace, Boston, MA (Sept. 4– Oct. 18). Artists: B. Bally, Eisler, S. Enterline, Gentille, Gralnick, Hamlet, J. Iversen, Jocz, A. MacGeorge, Opočenský, J. Parcher, C. Sanford, J. Slosburg-Ackerman, L. Spiros, D. Suydam, A.B. Thompson, J. Wood.

Lapponia Jewelry: International Jewelry from Finland, 30th-anniversary exhibition of Lapponia jewelry, Taideteollisuusmuseo, Helsinki, Finland (Aug. 24– Sept. 30).

L'Arte della Gioia, Pedrocchi, Padua, Italy. Artists: Bakker, Derrez, Peters, Sajet, Smit.

Metalwork from Barcelona, Southwest Texas University State Art Gallery, San Marcos, TX, USA.

News from the Netherlands: A Jewelry Survey, Fundacao Calouste Gulbenkian, Lisbon, Portugal; Slovak National Gallery, Bratislava, Slovakia; Dutch Form Foundation, Amsterdam, The Netherlands. Artists: Bakker, Boekhoudt, Derrez, P. Hartman, Hees, Herbst, R. de Jong, B. Kessler, Laken, N. Linssen, L. Martin, Peters, A. Planteydt, L. Sarneel, L. de Wolf.

NFS Föringen för Nutida Svenskt Silver, Röhsska Konstslöjdmuseet, Gothenburg, Sweden. Participating artists: Peter De Wit, Margareth Sandstrom.

Primary Visions and Mannerisms, University of the Arts, Philadelphia, PA, USA. Participating artists: Bennett, Church, Opočenský, Slosburg-Ackerman, T. Vigeland.

Schmuck + Gerät – Bund der Kunsthandwerker Baden-Württemberg, Symposium, Schmuckmuseum, Pforzheim, Germany (April 21– June 10). Moderator: Vanessa Lynn.

Schmuckszene '90, Internationalen Handwerksmesse, Munich, Germany (March 10–18).

Signaturen Using Gold and Silver, International Jewelry Competition and Traveling Exhibition, Stadtischen Museum, Wettbewerb, Schwäbisch Gmünd, Germany.

Sinnesfröjd (A Joy of Mind), Liljevalchs Konsthall, Stockholm, Sweden.

Triennale du Bijou, Musée du Luxembourg, Paris. Artists include: Babetto, M. Becker, L. Blåvarp, Derrez, Heindl, Peters, H. S. Pijanowski, Ramshaw, Sajet, D. Schocken, Skubic, R. Smit, J. Syvanoja, Watkins.

US Metal/NW Metal, Cheney Cowles Museum, Spokane, WA, USA.

1991

1st Australian Contemporary Jewellery Biennial, Jam Factory, Adelaide, Australia, travelled. Participating Pierre Cavalan, Carlier Makigawa, Margaret West.

The 20th Anniversary Show, Electrum Gallery, London, England.

Americky Sperk, Umeleckoprumyslove Muzeum, Prague, Czechoslovakia.

Arsenale: Aggression im Schmuck, Germany: Museum für Kunsthandwerk, Frankfurt a.M., (Nov. 11– Dec. 12); Deutsches Klingenmuseum, Solingen, (Jan. 5– Feb. 16, 1992); Konzert- und Bühnenhaus, Kevelaer, (March 1992); Kunstmuseum, Schwäbisch-Gmünd; Switzerland: National Museum, Zurich.

Beauty is a Story, Museum Voor Hedendaagse Kunst, Het Kruithuis, 's-Hertogenbosch, The Netherlands (Feb. 24– April 7); Landcommanderij Alden Biesen, Bilzen-Rijkhoven, Belgium (April 14– June 2). Artists: Batal, Bischoff, Heindl, D. Kruger, W. Krüger, L. Liket, P. Muff, Overstreet and Kranitzky, Sajet, L. Sarneel, Scott, D. Thomas, M. Wong.

Carin Delcourt van Krimpen Gallery established, Rotterdam, The Netherlands (Dec.).

Copper III, 1991 National Metal Competition, Old Pueblo Museum, Tucson, AZ, USA (Dec. 10, 1991– Jan. 31, 1992). Jurors: Dr. Robert L. Cardinale, Eleanor Moty and David Pimentel.

Elsa Freund: American Studio Jeweler, Arkansas Arts Center Decorative Arts Museum, Little Rock, AK, USA (Sept. 8– Oct. 6).

Exhibition of Platinum Jewellery, Goldsmiths' Hall, London. Participating artist: Wendy Ramshaw.

Jehi or, Jewish Museum, Frankfurt, Germany.

Jewellery of the Twentieth Century, Museum für Kunst und Gewerbe, Hamburg, Germany; also, Koblenz, Ausburg, Wiesbaden in Germany.

Metals Expressions II, Appalachian Center for Crafts, Smithville, TN, USA; National Ornamental Metals Museum, Nashville, TN, USA.

More than a Maker: Recent Jewellery and Objects by David Walker, Erica Underwood Gallery, Curtin University Campus, Perth, Australia (Aug. 6–29).

Naakte Schoonheid, Museum van Hedendaagse Kunst, Antwerp, Belgium.

Otto Künzli: The Third Eye – Solo Exhibition, Stedelijk Museum, Amsterdam, The Netherlands; Museum Bellerive, Zurich, Switzerland, 1992.

Schmuck der Avantgarde aus der Sammlung Teunen, Wilhelm-Hack-Museum, Ludwigshafen, Germany.

Schmuckszene '91, Internationale Handwerksmesse Munich, Germany (March 16–24).

1992

IIIème Triennale du Bijou, Musée des Arts Décoratifs, Paris, France. Artists: Babetto, Bischoff, Chang, Puig Cuyàs, De Wit, Heindl, Knobel, D. Kruger, B. Laken, Pavan, Peters, Ramshaw, Sajet, D. Schocken, Smit, J. Syvänoja, Tamminen, T. Vigeland, Watkins.

Brilliant Stories: American Narrative Jewelry, USIS Exhibition Hall, Amman, Jordan; Riyadh, Saudi Arabia; Jeddah, Saudi Arabia; Musée des Beaux-Arts, Algiers, Algeria; Oudais Museum, Casablanca, Morocco; Karachi, Pakistan; Lahore, Pakistan; Cairo, Egypt; travelled throughout Middle East, Africa and USA until 1994.

British Goldsmiths of Today, Worshipful Company of Goldsmiths, London, England.

Design Visions, the Australian International Crafts Triennial, Art Gallery of Western Australia, Perth, Australia (Aug. 13 – Oct. 4); American Goldsmiths Exhibit.

Françoise van den Bosch Prize, Seventh Recipient: Manfred Bischoff.

Interstices: Works by Margaret West from 1981–1992, curated by Julie Ewington; Canberra School of Art Gallery, Canberra, Australia; travelled throughout Australia until 1994.

Joies Indissenyables: Exposició Internacional de Joieria Contemporània, Escola Massana, Capella de l'Antic Hospital de la Santa Creu, Barcelona, Spain (Feb. 20– March 18); conceived by Xavier Domenech, Ramón Puig Cuyás.

Klaus Ullrich-Schmuckgestalter seit 1955, Schmuck-museum, Pforzheim, Germany.

Korun Kieli, The Helen Williams Drutt Collection, Taideteollisuusmuseo, Helsinki, Finland; Röhsska (March 12 – April 12, 1995); Konstslöjdmuseet, Gothenburg, Sweden (Nov. 28, 1992– Jan. 10, 1993).

Of Magic, Power and Memory: Contemporary International Jewelry, Bellevue Art Museum, Bellevue, WA, USA (April). Artists: Beuhler, Ebendorf, Hall, Harper, Ho, Kranitzky and Overstreet, Mawdsley, Scott, Slemmons, Solberg.

Marijke Studio established, Padua, Italy (Nov.) Founder: Marijke Vallanzasca. Exhibits European jewelry.

Neckworks, Fremantle Art Centre, Perth, Australia.

Neotoric Jewelry, Snug Harbor, Cultural Center, Staten Island, NY, USA.

Repair Days Reunion, National Ornamental Metal Museum, Memphis, TN. Mary Lee Hu, Helen Shirk.

Schmuckkunst Aus Amerika, Galerie für Moderne Kunst, Vienna, Austria.

Schmuckszene '92, Internationalen Handwerksmesse, Munich, Germany (March 14–22).

Sieraad en sieraad, Kritzraedthuis, Sittard, The Netherlands.

Sieraden, Centrum Beeldende Kunst, Groningen, The Netherlands.

Stone-Touch-Jewelry, Oppenheimer Diamond Museum, Ramat Gan, Israel.

Treasures: Jewelry and Other Metalwork from the Permanent Collection of the American Craft Museum, American Craft Museum, (Jan. 20– Aug. 2). Artists include: Brynner, Colette, DePatta, Fike, Fisch, Hu, A. Hutchins, Jerry, Kington, S. Kramer, LaPlantz, Lechtzin, Loloma, B. Martin, J. P. Miller, Paley, E. Pardon, R. H. Pearson, L. B. Peck, Renk, Scherr, R. Senungetuk, A. Shannon, A. Smith, L. Watson-Abbott.
Wearable Glass, Jam Factory, Adelaide, SA, Australia.

1993

10 American Jewelers, Perimeter Gallery, Chicago, IL (Oct. 8–31); Charles A. Wustum Museum of Fine Arts, Racine, WI, USA (Nov. 14– Dec. 19).
13 Goldschmiede: Von Amsterdam bis Tokyo, Bayerische Akademie der Schönen Künste, Munich, Germany (March 4 – April 11). Artists: Babetto, F. Becker, C. Bury, Cepka, Hiramatsu, Martinazzi, E. R. Nele, Pavan, A. Pomodoro, Reiling, Schmölzer, R. Smit, J. Symon.
2nd Australian Jewellery Biennial, Jam Factory, Adelaide, SA, Australia.
The Art of Jewellery, Setagaya Art Museum, Tokyo, Japan. Artists: Puig Cuyàs, L. de Wolf, Heindl, Makigawa, Metcalf, Schick, T. Vigeland, M. West.
The Arts & Crafts Metalwork of Janet Payne Bowles, Munson-Williams-Proctor Institute Museum of Art, Utica, NY, USA (Sept. 4, 1993 – Jan. 3, 1994); Indianapolis Museum of Art, Indianapolis, Indiana (April 9– May 22, 1994).
The Body Adorned, University of Texas, El Paso (Feb. 25– March 19); organized by Rachelle Thiewes. Artists include: Batal, Friedlich, Schick, Slemmons, J. Wood.
Broken Lines: Emmy van Leersum, 1930–1984, Museum Voor Hedendaagse Kunst, Het Kruithuis, 's-Hertogenbosch, The Netherlands (April 4– June 13); toured Europe and North America until April/May 1995.
Burg Giebichenstein: Die hallesche Kunstschule von den Anfangen bis zur Gegenwart, Staatliche Galerie Moritzburg, Halle, Germany (March 20 – June 13); Badisches Landesmuseum, Karlsruhe, Germany (June 25 – Sept. 12).
Contemporary Jewellery, 1964–1993: Selected Works, Helen Williams Drutt Collection, Arkansas Arts Center Decorative Arts Museum, Little Rock, AK, USA.
Contemporary Metal: Form and Narrative, invitational, Krannert Art Museum, University of Illinois, Urbana-Champaign; I-Space, Chicago, IL, USA. Participating artists: Laskin, Mawdsley, Metcalf, Schick, Shirk.
Documents Northwest, The Poncho Series: Six Jewelers, Seattle Art Museum, Seattle, WA, USA (April 22–

June 27). Participating artists: F. Book, Cory, R. Davidson, Hu, Slemmons, Solberg.
Ebbe Weiss-Weingart-Schmuck und Objekte 1946-1993, Schmuckmuseum, Pforzheim, Germany.
Elsa Freund: Modern Pioneer, Florida Craftsmen Gallery, St Petersburg, FL, USA (Sept. 17– Oct. 27), travelled throughout USA until Oct. 1994.
Facet I: Internationale sieradenbiënnale/International Jewellery Biennale, Kunsthal, Rotterdam, The Netherlands (May 1– July 7). Artists: Babetto, Becker, Bennett, Bischoff, J. Capdevila, Cepka, Chang, G. Corvaja, X. Domenech, Harper, Hiramatsu, Marx, Metcalf, M. Nisslmüller, B. Paganin, H. S. and E. M. Pijanowski, Puig Cuyàs, Sajet, L. Sarneel, Schobinger, Skubic, R. Smit, D. Thomas, S. Walz.
Gold oder Leben!, Akademie der Bildenden Künste, Munich, Germany (March 1–31).
Goldschmiede Silberschmiede. Drei Generationen: Franz Rickert, Hermann Jünger, Erhard Hössle, Ulla Mayer, Otto Künzli, Galerie für angewandte Kunst, Munich, Germany (March 3– May 31).
Holography in Jewellery Design, Museum für angewandte Kunst, Cologne, Germany.
Jewelryquake: International Three Schools Jewelry Collaboration, Hiko Mizuno College of Jewelry, Tokyo (Sept.); Galerie für angewandte Kunst, Munich (Feb. 1994); Gerrit Rietveld Akademie, Amsterdam (March 1994). Participating: Akademie der Bildende Künste, Munich; Gerrit Rietveld Akademie, Amsterdam; Hiko-Mizuno College of Jewelry, Tokyo.
Kosmos/Kosmetika, Nordic Jewelry Exhibition, Form/Design Centre, Malmö, Sweden.
Kunststoff Schmuck Kunst: 1923–1993, Galerie Biró, Munich. Artists include: Appenzeller, Babetto, Bakker, Chang, Derrez, Jünger, Künzli, Van Leersum, Puig Cuyàs, Rothmann, Watkins.
Lifetime Achievements: The American Craft Council College of Fellows in Metal, National Ornamental Metal Museum, Memphis, TN, USA (Jan. 31–March 28). Artists: Husted-Andersen, Christensen, M. Craver, Eikerman, Fike, Fisch, C. Carl Jennings, Kington, Lechtzin, Loloma, K. Matzdorf, F. A. Miller, J. P. Miller, Pearson, R. Penington, Prip, M. A. Scherr, Seppä, Solberg, R. Thomas, F. Whitaker.
Mag Het Iets Meer Zijn?: Marion Herbst, 1968–1993, Stedelijk Museum, Amsterdam, The Netherlands.
Müncher Goldschmiede: Schmuck und Gerät 1993, Müncher Stadtmuseum, Munich, Germany (March 26 – May 23); Bischoff, Hilbert, Jünger, D. Kruger, Künzli, Nagai, Von Skal.
Renate Heintze Schmuck: Staaliche Galerie Moritzburg Halle, Germany (March 7– June 13); Deutsches Gold-schiedehaus, Hanau (Sept. 19– Nov. 11).
Schmuck: Die Sammlung der Danner-Stiftung, Galerie für angewandte Kunst, Munich, Germany (March 12–

Ramona Solberg and Ron Ho in Seattle, 1994, for their exhibition *Two Friends*

May 15); among artists collected: Babetto, F. Becker, M. Becker, Bischoff, Corvaja, Dobler, Dziuba, Hilbert, Jünger, D. Kruger, Künzli, Lorenzen, Martinazzi, Nagai, Pavan, H. S. and E. M. Pijanowski, Puig Cuyàs, Pinton, Rothmann, Von Skal, Smit, Spiller, Symon, Thomas, Treykorn, Visintin, Wehrens.
Schmuckszene '93, Internationalen Handwerksmesse, Munich, Germany (March 13–21).
Sculptural Concerns: Contemporary American Metalworking, organized by Fort Wayne Museum; Contemporary Arts Center, Cincinnati, OH, USA (May 29 – Aug. 21); Fort Wayne Museum of Art, Fort Wayne, IN, USA (Sept. 11 – Nov. 7); travelled nationally. Artists include: C. Dinsmore, Bennett, Harper, Jocz, Metcalf, Moty, H. S. Pijanowski, Shirk.
Silver till nytta och lust, Nationalmuseum, Stockholm, Sweden.
Subjects: International Jewelry Exhibition, invitational, Design Forum, Helsinki, Finland. Artists include: Bakker, Derrez, Dobler, M. Herbst, Itoh, Novak, Puig Cuyas, Schick, Skubic, J. Syvänoja, Tamminen, Watkins.
Tekens & Ketens, Gemeentemuseum, Arnhem, The Netherlands; Museum Van Der Togt, Amstelveen, The Netherlands.
Tone Vigeland – Solo Exhibition, Kunstnerforbundet, Oslo, Norway.
A Tribute to Earl Pardon, Connell Gallery, Atlanta, GA; 'Fourteen former students exhibit their work as a tribute to a man whose life was an embodiment of grace, imagination and good humor.'
Voorzien: Benno Premsela Applied Art Collection, Stedelijk Museum, Amsterdam, The Netherlands (Jan. 16 – March 7). Artists: Appenzeller, Babetto, Bakker, Van Beek, Van den Bosch, Broadhead,

M. Herbst, Heron, Hiramatsu, Honing, V. Kaminski, B. Kessler, Knobel, Künzli, Van Leersum, L. Martin, F. Morellet, Peters, A. del Ponte, J. Syvänoja, K. Winterman.

Yasuki Hiramatsu Retirement Exhibition, Tokyo National University of Fine Arts and Music, Tokyo, Japan.

Your Heart in a Box: New Jewellery in Mixed Metals, Midlands Arts Centre, Birmingham, England; travelled.

1994

Brooch: The Subject, Tempe Arts Center, Tempe, AZ, USA.

Carin Delcourt van Krimpen Gallery establishes Space in Amsterdam (Sept.).

Contemporary Metalsmithing: Behind and Beyond the Bench, Craft Alliance, St Louis, MO, USA (June 10– July 23).

Exhibition of Platinum Jewellery, Worshipful Company of Goldsmiths, London.

Françoise van den Bosch Prize, Eighth Recipient: Esther Knobel.

Esther Knobel: Sketches in Raw Material. Galerie Ra, Amsterdam , the Netherlands.

Golden Ring of Honour of the Association for Goldsmiths' Art (created by Anton Cepka '90), recipient: Yasuki Hiramatsu, Deutsches Goldschmiedehaus, Hanau, Germany.

Harakan korut, Helsinki, Finland (Aug. 27 – Sept. 17). 35 Finnish artists participated.

Hermann Jünger, Kent State University Art Galleries, Kent State University, Kent, OH, USA; The Canadian Clay and Glass Museum, Toronto, Ontario, Canada.

In Touch: Nytt Kunsthåndverk, Maihaugen, De Sandvigske Samlinger, Lillehammer, Norway. Jewellery artists: Babetto, Bennett, Blavarp, Puig Cuyas, Gentille, I. Hanevold, W. Mattar, K. Mehus, Metcalf, H. Sand, T. Vigeland.

Jewels and Gems: Collecting California Jewelry, Oakland Museum, Oakland, CA, USA (July 9 – Oct. 2); organized by Kenneth Trapp.

Jang Sin Goo-zeitgenössische Schmuckkunst in Korea, Schmuckmuseum, Pforzheim, Germany (Nov.).

Jung-Gyu Yi: Art Jewelry Exhibition, Hyundai Art Gallery, Seoul, Korea (Aug. 9–14); Hongin Art Gallery, Dae Jean, Korea (Aug. 18–28).

Local Goddesses, David Tower Museum, Jerusalem, Israel. Artists: Knobel, Schocken.

Monika Winkler: Schmuck, Grassimuseum Leipzig-Museum für Kunsthandwerk, Leipzig.

A Moveable Feast: HWD Collection 1964–1994; Stedelijk Museum Amsterdam (Nov. 18, 1994– Jan. 8, 1995).

A New Century in European Design, Tokyo Metropolitan Teien Art Museum, Tokyo, Japan (June 11– July 13);

Onno Boekhoudt, Liesbeth Biesten, Appenzeller, Gert Staal and Helen W. Drutt English (left to right), Symposium, Stedelijk Museum, Amsterdam, January, 1995

travelled throughout Japan until 1995; participating artists: Künzli, Tamminen, T. Vigeland, Watkins.

Nordiska Profiler, Kunstindustrimuseet, Stockholm, Sweden; travelled through Scandinavia. Also: Copenhagen, Gothenberg, Oslo, Bergen, Trondheim, Helsingfors.

Op Art: Eyeglasses by Jewelers, Hoffman Gallery, Oregon School of Arts and Crafts, Portland, OR, USA (March 3 – April 3), travelled throughout USA until May 1995. Curated by Deb Stoner. Artists include: Dobler, Ebendorf, Fisch, Hall, M. Hees, Peters.

Schmuck und Gerät, Deutsches Goldschmiedehaus, Hanau, Germany, toured Europe until May 1995. Artists include: Babetto, F. Becker, R. Bott, Cepka, C. F. Dau, Fröhlich, Hiramatsu, Holder, Jünger, Martinazzi, Persson, Pinton and Weiss-Weingart.

Schmuck Unserer Zeit, 1964–1994: Sammlung Helen Williams Drutt USA, Museum Bellerive Zurich, Switzerland (Feb. 10– May 1).

Schmuckszene '94, Internationalen Handwerksmesse, Munich, Germany.

Sigurd Persson, Retrospective, Prince Eugen's Waldemarsudde, Stockholm, Sweden.

Space for Jewelry: National Exhibition of Czech and Slavic Jewellery; organized by Pavel Opočenskỳ, Manes, Prague, Czech Republic.

Symfonie voor solisten, Gemeentemuseum, Arnhem, The Netherlands (Feb. 12–May 15). Gijs Bakker and students.

Symposium, Massachusetts College of Art, Boston, Massachusetts. Organized by Jill Slosburg-Ackerman and Joe Wood. Moderators: Clive Dilnot, Professor of Philosophy, Harvard; Bruce Metcalf; Joyce Scott; Susan G. Lewin.

Vessels and Parures: Vessels and Jewellery Ensembles from Pierre Cavalan, Jam Factory, Adelaide, Australia (Feb. 18 – April 3).

What is Jewellery?, curated by David Poston, Crafts Council Gallery, London, England.

1995

The Art of Jewellery, 30th Anniversary Exhibition of the-founding of the Japan Jewellry Designers Association Inc., Itami City Craft Center, Itami Hyogo, Japan. (May 21).

Breon O'Casey, Sligo Art Gallery, Yeats Memorial Building, Hyde Bridge, Sligo (May 25– June 23).

Dinner/Symposium, at closing of *A Moveable Feast: Helen Williams Drutt Collection*, Stedelijk Museum, Amsterdam, The Netherlands. Organized by Gert Staal, Vormgevingsinstituut (Netherlands Design Institute) and Liesbeth Crommelin, Stedelijk Museum (Jan. 9).

Jewelry from the Permanent Collection, American Craft Museum (March 16 – June 25).

Mario Pinton: Retrospective, L'Oreficeria, Sala Rossini dello Stabilimento Pedrocchi, Padua, Italy (March 11– April 30).

A Moveable Feast: Helen Williams Drutt Collection 1964–1994; Museum voor Moderne Kunst, Ostend, Belgium (June 17– Sept. 24).

Schmuckszene '95, Internationale Handwerksmesse, Munich, Germany (March 11–19).

Tone Vigeland: Retrospective, Kunstindustrimuseet, Oslo, Norway (Nov.); USA Tour, American Federation of Arts, New York, USA, through to 1997.

Uta Feiler/Hermann Jünger/Rolf Lindner, Galerie am Fischmarkt, Erfurt, Germany.

bibliography

Selected Books

Anderson, Patricia. *Contemporary Jewellery: The Australian Experience, 1977–1987.* Newtown, Australia: Millennium, 1988.

Bates, Kenneth F. *Enameling: Principles and Practice.* Cleveland and New York: The World Publishing Company, 1951.

Black, J. Anderson. *Storia Dei Gioielli.* Novara: Istituto Geografico de Agostini, 1973.

——. *The History of Jewelry, 5000 Years.* Park Lane, New York: Crown Publications, 1981.

Blauer, Ettagale. *Contemporary American Jewelry Design.* New York: Van Nostrand Reinhold, 1991.

Bott, Gerhard. *Schmuck als künstlerische Aussage unserer Zeit.* Königsbach/Pforzheim: Hans Schöner, 1971.

Cartlidge, Barbara. *Twentieth-Century Jewelry.* New York: Harry N. Abrams, 1985.

Chadour, Anna Beatriz and Andreas Freisfeld. *SchmuckStücke: Der Impuls der Moderne in Europa.* Munich: Klinkhardt and Biermann, 1991.

—— and Rüdiger Joppien. *Kunstgewerbemuseum der Stadt Köln: Schmuck II, Fingerringe.* Cologne, 1985.

——, Barbara Deppert-Lippitz, Judy Rudoe and Diana Scarisbrick. *Rings: The Alice and Louis Koch Collection.* Leeds: W. S. Maney and Son., 1994.

Coyne, John, ed. *The Penland School of Crafts Book of Jewelry Making.* Indianapolis and New York, 1975.

Dormer, Peter and Ralph Turner. *The New Jewelry: Trends and Traditions.* London: Thames and Hudson, 1985.

Dubin, Lois Sherr. *The History of Beads from 30,000 B.C. to the Present.* New York: Harry N. Abrams, 1987.

Evans, Chuck. *Jewelry: Contemporary Design and Technique.* Worcester, MA: Davis Publications, 1983.

Falk, Fritz. *Schmuck aus dem Schmuckmuseum Pforzheim.* Pforzheim, Schmuckmuseum, 1977.

Fisch, Arline M. *Textile Techniques in Metal for Jewelers, Sculptors, and Textile Artists.* New York: Van Nostrand Reinhold, 1975.

Fitch, Janet. *The Art and Craft of Jewelry.* London: Reed International Books. 1992. San Francisco: Chronicale Books, 1994.

Formanek, Verena. *Wiener Schmuck: Tendenzen 1936–1991.* Vienna, 1991.

Gentille, Thomas. *Step-by-Step Jewelry.* New York: Golden Press, 1968.

Haynes, Peter. *Craft Australia: A Portable Treatise.* 1987.

Heiniger, Ernst A. and Jean. *The Great Book of Jewels.* Boston: New York Graphic Society, 1974.

Hinks, P. *20th Century British Jewellery 1900-1980.* London: Faber and Faber, 1983.

Hollander, H. B. *Plastics for Artists and Craftsmen.* London: Pitman; New York: Watson-Guptill, 1972.

Howell-Koehler, Nancy. *Soft Jewelry.* Worcester, MA: Davis Publications, 1976.

Hughes, Graham. *The Art of Jewelry.* New York: The Viking Press, 1972.

——. *Modern Jewelry: An International Survey 1890–1963.* New York: Crown Publishers, 1963.

Kuhnen, Johannes, ed. *Directions – Silversmithing.* Canberra: Crafts Council, 1990.

Lewin, Susan Grant. *One of a Kind: American Art Jewelry Today.* New York: Harry N. Abrams, 1994.

Linzer Institut für Gestaltung. *Zeichen am Körper.* Vienna: Falter, 1987.

Mascetti, Daniela, and Triossi, Amanda. *Earrings: From Antiquity to the Present.* New York: Rizzoli, 1990.

Matthews, Glenice Lesley. *Enamels Enameling Enamelists.* Radon, PA: Chilton Book Company, 1984.

McCreight, Tim. *The Complete Metalsmith: An Illustrated Handbook* (revised edn). Worcester, MA: Davis Publications, 1991.

——, ed. *Metals Technic, A Collection of Techniques for Metalsmiths.* Cape Elizabeth, Maine: Brynmorgen Press, 1992.

McNeil, Donald S., ed. *Jeweler's Dictionary.* 3rd edn. Radnor, PA.: Jewelers Book Club, 1979.

Meyerowitz, Patricia. *Jewelry and Sculpture Through Unit Construction.* New York: Bonanza Books, 1967.

Moe, Karin. *Kvinne og Kunstnar.* Oslo: Det noske Samlaget, 1983.

Morton, Philip. *Contemporary Jewelry: A Studio Handbook.* 2nd edn. New York: Holt, Rinehart and Winston, 1976.

Moss, Kathlyn and Alice Scherer. *The New Beadwork.* New York: Harry N. Abrams, 1988.

Von Neumann, Robert. *The Design & Creation of Jewelry.* 2nd edn. Philadelphia: Chilton Book Company, 1972.

O'Connor, Harold. *The Jeweler's Bench Reference.* Taos, NM: Dunconor Books, 1978.

Opstad, Jan Lauritz. *Ny norsk gullsmedkunst.* Oslo: C. Huitfeldt, 1981.

Polak, Ada. *Gullsmedkunst i Norge for og na.* Oslo: Norwegian Jewelers Association, 1970.

Praddow, Penny and Debra Healy. *American Jewelry: Glamour and Tradition.* New York: Rizzoli, 1987.

Pullee, C. *20th Century Jewellery.* London: Quintet, 1990.

Radice, Barbara. *Jewelry by Architects.* New York: Rizzoli, 1987.

Reiling, Reinhold. *Goldschmiedekunst Arbeiten von 32 Europäischen goldschmieden.* Königsbach-Pforzheim: Hans Schöner, 1978.

Revere, Alan. *Professional Goldsmithing: A Contemporary Guide to Traditional Jewelry Techniques.* New York: Van Nostrand Reinhold, 1991.

Scarisbrick, Diana, ed. *Jewellery: Makers. Motifs. History. Techniques.* London: Thames and Hudson, 1989.

——. *The Jewelry Design Source Book.* New York: Van Nostrand Reinhold, 1989.

Schollmayer, Karl. *Art Contemporain du Bijou.* Paris: Dessain et Tolra, 1974.

——. *Neuer Schmuck.* Tübingen, Germany: Ernst Wasmuth, 1974.

Schofield, Anne and Fahy, Kevin. *Australian Jewellery, 19th and Early 20th Century.* Sydney: David Ell Press, 1991.

Seedam-Kulturzentrum. *Moderne Kunst – unsere Gegenwart 2.* Pfaffikon: Seedamm-Kulturzentrum, 1993.

Seeler, Margaret. *The Art of Enameling.* New York: Van Nostrand Reinhold, 1969.

Seppä, Heikki. *Form Emphasis for Metalsmiths.* Kent, OH: Kent State University Press, 1978.

Solberg, Ramona. *Inventive Jewelry Making.* New York: Van Nostrand Reinhold, 1972.

Sprintzen, Alice. *The Jeweler's Art: A Multimedia Approach.* Worcester, MA: Davis Publications, 1995.

Tait, Hugh, ed. *Jewelry: Seven Thousand Years.* New York: Harry N. Abrams, 1987.

Thompson, Bob, ed. *Jewellery: Australia Now.* Sydney: Crafts Council of Australia, 1989.

Turner, Ralph. *Contemporary Jewelry: A Critical Assessment 1945–1975.* London: Studio Vista; New York: Van Nostrand Reinhold, 1976.

Untracht, Oppi. *Jewelry: Concepts and Technology.* Garden City, NY: Doubleday, 1982.

——. *Metal Techniques for Craftsmen.* Garden City, NY: Doubleday, 1968.

Ward, Anne, et al. *Rings Through the Ages.* New York: Rizzoli, 1981.

Watkins, David. *The Best in Contemporary Jewellery.* Mies, Switzerland: Rotovision, 1993.

Wilcox, Donald J. *Body Jewelry: International Perspectives.* Chicago: Henry Regnery, 1973.

Worshipful Company of Goldsmiths. *Modern British Jewellery.* London: Worshipful Company of Goldsmiths, 1963.

Selected Monographs

In alphabetical order by artist's last name
Ex. cat. = Exhibition catalogue
Ex. br. = Exhibition brochure

Hans Appenzeller: 20 Years. Artists's foreword. Intro. Helen W. Drutt English. Amsterdam/New York: Hans Appenzeller, 1989.

Hans Appenzeller: Sieraden/Jewelry. Intro. Gert Staal. Amsterdam, Hans Appenzeller, 1982.

Giampaolo Babetto. Ex. cat. Text Philip Peters. The Hague: Galerie Nouvelles Images, 1977.

Babetto. Text by Japp Bolten. Padua: Giampaolo Babetto, 1980.

Giampaolo Babetto. Contemporary Gold Jewellery Artists, 1. Zurich: Aurum Publishing AG, 1993.

Giampaolo Babetto: Ritratti. Ex. cat. Ingolstadt: Museum für Konkrete Kunst (June 17– Sept.12, 1994).

Alexandra Bahlmann. Munich: Galerie Spectrum and Alexandra Bahlmann. 1990

Ulrike Bahrs. Ex. br. London: Electrum Gallery (Oct.8–26, 1985).

Gijs Bakker, vormgever: Solo voor een solist. Ex. cat. By Gert Staal. Utrecht: Centraal Museum (Sept.22– Nov.5, 1989). New York: Helen Drutt Gallery (Dec.7, 1989– Jan.6, 1990).

Gijs Bakker. Ex. cat. Interview Renny Ramakers. Munich: Galerie Spektrum (Oct.14– Nov.11, 1993). Amsterdam: Galerie Ra Nov.13– Dec.8, 1993). Padua: Marijke Studio (April 1994). Philadelphia: Helen Drutt Gallery (Spring 1994).

Frank Bauer. Ex. cat. London: Victoria and Albert Museum (Jan.18– March 13, 1986). 1985.
Friedrich Becker. Ex. cat. Intro. Graham Hughes and Hans Georg Lenzen. London: Worshipful Company of Goldsmiths (Oct.4–19, 1966).
Friedrich Becker: Schmuck- und kinetische Objekte. Ex. cat. Text Paul Luchtenberg, Graham Hughes and Karl Schollmayer. Hanau: Deutsches Goldschmiedehaus (Oct.8–29, 1972).
Friedrich Becker: Schmuck, Silbergerait, Kinetische Objekte (1951–1983). Ex. cat. Foreword Gerd Schäfer and Karl-Heinz Hering. Essays Inge Asenbaum, Fritz Falk, and Curt Heigl. Düsseldorf: Kunstrverein für die Rheinlande und Westfalen and Düsseldorf Grabbeplatz Kunsthalle (Feb.10– April 1, 1984).
Michael Becker: Works on Architecture. Ex. cat. Text Ton Berends and artist. Amsterdam: Galerie Louise Smit; The Hague: Studio Ton Berends; New York: Helen Drutt Gallery (1990).
Bischoff, Manfred. *übersetzen*. Ed. Yvonne G. J. M. Joris. Essay Gert Staal. 's-Hertogenbosch: Museum Het Kruithuis, 1993.
Françoise van den Bosch. Text Liesbeth Crommelin, Judith Cahen and Jerven Ober. Amsterdam: De Nederlandse Kunststichting, 1978.
Stichting: Françoise van den Bosch. Essays Victoria Bisschop van Tuinen and Jerven Ober. Amsterdam: The Françoise van den Bosch Foundation, 1987.
Françoise van den Bosch (1944–1977). Essays Jerven Ober (ed) and Liesbeth Crommelin. Naarden: The Françoise van den Bosch Foundation, 1990.
Caroline Broadhead. Text Jerven Ober (ed.), Jan Aarntzen, Paul Derrez and Ralph Turner. Apeldoorn: Gemeentelijke Van Reekumgalerij, 1980.
Caroline Broadhead. Text Griselda Gray and artist. Bristol: Arnolfini, 1981
Caroline Broadhead: Jewellery in Studio. By John Houston. London: Bellew Publishing, 1990.
Brynner, Irena. *Jewelry As An Art Form*. New York: Van Nostrand Reinhold, 1979.
Claus Bury: Schmuck Zeichnungen Objekte. Ex. cat. Essays Gerhard Bott and Fritz Falk. Pforzheim: Schmuckmuseum (April 17– June 3, 1974). Hanau: Deutsches Goldschmiedehaus (June 16– July 14, 1974).
Claus Bury: Drawings and Objects 1976–1978. Ex. cat. Foreword Gerhard Bott. Intro. Rex Keogh. Melbourne: National Gallery of Victoria (April 3– 29, 1979): Sydney: Art of Man Gallery (May 8–26, 1979).
Claus Bury. Ex. cat. Organized Helen Williams Drutt. Text Gerhard Bott and artist. Philadelphia: Moore College of Art (March 19– April 24, 1982).
Claus Bury: Architektonische Skulpturen 1978–1986. Ex. cat. Essays Hans M. Schmidt and Christoph Brockhaus. Duisberg: Wilhelm-Lehmbruck-Museum der Stadt Duisberg, 1986.
Claus Bury: Architectonic Sculptures/Arkitecktonische Skulpturen 1979–1993. Ex. cat. Text Uwe Wieczorek and Gerhard Kolberg. Ostfildern: Cantz Verlag, 1994.
Pierre Cavalan: Bijoux, Jewellery. Essay Robert Nelson. New South Wales: Pierre Cavalan and the Australia Council, 1994.
Kai Chan: New Works. Ex cat. Essays Alan C. Elder, Anne West, Helen Duffy. Toronto: Ontario Crafts Council, 1987.
Pierre Degen: New Work. Ex. cat. Intro. Ralph Turner. Text Rory Spence, Christopher Reid, Paul Derrez, Danielle Keunen, Bernard François and Paul Filmer. London: Crafts Council, 1982.
Bettina Dittlmann. Text Jason Blickstein. Dachau: Sabine Zauner, 1994.
Zeichen Schmuck: Dobler. Ex. cat. Vienna: Galerie V & V, 1983.
Georg Dobler: Abstraktion und Kürperform als Synthese. Ex. cat. Vienna: Galerie V & V (Sept.24– Oct.24, 1987).
Robert Ebendorf. Ex. cat. Text Heikki Seppä and Robert Ebendorf. New York: Florence Duhl Gallery (Feb.7, 1980); Grand Forks, University of North Dakota (March– April 1980).
Robert Ebendorf Retrospective Exhibition. Ex. cat. Text David Revere McFadden and Vanessa S. Lynn. New Paltz, NY: College Art Gallery, State University of New York (April 4–26, 1989).
Gry Eide: The Past into the Future. Text Paul Derrez. Oslo: Royal Norwegian Ministry of Foreign Affairs, 1989.
Bianca Eshel-Gershuni. Ex. cat. Text Yona Fischer. Jerusalem: The Israel Museum (Feb.– March 1977).
Uta Feiler: Schmuck. Ex. cat. Erfurt: Museen der Stadt Erfurt, 1986.
Fisch, Arline. Woven Gold. Ex. cat. Text Douglas Steakley, Fritz Falk, Barbara Cartlidge and the artist. Carmel: Concepts Gallery (May 1–31, 1987); Palo Alto (July 10– Aug.7, 1987); San Diego: Wita Gardiner Gallery (Sept.12– Oct.24, 1987); London: Electrum Gallery (Nov. 1987); Vienna: Galerie am Graben (Jan. 1988).
Arline M. Fisch. Ex. cat. Text Carl Auböck, Anton Porhansi and the artist. Vienna: Museum für angewandte Kunst, 1982.
Elsa Freund: American Studio Jeweler. Ex. cat. Little Rock: The Arkansas Arts Center Decorative Arts Museum (Sept.8– Oct.6, 1991).
Elsa Freund: Modern Pioneer. Ex. cat. Text Alan DuBois. St Petersburg, FL: Florida Craftsmen, Inc., 1993.
Max Fröhlich: Silber- und Goldschmiedearbeiten. Ex. cat. Text Margit Weinberg-Staber, Elena Fischli-Dreher and the artist. Vienna: Galerie am Graben (Sept.6– Oct.2, 1982); Zurich: Kunstgewerbemuseum (Jan./Feb. 1983).
Max Fröhlich: Silverware and Jewelry 1982–1988. Ex. cat. Foreword Elena Fischli. New York: Helen Drutt Gallery (Dec.3, 1988–Jan.7, 1989).
Lisa Gralnick. Ex. cat. Foreword Henry P. Raleigh. Text Michael Dunas and Sarah Bodine. Amsterdam: Galerie Ra (Dec.10, 1988– Jan.15, 1989); New York: CDK Gallery (April 4– May 6, 1989).
William Harper. Ex. cat. Preface Elayne H. Varian. Intro. Albert Steward. Tallahassee, FL: University Fine Arts Galleries (Nov.14– Dec.4, 1980).
The Art of William Harper: Enameled Jewelry and Objects. Ex. cat. Text by the artist. New York: Kennedy Galleries (June 2– July 3, 1981).
Saints Martyrs and Savages: Enameled Jewelry by William Harper. Ex. cat. Text by the artist. New York: Kennedy Galleries (Nov.29, 1982– Jan.7, 1983).
William Harper: Jasper's Variations and Faberge's Seeds . Ex. cat. Intro. Arthur Danto. New York: Peter Joseph Gallery (Dec.1, 1994– Jan.14, 1995).
William Harper: The Artist as Alchemist. Ex. cat. Curated Thomas A. Manhart. Orlando: Orlando Museum of Art (Nov.4– Dec.10, 1989).
William Harper: Recent Works in Enamel. Ex. cat. Text Michael Monroe. Washington, DC: Renwick Gallery, NCFA, Smithsonian Institution (Nov.24, 1977– March 26, 1978).
William Harper: Self-Portraits of artist, sacred and profane. Ex. cat. Essay Jane Addams Allen. New York: Franklin Parrasch Gallery [1990].
Anna Heindl: Schmuckarbeiten 1982–83. Ex. cat. Text Erwin Wurm. Vienna: Galerie am Graben (May 1983); Steyr: Galerie Schnittpunkt (Oct. 1983); Dortmund: Galerie Voss (Nov.15– Dec.24, 1983).
Anna Heindl: Schmuck. Ex. cat. Text Wilfred Skreiner and Gerti Draxler. Vienna: Anna Heindl, 1986.
Anna Heindl: Ears and Tears. Ex. cat. Text Armin Thurnher. Vienna: Anna Heindl, 1992.
Rahmen und Ornament: Schmuck Anna Heindl. Ex. cat. Foreword Wilfried Skreiner. Zurich: Galerie Zaunschirm, 1989.
Renate Heintze: Schmuck. Ex. cat. Essay Christiane Keisch. Halle: Staatliche Galerie Moritzburg (March 7– June 13, 1993). Hanau: Deutsches Goldschmiedehaus (Sept.19– Nov.21, 1993).
Marion Herbst 1968-1993: Mag het iets meer zjin?. Text Liesbeth Crommelin, Ans van Berkum and Martijn van Ooststroom. Aalburg,: Pictures Publishers, 1993.
Marion Herbst: Een Overzicht 1969–1982. Intro. Jerven Ober. Amsterdam: Stichting van den Bosch, 1982.
Herman Hermsen: Jewellery Schmuck Sieraden. Ex. cat. Text Egon Kuhn. Nimwegen: Herman Hermsen, 1989.
Herman Hermsen: Werk. Ex. cat. Text Egon Kuhn; 1984.
Susanna Heron: Bodywork Exhibition. Ex. cat. Foreword Ralph Turner. Text Sarah Osborn, David Ward and artist. London: Crafts Council Gallery (April 16– May 31, 1980).
The Recurring Theme: Susanna Heron. Ex. cat. Text Jerven Ober (ed) and the artist. Apeldoorn: Gemeentelijke Van Reekumgalerij, 1982.
Johanna Hess-Dahm. Ex. cat. Text Gundel Bernimoulin and artist. Berne: Galerie Michele Zeller (May 6– June 25, 1983).
Johanna Hess-Dahm: Schmuck/Jewellery. Ex. cat. Text Paul Derrez. Amsterdam: Galerie Ra (Dec.13, 1986– Jan.17, 1987); Munich: Galerie Spektrum (Feb.17– March 15, 1987); Berne: Galerie Michele Zeller (Nov.5–28, 1987); Zurich: Museum Bellerive (Dec.12, 1987– Feb.2, 1989); Salzburg: Kunstformen Jetzt (July 27– Aug.8, 1988).
Therese Hilbert. Ex. cat. Text Wolfgang Wunderlick and Helmut Friedel. Pforzheim: Schmuckmuseum (Sept.15– Oct.28, 1979); Hanau: Deutsches Goldschmiedehaus (Jan.20– March 2, 1980); Graz: Galerie Alberstrabe (May 18– April 18, 1980); Vienna: Loft Wien (Oct.1–31, 1980).
Therese Hilbert: Schmuck. Graz: Verlag Droschl, 1985.
Prof. Yasuki Hiramatsu Retirement Exhibition. Tokyo: National University of Fine Arts and Music. 1993.
Saara Hopea-Untracht: Elämä Ja Työ/ Life and Work. By Oppi Untracht. Porvoo, Helsinki and Juva: Werner Söderström Osakeyhtiö, 1988.
Annette Juel. Ex. cat. Text Jørgen Schou-Christensen. Copenhagen: Stensalen Kunstindustrimuseet, 1990.
Jünger, Hermann. Herbei, herbei, was Löffel sei... Geiben: Anabas-Verlag, 1993.
Hermann Jünger: Goldschmiede Arbeiten. Ex. cat. Intro. Inge Asenbaum. Essays Helmut Friedel and the artist. Vienna: Galerie am Graben (Oct. 12– Nov.7, 1981); Düsseldorf: Galerie Orfèvre (1982); Augsburg: Galerie Rehklau (1982).
Contemporary German Jewellery: Hermann Jünger. Ex. cat. Text Helmut Friedel and the artist. Melbourne: The Goethe Institute and The Craft Board of the Australia Council, 1982.
Hermann Jünger: Schmuck nach 1945. Ex. cat. Essays Gerhard Bott, Fritz Falk, Hildegard Hoos, Rüdiger Joppien, Otto Künzli, Bernhard Lypp and the artist. Nuremberg: Germanisches Nationalmuseum (June 26– Aug.21, 1988); Frankfurt a. M.: Museum für Kunsthandwerk (Sept.15– Oct.30, 1988); Hamburg: Museum für Kunst und Gewerbe (Nov.10, 1988–Jan.22, 1989); Pforzheim: Schmuckmuseum (Feb.18– April 9, 1989).
Beppe Kessler. Text Maggie Laszlo, Marjan Unger, Hans-Jorg Ammann. Amsterdam: Beppe Kessler, 1992.
Kim, Jung Hoo. Ex. cat. Text Jeannine Falino and Jamie Bennett. Seoul: Gallery Seomi (Aug.20– 29, 1992).
Grete Prytz Kittelsen: Emaljekunst og Design. Ex.cat. Text Jan-Lauritz Opstad. Oslo: Kunstindustrimuseet, 1978.
Esther Knobel: Sketches in Raw Material. Ex. cat. On the occasion of Françoise van den Bosch Prize, 1994. Amsterdam: Galerie Ra (Dec.3– Jan.11, 1994).
Friedrich Knupper: Schmuck und Objekte. Text Claus Pese, Peter Schmitt, and Rüdiger Joppien. Nuremberg: Verlag des Germanischen Nationalmuseums, 1990.
Daniel Kruger: Sieraden. Ex. br. 's-Hertogenbosch: Museum Het Kruithuis (June 20– Aug.2, 1980).
Daniel Kruger. Ex cat. Intro. Hermann Jünger. Pforzheim: Schmuckmuseum (Jan. 14– March 11, 1984); Hanau: Deutsches Goldschmiedehaus (May 6– June 10, 1984); Vienna: Galerie am Graben (Sept.3–29,1984); Amsterdam: Galerie Ra (Nov. 10– Dec.8, 1984).
Daniel Kruger: Vijf Stenen en een Kleine Schijnbeweging. Ex. cat. Foreword Yvonne Joris. Essay Gert Staal. 's-Hertogenbosch: Museum Het Kruithuis, 1994.
Winfried Krüger. Ex. cat. Text Thomas Werneke. Pforzheim: Reuchlinhaus Pforzheim (Sept.1– Oct.6, 1982).
Otto Künzli. Ex. cat. Essays Wolfgang Wunderlich and Helmut Friedel. Pforzheim: Schmuckmuseum (Sept.15– Oct.28, 1979). Hanau: Deutsches Goldschmiedehaus (Jan.20, 1979– March 2, 1980).
Kollektion Künzli 1983. Ex. cat. Kassel: Deutsches Tapetenmuseum (June 30– Aug.28, 1983).
Otto Künzli: Ein Dach über dem Kopf. Munich: Förderprreise, 1987.
Otto Künzli: Oh, say! Ex. cat. Intro. Klaus Ottmann. Middletown, Connecticut: Ezra and Cecile Zilkha Gallery, Center for the Arts, Wesleyan University (May 5– June 7, 1992).
Otto Künzli: Das dritte Auge/The Third Eye/Het derde oog. Ex. cat. Intro. Maribel Königer. Amsterdam: Stedelijk Museum, 1991. Zurich: Museum Bellerive, 1992.
Birgit Laken: Metal in Motion. Text Hendrik van Delft. Haarlem: Birgit Laken, 1990.
Lee, Jeong-Lim Metal and Enamel Exhibition. Ex. cat. Text Lee, Jae-Eon. Seoul: Gallery Bing, 1993.
Emmy van Leersum. Ex. cat. Intro. Wil Bertheux and Liesbeth Crommelin. Essays Ralph Turner, Frans Haks, Jerven Ober, Benno Premsela and artist. Amsterdam: Stedelijk Museum (Nov.23, 1979– Jan.6, 1980).
Emmy van Leersum: systeemen in sieraden, sculpturen en breisels. Ex. br. Utrecht: Zwolsche Algemeene Verzeeringen (Jan.13– Feb.11, [1983]).
Emmy van Leersum (1930–1984): Gebroken Lijnen/ Broken Lines. Ex. cat. Foreword Yvonne G. J. M. Joris. Essays Antje von Graevenitz, Gert Staal and Wim van Bergen. 's-Hertogenbosch: Museum Het Kruithuis (April 4–June 13, 1993).
Erika Leitner: Schmuck. Ex. cat. Text Carl Auböck and artist. Vienna: Galerie am Graben (June 17– July 3, 1977).
Erika Leitner. Text Herbert Fux. Vienna: Erika Leitner, [1982].
Nel Linssen: Papieren sieraden/Paper Jewelry, 1986–1991. Intro. Paul Derrez. Amsterdam: Nel Linssen, 1991.
Lorenzen, Jens-Rüdiger. Schmuck/Objeckte. Ex. cat. Foreword Curt Heigl. Nuremberg: Kunsthalle

Nürnberg-Studio (Dec.8, 1982– Jan.30, 1983); Hanau: Deutsches Goldschmiedehaus (June 5– July 10, 1983).
Rüdiger Lorenzen – Miniaturen und Objekte. Ex. cat. Pforzheim: Schmuckmuseum, 1972.
Fritz Maierhofer: Arbeiten und Zeichnungen. Ex. cat. Vienna: Galerie Kaiser (Nov.11– Dec.12, 1974) and Galerie am Graben (Dec.12–24, 1974).
Fritz Maierhofer: Gold- und Silverschmied. Ex. cat. Ed. Inge Asenbaum. Vienna: Galerie am Graben (Nov.2–20, 1982).
Fritz Maierhofer. Ex. cat. Berne: Galerie Michele Zeller (Oct.7– Nov.5, 1983).
Carlier Makigawa. Ex. cat. Text Jenny Zimmer. Australia Council for the Arts, Carlier Makigawa, 1993. Philadelphia: Helen Drutt Gallery. Sydney: Sherman Gallery; Melbourne: Christine Abrams Gallery; Amsterdam: Galerie Ra.
Wire Wear: Julia Manheim. Ex. cat. Text Barbara Taylor, Sharon Plant, Ralph Turner and John Millard. Newcastle: Newcastle Polytechnic, [1983].
Martinazzi, Bruno and Carla Gallo Barbisio. *La Lavorazione Deo Metallo Prezioso.* Turin: Daniela Piazza Editore, 1983.
Martinazzi, Bruno. *I cieli e la terra e tutte le tue creature.* Turin: Noire Editore, 1988.
Martinazzi: Materia e tempo. By Francesci de Bartolomeis. Biella: Editore Stampatore, 1977.
Martinazzi. Ed. Carla Gallo Barbisio. Intro. Paolo Fossati. Turin: Stamperia Artistica Nazionale in association with Helen Drutt Gallery, Philadelphia and New York, (Oct.11– Nov.11, 1990).
Jewelry by Bruno Martinazzi. Ex. cat. Intro. Graham Hughes. London: Worshipful Company of Goldsmiths, 1964.
Paul McClure: Corpus. Ex cat. Montreal: Galerie Jocelyne Gobeil (Sept.11– Oct.12, 1991).
Gert Mosettig: Jewelry. Ex. cat. Text Klaus Remer. Hanau: Deutsches Goldschmiedehaus (Sept.10– Nov.29, 1989).
Melitta Moschik: Daten Skulpturen – Schmuck Subjekte. Ex. cat. Vienna: Galerie V & V (Jan.25– March 3, 1990).
Enrico Nagai. Contemporary Gold Jewellery Artists, 2. Zurich: Aurum Publishing AG, 1993.
Manfred Nisslmüller: Taschenrecorder. Text Désirée Schellerer. Graz: Werkstadt Graz, 1993.
Vratislav Karel Novák. Text Jan Kříz. Prague: Atrium, 1985.
Breon O'Casey. Ex. br. Text Margaret Gardiner and Christopher Reid. New York: Helen Drutt Gallery (April 6–29, 1989).
Judyland: The Art of Judy Onofrio. Ex. cat. Text Laurel Reuter. Grand Forks: North Dakota Museum of Art, 1993.
The Metalwork of Albert Paley. Ex. cat. Essay Robert A. Sobieszek. Chronology and Bibliography Helen Williams Drutt. Sheboygen, WI: John Michael Kohler Arts Center (April 13– June 1, 1980).
Albert Paley: The Art of Metal. Ex. cat. Text Richard Mühlberger, Penelope Hunter-Stiebel, Claude Blair and the artist. Springfield, MA: Museum of Fine Arts, 1985.
Albert Paley: Sculptural Adornment. Ex. cat. Intro. Edward Lucie-Smith. Essays Deborah L. Norton and Matthew Drutt. Washington, DC: Renwick Gallery, NMAA, Smithsonian Institution, 1991.
Baroque Modernism: New Work by Albert Paley. Ex. cat. Essays Peter T. Joseph, J. Richard Gruber and Marcia Westby. New York: Peter Joseph Gallery, 1992.
Albert Paley: Organic Logic. Ex. cat. Foreword Peter T. Joseph. Essay Penelope Hunter-Stiebel. New York: Peter Joseph Gallery (March 1994).
Inspiration & Context: The Drawings of Albert Paley. Ex. cat. Text Mildred E. Schmertz. Rochester: Memorial Art Gallery, University of Rochester, 1994.
Earl Pardon: Retrospective Exhibition. Ex. cat. Intro. Joseph C. Palamountain, Jr. Essay the artist. Saratoga Springs, NY: Skidmore College Art Gallery (Nov.6–25, 1980).
The Jewelry of Margaret de Patta: A Retrospective Exhibition. Ex. cat. Intro. Hazel Bray. Essays Yoshiko Uchida and Eugene Bielawski. Oakland: Oakes Gallery, Oakland Museum (Feb.3– March 28, 1976).
Pavan. Padua: Francesco Pavan, 1987.
Ros Perry. Ex. br. Text Helen Craven. Bristol: Arnolfini, 1983.
Ruudt Peters. Intro. Ans van Berkum. Amsterdam: Art-Edition met Sieraad, 1989.
Ruudt Peters: Passio. Intro. Marjan Unger. Amsterdam: Uitgeverij Voetnoot, 1992.
John Prip: Master Metalsmith. Ex. cat. Foreword Christopher Monkhouse. Text Paul J. Smith and Tim McCreight. Providence: Museum of Art, Rhode Island School of Design (Oct.9– Dec.20, 1987); New York: American Craft Museum (Jan.29– April 28, 1988).
Wendy Ramshaw: A Retrospective Survey 1969–1981. Ex. cat. Foreword Sir Roy Strong; essay by the artist. London: Victoria and Albert Museum (Oct.6, 1982– Jan.16, 1983).
Wendy Ramshaw: Gebreide vormgeving/Knitted Outfits. Ex. cat. Intro. Barbara Cartlidge. Leeuwarden: Museum het Princessehof (Sept.30– Nov.13, 1988).
Wendy Ramshaw: Jewellery 1988. Ex. cat. Intro. Peter Dormer. Scottsdale, AZ: Joanne Rapp Gallery/ The Hand and The Spirit, (Feb.1– March 31, 1989).
Wendy Ramshaw: Picasso's Ladies. Ex. cat. Text Marina Vaizey. London: The British Council, 1989. [bound together with *David Watkins: Xingu.*]
Reinhold Reiling, Goldschmied. Ex. cat. Pforzheim: Schmuckmuseum, 1982.
Richard H. Reinhardt: Recent Work 1987. Ex. cat. Text Sharon Church and Peter Solmssen, Philadelphia: Swan Gallery and University of the Arts, 1987.
Suzan Rezac. Ex. cat. Statement by artist. Philadelphia: Helen Drutt Gallery (April 3– May 5, 1984).
Gerhard Rothmann: Goldschmiedearbeiten und Zeichnungen. Ex. cat. Oldenburg: Landesmuseum für Kunst (April 6– May 2, 1976); Hanau: Deutsches Goldschmiedehaus (May 8– June 2, 1976); Pforzheim: Schmuckmuseum (June 4– July 7, 1976) Gmünd: Städtischen Museum (Aug.7– 15, 1976).
Musterbuch: Gerd Rothmann, Ex. cat. Munich: Galerie Spektrum (May 2–30, 1984); Arnhem: Gemeentmuseum (June 9– July 22, 1984); Zurich: Museum Bellerive (Dec.5, 1984– Feb.3, 1985); Darmstadt: Hessisches Landesmuseum (March 14– April 15, 1985).
Körpersensationen: Gerd Rothmann. Text Christoph Blase, Lali Johne, Theresa Iten, Manfred Nisslmüller, Wolfgang Wunderlich, Hans Jörg Mayer, Felicitas Frischmith, H. O. Sykan, Friedrich G. Scheuer, Alexeij Sagerer, Maria Vok, Christian Israel, Helmut Eisendle, Werner Lubitz, Stephan Huber, Inge Asenbaum, Philipp Benke and Christian Nagel. Vienna: Galerie am Graben, 1987.
Philip Sajet: Elf Colliers. Ex. cat. Essay Mariam Unger. Amsterdam: Stedelijk Museum (Dec.9, 1994– Jan.18, 1995).
Hermann Schafran: Arbeiten 1976-84. Text Manfred Fath and Rolf-Gunter Dienst: Mannheim: Stadt. Kunsthalle (Nov.24, 1984–Jan.27, 1985).
Otto und Gertrud Schamschula: Schmuck/Gerät/Objekte 1954–1988. Ex. cat. Essay Sabine Runde. Frankfurt: Museum für Kunsthandwerk (May 19– July 17, 1988).
Anneke Schat: Edelsmeedkunst–Modern Jewellery. By Monique Mokveld. Amsterdam: Ploegsma, 1987.
Mary Ann Scherr Retrospective. Intro. Alfred G. Radloff. Akron, OH: Akron Art Institute (Nov.21, 1971– Jan.2, 1972).
Marianne Schliwinski: Schmuck in Kupfer und Silber. Text Ulla Stöver. Munich: Anderland-Verlagsgesellschaft mbH, 1980.
Schobinger, Bernhard. *Landscape with Diamonds.* Zurich: Bernhard Schobinger, 1984.
——. *Objekte.* Photographs Annelies Stŕba. Zurich: Bernhard Schobinger and Stŕba, 1988.
Deganit Stern Schocken. Essay Rachel Sukman, Tel Aviv, 1995.
SchockenArbeiten Seit 1948 + 1977–978: Auswahl aus 2 Jahren, Bernhard Schobinger. Zurich: Museum Bellerive (Dec.5, 1978– Feb.4, 1979).
Bernhard Schobinger: Eiszeit – Juwelentraum. Richterswil: Bernhard Schobinger, 1981.
Bernhard Schobinger/Annelies Sŕba. Ex. cat. Essay Christoph Blase. Lucerne: Galerie Meile, 1993.
Mariannne Schliwinski: Schmuck. Essay Ulla Stover, Munich, 1980.
Stephan Seyffert: Ringbuch. Karlsruhe: Stephan Seyffert, 1994.
Helen Shirk: 20 Years. Ex. cat. Text Helen W. Drutt English and the artist. Memphis, TN: National Ornamental Metal Museum., Sept. 17– Oct.29th, 1989.
Hubertus von Skal. Wirfeingesicht. Ex. cat. Text Armin Zweite. Munich: Stadtische Galerie in Lenbachhaus, Prestel Verlag (30 Nov. 1983– 8 Jan. 1984).
Olaf Skoogfors. Ex. br. Text Helen Drutt. Seattle: Henry Gallery, University of Washington (June 23– July 24, 1977).
Olaf Skoogfors: Twentieth-Century Goldsmith 1930–1975. Ex. cat. Foreword Helen Williams Drutt. Text Richard H. Reinhardt, John Prip, Claus Bury and the artist. Philadelphia: The Falcon Press, 1979.
Skubic: Halbzeit. Ex. cat. Intro. Inge Asenbaum. Vienna: Galerie am Graben, 1985.
Kiff Slemmons. Ex. cat. Statement by the artist. Cambridge, MA.: Mobilia Gallery (May 14– July 30, 1994).
Robert Smit: Towards the Liberation of Drawings. The Hague: Orez Mobiel, 1979.
Robert Smit: Beyond Reach/Buiten bereik. Ex. cat. Text Frank Gribling, Ineke Spaander and Angelo Tasso. Delft: Stedelijk Museum 'Het Prinsenhof', 1987.
Robert Smit: Bijoux. Ex. cat. Nice: Musée d'Art Moderne et d'Art Contemporain, 1994
Robert Smit. Contemporary Gold Jewellery Artists, 3. Zurich: Aurum Publishing AG, 1993.
Chris Steenbergen. Ex. cat. Text D.U. Kuyken-Schneider: Rotterdam: Museum Boymans-van Beuningen, (Nov.16, 1985– Jan. 5, 1986).
Peter Tully. Text John McPhee. Canberra: Australian National Gallery, 1991.
Klaus Ullrich. Ex. cat. Rotterdam: Galerie Delta (May 21–23, 1965).
Klaus Ullrich – Schmuckgestalter seit 1955. Ex. cat. Pforzheim: Schmuckmuseum, 1992.
Ventrella, Roberto. *Labirinti (Impronte 1978–82).* Naples: Roberto Ventrella, 1982.
Tone Vigeland. Intro. Anniken Thue. Oslo: Royal Norwegian Ministry of Foreign Affairs, [1991].
More Than a Maker: Recent Jewellery and Objects by David Walker. Text Dorothy Erickson and the artist. Perth: Erica Underwood Gallery, Curtin University (Aug.6–29, 1991).
David Watkins: Jewellery and Sculpture. Ex. cat. Text Peter Dormer, Helen W. Drutt English and Gert Staal. Leeds City Art Galleries; London: Crafts Council Gallery; Amsterdam: Stedelijk Museum, 1985.
David Watkins: Xingu. Text Marina Vaizey. London: The British Council, 1989. [Bound with Wendy Ramshaw: *Picasso's Ladies.*]
Interstices: Works by Margaret West from 1981–1992. Ex. cat. Curated Julie Ewington. Canberra School of Art, 1992.
Jewelry by Ed Wiener. Ex. cat. Text Milton W. Brown and Blanche R. Brown. New York: Fifty/50 Gallery (Dec.1, 1988– Jan.7, 1989).
Ebbe Weiss-Weingart – Schmuck und Objekte 1946–1993. Ex. cat. Pforzheim: Schmuckmuseum, 1993.
Peter de Wit: Sieraden/Jewellery/Schmuck. Ex. cat. Interview by Paul Derrez. Amsterdam: Galerie Ra (Dec. 14, 1985– Jan. 11, 1986); London: Electrum Gallery (Feb. 11– March 4, 1986); Vienna: Galerie Am Graben (April 7– April 26, 1986).
Lam de Wolf. Amstelveen: Lam de Wolf Edities, 1991.
Helga Zahn: a Retrospective Assessment 1960–1976 of Jewellery, Prints and Drawings. Ex. cat. Intro. Ralph Turner. London: Crafts Advisory Committee Gallery (April 14– June 12, 1976).
Tomasz Zaremski. Ex. br. Text Irena Huml. Warsaw: Galeria Zapiecek (March 1979).
Alberto Zorzi. Ex. cat. Text Giorgio Segato and Enrico Crispilti. Padua: Fioretto Galleria D'Arte (Dec.3– 31, 1988); Milan: Galleria Schubert (June 17–28, 1989); Salzburg: Kunstformen Jetzt (March 1– April 25, 1989); Berne: Galerie Michele Zeller (Oct.12– Nov.4, 1989).
Der Goldschmied Othmar Zschaler. Ex. cat. Pforzheim: Schmuckmuseum, 1972.
Der Goldschmied Othmar Zschaler The Goldsmith: Foreword Egbert Moehsnang. Essays Peter Friedli and Fritz Falk. Berne: Paul Haupt, 1984.

Selected Exhibition Catalogues

The American Contemporary Jewelry Exhibition. Tokyo: Yomiuri Shimbun, 1968.
American Craft Today: Poetry of the Physical. Text Paul J. Smith and Edward Lucie-Smith. New York: American Craft Museum, 1987.
American Dreams/American Extremes. Foreword Yvonne G. J. M. Joris. Text Gert Staal. 's-Hertogenbosch: Museum Het Kruithuis (April 28– June 19, 1990). Romestraat: Provinciaal Museum voor Moderne Kunst (July 7– Aug.27, 1990).
American Jewelry and Related Objects. Jury: David Campbell, John Paul Miller and Grace McCann Morley. Foreword Gertrude H. Moore. Rochester: Memorial Art Gallery, 1957.
American Jewelry Today. Scranton, PA: Everhart Museum (Nov.1–30, 1965, and 1967).
American Metal Work, 1976. Intro. Jon Nelson. Lincoln, NB: Sheldon Memorial Art Gallery, University of Nebraska (July 12– Aug.31, 1976)
American Metalsmiths 1974. Foreword Carlo M. Lamagna. Lincoln, MA: DeCordova Museum (April 7– June 9, 1974).
Amulet. Text Lotte Menkman and Maarten Beks. Nimwegen, Holland: Galerie Marzee, [nd].
Anton Cepka/Jana Cepková: Sperky a Emaily. Brno: Moravska Galerie; Jablonec nad Nisou: Museum Skla a Bizuterie. 1988.
Anton Cepka and Vratislav Novák. Pforzheim: Schmuckmuseum (Dec.10, 1988– Feb.5, 1989). Hanau: Deutsches Goldschmiedehaus (Feb. 26– March 27, 1989).
Arsenale: Aggression im Schmuck. Text Wolfgang Schepers, Petra von Trott zu Solz, Eberhard

Keller and Heiner Treinen. Frankfurt: Museum für Kunsthandwerk (Nov.11– Dec.12, 1991); Solingen: Deutsches Klingenmuseum (Jan.5–Feb.16, 1992); Kevelaer: Konzert und Bühnenhaus (March 1992).
An Art Collection of Combs. Ed. Marie-José van den Hout. Text Marjan Unger and Pieter Seuren. Nimwegen: Galerie Marzee, 1989.
Art Exhibition from the Bezalel Academy, Jerusalem. Tokyo: Mikimoto Hall (Sept.3–12, 1982).
Art in Jewelry. Foreword Elaine H. Varian. New York: Finch College Museum of Art, 1966.
The Art of Enamels. Foreword Kurt J. Matzdorf. Text Jamie Bennett, Mark D. Cooper, Robert W. Ebendorf and Susan J. Slack. New Paltz, NY: State University College (Sept.10–30, 1973).
The Art of Personal Adornment. Intro. Paul J. Smith. Essays Robert Riley, Paul S. Wingert, Oppi Untracht, Diane Lee Carroll, Frederick J. Dockstader and Diane Waldman. New York: Museum of Contemporary Crafts (Sept.24–Nov.7, 1965)
Arte Italiana: aspecten van hedendaagse Italiaanse kunst. Intro. Ton Berends. Text Tomasso Trini and Flamino Gualdoni, and Alessandro Mendini. The Hague: Galerie Nouvelles Images (July 4–Aug.30, 1987).
Artists and Language. Pittsburgh: The Society for Contemporary Crafts (Feb.5– April 18, 1993).
Artists in Metal: A National Invitational Jewelry Exhibition. Intro. Hudson Roberts. Los Angeles: Fine Arts Gallery, California State University (Feb.4–22, 1973).
Austellung: Schmuck Jewellery Bijoux. Intro. Gerhard Bott. Darmstadt: Hessisches Landesmuseum (Dec.10, 1964– Feb.14, 1965).
Ausstrahlungen: Schmuck 1936–1991. Text Erika Patka. [Vienna]: Niederösterreich-Gesellschaft für Kunst und Kultur, 1991.
4 Australian Jewellers. Intro. Judith O'Callaghan. Melbourne: National Gallery of Victoria, 1987.
Australian Jewellery. By Dick Richards. Text Anne Schofield and Helge Larsen. Sydney: Crafts Board of the Australia Council, 1982.
Autori del Gioiello Olandese Contemporaneo. Text Liesbeth Crommelin and Ennio Chiggio. Vicenza: Torri di Arcugnano, 1990.
Beauty is a Story. Foreword Yvonne Joris. Essay Gert Staal. 's-Hertogenbosch: Museum Het Kruithuis (April 14– June 2, 1991).
Belgian Jewels Today. Text Albert Bontridder. Antwerp: Provincial Museum, 1983.
Benson & Hedges Gold: Art and Design. Hamburg: BAT Cigarettenfabriken GmbH, 1988.
Besteck. Text Anna Schreurs. Bonn: Knauth & Hagen, 1992.
Bezalel Academie, Jeruzalem. Amersfoort, Holland: De Zonnehof (Nov.13– Jan.4, 1982).
Bezalel Acamemie, Jerusalem: Edeslmeedkunst Orfèvrerie. Brussels: Maison des amis belges de l'université hébraïque de Jérusalem (March 10–20, 1982). Antwerp: Maison des bouchers (April 1–30, 1982).
Bezalel Academy Jerusalem. Intro. Arie Ofir. Pforzheim: Schmuckmuseum, 1978.
Bezalel 70+. Tel Aviv: Tel Aviv Museum of Art, 1976.
Bezalel Graduates. Jerusalem: Israel Museum, 1988.
Bijou Frontal: Neue Tendenzen Der Schmuck-gestaltung in der Schweiz. Text Bruno Haldner, Beat Wyss, and May B. Broda. Basle: Gewerbemuseum, Museum für Gestaltung (March 26– May 19, 1985).
The Body Adorned: An Exhibition of Jewelry. Curated Rachelle Thiewes. Intro. Stephen Vollmer. El Paso: Fox Fine Arts Center, University of Texas at El Paso (Feb.25– March 19, 1993).
Brilliant Stories: American Narrative Jewelry. Curated Lloyd E. Herman. Washington: Arts America Program, the United States Information Agency, [1992].
British Jewellery. Text Ralph Turner. Hanau: Deutsches Goldschmiedehaus (July 29– Aug.26, 1973).
British Jewellers: On Tour in Holland. Text Jerven Ober, Ralph Turner. Apeldoorn: Gemeentelijke van Reekumgaieri, 1978.
British Jewellery. Text Ralph Turner, Graham Hughes and Peter Dormer with Jan Burney. London: Crafts Council Gallery (April 19– July 16, 1989)
Burg Giebichenstein: Die hallesche Kunstschule von den Anf[a]ngen bis zur Gegenwart. Halle: Staatliche Galerie Moritzburg (March 20– June 13, 1993). Karlsruhe: Badisches Landesmuseum (June 25–Sept.12, 1993).
Claus Bury/Fritz Maierhofer/Gerd Rothmann. Text Hermann Jünger. London: Electrum Gallery (June 28– July 29, 1979).
Color and Image: Recent American Enamels. Text Lloyd E. Herman. Hamilton, NY: Gallery Association of New York State, 1988.
Concepts Comments Process: Dutch Jewellery 1967–1987. Text Evert Rodrigo. Amsterdam: Rijksdienst Beeldende Kunst, 1987.
Contemporary Jewellery: The Americas, Australia, Europe and Japan. Kyoto: The National Museum of Modern Art, 1984.
Contemporary Jewelry from the Federal Republic of Germany. Essays Erika Billeter, Fritz Falk, Jens-Rüdiger Lorenzen and Sabine Strobel. Stuttgart: Institute for Foreign Cultural Relations, 1989.
Contemporary Jewellery 1964-1993: Selected Works, Helen Williams Drutt Collection. Text Peter Dormer. Arkansas: The Arkansas Arts Center, Decorative Arts Museum. (Oct.8– Nov.21, 1993).
Contemporary Metal. Curated Richard Helzer. Billings, Montana: Yellowstone Art Center (June 18– Aug.30, 1981).
Contemporary Metals: Focus on Idea. Text Sanford Sivitz Shaman, Patricia Grieve Watkinson and Jane S. Weintraub. Pullman, WA: Washington State University Museum of Art (April 13– May 3, 1981).
Copper Brass Bronze Exhibition. Jury: Robert Ebendorf, William Harper and Stephen Prokopoff. Text Robert Cardinale and Adria Arch. Tucson: University of Arizona Museum of Art (April 3– May 15, 1977).
Copper 2: The Second Copper, Brass, and Bronze Exhibition. By Robert L. Cardinale and Lita S. Bratt. Preface Peter Bermingham. Foreword Michael F. Croft. Tucson: University of Arizona Museum of Art (March 2– April 6, 1980).
Cross Currents: Jewellery from Australia, Britain, Germany, and Holland. Text Tom Arthur and Helge Larsen. Sydney: Museum of Applied Arts and Sciences, Power House Museum, 1984.
Crossroads. Text Robert Lee Morris. New York: Artwear (May 14– June 14, 1992).
Dänisches Silber und Handwerk. Intro. Anders Hostrup Pedersen. Text Hans Lassen and Ibi Trier Morch. Zurich: Dämischen Wochen (Jan.26– Feb.25, 1962).
Danner Stiftung. Text Rolf Rüdiger Maschke. Munich: Benno and Therese Dannersche, Kunstgewerbestiftung, 1990.
Der Ri Der Ring. Foreword Hans Martin. Hanau: Deutsches Goldschmiedehaus (Nov.26, 1978–Jan.14, 1979).
Dieci Orafi Padovani – moderne Goldschmiedekunst aus Italien. Pforzheim: Schmuckmuseum, 1983.
Documents Northwest: Six Jewelers. Ex. br. Essay Vicki Halper. Seattle: Art Museum (April 22–June 27, 1993).
Double Vision: Collaborations by Forty-Nine North American Metal Artists. Essay Bruce Pepich and Caren Heft. Racine, WI: Charles A. Wustum Museum of Fine Arts, 1995.
13 Goldschmiede von Amsterdam bis Tokyo: Babetto, Becker, Bury, Cepka, Hiramatsu, Martinazzi, Nele, Pavan, Pomodoro, Reiling, Schmömlzer, Smit, Symon. Munich: Bayerische Akademie der Schönen Kunste (March 4– April 11, 1993).
Electronic Jewelry. Curated Chad Lynde. Text Chad Lynde and Bob Duckson. San Bernadino: Art Gallery, California State College (Jan.14– Feb.24, 1983).
Electrum Gallery – The Tenth Year 1971–1981. Intro. Barbara Cartlidge. Text Arline Fisch. London: Electrum Gallery (June 9–27, 1981).
Email: Schmuck und Gerät in Geschichte und Gegenwart. Foreword Inge Asenbaum. Text Otto Nedbal, Manfred Leithe-Jasper and Fritz Falk. Pforzheim: Schmuckmuseum (Jan.19– March 2, 1980).
Enamelists: Established and Emerging. Text Deaux Kranzberg. Atlanta: Chastain Arts and Crafts Center (May 22– June 18, 1977).
Enamelists: Vera Ronnen-Wall, June Schwarcz, William Harper. Intro. Sharon K. Emanuelli. Los Angeles: Craft and Folk Art Museum (March 17–April 18, 1982).
Enamelists and the Students. Foreword Margaret Fischer. Cleveland, OH: Mather Gallery, Case Western Reserve University (Feb.27– March 19, 1976).
Enamels. New York: Museum of Contemporary Crafts (Sept.18– Nov.29, 1959).
Enamels 50/80. Curated Margaret Seeler and Judith Daner. Brookfield, CT: Brookfield Craft Center, 1981.
Enamels '70. Intro. Charles Bartley Jeffery. St. Louis, MO: Craft Alliance Gallery, (March 1– 26, 1970).
Enamels '82. Intro. Harry Weiss. Jury: Jamie Bennett, Constance Costigan and William Harper. Washington, DC: George Washington University (Oct.– Nov. 1982).
Europäisches Email. Hanau: Deutsches Goldschmiedehaus, 1960.
Experimental Metalsmithing: Carnegie Grant Project. Text Albert E. Elsen and Alma Eikerman. Bloomington, Indiana University, 1968.
Facet I: Internationale sieradenbiënnale/International Jewellery Biennale. Intro. Tracy Metz. Rotterdam: Kunsthal (May 1– July 7, 1993).
Fachhochschule Düsseldorf, Fachbereich Design: Studienschwerpunkt Schmuck – Design. Foreword Hans Albert Klüfer. Hanau: Deutsches Goldschmiedehaus (April 2– May 8, 1977).
56 Bracelets 17 Rings 2 Necklaces. Intro. Evert van Staaten. Essays Marga Bijvoet, Liesbeth Hesselink and artists. Apeldoorn, Gem van Reekumgalerij, 1979.
5 x Österreicher Schmuck. Text Birgitt Jürgenssen. Munich: Galerie Spektrum, 1983.
First Australian Contemporary Jewellery Biennial. Adelaide, South Australia: Jam Factory, 1991.
Form/Formel/Formalismus: Schmuck 1985. Munich: Sonderschau der Internationalen Handwerksmesse (March 9–17, 1985).
Forms in Metal: 275 Years of Metalsmithing in America. Text Robert H. Luck and Paul J. Smith. New York: Museum of Contemporary Crafts of the American Crafts Council and Finch College Museum of Art, 1975.
Fragments: Therese Hilbert and Otto Künzli Jewellery 1976–1986. Text Beat Wyss and artists. Interview Franz G. Gold. Philadelphia: Helen Drutt Gallery (April 5– May 3, 1986).
Fremd-Körper: Schmuck der Avantgarde aus de Sammlung Teunen. Intro. Lida von Mengden. Ludwigshafen/Rhein: Wilhelm-HackMuseum, 1990.
Friedrich Wilhelm Müller Wettbewerb 1992: Schmückendes für Hand und Ohr. Schwäbisch Gmünd: Wilhelm Müller GmbH & Co. and Museum für Natur and Stadtkultur; Hanau: Gesellschaft für Goldschmiedekunst e.V., 1993.
Gabriele Dziuba/Manfred Bischoff. Vienna: Galerie V & V; Graz: Galerie Droschl; Munich: Galerie Cada, 1984.
Galerie Metal. Text Lise Funder and Jan Lohmann. Copenhagen: Galerie Metal, 1988.
Galerie Carin Delcourt van Krimpen. Preface Carin van Krimpen. Rotterdam: Carin Delcourt van Krimpen, 1993.
Gioiello, Arte Contemporanea D'Austria/ Jewellery, Austrian Contemporary Art/Schmuck, Zeitgenössische Kunst aus Österreich, Biennale di Venezia 1984. Text Maurizio Calvesi, Helmut Zilk, Inge Asenbaum, and Peter Baum. Venice: Ateneo San Basso (June 9– Aug.19, 1984).
Gioiello: Biennale Svizzera del Gioiello d'Arte Contemporaneo. Text E. Bellati and Alban Hürlimann. Lugano: Villa Malpensata (March 5–April 10, 1988).
Gioiello e Legature: Artisti del XX Secolo. Text Graziella Folchini Grassetto, Giorgio Segato, Giulia Bologna and Marcel Garrigou. Padua: L'Orafo Italiano Editore, 1990.
Gold+Silber Schmuck + Gerät: Von Albrecht Dürer bis zur Gegenwart. Text Curt Heigl, Elisabeth Treskow, Hubertus von Skal, Friedrich Becker, Arnaldo Pomodoro, Margit Staber, Erhard Hössle, and Wilhelm Wagenfeld, Nuremberg: Norishalle (March 19– Aug.22, 1971).
Gold und Silberschmiedearbeiten Klasse H. Markl Akademie für Werkkunst und Mode Berlin. Intro. Hans Markl. Hanau: Deutsches Goldschmiedehaus (May 24– June 14, 1970).
Goldschmiede dieser Zeit. Text Helmut Friedel, Hermann Jünger, Peter Cornelius Claussen, Wolfgang Wunderlich, Cornelia Vogelsanger and Katharina Issler. Hanover: Kestner-Gesellschaft (Oct.19– Nov.25, 1979).
Goldschmiede Silberschmiede: Von der Weimar Zeit bis heute: Franz Rickert, Hermann Jünger, Erhardd Höble, Ulla Mayer, Otto Künzli. Text Ursula Keltz, Franz Rickert, Hermann Jünger and Gerhard Glüder. Munich: Staatliches Museum für angewandte Kunst (March– May 1993).
Goldschmiedekunst: Renzo Pasquale, Francesco Pavan, Diego Piazza, Giuliano Reveane, Graziano Visintin. Text Lina Ossi. Basle: Galerie Atrium (May 5– June 5, 1981); Vienna: Galerie Am Graben (June 15– July 7, 1981).
The Goldsmith. Jury: Arline Fisch, Lloyd Herman and William E. Woolfenden. Text Harry Bober. Washington, DC: Renwick Gallery, NCFA, Smithsonian Institution (May 17– Aug.18, 1974).
Goldsmith '70. Text Malcolm E. Lein, Stanley Lechtzin, and John Prip. St Paul, MI: Minnesota Museum of Art, 1970.
Good as Gold: Alternative Materials in American Jewelry. Curated Lloyd E. Herman. Washington, DC: Smithsonian Institution Traveling Exhibition Service, 1981.
Impulse & Form, Text Robert Bell. Perth: Art Gallery of Western Australia, 1985.
In Praise of Hands: Contemporary Crafts of the

World. Text Octavio Paz. Toronto: World Crafts Council, 1974.
In Touch: Nytt Kunsthåndverk. Foreword Jan-Lauritz Opstad. Essays Peter Dormer and Jørgen Schou-Christensen. Lillehammer: Maihaugen, De Sandvigske Samlinger, 1994.
Infinite Riches: Jewelry Through the Centuries. By Cynthia Duval. St Petersburg, FL: Museum of Fine Arts (Feb.19– April 30, 1989).
Inno Alla Gioia. Organized Marijke Vallanzasca Bianchi. Padua: Galleria Tot, 1983.
Instant: Frankworks. Frankfurt a. M.: Messe Frankfurt (Aug.22–28, 1992).
International Exhibition of Modern Jewellery: 1890-1961. 2 vol. Intro. Graham Hughes. London: Worshipful Company of Goldsmiths (Oct.26–Dec.2, 1961).
International Festival of Enamels. Text Emily Beebee and Kay Whitcomb. Laguna Beach, CA: Laguna Beach Museum of Art (Sept.1976).
Invitational Exhibition of Enamels. Intro. Dorothy Sturm. Memphis: Memphis Academy of Arts (Feb.6–27, 1972).
Invitational Jewelry Exhibition. Foreword Allan Peterson. Pensacola, FL: Visual Arts Gallery, Pensacola Junior College (March 4–21, 1975).
Israeli Contemporary Crafts. Kyoto: National Museum of Modern Art, 1994.
Itoh, Kruger, Mattar, Pasquale. Cologne: Galerie Mattar (May 15– June 12, 1986).
Jang Sin Goo: Zeitgenössische Schmuckkunst in Korea, Ex. cat. Text Jamie Bennett and Chan Kyun Kang. Pforzheim: Schmuckmuseum, 1994.
Japan Jewellery Designers Association, Tokyo:
Tokyo Triennials: International Jewellery Arts Exhibitions: 1970, '73, '76, '79. '86
Japan Jewellery Exhibitions: 1979, '83. '86. '88. '89
Japan Jewellery Designers Association: Schmuck aus dem Modernen Japan. Text Fritz Falk, Shu Eguchi and Yasuki Hiramatsu. Pforzheim: Schmuckmuseum, 1983.
Jeweelkunst in België van gotiek tot heden. Text F. Norman, Lieven Daenens, A. M. Claessens-Peré and Johan Valcke. Ghent: Museum voor Sierkunst (June 28– Oct.15, 1986).
Jewelers, USA. Organized Dextra Frankel. Intro. Arline Fisch. Fullerton, CA: California State University Art Gallery (Feb.27– March 25, 1976).
Jewellery Australia Now. Ed. Bob Thompson. Text Bruce Metcalf, Nola Anderson, Anna Griffiths, Anne Brennan, Glenda King, Adam Geczy, Anna Burch, David Walker. Sydney: Crafts Council of Australia, [1988.]
Jewellery from Britain. Text Johan Valcke, Hermann Jünger, Paul Derrez and Ralph Turner. Antwerp: International Cultureel Centrum (May 25– June 23, 1985).
Jewellery in Europe. Selected Ralph Turner. Text Ralph Turner and Gerhard Bott. Edinburgh: The Scottish Arts Council and the Crafts Advisory Board (Dec.20, 1975– Jan.18, 1976).
The Jewellery Project. Text Ralph Turner, Alfred Knapp, Susanna Heron, Griselda Gilroy and David Ward. London: Crafts Council Gallery (April 20– June 26, 1983).
Jewellery Redefined. Text Diana Hughes and Sarah Osborn. London: British Crafts Centre, 1982.
Jewellery '71: An Exhibition of Contemporary Jewellery. Intro. Renée S. Neu. Ontario: Art Gallery of Ontario (Nov.6– Dec.5, 1971).
Jewelries/Epiphanies. Curated Catherine Mayes, Daniel Jocz and Joe Wood. Text James S. Ackerman, Sarah Bodine and Michael Dunas. Boston: Artists Foundation's Gallery at CityPlace (Sept.4– Oct.18, 1990).
Jewelry '63: An International Exhibition. Intro. Paul J. Smith and William Benson. Plattsburg, NY: State University College (April 17– May 7, 1963).
Jewelry '64: An International Exhibition. Judge: Earl Pardon. Foreword William Benson. Plattsburg, NY: State University College (April 15– May 8, 1964).
Jewelry '76. Coordinated Richard Mafong and Jem Freyaldenhoven. Atlanta: Georgia State University, 1976.
Jewelry and Beyond: Recent Metalwork by Distinguished Members of the Society of North American Goldsmiths. Essay Arline M. Fisch. Mount Vernon, IL: Mitchell Museum (April 21– May 20, 1984); New York: Fashion Institute of Technology (June 7–17, 1984).
Jewelry and Hollowware: Invitational: '72. Ames, IA: Design Center Gallery (Feb.1–29, 1972).
Jewelry for Head and Hair. Pforzheim: Schmuckmuseum, 1985.
Jewelry International: Contemporary Trends. Text Helen Williams Drutt. New York: American Craft Museum II (May 25– Sept.1, 1984).
Jewelry: Means: Meaning. Text Michael Tomlinson. Knoxville, TN: Ewing Gallery of Art and Architecture, University of Tennessee, 1989.
Jewelry USA. New York: American Craft Museum II (May 25– Sept.1, 1984).
Jewelryquake: International Three Schools Jewelry Collaboration – Akademie der Bildende Künste, Munich, Gerrit Rietveld Academie, Amsterdam, Hiko-Mizuno College of Jewelry, Tokyo. Intro. Joke Brakman, Kazuhiro Itoh, Otto Künzli and Takahiko Mizuno. Tokyo: Hiko Mizuno College of Jewelry (Sept.1–10, 1993); Munich: Galerie für angewandte Kunst (Feb.8–22, 1994); Amsterdam: Gerrit Rietveld Academie (March 6–12, 1994).
Joieria Europea Contemporània. Text Friz Falk, Francesco Miralles, Daniel Giralt-Miracle and Peter Dormer. Barcelona: Fundació Caixa de Pensions, 1987.
Joies de Catalunya/Schmuck Aus Katalonien. Text Daniel Giralt-Miracle and Fritz Falk. Pforzheim: Schmuckmuseum, 1985.
Joies Indissenyables. Text Xavier Domenech and Ramón Puig I. Cuyàs. Barcelona: Capella de l'Antic Hospital de la Santa Creu (Feb.20– March 18, 1992).
Jugend Gestaltet, Sonderschau der Internationalen Handwerksmesse. Foreword Peter Nickl. Munich: Bayerischer Handwerkstage (March 4–12, 1989).
Karl F. Schobinger, Bernhard Schobinger, and Martin Bruggmann: Zeichnungen und Schmuck. Essay Curt Burgauer. Aarau: Aargauer Kunsthaus (April 25– May 24, 1981).
Konzepte: 3 Goldschmiede. Bury, Jünger, Rothmann. Darmstadt: Hessisches Landesmuseum (March 3– April 30, 1978).
Körper-Zeichen. Munich: Städtische Galerie im Lenbachhaus (July 12– Aug.15, 1979).
Körperkultur: Otto Künzli and Gerd Rothmann. Text Dorothea Baumer and Helmut Friedel. Vienna: Galerie am Graben and Oldenburg: Landesmuseum, 1982.
Kunststoff Schmuck Kunst 1923–1993. Text Olga Zobel-Biró and Christianne Weber-Stöber. Munich: Galerie Biró, 1993.
L'Art de L'Email. Intro. Georges Magadoux. Essays Georges-Emmanuel Clancier and René Blanchot. Limoges: Chapelle du Lycée Gay-Lussac (July 8– Sept.8, 1975).
L'Art de L'Email. Jury: Jean-Jacques Prolongeau, Paul Riche, Joël Gauvin and Georges Chazaud. Limoges: Chapelle du Lycée Gay-Lussac (July 12– Sept.10, 1978).
L'Immaginazione Costruttiva. Curated Giorgio Segato. Text Licisco Magagnato and Lionello Puppi. Padua: Civica Galleria Piazza Cavour (April 30– May 31, 1987).
Le Bijou 1900: Modern Style-Juwelen. Foreword François Mathey. Text Y. Oostens-Wittamer. Brussels: Hotel Solvay, Brussels, 1965.
Local Goddesses. Jerusalem: David Tower Museum, 1994.
London Amsterdam: New Art Objects from Britain and Holland. Text Gert Staal and Martina Margetts. London: Crafts Council Gallery (July 13– Sept.18, 1988); Amsterdam: Galerie Ra and Galerie de Witte Voet (Oct.15– Dec.4, 1988).
Loot VII. Intro. Brian Beaumont-Nesbitt. London: Goldsmiths' Hall (Nov.2–21, 1981).
Loot & Superloot. Foreword Graham Hughes. Minneapolis: Minneapolis Institute of Art (July 9– 28, 1978).
The Maker's Eye. London: Crafts Council, 1982.
Masterworks of Contemporary American Jewelry: Sources and Concepts. Text Graham Hughes, Oppi Untracht and Toni Lesser Wolf. London: Victoria and Albert Museum (May 11–June 27, 1985).
Masterworks/Enamel/87. Intro. Bill Helwig. Cincinnati: Taft Museum (July 23– Aug.31, 1987)
Matter/Anti-Matter. [Eva Eisler, Thomas Gentille, John Iversen, Pavel Opo˘censk`y and Lisa Spiros]. Nimwegen: Galerie Marzee (Jan.1991); Ghent: Galerie Sofie Lachaert (April 1991); Berlin: Treykorn (Sept. 1991); Frankfurt: Galerie für modernen Schmuck (Nov. 1991); Vienna: Galerie V & V (Nov. 1991).
Metaal & Kunst: Sculpturen/Jewelen. Text M.-R. Bentein. Zwevegem, The Netherlands: Gemeentelijk Park Zwevegem (June 5– July 6, 1980).
Metal '74. Organized Thomas Markusen and Albert Paley. Brockport, NY: Fine Arts Gallery, State University College (Nov.17– Dec.20, 1974).
Metal Experience. Intro. Hazel Bray. Oakland, CA: The Oakland Museum (June 5– July 4, 1971).
Metal: Germany. Cologne: Arbetisgemeinschaft des Deutschen Kunsthandwerks e. V.
metal: germany. Intro. Erich Köllmann. New York: Museum of Contemporary Crafts (Jan.20– March 5, 1967).
Metals Invitational, 1975 AD. Foreword Kurt Matzdorf. New Paltz, NY: College Art Gallery, State University College (Oct.8–29, 1975).
Metals Invitational '94. Akron, OH: Emily Davis Gallery, The University of Akron (April 4–23, 1994).
The Metalsmith: Society of North American Goldsmiths Exhibition. Foreword Ronald D. Hickman. Phoenix: Phoenix Museum of Art (Jan.14– Feb.20, 1977).
Metalsmith 1981. Jury: Paul J. Smith. Curated Jon Havener, Gary Nemchock and Olli Valanne. Lawrence: Visual Arts Exhibition Gallery, The University of Kansas (June 5– July 5, 1981).
Modern Scandinavian Jewels: Denmark, Finland, Norway, Sweden. Intro. Ibi Trier Morch. New York: Georg Jensen Inc., 1963.
Moderne Engelse Sieraden: British Jewellers on Tour in Holland. Intro. Jerven Ober. Apeldoorn, Holland: Gemeentelijke Van Reekumgalerij, 1978.
Müncher Goldschmiede: Schmuch und Gerät 1993. Organized Helmut Bauer. Munich: Müncher Stadtmuseum, 1993.
National Invitational Exhibition in Contemporary Jewellery. Foreword Richard Mafong and Jem Freyaldenhoven. Atlanta, GA: Department of Art, Georgia State University, 1974.
National Jewelry Competition. Sponsored by the Department of Art and the International Center for Arid and Semi-Arid Land Studies. Jury: Robert von Neumann. Lubbock: Texas Tech University, Lubbock (March 22– April 19, 1970).
Neues Bergreifen/Uuden Ymmärtäminen. Helsinki: Taideteollisuusmuseo Konstindustrimuseet (Aug. 11– Sept.13, 1992). Hameln: Galerie Unique (Oct.9 –30, 1992). Düsseldorf: Galerie Cebra (Jan.22– Feb.9, 1993).
New Departures in British Jewellery. Selected by Eric Spiller. Intro. Ralph Turner. London: Crafts Council, 1983.
New Gold, Silver and Jewels Commissioned by Industry. Foreword Viscount Boyd of Merton. London: Worshipful Company of Goldsmiths, 1965.
NHGCA Metals Invitational 1984. New Harmony, IN: New Harmony Gallery of Contemporary Art (Nov.18, 1984– Jan.6, 1985).
New Tradition: The Evolution of Jewellery 1966–1985. By Caroline Broadhead. London: British Crafts Centre, 1985.
Niet Alleen Voor de Sier. Essay Huub Mous. Leeuwarden: keunstwurk, 1994.
1971–1991 Four Artists Reflect: Robert Ebendorf, Ferne Jacobs, Mary Ann Scherr, Joyce Scott. Intro. Ralph Turner. Pittsburgh: The Society for Arts and Crafts (May 3– Aug.17, 1991).
1975 Jewelry Invitational 'Symbolism & Imagery'. Ellensburg,: Fine Arts Gallery, Central Washington State College (Feb.1975).
New Jewellery. Stockholm: Kulturhuset, 1985.
Nine North Carolina Jewelers. Intro. Ray Menze. Cullowhee, NC: Western Carolina University Art Gallery (April 18–29, 1977).
Norsk Emaljekunst: I Lyset. Foreword Thor Kielland. Oslo: Kunstindustrimuseet (June– Aug., 1952).
Norwegian Jewellery. Text Jan-Lauritz Opstad, Robert Ebendorf and Paul Derrez. Oslo: Royal Norwegian Ministry of Foreign Affairs, 1987.
Objects of Adornment: Five Thousand Years of Jewelry from the Walters Art Gallery, Baltimore. Intro. Robert P. Bergman. Text Jeanny Vorys Canby, Diana M. Buitron, Andrew Oliver, Jr., Richard H. Randall, Jr., Diana Scarișbrick and William R. Johnston. New York: Walters Art Gallery and the American Federation of Arts, 1984.
Objects One: An Account of Danish Arts and Crafts 1985/86. Text Per Mollerup, Kristen Bjørnkjær, Ursula Munch-Petersen, Finn Lyngaard, Ole Bent Petersen and Dan Svarth. Copenhagen: The Objects Group, 1986.
Objects to Human Scale: Contemporary Australian Jewellery. Text Helge Larsen. Tokyo: Reine Publishing Co., 1980.
Objects: USA. By Lee Nordess. New York: The Viking Press, 1970.
The Observer Jewellery Exhibition. Text Ken Baynes and Brian Beaumont-Nesbitt. Cardiff: National Museum of Wales (Sept.1– Oct.27, 1973).
Ohio Metals: A Legacy. Text JoAnn Stevens, Susan Ewing, Ulysses G. Dietz, and Sarah Bodine and Michael Dunas. Columbus: Ohio Designer Craftsmen and Internalia/Design Books, 1993.
Op Art: Eyeglasses by Jewelers. Curated Deb Stoner. Portland: Hoffman Gallery, Oregon School of Arts and Crafts (March 3– April 3, 1994).
Orfebres FAD. Barcelona: Orfebres FAD, 1980.
Organic Jewellery. Foreword Sarah Hosking and Jan Dawson. Essays John Houston and Jan Dawson. Leicestershire Museums, 1975.
Ornamenta 1: Internationale Schmuckkunst. Foreword Michael Erlhoff. Text Claude Levi-Strauss, Fritz Falk, Sarah Bodine, Manfred Schmalriede, Uta

Brandes, Wilhelm Mattar, Stanley Lechtzin, Axel Wirths and Günter Zamp Kelp. Pforzheim: Schmuckmuseum (Sept.30– Nov.19, 1989).

Parures de Pacotille. Preface Claude Ritschard. Essays Claude Ritschard, Jérôme Baratelli and Marianne Mattey with Isabelle Utz. Geneva: Ecole des arts décoratifs (March 9– April 21, 1989).

Personal Expression: Schmuck und Objekte Aus Israel. By Alex Ward. Cologne: Museum für angewandte Kunst, 1989.

Perth International Crafts Triennial. By Robert Bell, contributions Matthew Kangas, Ralph Turner, Désirée Schellerer, Kiyoji Tsuji, Michael Bogle and Julie Ewington. Perth: Art Gallery of Western Australia (Oct.14– Dec.3, 1989).

Point of View: Dutch Contemporary Jewelry and Design. Curated Charon Kransen. Text Paul Derrez, Susan Grant Lewin and Douglas Steakly. New York: Charon Kransen, 1990.

Precious Metals: The American Tradition in Gold and Silver. Essays Peter Bohan, Bob Ebendorf and Henry P. Raleigh. Coral Gables, FL: Lowe Art Museum, University of Miami (Nov.20, 1975– Jan.11, 1976).

1ère Biennale du Bijou, Paris 1987. Text Françoise-Claire Prodhon. Paris: Hôtel de Sens, Bibliothèque Forney (Sept.8– Nov.12, 1987).

Present Tense. Curated Leslie Vansen. Milwaukee: The University of Wisconsin-Milwaukee (Jan.22– Feb.23, 1992).

Rattlesnakes: an Exhibition of Modern American Jewellery. Intro. Graham Hughes. London: Goldsmiths' Hall (July 5–28, 1978).

Ready made: Schmuck aus Fertigteilen. Text Wilhelm Mattar, Jiř Švestka, and Heiner Treinen. Cologne: Atelier Mattar, [nd].

Reprise. Intro. Richard Thomas. Bloomfield Hills, MI: Cranbrook Academy of Art Museum (Sept. 28– Nov.9, 1975).

Scandinavian Craft Today. Tokyo: Seibu Museum of Art, 1987.

Schmuck. Wasserburg am Inn: Galerie im Ganserhaus, 1984

Schmuck. Berne: Galerie Michele Zeller (July 5– Aug.25, 1985).

Schmuck 70 – Tendenzen. Intro. Fritz Falk. Pforzheim: Schmuckmuseum, 1970.
Also: *Schmuck 73, Schmuck 82*

Schmuck aus den Niederlanden. Munich: Galerie Spektrum (Oct.6– Nov.6, 1982).

Schmuck aus Stahl. By Karl Bernd Heppe. Dusseldorf: Wirtschaftsvereinigung Stahl, 1989.

Schmuck: Berlin West. Text Reinhold Ludwig. Berlin: Kunsthandwerk Berlin e. V., 1988.

Schmuck: Burg Giebichenstein. Text Peter Skubic, Andrea Richter, Dorothea Prühl and Heinz Schönemann. Stuttgart: Arnoldsche, 1992.

Schmuck: Die Sammlung der Danner-Stiftung. Foreword Hebert Rüth. Text Michael Koch, Otto Künzli and Beat Wyss. Munich: Galerie für angewandte Kunst (March 12– May 15, 1993).

Schmuck 77 – Tendenzen. Intro. Fritz Falk. Pforzheim: Schmuckmuseum (July 16– Sept.11, 1977).

Schmuck '86. Munich: Haus der Kunst (Oct.1–5, 1986).

Schmuck für Kopf und Haar. Text Fritz Falk. Pforzheim: Schmuckmuseum (Dec.1, 1985– Jan.26, 1986).

Schmuck International 1900–1980. Text Helmut Zilk, Dieter Ronte, Friedrich Becker, Eugen Mayer, Vľea Vokáčová and Peter Skubic. Vienna: Kunstlerhaus (June 26– Aug.17, 1980).

Schmuck Konzentriert. Berlin: Galerie V.F.K. E.V. (Oct.11– Nov.13, [1983]).

Schmuck-Objeckte: Goldschmiede finden neue Formen. Intro. Erika Billeter. Text Jerven Ober. Zurich: Museum Bellerive (Sept.24– Nov.14, 1971).

Schmuck-Tischgerät aus Österreich 1904/08–1973/77. Text Elisabeth Rücker and Inge Asenbaum. Vienna: Galerie am Graben, 1978.

Schmuck und Gerät: 1959–1984. Munich: Sonderschau der Internationalen Handwerksmesse (March 10– 18, 1984).

Schmuck + Gerät – Bund der Kunsthandwerker Baden-Württemberg. Pforzheim: Schmuckmuseum (April 21– June 10, 1990).

Schmuck und Gerät: Eine Austellung der Gesellschaft für Goldschmiedekunst. Christianne Weber-Söber (ed.). Munich: Klinkhardt and Biermann, 1994.

Schmuck und Gerät von 1800 bis heute. Hanau: Deutsches Goldschmiedehaus, 1958.

Schmuck und Objekt Kunst. Foreword Frank Nolde. Text Karola Weidenmüller, Claudia Baugut, Barbara Jacob, Rolf Lindner and Wilhelm Matter. Erfurt: Angermuseum (Aug.16– Oct.4, 1992)

Schmuck Unserer Zeit: 1964–1993. Text Sigrid Barten, Helen Williams Drutt English and Peter Dormer. Zurich: Museum Bellerive (Feb.10– May 1, 1994).

Schmuck: Zeichen Am Korper. Concept Helmut Gsoiipointer. Linz: Landesmuseum Francisco Carolinum (Sept.11, 1987– 10 Jan.,1988). Vienna: Falter Verlag, 1987.

Schmuckmuseum Pforzheim: Von der Antike bis zur Gegenwart, Intro. Fritz Falk. Pforzheim: Schmuckmuseum, 1980.

Schmuckszene '87: Internationale Schmuckschau. Munich: Bayerischer Handwerkstag e. V., 1987. Also: *Schmuckszene '89, '90, '91, '92, '93, '94, '95.*

Schrag. Text Klaus Honnef, Paul Donkerduyus, Lothar Romain, Evert Rodrigo, Gertjan Zuithof, Konrad Boehmer, Jaap Goedegebuure. Bonn: Rheinisches Landesmuseum, 1990.

Sculptural Concerns: Contemporary American Metalworking. Text Jeannine Falino and Ian Brooks Loyd. Fort Wayne, IN: Fort Wayne Museum of Art; Cincinnati, OH: Museum of Art and the Contemporary Arts Center, 1993.

Second Annual Jewelry Invitational. Foreword Ken Cory. Ellensburg, WA: Central Washington State College Fine Arts Gallery, 1976.

Second Annual National Exhibition in Contemporary Jewelry. Intro. Ricka Feeley. Atlanta: Fulton Federal Savings and Loan Association (April 8– 18, 1975).

Second International Enamel Art Exhibition. Schirmherr: Wolfgang Wild. Foreword Kurt Neun. Jury: Kenneth F. Bates, Maureen Carswell, Curt Heigl and Andreu Vilasis. Text Edmund Massow, Frauke Wever, Sigrid Delius and Sylke Klopsch. Coburg, Germany: Kunstverein Coburg Druckhaus Neue Presse (June 27– Aug.30, 1987).

Second Triennale du Bijou. Paris: Musée du Luxembourg, 1990.

7 Goldschmiede 50 Schmuckstücke. Berlin: Staatliche Museen Preussischer Kulturbesitz (Sept.15– Nov.15, 1987).

Sieraden. Text Liesbeth Crommelin. The Hague: Galerie Nouvelles Images (Nov.16– Dec.24, 1973).

Sieraden/Schmuck/Jewellery Images. Text Marjan Unger, Renny Ramakers, Monique Mokveld and Jerven Ober. Amsterdam: VES (Society of Jewellery Makers and Designers), 1985.

Un Siglio de Joyeria y Bisuteria Española 1890–1990. Govern Balear: Lonja Conselleria de Cultura, Educació i Esports, (July– September, 1991).

Signaturen. Text Max Fröhlich, Brigitte von Savigny. Schwäbisch Gmünd: Siftung Gold- und Silberschmiedekunst (June 26– Sept.2, 1990).

Silver: New Forms and Expressions II. Text David R. McFadden, Ronald Pearson, Helen Shirk and Jack Lenor Larsen. New York: Fortunoff (Oct.1– 21, 1990).

Silver in Silver City. Foreword Cecil Howard. Silver City: Francis McCray Gallery, Western New Mexico University (March 19– April 16, 1978).

Silverschmiede. Foreword Wolfgang Schepers. Düsseldorf: HWK Galerie; Hanover: Handwerksform; Berlin: Kunstgewerbemuseum; Oldenburg: Landesmuseum für Kunst und Kulturgeschichte; Munich: Galerie Handwerk; Stuttgart: Landesgewerbeamt, 1985–86.

Skidmore College: Five Goldsmiths. Text Helen W. Drutt English and Eleanore Galant. Philadelphia: Helen Drutt Gallery (March 10– April 15, 1989).

SNAG: Society of North American Goldsmiths. Foreword Fritz Falk. Text Thomas R. Markussen. Pforzheim: Schmuckmuseum, 1979.

Sølv til Brug: Sølvsmeden Mogens Bjørn Andersen gennem 50 År. Ed. Erik Lassen. Oslo: Kunstindustrimuseet (Oct.30– Dec.6, 1981).

Southeastern Contemporary Jewelry. Intro. Jane Kessler. Charlotte, NC: Mint Museum (Nov.8 – Dec.31, 1981).

Stadtbildhauer, Skulpturenpark, Schloss Philippsruhe: Claus Bury, Edgar Gutbub, Dorothee von Windheim. Essays Mans M. Schmidt, Oscar Ackerman, Dorothee von Windheim. Hanau: Kulturdezement der Stadt, 1990.

Stadtgoldschmiede in Schwäbisch Gmünd: Schmuck und Gerät. Essay Brigitte von Savigny. Schwäbisch Gmünd: Museum für Natur und Stadtkultur (June 28– Aug.30, 1992).

Der Sumes ist das Herz des Schmuckes (von innen nach auben). Text Karola Grässlin. Munich: K-Raum Daxer (Dec.9– Jan.16, 1993).

The Sterling Craft: Five Centuries of Treasures from The Worshipful Company of Goldsmiths London and Ancient and Modern Masterpieces of British Gold, Silver and Jewelry. Intro. Graham Hughes. San Francisco: M.H. de Young Memorial Museum (June 21– Aug.7, 1966).

Stone – Jewelry. Ramat Gan, Israel: Oppenheimer Diamond Museum, 1992.

Structure and Ornament, American Modernist Jewelry 1940–1960. Foreword Mark Foley. Preface Robert Cardinale. Intro. Mark Isaacson. New York: FIFTY/50 Gallery (Nov.29, 1984– Jan.12, 1985).

Structure and Surface: Beads in Contemporary American Art. Text Mark Richard Leach. Sheboygan, WI: John Michael Kohler Arts Center, 1990.

Subjects: International Jewelry Art Exhibition. Organized by Juhani Heikkilä and Petteri Ikonen. Helsinki: Design Forum Finland, 1993.

Symbolism and Imagery. Foreword Ken Cory. Ellensburg, WA: Fine Arts Gallery, Central Washington State College, 1975.

Symfonie voor solisten. Text Jeroen N.M. van den Eynde. Arnhem, Gemeentemuseum (Feb.12– May 15, 1994).

Tekens & Ketens/ Signs & Chains/ Zeichen & Ketten. Text Erik Beenker, Marjan Unger, Liesbeth Den Besten, and Henny Meijer. Amsterdam: Uitgeverij Voetndot, 1993.

Third National Student Metal Invitational. Intro. Stanley Lechtzin. Elkins Park, PA: Tyler School of Art, Temple University (Nov.25– Dec.17, 1972)

A Touch of Gold. Foreword Evan H. Turner. Philadelphia, PA: Philadelphia Museum of Art (Nov.23– Dec.15, 1974).

10 Jaar Ra. Text Liesbeth Crommelin. Amsterdam: Galerie Ra (Oct.1– Nov.1, 1986).

Tragezeichen: Schmuck von Giampaolo Babetto, Manfred Birschoff, Falko Marx, Manfred Nisslmüller, Francesco Pavan, Bernhard Schobinger, Peter Skubic, and Robert Smit. Essay

Christoph Blase. Leverkusen, Germany: Museum Morsbroich, [1988].

Treasures: Jewelry & Other Metalwork from the Permanent Collection of the American Craft Museum. Text Janet Kardon and John Perreault. New York: American Craft Museum (Jan.20– Aug.2, 1992).

Treasures of the USSR Diamond Fund. Moscow: USSR Diamond Fund, 1980.

Triennale du bijou 1990. Paris: Musée de l'art vivant (Sept.18– Oct.18, 1990).

IIIème Triennale du Bijou, Musée des arts décoratifs. Preface Danièle Giraudy, essays Jean-Yves Le Mignot, Chantal Bizot, Françoise-Claire Prodhon, David Watkins, Barbara Cartlidge. Paris: Editions du Mai, 1992.

20th Century Jewellery – From the Collection of the Schmuckmuseum Pforzheim. Intro. Fritz Falk. Pforzheim: Schmuckmuseum (July 22– Aug.3, 1977).

Two Decades of Metal. Text Arline Fisch. San Diego, CA: San Diego State University Gallery (Sept.12– Oct.10, 1981).

Uncommon Beauty in Common Objects: The Legacy of African American Craft Art. Ed. Barbara Glass. Text Nkiru Nzegwu. Wilberforce, OH: National Afro-American Museum and Cultural Center, 1993.

Using Gold and Silver. Schwäbisch Gmünd, Germany: Stadtisches Museum, 1990.

Uusinta Ruotsalaista Hopeaa/Svenskt Silver Idag. Text Åke H. Huldt. Helsinki: Taideteollisuusmuseo, and Konstindustrimuseet, 1984.

Variatienen in Metall und Porzellan: Gretchen Klunder Raber und Jolande Haas Goldberg. Pforzheim: Schmuckmuseum (Feb.23– April 14, 1985).

Vereiniging van Edelsmeden en Sieraadontwerpers. Text Paul Derrez and Riet Neerincx. Amsterdam: Stedelijk Museum (Sept.11– Oct.4, 1981).

VES Catalogues '82. Amsterdam: Vereiniging van Edelsmeden en Sieraadontwerpers, 1982.

VES View Review. Text Paul Winters, Letse Meij, and Ans van Berkum. Amsterdam: Vormgevers en Sieraadontwerpers, 1991.

Wally Gilbert/Thomas Gentille. Organized Richard Edgecumbe and Jane Stancliffe. London: Victoria and Albert Museum (June 17– Sept.2, 1973).

Was Ihr Wollt. Munich: Galerie Spektrum (Nov.24– Dec.29, 1993).

Wendy Ramshaw – David Watkins: Schmuck – Jewellery. Pforzheim: Schmuckmuseum (March 21– May 17, 1987); Hanau: Deutsches Goldschmiedehaus (May 24– July 5, 1988).

Werkstadt Graz: Schmölzer Skubic Schmeiser. Graz: Werkstadt Graz Galerie (March 21– April 11, 1988).

Young Americans 1953, fourth annual competitive exhibition, sponsored by American Craftsmen's Educational Council. New York: Gallery of America House (June 9– Sept.4).

Young Americans 1958. New York: Museum of Contemporary Crafts (Jan. 13– Sept.14, 1958).

Young Americans: Metal. Intro. Paul J. Smith. New York: American Craft Museum (Jan.18– March 16, 1980).

Zeitgenössischer Schmuck aus Polen. Foreword Fritz Falk. Essays Sylvia-Monica Schmager and Marek Nowaczyk. Pforzheim: Schmuckmuseum (Sept.20– Nov.2, 1980).

Zeitgenössisches deutsches Kunsthandwerk. 5. Triennale. Text Sabine Runde, Helga Hilschenz-Mlynek. Munich: Prestel Verlag, 1990/91.

Zunft Turm – Zunft Jungkunst. Text Dr Weigelt, Jürgen Hildebrandt, Walter Huber, Heinz Seeherr and Reinhold Bothner. Pforzheim: Pforzheim Reuchlinhaus (Sept.11– Oct.9, 1977).

sources of illustrations

Photographic credits and acknowledgments
are listed by name, with illustrations identified
by page number and the following abbreviations:
a (above), *b* (below), *c* (centre), *l* (left)
and *r* (right).

Photo Hans-Jørgen Abel: 131; 326*a* all; 326*c* all.
Photo ©Taco Anema fotograf: 258.
Photo James Arnofsky: 301*cc*.
Jean Barbier, Courtesy Taideteollisuusmuseo, Helsinki: 206*b*; 290*bl*.
Diane Baskin: 282*l*.
Photo Karen Bell: 95*bl*; 232*al*; 301*cr*; 301*cl*.
Peter Blodgett: 293*cr*; 293*cl*.
Sheila Bohlin: 287.
Photo Ferdinand Bosch: 299*bl*.
Marta Breis: 293 bl; 293*br*.
Photo ©Thomas Brummett: 296*al*; 296*ar*; 301*ar*.
Courtesy Claus Bury: 294*bl*; 294*br*.
Peter Chang: 295*b* all.
Ken Cory: 325*al*; 325*cl*.
Courtesy Ken Cory Estate: 333*ar*.
Photo ©Annaleen Couwes: 263*r*.
Bob Cramp: 91.
Photo Anthony Cuñha: 292*br*; 311*cr*.
Guri Dahl: 132
Georg Dobler: 298*al*; 298*c* all; 133*c*.
Helen Drutt: 340*al*.
Courtesy Helen Drutt Gallery: 335*l*.
Courtesy Robert Ebendorf: 335*r*.
David Egan: 307*ar*
Photo ©Foto Mara Eggert: 219
Photo George Erml: 101*l*; 102; 299*cl*; 302*ar*.
Photo Dana Fischer: 275.
Peggy Fox: 273*l*.
Jan Frank: 260*r*.
Jem Freyaldenhoven: 300*a* all.
Max Fröhlich: 300*br*.
Photo Ralph Gabriner: 297*b* all.
Photo Courtesy Galerie Ra: 297*cl*; 297*cr*.
Jzika Gaon: 244*ar*.
Elizabeth Garrison: 301*al*.

Kate Gollings: 251; 310*b* all.
Photo Rainer Griese: 321*bl*.
Photo Gary Griffin; 302*c* all.
Copyright *The Guardian*: 267.
Photo Tom Haartsen: 224.
Mike Hallson: 90*r*.
Photo Lynn Hamrick: 188; 191*ar*; 296*c* all; 296*b* all; 324*cl*; 324*cr*; 324*b* all.
Photo Bobby Hansson: 101*r*.
Photo Bobby Hansson, The Society of North American Goldsmiths: 33; 34 all; 36 all; 38 all; 39; 40; 41; 43 all; 44 all; 45; 46 all; 47 all; 48 all; 49; 53 all; 56 all; 59; 60; 61*a*; 63*ar*; 90*l*; 93 all; 100*b*; 123*c*; 124 all; 125; 126*bl*; 126*br*; 129; 133*b*; 140 all; 142 all; 146*b*; 147; 159; 194 all; 199*l*; 291*cl*; 298*ar*; 301*b*; 303*bl*; 307*cr*; 309*bl*; 317*cl*; 317*br*; 318*cl*; 320*c*; 321*al*; 321*ac*; 323*al*; 324*al*; 324*ar*.
Photo Kurt Hess: 297*al*.
Photo Eva Heyd: 299*cr*.
Photo Bob Hirsch: 303*cr*.
Photo Tom Hodge: 307*al*
Photo ©1990 Hok: 308*ar*; 308*al*.
Photo William Hans van de Kerck Hove: 310*cr*.
Mary Lee Hu: 304*b* all; 305*ar*; 305*al*.
Kazuhiro Itoh: 305*c* all.
Gerhard Jaeger: 210; 289*al*; 289*ar*.
Photo Lief R. Jansson, Courtesy Svensk Press: 340*ar*.
Photo Mark Johann: 303*br*.
E. Jünger: 306*al*.
E. and L. Jünger: 11; 306*ar*; 306*cl*.
Courtesy Hermann Jünger: 306*ac*; 306*cr*; 330.
Photo Mathilde Jurrissen: 105.
Photo Ruthe Karlin: 292*al*.
Peer van der Kruis, Heeze, Courtesy Museum Het Kruithuis, 's-Hertogenbosch, The Netherlands: 310*a* all.
Otto Künzli: 292*cr*; 292*bl*; 304*a* all; 308*br*; 308*bl*.
Rebekah Laskin: 309*al*; 309*ar*.
Photo Oded Lebel: 65.
Stanley Lechtzin: 309*c* all; 309*br*.
Photo John Lenz: 150*r*; 151; 291*bl*; 291*br*.

Photo Leonberg-Ramtel: 322*c* all.
Photo Casey McNamara: 305*br*.
Courtesy Fritz Maierhofer: 333*al*.
Bruno Martinazzi: 103*ar*; 311*ac*; 311*ar*.
Richard Mawdsley: 311*b* all.
Photo Hans Mayr: 321*cl*.
Bruce Metcalf: 312*ar*; 312*al*.
Bruce Miller: 261; 314*b* all.
Photo J. Milmoe: 298*br*.
Photo Jeroen Miltenburg: 134*a*.
Eric Mitchell: 57*l*; 121.
Photo Nicolas Monkewitz: 300*bl*.
Photo Müller-Doldi: 339.
Photo ©Per Myrehed: 286*r*.
Photo T. Nakamura: 226; 298bl.
Photo Richard Nicol: 302*b* all, 303*al*; 303*ar*.
Peter Olsen: 123*a*; 161; 311*cl*.
Pavel Opočenský: 314*c* all.
Photo Jan Otsen: 318*br*.
Ulla Paakkunainen: 35; 37 all; 50; 51; 52 all; 54*a*; 54*b*; 55; 57*r*; 58; 61*b*; 62; 63*bl*; 64; 82*b*; 84 all; 85 all; 86 all; 87; 88*b*; 92*r*; 94 all; 96*a*; 97 all; 98 all; 100*a*; 100*c*; 103*al*; 103*b*; 122; 126*ar*; 127; 130*b*; 134*c*; 134*b*; 136, 137*ar*; 137*cr*; 137*br*; 138; 139 all; 141; 143; 144; 145; 146*a*; 148*r*; 149 all; 152*r*; 154*al*; 156 all; 157; 158 all; 187; 190*b*; 191*br*; 195 all; 196 all; 197; 198; 199*r*; 200 all; 201; 202 all; 204*al*; 205; 206*a*; 207; 208; 289*b*; 290*a* all; 290*c* all; 290*br*; 299*br*; 300*cr*; 302*al*; 306*bl*; 306*br*; 308*cl*; 308*c*; 311*al*; 312*c*; 312*br*; 315*a*; 315*br*; 320*ar*; 321*ar*; 323*c*; 323*b* all; 326*b*; 327*ar*; 327*cr*.
Pacific Stars and Stripes Photo: 331.
Courtesy Estate of Earl Pardon: 315*c* all.
Jackie Pardon: 262*l*.
Photo Kim Paterson: 225*l*.
Photo Frøde Pedersen: 283.
Marlen Perez (Museum Bellerive, Zurich, Switzerland): 42; 99; 123*b*; 133*a*; 137*b*; 137*bl*; 148*l*; 153; 189; 308*cr*.
Photo Chris Pfaff: 321*br*.
Photo Courtesy Philadelphia Museum of Art: 332.

Photo Joel Pieper: 314*ar*.
Gary Pollmiller: 319*al*; 319*ar*.
Photo Dean Powell: 150*l*; 291*cr*; 305*bl*.
Photo Sjaak Ramakers: 250.
Jack Ramsdale: 54*ar*; 81; 82*a*; 83; 88*a*; 92*a*; 92*bl*; 95*al*; 95*ar*; 96*b*; 104; 152*l*; 185; 186 all; 190*ar*; 191*cl*; 192 all; 193 all; 203; 222; 292*cl*; 295*cr*; 313*c* all; 325*ar*.
Marylu Raushenbush: 256.
Photo Richard Reinhardt: 318*a* all.
Photo Murray Riss: 316*al*.
Photo Brad Rogers: 218*r*.
Photo Rosa ©Netherlands Design Institute: 344.
Gerd Rothmann: 154*cl*;154*br*; 155.
Photo Jos Ruijssenaars: 135.
Foto ©Dietmar Schneider: 253*ar*; 340*b*.
Courtesy Bernhard Schobinger: 204*bl*; 204*r*; 319*c* all.
Photo ©1983 Roger Schreiber: 303*ac*; 304*cl*.
Helen Shirk: 320*b* all.
Olaf Skoogfors: 2.
Rod Slemmons: 322*al*; 322*ar*; 343.
Robert Smit: 322*b* all.
Photo Jane Sonet-Glazer: 232*br*.
Photo Annelies Štrba: 271.
Sun Photo: 316*cr*.
Photo Tim Sylvia: 303*cl*.
Kanji Taken: 320*al*.
Photo Brigit Takur: 247*ar*.
Merrily Tompkins: 281*b*.
Jo Touro ©Nov '92: 220.
Photo Michael Tropea: 292*ar*.
Courtesy Estate of Peter Tully, Mrs M. Gibson: 282.
Photo Malcolm Turner: 319*ar*.
Saundra Valencia: 278*r*.
Photo ©Rob Versluys, Amsterdam: 316*ar*.
Photo David Ward: 294*cl*.
David Watkins: 317*cr*; 327*al*; 327*ac*.
Jessica White: 249.
J. Fred Woell: 328*c* all.
Photo Reinhard Zimmermann: 160; 297*ar*.

index of names